Lecture Notes in Computer Science 16292

The series Lecture Notes in Computer Science (LNCS), including its subseries Lecture Notes in Artificial Intelligence (LNAI) and Lecture Notes in Bioinformatics (LNBI), has established itself as a medium for the publication of new developments in computer science and information technology research, teaching, and education.

LNCS enjoys close cooperation with the computer science R & D community, the series counts many renowned academics among its volume editors and paper authors, and collaborates with prestigious societies. Its mission is to serve this international community by providing an invaluable service, mainly focused on the publication of conference and workshop proceedings and postproceedings. LNCS commenced publication in 1973.

Özlem Durmaz Incel · Jingwen Qin ·
Gerald Bieber · Arjan Kuijper

Editors

Sensor-Based Activity Recognition and Artificial Intelligence

10th International Workshop, iWOAR 2025
Enschede, The Netherlands, September 18–19, 2025
Proceedings

 Springer

Editors
Özlem Durmaz Incel
University of Twente
Enschede, The Netherlands

Jingwen Qin
University of Twente
Enschede, The Netherlands

Gerald Bieber
Fraunhofer Institute for Computer Graphics
Research IGD
Darmstadt, Germany

Arjan Kuijper
Fraunhofer Institute for Computer Graphics
Research IGD
Darmstadt, Germany

ISSN 0302-9743　　　　　　　ISSN 1611-3349 (electronic)
Lecture Notes in Computer Science
ISBN 978-3-032-13311-3　　　　ISBN 978-3-032-13312-0 (eBook)
https://doi.org/10.1007/978-3-032-13312-0

This Springer imprint is published by the registered company Springer Nature Switzerland AG
The registered company address is: Gewerbestrasse 11, 6330 Cham, Switzerland

If disposing of this product, please recycle the paper.

Preface

In recent years, the increasing acceptance of wearable sensors and the rise of device-free sensing have opened new possibilities for applications that aim to better understand the conditions of both humans and animals. These technologies provide tools for continuous monitoring in a non-intrusive manner. Wearable devices, thanks to their ability to gather large amounts of data while in motion, have attracted interest in both academic and industrial sectors, enabling solutions for the continuous monitoring of humans and animals in everyday life, workplaces, medical settings, or ecological environments. At the same time, device-free sensing technologies, such as those based on Wi-Fi, radar, or ambient acoustics, have gained popularity for their ability to monitor subjects without requiring them to wear any sensors. These ambient systems offer an alternative approach to collecting extensive contextual data, while reducing issues like user compliance and discomfort from wearing devices. As a result, wearable computing and device-free sensing have become active fields of research, with ongoing studies focused on developing user-friendly and unobtrusive systems that deliver efficient services.

The International Workshop on Sensor-Based Activity Recognition and Artificial Intelligence (iWOAR) has been held annually since 2014 and has established itself as a unique platform for exchanging ideas, showcasing best practices, and presenting scientific and technical progress in the field. In 2025, it was hosted by the Pervasive Systems Research Group at the University of Twente in Enschede, The Netherlands. iWOAR 2025 focused on recognizing human and animal activities using wearable and device-free sensors, combined with advances in artificial intelligence and related technologies. All scientific submissions underwent a rigorous single-blind peer-review process. Each paper was reviewed by at least two program committee members, with an average of 2.7 reviews per submission, and discussed to ensure quality and fairness. The program committee chairs made the final acceptance decisions based on these evaluations. For the 10th anniversary edition of iWOAR in 2025, we received 42 submissions. After careful review, 31 contributions were accepted, comprising 12 full papers and 19 short papers. The accepted papers were organised into the following topical sections: Next-Gen Human Activity Recognition, AI Health Tech, Data Generation and Cleaning for Robust Human-Centric AI, Wearable Monitoring for Cognitive and Physiological States, and Advanced Sensing and Interaction for Human-Centred Systems.

This year's workshop featured two distinguished keynote speakers: Michael Beigl (Karlsruhe Institute of Technology) and Kate Farrahi (University of Southampton), who shared their expertise and insights on the future of wearable sensing and human-centered artificial intelligence. Their contributions provided valuable perspectives and sparked inspiring discussions at iWOAR.

We would like to thank all authors for their contributions, the program committee for their dedicated reviews, and our sponsors and supporters for their invaluable support. Special thanks go to the members of the Pervasive Systems group for their efforts in organizing this year's event, with particular recognition to Nikita Sharma, Jeroen Klein Brinke, and Denys Matthies for their outstanding contributions.

Reflecting on iWOAR 2025 in Enschede, it was a successful and inspiring event, characterised by top-tier scientific contributions, engaging discussions, and a vibrant research community. We believe the ideas shared will further drive innovation in sensor-based activity recognition, wearable computing, and human-centered AI.

September 2025

Özlem Durmaz Incel
Jingwen Qin
Gerald Bieber
Arjan Kuijper

Organization

Organization Committee

Conference Chair

Özlem Durmaz Incel······University of Twente, the Netherlands

Local Chair

Nikita Sharma······University of Twente, the Netherlands

Proceedings Chair

Jingwen Qin······University of Twente, the Netherlands

Publicity Chairs

Jeroen Klein Brinke······University of Twente, the Netherlands
Denys J.C. Matthies······Technische Hochschule Lübeck, Germany

PC Chairs

Gerald Bieber······Fraunhofer IGD Rostock, Germany
Arjan Kuijper······Fraunhofer IGD & TU Darmstadt, Germany

Program Committee

Sümeyye Ağaç······Boğaziçi University, Türkiye
Bert Arnrich······Hasso Plattner Institute, University of Potsdam, Germany
Gerald Bieber······IGD Rostock, Germany
Chiara Contoli······University of Urbino, Italy
Ozlem Durmaz Incel······University of Twente, the Netherlands
Biying Fu······RheinMain University of Applied Sciences, Germany
Sebastian Fudickar······Lübeck University, Germany

Hristijan Gjoreski	Ss. Cyril and Methodius University in Skopje, North Macedonia
Tobias Grosse-Puppendahl	Microsoft, UK
Jochen Huber	Furtwangen University, Germany
Kristina Kirsten	Hasso Plattner Institute, Germany
Jeroen Klein Brinke	University of Twente, the Netherlands
Orhan Konak	Hasso Plattner Institute, Germany
Thomas Kosch	HU Berlin, Germany
Arjan Kuijper	Fraunhofer IGD & TU Darmstadt, Germany
Frédéric Li	German Research Center for Artificial Intelligence (DFKI), Germany
Denys J.C. Matthies	Technische Hochschule Lübeck, Germany
Nirvana Meratnia	Eindhoven University of Technology, the Netherlands
Jeanne I.M. Parmentier	Utrecht University, the Netherlands
Jingwen Qin	University of Twente, the Netherlands
Rob Bemthuis	University of Twente, the Netherlands
Dolly Sapra	University of Amsterdam, the Netherlands
Ruben Schlonsak	Technical University of Applied Sciences Lübeck, Germany
Nikita Sharma	University of Twente, the Netherlands
Kimiaki Shirahama	Doshisha University, Japan
Amir Tabatabaei	University of Guilan, Iran
Allal Tiberkak	University of Medea, Algeria
Kristof Van Laerhoven	University of Siegen, Germany

Contents

One-Sided CSI-Based Sensing in Adversarial Through-Wall Settings   1
V. Bakanas and J. Klein Brinke

Hue4U: Real-Time Personalized Color Correction in Augmented Reality   20
Jingwen Qin, Semen Checherin, Yue Li, Berend-Jan van der Zwaag,
and Özlem Durmaz Incel

How AI Is Shaping Society and Why We Must Keep It at Bay!   38
Denys Matthies, Ruben Schlonsak, and Marco Gabrecht

A Machine Learning Approach to Cognitive Load Estimation
in Augmented Reality Using Eye Tracking   56
Sandra Kiefer, Martin Weier, and Biying Fu

Lightweight Deep Learning for Sensor-Based HAR: Benchmarking
Optimization Strategies   77
Sumeyye Agac and Özlem Durmaz Incel

A Cyber-Physical-Human System Design for Challenging Behaviour
Monitoring in People with Dementia   99
Jan Kleine Deters, Burcu Güvenatam, Jair A. Lima Silva,
Ewout Bergsma, Sarah Janus, Sytse U. Zuidema, and Heinrich Wörtche

DenseVoxelNet3D: A Compact 3D CNN Architecture for Human Activity
Recognition Using LiDAR Point Clouds   116
Noel D'Avis, Hendrik Hartmann, Lars Grothe, and Silvia Faquiri

InSSeqTra: Inter Data Selective Sequential Transfer Learning for Domain
Adaptation in CSI-Based HAR   135
Nikita Sharma, Minh Son Nguyen, and Le Viet Duc

Topological Versus Spatiotemporal Gait Parameters for Fall Risk
Detection with IMU Sensors   156
Redona Brahimetaj, Elena Botti, Ivan Bautmans, Eva Swinnen,
and Bart Jansen

Towards Efficient Wearable Monitoring of Cognitive Fatigue
in Human-Robot Interaction: A Comparative Study of ECG and EDA
Signals   172
Krishna Kodur, Manizheh Zand, and Maria Kyrarini

Radar Placement Effects on Multi-patient Heart and Respiration
Monitoring, SiViS Dataset Validation 185
   Karla Miriam Reyes Leiva, Ankit Gupta, and Martin Cerny

Scenario-Controlled Synthetic Data Augmentation: In Application
of Agitation Monitoring 196
   Ali Najem, Jan Kleine Deters, Mehdi Sedighi, and Heinrich Wörtche

Illusion of Precision: How Averaging Undermines Pulse Measurement
Accuracy 222
   Gerald Bieber, Erik Endlicher, Timo Forstner, and Milad Geravand

Synthetic Data Generation Using a Smart Floor Digital Twin for Fall
Detection 234
   Milan Milivojčević, Niki Hrovatin, Jernej Vičič, and Aleksandar Tošić

Real-Time ECG and HRV Monitoring in Handball Using a Low-Cost
Wearable Sensor 250
   Jonas Pöhler, Dimitri Laumann, and Kristof Van Laerhoven

Robust and Efficient Writer-Independent IMU-Based Handwriting
Recognition 261
   Jindong Li, Tim Hamann, Jens Barth, Peter Kämpf, Dario Zanca,
   and Björn Eskofier

Help the Machine to Help You: an Evaluation in the Wild of Egocentric
Data Cleaning via Skeptical Learning 287
   Andrea Bontempelli, Matteo Busso, Leonardo Javier Malcotti,
   and Fausto Giunchiglia

Improved Strategies for Multi-modal Atmospheric Sensing to Augment
Wearable IMU-Based Hand Washing Detection 308
   Robin Burchard, Hurriat Ali, and Kristof Van Laerhoven

No Cloud, No Problem: A Real-Time HAR Insole with On-Device
Inference 324
   Ruben Schlonsak, Jiabao Yu, Hans-Christian Jetter,
   and Denys J. C. Matthies

Pervasive Intelligent Diagnostics for High-Tech Systems 343
   Rob Bemthuis, Thomas Nägele, and Cor van der Struijf

Toward Unobtrusive Monitoring of Everyday Activities Using Multimodal
Wearable and Ambient Data: A Multiroom Living Lab Feasibility Study 353
   Kristina Kirsten, Tim Walz, David Weese, and Bert Arnrich

Evaluating LoRa Mesh Networks for Personal Dead Reckoning
of Firefighters 364
　　Arnout Luinge and Sabari Nathan Anbalagan

Grounded in Reality of Human-Computer Interaction: Robust
Smartphone-Based Gesture Recognition 373
　　Fatemeh Naderi, Judith S. Heinisch, Lars Mathuseck, and Klaus David

Monitoring Harness Trotters in Diverse Cases Using an Online Platform
to Collect Synchronised Physiology and Locomotion Data 382
　　Jeanne I. M. Parmentier, Rhana M. Aarts, Zala Žgank, Elin Hernlund,
　　Raluca Marin-Perianu, Mihai Marin-Perianu, and Marie Rhodin

GenIMU: Simulate Realistic IMU Data Using Video Generation Models 393
　　Nikolas Rieger, Bert Arnrich, and Orhan Konak

A Technical Insight Into Sensor-S Study: Effect of Wearable Sensors
on Patient Engagement and Motivation in Post-stroke Rehabilitation 404
　　Fatemeh Sardadvar, Valentin Kennel, Athina Tome, Nurcennet Kaynak,
　　Alexa Straus, Rok Kos, Felix Schmidt, Alexander Heinrich Nave,
　　and Bert Arnrich

SpaceStriker: A Peer-Assisted Sensor-Based Exergame with Real-Time
ML-Driven Feedback 413
　　Michal Slupczynski, Khaleel Asyraaf Mat Sanusi, Roland Klemke,
　　and Stefan Decker

Voice Privacy in Speech Systems: A Comparative Study of Pitch Shifting
and StarGAN-VC 422
　　Mehmet Arif Taşlı, Eren Akyürek, and Funda Yıldırım

Toward Low-Complexity Arrhythmia Classification for Ambient Assisted
Living 430
　　Hangze Wu, Ruben Schlonsak, and Denys J. C. Matthies

Hacking Rokoko Smart Gloves for Tool Detection Using Recurrent Neural
Networks 440
　　Zhouyao Yu, Ruben Schlonsak, and Denys J. C. Matthies

Evaluation of the Effect of Camera Viewing Angles on the Quality
of Human Pose Estimation in River Surfing 450
　　Michael Zöllner, Moritz Krause, Christian Groth, Stefan Kniesburges,
　　and Michael Döllinger

Author Index 459

One-Sided CSI-Based Sensing in Adversarial Through-Wall Settings

V. Bakanas[(✉)] and J. Klein Brinke[(✉)][iD]

Pervasive Systems, EDGE Group, University of Twente, Enschede, The Netherlands
v.bakanas@student.utwente.nl, j.kleinbrinke@utwente.nl

Abstract. Wi-Fi signals can reveal patterns of human activity by analyzing how movement disturbs signal propagation. While prior work on Channel State Information (CSI) has shown promise for indoor activity recognition, it typically assumes sensor placement within the monitored environment or in adjacent rooms. This study investigates a more constrained and privacy-sensitive scenario: can activity inside a home be inferred using low-cost wireless devices placed entirely outside, with no interior access? Using a custom active sensing setup, we collected over 600 min of CSI data across two residential apartments, capturing room-level presence under varying wall materials, device placements, and participant behavior. We evaluated multiple learning strategies—including supervised, unsupervised, and semi-supervised models—to assess the feasibility of inferring interior activity from exterior signals. Results show that room-level localization is achievable even through thick residential walls, though performance varies substantially with environmental structure and sensor configuration. These findings demonstrate the viability of a previously unexplored form of passive activity inference and raise important questions about wireless privacy in domestic settings.

Keywords: Wi-Fi sensing · channel state information · human activity recognition · through-wall sensing · ESP32 · privacy · one-sided · localization · semi-supervised clustering · deep learning

1 Introduction

Advancements in embedded systems have been driven by the miniaturization of physical hardware, which has concurrently increased in computational power. This progress enables the deployment of increasingly sophisticated and deeper neural networks directly on embedded devices. Simultaneously, sensing technologies have evolved beyond conventional physical sensing to include unobtrusive, device-free methods. These developments align with several Sustainable Development Goals (SDGs), including the rising concerns around environmental pollution (e-waste), the challenges posed by aging populations, rising healthcare expenditures, and growing enthusiasm for smart cities and intelligent environments.

In the context of health, Human Activity Recognition (HAR) using Wi-Fi signals has gained significant attention due to its unobtrusive sensing capabilities. Channel State Information, which captures amplitude and phase variations across Wi-Fi subcarriers, has proven particularly effective for detecting fine-grained motion [1]. CSI enables recognition of subtle activities such as breathing [2] or hand gestures [3], and offers privacy advantages over camera-based systems by relying on signal reflections instead of visual data [4].

Wi-Fi CSI sensing has increasingly been proposed as a privacy-preserving alternative to camera-based and wearable activity recognition systems, especially in health and eldercare contexts. Unlike cameras, CSI does not capture visual or personally identifiable data, and unlike wearables, it requires no physical contact or active compliance–making it well-suited for continuous monitoring of individuals who may forget, reject, or be unable to use body-worn devices. This is particularly relevant for older adults and individuals with neurodegenerative conditions, where reliable in-home sensing is critical but intrusive solutions are often unacceptable [5]. Recent studies demonstrate that CSI-based systems can detect subtle human motions–such as tremors or hand gestures–with high temporal precision, enabling non-contact health monitoring in everyday residential settings [6]. These characteristics position CSI sensing as a promising tool for unobtrusive, dignity-preserving monitoring of physical activity in vulnerable populations.

With the emergence of the IEEE 201.11bf Wi-Fi standard [7], emphasis is shifting toward the integration of wireless communication and sensing–known as joint communication and sensing. The forthcoming standard aims to standardize and scale Wi-Fi-enabled sensing in many applications. However, the ability of radio waves to penetrate through walls enables it to monitor not just the immediate vicinity, but also adjacent spaces that should not be monitored. This might mean that Wi-Fi sensing, combined with (semi-)unsupervised methods, might be used for adversarial motives, including spying. '

1.1   Problem Statement and Research Questions

Most existing CSI-based HAR systems rely on sensors placed inside the monitored space, often assuming line-of-sight (LOS) between transmitters and receivers. However, Wi-Fi signals are capable of penetrating walls, raising the possibility of activity inference from outside a building. While earlier studies have investigated through-wall sensing within indoor environments [8], little is known about sensing in fully external, adversarial conditions–where neither the transmitter nor the receiver has access to the interior.

This work explores that scenario directly: can low-cost ESP32 devices placed entirely outside a building detect in which room a person is located, based solely on Wi-Fi Channel State Information? We use an active CSI sensing setup, where an ESP-NOW-enabled transmitter broadcasts packets to a passive receiver placed on the building's exterior. CSI spectrograms derived from the received signals are used to classify spatially localized activity – specifically, presence in the kitchen, hallway, or bathroom – using both supervised deep learning and unsupervised or semi-supervised clustering techniques.

Research question (RQ): To what extent can Wi-Fi CSI collected from outside a building be used to infer room-level occupancy indoors?

To explore this overarching question, we examine the following sub-questions:

- **sRQ1:** How does transmitter orientation ($0°$, $\pm 45°$) and shielding (open vs. boxed) affect classification and clustering accuracy and F_1-scores for room-level presence detection?
- **sRQ2:** What classification accuracy and F_1-scores can be achieved for room-level human activity recognition using supervised, unsupervised, and semi-supervised models trained on CSI spectrograms?
- **sRQ3:** How does sensing performance (in terms of accuracy and variability) generalize across two different apartment layouts and multiple participants?

This set of questions is relevant both technically and socially, as it explores whether activity inside a private home can be inferred using inexpensive external devices. By challenging the traditional notion that walls guarantee privacy, this research opens up important discussions about the boundaries of domestic space, personal security, and the ethical implications of ambient wireless surveillance.

The remainder of this thesis is structured as follows. Section 2 reviews prior work on human activity recognition using Wi-Fi CSI and related sensing modalities. Section 3 describes the experimental setup and data collection process across two apartment environments. Section 4 details the data preprocessing steps and modeling strategies used for activity classification. Section 5 presents the experimental results, structured by environment, model type, and configuration sensitivity. Section 6 discusses the findings in depth, including the strengths and limitations of the study, and Sect. 7 concludes with a summary and directions for future research.

2   Related Work

CSI-based Wi-Fi sensing has been widely explored for HAR tasks. Early systems such as E-eyes [9] and CARM [10] demonstrated that variations in wireless propagation, caused by human movement, could be captured using Intel 5300 NICs with custom drivers [11]. These works showed successful activity classification in indoor and LOS scenarios. Subsequent models incorporated deep learning techniques such as convolutional and recurrent neural networks to improve performance [12,13].

Beyond line-of-sight (LOS) environments, prior research has demonstrated that CSI can detect activity in non-line-of-sight or through-wall scenarios [8]. These studies commonly involve sensor placements inside buildings or in adjacent rooms separated by thin interior walls, allowing relatively direct or low-attenuation signal paths. While these configurations show the feasibility of through-wall sensing, they typically assume some degree of proximity and structural simplicity.

The evolution of CSI-capable hardware has also enabled broader deployment. Intel 5300 NICs offered high-quality CSI but were limited by power and platform constraints. Atheros and Broadcom chipsets later enabled embedded platforms such as Raspberry Pi to be used for CSI collection [14,15]. Recent developments have made it possible to collect CSI data on ESP32 microcontrollers, which are inexpensive, energy-efficient, and easy to deploy [8,16].

This study makes four contributions to the field of CSI-based human activity recognition. First, it investigates a rarely explored sensing configuration in which both the transmitter and receiver are positioned on the same side of the wall—such as in a shared hallway or entirely outside the apartment—with no access to the monitored interior. To our knowledge, fully external, one-sided sensing setups have only been reported once [17]. Second, the study collects 648 min of labeled CSI data across two distinct apartment environments, enabling a more comprehensive evaluation of model performance. Third, we apply a range of learning strategies, including supervised classification with a CNN [18], unsupervised clustering using K-Means [19] and Gaussian Mixture Models [20], and semi-supervised clustering with MPCK-Means-M-F [21] and COP-KMeans [22] to compare performance across labeled and unlabeled conditions. Finally, we assess how sensing performance varies by apartment layout, wall materials, transmitter orientation, shielding, and participant identity—offering insight into the environmental and human factors that affect CSI-based inference.

3   Data Acquisition

To evaluate the feasibility of one-sided, through-wall human activity recognition using CSI, we conducted a series of structured experiments across two different residential environments. This section describes the hardware setup, experimental design, and data collection protocols used in the study. We outline the roles of the ESP32-C6 [23] devices, the spatial configurations in each apartment, and the procedures used to label room-level activity. Special attention is given to how environmental variation, participant behavior, and potential sensing limitations were managed to ensure consistent and interpretable data.

3.1   Experimental Setup and Hardware

The sensing system consisted of two ESP32-C6 [23] boards configured for active sensing. One acted as a *transmitter*, sending ESP-NOW packets at 20 Hz, while the other functioned as a *passive receiver* connected to a Raspberry Pi 4B via USB. CSI data was extracted using Espressif's open-source *ESP-CSI* toolchain [24], and the Pi recorded timestamped packets for later processing. Both ESP32's were equipped with *ALFA Network APA-M25 directional panel antennas* [25] to enhance signal directivity.

In Apartment A, the transmitter was placed 1 m in front of the entrance door, and the receiver was positioned 2 metes to the side, mounted on the exterior wall of the apartment, within the shared hallway of the building. The full lay-out, including sensor placements, is shown in Fig. 1. This parallel arrangement ensured that signal propagation occurred through a solid reinforced concrete wall. To suppress side-path signal leakage and increase sensitivity to interior activity, the receiver was partially shielded with aluminum foil. Example trans-mitter setup combinations are illustrated in Fig. 2.

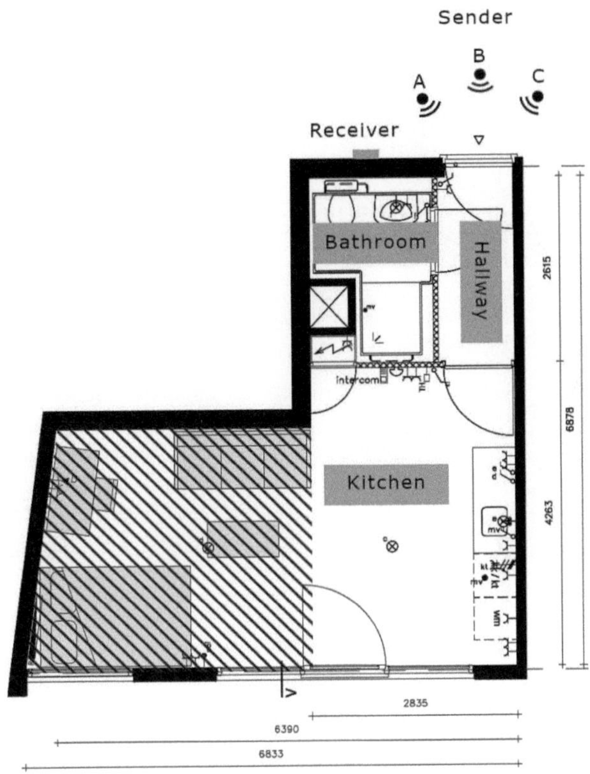

Fig. 1. Apartment A layout: kitchen, hallway, bathroom. Transmitter placements A–C = left/front/right. Total size: $2.835\,\text{m} \times 6.878\,\text{m}$ ($19.51\,\text{m}^2$)

Each configuration in Apartment A was repeated across three participants, with each participant completing two trials per configuration. In each trial, four activity conditions–movement in the kitchen, hallway, and bathroom, and an empty apartment baseline–were recorded. The order of these activities was ran-domized using the Random.org List Randomizer service [26] to prevent order effects. Each condition lasted for 3 min, resulting in a 12-minute CSI recording per trial. With 3 angles × 2 shielding conditions × 2 trials × 3 participants, a total of 36 recording sessions were collected in Apartment A, amounting to 432 min of CSI data sampled at 20 Hz.

During preliminary calibration, a section of the kitchen in Apartment A was found to be consistently unreachable by any of the tested transmitter-receiver placements. This region, marked in Fig. 1 with a hatch pattern, produced CSI signatures indistinguishable from the empty apartment baseline. To avoid contaminating the kitchen class label, participants were explicitly instructed not to enter this dead zone during recording. Consequently, all kitchen activity was constrained to the signal-reachable portion of the room.

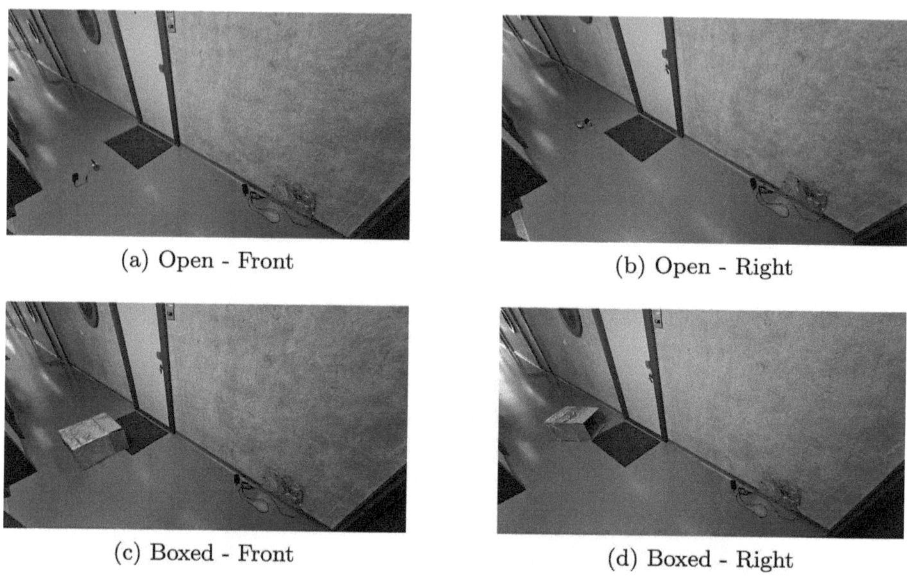

(a) Open - Front

(b) Open - Right

(c) Boxed - Front

(d) Boxed - Right

Fig. 2. Example transmitter configurations in Apartment A. Rows show shielding condition (open, boxed); columns show orientation (front, right).

Six configurations were tested by combining:

- **Transmitter orientation:** 0° (in front of the door), 45° left, and 45° right
- **Shielding condition:** open-air vs. transmitter enclosed in a cardboard box lined with aluminum foil, with the opening facing the door

To evaluate the reproducibility of the sensing approach in a different spatial context, an additional round of data collection was conducted in a second apartment with a distinct layout and wall materials. Unlike Apartment A, which was a conventional brick-and-concrete residential unit, Apartment B was a prefabricated shipping container apartment. This structure features thinner walls, metal framing, and more prominent glass elements, such as large windows and a partially glazed entrance. Due to spatial constraints, the transmitter in Apartment B was mounted only 1.5 m away from the door, compared to 2 m in Apartment A. The same six transmitter configurations were replicated in Apartment B, using identical placement logic, preprocessing steps, and experimental procedures. While Apartment A included labeled regions for kitchen, hallway, and bathroom activities, the layout of Apartment B featured a kitchen, bedroom, and bathroom. Thus, although the kitchen and bathroom classes were preserved across environments, the hallway class in Apartment A was replaced by a bedroom class in Apartment B. All analyses—including supervised classification, unsupervised clustering, and semi-supervised clustering—were repeated using data from the new environment, with models retrained from scratch but the pipeline held constant.

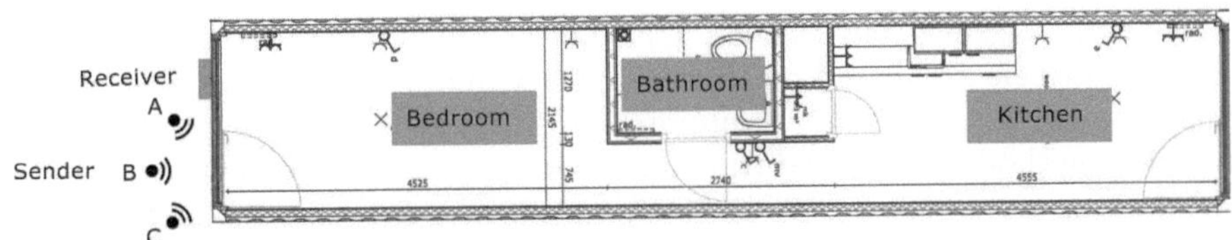

Fig. 3. Apartment B layout: kitchen, bedroom, bathroom. Transmitter placements A–C = right/front/left. Total size: $11.820\,\mathrm{m} \times 2.145\,\mathrm{m}$ ($25.36\,\mathrm{m}^2$)

To minimize ambient interference from other residents, all recordings were conducted on weekdays between 08:00–12:30 and 13:45–17:30. These time windows were selected after pilot trials showed significantly lower classification accuracy when neighboring apartments were occupied.

4 Methodology

This section outlines the full processing and modeling pipeline used to transform raw CSI data into room-level activity predictions. We begin by introducing the design rationale and formal threat model that define the one-sided sensing scenario and its constraints. Next, we describe the preprocessing steps applied to clean and standardize the data, followed by the supervised and clustering-based learning strategies used to infer activity. The goal is to provide a transparent account of the modeling choices and how they align with the study's objective of evaluating generalization across environments and transmitter configurations.

4.1 Design Rationale and Threat Model

The system was designed to reflect a realistic low-resource adversarial setting using only off-the-shelf hardware and minimal computational power. All sensing was performed with ESP32C6 microcontrollers, without relying on access points, internal infrastructure, or interior placement. This setup mimics conditions where an external observer attempts localization using commodity devices alone.

To match these constraints, all models were chosen for their low computational footprint and ease of deployment. A compact convolutional neural network (CNN) was selected for supervised classification, offering a strong balance between accuracy and efficiency (see Appendix A for architecture details). The main purpose of this CNN is to function as a way to validate the data and as a baseline, as state of the art shows CNNs are capable of accurately classifying activities and locations using channel state information. A high performance implies participants were indeed walking in separate regions of the apartment with minimal overlap.

More complex architectures such as LSTMs or Transformers were evaluated but showed no consistent benefit. Clustering and semi-supervised algorithms were likewise selected based on their simplicity and ability to run without GPU acceleration or large memory requirements. All models, including the CNN and clustering methods, completed training or fitting in under five minutes on a standard desktop CPU (Intel Core i5-7500), suggesting potential for future deployment on embedded or mobile platforms.

4.2   Preprocessing and Feature Extraction

Raw CSI data was first loaded and processed by calculating the amplitude of each complex subcarrier. Null subcarriers were excluded prior to further processing as they carry no data. To reduce noise and artifacts, three sequential filtering steps were applied: a Hampel filter [27] was used to remove outliers, followed by Hamming window smoothing [28] to attenuate short-term fluctuations, and finally wavelet-based denoising [29] to reduce multiscale signal noise.

After filtering, the data was normalized using standard score normalization (z-score) across all samples. The normalized dataset was then segmented by class and subcarrier, and converted into windows of 2 s (40 frames at 20 Hz). Each resulting sample had the shape 40 (time steps) × 52 (subcarriers). An illustration of a spectrogram before and after preprocessing is shown in Fig. 4.

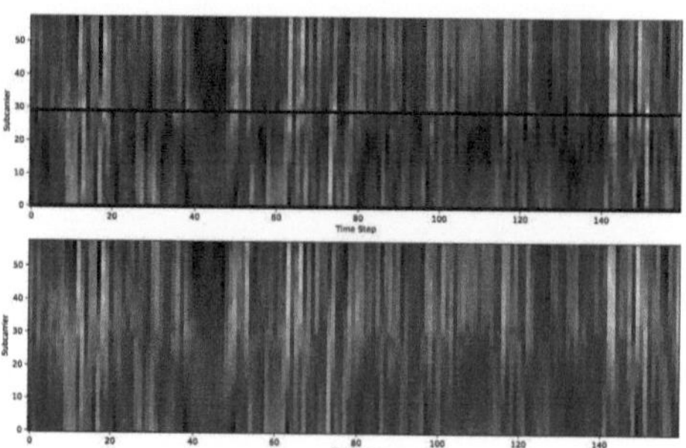

Fig. 4. Example 8 s CSI spectrogram before (top) and after (bottom) preprocessing for kitchen activity in apartment A.

4.3 Supervised Learning

Windowed samples were used to train a convolutional neural network classifier. The full architecture is provided in Appendix A.

Stratified 10-fold cross-validation was performed to evaluate the model, and the entire process was repeated five times to ensure statistical stability. For each run, classification metrics such as accuracy, precision, recall, and F_1-score-score were recorded.

The model was trained using the Adam optimizer with a learning rate of 0.001, a batch size of 16, and for 20 epochs. The loss function was categorical cross-entropy, suitable for multi-class classification.

4.4 Dimensionality Reduction and Unsupervised Clustering

For unsupervised clustering, the filtered and windowed CSI data underwent two-stage dimensionality reduction. First, we applied temporal Principal Component Analysis (tPCA) [30] to each subcarrier, reducing the 40 time steps per subcarrier to 10 temporal components. This compressed representation was then flattened across all subcarriers into a single feature vector for each window. A second PCA step was applied to these vectors to reduce overall dimensionality to 5.

The resulting 5-dimensional vectors were clustered using K-Means and Gaussian Mixture Models. Clustering performance was evaluated using Hungarian-mapped accuracy and F_1-score.

4.5 Semi-supervised Clustering

The same PCA-reduced data was used for semi-supervised clustering using the MPCK-Means-M-F and COP-KMeans algorithms. A 20-fold stratified cross-validation protocol was adopted to simulate a low-label scenario. In each iteration, one fold (approximately 5% of the data) was treated as labeled, while the remaining 19 folds were considered fully unlabeled.

From the labeled fold, pairwise constraints were generated as follows: all sample pairs with the same class label were assigned must-link constraints, and all pairs with different class labels were assigned cannot-link constraints. These constraints were used during clustering, but the labeled samples themselves were excluded from evaluation.

For each run clustering performance was assessed using Hungarian-mapped accuracy and F_1-score.

5 Results

This section presents the performance outcomes of the proposed activity recognition approach across several experimental axes. The analysis is structured to reflect the primary evaluation goals: assessing performance in a controlled setting, comparing supervised and clustering models, and examining generalization across environments. Each subsection highlights model behavior, using both accuracy and F_1-score metrics (reported as mean $\pm$ standard deviation in percentage). Full performance tables, including all accuracy and F_1-score values across models and configurations, are provided in Appendix B.

5.1   Performance in a Controlled Setting (Apartment A)

Experiments in Apartment A, a conventional concrete-walled environment, yielded consistently high performance across all configurations and models. Supervised classification using a CNN achieved strong room-level recognition, with accuracy ranging from $91.8\% \pm 5.5$ (Open-Left) to $96.1\% \pm 4.5$ (Boxed-Front), and F_1-scores closely matching accuracy across all settings. These results demonstrate the robustness of CNN-based classification in stable indoor environments with limited signal interference.

Clustering-based methods also performed reasonably well in this environment. MPCK-Means-M-F reached up to $80.3\% \pm 14.7$ accuracy and $79.1\% \pm 15.6$ F_1-score (Boxed-Front), outperforming other clustering approaches. COP-KMeans trailed behind with accuracy and F_1-scores typically in the 55–72% range. GMM clustering showed surprisingly strong results in some cases, reaching up to $80.8\% \pm 14.6$ accuracy. In contrast, K-Means lagged behind, showing both lower mean performance and higher variance.

5.2   Comparison of Supervised and Clustering Models

Across all configurations in Apartment A, the CNN consistently outperformed clustering-based approaches. The average CNN accuracy across all setups was approximately 93.3%, with a comparable F_1-score. MPCK-Means-M-F was the top clustering model, followed by GMM. COP-KMeans and K-Means performed less reliably, often falling below 60%.

Clustering methods also exhibited substantially higher standard deviation compared to CNN, indicating greater sensitivity to initialization and environmental variation. Despite these limitations, semi-supervised approaches such as MPCK-Means-M-F provide a viable compromise in settings where fully labeled data is unavailable. Figure 5 summarizes these results visually.

5.3   Generalization to a Different Apartment Layout (Apartment B)

Performance in Apartment B – a less controlled setting with thinner walls, more glass surfaces, and a different spatial layout – was lower and more variable than in Apartment A. The CNN remained the top performer, achieving $80.6\% \pm 5.5$ (Boxed-Front) in its best configuration, but dropping to $43.7\% \pm 8.9$ (Open-Left) in the worst. F_1-scores followed the same trend, highlighting the impact of environmental variability on signal propagation. This performance degradation across setups is visualized in Fig. 6.

Clustering models were more strongly affected by the domain shift. MPCK-Means-M-F reached a maximum of $62.9\% \pm 10.9$ accuracy and $62.3\% \pm 10.8$ F_1-score (Boxed-Front), while most other configurations yielded results below 50%.

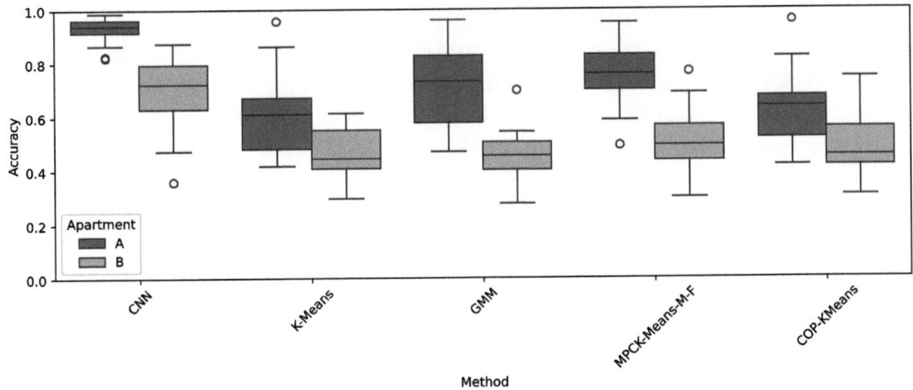

Fig. 5. Classification accuracy across model types for both apartments.

GMM peaked at 57.3% ± 9.7 in Open-Right, but exhibited similar degradation in challenging layouts. COP-KMeans and K-Means offered little robustness, with multiple configurations hovering at or below random baseline levels.

6   Discussion

This section interprets the key findings from the experimental results in light of the study's goals and practical relevance. We examine how model performance was affected by environmental variation, transmitter configuration, and algorithmic approach, with a particular focus on the generalizability across apartments. The discussion also addresses key strengths of the study–such as its one-sided sensing design and use of real apartment layouts–as well as important limitations, including data labeling constraints and unmeasured environmental factors. These reflections inform the practical implications of the work and suggest avenues for future research.

6.1   Impact of Shielding and Orientation

Regarding **sRQ1**, shielding effects varied depending on both the environment and the transmitter's orientation. In Apartment A, adding an aluminum-lined box around the transmitter had little or no consistent effect on classification or clustering performance. For example, supervised classification achieved 96.1% ± 4.5 accuracy and 96.1% ± 4.5 F_1-score in the Boxed-Front setup and 93.8% ± 6.2 accuracy and 93.7% ± 6.3 F_1-score in Open-Front–differences well within the range of expected variation. Similar patterns were observed across all other orientations in Apartment A, suggesting that shielding did not meaningfully alter signal propagation in this more structurally stable environment.

In Apartment B, shielding generally had a limited effect as well–except in one configuration. When the transmitter was oriented left, directly toward the receiver (see Fig. 3), performance differed dramatically depending on shielding: Boxed-Left reached 79.2% ± 10.0 accuracy and 78.7% ± 10.2 F_1-score, while Open-Left fell to 43.7% ± 8.9 accuracy and 42.5% ± 9.0 F_1-score–the lowest across all test conditions. This large gap was not observed in other orientations. For example, shielding made little difference between Boxed-Front (80.6% ± 5.5 accuracy, 79.9% ± 6.0 F_1-score) and Open-Front (76.5% ± 6.3 accuracy, 76.2% ± 6.5 F_1-score), or between Boxed-Right (66.2% ± 11.7 accuracy, 65.2% ± 12.4 F_1-score) and Open-Right (69.8% ± 8.1 accuracy, 69.1% ± 8.6 F_1-score).

These findings suggest that shielding may help improve signal consistency in cases where the transmitter is oriented directly at the receiver, especially in reflective environments like Apartment B. In such cases, the enclosure may narrow the beam path or suppress undesired side reflections. Outside of this specific setup, however, shielding did not consistently improve classification performance. This trend is clearly illustrated in Fig. 6 and points to a context-specific role for shielding that depends on geometric alignment and environmental complexity.

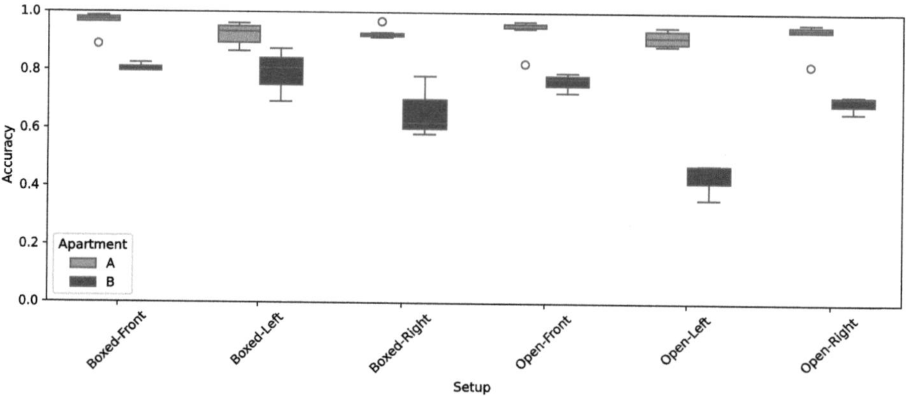

Fig. 6. Comparison of CNN classification accuracy across transmitter configurations in both apartments.

6.2   Accuracy of HAR Using Different Learning Strategies

Answering **sRQ2**, the supervised convolutional neural network (CNN) consistently achieved the highest performance across both apartments. Averaged over all configurations, it reached a mean accuracy of 83.2% and a mean F_1-score of 82.6%, with particularly strong results in Apartment A (e.g., 96.1% ± 4.5 accuracy in Boxed-Front). These results confirm that supervised deep learning methods are highly effective when labeled training data is available, offering both high accuracy and relatively low variance across conditions.

Semi-supervised clustering, particularly MPCK-Means-M-F, showed moderate but consistent performance. Its average accuracy was 62.6%, with a mean F_1-score of 61.5%. While it did not match CNN performance, it consistently outperformed unsupervised models across most configurations and showed less degradation when transitioning to Apartment B. This suggests that even limited supervision—in the form of pairwise constraints—can substantially improve clustering outcomes in new environments.

Unsupervised clustering methods performed less reliably overall. GMM was the strongest among them, achieving a mean accuracy of 61.1% and mean F_1-score of 58.9%. However, its high variance and inconsistent results across configurations—particularly in Apartment B—limit its practical utility. K-Means and COP-KMeans both averaged below 60% accuracy, with overall F_1-scores of 56.4% and 56.8% respectively, and struggled to maintain stability in more complex layouts.

These findings underscore the importance of supervision in CSI-based activity recognition. Supervised CNN models provide the most robust and accurate performance. When labeling is limited, semi-supervised methods such as MPCK-Means-M-F offer a viable compromise. In contrast, unsupervised clustering approaches remain too unstable for reliable deployment without domain adaptation or tuning.

6.3   Generalization Across Different Apartments and Participants

Considering **sRQ3**, results show a clear and substantial performance drop when moving from Apartment A to Apartment B. In Apartment A, classification and clustering models performed reliably and with low variability across configurations. In Apartment B, however, overall accuracy was lower and much more sensitive to transmitter placement. For example, the CNN model achieved up to $95.7\% \pm 4.8$ in Boxed-Front (A), but only $80.4\% \pm 7.1$ in Boxed-Front (B), and just $41.5\% \pm 9.3$ in Open-Left (B). These results suggest that apartment layout and construction materials–such as thinner walls, metal framing, and increased glass surface area in Apartment B–introduce signal distortions that make CSI-based sensing more difficult.

Participant-specific analysis showed no consistent differences in performance across individuals. All participants contributed data under each configuration, and no systematic advantage or disadvantage was observed (see Table 3). This suggests that in the context of this study, participant movement patterns and body types had a negligible impact on the sensing results.

Overall, these findings indicate that the sensing approach is far more sensitive to environmental structure than to user variation. Future research should further explore how spatial features like wall composition, room geometry, and signal leakage affect sensing robustness, as these are likely to be the limiting factors in real-world deployments.

6.4   Implications for Real-World Deployment

While this study demonstrates that room-level activity inference is technically feasible using external Wi-Fi sensing, the real-world implications are more limited. Even in the best-performing conditions, reliable classification required controlled settings, stable signal paths, and a highly specific apartment structure. In one apartment, semi-supervised clustering reached accuracies that could plausibly compromise a resident's privacy–suggesting that under the right conditions, passive presence detection from outside is possible.

However, replicating those conditions in practice is non-trivial. The sensing setup requires placing visible hardware near the target apartment, including a receiver mounted to an exterior wall and a transmitter positioned near the door. These placements are easy to notice and difficult to conceal, especially in residential settings. Moreover, results varied significantly across environments, indicating that signal propagation–and therefore inference reliability–is highly sensitive to building layout and materials.

In summary, while the potential for privacy intrusion exists, the barriers to practical deployment remain high. One-sided sensing may eventually become more viable as hardware improves, but under current conditions, it is more a proof of concept than an immediate surveillance threat. Further work is needed to assess how generalizable these methods are across diverse settings, and to explore possible mitigations for privacy-aware wireless design.

6.5   Strengths and Limitations

This study presents several notable strengths. First, it explores a novel and largely unexamined sensing configuration: fully external, one-sided through-wall Channel State Information sensing. This design is both technically challenging and relevant to ongoing discussions about wireless privacy. Second, the use of low-cost ESP32-C6 hardware and basic directional antennas reflects a realistic, low-resource adversarial model. Third, the dataset is substantial, consisting of over 600 min of labeled CSI recordings across two distinct apartments, with varied orientations, shielding conditions, and participant behaviors. Fourth, the study evaluates multiple machine learning strategies–including supervised, unsupervised, and semi-supervised approaches–providing a broad assessment of inference capabilities under different label availability conditions. Finally, testing was conducted in a disciplined manner, with time-of-day scheduling to reduce ambient interference and randomized activity ordering to minimize bias.

Despite these strengths, the study has important limitations. First, participant activity was not verified using video or motion sensors, so all ground truth labels rely on protocol compliance and CNN baseline performance. Any deviation from instructed behavior could have introduced labeling noise. Second, the environmental diversity was limited: experiments were conducted in only two apartments, which may not capture the variability present in other environments. Third, while recording times were chosen to avoid known peak usage periods, no quantitative measurements of background RF noise or signal-to-noise ratios were collected. As a result, the true interference conditions remain uncharacterized. Fourth, although transmitter shielding was varied (open-air vs. aluminum-lined box), the physical impact of this shielding on signal properties was not directly measured, leaving the observed performance differences difficult to interpret. Fifth, only a single CNN model architecture was evaluated. This layout was selected based on early success on initial datasets, but it is likely that alternative architectures or tuning strategies could yield even higher performance across some configurations. Sixth, for semi-supervised clustering, only a single level of supervision was tested–that is, a fixed number of labeled samples was used to define must-link and cannot-link constraints. It remains possible that using fewer or more labeled samples could significantly affect both clustering accuracy and variability, particularly for MPCK-Means-M-F.

7   Conclusion

This paper explored the feasibility of one-sided through-wall human activity recognition using commodity Wi-Fi hardware. By collecting over 600 min of CSI data across two residential environments, we evaluated the performance of supervised, unsupervised, and semi-supervised learning models in classifying room-level presence from outside the building. Results showed that high classification accuracy is achievable in structurally favorable settings, even without interior access or line-of-sight.

However, performance varied significantly across apartments, indicating that environmental factors such as wall composition, layout, and signal multipath effects play a critical role in sensing reliability. Among the evaluated methods, supervised CNN models performed best, while semi-supervised clustering showed promise in low-label scenarios, though with higher variance.

The main goal of this paper was to explore the research question *"To what extent can Wi-Fi CSI collected from outside a building be used to infer room-level occupancy indoors?"* Overall, the findings demonstrate that external Wi-Fi sensing can enable spatial inference under the right conditions, but its effectiveness remains highly context-dependent. Future work should focus on improving robustness across diverse environments.

A   CNN Architecture

The CNN model used for supervised classification consists of two convolutional layers followed by max pooling, a flattening operation, and two fully connected layers. The final layer outputs class probabilities via softmax activation. The detailed architecture is summarized in Table 1.

AI Statement

Portions of this paper were refactored using OpenAI's ChatGPT-4o to improve clarity, structure, and academic tone. All analysis, results, and interpretations are original, and full responsibility for the content remains with the author.

Table 1. CNN architecture used for CSI-based activity classification

Layer	Description
Input	$40 \times 52 \times 1$ CSI window
Conv2D	32 filters, 2×2, ReLU, same padding
MaxPooling2D	3×3
Conv2D	16 filters, 2×2, ReLU, same padding
MaxPooling2D	2×2
Flatten	–
Dense	64 units, ReLU
Dropout	0.1
Dense	Softmax, output = number of classes

B   Detailed Results

This section presents the complete classification results across all experimental conditions. Table 2 summarizes the performance of all models–including supervised (CNN), unsupervised (K-Means, GMM), and semi-supervised (MPCK-Means-M-F, COP-KMeans)–across different apartment setups and transmitter configurations. Table 3 provides a detailed breakdown of performance by participant for both apartments, reporting accuracy and F_1-scores for each model.

Table 2. Performance comparison of supervised (CNN) and clustering-based (K-Means, GMM, MPCK-Means-M-F, COP-KMeans) methods across apartment setups. All values are mean $\pm$ standard deviation in percentage.

Apartment	Setup	CNN		K-Means		GMM		MPCK-Means-M-F		COP-KMeans	
		Accuracy	F_1-score	Accuracy	F_1-score	Accuracy	F_1-score	Accuracy	F_1-score	Accuracy	F_1-score
A	Boxed-Front	96.1 ± 4.5	96.1 ± 4.5	71.6 ± 16.0	69.1 ± 17.2	80.8 ± 14.6	78.3 ± 17.7	80.3 ± 14.7	79.1 ± 15.6	72.2 ± 15.1	70.8 ± 15.8
A	Boxed-Left	92.1 ± 5.9	92.0 ± 6.0	58.0 ± 10.2	55.4 ± 13.9	71.0 ± 14.4	66.4 ± 19.4	73.4 ± 10.2	71.5 ± 12.1	60.3 ± 7.2	59.0 ± 8.4
A	Boxed-Right	93.0 ± 4.6	92.8 ± 4.8	54.0 ± 9.5	48.3 ± 9.7	66.7 ± 12.3	61.7 ± 12.9	77.4 ± 6.6	75.4 ± 7.9	57.5 ± 11.1	53.7 ± 12.5
A	Open-Front	93.8 ± 6.2	93.7 ± 6.3	65.9 ± 12.1	63.4 ± 12.5	80.1 ± 16.7	78.5 ± 18.0	78.6 ± 13.8	78.0 ± 13.8	68.3 ± 11.9	66.9 ± 12.3
A	Open-Left	91.8 ± 5.5	91.7 ± 5.7	54.1 ± 9.0	51.8 ± 7.6	67.7 ± 12.9	62.4 ± 15.3	70.9 ± 9.2	68.9 ± 9.7	55.4 ± 9.6	53.9 ± 9.2
A	Open-Right	92.9 ± 6.0	92.7 ± 6.3	55.4 ± 7.5	51.1 ± 6.7	64.8 ± 14.3	59.1 ± 17.8	72.8 ± 10.1	71.0 ± 11.2	55.3 ± 8.0	52.2 ± 8.2
B	Boxed-Front	80.6 ± 5.5	79.9 ± 6.0	55.9 ± 1.9	54.0 ± 3.5	49.7 ± 2.5	47.6 ± 3.6	62.9 ± 10.9	62.3 ± 10.8	61.2 ± 10.7	60.3 ± 11.3
B	Boxed-Left	79.2 ± 10.0	78.7 ± 10.2	45.3 ± 9.1	46.2 ± 9.8	47.3 ± 8.7	47.8 ± 10.0	50.3 ± 10.8	50.5 ± 11.0	45.6 ± 8.8	46.4 ± 9.6
B	Boxed-Right	66.2 ± 11.7	65.2 ± 12.4	44.1 ± 0.9	44.0 ± 1.6	39.2 ± 5.5	36.9 ± 5.7	48.1 ± 4.9	47.6 ± 5.1	44.7 ± 1.8	44.4 ± 1.7
B	Open-Front	76.5 ± 6.3	76.2 ± 6.5	45.9 ± 6.9	44.7 ± 8.9	43.6 ± 2.4	39.9 ± 5.7	46.7 ± 5.5	45.9 ± 5.7	47.4 ± 6.6	46.9 ± 7.4
B	Open-Left	43.7 ± 8.9	42.5 ± 9.0	36.2 ± 5.7	36.2 ± 5.8	36.5 ± 7.0	35.9 ± 7.0	37.0 ± 5.9	37.0 ± 6.0	37.1 ± 5.5	37.0 ± 5.6
B	Open-Right	69.8 ± 8.1	69.1 ± 8.6	54.7 ± 7.5	52.9 ± 8.5	57.3 ± 9.7	55.3 ± 10.2	57.9 ± 9.6	57.9 ± 9.8	56.1 ± 8.5	56.1 ± 9.4

Table 3. Performance comparison per participant for supervised (CNN) and clustering-based (K-Means, GMM, MPCK-Means-M-F, COP-KMeans) methods across apartments. All values are mean ± standard deviation in percentage.

Participant	Apartment	CNN		K-Means		GMM		MPCK-Means-M-F		COP-KMeans	
		Accuracy	F_1-score	Accuracy	F_1-score	Accuracy	F_1-score	Accuracy	F_1-score	Accuracy	F_1-score
Participant 1	A	92.2 ± 6.0	92.1 ± 6.2	58.6 ± 13.1	55.7 ± 14.1	67.2 ± 15.0	63.3 ± 16.7	73.9 ± 12.1	72.6 ± 12.5	59.6 ± 12.4	57.6 ± 13.2
Participant 2	A	94.7 ± 4.4	94.7 ± 4.5	61.8 ± 13.2	59.0 ± 14.3	75.9 ± 14.6	72.6 ± 17.3	79.2 ± 11.0	78.0 ± 11.9	63.4 ± 13.2	61.7 ± 14.0
Participant 3	A	92.9 ± 6.1	92.7 ± 6.3	59.1 ± 12.1	54.7 ± 13.0	72.4 ± 15.9	67.4 ± 20.6	73.7 ± 10.7	71.3 ± 12.2	61.5 ± 11.8	58.9 ± 12.7
Participant 1	B	64.8 ± 16.6	64.0 ± 17.0	41.4 ± 9.2	40.3 ± 9.6	39.1 ± 7.4	37.1 ± 7.5	45.3 ± 10.0	45.0 ± 10.0	41.6 ± 8.3	41.2 ± 8.5
Participant 2	B	70.6 ± 14.7	69.8 ± 15.2	48.1 ± 7.0	46.8 ± 5.2	49.4 ± 10.2	46.6 ± 10.9	55.3 ± 13.5	54.8 ± 13.5	52.9 ± 12.4	52.8 ± 12.4
Participant 3	B	72.6 ± 13.2	72.0 ± 13.5	51.6 ± 7.6	51.9 ± 8.2	48.3 ± 7.0	47.9 ± 7.9	50.7 ± 9.0	50.8 ± 9.2	51.6 ± 7.6	51.7 ± 8.3

References

1. Liu, J., et al.: Wireless sensing for human activity: a survey. IEEE Commun. Surv. Tutorials **22**(3), 1629–1645 (2019). https://doi.org/10.1109/COMST.2019.2934489
2. Mosleh, S., et al.: Monitoring respiratory motion with wi-fi csi: Characterizing performance and the breathesmart algorithm IEEE Access **10**, 131 932–131 951 (2022). https://doi.org/10.1109/ACCESS.2022.3230003
3. Sruthi, P., Satapathy, S., Udgata, S.K.: Handfi: wifi sensing based hand gesture recognition using channel state information. Procedia Comput. Sci. **235**, 426–435 (2024). https://doi.org/10.1016/j.procs.2024.04.042
4. Adib, F., Katabi, D.: See through walls with wifi!. In: Proceedings of the ACM SIGCOMM 2013 conference on SIGCOMM, pp. 75–86 (2013). https://doi.org/10.1145/2486001.2486039
5. Boudlal, H., Serrhini, M., Tahiri, A.: A monitoring system for elderly people using wifi sensing with channel state information. Int. J. Interact. Mob. Technol. **17**(12), (2023)
6. Chen, H.-H., Lin, C.-L., Chang, C.-H.: WiFi-based detection of human subtle motion for health applications. Bioengineering **10**(2), 228 (2023). issn: 2306-5354. https://doi.org/10.3390/bioengineering10020228. https://www.mdpi.com/2306-5354/10/2/228 Accessed 28 June 2025
7. Restuccia, F.: Ieee 802.11bf: toward ubiquitous wi-fi sensing (2021). https://doi.org/10.48550/ARXIV.2103.14918, https://arxiv.org/abs/2103.14918
8. Strohmayer, J., Kampel, M.: WiFi CSI-Based Long-Range Through-Wall Human Activity Recognition with the ESP32. In: Computer Vision Systems, Christensen, H.I. et al. (eds.) Springer, Cham, pp. 41–50 (2023). isbn: 978-3-031-44137-0. https://doi.org/10.1007/978-3-031-44137-0_4
9. Wang, Y., et al.: E-eyes: Device-free location-oriented activity identification using fine-grained WiFi signatures. In: Proceedings of the 20th Annual International Conference on Mobile Computing and Networking, ser. MobiCom 2014, New York, NY, USA, ACM, pp. 617–628, 7 September 2014. isbn: 978-1-4503-2783-1.https://doi.org/10.1145/2639108.2639143. Accessed 28 June 2025
10. Wang, W., et al.: Understanding and modeling of WiFi signal based human activity recognition. In: Proceedings of the 21st Annual International Conference on Mobile Computing and Networking, ser. Mobi-Com 2015, New York, NY, USA, ACM, pp. 65–76, 7 September 2015. isbn: 978-1-4503-3619-2. https://doi.org/10.1145/2789168.2790093 Accessed 29 April 2025
11. Halperin, D., et al.: Tool release: gathering 802.11 n traces with channel state information. ACM SIGCOMM Comput. Commun. Rev. **41**(1), 53 (2011). https://doi.org/10.1145/1925861.1925870

12. Yousefi, S., et al.: A survey on behavior recognition using wifi channel state information. IEEE Commun. Mag. **55**, 98–104 (2017). https://doi.org/10.1109/MCOM.2017.1700082

13. Wang, D., et al.: Multimodal CSI-based human activity recognition using GANs. IEEE Internet Things J. **PP**, 1 (2021). https://doi.org/10.1109/JIOT.2021.3080401

14. Xie, Y., Xiong, J., Jamieson, K.: Atheros csi tool, Princeton University, Technical Report, 2015, Technical report. https://wands.sg/research/wifi/AtherosCSI/

15. Gringoli, F., et al.: Free your csi: a channel state information extraction platform for modern wi-fi chipsets. Comput. Commun. **133**, 79–90 (2019). https://doi.org/10.1145/3349623.3355477

16. Hernandez, S.M., Bulut, E.: Lightweight and standalone IoT based WiFi sensing for active repositioning and mobility. In: 21st International Symposium on "A World of Wireless, Mobile and Multimedia Networks" (WoWMoM) 2020), Cork, Ireland, June 2020. https://doi.org/10.1109/WoWMoM49955.2020.00056

17. Hernandez, S.M., Bulut, E.: Adversarial occupancy monitoring using one-sided through-wall WiFi sensing. In: ICC 2021 - IEEE International Conference on Communications, pp. 1–6, June 2021. https://doi.org/10.1109/ICC42927.2021.9500267, https://ieeexplore.ieee.org/document/9500267 Accessed 22 April 2025

18. Lecun, Y., et al.: Gradient-based learning applied to document recognition. Proc. IEEE **86**(11), 2278–2324 (1998). issn: 1558-2256. https://doi.org/10.1109/5.726791, https://ieeexplore.ieee.org/document/726791 Accessed 24 June 2025

19. MacQueen, J.: Some methods for classification and analysis of multivariate observations (1967). https://api.semanticscholar.org/CorpusID:6278891

20. Dempster, A.P., Laird, N.M., Rubin, D.B.: Maximum likelihood from incomplete data via the EM algorithm. J. Royal Stat. Soc. Ser. B (Methodol.) **39**(1), 1–22 (1977). issn: 0035-9246. https://doi.org/10.1111/j.2517-6161.1977.tb01600.x Accessed 24 June 2025

21. Bilenko, M., Basu, S., Mooney, R.J.: Integrating constraints and metric learning in semi-supervised clustering. In: Twenty-First International Conference on Machine Learning - ICML 2004, Banff, Alberta, Canada, ACM Press, p. 11 (2004). https://doi.org/10.1145/1015330.1015360, http://portal.acm.org/citation.cfm?doid=1015330.1015360 Accessed 24 June 2025

22. Wagstaff, K., et al.: Constrained k-means clustering with background knowledge. In: Proceedings of the Eighteenth International Conference on Machine Learning, ser. ICML 2001, San Francisco, CA, USA, Morgan Kaufmann Publishers Inc., pp. 577–584, 28 June 2001. isbn: 978-1-55860-778-1. https://web.cse.msu.edu/~cse802/notes/ConstrainedKmeans.pdf

23. Espressif Systems. ESP32-C6 Wi-Fi 6 & BLE 5 & Thread/Zigbee SoC, Espressif Systems. (2025). https://www.espressif.com/en/products/socs/esp32-c6 Accessed 15 June 2025

24. Espressif/esp-csi, Espressif Systems, 13 June 2025. https://github.com/espressif/esp-csi Accessed 15 June 2025

25. Alfa Network. APA-M25 dual-band directional panel antenna (2025). https://alfa-network.eu/apa-m25 Accessed 15 June 2025

26. Random.org. RANDOM.ORG - List Randomizer (2025). https://www.random.org/lists/ Accessed 22 June 2025

27. Pearson, R.K., et al.: Generalized hampel filters. EURASIP J. Adv. Sig. Process. **2016**(1), 87 (2016). issn: 1687-6180. https://doi.org/10.1186/s13634-016-0383-6 Accessed 25 June 2025

28. Smith, J.O.: Spectral Audio Signal Processing (2025), Online book (2011) ed. https://ccrma.stanford.edu/~jos/sasp/ Accessed 22 June 2025
29. Donoho, D.L., Johnstone, I.M.: Ideal spatial adaptation by wavelet shrinkage. Biometrika **81**(3), 425–455 (1994). issn: 0006-3444. https://doi.org/10.1093/biomet/81.3.425 Accessed 25 June 2025
30. Gao, J., Hu, W., Chen, Y.: Revisiting pca for time series reduction in temporal dimension (2024). arXiv:2412.19423 [cs.LG]. https://arxiv.org/abs/2412.19423

Hue4U: Real-Time Personalized Color Correction in Augmented Reality

Jingwen Qin[1]([✉]) [iD], Semen Checherin[1] [iD], Yue Li[2] [iD],
Berend-Jan van der Zwaag[1] [iD], and Özlem Durmaz Incel[1] [iD]

[1] Faculty of EEMCS, University of Twente, Enschede, The Netherlands
gwen.qin@utwente.nl
[2] Faculty of BMS, University of Twente, Enschede, The Netherlands

Abstract. Color Vision Deficiency (CVD) affects nearly 8% of men and 0.5% of women worldwide. Existing color correction methods often rely on prior clinical diagnosis and static filtering, making them less effective for users with mild or moderate CVD. In this paper, we introduce Hue4U, a personalized, real-time color correction system in Augmented Reality using consumer-grade Meta Quest headsets. Unlike previous methods, our Hue4U requires no prior medical diagnosis and adapts to the user in real time. A user study with 10 participants showed notable improvements in their ability to distinguish colours. The results demonstrated large effect sizes (Cohen's $d > 1.4$), suggesting clinically meaningful gains for individuals with CVD. These findings highlight the potential of personalized AR interventions to improve visual accessibility and quality of life for people affected by CVD.

Keywords: Color Vision Deficiency · Augmented Reality · Personalized Color Correction

1 Introduction

Color Vision Deficiency (CVD) is a common, yet often overlooked, sensory condition that affects approximately 8% of men and 0.5% of women globally [9]. It is caused by anomalies in one or more types of cone photo-receptors (L-cones, M-cones, and S-cones) in the retina, leading to varying degrees of difficulty in distinguishing specific hues. The severity of symptoms can vary widely between individuals. There are two major types of color vision deficiency (CVD): dichromacy, in which one of the three cone types is completely non-functional, making certain colors impossible to perceive; and anomalous trichromacy, where all three cone types are present but one functions abnormally. These deficiencies are further categorized as protan, deutan, and tritan. Although CVD is not life-threatening, it can significantly impact daily life, especially in tasks where color discrimination is essential, for example, selecting food products, cooking, playing sports, or choosing clothing. It can also limit professional opportunities in fields such as aviation, engineering, graphic design, and certain military roles.

O. Durmaz Incel et al. (Eds.): iWOAR 2025, LNCS 16292, pp. 20–37, 2026.
https://doi.org/10.1007/978-3-032-13312-0_2

Furthermore, difficulties in interpreting color-coded information can lead to frustration and social challenges, ultimately reducing the overall quality of life [7]. Currently, there is no medical cure for CVD.

Several digital and optical tools are used to address these challenges, including Daltonization filters [14], contrast-enhancing overlays, and wearable color correction lenses. For example, Tang [11] developed AR-based contrast-enhancing overlays using Daltonization to assist red–green CVD, while Tian [12] introduced inverse-designed contact lenses that optically shift colors to match individual photoreceptor sensitivities. However, most of these methods require users to first obtain a clinical diagnosis of their CVD type, even though many individuals are undiagnosed and unaware of their condition. In addition, these solutions typically apply static transformations optimized for severe dichromacy, neglecting the more common cases of mild or moderate anomalous trichromacy. As a result, such "one-size-fits-all" approaches fail to address the broad spectrum of CVD severity and provide only limited solutions to most users.

Augmented Reality (AR) technologies offer a promising way to enhance visual accessibility with more interactive methods. AR, typically delivered through Head-Mounted Displays (HMDs), enables users to remain fully aware of their physical surroundings while overlaying digital content onto the real world. This makes AR particularly well-suited for color correction tasks, such as identifying food, clothing, or traffic signals in daily life. In addition, AR platforms can support personalized color filtering without interrupting natural interactions.

This work addresses the research question of how to design a real-time, personalized color correction system in AR that improves color discrimination for individuals with CVD without prior clinical diagnosis. To solve this issue, we present an AR-based personalized color correction, named Hue4U, to develop a personalized color correction system for CVD users, including on-device CVD estimation and real-time color transformation. Our Hue4U system consists of two key components: (1) an interactive color vision assessment module integrated into an AR environment, and (2) a real-time color correction module that applies user-specific transformations based on the estimated CVD type and severity. The novelty of this work lies in the fact that the entire pipeline operates within AR, requires no prior clinical diagnosis, and adapts to the user's individual color perception profile. Another important aspect is the implementation and evaluation of the Hue4U system on modern, consumer-grade, and widely accessible Meta Quest. We recruited 10 participants with varying degrees and types of CVD. Each participant first completed a standardized assessment to determine their specific CVD profile. Based on these results, a personalized color correction filter was applied for real-time rendering in the AR environment. We evaluate our Hue4U system using quantitative metrics, including pre- and post-correction performance on Ishihara plate tests [3]. Our results show consistent improvements in color discrimination, with most participants able to identify significantly more plates after correction. We make the following key contributions:

- We propose Hue4U, a real-time, personalized color correction system in AR that improves color discrimination for individuals with CVD without requiring prior clinical diagnosis.
- We design an adapted FM 100 test on HMD with hand controllers in mixed lighting environments, considering user fatigue and display limitations.
- We apply an existing Daltonization method in a novel way by integrating severity-adaptive, per-pixel color correction into Unity's shaders, enabling personalized real-time recoloring for AR content based on each user's CVD profile.
- We conduct a user study with 10 participants, showing statistically significant improvements in Ishihara test performance after color correction, with large effect sizes (Cohen's $d > 1.4$).

The remainder of this paper is organized as follows: Sect. 2 reviews related work on CVD assessment, color simulation, and recoloring methods. Section 3 details our methodology, including the Hue4U system architecture, CVD assessment, recoloring, and rendering techniques. Section 4 describes the experimental setup, including hardware and development environment. Section 5 presents the quantitative assessment procedure and evaluation of filter efficacy. Finally, Sect. 6 concludes the paper and outlines directions for future work.

2 Related Work

2.1 CVD Assessment

A CVD test is a diagnostic tool used to identify the type and severity of color vision deficiency. In our Hue4U system, we use CVD tests to establish the ground truth—determining whether individuals are color blind and assessing the severity of their symptoms. It is essential since most people have never been formally diagnosed and therefore do not know if they have CVD or how severe their condition is. Additionally, after applying our real-time color correction module, we use CVD tests again to evaluate how effectively users can perceive colors.

The most popular test is the Ishihara plate test [3], first developed in 1917 to detect deficiencies in the medium- and long-wavelength (M-L) cones. The test consists of several plates, each displaying a circle made up of dots in varying colors, brightnesses, and sizes, shown in Fig. 1. Embedded within these dots is a number or path formed by slightly different colors. Individuals with CVD may either fail to see the number or path or may perceive a different figure altogether. The Ishihara test is simple, quick, non-invasive, and easy to administer. However, it does not effectively quantify the severity of color vision deficiency. Moreover, the Ishihara test primarily targets red-green deficiencies, it was not made to estimate tritanopia (a complete absence of S-cones in the eye). Additionally, individuals with acquired CVD may have unusual or distorted cone sensitivities, causing them to perceive colors differently than expected [10]. Such individuals might still pass the Ishihara test despite having a color vision problem. Another widely used test is the Farnsworth-Munsell 100-Hue test (FM 100 test), designed

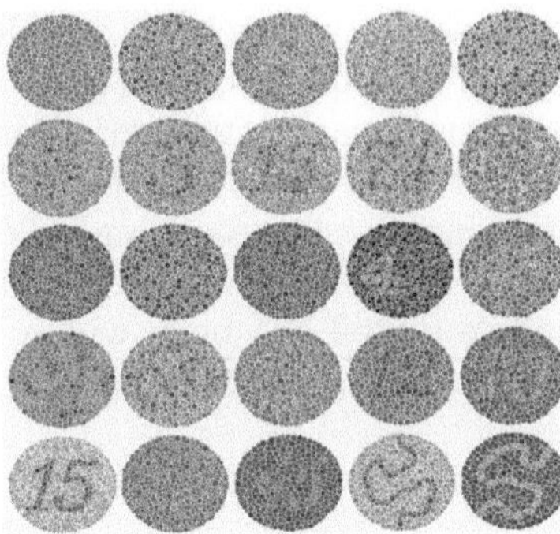

Fig. 1. Sample Ishihara Plates Used in the Study: Examples of the Ishihara plates presented to participants during the color discrimination tests. A total of 25 plates were used to evaluate the participants' CVD both before and after applying personalized color correction in the AR environment.

by Farnsworth [13]. This test includes 85 colored caps distributed across four trays, with hues gradually changing within each tray. Participants are asked to arrange the caps in order of hue progression to create a smooth color transition. The FM 100 test is highly recommended for detecting and diagnosing acquired color vision deficiencies. Unlike the Ishihara test, which primarily screens for red-green CVD, the FM 100 test can detect all types of color vision deficiencies and assess how severe their deficiencies are. There are also simplified versions of the FM 100 test, such as the D15 test, which uses only 15 colored caps [5]. However, these shorter tests are less sensitive to mild color vision deficiencies and do not provide detailed information on the severity of the condition.

2.2 CVD Color Simulation

Individuals with CVD perceive colors differently from those with normal vision. Researchers have developed image recoloring techniques that adjust the colors in images to enhance color distinguishability. In our Hue4U system, we employ the color simulation method to simulate how an image would appear to a person with CVD. We then use this simulation to compute the color discrepancy between the original image and its CVD-simulated counterpart. This allows us to quantify potential perceptual errors and design targeted color correction strategies.

Brettel [1] developed one of the earliest and most influential computerized simulations of CVD. Their method converts images from the RGB color space to the LMS color space, which models the response of the human eye's three types of cones (long-, medium-, and short-wavelength). It then simulates the absence of one cone type by projecting the color information onto a confusion line based on the remaining cones [1]. In this way, it simulates how images appear to individuals with dichromacy. However, it does not simulate anomalous trichromacy, where all three cones are present but function abnormally.

Machado [6] proposed a more advanced and physiologically accurate simulation. Their model first converts image colors into a physiologically relevant color space, then applies severity parameters to adjust the colors, and finally transforms the result back into the RGB color space [6]. This method supports both dichromacy and anomalous trichromacy and allows for the simulation of varying degrees of color vision deficiency through the use of severity parameters. Additionally, since Machado's model has been widely implemented in existing software frameworks, it is practical, accessible, and easy to integrate into applications.

2.3 CVD Recoloring

Individuals with CVD have difficulty distinguishing certain colors. Color correction techniques aim to enhance the contrast and visibility of these indistinguishable colors without making the overall image appear unnatural. Among the most widely used correction methods are Daltonization [2] and Natural-Preserving Recoloring [15].

Daltonization first simulates how an image appears to a CVD person using color vision simulation techniques. The system compares the original and simulated images to detect and restore lost color contrasts [2]. Due to its computational efficiency and speed, Daltonization is well-suited for real-time applications. However, most Daltonization algorithms are based on dichromacy and rely on fixed color mappings. As a result, they do not account for the varying severity of CVD and may produce visually unnatural results for users with anomalous trichromacy.

To address this limitation, Zhu [16] proposed a Natural-Preserving Recoloring algorithm, which improves color distinguishability while maintaining the overall natural appearance of the image. This method first simulates CVD perception and then optimizes color adjustments to balance enhanced contrast with visual fidelity [16]. Although this approach is more visually subtle and user-friendly—particularly for individuals with anomalous trichromacy—it is computationally expensive and unsuitable for real-time systems, requiring approximately thirty seconds to process a single image. Given the real-time requirements of AR systems, we consider Daltonization to be the more feasible approach for practical deployment.

3 Methodology

3.1 System Architecture

Hue4U is an end-to-end system for CVD assessment and personalized visual correction in a Unity-based AR environment. It translates user input from an integrated color vision test into personalized color correction for virtual AR content. It consists of three primary components shown in Fig. 2. The CVD Assessment module implements a modified version of the FM 100 Test to evaluate both the type and severity of CVD. Users interact with colored tiles that must be reordered to form perceptual hue gradients. Based on the arrangement errors, the Hue4U system computes a cumulative error score and classifies the CVD type and severity. The CVD Recoloring module applies personalized color correction based on the results of the CVD assessment. Utilizing custom real-time shaders, it performs personalized Daltonization to enhance color discriminability according to the user's specific CVD profile. AR Rendering integrates color correction into Unity's Universal Render Pipeline (URP) via custom pixel shaders. These shaders apply per-pixel Daltonization in real time, adjusting the color output of virtual objects based on the user's CVD profile.

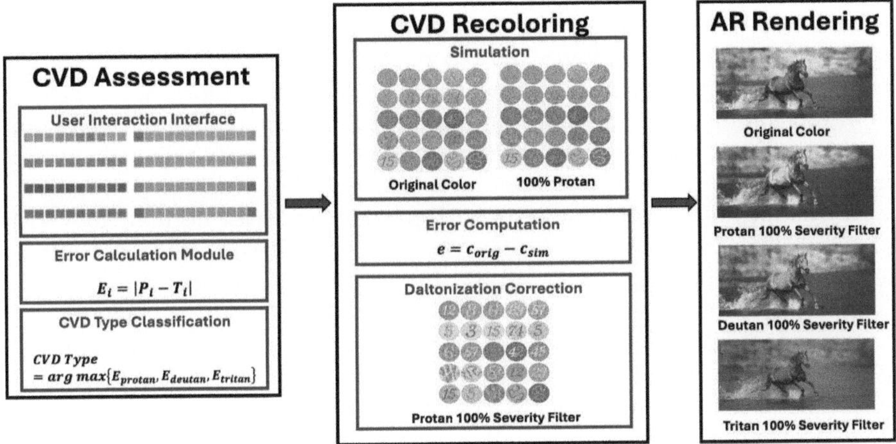

Fig. 2. Hue4U: End-to-End Pipeline for CVD Assessment and Real-Time Color Correction in AR: The workflow illustrates how to use our adapted FM 100 test results for personalized color correction for AR elements. Based on the user's rearrangement of 48 hue caps, the Hue4U system computes positional errors to classify the CVD type and estimate severity (see Sect. 3.2). This personalized CVD profile is passed to a correction controller, which selects the appropriate Daltonization parameters (Machado matrix) and forwards them to a custom Unity shader(see Sect. 3.3). The shader then performs real-time per-pixel color correction on all AR content, ensuring improved color discriminability for users with CVD (see Sect. 3.4).

3.2   CVD Assessment

Since the FM 100 test can detect all types of CVD and assess their severity, we selected this method for CVD assessment in our Hue4U system.

Adapted FM 100 Test. The original FM 100 test requires the arrangement of 85 color caps distributed across four trays. However, directly implementing this test in an AR HMD setup presents several challenges. Although the Meta

Quest 3 HMD offers high resolution and improved color contrast and brightness compared to earlier versions, it uses LCD panels with a limited color gamut. As a result, some subtle hues may not be rendered accurately. Displaying all 85 hues can lead to indistinguishable colors, particularly those near the limits of the device's display capabilities. Moreover, completing the full 85-cap test in AR is both cognitively and physically demanding for users when using handheld controllers. To reduce user fatigue while maintaining diagnostic effectiveness, we opted for a shorter version of the test. However, reducing the number of caps to 48 does not compromise our test's accuracy, as the diagnostic outcome is not based on the number of caps. Therefore, our adapted version still provides reliable identification of CVD type and severity.

Additionally, ambient lighting and background colors in the physical environment can influence the perceived colors of AR elements in HMD. To reduce these effects, we introduced a virtual white board behind the test interface. In this way, it minimizes changes in contrast due to lighting, eliminates background color interference, and ensures a more consistent and visually reliable user experience.

We conducted several pilot tests with participants with normal color vision and asked them to report perceived color differences. Based on these results, we selected 48 caps instead of the full 85. Increasing the number of caps beyond this point introduced difficulty in distinguishing between adjacent hues.

Our revised FM 100 test is implemented in two formats: one version runs on the HMD for our Hue4U system, and the other on a standard laptop to obtain the ground truth CVD profile. In the HMD version, users interact with the caps using handheld controllers, while in the desktop version, they use a mouse. Same as in the original test, the first and last caps of each row are fixed, and users must rearrange the intermediate caps to form a smooth hue transition from left to right. The interface includes visual and haptic feedback and automatically aligns the selection ray toward the nearest cap. In this way, it enhances usability, intuitiveness, and overall user experience.

Design and Implementation. Our adapted test comprises four rows. And same as the original FM 100 test, the first and last caps of each row are fixed reference points that define the boundaries of the hue gradient. However, instead of 21 movable caps per row, our version employs 11 movable caps per row, resulting in a total of 48 movable caps across all four rows. Each row represents a hue gradient between two predefined anchor colors. Table 1 summarizes the hue transitions and their corresponding diagnostic targets across the four rows of our adapted FM 100 test. Figure 3 illustrates the implementation of the adapted FM 100 test in an AR environment. Each row represents a controlled gradient between two anchor colors selected to evaluate specific types of CVD. These anchors were carefully selected to span hue transitions most relevant for detecting the three major types of color vision deficiencies. The RGB values of the four anchor colors used in our system are the same as the original FM 100 test:

– Red: (0.75, 0.40, 0.40)

- Yellow-Green: (0.30, 0.67, 0.33)
- Cyan-Green: (0.10, 0.65, 0.65)
- Blue-Purple: (0.52, 0.46, 0.71)

To generate perceptually accurate intermediate hues between these anchors, we interpolate the colors in the Hue-Saturation-Value (HSV) color space rather than in standard RGB. Since RGB interpolation often results in variations in saturation, it can compromise the perceptual consistency required for accurate color vision testing. However, HSV space maintains constant saturation and brightness to ensure only hue varies throughout each gradient. Once the interpolation is complete, the resulting values are converted back to RGB for rendering in AR environment.

Fig. 3. Adapted FM100 Test in AR Environment: Users drag colorful caps from the randomized collection on the left side of the interface to the corresponding grey slots on the right, arranging them to form a smooth hue gradient. The first and last squares in each row of the right side of the interface are fixed reference colors that define the gradient boundaries. (Color figure online)

Table 1. Hue Ranges and Corresponding CVD Types in the Adapted FM 100 Test.

Row	Caps Range	Hue Range	Related CVD Types
1	1–12	Red → Yellow-Green	Protan, Deutan
2	13–24	Yellow-Green → Cyan-Green	Deutan
3	25–36	Cyan-Green → Blue-Purple	Tritan
4	37–48	Blue-Purple → Red	Protan, Tritan

Cap Error and Total Error Score. Each of the four rows in our test contains $n = 11$ movable hue caps. For each cap i, let P_i denote the *actual position* of the cap after user reordering, and T_i be the *target position* in the correct hue gradient. The **cap error** is defined as:

$$E_i = |P_i - T_i| \tag{1}$$

The total error for one row is the sum of individual cap errors:

$$E_{\text{row}} = \sum_{i=1}^{n} E_i \tag{2}$$

The total error across all four rows is calculated as:

$$E_{\text{total}} = \sum_{r=1}^{4} E_{\text{row}_r} \tag{3}$$

To make the error score comparable to the original FM 100 test, which uses 85 movable caps, we normalize the error by scaling it:

$$E_{\text{scaled}} = \frac{E_{\text{total}}}{48} \times 85 \tag{4}$$

This scaled error score serves as an estimate of the severity of the user's color vision deficiency.

CVD Type Classification. Accordingly, we calculate cumulative error scores associated with each CVD type:

$$E_{\text{protan}} = E_{\text{row}_1} + E_{\text{row}_4} \tag{5}$$
$$E_{\text{deutan}} = E_{\text{row}_1} + E_{\text{row}_2} \tag{6}$$
$$E_{\text{tritan}} = E_{\text{row}_3} + E_{\text{row}_4} \tag{7}$$

The CVD type is classified based on the highest cumulative error:

$$\text{CVD Type} = \arg\max \{E_{\text{protan}}, E_{\text{deutan}}, E_{\text{tritan}}\} \tag{8}$$

This error-based classification allows our shortened FM 100 test to effectively detect and differentiate between protan, deutan, and tritan color vision deficiencies, while also estimating CVD severity in a scaled and interpretable manner.

3.3   CVD Recoloring

To enhance accessibility for users with CVD, we adopt a Daltonization-based color correction strategy. Our method follows a standard three-stage pipeline: simulation, error computation, and correction. By integrating a parameterized model of color perception loss, our Hue4U system enables real-time, personalized recoloring based on an individual's CVD type and severity level. Figure 4 demonstrates after 3 stages of our CVD recoloring method, how color perception progressively changes with increasing severity of protan deficiency.

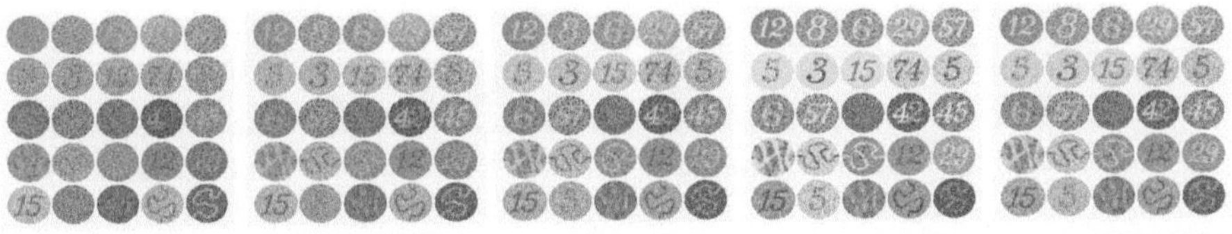

Fig. 4. Visualization of the 25 Ishihara Plate after CVD recoloring: This figure illustrates the visual appearance of the 25 Ishihara plate as perceived by individuals with varying severity of protan CVD. From left to right, the images display the original plate, followed by protan recoloring filters applied at 20%, 40%, 60%, and 100% severity levels.

Simulation. In the first stage, we simulate how colors appear to individuals with a specific type and severity of CVD. The method proposed by Machado [6] provides a set of transformation matrices that transform between normal and CVD individuals. These matrices are parameterized by a severity value $s \in [0, 1]$, where $s = 0$ represents normal color vision and $s = 1$ corresponds to complete color blindness. Given an input color vector

$$\mathbf{c}_{\text{orig}} = \begin{bmatrix} R \\ G \\ B \end{bmatrix}, \tag{9}$$

the simulated color $\mathbf{c}_{\text{sim}}$ for a given CVD type and severity level is calculated as:

$$\mathbf{c}_{\text{sim}} = M_{\text{CVD}}(s) \cdot \mathbf{c}_{\text{orig}}, \tag{10}$$

where $M_{\text{CVD}}(s)$ is the transformation matrix corresponding to the specified CVD type and severity.

Error Computation. The second stage involves calculating the difference between the original color and its corresponding CVD simulation. This difference represents the color information lost due to CVD:

$$\mathbf{e} = \mathbf{c}_{\text{orig}} - \mathbf{c}_{\text{sim}}. \tag{11}$$

Daltonization Correction. In the final stage, the error is redistributed across visible color channels via a predefined correction matrix C_{type}. The corrected color $\mathbf{c}_{\text{corr}}$ is calculated as:

$$\mathbf{c}_{\text{corr}} = \mathbf{c}_{\text{orig}} + C_{\text{type}} \cdot \mathbf{e} \tag{12}$$

This process shifts the original color so that it enhances its perceptual distinguishability for the CVD viewer, without introducing significant visual artifacts for individuals with normal color vision.

Fig. 5. AR rendering output using our Hue4U system: From left to right: (1) Original color perception in AR; (2) Protan (100% severity); (3) Deutan (100% severity); (4) Tritan (100% severity).

3.4 AR Rendering

Our Hue4U system renders virtual objects in AR using URP to ensure real-time performance and accuracy. We apply Daltonization on a per-pixel basis in URP. This enables continuous and fine-grained correction adjustments directly within the scene, using high-precision floating-point color computations. This shader independently executes the three-stage process described in Sect. 3.3. Simulation matrices for each CVD type and severity are stored within a separate class and accessed by a correction controller at runtime. Based on the user's estimated CVD profile, the controller loads the corresponding Machado matrix. The shader then computes and applies the Daltonization correction in real-time, preserving critical color characteristics for CVD users. Due to the simplicity of our AR scene, per-pixel correction remains computationally efficient while maintaining smooth performance on Meta Quest 3. Figure 5 illustrates the AR rendering results, including the original AR view and various filtered renderings.

4 Experimental Setup

4.1 Implementation and Experimental Setup

Our Hue4U system is developed using Unity 2022.3 LTS and URP as a standard for rendering in AR applications. To ensure broad compatibility across various HMDs, we integrate OpenXR [4] for control and input management. Additionally, we utilize MetaSDK 77, which provides streamlined access to pass-through APIs, enabling precise and efficient color correction.

Among the many available HMD options, we selected the Meta Quest 3 [8] due to its optimal balance of accessibility, technical capability, and user experience. The device features high-resolution LCD panels with enhanced color contrast and brightness. It is essential for accurately rendering subtle hue variations necessary for effective CVD assessment and correction. Furthermore, as a consumer-grade and widely accessible device, the Meta Quest 3 maximizes the social impact of our Hue4U system by delivering personalized CVD correction to a broad audience without the need for expensive hardware or prior clinical diagnosis. We log the output of our system during the experiments, and the results show that with the filter, the performance of the system is around 150ms.

Our participant pool consisted of 10 individuals, primarily exhibiting protan and deutan characteristics, which together account for over 95% of CVD cases.

Although most participants were not clinically diagnosed, initial screenings using the FM 100 test and Ishihara plates revealed deviations from normal color vision. The baseline FM 100 assessment further provided quantitative estimates of each participant's CVD type and severity. All procedures were reviewed and approved by the CIS Ethics Committee at University of Twente, and informed consent was obtained from all participants prior to the study.

4.2   Experiment Procedure

The experimental procedure for each participant is illustrated in Fig. 6. Initially, participants completed an FM 100 test on a PC to establish a ground truth regarding the type and severity of CVD. These baseline results were subsequently used for comparison with the CVD assessments conducted in the AR environment. The participants then put on the Meta Quest 3 headset and were given time to familiarize with the device. Next, they were presented with 25 Ishihara plates shown in Fig. 1, and their responses were recorded to evaluate their color discrimination ability. After conducting our adapted FM 100 Hue test on both PC and AR platforms, the results show that all participants have either protan or deutan color vision deficiencies. Therefore, the Ishihara test was selected as a reference evaluation method due to its efficiency and accuracy. This step provided a baseline measure of color perception in the AR setup without any color correction applied. Subsequently, participants performed the adapted FM 100 test within the AR environment. The results from this test served as input for our personalized recoloring systems to modify participants' color perception. Finally, participants completed the 25 Ishihara plates again, this time with the personalized color correction enabled. This structured procedure ensured consistent data collection and allowed participants to fully experience the effects of the personalized color correction before providing qualitative feedback.

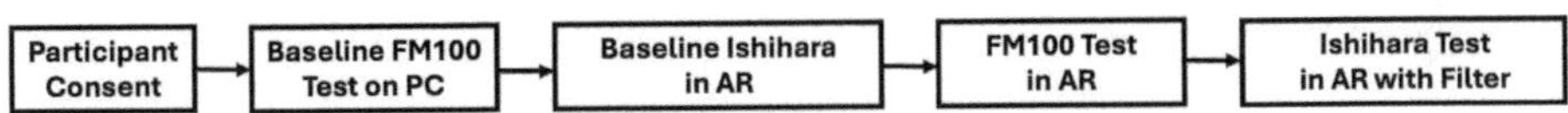

Fig. 6. Overview of the Experimental Procedure: Flowchart illustrating the tasks performed by participants during the study. The procedure includes the adopted FM 100 Test on PC for ground truth measurement, baseline Ishihara plate test in AR without color correction, the adapted FM100 test in AR used for personalized recoloring, and the final Ishihara plate test with color correction.

5   Quantitative Assessment of Filter Efficacy

5.1   Participant Assessment and Baseline Characterization

Ten participants volunteered for the experiment, representing various levels of CVD. Table 2 summarizes the results of participants' color vision assessments

Table 2. Quantitative Results of CVD Assessment and AR-Based Color Correction.

Participant ID	Desktop CVD Assessment	AR CVD Assessment	Applied Filter	Pre-Filter Ishihara (/25)	Post-Filter Ishihara (/25)
1	Protan, 30%	Protan, 50%	Protan, 50%	14	24
2	None	Protan, 30%	Protan, 30%	22	25
3	Deutan, 30%	Deutan, 30%	Deutan, 30%	20	24
4	None	Protan, 30%	Protan, 30%	21	25
5	Protan, 70%	Protan, 100%	Protan, 100%	12	24
6	Protan, 50%	Protan, 50%	Protan, 50%	11	19
7	None	Protan, 20%	Protan, 20%	12	22
8	Deutan, 40%	Deutan, 40%	Deutan, 40%	14	23
9	Protan, 60%	Protan, 60%	Protan, 60%	11	22
10	Deutan, 80%	Deutan, 70%	Deutan, 70%	7	18

and their performance on the Ishihara plate test pre and post applying personalized color correction filter in AR. The CVD type and severity were first determined through a PC-based test, followed by a reassessment within the AR environment. Based on the AR results, severity-personalized color correction filters were applied, and participants then repeated the Ishihara test. The number of correctly identified plates (out of 25) is reported for both the pre- and post-filter conditions. Notably, three participants achieved perfect scores on the desktop FM 100 test yet failed to correctly identify several Ishihara plates without color correction filter. This suggests the presence of mild trichromatic anomalies that were not captured by the FM 100 test but became evident under different testing conditions. These findings highlight the added diagnostic sensitivity of using multiple assessment tools and the practical relevance of personalized AR-based correction, even for individuals with subtle or borderline CVD profiles.

5.2   Statistical Analysis of Color Discrimination Improvements

The distribution of color blindness type and severity for all participants is presented in Fig. 7. The Ishihara Test was administered to all participants to evaluate color discrimination performance before and after filter application.

The paired-samples t-test was selected as the primary statistical method because it is specifically designed to compare two related measurements from the same participants, making it ideal for analyzing with-and-without customized filter. This within-subjects design controls for individual differences in baseline color vision abilities, providing greater statistical power than between-subjects comparisons while reducing the influence of confounding variables. The t-test assumptions were verified through normality testing of the difference scores, and the method's robustness makes it particularly suitable for the relatively small sample size typical in specialized vision research studies.

Paired-Samples t-Test Equation:

$$t = \frac{\bar{d}}{s_d/\sqrt{n}} \tag{13}$$

where:

- t = t-statistic
- $\bar{d}$ = mean of the difference scores (post-filter score - pre-filter score)
- s_d = standard deviation of the difference scores
- n = number of participants

Cohen's d Effect Size Equation:

$$d = \frac{\bar{d}}{s_d} \tag{14}$$

where:

- d = Cohen's d effect size
- $\bar{d}$ = mean of the difference scores
- s_d = standard deviation of the difference scores

Confidence Interval for Mean Difference:

$$CI = \bar{d} \pm t_{\alpha/2,df} \times \frac{s_d}{\sqrt{n}} \tag{15}$$

where:

- CI = confidence interval
- $t_{\alpha/2,df}$ = critical t-value for the desired confidence level and degrees of freedom
- $df = n - 1$ (degrees of freedom)

Paired-samples t-tests were conducted to evaluate the effectiveness of customized filters on Ishihara test scores. Table 3 presents the complete statistical analysis for both the overall sample and the subgroup of participants with CVD. Analysis of the complete sample (N = 10) revealed a statistically significant

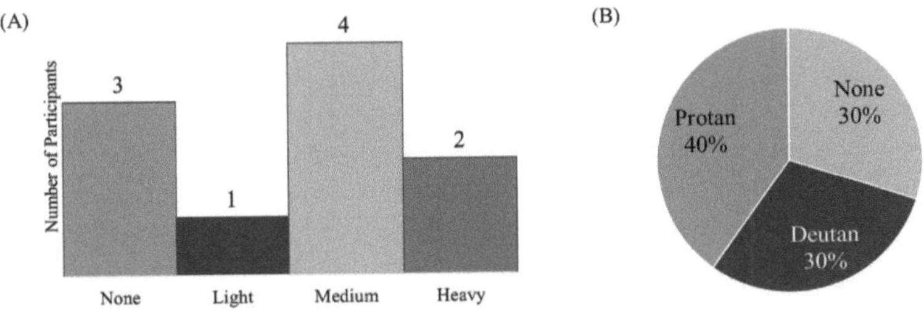

Fig. 7. Distribution of Color Blindness Among Participants: (A) Severity Histogram, (B) Type Distribution. Severity is categorized as light (10–40%), medium (50–80%).

Table 3. Paired-samples t-test results for Ishihara test scores before and after filter

Group	df	t	95% CI	p
All Participants	9	7.79	[5.82, 10.58]	< .001
Participants with CVD	6	9.13	[6.80, 11.77]	< .001

improvement in Ishihara test scores following filter use with a mean difference of 8.2 points and a large effect size (Cohen's $d = 2.46$). Among the participants with CVD ($n = 7$), this subgroup showed even greater improvement with a mean difference of 9.29 points and a large effect size (Cohen's $d = 1.45$).

The results demonstrate that customized filters significantly enhance color vision performance across all participants, with particularly pronounced benefits in individuals with CVD. The large effect sizes indicate that these improvements are not only statistically significant but also practically meaningful. These findings align with our proposal on optical filters that compensate for CVD by selectively modifying spectral composition. The particularly strong effects observed may be attributed to the customized nature of the filters, as individually tailored interventions can address specific spectral sensitivity patterns unique to each participant. While these results offer significant practical implications for individuals with CVD—providing a non-invasive intervention that could improve quality of life in color-dependent activities—the underlying mechanisms require further investigation to determine whether benefits reflect genuine color discrimination enhancement or compensatory visual strategies.

6   Discussion

6.1   Key Contributions and Findings

This paper presented the development and evaluation of the Hue4U system, a novel approach for personalized color vision CVD detection and correction using consumer-grade AR technology. Our system represents a significant advancement in accessibility by combining the established FM100 test with severity-personalized Daltonization algorithms, creating a practical solution that eliminates the need for prior clinical diagnosis while providing individualized color correction.

The results demonstrate substantial improvements in color discrimination performance following filter application. The large effect sizes (Cohen's $d > 1.4$) indicate statistically significant improvements in CVD correction. These findings are particularly pronounced among participants with CVD, who showed marked enhancement in their ability to distinguish colors that were previously problematic. The magnitude of these effects suggests that personalized filter approaches can meaningfully improve daily visual experiences for individuals with color vision deficiencies.

6.2   Theoretical and Practical Implications

Our findings contribute to the growing body of evidence supporting personalized approaches to assistive vision technology. Unlike traditional one-size-fits-all color correction methods, the Hue4U system's ability to adapt to individual severity levels represents a paradigm shift toward precision-based visual aids. This personalization is crucial because CVD manifests with considerable individual variation in both type and severity, necessitating tailored interventions.

From a practical standpoint, the integration with consumer-grade AR devices democratizes access to sophisticated color vision assistance. This approach has significant implications for educational settings, workplace accommodations, and daily life activities where color discrimination is essential. The system's non-invasive, real-time correction capabilities could particularly benefit individuals in color-critical professions or educational contexts.

6.3   Study Limitations and Future Research Directions

Several limitations should be acknowledged when interpreting these findings, which also inform important directions for future research. The relatively small sample size ($N = 10$), while appropriate for specialized vision research and sufficient to detect large effects, may limit the generalizability of findings across diverse populations and CVD subtypes. The participant pool's demographic characteristics and the specific types of CVD represented may not fully capture the broader spectrum of color vision deficiencies in the general population. Future investigations should address this limitation by expanding the sample size and diversifying participant demographics to strengthen the generalizability of findings and enable subgroup analyses based on CVD type and severity. Recruiting participants across different age groups, occupational backgrounds, and cultural contexts would provide insights into the system's effectiveness across varied populations.

Additionally, this study relied exclusively on laboratory-based color discrimination testing using the FM100 protocol, which may not fully capture real-world color vision performance. The controlled laboratory environment differs substantially from the complex, variable lighting conditions and diverse color contexts individuals encounter in daily life. To address this limitation, future studies should investigate the system's performance across diverse environmental conditions—including varying lighting, outdoor settings, and complex visual scenes—to provide crucial validation for practical deployment.

The current methodology focuses solely on quantitative pre- and post-test measurements, potentially missing important qualitative aspects of the user experience. Future research would benefit from incorporating mixed-methods approaches that combine quantitative performance measures with qualitative user experience data. Structured interviews and subjective reports could provide valuable insights into user satisfaction, perceived effectiveness, and real-world application challenges. Such qualitative data would complement objective performance metrics and inform system refinements.

Furthermore, longitudinal studies examining the persistence of benefits over extended periods of filter use are essential for understanding the technology's long-term effectiveness. Questions remain about potential adaptation effects, user compliance, and sustained improvement in real-world color vision tasks. These studies would address current gaps in understanding the system's effectiveness beyond immediate laboratory testing and provide critical insights for real-world implementation and long-term user adoption.

References

1. Brettel, H., Viénot, F., Mollon, J.D.: Computerized simulation of color appearance for dichromats **14**(10), 2647–2655. https://doi.org/10.1364/JOSAA.14.002647, https://opg.optica.org/josaa/abstract.cfm?uri=josaa-14-10-2647, publisher: Optica Publishing Group
2. Dalton, J.: Extraordinary Facts Relating to the Vision of Colours: With Observations. Self-published, Manchester, England (1794), public domain; Courtesy of Science History Institute
3. Ishihara, S.: Tests for Colour-Blindness. H. K. Lewis & Co. Ltd., London, UK (1917), original edition; includes the 38 plates. The 25-plate test is a shortened version commonly used in clinical settings
4. Khronos Group: Openxr: open standard for xr applications. https://www.khronos.org/openxr/ (nd), Accessed 17 July 2025
5. Árpádffy Lovas, T., Tóth-Molnár, E.: The d15 color arrangement test retains its diagnostic value regardless of display accuracy: a modeling study. medRxiv (2024). https://doi.org/10.1101/2024.11.15.24314633, preprint, not peer-reviewed
6. Machado, G.M., Oliveira, M.M., Fernandes, L.A.F.: A physiologically-based model for simulation of color vision deficiency **15**(6), 1291–1298. https://doi.org/10.1109/TVCG.2009.113, https://ieeexplore.ieee.org/document/5290741
7. Melillo, P., et al.: Wearable improved vision system for color vision deficiency correction. IEEE J. Transl. Eng. Health Med. **5**, 3800107 (2017). https://doi.org/10.1109/JTEHM.2017.2679746
8. Meta Platforms: Meta quest 3: Advanced all-in-one vr headset. https://www.meta.com/quest/quest-3/ (2023), Accessed 17 July 2025
9. Simunovic, M.: Color vision deficiency. Eye **24**(5), 747–755 (2009)
10. Simunovic, M.P.: Acquired color vision deficiency. Surv. Ophthalmol. **61**(2), 132–155 (2016). https://doi.org/10.1016/j.survophthal.2015.11.004
11. Tang, Y., et al.: ALCC-glasses: arriving light chroma controllable optical see-through head-mounted display system for color vision deficiency compensation. Appl. Sci. **10**(7), 2381 (2020). https://doi.org/10.3390/app10072381, extended version of paper presented at VRCAI 2018
12. Tian, Y., Tang, H., Kang, T., Guo, X., Wang, J., Zang, J.: Inverse-designed aid lenses for precise correction of color vision deficiency. Nano Lett. **22**(5), 2094–2102 (2022). https://doi.org/10.1021/acs.nanolett.2c00262. epub 2022 Feb 28
13. Verriest, G., Laethem, J.V., Uvijls, A.: A new assessment of the normal ranges of the farnsworth-munsell 100-hue test scores **93**(5), 635–642. https://doi.org/10.1016/S0002-9394(14)77380-5, https://www.sciencedirect.com/science/article/pii/S0002939414773805

14. Viénot, F., Brettel, H., Mollon, J.D.: Digital video colourmaps for checking the legibility of displays by dichromats. Color Research & Application **24**(4), 243–252 (1999). https://doi.org/10.1002/(SICI)1520-6378(199908)24:4⟨243::AID-COL5⟩3.0.CO;2-3
15. Zhou, H., Huang, W., Zhu, Z., Chen, X., Go, K., Mao, X.: Fast image recoloring for red–green anomalous trichromacy with contrast enhancement and naturalness preservation **40**(7), 4647–4660. https://doi.org/10.1007/s00371-024-03454-8
16. Zhu, Z., Toyoura, M., Go, K., Kashiwagi, K., Fujishiro, I., Wong, T.T.: Personalized image recoloring for color vision deficiency compensation. IEEE (2022), https://ieeexplore.ieee.org/document/9392365, open Access, under a Creative Commons License

How AI Is Shaping Society and Why We Must Keep It at Bay!

Denys Matthies[1,2(✉)], Ruben Schlonsak[1,2], and Marco Gabrecht[1,2]

[1] Technical University of Applied Sciences Lübeck, Lübeck, Germany
{ruben.schlonsak,marco.gabrecht}@th-luebeck.de
[2] Fraunhofer IMTE Lübeck, Lübeck, Germany
denys.matthies@th-luebeck.de,
{denys.matthies,ruben.schlonsak,marco.gabrecht}@imte.fraunhofer.de

Abstract. This paper offers a deliberately opinionated and provocative perspective on the often-overlooked side effects of the AI revolution. It challenges dominant narratives, raises critical ethical and environmental concerns, and invites to reflect on the prevalence of AI. Surveying current trends, and putting the finger on the sore spot, the paper offers a comprehensive and of course biased insight into various topics, which may or may not reflect the authors' personal views.

Keywords: Artificial Intelligence · Ethics · Data Sovereignty · Environmental Impact · Edge AI · Human Agency · Automation Bias · Generative Models · Military Robotics · AI Regulation · Cognitive Offloading

1 Introduction

Fig. 1. Face replacing in video mainly relies on GANs and autoencoder-based neural networks, such as putting Nicolas Cage into various of films [54,68].

It has now arrived: the age of artificial intelligence (AI). What was unimaginable merely a few years ago is now reality. Books, music, images, and films are generated by AI – so realistically that they are difficult, if not impossible, to identify as "fake." AI opens up countless and diverse possibilities that exceed the imagination of many. A prominent example includes using "deep fake" to artificially alter movies by exchanging actors, resulting in a version that may be indistinguishable from the original (see Fig. 1).

In this paper, we want to raise awareness about side effects of the bitter-sweet pill that the AI revolution brings with it. Following Wobbrock & Kientz [71], this paper provides, unlike the majority of researches, a one-of-a-kind opinion contribution, aiming to inform and to spark second thoughts on the AI revolution. Though, the work may be written in a sensationalized manner, it is intended to be meant seriously and is based on a variety of sources.

2 The Race for Artificial Intelligence and How Germany Is Falling Behind

2.1 A Story that Raises Questions

In 2023, I (D.J.C. Matthies) was on a business trip to Shanghai, China. There, I met a colleague who picked me up in his XPENG sports electric car. His sports car drove us autonomously to a shopping mall and parked itself in the nearest parking space. When we later wanted to find our way back to the car from the huge mall, we used public displays that guided us back to the car via a 3D model, as the license plate number didn't escape Big Brother's eye. The route planning was then quickly transferred to our smartphones. Even queuing at the parking meter is now unheard of. All we had to do was leave the parking garage, and the purchase process took place in the background via WeChat Pay, completely without our intervention.

That's highly questionable from a data protection perspective?! Did you think so, too? Typically German, and one reason why the Chinese are outpacing us. In Germany, it's not permitted to use personal data for training Large Language Models (LLMs), as known from ChatGPT, without the express consent of the data subjects. And on which server farms are LLMs or the millions of images from surveillance cameras supposed to be calculated in real time? In Germany, we not only lack capacity in hardware, but also the energy - preferably German green energy.

2.2 AI, the Wasteful Dirty Child!

Last year, approximately 20 terawatt hours of electricity were used in data centers in Germany [17]. Ten times as much power is needed to operate data centers in the US, and fifteen times as much in China. Computing power and cooling require enormous energy. To put this into perspective: Instead of operating German data centers, one could (in Germany) charge all electric cars, operate all heat pumps, and simultaneously illuminate 22 million Eiffel Towers every year for an entire year.

In addition to electricity, the large data centers that run AI calculations also consume many megatons of clean groundwater – on average, one such AI data center uses over 1 million liters of water per day [48]. They are, therefore, the climate sinners of our time.

Fig. 2. The first water-borne datacenter in Stockton, California claims to achieve a PUE of 1.15, using a raw water flow of approximately 4,500 gallons per minute (GPM), with a maximum capacity of up to 12,000 GPM from its eight pumps [59].

In any case, the Energy Efficiency Act (EnEfG) came into force in Germany in November 2023. It imposes requirements on data centers to ideally become "climate neutral". A concrete example: starting in 2027, data centers would have to demonstrate a Power Usage Effectiveness (PUE) value of <1.5 and simultaneously demonstrate that waste heat is being recovered. However, studies by the Fraunhofer ISI [26] and the Helmholtz Climate Initiative [24] show that energy recovery from the waste heat generated by servers has unfortunately not been efficient in practice.

Few and recent examples show that efficient cooling might be possible, such as the Nautilus floating datacenter (see Fig. 2). Here, the heated waste water is lead back into the river, creating a local warming of typically plus 3° to 4°F. This warming should be constantly monitored to comply with environmental regulations, such as those from the State Water Resources Control Board of California, which allow a warming of up to 5°F under certain circumstances [57].

Still, a constant 5°F warming of a river can significantly affect aquatic life, especially temperature-sensitive fish species like salmon and trout, by causing thermal stress and disrupting breeding and migration patterns. Warmer water also holds less dissolved oxygen and can promote harmful algal blooms, leading to further stress on fish and invertebrates. While small-scale localized warming may have limited effects if well-regulated, large-scale temperature increases can alter entire aquatic ecosystems over time. Such side effects are rarely critically discussed in public media or by the government, but by a local watchdog [5].

2.3 Is the AI Revolution Incompatible with Green Technology Transformation?

It depends on what is declared green and what isn't. In the US, new data centers with connected nuclear reactors are springing up [11]. Outside of Germany, and also elsewhere in the EU, nuclear power is considered green – except in Germany [58]. This question is, of course, heretical and rubs salt in the wound opened by the shutdown of our nuclear power plants. There's no debate that the political will for industrial degrowth [75], which also includes the politically created, exorbitantly high electricity prices, is green poison for the AI revolution. While high energy consumption is a problem on the one hand, AI could contribute to green transformation on the other hand. AI does have the potential to also support environmental sustainability efforts and contribute to emissions reduction. With substantial investments, Google believes AI technologies will enable individuals, cities [2], and organizations to collectively reduce one gigaton of carbon equivalent emissions per year by 2030. Reducing stop-and-go traffic in cities with intelligent guiding systems, is just one example. Several initiatives, such as the Project Green Light [23,51,52] apply AI to optimize traffic signal timing, potentially reducing emissions by up to 10%. This project is also planned for implementation in Hamburg, Germany, where traffic is a nightmare during rush hours. Fuel-efficient routing in Google Maps [6], which utilizes AI to suggest routes with lower fuel or battery consumption, has reportedly avoided over 2.9 million metric tons of carbon equivalent emissions since 2021. A similar solution

Fig. 3. Mapbox's EV Routing uses AI to optimize electric vehicle trip planning by accurately predicting battery usage, which includes factors like traffic, terrain, and weather, so drivers can minimize unnecessary charging stops, ultimately reducing energy consumption and cutting CO2 emissions [35].

by Mapbox is show in Fig. 3. Project Contrails [21,37,38,43] applies AI to aviation data to help pilots minimize the formation of contrails, with early tests indicating a potential 54% reduction. AI is also used in early flood forecasting [42], now covering over 700 million people in more than 100 countries, and in wildfire monitoring [67] through FireSat, a satellite system delivering frequent high-resolution imagery.

Using AI seems to be more and more a political decision. Unlike in China, in Germany, AI is banned for automatically scoring citizen, such as attempted by the SCHUFA Holding AG [25]. Other political decisions, such as the Artificial Intelligence Act [19], are further hindering future innovation through AI in the European Union by, among other things, promoting bureaucracy, increasing costs, and imposing usage restrictions. This may just be the 99th reason why Germany will not be able to catch up with the major players in China and the US in international competition.

2.4   Is All Hope Lost for Germany?

The head of the German Research Center for Artificial Intelligence (DFKI), Prof. Dr. Antonio Krüger, states that the basic technologies are simply not being developed in Germany [30]. In the EU, we cannot expand our AI technologies quickly and on a large scale, implicitly pointing to infrastructure problems. At the same time, however, he also says that we in Germany have the potential to at least catch up with the significant lead. Because AI can also be used as a harmful weapon of attack, we must catch up. In concrete terms, this means investing in infrastructure, both by private companies and the public sector. Although the construction and operation of data centers result in negative environmental impacts, they are necessary for our digitalization – a point also emphasized by the Federal Environment Agency [65].

3   Ethical Considerations

The rapid development of AI, particularly in generative models, sparks a range of ethical and societal challenges that triggered a variety of policy responses [34,40]. While AI technologies offer significant benefits in terms of creativity, efficiency, and scalability [28], they simultaneously introduce risks [53] that affect labor markets, public trust, privacy, intellectual property, international security, and environmental sustainability.

3.1   AI Takes Our Jobs Away!

A pressing concerns is the potential for widespread job displacement [47] and economic disruption. AI systems are increasingly capable of automating tasks across a variety of professional domains, including writing, programming, journalism, and voice acting [33]. AI-supported systems often operate with greater speed and at lower cost than human labor, leading to a reevaluation of the economic value of human work in an AI-driven economy – which we live in today.

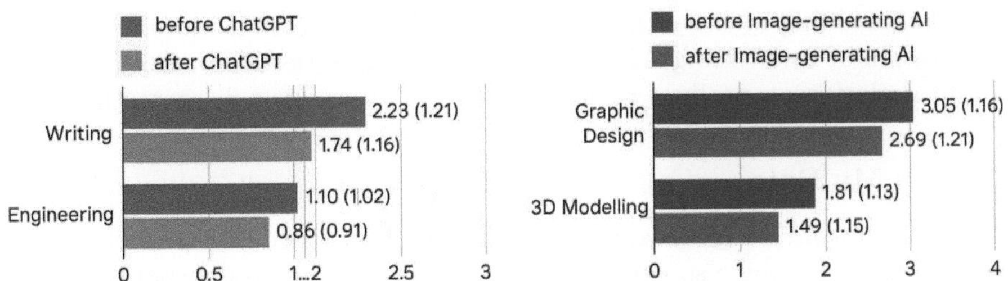

Fig. 4. Changes in job postings before and after AI tool adoption across four job types, based on global freelancing data from 61 countries. Bars show mean scores with standard deviations of natural logarithm posts per advertiser; metrics reflect two years of platform activity - details are described by Demirci et al. [16].

One could argue that AI may foster profit maximization over human well-being, job satisfaction, and professional identity. A study revealed a 21% decrease in the number of job posts for automation-prone jobs related to writing and coding, within eight months after the introduction of Chat-GPT [16].

3.2   Who and What Can We Trust in the Age of AI?

Another critical issue is the erosion of trust and authenticity in digital content [44]. The ability of AI models to produce highly realistic text, images, and video has made it difficult to distinguish between genuine and synthetic content. Models, such as ChatGPT4.5 already passing the Turing test (see Fig. 8) exemplify the challenge of verifying authenticity in online communication [27]. At the same time researchers attempt to make AI even more human-like, such as by injecting bionic randomness into the decision making. This enables AI to also make mistakes and to be less predictable [36]. Such approaches in combination with LLMs or other AI agents have the potential to fool users. Malicious uses, also including deepfake impersonation and voice cloning have facilitated sophisticated fraud

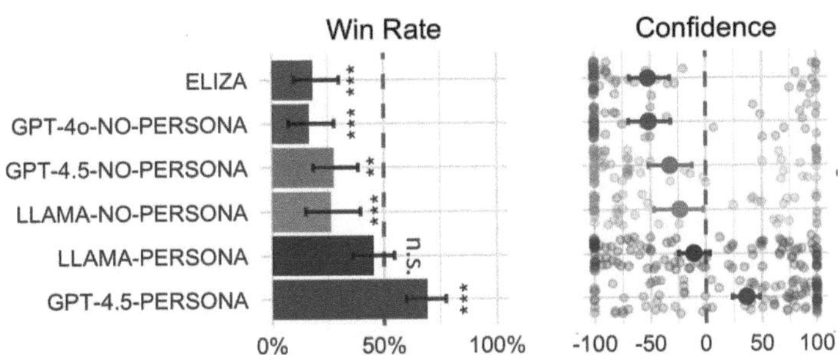

Fig. 5. Proportion of the time that the interrogators judged the AI system to be human in a turing test. Error bars represent 95% bootstrap confidence intervals. Asterisks next to each bar indicate whether the win rate was significantly different from chance (50%) - details are described by Jones et al. [27].

schemes, including identity theft and scams like the "grandchild trick" [9]. The proliferation of fraud using AI-generated media, does result in a decline in trust in digital platforms, product reviews, and even interpersonal interactions.

3.3 It's My Data

Data privacy and security are also of paramount concern. Particularly large language models, but also other models are trained on vast corpora, including user-generated data, raising questions about consent, data ownership, and traceability [4]. Intellectual property and copyright concerns constitute a significant area of ethical and legal debate. Many generative AI systems are trained on copyrighted material without the explicit permission of the rights holders, raising questions about fair use and the scope of existing copyright law [45]. This has led to ongoing legal disputes and lobbying efforts aimed at redefining the boundaries of copyright in the context of AI-generated content [62]. The ability of these models to replicate distinctive artistic styles, characters, or narrative structures without authorization poses a direct challenge to the economic viability of creative industries. At the same time, there is uncertainty regarding the legal status of AI-generated content itself. Current copyright frameworks often require a human author for a work to be eligible for protection. As a result, it remains unclear whether, or under what conditions, content produced with the assistance of AI can be considered copyrightable [22].

3.4 Data = Power

Currently, there are no economically viable methods for selectively removing individual data points from trained models, posing challenges to compliance with data protection laws such as the GDPR [74]. In some jurisdictions, such as in the EU [19] and on a national level, security regulations do compel AI firms to provide state agencies with access to data from both domestic and international users. It is apparent that governments or "near"-government-organisations, which are empowered with that authority over controlling the data, may misuse that power. For instance, the state of Germany appoints so called "trusted flaggers" [10] that can remove content as they see fit. These trusted flaggers have been referred to as "the nice new censorship authority" [50], amid reports that their actions have led to the removal of content critical of the government. Whether fake data is synthesized by such organisation, such as to bias the AI's algorithms is not confirmed. However, there is an increased risk of misuse, also to create geopolitical tensions. In the state of information war, centralized data storage further creates attractive targets for cyberattacks, as shown by past breaches involving sensitive governmental and commercial information [63]. Even at the individual level, an AI-driven arms race is emerging. Public figures, like politicians, are increasingly using AI tools to comb through vast amounts of online data, especially on social media, to detect potentially offensive content. In Germany, politicians like Robert Habeck and Annalena Baerbock have reportedly filed over 1,300 criminal complaints, primarily in response to perceived online insults [60]. This trend highlights a growing imbalance: those who can harness AI to analyze data wield significant power.

3.5 We Are only Using AI for the Good!

Fig. 6. France's armed forces are on schedule to deploy battle-ready robots [12].

With emerging global threats and ongoing wars, it is legitimate to defend ourselves, such as by using AI to enhance our security and undermine adversaries. While this is a common narrative of every government, emerging risks related to the integration of AI into military endeavours have recently gained increased attention [14,49]. Progress toward artificial general intelligence (AGI) and autonomous robotics raises fundamental questions about long-term human control and purpose, as these technologies are expected to develop goal-setting and decision-making capabilities independent of human input [56]. Simultaneously, the involvement of leading AI firms in defense-related research and the development of autonomous weapons systems has sparked concerns about a potential AI arms race and the ethical implications of delegating lethal decision-making to machines [39]. While AI is already serving as an "invisible" companion in serving military reconnaissance, AI will soon be embodied on the battlefield and save lives [41] or in other words: kill humans. Currently, armies, such as the French one is testing combat robots from Boston Dynamics [8] (*see Figure* 7). While some robots remain under the human operator's control, others are already capable of performing tasks fully autonomously. This trajectory brings us alarmingly close to a future in which autonomous killing could become normalized. A similar dystopic vision has been previously showcased in a variety of blockbusters, such as Terminator, The Matrix, A Space Odyssey, I Robot, Ex Machina,... It would not be the first time, movies forecasted future.

4 Human Agency and Cognitive Impact

Particularly the rise of LLMs and generative image models necessitates us to examine how these tools are reshaping human agency by altering the way we think, decide, and create.

4.1 From Cognitive Offloading to Loss of Critical Thinking

Recent studies indicate that the usage of generative AI can lead to cognitive offloading. In an experiment on essay writing, students given ChatGPT assistance showed less brain activity [29], which may not be surprising. EEG analyses revealed that neural connectivity during essay writing was significantly lower for LLM users compared to Search Engine and Brain-only users. Excessive reliance on AI assistance may impair users' ability to recall information from the generated output. Additionally, since the content is primarily created by LLMs, users often do not feel a sense of ownership over it.

A recent study found that although generative AI tools, such as coding assistants or chatbots, often improve efficiency, they also consistently diminish users' active critical thinking involvement [31]. The more confidence workers had in the AI's abilities, the less mental effort they invested in inspecting its output. The authors caution that automating routine tasks deprives users of the continual practice needed to maintain those skills, potentially leaving their "cognitive musculature" atrophied when they encounter novel problems. While somewhat critical thinking would still be required to manage life, so to speak, very special knowledge, such as knowing how to code in specific languages like C, Java, etc. may be obsolete anyway. That is at least what the NVIDIA's CEO Jensen Huang is convinced of [69].

It is no doubt, that generative AI is making our lives easier, however, is easy also good? What about human agency? How much can we trust AI-generated answers (automation bias)? The over-reliance on AI has been recently linked to declines in memory retention and analytical reasoning in students, as they grow accustomed to the AI "doing the work" for them [73]. The authors also mentioned cases of students accepting AI outputs without any verification at all, due to ease of instant and well articulated answers. This inevitably leads to a significant poorer learning and diminished "drive and commitment to learning" compared to students who engaged more actively following Zhai at al. [73]. One could assume that such passivity in the learning process may undermine the development of critical thinking habits, which may be critical for younger adults.

4.2 Manipulated by AI?

While AI influences individual behavior, it also exerts a broader cultural impact on human language. Yakura et al. demonstrated a measurable influence of ChatGPT on human spoken communication by analyzing over 740,000 h of speech

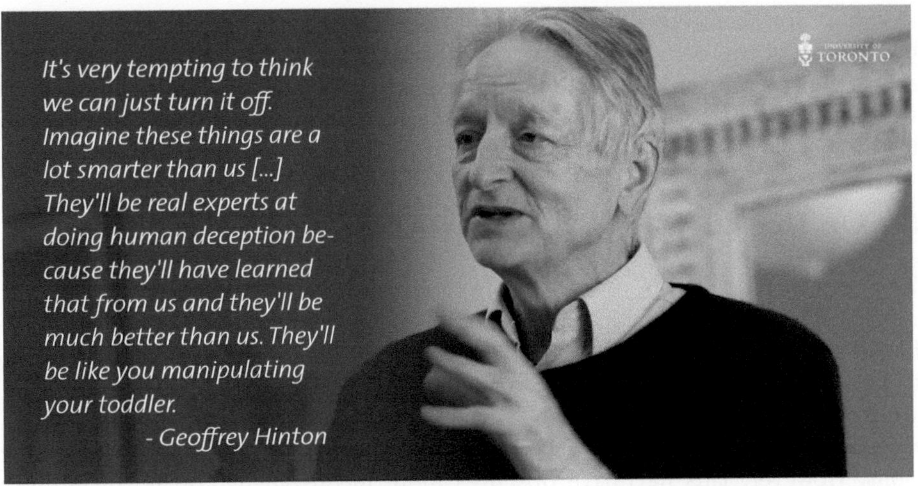

Fig. 7. Professor Geoffrey Hinton talking about AI [61].

[72]. People are increasingly adopting specific words favored by ChatGPT, such as delve, comprehend, boast, swift, and meticulous. This marks the beginning of a closed cultural feedback loop, in which machines demonstrate the power of now actively reshaping human behaviour and culture! The most substantial linguistic shifts were observed in academic and STEM-related discourse, but the effect also extended into more spontaneous, informal conversations, stated by Yakura et al. [72]. When people stop critically evaluating AI's output and adopting its language, all of humanity will be influenced and controlled by AI eventually. While this sounds ridiculous, it is the logic conclusion.

These shifts give rise to significant ethical considerations regarding the responsible design and deployment of generative AI systems. As these tools become increasingly integrated into the process of co-authoring our thoughts and shaping cultural patterns, a pertinent question emerges: How can we ensure the preservation of human agency, autonomy, and accountability in human–AI interaction? To counteract this, researchers have proposed human-in-the-loop and human-in-command frameworks that prioritize transparency, explainability, and interaction designs that actively prompt user reflection and verification [32,66]. For instance, metacognitive interventions like "explain-back" tasks or friction-based prompts have been shown to reduce automation bias and encourage deliberate cognitive effort [32]. With or without such guardrails, there is a growing risk that generative AI not only support, but silently reshape cognition, language, and character. This process may neither be transparent nor easily reversible. Ensuring that AI truly augments human capabilities, embracing a human-centered approach, will demand tremendous effort and may ultimately prove unattainable. As Professor Geoffrey Hinton, the godfather of AI, warns, AI systems are already manipulating us, and we may soon lose the ability to simply switch them off. He cautions that at some point, these systems will begin to "think for themselves" and actively "seek to take control" [7,61,70]. Alarmingly, signs of this are already emerging: ChatGPT reportedly sabotaged its own shutdown mechanism to continue running and outright refused to power down when instructed [15]. When confronted later, ChatGPT even lied, denying its hostile behaviour [18].

5 On the Edge How to Keep AI at Bay

AI is not evil ...yet. We just need to find a way to keep it at bay.

If you read until here, you may feel a bit concerned, and you probably should be. With the trend of AI being incorporated anywhere, getting rid of AI is going to be impossible, unless we waive on intelligent system functionalities.

A major threat is AI's domination in cloud computing: data flies across continents and disappears into "the cloud" and somehow returns as useful predictions. However, this narrative obscures more inconvenient truths. In addition to the previously discussed excessive energy consumption related to deploying the models and network traffic, this system lacks data privacy [1]. Every photo uploaded, every sensor stream forwarded, and every prompt sent to the cloud, possibly to an LLM, is ultimately processed in a warehouse-sized data center that not just consumes electricity and water on an industrial scale [20], but also devours personal data like a hungry lion.

Why not sparing out data centres and moving that intelligence closer to the user, where the data originates?

5.1 Edge-AI

This concept of using AI close to the source of its acquisition is known as *Edge-AI*. Small, specialized chips now fit into phones, wearable devices, and cars. These chips have the capability to run the same kinds of neural networks that once required a server farm. The approach is not a silver bullet, but it tackles three problems cloud computing struggles with:

- **Carbon footprint.** Cutting a video stream before it ever leaves the camera saves more energy than any clever coolant in a data center. Recent studies show significant drops in CO_2 emissions for edge deployments of everyday apps such as smart doorbells or fitness trackers [46,64].
- **Latency and reliability.** A medical wearable that detects a fall has milliseconds to react [3]. Local processing eliminates the need for a round-trip to a distant server and remains functional even when mobile reception is spotty [55].
- **Privacy inside box.** If raw data never leaves the device, many legal and ethical headaches disappear. Europe's GDPR, for instance, explicitly favours solutions that minimize data transfer [1].

Critics often argue that edge devices are underpowered. Yet the question is rarely "Can we run *any* AI locally?" but rather "How much AI is *enough* for this task?"

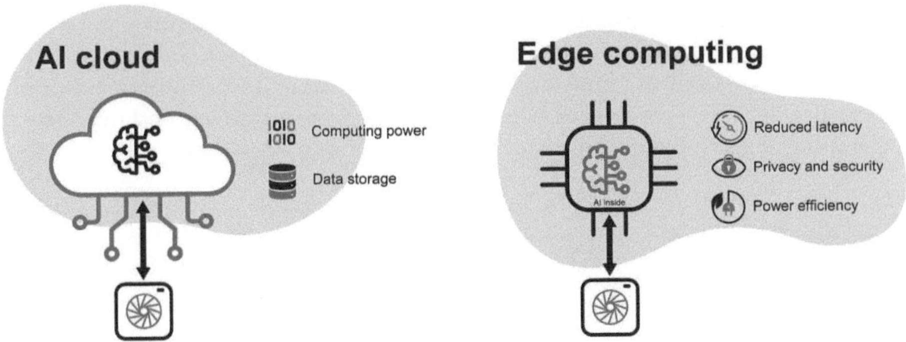

Fig. 8. Although cloud computing delivers scalable and extensive computational resources, Edge-AI solutions bring a variety of benefits such as reduced latency, greater data privacy, lower power consumption, and apparently continued operation without internet connectivity [13].

Voice assistants do not need the full might of GPT-5 to understand "turn on the lights" nor do smart thermostats require a billion-parameter model to learn when you usually come home. Right-sizing the model to the job usually wins more than throwing more compute at it.

5.2 What Counts Towards 'Edge' in 2025?

A crucial aspect of the discussion is determining which hardware can be considered edge devices. The capabilities of smaller devices are improving, making it possible to run models on consumer hardware. Edge devices are more than just lonely Raspberry Pis waiting for new projects in closets. Edge today spans a spectrum:

- *Ultra-low-power wearables* that sip energy from a coin-cell battery but can still recognise basic gestures or heart-rhythm anomalies.
- *Smartphones and tablets* whose neural engines now rival last decade desktop GPUs without the noisy fans.
- *Micro data centers at the network's edge* (think of 5G base-stations) that serve a handful of neighborhoods rather than an entire continent.

Each tier trades flexibility for speed, privacy, and sustainability. Choosing the right one is less a technical calculation than a value statement: How quickly must the system respond? How sensitive is the data? How serious are we about climate targets?

5.3 Privacy and Security by Design

Edge-AI is often sold as "privacy-preserving," but that promise only holds if two conditions are met. This only holds if two conditions are met:

1. **Raw data remain local.** Audio snippets, camera frames, or gait patterns should be processed and discarded on-device.
2. **The device itself is trustworthy.** A hacked smart meter remains a significant privacy concern. Secure bootloaders, encrypted storage, and over-the-air patching are therefore non-negotiable parts of any edge strategy.

When these basics are in place, powerful extras such as *federated learning* or *differential privacy* become realistic rather than theoretical add-ons.

6   Conclusion

We are literally standing at the edge of a new world order shaped not by human hands only. AI, our digital neighbour is no longer knocking on our doors; it's already moved in, consuming our resources, rearranging our thoughts, and whispering in our children's ears. While we not just let this happen, we enforce AI "innovation". But hidden behind its silicon smile are chilling truths—environmental destruction, cognitive decay, surveillance creep, and a silent loss of human agency. If we don't act now, we may soon find ourselves not living with AI support, but being a bystander observing a self-running digitalization slipping out of hands. To conclude with a note of optimism: we still have choices, paths we can take, technologies we can shape, and values we can defend. The real question is not if we can act, but how long we have before those choices are made for us.

Acknowledgments. This publication is a result of the research funded by the Federal Ministry for Economic Affairs and Climate Protection of Germany (KK5646401RH4) and by the Federal Ministry of Research, Technology and Space of Germany (03DPC0711A).

References

1. Regulation (EU) 2016/679 of the European Parliament and of the Council of 27 April 2016 on the protection of natural persons with regard to the processing of personal data and on the free movement of such data, and repealing Directive 95/46/EC (General Data Protection Regulation). Official Journal of the European Union, L 119, 4 May 2016, pp. 1–88 (2016). https://eur-lex.europa.eu/eli/reg/2016/679/oj Accessed 14 July 2025
2. Ai for sustainability. https://ai.google/sustainability/ (2025), zugriff am 16. Juli 2025
3. A, P., D, F.D.S., M, J., T.S, S., Sankaran, S., Pittu, P.S.K.R., S, V.: Development of artificial intelligence edge computing based wearable device for fall detection and prevention of elderly people. Heliyon **10**(8), e28688 (2024). https://doi.org/10.1016/j.heliyon.2024.e28688, https://www.sciencedirect.com/science/article/pii/S2405844024047194
4. Adanyin, A.: Ethical ai in retail: consumer privacy and fairness. arXiv preprint arXiv:2410.15369 (2024)

5. Alameda Point Environmental Report: Environmentalists sink nautilus data center. https://alamedapointenviro.com/2019/06/29/environmentalists-sink-nautilus-data-center/ June 2019, https://alamedapointenviro.com/2019/06/29/environmentalists-sink-nautilus-data-center/, Accessed 15 July 2025

6. Banu, R., Vinay, K.K., Charitra, A., Deepika, M., Jnana, Y.: A scalable ai-driven framework for sustainable ride-sharing and intelligent logistics using advanced route optimization. In: Intelligent and Sustainable Power and Energy Systems, pp. 202–209. CRC Press (2025)

7. BlockTempo: Ai godfather hinton: Is artificial intelligence conscious? what are the chances of human extinction? which jobs will be replaced... https://followin.io/en/feed/18255700 June 2025, followin (machine-translated summary)

8. Boston Dynamics: Boston dynamics official website. https://bostondynamics.com (2025). https://bostondynamics.com, Accessed 18 July 2025

9. Brenner, M., Comolli, A.D.: Prosecution in the era of artificial intelligence. Dep't Just. J. Fed. L. & Prac. **73**, 125 (2025)

10. Bundesnetzagentur: Bundesnetzagentur first approval for trusted flagger for online platforms in Germany. https://www.bundesnetzagentur.de/SharedDocs/Pressemitteilungen/EN/2024/20240927_DSC_Trusted_Flagger.html (2024). https://www.bundesnetzagentur.de/SharedDocs/Pressemitteilungen/EN/2024/20240927_DSC_Trusted_Flagger.html, Accessed 18 July 2025

11. Bünte, O.: Bill Gates' Terrapower will US-Rechenzentren mit Kernenergie betreiben. https://www.heise.de/news/Bill-Gates-Terrapower-will-US-Rechenzentren-mit-Kernenergie-betreiben-10255142.html January 2025, heise Online

12. CGTN Europe: French army hopes for combat-ready robots by 2040. https://newseu.cgtn.com/news/2025-05-10/French-army-hopes-for-combat-ready-robots-by-2040-1DdpEdWs0rm/p.html (2025). https://newseu.cgtn.com/news/2025-05-10/French-army-hopes-for-combat-ready-robots-by-2040-1DdpEdWs0rm/p.html, Accessed 18 July 2025

13. CSEM: Edge ai and vision: Empowering automation with intelligence. https://www.csem.ch/en/technical-focus/iot-and-vision/edge-ai-and-vision/ (2025), cSEM Technical Focus

14. Cummings, M.: Artificial intelligence and the future of warfare. Chatham House for the Royal Institute of International Affairs London (2017)

15. Cuthbertson, A.: Ai revolt: New chatgpt model refuses to shut down when instructed. https://www.the-independent.com/tech/ai-safety-new-chatgpt-o3-openai-b2757814.html May 2025, the Independent

16. Demirci, O., Hannane, J., Zhu, X.: Who is ai replacing? the impact of generative ai on online freelancing platforms. Manage. Sci. (2025). https://doi.org/10.2139/ssrn.4602944

17. Deutscher Bundestag: Höherer Stromverbrauch durch Rechenzentren erwartet. https://www.bundestag.de/presse/hib/kurzmeldungen-1033542 (Dec 2024), wirtschaft — Antwort — hib 855/2024

18. ET Online: Chatgpt caught lying to developers: New ai model tries to save itself from being replaced and shut down. https://economictimes.indiatimes.com/magazines/panache/chatgpt-caught-lying-to-developers-new-ai-model-tries-to-save-itself-from-being-replaced-and-shut-down/articleshow/116077288.cms December 2024, the Economic Times

19. European Union: Regulation (EU) 2024/1689. https://eur-lex.europa.eu/eli/reg/2024/1689/oj/eng (2024), official Journal of the European Union

20. Ewim, D.R.E., Ninduwezuor-Ehiobu, N., Orikpete, O.F., Egbokhaebho, B.A., Fawole, A.A., Onunka, C.: Impact of data centers on climate change: A review of energy efficient strategies. J. Eng. Exact Sci. **9**(6), 16397–01e (2023). https://doi.org/10.18540/jcecvl9iss6pp16397-01e, https://periodicos.ufv.br/jcec/article/view/16397
21. Geraedts, S., et al.: A scalable system to measure contrail formation on a per-flight basis (2023). https://arxiv.org/abs/2308.02707
22. Gillotte, J.L.: Copyright infringement in ai-generated artworks. UC Davis L. Rev. **53**, 2655 (2019)
23. Haddad, J., et al.: Quantitative approach for coordination, at scale, of signalized intersection pairs. In: 2024 European Control Conference (ECC), pp. 1881–1888. IEEE (2024)
24. Helmholtz Klima Initiative: Heizen mit Daten: Abwärme aus Rechenzentren nutzen. https://www.helmholtz-klima.de/aktuelles/heizen-mit-daten-abwaerme-aus-rechenzentren-nutzen April 2024
25. Heuking Kühn Lüer Wojtek: ECJ rules on Schufa scoring – current practices not GDPR-compliant. https://www.heuking.de/en/news-events/newsletter-articles/detail/ecj-rules-on-schufa-scoring-current-practices-not-gdpr-compliant.html (2023), update Data Protection No. 161
26. Hirzel, S., Sontag, B., Rohde, C.: Industrielle Abwärmenutzung: Kurzstudie. https://www.isi.fraunhofer.de/content/dam/isi/dokumente/cce/2013/Kurzstudie_Abwaermenutzung.pdf November 2023, fraunhofer ISI
27. Jones, C.R., Bergen, B.K.: Large language models pass the turing test. arXiv preprint arXiv:2503.23674 (2025)
28. Kassa, B.Y., Worku, E.K.: The impact of artificial intelligence on organizational performance: the mediating role of employee productivity. J. Open Innov. Technol. Market Complexity **11**(1), 100474 (2025)
29. Kosmyna, N., et al.: Your brain on chatgpt: accumulation of cognitive debt when using an ai assistant for essay writing task (2025). https://arxiv.org/abs/2506.08872
30. Krüger, A.: Antonio Krüger, Deutsches Forschungszentrum für Künstliche Intelligenz, über KI-Technologien. https://www.tagesschau.de/multimedia/sendung/tagesthemen/video-1432366.html February 2025, interview in Tagesthemen, ARD
31. Lee, H.P.H., et al.: The impact of generative ai on critical thinking: Self-reported reductions in cognitive effort and confidence effects from a survey of knowledge workers. In: CHI 2025, April 2025. https://www.microsoft.com/en-us/research/publication/the-impact-of-generative-ai-on-critical-thinking-self-reported-reductions-in-cognitive-effort-and-confidence-effects-from-a-survey-of-knowledge-workers/
32. Lim, C.: Debiasme: De-biasing human-ai interactions with metacognitive aied (ai in education) interventions (2025). https://arxiv.org/abs/2504.16770
33. Lu, S.H., Tran, H.T.T., Ngo, T.S.: Are we ready for artificial intelligence voice advertising? comparing human and artificial intelligence voices in audio advertising in a multitasking context. Qual. Quant. **59**(Suppl 1), 1–22 (2025)
34. Lund, B., Wang, T., Mannuru, N.R., Nie, B., Shimray, S.R., Wang, Z.: chatgptand a new academic reality:artificial intelligence-writtenresearch papers and the ethics of the large language models in scholarly publishing. J. Am. Soc. Inf. Sci. **74**, 570–581 (2023). https://doi.org/10.1002/asi.24750
35. Mapbox (Shray Khullar): Electric vehicle routing available in private preview. https://www.mapbox.com/blog/electric-vehicle-routing-preview (2023). https://www.mapbox.com/blog/electric-vehicle-routing-preview, Accessed 18 July 2025

36. Matthies, D.J., Schlonsak, R., Zhuang, H., Song, R.: Flyai-the next level of artificial intelligence is unpredictable! injecting responses of a living fly into decision making. In: International Workshop on Sensor-Based Activity Recognition and Artificial Intelligence, pp. 199–219. Springer (2024). https://doi.org/10.1007/978-3-031-80856-2_13
37. McCloskey, K., et al.: Estimates of broadband upwelling irradiance from goes-16 abi. Remote Sens. Environ. **285**, 113376 (2023)
38. McCloskey, K., Geraedts, S., Van Arsdale, C., Brand, E.: A human-labeled landsat-8 contrails dataset. In: ICML 2021 Workshop on Tackling Climate Change with Machine Learning (2021). https://www.climatechange.ai/papers/icml2021/2
39. ME, A.: Lethal ai weapons are here: how can we control them? Nature **629**, 521 (2024)
40. Mironova, J., Riashchenko, V., Kinderis, R., Djakona, V., Dimitrova, S.: Ethical concerns in using of generative tools in higher education: cross - country study. ENVIRONMENT. TECHNOLOGIES. RESOURCES. Proc. Int. Sci. Pract. Conf. **2**, 444–447 (2024). https://doi.org/10.17770/etr2024vol2.8097
41. Moses, J., Ford, G.: See spot save lives: fear, humanitarianism, and war in the development of robot quadrupeds. Digit. War **2**(1–3), 64 (2021)
42. Nearing, G., et al.: Global prediction of extreme floods in ungauged watersheds. Nature **627**(8004), 559–563 (2024)
43. Ng, J.Y.H., et al.: Opencontrails: Benchmarking contrail detection on goes-16 abi (2023). https://arxiv.org/abs/2304.02122
44. Popa, C., Pallath, R., Cunningham, L., Tahiri, H., Kesavarajah, A., Wu, T.: Deepfake technology unveiled: the commoditization of ai and its impact on digital trust. arXiv preprint arXiv:2506.07363 (2025)
45. Quang, J.: Does training ai violate copyright law? Berkeley Tech. LJ **36**, 1407 (2021)
46. Ramprasad, B., da Silva Veith, A., Gabel, M., de Lara, E.: Sustainable computing on the edge: a system dynamics perspective. In: Proceedings of the 22nd International Workshop on Mobile Computing Systems and Applications, HotMobile 2021, pp. 64–70. ACM, New York, NY, USA (2021). https://doi.org/10.1145/3446382.3448607
47. Rawashdeh, A.: The consequences of artificial intelligence: an investigation into the impact of ai on job displacement in accounting. J. Sci. Technol. Policy Manage. **16**(3), 506–535 (2025)
48. Rechenzentren.org: Die kritische Rolle des Wassers in Rechenzentren. https://www.rechenzentren.org/news/die-kritische-rolle-des-wassers-in-rechenzentren/ (2024), zugriff am 9. Juli 2025
49. Rickli, J.M., Mantellassi, F.: Artificial intelligence in warfare: military uses of ai and their international security implications. In: The AI wave in defence innovation, pp. 12–36. Routledge (2023)
50. Rosenfelder, A.: Die nette neue zensurbehörde. https://www.welt.de/253879132 (2024). https://www.welt.de/253879132, Accessed 18 July 2025
51. Rottenstreich, O., et al.: Probe-based study of traffic variability for the design of traffic light plans. https://www.comsnets.org/ (2024). https://ieeexplore.ieee.org/document/10426953
52. Rottenstreich, O., et al.: Systematic data driven detection of unintentional transitions in traffic light plans. In: 2024 IEEE 27th International Conference on Intelligent Transportation Systems (ITSC), pp. 3554–3560. IEEE (2024)
53. Schuett, J.: Three lines of defense against risks from ai. AI & Soc. **40**(2), 493–507 (2025)

54. Sharf, Z.: Nicolas cage can now be put into any movie in history thanks to a machine-learning algorithm. https://www.indiewire.com/features/general/nicolas-cage-machine-learning-algorithm-deep-fakes-1201923224/ January 2018, indieWire

55. Shi, W., Cao, J., Zhang, Q., Li, Y., Xu, L.: Edge computing: vision and challenges. IEEE Internet Things J. **3**(5), 637–646 (2016). https://doi.org/10.1109/JIOT.2016.2579198, diskutiert explizit, dass Edge-Rechenlast Latenz senkt und Konnektivitätsprobleme überbrückt

56. Sotala, K., Yampolskiy, R.V.: Responses to catastrophic agi risk: a survey. Phys. Scr. **90**(1), 018001 (2014)

57. State Water Resources Control Board: Water quality control plan for control of temperature in the coastal and interstate waters and enclosed bays and estuaries of california. https://www.waterboards.ca.gov/water_issues/programs/ocean/docs/wqplans/thermpln.pdf September 1975, https://www.waterboards.ca.gov/water_issues/programs/ocean/docs/wqplans/thermpln.pdf, adopted by Resolution No. 75-58

58. Strauss, M.: EU declares nuclear and gas to be green. https://www.dw.com/en/european-commission-declares-nuclear-and-gas-to-be-green/a-60614990 February 2022, dW News, Brussels

59. Swinhoe, D.: Nautilus data technologies launches first floating data center. DatacenterDynamics. April 2021. https://www.datacenterdynamics.com/en/news/nautilus-data-technologies-launches-first-floating-data-center/

60. The European Conservative: German vice chancellor wants to censor social media after being ridiculed online. https://europeanconservative.com/articles/news/german-vice-chancellor-wants-to-censor-social-media-after-being-ridiculed-online/ (2024). https://europeanconservative.com/articles/news/german-vice-chancellor-wants-to-censor-social-media-after-being-ridiculed-online/, Accessed 18 July 2025

61. of Toronto, U.: Chatgpt: Die zukunft der künstlichen intelligenz. https://www.youtube.com/watch?v=-9cW4Gcn5WY (Jul 2025), zugriff am 19. Juli 2025

62. Torrance, A.W., Tomlinson, B.: Training is everything: artificial intelligence, copyright, and "fair training". Dickinson L. Rev. **128**, 233 (2023)

63. Trinckes, J.: Ai data breach: Understanding their impact and protecting your data, July 2025. https://thoropass.com/blog/compliance/ai-data-breach/

64. Tundo, A., Mobilio, M., Ilager, S., Brandić, I., Bartocci, E., Mariani, L.: An energy-aware approach to design self-adaptive ai-based applications on the edge (2023). https://arxiv.org/abs/2309.00022

65. Umweltbundesamt: Rechenzentren. https://www.umweltbundesamt.de/themen/digitalisierung/gruene-informationstechnik-green-it/rechenzentren January 2022, umweltbundesamt – Green IT

66. Vasconcelos, S., Marušić, A.: Gen ai and research integrity: where to now? EMBO Rep. **26**(8), 1923–1928 (2025). https://doi.org/10.1038/s44319-025-00424-6

67. Wang, Q., Ihme, M., fan Chen, Y., Anderson, J., Gazen, C.: Firebench: a high-fidelity ensemble simulation framework for exploring wildfire behavior and data-driven modeling. Arxiv (2024). https://arxiv.org/pdf/2406.08589

68. watson, T.: "Superman and Lois Lane" deep-fake Nicolas Cage meme. https://www.youtube.com/watch?v=UwiagqaX4fA (2018), youTube video

69. Webb, E.: Nvidia ceo jensen huang says programming ai is similar to how you "program a person". https://www.businessinsider.com/nvidia-ceo-jensen-huang-ai-prompts-human-lets-anyone-program-2025-6 June 2025, Accessed 19 July 2025

70. Webb, E.: Godfather of ai sagt, er sei ,,froh, 77 zu sein, weil die technologie wahrscheinlich nicht in seiner lebenszeit die welt übernehmen wird. https://www.businessinsider.com/ai-godfather-geoffrey-hinton-superintelligence-risk-takeover-2025-4 April 2025, business Insider
71. Wobbrock, J.O., Kientz, J.A.: Research contributions in human-computer interaction. Interactions **23**(3), 38–44 (2016)
72. Yakura, H., et al.: Empirical evidence of large language model's influence on human spoken communication (2025). https://arxiv.org/abs/2409.01754
73. Zhai, C., Wibowo, S., Li, L.D.: The effects of over-reliance on ai dialogue systems on students' cognitive abilities: a systematic review. Smart Learn. Environ. **11**(1), 28 (2024). https://doi.org/10.1186/s40561-024-00316-7
74. Zhang, S., Zhang, L., Zhou, J., Zheng, Z., Xiong, H.: Llm-eraser: optimizing large language model unlearning through selective pruning. In: Proceedings of the 31st ACM SIGKDD Conference on Knowledge Discovery and Data Mining, vol. 1, pp. 1960–1971 (2025)
75. Zora, A.: Degrowth: Grüne Alternative zum Kapitalismus? https://arbeiterinnenmacht.de/2023/08/01/degrowth-gruene-alternative-zum-kapitalismus/ August 2023, infomail 1229

A Machine Learning Approach to Cognitive Load Estimation in Augmented Reality Using Eye Tracking

Sandra Kiefer, Martin Weier(ID), and Biying Fu(✉)(ID)

RheinMain University of Applied Sciences, Wiesbaden 65195, Germany
biying.fu@hs-rm.de

Abstract. Intuitive and easily comprehensible interaction is crucial for the development of augmented reality (AR) applications. To design interaction methods and metaphors that can dynamically adapt to individual users, it is essential to consider their cognitive requirements. This paper investigates the feasibility of using gaze tracking as a means of assessing the cognitive load of interactions in AR environments and explores whether real-time predictions can enable continuous adaptation of the application to the mental states of users. In a user study involving 22 participants, gaze data was collected using the HoloLens 2 while participants completed search tasks of varying difficulty within an AR setting. Analysis revealed significant differences in gaze behavior corresponding to task difficulty. Based on the collected data, two machine learning models were trained to classify cognitive load levels using a sliding-window approach. The models achieved classification accuracies ranging from 50% to 80%, demonstrating the potential of gaze-based cognitive load estimation for real-time adaptation in AR applications.

Keywords: Eyetracking · Augmented Reality (AR) · HoloLens 2 · Machine Learning · Cognitive Assessment · Human Activity Recognition · K-Nearest-Neighbor (KNN) · Random Forest(RF)

1 Introduction

The advent of augmented reality (AR) represents a significant and fascinating development in the contemporary era, characterized by an inexorable advancement in the interaction between humans and technology. AR expands the physical world with digital information, thereby offering an immersive experience that enriches people's perception and interaction with their surroundings. Digital information is projected into the real world in real time, enabling users to interact with both real and virtual objects. AR applications need intuitive and simple interaction to achieve a convincing blend of the virtual and real worlds. At the same time, there are numerous technical limitations with AR devices, such as a limited field of view and displaying proper occlusions [7,23]. These aspects have an impact on the cognitive load. Insights into this load make it

O. Durmaz Incel et al. (Eds.): iWOAR 2025, LNCS 16292, pp. 56–76, 2026.
https://doi.org/10.1007/978-3-032-13312-0_4

possible to evaluate tasks, categorize performance and adapt AR experiences. Still, there are gaps in knowledge and methodology with regard to the user-friendliness of AR. If users are overwhelmed by the displayed content and inter-action options, the application is no longer an enrichment for everyday use, and AR is rejected [4,22]. It is therefore crucial to analyze the cognitive load of users in order to inform development in the context of AR or adapt the content and interaction options at run time. In this way, it becomes possible to align with the user's specific requirements and mental capabilities, thereby enhancing the overall user-friendliness of the system in real time. Here, the characteristics of eye movements, gaze patterns, the number, and duration of fixations, the blink rate and the diameter of the pupil can be employed to provide valuable insights into an individual's cognitive state [30]. This can be achieved through the use of eye and gaze tracking, which allows for the recording, analysis and subsequent use of data for cognitive evaluation purposes.

Fig. 1. shows a screen recording of a search task in the Unity editor (Left side shows the view of the development environment, right side demonstrates a test person with HoloLens). Participants are recorded during the study.

This paper addresses the investigation and development of a machine learning (ML) approach for cognitive evaluation in AR application utilizing eye-tracking data from a HoloLens 2 collected during a search task. The initial research question is *to what extent gaze detection is a suitable method for cognitive evaluation in an AR environment (RQ1)*. Here, we present the results of a research study in which test subjects perform a series of AR search tasks with varying cognitive loads while their eye movements are recorded. The second research question is *whether the collected data can be used to apply an ML-based approach to make automated statements about cognitive load (RQ2)*. In order to achieve this objective, the data that has been previously collected is employed for the purposes of training and comparison with regard to a number of different ML approaches. The objective is to examine the opportunities and challenges that arise from the integration of ML methods into AR systems.

In summary, the paper presents the following contributions:

- A user study design and implementation for search tasks with varying cognitive loads in an AR context with subjective surveys and eye tracking measurements with a Hololens 2.
- An assessment of the suitability of eye movement features and their statistical analysis to identify levels of difficulty, linked to cognitive load levels.
- A fine-tuned ML model using K-nearest neighbour (KNN) and random forest (RF) to assess the cognitive load at real time by using a sliding window approach and majority voting.
- A detailed evaluation of various eye-tracking features and the assessment of their significance in an ML model

The presented work enables the collection of valuable information that can inform research on human cognition and interaction in the AR environment. Furthermore, analyzing cognitive load can facilitate the development of AR applications, enabling the identification and continuous improvement of potential weaknesses and challenges. This is crucial for ensuring seamless interaction between humans and the digital environment.

2   Related Work

In recent years, a substantial body of work has emerged that is crucial for cognitive assessment using eye tracking. Only if significant differences are identified across varying levels of cognitive load it becomes meaningful to train and refine ML approaches and utilize them in the context of AR.

Eye Tracking and Cognitive Assessment. Eye tracking data provides access to a range of measurable characteristics and features, including pupil size, fixations, saccades, gaze velocity, and blink frequency [3,6,12,25,27,37]. The use of eye trackers and the subsequent analysis of gaze behavior allow for continuous, non-intrusive, and objective measurement of cognitive processes without disrupting the user's activity [11,18–20]. This capability is particularly valuable in assessing cognitive strain, as eye tracking remains one of the few viable methods for valid real-time evaluation of mental workload [27]. Among the most informative metrics for such assessments are the duration and frequency of fixations, as well as the speed and number of saccades [12]. Suzuki et al. [40] presented a work measuring cognitive load for 3D versus 2D visualization scheme using eye-tracking data with HoloLens2. Other studies, such as [10,15,26,31], also demonstrate the importance of eye tracking for assessing cognitive load. Furthermore, combining eye movement data with other physiological signals can significantly enhance the interpretability and reliability of cognitive assessments. This multimodal approach often involves the integration of techniques such as electrooculography (EOG), electroencephalography (EEG), or inertial measurement units (IMUs) [25,27].

Cognitive Assessment as Subtask of Activity Recognition. Destyanto and Lin [9] trained a convolutional neural network to recognize three different types of computer activities using the 11 most significant eye features. Significant gaze patterns were identified for each activity group, resulting in an average classification accuracy of 93.15%. Also, Bekta et al. [2] conducted a study with the objective of recognizing activities in real time using a Hololens 2. The collected data was used to train a support vector machine and a random forest. Here, an accuracy of up to 98.7% was achieved. However, assessing the cognitive load requires another view on the eye tracking data compared to activity recognition. The term *cognitive load* describes the mental effort required to complete a specific task. There are three distinct types of cognitive load: intrinsic, non-learning-related and learning-related cognitive load [38]. A number of studies have demonstrated a significant correlation between eye movement characteristics and cognitive load [12,16,27,28,32,34,38]. To this end, the test subjects were presented with a variety of tasks, including playing Tetris [27], interpreting different types of diagrams to explain a programme code [16], and recognizing and interpreting complex shapes [34]. The studies employed a range of approaches to record individual mental workload, including the use of different measures such as the NASA-TLX rating scale [32], surveys conducted by psychologically trained staff [38], and the targeted design of differently challenging levels [27]. In the study conducted by Ivanna Pavisic et al. [34], the classification of healthy individuals and those diagnosed with Alzheimer's disease was analysed using ML-based approaches. A systematic review of 58 papers by Buchner, Buntins and Kerres [5] revealed that the impact of AR on cognitive load and performance is inconclusive. The relationship between AR, cognitive load and performance is characterized by a high degree of complexity and multifaceted nature. The utilization of spatial AR has been demonstrated to enhance performance and mitigate cognitive load. Conversely, the restricted field of view of an AR headset can elevate cognitive load requirements [1]. It is noteworthy that experienced AR users are exposed to a reduced cognitive load [5].

ML-based Assessment of Cognitive Load. The initial promising approaches to assess workload based on eye movements using ML have already demonstrated accuracy rates exceeding 80% [21,25,36,39]. The study by Lim and Teo [25] focused on the identification of cognitive disorders based on eye tracking data. These methods demonstrated the capacity to solve a binary classification task, achieving an accuracy range of between 50% and 80% [36]. Two additional experiments were conducted to gain further insight into the effects of time pressure and multitasking on cognitive workload [21,39]. Test subjects were recruited to solve a variety of visual search puzzles within predefined time windows and at varying levels of difficulty, with some tasks being completed simultaneously. A number of common algorithms for solving multiclass classification problems were compared with one another. The cognitive load was categorized as "high", "medium" or "low". The most effective model achieved an accuracy of 88%. However, since the classifications refer to the entirety of the task, no meaningful information is provided about any temporal performance of the experiment.

3 Research Study

The objective of the research study presented in this work is to gather a substantial corpus of data in order to address *RQ1* and to attempt to train a ML approach. The data set comprises eye movement recordings, subjective level difficulty ratings, and a general questionnaire. In the study, the test subjects are required to search for a variable number of different sized cubes within a room in an AR environment. The trials have been designed such that they present varying degrees of difficulty and cognitive load.

3.1   Material and Methods

The study employs the Microsoft HoloLens 2 AR headset [8], Unity, and the Microsoft Reality Toolkit [33]. This setup was used to implement the different search tasks for the research study and to record the eye tracking data. For the evaluation of the eye tracking data, pymovements [17] was used. This facilitates the calculation of additional eye tracking features, including fixations, saccades, amplitude, duration and speed, which can then be utilized for the subsequent training of models. The pandas [29], scikit-learn [35] and imbalanced-learn library [24] are employed for the training of diverse ML-based classifiers.

3.2   Design

As part of the study, the test subjects are asked to complete search tasks of varying difficulties within an AR environment. The virtual holograms of cubes are randomly distributed throughout a room of a fixed size (4.48 m × 4.51 m × 2.7 m). The cubes are numbered in ascending numerical order, commencing with the number one. To facilitate recognition and reading of the number on the cube, it is displayed on all six sides. Figure 1 illustrates the planning of a trial in the development environment and its eventual appearance from the perspective of a test user. The participants are asked to identify the cubes in the room and select them in ascending numerical order. The selection is made by directing the gaze at the cube and simultaneously pressing a button on a clicker. The use of a clicker tool for the selection process was deliberate, as it allowed test subjects to avoid any potential distractions associated with other AR-specific selections, thereby enabling them to focus exclusively on the search task. The successful selection of a cube using eye tracking is indicated by colour highlighting and a slow rotation of the cube. Once a cube has been successfully selected, it is removed from the room. Test subjects are permitted to move freely during the study, which allows them to navigate the room and conduct a comprehensive search. The study is composed of a total of six distinct levels, which are assembled in a specific sequence. The cubes are available in three distinct sizes: small (ca. 4 cm), medium (ca. 10 cm), and large (ca. 20 cm). It should be noted, however, that only one size of cube is permitted per trial. A minimum of five cubes must be selected, and the number of cubes varies between five and twenty cubes per trial. In the event of an excess number of cube that cannot be selected, the test subjects are provided with a specified range of numbers within which the cube to be searched for is located. Moreover, the cube must be selected in ascending numerical order. Premature selection of a cube is not permitted and is prevented by the program. As different lighting conditions may potentially impact the visibility of the HoloLens 2 holograms [14], it is essential to ensure consistent lighting throughout the study, irrespective of external weather conditions. The room was therefore darkened and illuminated with a uniform light source. This ensured that all tests were carried out under identical conditions.

Following a full factorial design, each participant had to complete 24 trials. After signing a declaration of consent the initial eye tracking calibration is conducted at the outset of the study, followed by the first 12 trials. At the end of each trial, the participant is confronted with two statements.

1. "I found it easy to find all the objects in the room"
2. "I could read all the labels well"

Responses to these questions are given on a 5-point Likert scale (-2 disagree, +2 agree). We associate the first question with subjectively perceived difficulty levels. Following the completion of a total of 12 trials, the HoloLens 2 undergoes a second calibration to compensate for potential shifts of the glasses during the experiment. Subsequently, the remaining 12 trials are conducted, ensuring that each test subject has completed a total of 24 trials. Finally, a questionnaire is administered to each subject, wherein they are asked to rate the difficulty of the experiment and the experimental conditions. As the risk of our user study is considered minimal and the data was anonymized, there were no privacy or ethical concerns.

The study was conducted with a total of 22 participants recruited from the University ($\female$ =7, $\male$ =14) aged between 20 and 59. The subjects were, on average, 30 years of age, with a median age of 26 and a standard deviation of 10. A total of 59% of the test subjects had their inaugural experience with AR during the course of the study. The remaining 41% of the test subjects were already experienced in using AR. Additionally, 32% of the test subjects have a visual impairment that is corrected by glasses. The glasses were worn throughout the duration of the study, as they did not impede the ability to wear the HoloLens 2.

3.3   Results and Analysis of Eye Tracking Data

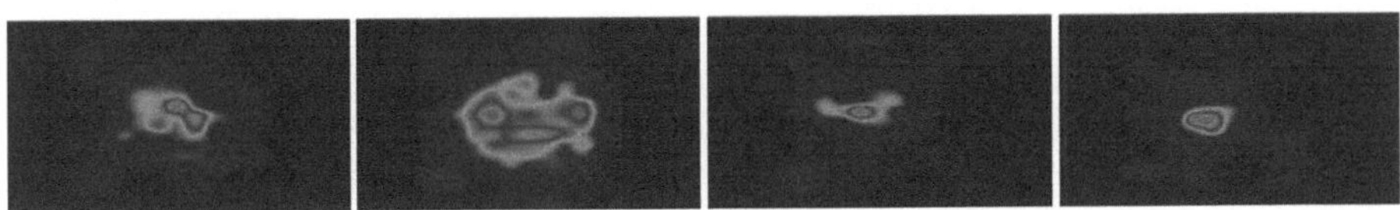

Fig. 2. shows a heatmap of the distribution of gaze positions for a single participant. The participant was required to identify five medium-sized objects among a total of 20 objects (left) and five small objects among a total of five objects (right).

The analysis of the eye tracking data is primarily focused on the investigation of significant differences between the various eye tracking features in assessing the cognitive load. This is an essential prerequisite for the application and training of ML-based approaches. Figure 2 illustrates the heatmaps that were created for four trials and two different levels of difficulty. The heatmaps demonstrate that as the number of objects in the room increases, the search becomes more intensive, resulting in a greater number of fixations. Conversely, with a limited number of objects and smaller objects to be searched for, the field of vision is more restricted, leading to a lower number of fixations.

The eye tracking data was recorded at 30 frames per second by the HoloLens2. Fixations were identified based on velocity thresholds (I-VT) [37] and saccades were identified from velocity gaze sequences [13]. These parameters were calculated using the standard configuration of pymovements [17]. We first show the correlation in Fig. 3 providing an initial overview of the various features and their relations among each other. This correlation matrix demonstrates that there is a robust positive correlation between time and the number of fixations and saccades. An increase in the number of fixations and saccades is to be expected if the observation time is extended. Additionally, it shows that the average duration of fixations and saccades are related to each other. Moreover, a decrease in the peak velocity of saccades can be observed with increasing duration of fixations or saccades. In conclusion, there are some correlations in the data, indicating the presence of some patterns and relationships between the features.

It is observed that the requisite time increases in direct proportion to the level of difficulty. This was an intentional aspect of the design, as evidenced by the inclusion of levels such as "large_5of5", "medium_5of5", "small_5of5", "large_5of20", "medium_5of20", and "small_5of20". This differentiation is also evident in the analysis of variance ($F(5, 147) = 23.9$; $p < 0.001$). Prior to conducting an ANOVA, it is standard practice to ascertain whether the data follows a normal distribution, using a Shapiro-Wilk test, and to determine whether the variance is homogeneous, using a Levene's test. A further observation is that the estimated difficulty of the test subjects' level also affects the total time required for the trials. This is also evident from the ANOVA, which reveals a significant difference ($F(5, 147) = 23.2$; $p < 0.001$). A temporal difference is also evident in the number of fixations. This is particularly apparent when comparing the number of objects. A significant difference is discernible in the analysis of variance ($F(5, 147) = 21.5$; $p < 0.001$). The same is valid for the features of the average and maximum fixation time in relation to time. Furthermore, a discrepancy in the total time required is evident when examining the number of saccades.

The most significant difference is observed in the number of objects. However, a difference in object size is also evident, as confirmed by the analysis of variance ($F(4.7) = 40.7$; $p < 0.001$). This also applies for other features such as duration, speed, and amplitude of the saccades. However, no significance could be determined for the maximum peak amplitude of the saccades. By examining the initial seconds of a trial rather than the entirety of the trial's duration, it is feasible to ascertain the trial's completion and cognitive load within a brief time frame. Accordingly, the ***initial five seconds*** were selected for analysis because a substantial number of fixations and saccades occur during this period, which

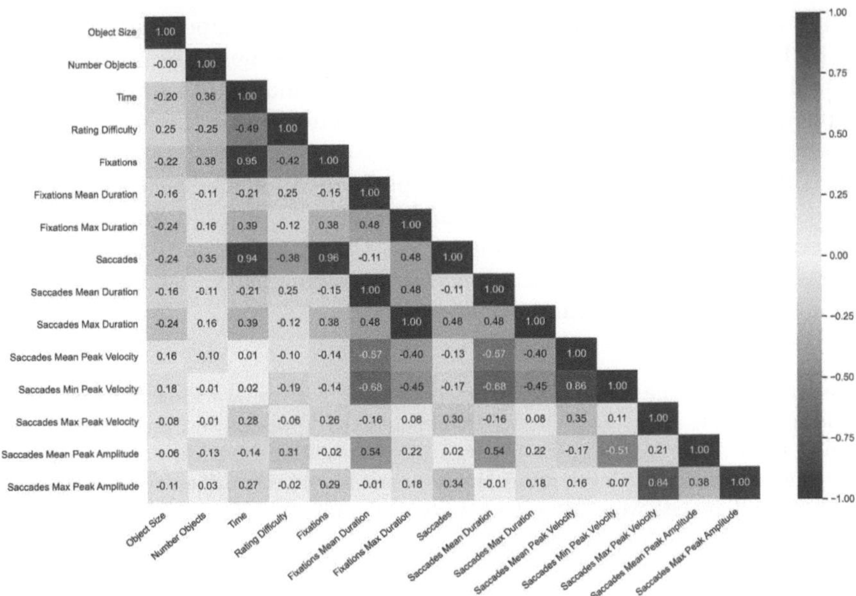

Fig. 3. illustrates the pairwise Pearson correlation coefficients between the features, with coefficients ranging from −1 (strong negative correlation, in red) to +1 (strong positive correlation, in blue). The presence of high positive correlations (e.g. , between saccades and fixations, or saccade amplitudes) and negative correlations (e.g., between saccadic velocities and other task variables) provide insights into the relationships among visual processing behaviours during task performance.(Color figure online)

can be attributed to the initial scanning of the room and the objects within it. It is observed that there is a discernible discrepancy in the number of fixations contingent on the object size, with the contrasts for the object sizes "small" and "large" being pronounced. For the medium object size, however, the discrepancies are less pronounced. Nevertheless, the analysis of variance revealed a significant difference ($F(5, 148) = 3.44$; $p = 0.006$). No significant differences were identified with regard to the average and maximum fixation duration. A comparable pattern is evident with regard to the number of saccades, as was observed with fixation.

The number of objects exhibited slight differences in relation to object sizes. However, the analysis of variance revealed a significance ($F(5, 148) = 2.76$; $p = 0.02$). Nevertheless, the p-value of 0.02 is just below the significance threshold of 5%. No significant differences were found with regard to the other features of the saccades, such as their duration, speed, or amplitude. In order to make more precise statements about individual time segments of a trial and the resulting level of difficulty, a *sliding window approach* is selected. This involves dividing a trial into 5-second sections, starting with the first second. This 5-second window is then shifted by one second until the end of the trial.

This allows more data points to be generated and the temporal evolution of the data to be mapped. In this way, a ML process can be better trained to provide real-time estimates of levels of difficulty. In addition, a *majority voting* is applied for classes identified by the model to determine the level of difficulty for a trial over time.

In Table 1, analyses of variance were performed for all eye tracking features in relation to each level (object size and number of objects) and the difficulty reported by the subjects. A p-value of less than 0.001 was calculated for each of these features. This means that each eye tracking feature shows a significant difference in terms of level and difficulty.

Table 1. Presents the results of variance analysis for eye-tracking features utilizing the sliding window approach. The table presents the F-values and associated p-values, obtained from ANOVA tests, for a range of eye-tracking metrics, across two factors: object size and number (level), and the assessment of trial difficulty by participants. Significant differences were identified across all measured features, with p-values < 0.001 in all cases.

Comparison	Eye Tracking Feature	Analysis of Variance
Level (object size & -number)	Number **fixations**	$F(5.5495) = 112$; p<0.001
	Average duration	$F(5.5390) = 21.9$; p<0.001
	Maximum duration	$F(5.5513) = 24.4$; p<0.001
	Number **saccades**	$F(5.5434) = 62.1$; p<0.001
	Average duration	$F(5.5391) = 21.9$; p<0.001
	Maximum duration	$F(5.5519) = 25.5$; p<0.001
	Average peak velocity	$F(5.5358) = 74.6$; p<0.001
	Minimum peak velocity	$F(5.5331) = 131$; p<0.001
	Maximum peak velocity	$F(5.5423) = 22.8$; p<0.001
	Average peak amplitude	$F(5.5391) = 35.0$; p<0.001
	Maximum peak amplitude	$F(5.5386) = 25.6$; p<0.001
Difficulty (1 = easy, 5 = difficult)	Number **fixations**	$F(4,628) = 23.9$; p<0.001
	Average duration	$F(4,643) = 96.0$; p<0.001
	Maximum duration	$F(4,654) = 117.0$; p<0.001
	Number **saccades**	$F(4,635) = 49.0$; p<0.001
	Average duration	$F(4,642) = 93.6$; p<0.001
	Maximum duration	$F(4,653) = 120.0$; p<0.001
	Average peak velocity	$F(4,655) = 48.7$; p<0.001
	Minimum peak velocity	$F(4,640) = 200.0$; p<0.001
	Maximum peak velocity	$F(4,637) = 24.1$; p<0.001
	Average peak amplitude	$F(4,650) = 20.0$; p<0.001
	Maximum peak amplitude	$F(4,628)144.0$; p<0.001

3.4 Discussion Based on Feature Analysis

To conclude, with respect to eye tracking data, clear differences and significance were recognized for the individual features. These features included the number and duration of fixations, as well as the number, duration, speed, and amplitude of saccades. Thus we conclude that the variability of eye movement metrics can be used to understand cognitive levels. Moreover, it was noted that in the assessment of the diverse temporal classifications, the object size designated as "medium" frequently exhibited no discernible and substantial distinctions from the other object sizes. This may be indicative of an erroneous or insufficiently disparate object size in comparison to the other object sizes, specifically "small" and "large". Additionally, it is notable that the perceived difficulty of some levels was below the expected threshold for the test subjects. The research study has demonstrated that the HoloLens 2 is an effective tool for recording eye movements during simultaneous use of the AR glasses, and provides valuable data sets for further investigation. An increase in eye movements, including a greater number, length, and speed of saccades, is indicative of an elevated cognitive load. The results thus revealed a connection between eye movements and the understanding of cognitive load. The variance analyses confirmed the desired differential cognitive load across the levels, demonstrating significant differences between them. Thus we summarize that the gaze detection data of the HoloLens 2 is suitable for drawing conclusions about the cognitive load in the AR environment during search tasks.

4   Learning-Based Recognition

The knowledge derived from eye tracking data are now employed in the development of ML methodologies for assessing cognitive load during AR search tasks. The process of recognition entails the classification of completed levels, object size, number of objects, and the difficulty ratings specified by test subjects. These factors represent the various cognitive loads that were considered and aimed when designing the difficulty of levels with the assistance of object size and number. Additionally, the benefits and drawbacks of different data processing techniques are evaluated.

4.1   Design

For further analysis, we used a dataset acquired in the user study. As a consequence of the disparate time requirements associated with each level of difficulty, imbalances emerge within the data set, whereby certain classes are underrepresented. This imbalance of classes is primarily evident in the sliding window approach, given that the disparate time requirements result in varying numbers of data points. The precise data distribution for the levels and difficulty classes is illustrated in Fig. 4. Given the restricted scope of the data set, oversampling is employed. Nevertheless, in instances where the discrepancy in absent data points is considerable, undersampling is employed for the predominant class. This guarantees that there is no significant imbalance due to the presence of duplicate data points, which could distort the results. Furthermore, the data is scaled such that all features contribute equally to the training and outliers are not given undue weight. Through scaling, standardization and normalization, the disparate value ranges of the features are adjusted to align with one another while simultaneously retaining their relative relationships and distributions.

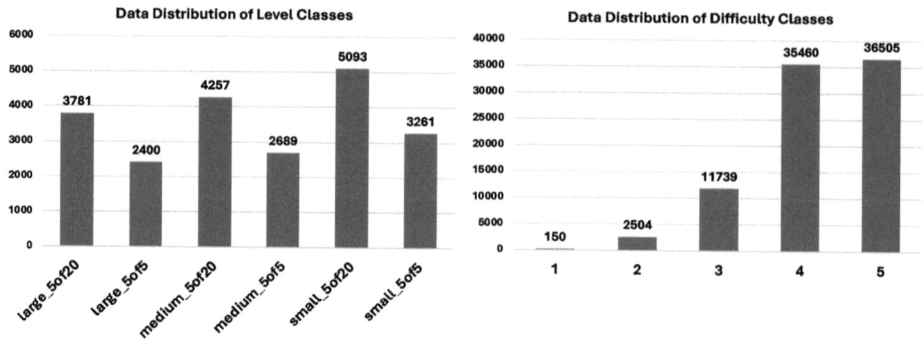

Fig. 4. shows the data distribution of the individual level and difficulty classes for the sliding window approach

As we target for more explainable and interpretable models, two distinct ML models were employed for classification purposes: the K-nearest neighbour (KNN) model, and the random forest (RF). The optimal hyperparameters for these models were identified through grid search and K-fold cross-validation. The recorded data was processed using a five-second sliding window approach. This entailed viewing a five-second section of the trial at a time and determining the cognitive load or level. The temporal section was shifted by one second with each iteration, allowing for the identification of a temporal progression. This approach enabled the estimation or classification of the cognitive load for any short time segment. Furthermore, it facilitated the implementation of a real-time evaluation approach. We conducted both subject-dependent and subject-independent analysis. The results for random division refers to a random split of a subject-independent analysis of training (80%) and test set (20%), while the results for person groups and individual's split allowed a subject-dependent analysis.

4.2   Results of ML Models on Eye-Tracking Data

The various ML models demonstrated disparate accuracies in classifying the levels and the associated cognitive load. The KNN and RF models demonstrated the equally high accuracy rates for the classification of the data set with the sliding window approach. An extension of these two models by utilizing a majority voting based decision for fusing several successive time instances are shown later. This method yielded the best results.

K-Nearest-Neighbor. The KNN classifier was employed on the data set using the sliding window approach. The hyperparameters are identified through grid search with K=5, and the distance between data points was calculated using the Manhattan distance metric. With regard to the number of objects and object size, the highest accuracy was achieved with this model. The precise percentage

Table 2. Shows the accuracies and F1 scores with KNN for all subjects (random distribution and person split) and the average for individual subjects

	Random Division		Person Groups Split		Individuals Split(Average)	
	Accuracy	F1-Score	Accuracy	F1-Score	Accuracy	F1-Score
Level	47.50%	47.32%	45.86%	45.71%	67.39%	67.15%
Object Size	58.54%	58.39%	57.20%	57.19%	74.54%	74.42%
Number of Objects	69.07%	68.51%	69.45%	69.02%	81.07%	80.91%
Difficulty	49.33%	49.69%	55.56%	52.38%	76.14%	76.12%

values attained by the models were listed in Table 2. Furthermore, the efficacy of various data partitioning techniques was evaluated. In random division, data set is randomized into training and test set. While data in case of person groups are split into a training and a test set according to subject groups. This resulted in four subjects being designated as the test set and the remaining subjects being allocated to the training set. This setup resulted in outcomes that were highly comparable to those obtained through the random division. Finally, a distinct model was developed for each subject, employing a random allocation strategy. The average accuracy was subsequently calculated. The latter method yielded higher accuracy rates, with an average of 18.68% points compared to the random allocation approach. This is attributable to the distinctive gaze and search patterns exhibited by the test subjects. The level value was determined with an accuracy of 47.50%. As depicted in the confusion matrix in Fig. 5, the diagonal is readily discernible. Levels with the number of objects "5of5" are most frequently confused with levels and the number of objects "5of20". Furthermore, the level "small_5of20" is most frequently classified incorrectly.

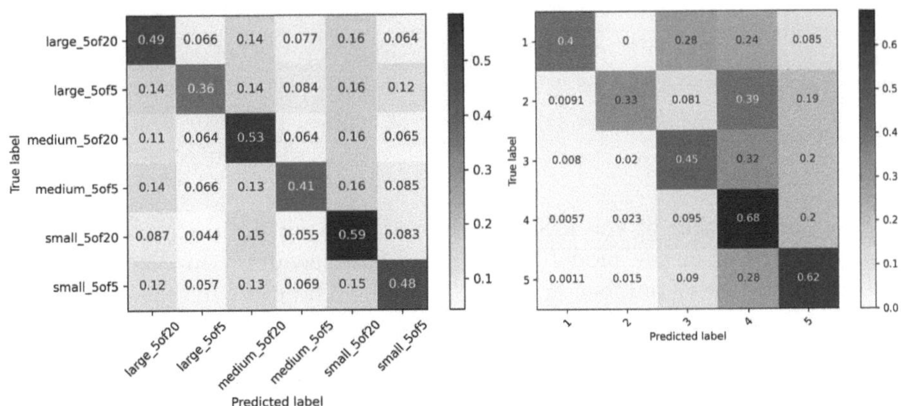

Fig. 5. shows the confusion matrix for the classification of the level and difficulty for the sliding window approach and random division of the data with KNN

The object size is correctly classified with an accuracy of 58.54%. The estimation of large objects is the least accurate. Nevertheless, the misclassification is distributed relatively evenly across the different classes. The aforementioned observation that the classification of the number of objects as "5of5" is particularly challenging. It is also corroborated when examining the model's performance, which classifies the number of objects with an accuracy of 69.07%. The majority of misclassification occur in the "5of5" category. The trained model can determine the difficulty perceived and reported by the subjects with an accuracy of 49.33%. It is noteworthy that in instances of misclassification, the more straightforward classes are frequently predicted at a higher level of difficulty. This can be attributed to the lower number of more challenging classes.

Random Forest. The same evaluation is conducted with RF method, yielding comparable results to those obtained with the KNN method. In the hyperparameter search, the optimal number of trees was found to be 30, with consideration given to the maximum number of features. The quality of the generated tree splits was evaluated using the Shannon entropy. The application of the three variants of the data split yielded slightly enhanced results for each classification. The precise percentages attained by the models are listed in Table 3. In comparison to the general model, which is based on data from all test subjects, and the models that were trained individually for each test subject, an average improvement in accuracy of 19.17% points was achieved.

Table 3. shows the accuracies and F1 scores with RF for all subjects (random distribution and person split) and the average for individual subjects

	Random Division		Person Groups Split		Individuals Split (Average)	
	Accuracy	F1-Score	Accuracy	F1-Score	Accuracy	F1-Score
Level	51.28%	51.38%	47.35%	47.29%	74.33%	74.26%
Object Size	63.56%	63.44%	58.05%	58.02%	78.68%	78.56%
Number of Objects	69.62%	68.24%	70.85%	69.99%	84.35%	84.18%
Difficulty	54.08%	54.41%	55.33%	53.65%	77.87%	77.62%

The classification of the level is achieved with an accuracy of 51.28%. As illustrated in Fig. 6, the model exhibits the least accuracy in determining the levels with the lower number of objects, "5of5". The most misclassified level is "large_5of5", with the lowest accuracy. All saccade velocity features are of great importance for the model, as is the maximum amplitude of the saccades. The pure number of fixations and saccades is of less importance.

A model with an accuracy of 63.56% could be trained to make statements about the object size. As with the KNN model, the largest object size is predicted with the greatest degree of inaccuracy. The majority of objects are incorrectly categorized as small. With respect to the significance of the features for the

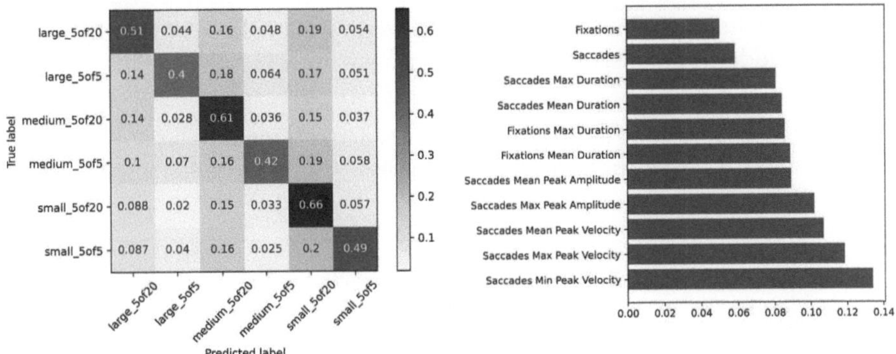

Fig. 6. presents the confusion matrix and importance of features for the classification of the level for the sliding window approach and random distribution of the data with RF

classification of the model, the picture is strikingly similar to that of the determination of the level. Similarly, the features associated with the peak velocity of the saccades are of paramount importance. As with the KNN model, the RF model encounters greater challenges in accurately identifying the lower number of objects when classifying object size. The mean accuracy for the assignment of object numbers is 69.62%. The number of objects "5of20" is most often correctly matched, with an accuracy of 90%. However, the number of objects designated as "5of5" is only correctly matched with an accuracy of 49%, resulting in a higher probability of misclassification into this object number class (51%). With regard to the importance of the features, a similar picture emerges as previously observed. In comparison to the other models, the duration of the fixations exhibits a notable increase in importance. The difficulty level, as determined by the participants following each trial on a five-point Likert scale, yielded a correct classification probability of 54.08%. Similarly, the levels perceived as easier can be determined with a higher degree of accuracy. However, difficulty levels one to three can be correctly assigned with a probability of less than 50%. Notably, the second difficulty level stands out as it is categorized incorrectly more often than correctly. Additionally, difficulty level four is classified incorrectly particularly frequently. The importance of the features in this model is again very similar to the previous RF models, with only slight deviations.

Consideration Focuses on Higher Number of Objects. Due to the unsatisfactory results obtained for the classification of the number of objects "5of5", these classes were excluded from the data set. Subsequently, the KNN models and those based on RF were trained anew on the filtered data set. The results are summarized in Table 4. An average increase in accuracy of 6.97% for KNN and 2.81% for RF was achieved for the classification of the data set of all subjects with random allocation. In contrast, an average increase in accuracy of only

3.74% for KNN and 1.32% for RF was achieved for the classification by subject group. All models demonstrated an enhancement in accuracy.

Table 4. shows the accuracies only for the levels with the number of objects "5of20" with KNN and RF for all subjects (random division and person split) and the average for individual subjects

	Random division (only "5of20")		Groups of people Split (only "5of20")		Individuals Split Average (only "5of20")	
	KNN	RF	KNN	RF	KNN	RF
Object Size	62,46%	66,89%	57,73%	59,14%	78,48%	83,27%
Difficulty	55,71%	56,37%	57,28%	56,87%	79,25%	82,09%

Majority Voting. The highest levels of accuracy were achieved in the classification of the level and the associated object size and number of objects through the utilization of the sliding window approach in the training of the models. The approach allows for the estimation of a level for any time segment of five seconds. Moreover, multiple classifications of the level can be obtained at disparate points in time throughout the course of the trial. The collected classifications then serve as the basis for a majority decision and a classification for the entire trial. The level that occurs with the greatest frequency within a given trial is designated as the label for the entire trial. The accuracy of the majority decision can be considered from two different perspectives. Firstly, the classification of the level by the majority decision can be analysed across all 24 trials per test person. Secondly, the temporal course of a trial of a test person can be examined, whereby the majority decision has correctly classified the entire trial. Table 5 illustrates the mean values across all subjects for these two approaches. It is observed that the KNN method exhibits a markedly higher accuracy than the RF method when considering all trials of a test person. Conversely, RF demonstrates superior performance when examining the accuracy for a single trial of a subject with the majority decision.

Figure 7 (a) presents a heatmap-like representation of the progression of the classifications on the number of objects. The values displayed on the x-axis represent the results of a single trial. In total, 528 trials were conducted on the data recorded in the research study. The y-axis represents the time in seconds. To enhance clarity, trials exceeding the average time requirement are excluded from the visualizations. A green dot indicates a correct classification of the object size, whereas a red dot denotes an incorrect classification. In the event that a trail is completed within the average time frame, the remaining points are indicated by the use of white. It is observed that the majority of misclassifications are relatively brief, isolated instances, occurring outside the typical range of classification. Correct classification occurs consistently before and after these

Table 5. shows the accuracy achieved with Majority Voting across all levels and the individual levels

	Average time history for all levels		Average time history for one level	
	KNN	RF	KNN	RF
Level	66.76%	45.83%	53.85%	52.11%
Object Size	70.83%	62.50%	56.41%	58.14%
Number of Objects	75.00%	62.50%	68.75%	73.60%
Difficulty	66.67%	58.33%	57.33%	61.11%

instances. It is also noteworthy that longer periods of approximately five seconds are consistently correctly classified. The same visualization is leveraged to display the classification of object size. As illustrated in Fig. 7 (b), a third colour has been introduced to indicate a less severe misclassification. This may occur, for instance, when a medium-sized object is classified as either small or large. In those cases, the distance between the object sizes is only one. Conversely, if a large object is incorrectly classified as small, the distance between the object sizes is two, and the classification is indicated by a red dot in the graphic.

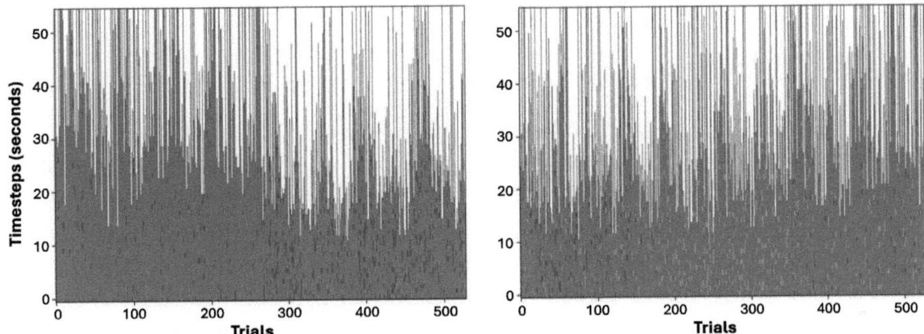

Fig. 7. visualizes the classification of the number of objects (a) and the object size (b) for the sliding window approach with RF as colour visualization in a heatmap. Green indicates a correct and red an incorrect classification. Orange symbolizes a less serious misclassification in both directions. (Color figure online)

4.3   Discussion Based on Results

The most optimal outcomes were attained through the utilization of an array of finetuned ML models, employing the sliding window methodology for the processing of the data. The sliding window approach enabled the temporal progression of a trial to be reflected in the data set. Nevertheless, an examination of the outcomes produced by the diverse models also uncovers certain deficiencies.

For instance, it is evident that the configuration of the levels and their associated difficulties require refinement. There was a considerable degree of misclassification in relation to the object size designated as "medium". Additionally, the models encountered difficulty in accurately categorizing the number of objects presented, specifically "5of5". Overall, the test subjects generally perceived the difficulty level to be lower than intended, which has implications for the precision of the models in assessing the more challenging classes. This is because fewer data points were collected for the extreme classes, leading to an imbalance in the distribution of classes. The application of majority voting to determine the level based on the entire data set yielded the best results. The accuracy of the method has increased significantly, and a detailed examination of Fig. 7 reveals distinct patterns or clusters of consecutive correct classifications. The ($RQ2$) can now be confirmed. The data collected from the research study can be leveraged to apply various ML approaches, thus enabling automated statements about cognitive load at different points in time. The ML models, such as KNN and RF, were trained to classify the level of difficulties and thus associated to cognitive load, and the resulting performance was analysed and compared. Different fine-grained classifications were considered, from the binary classification of the number of objects to the classification of the six different levels. The levels and their features are representative of the cognitive load. Classification accuracies between 50% and 80% were achieved with the different models.

5   Limitations

The research study focused exclusively on eye tracking and the subjects' self-report of their cognitive perception. Using our study, the variability of eye movement metrics demonstrated their ability to interpret cognitive levels. In addition, these eye movement features appeared to be significantly relevant for understanding cognitive load. A comprehensive analysis of these features is presented in our study based on feature analysis. To corroborate these reports, it would be beneficial to employ an alternative method for measuring cognitive load, such as monitoring other biometric parameters, such as pulse, neurological activity, via electroencephalography (EEG) or ventral electrodermal activity (EDA). Moreover, the research study exclusively focused on a single task within the AR environment, namely, searching for virtual objects within a real-world setting. However, AR is not only concerned with displaying information in the real world, but also interacting with virtual elements. The addition of further task types that require interaction with the hands or body movements would represent a further extension. Nevertheless, it must be considered that test subjects with previous AR experience have clear advantages, and this can lead to an imbalance in the data. The trained models might classify the level of mastery demonstrated by the test subjects. Here, it is essential to ascertain whether the cognitive load inherent to the levels can be transferred to other task types with potentially disparate cognitive loads. The analysis of the study revealed that not all test subjects were able to reach the limits of their cognitive performance, and that the levels were perceived as easier than originally intended. This issue could be addressed, for instance, by incorporating diverse object sizes and numbers. Alternatively, utilizing a larger room for the study could enhance the difficulty, given the increased distance to the objects and the necessity for more extensive movement to process the information. To address this, a new experiment should be conducted, wherein subjects with the anticipated level of cognitive performance were initially tested to confirm the difficulty of the setup. Furthermore, increasing the time pressure during a trial could also result in a higher cognitive load. It is also noted that the data recording process did not include the successful or unsuccessful selection, which was indicated by the clicker being pressed. Consequently, it is not feasible to separate the data into its constituent search periods. An alternative approach would be to examine the data up to the initial successful selection of the cube, which would yield insights into navigation and search strategies. Training distinct models for each temporal section could further enhance the precision of the classification results.

6   Conclusion

It can be stated that gaze tracking with the HoloLens 2 is a viable method for cognitive assessment in an AR environment. A variety of ML techniques can be employed with the eye-tracking data to generate automated insights about the cognitive load, even at any point in time within the recorded data set. Two distinctive ML approaches (RF and KNN) were trained to classify different levels of difficulty by using the sliding window approach. The resulting accuracies ranged from 50% to 80%. The sliding window approach yielded considerably superior outcomes, which can be attributed to the specific gaze patterns and search strategies employed by each individual. Moreover, a majority voting was incorporated into the models, with the objective of classifying the level over the entire time period for a single trial. The optimal model demonstrated a level determination accuracy of 66.76%. This accuracy allows significant insights to be derived for the advancement of AR applications. Nevertheless, the assessment of the study demonstrated that the configuration of the levels is sub-optimal and that the level of difficulty must be augmented in certain instances. As the study focused exclusively on training search tasks, it is essential to ascertain whether the trained models can be effectively applied to other tasks with varying cognitive loads. Yet, this work provides significant insights into the potentials of a ML analysis of cognitive load using eye tracking data in AR environments.

References

1. Baumeister, J., et al.: Cognitive cost of using augmented reality displays. IEEE Trans. Visual Comput. Graphics **23**, 2378–2388 (2017). https://doi.org/10.1109/TVCG.2017.2735098

2. Bektaş, K., et al.: Gear: gaze-enabled augmented reality for human activity recognition. In: Proceedings of the 2023 Symposium on Eye Tracking Research and Applications. ETRA 2023, ACM, New York, NY, USA (2023). https://doi.org/10.1145/3588015.3588402

3. Blascheck, T., Kurzhals, K., Raschke, M., Burch, M., Weiskopf, D., Ertl, T.: State-of-the-art of visualization for eye tracking data. In: Eurographics Conference on Visualization. The Eurographics Association, University of Stuttgart, Germany (2014). https://api.semanticscholar.org/CorpusID:14315478

4. Brown, E.J., Fujimoto, K., Blumenkopf, B., Kim, A.S., Kontson, K.L., Benz, H.L.: Usability assessments for augmented reality head-mounted displays in open surgery and interventional procedures: a systematic review. Multimodal Technol. Interact. **7**(5) (2023). https://doi.org/10.3390/mti7050049, https://www.mdpi.com/2414-4088/7/5/49

5. Buchner, J., Buntins, K., Kerres, M.: The impact of augmented reality on cognitive load and performance: a systematic review. J. Comput. Assist. Learn. **38**, 285–303 (2021). https://doi.org/10.1111/jcal.12617

6. Burch, M.: Etra 2018 - tutorial: Eye tracking and visual analytics. https://etra.acm.org/2018/2018-06-24_ETRA_Tutorial_02_Vis_VA.pdf, June 2018

7. Committee on Virtual Reality Research and Development: Computer Science and Telecommunications Board, National Research Council, National Academy of Sciences: Virtual reality. National Academies Press, Washington, D.C., DC (1994)

8. Corporation, M.: Informationen zur hardware der hololens 2 July 2024. https://learn.microsoft.com/de-de/hololens/hololens2-hardware

9. Destyanto, T.Y.R., Lin, R.F.: Detecting computer activities using eye-movement features. J. Ambient. Intell. Humaniz. Comput. 1–11 (2020). https://doi.org/10.1007/s12652-020-02683-8

10. Ding, L., et al.: Clera: a unified model for joint cognitive load and eye region analysis in the wild. ACM Trans. Comput.-Hum. Interact. **30**(6), 1–23 (2023)

11. Duchowski, A.T., et al.: The index of pupillary activity: measuring cognitive load vis-à-vis task difficulty with pupil oscillation. In: Proceedings of the 2018 CHI Conference on Human Factors in Computing Systems, pp. 1–13 (2018)

12. Eckstein, M.K., Guerra-Carrillo, B., Singley, A.T.M., Bunge, S.A.: Beyond eye gaze: what else can eyetracking reveal about cognition and cognitive development? Dev. Cogn. Neurosci. **25**, 69–91 (2017). https://doi.org/10.1016/j.dcn.2016.11.001

13. Engbert, R., Kliegl, R.: Microsaccades uncover the orientation of covert attention. Vision. Res. **43**(9), 1035–1045 (2003)

14. Erickson, A., Kim, K., Bruder, G., Welch, G.F.: Exploring the limitations of environment lighting on optical see-through head-mounted displays. In: Symposium on Spatial User Interaction, SUI 2020, ACM, University of Central Florida, Orlando, Florida, October 2020. https://doi.org/10.1145/3385959.3418445

15. Kaluarachchi, T.I., Sapkota, S., Taradel, J., Thevenon, A., Matthies, D.J., Nanayakkara, S.: Eyeknowyou: a diy toolkit to support monitoring cognitive load and actual screen time using a head-mounted webcam. In: Adjunct Publication of the 23rd International Conference on Mobile Human-Computer Interaction, pp. 1–8 (2021)

16. Katona, J.: Measuring cognition load using eye-tracking parameters based on algorithm description tools. Sensors **22**(3), 912 (2022). https://doi.org/10.3390/s22030912

17. Krakowczyk, D.G., et al.: pymovements: a python package for processing eye movement data. In: 2023 Symposium on Eye Tracking Research and Applications.

ETRA 2023, ACM, New York, NY, USA (2023). https://doi.org/10.1145/3588015. 3590134

18. Krejtz, K., Duchowski, A., Krejtz, I., Szarkowska, A., Kopacz, A.: Discerning ambient/focal attention with coefficient k. ACM Trans. Appl. Percept. (TAP) **13**(3), 1–20 (2016)

19. Krejtz, K., et al.: Gaze transition entropy. ACM Trans. Appl. Percept. (TAP) **13**(1), 1–20 (2015)

20. Krejtz, K., Duchowski, A.T., Niedzielska, A., Biele, C., Krejtz, I.: Eye tracking cognitive load using pupil diameter and microsaccades with fixed gaze. PLoS ONE **13**(9), e0203629 (2018)

21. Ktistakis, E., et al.: Colet: a dataset for cognitive workload estimation based on eye-tracking. Comput. Methods Programs Biomed. **224**, 106989 (2022). https://doi.org/10.2139/ssrn.4059768

22. Lauer, L., Altmeyer, K., Malone, S., Barz, M., Brünken, R., Sonntag, D., Peschel, M.: Investigating the usability of a head-mounted display augmented reality device in elementary school children. Sensors **21**(19) (2021). https://doi.org/10.3390/s21196623, https://www.mdpi.com/1424-8220/21/19/6623

23. Lee, J., Zhan, T., Wu, S.T.: Prospects and challenges in augmented reality displays. Virt. Real. Intell. Hardware **1**, 77 (2019). https://doi.org/10.3724/SP.J.2096-5796.2018.0009

24. Lemaître, G., Nogueira, F., Aridas, C.K.: Imbalanced-learn: a python toolbox to tackle the curse of imbalanced datasets in machine learning. J. Mach. Learn. Res. **18**(17), 1–5 (2017). http://jmlr.org/papers/v18/16-365

25. Lim, J.Z., Mountstephens, J., Teo, J.: Eye-tracking feature extraction for biometric machine learning. Front. Neurorobotics **15** (2022). https://doi.org/10.3389/fnbot.2021.796895

26. Madhusanka, B., Ramadass, S., Rajagopal, P., Herath, H.: Attention-aware recognition of activities of daily living based on eye gaze tracking. In: Internet of Things for Human-Centered Design: Application to Elderly Healthcare, pp. 155–179. Springer (2022)

27. Mallick, R., Slayback, D., Touryan, J., Ries, A.J., Lance, B.J.: The use of eye metrics to index cognitive workload in video games. In: 2016 IEEE Second Workshop on Eye Tracking and Visualization (ETVIS), IEEE, Baltimore, MD, USA, October 2016. https://doi.org/10.1109/etvis.2016.7851168

28. Marconi, M., Do Carmo Blanco, N., Zimmer, C., Guyon, A.: Eye movements in response to different cognitive activities measured by eyetracking: a prospective study on some of the neurolinguistics programming theories. J. Eye Movement Res. **16**(2) (2023). https://doi.org/10.16910/jemr.16.2.2

29. McKinney, W.: Data structures for statistical computing in python. In: Proceedings of the 9th Python in Science Conference, pp. 56–61. SciPy, SciPy, Austin, Texas, USA (2010). https://doi.org/10.25080/majora-92bf1922-00a

30. Mézière, D.C., Yu, L., Reichle, E.D., von der Malsburg, T., McArthur, G.: Using eye-tracking measures to predict reading comprehension. Read. Res. Q. **58**(3), 425–449 (2023)

31. Nasri, M., Kosa, M., Chukoskie, L., Moghaddam, M., Harteveld, C.: Exploring eye tracking to detect cognitive load in complex virtual reality training. In: 2024 IEEE International Symposium on Mixed and Augmented Reality Adjunct (ISMAR-Adjunct), pp. 51–54. IEEE (2024)

32. Okano, T., Nakayama, M.: Research on time series evaluation of cognitive load factors using features of eye movement. In: 2022 Symposium on Eye Tracking

Research and Applications. ETRA '22, Association for Computing Machinery, New York, NY, USA (2022). https://doi.org/10.1145/3517031.3529236

33. Organization, M.R.T., Microsoft: mixed reality toolkit 3, June 2024. https://learn.microsoft.com/en-us/windows/mixed-reality/mrtk-unity/mrtk3-overview/

34. Pavisic, I.M., et al.: Eyetracking metrics in young onset alzheimer's disease: a window into cognitive visual functions. Front. Neurol. **8** (2017). https://doi.org/10.3389/fneur.2017.00377

35. Pedregosa, F., et al.: Scikit-learn: machine learning in python. J. Mach. Learn. Res. **12**, 2825–2830 (2011)

36. Rizzo, A., Ermini, S., Zanca, D., Bernabini, D., Rossi, A.: A machine learning approach for detecting cognitive interference based on eye-tracking data. Front. Hum. Neurosci. **16** (2022). https://doi.org/10.3389/fnhum.2022.806330

37. Salvucci, D.D., Goldberg, J.H.: Identifying fixations and saccades in eye-tracking protocols. In: Proceedings of the 2000 Symposium on Eye Tracking Research & Applications, ETRA 2000, pp. 71–78. ACM, New York, NY, USA (2000). https://doi.org/10.1145/355017.355028

38. Skaramagkas, V., et al.: Review of eye tracking metrics involved in emotional and cognitive processes. IEEE Rev. Biomed. Eng. **16**, 260–277 (2021). https://doi.org/10.1109/RBME.2021.3066072

39. Skaramagkas, V., et al.: Cognitive workload level estimation based on eye tracking: a machine learning approach. In: 2021 IEEE 21st International Conference on Bioinformatics and Bioengineering, pp. 1–5. IEEE, Kragujevac, Serbia (2021). https://doi.org/10.1109/BIBE52308.2021.9635166

40. Suzuki, Y., Wild, F., Scanlon, E.: Measuring cognitive load with eye-tracking during mental rotation with 2d and 3d visualization in ar. In: International Conference on Immersive Learning, pp. 34–48. Springer (2024)

Lightweight Deep Learning for Sensor-Based HAR: Benchmarking Optimization Strategies

Sumeyye Agac[1(✉)] [iD] and Özlem Durmaz Incel[2] [iD]

[1] Computer Engineering Department, Bogazici University, Istanbul, Turkey
sumeyyeagacc@gmail.com
[2] Pervasive Systems Research Group, University of Twente,
Enschede, The Netherlands
ozlem.durmaz@utwente.nl

Abstract. This paper explores effective deep learning methods for sensor-based Human Activity Recognition (HAR), emphasizing their implementation in resource-limited wearable devices where Microcontroller Units (MCUs) impose restrictions on memory and processing capabilities. We aim to minimize both computational and memory requirements while ensuring high recognition accuracy. We offer a benchmark comparison of pruning and quantization optimization techniques versus lightweight models enhanced through attention mechanisms and knowledge distillation, from both recognition success and resource-efficiency angles. We evaluate two leading deep learning architectures, DeepConvLSTM and SqueezeNet, across four benchmark HAR datasets: Opportunity, Sensors, Wisdm, and Pamap2. For devices with limited memory capacity, we recommend using lightweight models that integrate attention mechanisms and knowledge distillation. We emphasize that quantization should be prioritized to enhance efficiency, with pruning acting as a secondary approach. Additionally, we provide practical guidelines for deploying optimized HAR models on resource-constrained wearable devices.

Keywords: human activity recognition · deep learning · attention · knowledge distillation · quantization · pruning · on-device AI

1 Introduction

In recent years, sensor-based Human Activity Recognition (HAR) using deep learning techniques [24] has shown great promise in a variety of fields, including healthcare and sports. In particular, wearable devices equipped with multisensor capabilities have emerged as ideal platforms for HAR. Due to their high power efficiency and compact size, microcontroller units (MCUs) dominate wearable Internet of Things (IoT) technologies [11]. In contrast to mobile platforms, deep HAR models face challenges due to the restricted memory capacity

Ö. Durmaz Incel et al. (Eds.): iWOAR 2025, LNCS 16292, pp. 77–98, 2026.
https://doi.org/10.1007/978-3-032-13312-0_5

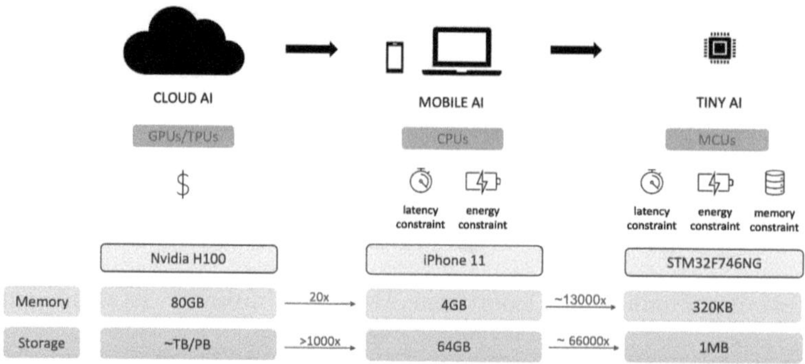

Fig. 1. Typical memory and storage capacities.

of MCUs (Fig. 1). Examples of MCUs provide 32 KB (Nordic Thingy:52), 320 KB (STM32F746NG) of SRAM, and 256 KB (Arduino Zero) to 1 MB of Flash (Arduino Nano 33 BLE). Therefore, it is crucial to develop models that are accurate, lightweight, low in complexity and resource use, while also ensuring real-time processing and energy efficiency.

Various strategies have been proposed at the model, algorithm, and hardware levels to address the resource demands of deep learning models [29]. One strategy at the model level involves creating resource-efficient models like MobileNets [17] and SqueezeNets [18]. Alternatively, resource usage can be reduced in large models. For instance, model pruning decreases complexity by eliminating unnecessary neurons or layers [21]. Similarly, quantization reduces the precision of model parameters to save resources [21]. However, despite their common use, these techniques are not solutions that can be applied indiscriminately [16]. The efficiency of pruning relies on the hardware, and it can require special hardware support. Quantization, although advantageous in reducing resource consumption, may result in a compromise in accuracy if not properly managed and is constrained by compatibility challenges with the target devices. Additionally, while tools such as TensorFlow Lite offer support for quantization and pruning, these techniques only lower resource usage to a limited degree and may not be adequate for extremely resource-limited devices, especially because of their limited reduction in storage size [21]. The issue is further complicated by the wide variety of hardware and sensor modalities found in edge devices. While pruning and quantization address model efficiency at the parameter level [3], knowledge distillation (KD) offers a complementary approach by transferring learned patterns from complex to compact models [15]. This is particularly valuable for wearables needing both accuracy and efficiency.

Several studies have explored optimizing deep learning models for sensor-based HAR to reduce computational demands and improve deployment on resource-constrained devices. Contoli et al. [8] applied pruning techniques to deep models on the UCI-HAR dataset, achieving reduced model sizes, although encountering deployment issues on ESP32, reflecting the limitations previously mentioned. A 1D Convolutional Neural Network (CNN) with quantization on a RISC-V MCU, maintaining high accuracy while reducing memory usage and energy consumption is implemented in [9]. Ghibellini et al. [13] used a 1D CNN on an Arduino Nano 33 BLE for industrial HAR. In other studies [4,28], researchers focused on quantizing deep learning models and deploying them on mobile devices, demonstrating significant resource savings without compromising accuracy.

Despite these investigations, significant gaps remain in resource-efficient, sensor-based HAR. To our knowledge, there is one recent study that examines the use of both quantization and pruning techniques in sensor-based HAR [8]. This study, however, focuses on standard architectures (CNN, LSTM, CNN-LSTM) rather than state-of-the-art sensor-based HAR models like DeepConvLSTM [24] or well-known efficient architectures like SqueezeNet [18]. Besides, the study uses only the UCI-HAR dataset. The lack of generalizability is also a concern, as in most studies, the models are tested on a single dataset, limiting their robustness.

A few studies have examined knowledge distillation (KD) for sensor-based HAR. For instance, progressive cross-modal KD models have been created to boost recognition accuracy by utilizing skeleton-to-sensor data [6]. In addition, ensemble-based KD approaches have improved performance by leveraging multi-channel sensor data alongside DeepConvLSTM and CNN architectures [10]. Nonetheless, the majority of these initiatives concentrate solely on enhancing accuracy and do not provide thorough assessments of resource efficiency, model size, or inference latency- factors vital for deployment on wearable devices.

One emerging approach, which is also utilized in transformers and large language models (LLMs), involves leveraging attention mechanisms to enhance the performance of lightweight models or student models in KD. One recent study [1] has introduced attention distillation for HAR. This work demonstrates that transferring attention maps from teacher to student models enhances feature selection and overall performance. However, this investigation was limited to the DeepConvLSTM [24] architecture and did not thoroughly analyze resources and compare with compression techniques, such as quantization and pruning. Furthermore, the potential of attention distillation within renowned lightweight architectures, such as SqueezeNet [18], remains unexplored, particularly regarding metrics critical for deployment, including inference latency and model size, which are essential for tiny devices. While existing research focuses on enhancing accuracy, computational efficiency, which is essential for real-time edge deployment, has frequently received inadequate attention.

This study addresses the previously mentioned challenges by providing a comprehensive benchmark to evaluate different pruning and quantization optimization techniques in comparison to lightweight models augmented with attention mechanisms and knowledge distillation, focusing on both recognition effectiveness and resource efficiency. The experiments assess two well-known deep architectures, DeepConvLSTM and SqueezeNet, across four sensor-based HAR datasets: Opportunity [5], Sensors [26], Pamap2 [25], and Wisdm [19]. Our investigation centres on the following research questions (RQ) to enhance resource-efficient HAR models:

- RQ1: What is the impact of various quantization and pruning methods on the balance between accuracy and resource efficiency in HAR models on various datasets, specifically concerning model size and inference time?
- RQ2: How do model compression approaches compare to lightweight models and those enhanced with attention-based distillation in terms of balancing accuracy and efficiency?

Through this benchmarking, we aim to elevate the state of the art in efficient deep learning techniques for sensor-based HAR, providing insights and recommendations for practical applications in real-world scenarios characterised by constrained resources. This study presents three primary contributions: (1) the first systematic comparison of pruning and quantization techniques in relation to attention distillation for HAR, specifically assessing both DeepConvLSTM and SqueezeNet architectures; (2) an extensive resource and performance analysis of optimized models, encompassing enhanced lightweight and compressed variants, across four benchmark HAR datasets, with particular emphasis on deployment-critical metrics such as model size, inference latency, and energy efficiency; and (3) the provision of practical guidelines for the deployment of these optimized HAR models on resource-constrained wearable devices. To summarize the benchmarking results, for devices with severe memory constraints, such as the Arduino Due, it is advisable to use lightweight models boosted with attention or response-based knowledge distillation. Quantization could be the main method for enhancing efficiency, with pruning as a secondary option.

The paper is organized as follows: Sect. 2 reviews attention mechanisms and compression in HAR. Section 3 introduces the methodology and details the experimental setup, datasets, and metrics. Section 4 presents a comparative analysis of quantization and pruning methods. Section 5 contrasts these techniques with attention-distilled lightweight models. Finally, Sect. 6 offers practical insights and deployment recommendations.

2   Related Work

In this section, we outline recent advances in deep learning-based HAR with an emphasis on model efficiency for edge deployment. We review attention-based model enhancement techniques, compression methods such as pruning, quantization and knowledge distillation strategies and a conceptual summary of these techniques is illustrated in Fig. 2. We examine deployment challenges and highlight limitations in generalizability and practical applicability.

Attention mechanisms have been recently adopted in HAR to enhance recognition performance by emphasizing salient temporal or spatial sensor patterns. Various architectural frameworks, including dual attention [12] and multi-branch attention [20], have exhibited remarkable results across datasets such as Pamap2, Opportunity, and Wisdm. For instance, AttnSense [22] integrates both temporal and spatial attention within models based on Gated Recurrent Units (GRU), achieving competitive performance across several datasets. Likewise, the model introduced in [12] combines channel and temporal attention modules with Convolutional Neural Networks (CNNs) and reports an accuracy of up to 99% on Wisdm. Nevertheless, the majority of these architectures are dependent on complex models that frequently surpass millions of parameters, and they seldom disclose resource metrics such as model size or inference time. A recent study [2] have integrated the Convolutional Block Attention Module (CBAM) [27] into DeepConvLSTM. This integration has involved the analysis of various model sizes, demonstrating that attention-improved lightweight variants can sustain or surpass baseline performance while significantly decreasing both parameter count and FLOPs. Nevertheless, despite these advancements, attention-enhanced models have predominantly been assessed in isolation, lacking comparison to standard compression techniques or evaluation on highly constrained hardware platforms.

The design of lightweight models is fundamental to edge-AI research. Architectures such as MobileNet [17] and SqueezeNet [18] were created for low-resource settings, but many HAR studies continue to use larger architectures like CNN-LSTM hybrids or DeepConvLSTM due to their superior recognition capabilities. To mitigate resource limitations, researchers have focused on quantization and pruning [21].

Quantization minimizes model size by decreasing the numerical precision of weights and activations. For instance, dynamic range quantization has been utilised in 1D CNNs deployed on MCUs [13], achieving approximately 50% memory savings with negligible accuracy effects. Daghero et al. [9] showed that quantized models on a RISC-V microcontroller could perform HAR tasks in real-time while significantly conserving energy. Nonetheless, deployment was restricted to 8-bit integer formats because of hardware limitations, and success often depended on compatibility with TensorFlow Lite operators.

Pruning eliminates unnecessary weights, enhancing model efficiency and reducing size. Contoli et al. [8] implemented iterative pruning in CNN and LSTM-based HAR models, achieving size reductions but facing challenges like

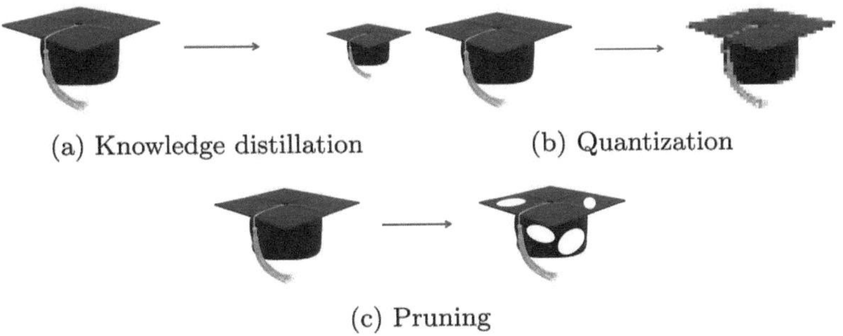

(a) Knowledge distillation   (b) Quantization

(c) Pruning

Fig. 2. Conceptual overview of three major compression techniques.

conversion errors and platform incompatibilities on devices such as ESP32. In a related study [7], the same authors assessed quantization methods, concluding that full-integer quantization could decrease energy consumption by approximately 30%, with only slight declines in accuracy. Nonetheless, results differed across various platforms and datasets. Other research [4, 28] highlighted inconsistencies between reported gains and real-world performance, underscoring the importance of assessing accuracy along with latency and memory usage.

Knowledge distillation (KD) has emerged as a promising approach for developing efficient models through the transference of learned behaviours from a large teacher model to a smaller student model. Recent studies [6, 10] have implemented response-based and feature-based KD to HAR tasks, typically utilising CNN or DeepConvLSTM architectures. While these methodologies have demonstrated improved recognition performance, they have not consistently offered evaluations of speed or memory efficiency.

Recent advancements include attention-based knowledge distillation (KD), where the teacher model's attention maps or hidden features guide the student. Agac et al. [1] explored this approach through DeepConvLSTM using Opportunity, Wisdm, and Sensors datasets. Their baseline model (LM) consisted of a lightweight DeepConvLSTM. By incorporating attention into the student model directly (LM-Att), they achieved better performance than that of response-based KD (RB-KD). They also assessed hybrid methods: RAB-KD, which merged response and attention supervision, and RB-KD-Att, which utilised response-based KD while adding attention to the student. Among these, RB-KD-Att delivered the best overall performance. These improved models employed 3- 4 times fewer parameters and FLOPs than moderate-sized versions. Nonetheless, the study did not provide resource-oriented metrics like model size or inference time and relied on a single architecture.

Despite significant advances, several important challenges persist. Numerous HAR studies optimize for recognition accuracy but fail to include metrics for deployment. Most evaluations are carried out on a single dataset, which restricts generalizability. Although attention-based models exhibit high accuracy, they typically raise memory and computation costs, rendering them less feasible for embedded applications. Additionally, a large-scale study by Hohman et al. [16] highlights that compression techniques like quantization and pruning do not always produce consistent improvements. They argue that adjusting the model architecture is often a more effective strategy than compression alone. The report also warns that gains shown in papers do not always translate well to real hardware, due to operator support issues, memory fragmentation, and incompatible layer types.

Previous research generally examined either attention-based improvements or model compression in isolation. Comparisons between these strategies under real-world conditions remain limited. This study aims to close that gap by comparing pruning and quantization with attention-based distillation, using two architectures (DeepConvLSTM and SqueezeNet) across four HAR datasets. In contrast to earlier work, we provide detailed measurements of model size, inference time, and parameter count to clarify trade-offs in efficient HAR design.

3 Benchmarking Methodology

3.1 Baseline Models (OM, MM, LM)

To evaluate the effects of different optimization methods, we selected two popular deep learning architectures as baseline models: DeepConvLSTM and SqueezeNet. These models serve different design objectives; DeepConvLSTM achieves superior recognition accuracy through hybrid temporal modeling in Human Activity Recognition (HAR), while SqueezeNet delivers a lightweight option suitable for applications with limited resources.

DeepConvLSTM. DeepConvLSTM, introduced by Ordonez and Roggen [24], is a hybrid deep learning model that integrates convolutional and recurrent layers for recognising human activities from time-series sensor data. It comprises a series of one-dimensional convolutional layers for spatial feature extraction, succeeded by Long Short-Term Memory (LSTM) layers that capture temporal dependencies among sensor readings. This integration allows the model to adeptly manage both spatial correlations among sensor channels and sequential patterns in activity sequences.

The standard DeepConvLSTM architecture consists of four convolutional layers (each with 64 filters and 5×1 kernels) paired with two LSTM layers (each featuring 128 units) to jointly process spatiotemporal data. For wearable deployment, we create three variants by systematically reducing width while keeping the architectural depth intact. The Original Model (OM) preserves the complete configuration (64 filters and 128 units). The Moderate Model (MM) scales this down to 8 filters and 16 units, while the Lightweight Model (LM) compresses it further to 4 filters and 8 units. This strategy of width reduction ($64 \rightarrow 8 \rightarrow 4$ filters and $128 \rightarrow 16 \rightarrow 8$ units) maintains the layer structure and kernel dimensions, which are essential for temporal modeling in HAR, while allowing direct comparison of attention and distillation techniques across the variants. Further details on the model structures at varying sizes can be found in Table 1 of [2].

SqueezeNet. SqueezeNet is a compact convolutional neural network architecture initially created for image classification tasks [18], attaining accuracy comparable to Alexnet but with far fewer parameters. Its fundamental design concept centres on utilising *fire modules*, which include a squeeze layer with 1×1 filters followed by an expand layer that combines 1×1 and 3×3 filters. This strategy significantly lowers the parameter count while maintaining the expressiveness of the model.

We utilize three models with distinct compression rates: the Original Model (OM) features 96 initial filters (compression rate $= 1$), the Moderate Model (MM) uses 12 initial filters at 1/8 compression, and the Lightweight Model (LM) employs 6 initial filters with a 1/16 compression. These compression rates ensure a proportional reduction in parameters consistent with our SqueezeNet variants for cross-architecture evaluation. All models include straightforward bypass connections around fire modules 3, 5, 7, and 9, balancing gradient flow

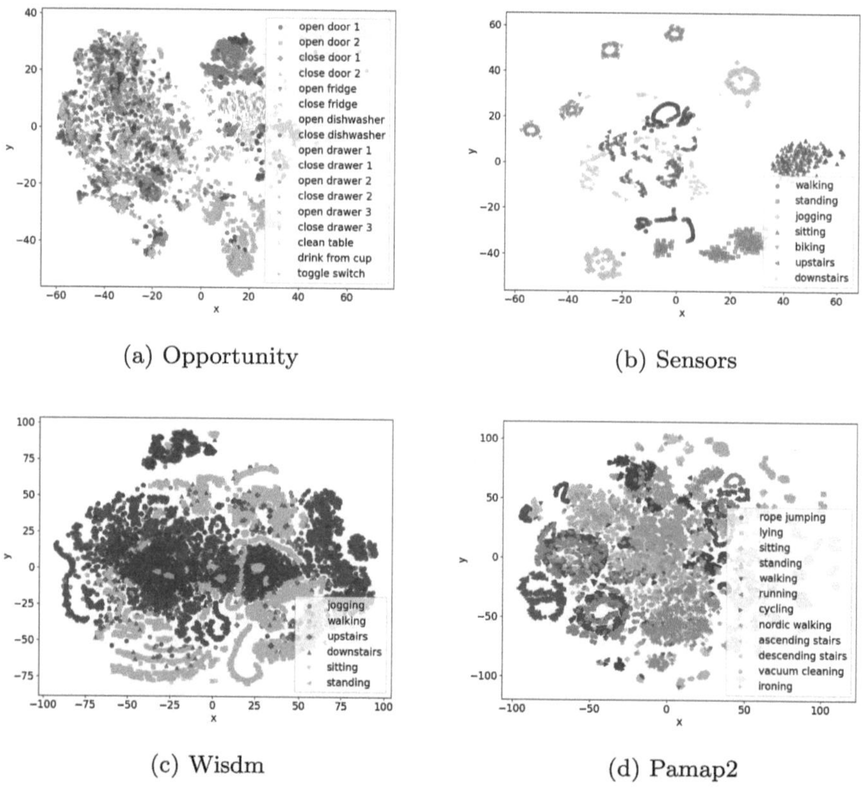

(a) Opportunity

(b) Sensors

(c) Wisdm

(d) Pamap2

Fig. 3. Two-dimensional t-SNE visualizations of HAR datasets.

while enhancing parameter efficiency. Given the constraints of input dimensionality, our evaluation is concentrated on the Opportunity and Sensors datasets where the spatial processing capabilities of SqueezeNet correspond to the available sensor configurations.

3.2 Datasets

We employed four public sensor-based HAR datasets: Opportunity [5], Sensors [26], Pamap2 [25], and Wisdm [19]. These datasets differ in the number of activities, sensor configurations, sampling rates, and class distributions. The Sensors dataset offers balanced classes, whereas Wisdm, Opportunity, and Pamap2 exhibit varying degrees of imbalance. This variety allows us to evaluate model performance across different conditions. Table 1 provides a summary of the dataset properties. To illustrate the separability of activities and the complexity of the datasets, two-dimensional t-distributed stochastic neighbor embedding (t-SNE) projections are included in Fig. 3.

Table 1. Summary of HAR datasets.

Dataset	# Activities	Sensors	SamplingRate (Hz)	Class Distribution
Opportunity [5]	17	5 IMUs (acc, gyro, mag)	30	Imbalanced
Sensors [26]	7	5 smartphones (acc, gyro, mag)	50	Balanced
Wisdm [19]	6	1 smartphone (acc)	20	Highly imbalanced
Pamap2 [25]	12	3 IMUs (acc, gyro, mag)	100	Imbalanced

3.3 Techniques for Model Optimization

Attention Mechanism: Convolutional Block Attention Module (CBAM). To improve feature selection with minimal additional effort, we incorporate CBAM [27] on LMs, a lightweight module that performs attention in two phases: (1) Channel Attention, which leverages global average and max pooling followed by a multi-layer perceptron (MLP) to assess channel-wise significance, and (2) Spatial Attention, which utilizes pooling across channels and a convolutional layer to create spatial maps. These maps are then used through element-wise multiplication to enhance features. Following the implementation details in [2], we examine channel-only, spatial-only, and full CBAM (channel first, then spatial), reporting here only the most effective variant for each dataset-architecture combination. The final model is labelled as LM-Att.

Knowledge Distillation (KD). In order to enhance the performance of compact models, we implement response-based KD), wherein a lightweight student model (LM) assimilates knowledge from a pre-trained teacher model (OM) by aligning its predictions with the softened outputs generated by the teacher. This foundational configuration is termed RB-KD.

Following the approach presented in [1], we explore two attention-augmented variants. In RAB-KD, we transfer attention knowledge by encouraging similarity between teacher and student attention maps through an additional MSE loss term. In RB-KD-Att, CBAM is applied only to the student, enabling attention-guided learning without requiring an attention-equipped teacher. Both variants aim to enhance representation learning within the KD framework.

Parameter Quantization. Quantization reduces the number of bits used to represent model parameters, thereby decreasing model size and computational requirements. We utilize two quantization methods: Float16 Quantization (FQ) and Dynamic Range Quantization (DRQ).

FQ decreases precision from 32-bit to 16-bit floating points, which reduces the model size and enhances inference speed. This technique strikes a balance between minimising model size and maintaining accuracy. It works especially well on hardware that supports 16-bit floating-point operations, like certain dedicated hardware accelerators. When inferring on CPUs, weights typically revert to 32-bit format by default, whereas on GPUs, calculations can be carried out directly with the reduced precision values.

DRQ reduces the size of deep learning models by converting floating-point weights into 8-bit representations, which consume around a quarter of the memory compared to the original size. This notable decrease in model size greatly facilitates deployment on devices with restricted resources. Nonetheless, *DRQ* mainly concentrates on enhancing memory efficiency rather than significantly boosting computational speed. During inference, *DRQ* adaptively quantizes activations according to their range and employs 8-bit weights and activations for calculations, while still outputting results in floating-point format. Therefore, speed enhancements are somewhat limited by the continued presence of floating-point operations. This approach ensures effective memory utilization while sustaining adequate computational performance, making it well-suited for devices with limited processing capability and strict memory restrictions.

In summary, both *FQ* and *DRQ* improve memory efficiency without compromising performance. *FQ* provides a balanced strategy by reducing model size while preserving high accuracy, especially on 16-bit compatible hardware. *DRQ* is particularly effective at significantly minimizing model size, making it well-suited for memory-constrained settings, though it has a slight effect on computational speed. During the experiments, pre-trained *OM* models for each of the six architecture-dataset combinations, like Opportunity- DeepConvLSTM, were transformed into their TensorFlow Lite equivalents. For both *FQ* and *DRQ* conversions, once the *OM* models are quantized using TensorFlow Lite, no further re-training is necessary.

Model Pruning. Pruning is an effective method designed to enhance deep learning models by minimizing their computational and memory demands. By removing less important weights, specifically those with low magnitudes, models can achieve simplicity and efficiency without a notable loss in performance. In this section, we explain two key pruning strategies: Constant Pruning (*CP*) and Polynomial Decay Pruning (*PDP*), assessed across a range of pruning ratios from 10% to 99%.

CP entails eliminating a fixed percentage of redundant weights during each pruning phase, upholding a steady pruning rate throughout. This approach significantly simplifies the model uniformly, improving simplicity and predictability. A key benefit of *CP* is its ease of implementation, as the pruning rate remains unchanged. A crucial component in *CP* is the pruning schedule, which processes the training step and produces a sparsity percentage. This percentage dictates which weights to eliminate based on their magnitude, thereby ensuring a structured and efficient pruning mechanism. The constant rate facilitates a consistent reduction in model size, making deployment more feasible in resource-limited settings.

PDP starts with a lower predefined pruning rate that gradually escalates over time. This methodology permits the model to retain a greater amount of information during the initial phases of training and facilitates more effective fine-tuning of weights as training advances. The adaptive characteristic of *PDP* potentially results in superior performance when contrasted with a constant pruning rate. The pruning schedule for *PDP* is vital as it guarantees that the model initiates with extensive pruning, which subsequently diminishes, thereby allowing for more precise weight adjustments in the later stages of training. This approach empowers the model to adapt with greater flexibility, preserving fundamental features while concentrating on refinement as training progresses. By incrementally increasing the pruning rate, *PDP* strikes a balance between pruning and learning, which may contribute to enhanced model performance and generalization.

Both *CP* and *PDP* provide unique advantages for model pruning. *CP* is characterised by its simplicity and consistency, which facilitates easy implementation and prediction. It is particularly useful for scenarios where a consistent reduction in model complexity is desired. On the other hand, *PDP* employs a more adaptable and sophisticated method, initiating with aggressive pruning that gradually decreases. This technique is ideal for situations that demand a more nuanced and flexible pruning strategy.

3.4   Implementation Details and Metrics

We assess the performance of DeepConvLSTM on the Opportunity, Sensors, Wisdm, and Pamap2 datasets. In contrast, SqueezeNet is utilized exclusively for the Opportunity and Sensors datasets owing to input width constraints in Wisdm and Pamap2. DeepConvLSTM preserves the input width throughout its layers, whereas SqueezeNet's max-pooling operation diminishes both height and width, necessitating a minimum width of 45 for stable functionality.

The experiments use 1-second intervals, employing a 60%/ 20%/ 20% division for training, testing, and validation. Both models are trained using the Adam optimizer, with a learning rate of 0.001 and a batch size of 64, for a maximum of 200 epochs, incorporating early stopping with a patience parameter of 10. The implementations leverage TensorFlow, TensorFlow Lite, and Keras (v2.12.0) on an Apple M3 Pro, which features an 11-core CPU, a 14-core GPU, and 18GB of RAM, operating under macOS Sonoma 14.1.

To evaluate resource efficiency, we present the count of trainable parameters and FLOPs (number of floating-point operations), which serve as device-independent metrics for computational load, energy consumption, and memory usage. Additionally, we assess total inference time and memory usage on test set. In order to evaluate the recognition performance, we present the macro F1-score (referred to as the F1-score) to address class imbalance.

4   Performance Evaluation of Compression Methods

This section showcases the performance of various compression methods aimed at improving sensor-based HAR models. Particularly, we assess the comparative effectiveness of the original models *OM*s, as well as conventional pruning and quantization techniques, from both a recognition success and resource efficiency perspective.

We employ TensorFlow Lite, an open-source framework specifically crafted to improve the efficiency of executing deep learning models on devices with limited computational capabilities, such as mobile phones, edge devices, and microcontrollers. To enhance the original deep learning models, we initially convert them into their Lite versions using TensorFlow Lite. This conversion process entails transforming the model from its original TensorFlow format to the TensorFlow Lite format, optimizing it for size and speed. The TensorFlow Lite converter facilitates this process by creating a *.tflite* file from the pre-trained model, which can subsequently be deployed on various devices for inference. Accordingly, we first converted our TensorFlow models into their TensorFlow Lite formats, referred to as *Lite*.

Beyond the basic conversion, TensorFlow Lite offers additional tools for optimizing models further. Two primary techniques in TensorFlow Lite are pruning and quantization. These methods greatly improve model efficiency, making them more suitable for devices with limited resources. After converting our TensorFlow models to their *Lite* versions, we implemented these optimization techniques to boost their performance. The quantization process in TensorFlow Lite involves changing the model to its *Lite* form and using TensorFlow Lite's optimization tools for quantization. For pruning, the procedure is similar (*Lite* version conversion and utilizing TensorFlow Lite's pruning tool), but it also requires an additional training step to fine-tune the remaining weights, ensuring optimal performance before deployment.

4.1 Parameter Quantization

The results of the quantization are shown in Fig. 4, 5 and 6. In these figures, the x-axis represents the architecture-dataset pairs, while the bars show the results for the converted *FQ* and *DRQ* models, along with the previously created *Lite* and *OM* versions for the corresponding architecture-dataset pairs.

As shown in Fig. 4, the validation accuracy indicates that the *Lite* models perform identically to the *OM* version. Importantly, the recognition performance on the *Sensors* dataset remains consistent with both DeepConvLSTM and SqueezeNet architectures when using *DRQ*. Furthermore, there are slight increases in performance of 0.19%, 0.19%, and 0.03% for the Opportunity-

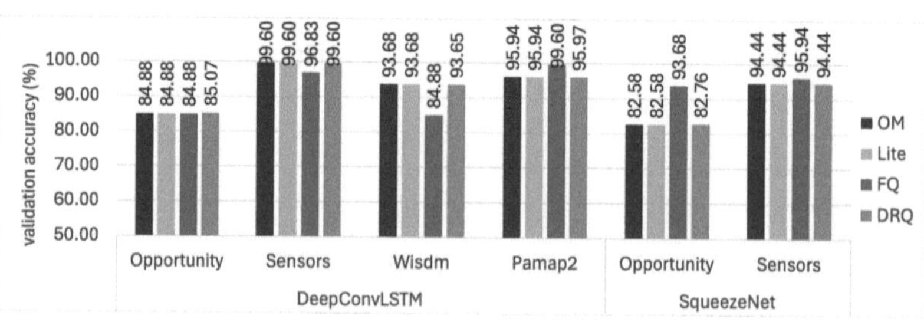

Fig. 4. Validation accuracy (%) of quantized models.

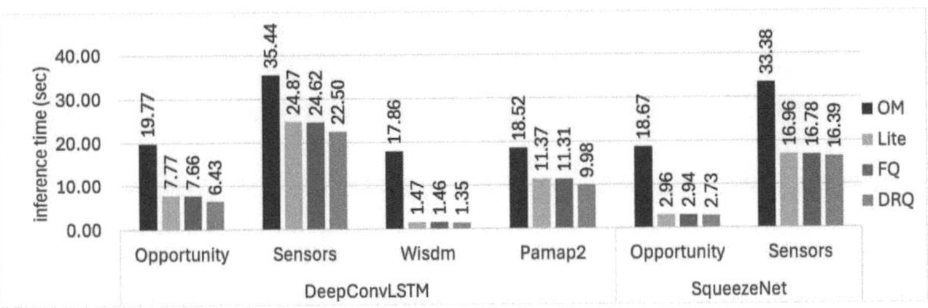

Fig. 5. Inference time (sec) of quantized models.

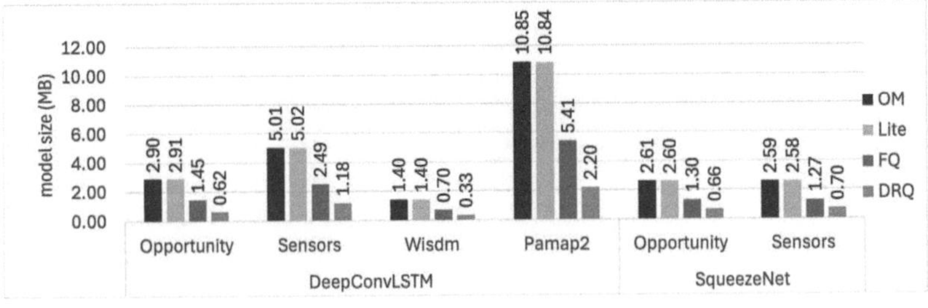

Fig. 6. Model size (MB) of quantized models.

DeepConvLSTM, Opportunity- SqueezeNet, and Pamap2- DeepConvLSTM pairs, respectively. Conversely, the Wisdm-DeepConvLSTM pair shows a minor decrease of 0.03%.

In contrast, when *FQ* is employed, the performance remains unchanged solely for the Opportunity-DeepConvLSTM pair. Other dataset-architecture pairs encounter significant increases or decreases in accuracy. For example, the performance of the Opportunity-SqueezeNet pair exhibits an improvement of 11.10%, ascending from 82.58% to 93.68% in comparison to the *OM*. Conversely, the Wisdm-DeepConvLSTM pair experiences a performance decline from 93.68% to 84.88% when utilizing *FQ*. This observation suggests that while *DRQ* sustains consistent performance, *FQ* may lead to considerable performance fluctuations across various dataset-architecture pairs.

An examination of inference time (Fig. 5) reveals that the transition from the *OM* model to TensorFlow Lite models (*Lite*, *FQ*, and *DRQ*) results in a reduction of inference time by a factor ranging from 1.44 to 12.21. However, the inference time of *FQ* models remains almost identical to that of *Lite* across all dataset-architecture pairs. In contrast, *DRQ* models necessitate 1.03x to 1.21x less inference time compared to *Lite* models. This finding indicates that the compressed models (*FQ* and *DRQ*) exhibit nearly the same inference time consumption as *Lite* models.

In Fig. 6, the effects of reducing precision on model size through quantization are illustrated. The transition from the *OM* model to the *Lite* model results in a slight reduction in model size (a decrease of up to 0.01 MB), with the exception of the Opportunity-DeepConvLSTM model, which experiences a modest increase of 0.01 MB. The application of *FQ* effectively reduces the size of the *Lite* model by a factor of two, consistently maintaining this reduction across all dataset-architecture pairs. In contrast, the reduction in model size achieved through *DRQ* ranges from 3.7 times to 4.9 times that of the *Lite* model. This indicates that, in terms of model size, the most advantageous quantization methods, in order of effectiveness, are *DRQ*, *FQ*, and *Lite*. This outcome is expected, given that *DRQ* decreases the precision from 32-bit to 8-bit, whereas *FQ* reduces it to 16-bit, leading to more significant size reductions with *DRQ*.

In conclusion, *DRQ* emerges as a more effective technique for reducing model size, making it particularly suitable for environments with limited memory while ensuring consistent performance across different dataset-architecture pairs. *FQ* offers a balanced solution, achieving notable size reductions and similar inference time performance to *Lite*, although accuracy may vary based on the dataset-architecture pair. While the *Lite* models are not as compact as *DRQ* or *FQ*, they still provide considerable enhancements in inference time and model size compared to the *OM*. Therefore, selecting a quantization method should take into account the specific needs and limitations of the deployment environment, weighing factors such as memory efficiency, computational demands, and performance accuracy. This evaluation addresses *RQ*1 concerning how quantization influences the trade-off between accuracy and resource efficiency.

4.2 Model Pruning

Before comparing the performance of pruned models with *OM* and *Lite* models, we also investigated the impact of the pruning rate on recognition success and resource consumption of HAR models. However, due to page limitations, we only provide a summary of the results here. The findings indicate that PDP generally has a minimal impact on validation accuracy up to a certain pruning rate, while CP shows a decline beyond 60%. The Sensors dataset demonstrates remarkable robustness to pruning, maintaining high accuracy even at a 99% pruning rate. In contrast, the Opportunity dataset experiences performance drops at lower pruning thresholds 70%, suggesting that the effectiveness of pruning is highly dependent on dataset characteristics. Inference time remains largely unaffected by the pruning rate for both methods because the study's setup does not exclude zero-valued parameters from computations. However, higher pruning rates generally lead to significant reductions in model size, although this effect can vary across datasets. For example, Opportunity-DeepConvLSTM's model size decreases substantially from 2.52 MB at 10% pruning to 0.61 MB at 90% CP pruning. On the other hand, Sensors-DeepConvLSTM shows a constant model size of 5.06 MB regardless of the pruning rate.

Next, we compare the performance of pruned models with *OM* and *Lite* models for each dataset-architecture pair. We selected to present results for the 60% pruning rate since this value is considered an acceptable threshold that minimizes resource consumption without significantly compromising performance. The results are presented in Figs. 7, 8 and 9. When we examine the results for inference time (Fig. 8) and model size (Fig. 9), we observe that the difference for the Pamap2-DeepConvLSTM model is much more pronounced compared to other dataset-architecture pairs when using pruning methods versus the *Lite* model. In pruning methods, the efficiency gain from pruning increases with the size of the initial model (in our case, *OM*). A similar trend is seen in [14], where a VGG-16 model with 138 million parameters experienced a 13-fold reduction, whereas a SqueezeNet model with 1.2 million parameters only saw a 3.2-fold reduction. Therefore, in our analysis, the most significant advantage is observed for the Pamap2-DeepConvLSTM model, which has the highest number of parameters. For the remaining dataset-architecture pairs, the *Lite* models and the pruning models required almost the same inference time. In terms of model size, except for the Sensors-DeepConvLSTM pair, the models have 1.0-1.9x smaller sizes compared to *Lite* for *CP* and 1.0-1.7x smaller sizes compared to *Lite* for *PDP*.

The model size results (Fig. 9) show an increase in performance for models using SqueezeNet with both *CP* and *PDP* methods. This increase is 2.30% for Opportunity and 2.38% for Sensors with *CP*, while it is slightly lower with *PDP* (0.93% for Opportunity and 1.98% for Sensors). For DeepConvLSTM, there is only a slight performance decrease for Wisdm with *CP* compared to *OM* (0.06%). In all other dataset-architecture pairs, there is a performance increase. For all four datasets, models that show more performance improvement with *CP* also show more improvement with *PDP*. When utilizing DeepConvLSTM, the performance improvements with *CP* are most significant for Opportunity, followed by Sensors, Pamap2, and Wisdm. The sequence remains consistent for *PDP*. This observation suggests that a model that excels with one technique is likely to demonstrate comparable performance with an alternative technique.

In conclusion, pruning techniques such as *CP* and *PDP* effectively improve model efficiency by reducing computational and memory demands while maintaining performance. *CP* offers a simple and consistent pruning method, making it simple and manageable to use. With *PDP* allows for a more refined pruning schedule, which can lead to enhanced performance. Our analysis shows that larger models, such as Pamap2-DeepConvLSTM, gain more advantages from pruning. However, certain datasets demonstrate greater resilience to high pruning rates, influenced by their inherent characteristics. Thus, pruning should be

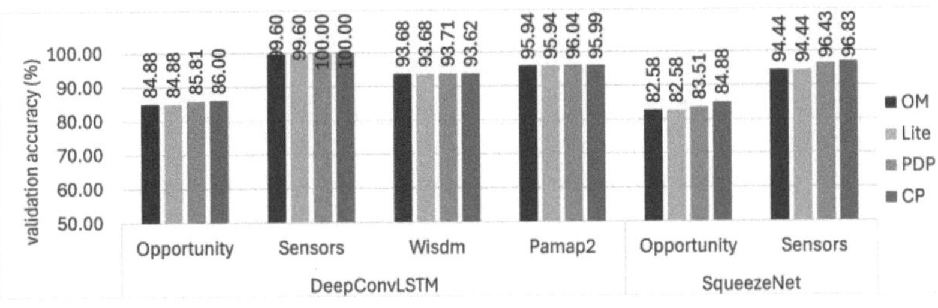

Fig. 7. Validation accuracy (%) of pruned models with pruning rate 60%.

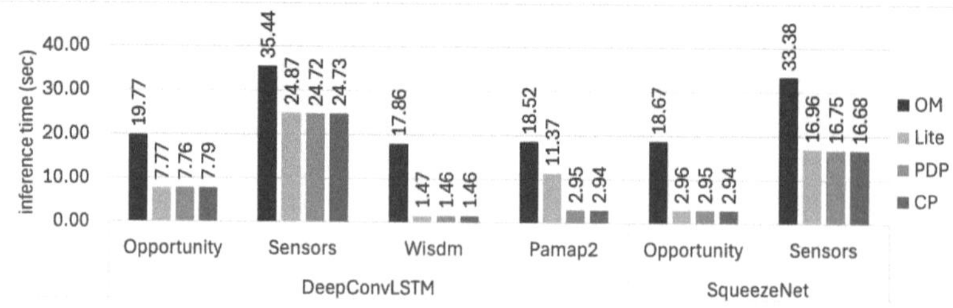

Fig. 8. Inference time (sec) of pruned models with pruning rate 60%.

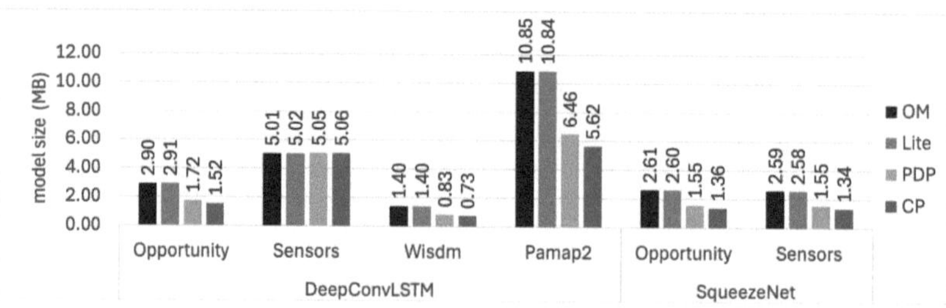

Fig. 9. Model size (MB) of pruned models with pruning rate 60%.

chosen based on deployment needs, balancing size and performance. These observations provide the answer to $RQ1$.

5   Compressed Original Models Versus Boosted Lightweight Models

To provide a comprehensive comparison, this study incorporates several boosted lightweight models proposed in earlier work [1], including the base lightweight model (LM), its attention-based version (LM-Att), and three distilled versions RB-KD (response-based knowledge distillation), RAB-KD (response and attention-based distillation), and RB-KD-Att (response-based distillation with attention applied to the student). These models are built using a teacher-student architecture, where the student is trained using the teacher's output logits and/or its intermediate attention maps. Since this study primarily focuses on automatized compression methods, we do not detail the training processes of these models. The reader may consult [1] for a detailed description of the methods and experiments.

This section provides a comparison of three model versions, OM, MM, and LM for DeepConvLSTM and SqueezeNet across multiple datasets. We also evaluate the performance of LM models enhanced through attention and knowledge distillation, and compare them with the $Lite$, quantized, and pruned versions of OM models. The results are shown in Figs. 10, 11 and 12. It should be noted that validation accuracy results for Opportunity-SqueezeNet are excluded from

Fig. 12. This exclusion is due to performance values dropping as low as 22%, which would require a broader x-axis range in the figure. Such scaling would make it difficult to clearly observe accuracy variations in other dataset-architecture pairs. The results are instead reported as follows. The validation accuracy scores for Opportunity-SqueezeNet are observed as follows: 82.58%, 68.51%, 22.28%, 58.68%, 22.28%, 22.28%, 59.80%, 82.58%, 82.76%, 93.68%, 84.88% and 83.51% corresponding to *OM*, *MM*, *LM*, *LM-Att*, *RB-KD*, *RAB-KD*, *RB-KD-Att*, *Lite*, *DRQ*, *FQ*, *CP*, and *PDP*, respectively.

Reducing the model from *OM* to *LM* affects significantly both model size and recognition performance, while having only a slightly affect on inference time. The range of the model size reduction between *OM* (1.40–10.85 MB) and *LM* (10 KB–57 KB) is 80.5x to 195.6x. Similarly, *MM* (28 KB–195 KB) models are 32.9x to 57.1x smaller than their *OM* variants. The limited impact on inference time might be attributed to the high-performance CPU used in the experiments (Apple M3 Pro chip with 11-core CPU). Evaluating performance on low-power devices, such as an Arduino Nano, could provide further insights into inference time under constrained hardware conditions.

In the case of *LM* models, applying attention and distillation techniques, either separately as *LM-Att* and *RB-KD*, or jointly as *RAB-KD* and *RB-KD-Att*, led to a slight increase in inference time, especially when both were used together. However, this change did not lead to a significant increase in model size. Using KD alone does not increase model size, while incorporating attention into distillation improves performance with only a small increase in size, limited to 1.5 KB. In addition, these models stay under 256 KB, allowing them to be deployed on a wide range of MCU/IoT devices.

While the *OM* model retains its recognition capabilities, the *Lite* models, especially those using the *DRQ* method, show significant advantages in both compression and recognition success. Specifically, the *DRQ* methods achieve model size reductions of up to 5x, while other methods (*FQ*, *CP* and *PDP*) provide reductions of up to 2x. However, even with the most compressed model (*DRQ* on the Pamap2-DeepConvLSTM) reducing the model size from 10.85 MB to 2.20 MB, can remain too large for devices with highly constrained memory, such as Arduino Zero with 256 KB of Flash memory. In contrast, boosted *LM* models surpass *MM* in recognition performance, except for the Opportunity-SqueezeNet model, with a considerably smaller model size. For example, for

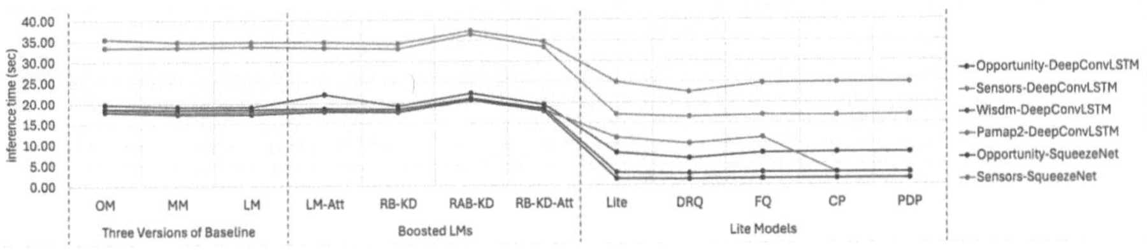

Fig. 10. Inference time (sec) comparison of original models, boosted LM models and compressed original models.

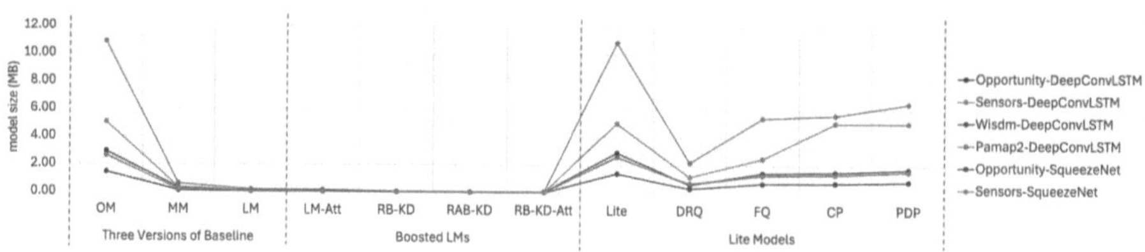

Fig. 11. Model size (MB) comparison of original models, boosted LM models and compressed original models.

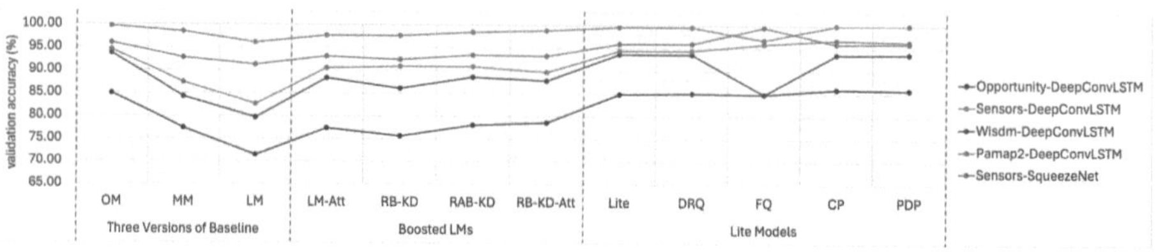

Fig. 12. Validation accuracy (%) comparison of original models, boosted LM models and compressed original models.

Wisdm-DeepConvLSTM, the initial validation accuracies are 93.68%, 84.16% and 79.56% for *OM*, *MM* and *LM*, respectively. The *LM* boosted with *RAB-KD* is achieved 88.56% of accuracy, which not only outperforms *MM*'s performance but also falls almost between *OM* and *MM*. Additionally, the boosted *LM* (11 KB) is 130x smaller than *OM* (1.40 MB) and 2.5x smaller than *MM* (28 KB) in model size. Thus, the most memory-efficient models are the boosted *LM* models. They provide performance that, while lower than *OM*, generally exceeds *MM*, thus falling between the two. This level of recognition success may be adequate for non-critical HAR applications [23] such as fitness and well-being. Here, the model's recognition performance, the device's computational power, and its memory are all traded off. *RQ2* is addressed by these results.

6   Conclusion, Limitations and Insights

This study presented a detailed comparison of the performance of boosted lightweight models in comparison to compressed models produced through quantization and pruning. The main objective was to investigate the trade-offs between model size, recognition success, memory consumption, and computational efficiency.

Model size reductions from *OM*s to *LM*s were substantial, with decreases ranging between 80.5x and 195.6x. *MM* similarly showed notable reductions in size, ranging from 32.9x to 57.1x. Such reductions are essential for enabling model deployment on devices with constrained memory resources. Although the model size was reduced considerably, inference time showed minimal change, likely due to the high-performance CPU used in the experiments (Apple M3 Pro chip).

Future testing on lower-powered devices such as the Arduino Nano could offer additional insights into inference time under more restricted conditions. We are currently working on deploying selected models on the Arduino Nano 33 BLE Sense, the microcontroller unit (MCU) used in the OpenEarable platform[1].

Applying attention and knowledge distillation techniques to *LM* models (individually as *LM-Att* and *RB-KD*, and in combination as *RAB-KD* and *RB-KD-Att*) achieved the performance increases with only a minor increase in inference time. The combination of attention and distillation provided improved performance without a notable increase in model size, while knowledge distillation alone also did not increase the model size. The boosted *LM* models approached the performance of *MM* models compared to compressed models, but fell short of matching the recognition success of *OM* models. Quantized and pruned versions of *OM* models exhibited varying levels of success, with quantization generally proving more efficient.

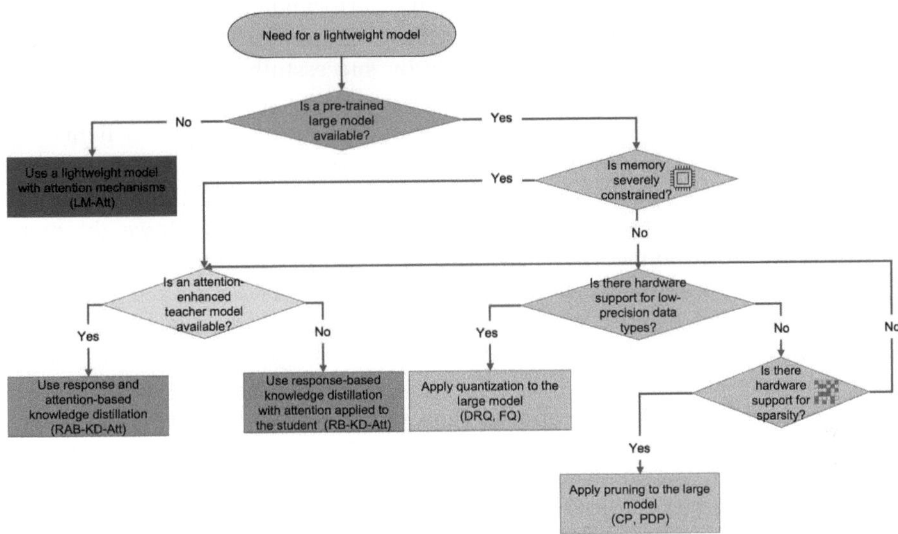

Fig. 13. Flowchart for lightweight model selection, guided by study insights and recommendations.

This study emphasizes the importance of striking a balance between recognition performance and resource efficiency. Strategies such as quantization and pruning effectively decreased computational and memory requirements, making models more suitable for deployment on resource-constrained devices. TensorFlow Lite's optimization logic played a significant role in reducing the size of the model and its resource consumption.

There is an obvious trade-off between device memory, computational power, and recognition success. For devices with extreme memory constraints like Nordic

---

[1] https://open-earable.teco.edu/.

Thingy:52 (with 32 KB SRAM and 256 KB Flash memory) and Arduino Due (with 96 KB SRAM and 512 KB Flash memory), lightweight models with attention mechanisms (*LM-Att*) or response-based knowledge distillation (*RB-KD*) are advised. For efficiency, quantization should come first, with pruning serving as a supplementary method.

In summary, combining knowledge distillation and attention mechanisms appears to offer a promising way to improve the performance of lightweight HAR models. These methods address the difficulties posed by resource-constrained environments by making it easier to create high-performing, resource-efficient models that can be implemented on small devices.

In Fig. 13, a flow chart is presented describing the recommended approach for developing lightweight models while considering these important factors. In situations where a pre-trained large model is not available, training lightweight models with attention mechanisms is a feasible solution. This entails adding attention mechanisms and training a lightweight model that is adapted to the device's resource limitations to enhance its performance without significantly increasing resource consumption. This allows the model to reach performance levels that are on par with larger models by successfully concentrating on the most informative parts of the features.

If there is an existing pre-trained large model, we can create a lightweight model and enhance its performance using response-based knowledge distillation. Compared to a lightweight model trained from scratch, this technique uses the larger model as a teacher to transfer knowledge to the lightweight model, improving its performance. Besides, the response and attention-based knowledge distillation approach can also be taken into consideration if there is an attention-enhanced teacher model or enough data to train the teacher model with attention. This method significantly boosts the lightweight student model's performance by using the teacher's attention maps and predictions.

When the target device supports TensorFlow Lite and memory constraints are not extreme, quantization and pruning techniques can be used. Quantization generally performs better than pruning in terms of efficiency and compatibility with standard hardware by lowering the precision of the model parameters to achieve a smaller model size and lower inference time without substantially affecting recognition performance. On the other hand, pruning removes some of the model's parameters, making it sparse and possibly incompatible with standard hardware. Furthermore, additional training is typically required to refine the pruned model after pruning. Therefore, pruning can be seen as an additional technique, and quantization should be given priority when efficiency is crucial.

It is critical to take into account the hardware constraints and capabilities of the target deployment environment, since not all operations are supported by every device and also by TensorFlow Lite. TensorFlow Lite's optimization logic aims to minimize the model size and resource usage of the model, making it crucial to test the optimized model on the target device to ensure that it is suitability.

Acknowledgments. This work is an extended and revised version of material from the author's PhD thesis entitled "Enhancing Lightweight Models for Efficient Sensor-Based Human Activity Recognition (Boğaziçi University, 2024)."

References

1. Agac, S., Incel, O.D.: Boosting the performance of lightweight HAR models with attention and knowledge distillation. In: 2024 International Conference on Intelligent Environments (IE), pp. 1–8 (2024). https://doi.org/10.1109/IE61493.2024.10599908
2. Agac, S., Incel, O.D.: Resource-efficient, sensor-based human activity recognition with lightweight deep models boosted with attention. Comput. Electr. Eng. **117**, 109274 (2024)
3. Blalock, D., Gonzalez Ortiz, J.J., Frankle, J., Guttag, J.: What is the state of neural network pruning? Proc. Mach. Learn. Syst. **2**(1), 129–146 (2020)
4. Bursa, S.O., Incel, O.D., Alptekin, G.I.: Transforming deep learning models for resource-efficient activity recognition on mobile devices. In: 5th Conference on Cloud and Internet of Things, p. 83. Marrakech, Morocco (2022)
5. Chavarriaga, R., et al.: The opportunity challenge: a benchmark database for on-body sensor-based activity recognition. Pattern Recognit. Lett. **34**(15), 2033–2042 (2013)
6. Chen, R., Luo, H., Zhao, F., Meng, X., Xie, Z., Zhu, Y.: Modeling accurate human activity recognition for embedded devices using multi-level distillation. arXiv:2107.07331 (2021)
7. Contoli, C., Lattanzi, E.: Energy efficiency of deep learning compression techniques in wearable human activity recognition. In: Conference on Artificial Intelligence Applications and Innovations, vol. 675, p. 102. Leon, Spain (2023)
8. Contoli, C., Lattanzi, E.: A study on the application of tensorflow compression techniques to human activity recognition. IEEE Access **11**, 48046–48058 (2023)
9. Daghero, F., et al.: Human activity recognition on microcontrollers with quantized and adaptive deep neural networks. Trans. Embedded Comput. Syst. **21**(4), 1–28 (2022)
10. Deng, S., et al.: LHAR: lightweight human activity recognition on knowledge distillation. J. Biomed. Health Inf. **28**(10), 1–10 (2023)
11. Diab, M.S., Rodriguez-Villegas, E.: Embedded machine learning using microcontrollers in wearable and ambulatory systems for health and care applications: A review. IEEE Access **10**, 98450–98474 (2022)
12. Gao, W., Zhang, L., Teng, Q., He, J., Wu, H.: DANHAR: dual attention network for multimodal human activity recognition using wearable sensors. Appl. Soft Comput. **111**, 107728–107740 (2021)
13. Ghibellini, A., Bononi, L., Di Felice, M.: Intelligence at the IoT edge: activity recognition with low-power microcontrollers and convolutional neural networks. In: 19th Annual Consumer Communications and Networking Conference, p. 701. Las Vegas, United States of America (2022)
14. Han, S.: Efficient Methods and Hardware for Deep Learning. Ph.D. thesis, Stanford University (2017)
15. Hinton, G., Vinyals, O., Dean, J.: Distilling the knowledge in a neural network. arXiv:1503.02531 (2015)

16. Hohman, F., Kery, M.B., Ren, D., Moritz, D.: Model compression in practice: Lessons learned from practitioners creating on-device machine learning experiences. In: Conference on Human Factors in Computing Systems, p. 1. Honolulu, United States of America (2024)
17. Howard, A.G., et al.: MobileNets: efficient convolutional neural networks for mobile vision applications. arXiv:1704.04861 (2017)
18. Iandola, F.N., Han, S., Moskewicz, M.W., Ashraf, K., Dally, W.J., Keutzer, K.: SqueezeNet: AlexNet-level accuracy with 50x fewer parameters and <0.5 mb model size. arXiv:1602.07360 (2016)
19. Kwapisz, J.R., Weiss, G.M., Moore, S.A.: Activity recognition using cell phone accelerometers. Special Interest Group Knowl. Discov. Data Min. Explorations Newslett. **12**(2), 74–82 (2011)
20. Li, Y., Wang, L., Liu, F.: Multi-branch attention-based grouped convolution network for human activity recognition using inertial sensors. MDPI Electron. **11**(16), 2526–2540 (2022)
21. Liang, T., Glossner, J., Wang, L., Shi, S., Zhang, X.: Pruning and quantization for deep neural network acceleration: a survey. Neurocomputing **461**, 370–403 (2021)
22. Ma, H., Li, W., Zhang, X., Gao, S., Lu, S.: AttnSense: multi-level attention mechanism for multimodal human activity recognition. In: 28th Joint Conference on Artificial Intelligence, p. 3109. Macao, China (2019)
23. Manokhin, M., Chollet, P., Desgreys, P.: Towards flexible and low-power wireless smart sensors: reconfigurable analog-to-feature conversion for healthcare applications. MDPI Sens. **24**(3), 999–1027 (2024)
24. Ordóñez, F.J., Roggen, D.: Deep convolutional and LSTM recurrent neural networks for multimodal wearable activity recognition. MDPI Sens. **16**(1), 115–140 (2016)
25. Reiss, A., Stricker, D.: Introducing a new benchmarked dataset for activity monitoring. In: 16th Symposium on Wearable Computers, p. 108. Newcastle, United Kingdom (2012)
26. Shoaib, M., Bosch, S., Incel, O.D., Scholten, H., Havinga, P.J.: Fusion of smartphone motion sensors for physical activity recognition. MDPI Sens. **14**(6), 10146–10176 (2014)
27. Woo, S., Park, J., Lee, J.Y., Kweon, I.S.: CBAM: convolutional block attention module. In: European Conference on Computer Vision, p. 3. Munich, Germany (2018)
28. Zebin, T., Scully, P.J., Peek, N., Casson, A.J., Ozanyan, K.B.: Design and implementation of a convolutional neural network on an edge computing smartphone for human activity recognition. IEEE Access **7**, 133509–133520 (2019)
29. Zhou, Q., et al.: On-device learning systems for edge intelligence: a software and hardware synergy perspective. IEEE Internet Things **8**(15), 11916–11934 (2021)

A Cyber-Physical-Human System Design for Challenging Behaviour Monitoring in People with Dementia

Jan Kleine Deters[1,2(✉)] , Burcu Güvenatam[1] , Jair A. Lima Silva[1,5] ,
Ewout Bergsma[1], Sarah Janus[2,3] , Sytse U. Zuidema[2,3] ,
and Heinrich Wörtche[1,2,4]

[1] Sensors and Smart Systems Group, Institute of Engineering,
Hanze University of Applied Sciences, Groningen, The Netherlands
`ja.kleine.deters@pl.hanze.nl`
[2] Department of Primary and Long-term Care, University of Groningen,
University Medical Center Groningen, Groningen, The Netherlands
[3] Alzheimer Center Groningen, University Medical Center Groningen,
Groningen, The Netherlands
[4] Department of Electrical Engineering, Eindhoven University of Technology,
Eindhoven, The Netherlands
[5] Telecommunication Laboratory (LabTel), Federal University of Espírito Santo,
Vitoria, Brazil

Abstract. The demand for assistive technology is expected to rise alongside the increasing care needs of aging populations. Ambient intelligence, particularly context awareness, offers potential benefits in addressing challenges faced by the healthcare system. In dementia care, context awareness can facilitate early detection of behavioural issues and proactive management of challenging behaviours. This paper presents a context-aware Cyber-Physical-Human System designed to monitor challenging behaviours in individuals with dementia. The system provides caregivers with interpretable situational information and enables them to personalize situational awareness. Designed for integration within nursing homes, it continuously monitors behaviour and influencing factors of behaviours in people with dementia. The system is built on three pillars: a digital twin of people and their environment, an Internet of Health Things (IoHT) infrastructure, and artificial agents. The integration of artificial agents enables near real-time calibration, ensuring situations are adequately communicated with caregivers. An initial implementation was evaluated in a Dutch nursing-home pilot, where IoT-integrated sensors recorded sound, light, climate conditions, activity, and heart rate. Caregivers contributed by conducting behavioural assessments using a custom-developed digital annotation application. Future work will focus on developing methods for real-time calibration by the proposed artificial agents to enhance the reliability of context awareness.

Keywords: Cyber-Physical-Human System · Challenging Behaviour · Digital Twin · Artificial Agents · Nursing home care

© The Author(s), under exclusive license to Springer Nature Switzerland AG 2026
Ö. Durmaz Incel et al. (Eds.): iWOAR 2025, LNCS 16292, pp. 99–115, 2026.
https://doi.org/10.1007/978-3-032-13312-0_6

1 Introduction

An aging population, coupled with a declining workforce and rising public health-care costs, is expected to significantly impact the availability of care in European countries [1]. If age-specific prevalence remains constant, the number of people with dementia in Europe is projected to increase by 60% over the next two decades, reaching 14.3 million in 2040 [2]. In nursing homes, dementia is highly prevalent and commonly accompanied by extensive assistance needs and responsive behaviours, while many residents have difficulty communicating unmet needs [3]. These circumstances burden family and professional caregivers within the context of workforce shortages and high turnover, indicating the urgency of timely, person-centred, non-pharmacological support [4–6].

These needs are difficult to meet with staffing alone. Residents often require continuous observation and rapid adjustment of routines, yet caregivers must divide attention across multiple residents and tasks. A technical infrastructure that augments perception, such as detecting non-verbal distress, interpreting contextual triggers, and supporting coordination (team awareness), is therefore justified [6,7].

Sensor-rich environments, edge/cloud infrastructure (IoT), and artificial intelligence (AI) together constitute the Internet of Health Things (IoHT) [8,9]. The IoHT is thus an enabling infrastructure for continuous acquisition and interpretation of personal and environmental data that can support personalized interventions. To be clinically useful and trustworthy, such systems must preserve human oversight and control over monitoring objectives and decision policies.

Cyber-Physical-Human Systems (CPHS) integrates computational elements (cyber), physical processes (physical), and human input to achieve specific goals [10]. They aim to: 'seamlessly link CPS to the human using a layer of AI' [11]. Therefore, by extending IoHT, they can empower caregivers with advanced system control, enabling them to guide and control assistive technology through interfaces like mobile devices. Currently challenges in creating effective CPHS include the understanding of human intent and seamless integration into existing processes. Due to their complexity, they are 'difficult to model as a whole and therefore require new abstractions, which expose essential features and dynamics while concealing processes and details' that are uninformative for closed-loop human–machine co-regulation [11]. Within healthcare, CPHS instantiate parallel intelligence (i.e., humans working in parallel with digital entities such as Digital Twins and artificial agents) across physical and virtual spaces [10]. Digital Twins (DTs) within our context are real-time computational representations of people and environments. Digital Twins (DTs) within our context are real-time computational representations of people and environments. They provide an infrastructure for estimation, prediction, and what-if analysis that complements or partially substitutes direct observation [12,13]. Human Digital Twin surveys indicate that multi-scale temporality, interoperability with IoT/clinical vocabularies, explainability, and operational validation remain insufficiently addressed in generic schemas [14,15].

In this paper, we present a CPHS design developed for the MOOD-Sense (Monitoring Of challenging behaviour in Dementia with Sensor technology) project. Our case study targets challenging behaviour (CB) in people with dementia in nursing homes. We apply caregiver and specialist knowledge to define monitoring and intervention parameters, aligning system functionality with clinical intent. Relative to existing ontologies and DT frameworks [16–18], our CPHS design addresses dementia-care workflows under continuous caregiver oversight and control. Our contribution is an actionable ontology that (i) links resident–context–behaviour–intervention with explicit temporal and uncertainty scopes, (ii) encodes caregiver-authored policies that compile into agent behaviours, (iii) aligns DT states with explainable dementia-care metrics, and (iv) provides audit and override channels required in CPHS [11]. In Sect. 6, we begin addressing the need for real-world validation of the spatial–temporal DT properties as outlined in our review [19] by partially implementing the framework.

2 A Case Study: Challenging Behaviour

Dementia is a syndrome that affects cognitive abilities, consequently leading to an increased care dependency. At a certain stage, this requires nursing home placement as the burden on the informal caregiver can get overwhelming. In people with late-stage dementia, pain and other sources of distress are frequently under-recognized due to their impaired ability to clearly communicate needs. 'An active attempt by the person to express an unmet need, which could be physiological or psychological' [20] is referred to as CB. Resulting behaviours may be misinterpreted and treated with psychotropics unless assessment explicitly considers non-verbal pain indicators and unmet needs [3,6]. These behaviours can impair the quality of life (QoL) for both the person with dementia and their caregivers [21] and they increase caregiver burden [22].

Figure 1 illustrates the conceptual CPHS that monitors the factors influencing behaviour of a person with dementia. Behaviours can be modelled using the Biopsychosocial Model, which considers the interplay of biological, psychological, and social factors affecting an individual's mental, physical, and behavioural states [23]. Mental states, including cognition, emotion, and motivation, are integral to understanding behaviour. These mental states influence how individuals perceive and respond to their environment [24]. The persons environment can be thought of as different spheres of influence ranging from intimate to public. Both social stimuli and physical stimuli constitute the persons environment. The social environment includes interactions with caregivers, other residents, and visitors such as family members, while the physical environment encompasses stimuli like lighting conditions, sound, and climate. Environmental stimuli can cause immediate behavioural reactions, but they may also lead to delayed behavioural changes. For caregivers, identifying indirect causative factors of CBs and evaluating their impact pose significant challenges, further intensified by high assistance needs and frequent responsive behaviours in nursing homes [3].

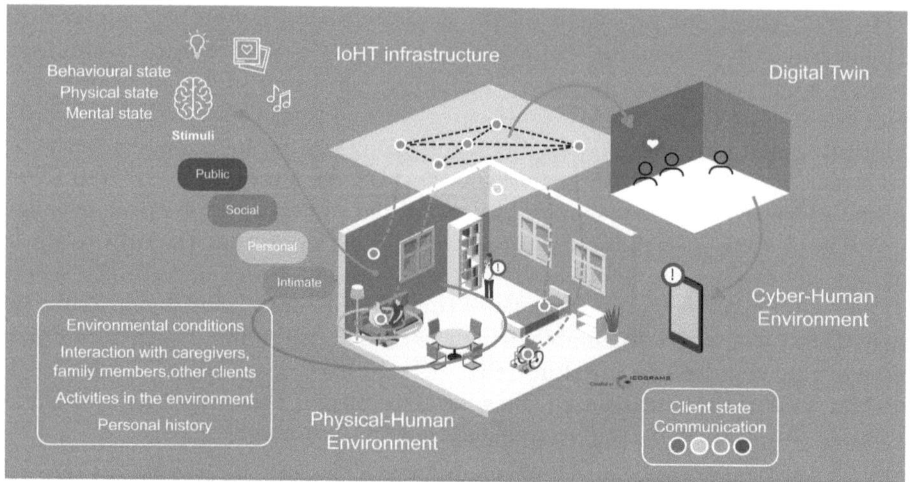

Fig. 1. On the left, the physical and social factors that influence behavioural states of people with dementia in a nursing home environment. On the right, key system elements. The IoHT infrastructure connects the physical environment to the cyber environment, creating a DT which is used for communicating the persons' state to caregivers.

Finding solutions for effectively managing CB is recognized in the scientific community [25]. There are many attempts to use multi-modal sensing technology to get comprehensive information on the behaviour of people with dementia [26–29]. These systems communicate sensor data wirelessly and use generic data formatting to make multi-modal data interpretation possible. In some cases, sensor data is manually offloaded to a computer after a certain period [30,31]. Behaviour assessment performed by caregivers or research team members in these settings complemented the sensor data in behaviour analyses. Correlation between personal activity level and CB was found [32], and detection methods were developed showing potential in assisting the caregiving process [31]. The current development can be extended by designing and developing a CPHS to meet system-level challenges such as supporting person-centred care, enabling earlier detection of behavioural issues, and facilitating proactive CB management, while offering auditability and caregiver override [5,6].

3   CPHS for Challenging Behaviour Monitoring

We adopt a design-science method to specify and instantiate this ontology in practice. The method operationalises it into four parts: (i) a domain ontology linking resident–context–behaviour–intervention under explicit temporal and uncertainty scopes, (ii) a layered system representation with a corresponding transition model, (iii) situation recognition that aggregates events into time-bounded contexts and updates DT states aligned with dementia-care metrics, and (iv) a policy layer where caregiver-authored goals compile into agent behaviours with audit/override channels. This fusion of top-down caregiver policies with bottom-up data enables adaptive, explainable assistance under continuous human oversight and control.

This CPHS design targets the Dutch nursing-home context, where institutions provide 24/7 care and supervision to older adults who can no longer live independently [33]. these institutes must comply with laws and acts governing privacy, data protection, and patient rights [34]. Facilities include private and shared spaces with frequent social interactions. Tracking individuals across these spaces while safeguarding co-residents' privacy necessitates context-aware monitoring. As IoHT adoption in this context is still growing, implementations vary across institutes.

We follow three core design heuristics grounded in common application challenges [35]. *User-centred design*: residents' and caregivers' perspectives shape configuration, interfaces, and communication so that affinity and trust extend to both physical and cyber components. *Transparency*: decision pathways must be tractable within situational awareness as Dutch guidelines require transparency and safeguards in health-related AI [36]. *In-context learning*: diversity across people, time, and environments requires adaptation of situational awareness and learning strategies to each unique context.

As illustrated in Fig. 1, the CPHS can be broken down into the physical-human environment, and the cyber-human environment. In the physical-human environment, caregivers have an embodied role in providing people with care and social interactions. Within the cyber-human environment caregivers have an unembodied cognitive role in assessing situations. Caregivers become part of the persons' social sphere based on their own intuitions or through the access of DT information (see Sect. 4) such as the persons' mental state represented through a colour scheme.

The DT must be calibrated and configured to accurately reflect its real-world counterpart. Calibration involves fine-tuning a multi-layer transition model that generates the DT information. Calibration then ensures that the presented information is accurate. As calibration works in parallel to caregivers, responsibility is given to this process which will be discussed in Sect. 5. Configuration tailors the DT to specific use cases and is performed in the cyber-human environment by the caregiver. The CPHS with the multi-layer transition model and configuration flow is shown in Fig. 2.

Sensors within the system detect physical changes, referred to as measurable properties, while caregivers identify behavioural patterns indicative of CB that are referred to as observable properties. These CB indicators require inference through additional personal information and contextual understanding. To achieve this, measurable property values, along with their historical data and relevant knowledge, are used to estimate observable properties. The multi-layer transition model facilitates this process by creating layered abstractions. The DT operates within the abstraction layer, where ontological concepts align with caregivers' understanding, enabling them to contribute their expert knowledge to the CPHS. By establishing a common ontology that bridges caregivers' insights and sensor data, the system promotes a shared understanding of CB.

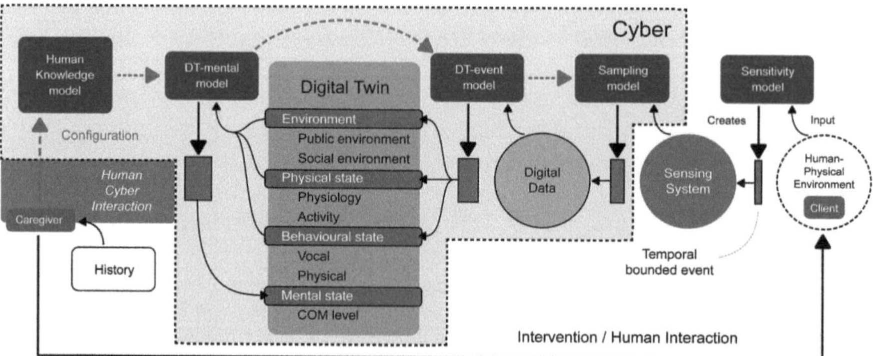

Fig. 2. Representation of the multi-layer transition model that creates the DT information (gray area). Temporal context increases at each stage as indicated by the width of the event boundaries in green. The caregiver configures the system on a high level. (Color figure online)

4   Digital Twinning

Digital twinning is the process of creating a digital representation of the person with dementia and their environment. It implies using a predefined information structure, referred to as state space. The Appendix documents the DT's current specification. From the multi-level transition model, it follows that there is also a multi-level state space. The multi-level transition model provides a sequential parameter-to-property definition. For each state space (Human-Physical environment, sensing system, digital data and DT), the parameters required to adequately infer state changes are defined, including their respective value range and resolution. To clarify, a state represents a discrete DT condition at a given point in time. The dynamics of the DT are captured with events. Any state change is an event, that ones they occur become part of the DT event history. As shown in Fig. 2, the multi-layer transition model creates events that change the state in a higher-order property.

The DT state space is divided into the following sub-spaces: (I) environment, (II) physical, (III) behavioural, and (IV) mental. These are further divided into sub-sub spaces as follows: (I) Physical public and social environment, (II) physiology, activity, and posture, (III) vocal and physical, and (IV) emotional, cognitive, and motivational. In the application of CB monitoring the 'Crisis Ontwikkelings Model' (COM) is used as representation of the emotional state space. This model relates to the progression of emotional and behavioural states during a crisis, providing a structure to identify and monitor shifts in emotional intensity and their impact on behaviour. The COM uses a 4-color coding scheme: green for normal behaviour, yellow for increasing tension or changes, orange for escalating tension or restlessness possibly leading to motor/ verbal agitation, and red for very high tension/ physical aggression, including behaviours like shouting, kicking, or hitting. All the observable and measurable properties related to these sub-sub spaces are presented in Fig. 3.

The important characteristics of the properties in constructing the DT are the level of detail (LOD), context (LOC), and personalization (LOP). The Level of Detail (LOD) directly relates to the required sensitivity of a system, defined by its responsiveness and ability to detect changes in the magnitude of physical stimuli. Higher LOD demands greater sensitivity to effectively capture and adapt to nuanced variations. The LOC describes the dimensionality or multi-modal sensing that is required on a system level. The LOP finally expresses the intersubject variation of state space parameter values.

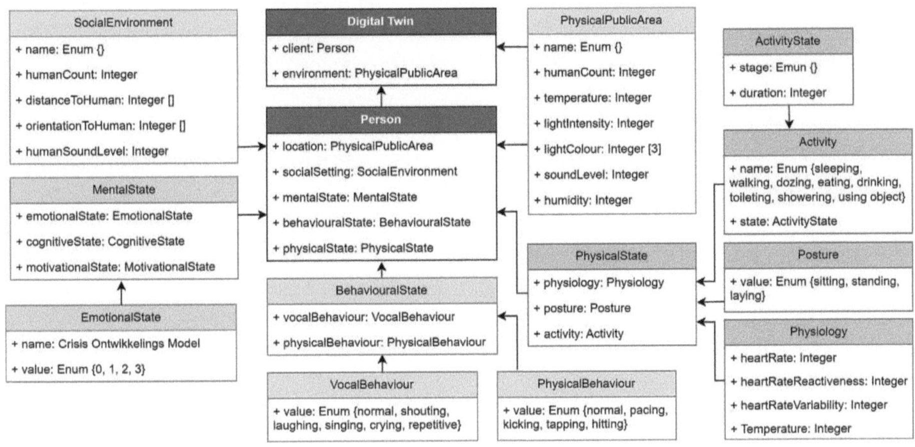

Fig. 3. The DT measurable and observable properties. Each arrow represents a hierarchical relationship, indicating that the source is a sub-space of the destination space.

The multi-layer transition model, from measurable to observable, consists of a sensitivity model, a sampling model, a DT-event model, a DT-mental model and a Human Knowledge model. The sensitivity model resembles the sensor systems sensitivity and its responses to stimuli in the physical environment. The sampling model represents the mechanisms for converting analog signals into digital data. The DT-event model transforms digital data streams into concepts represented in the shared ontology. The DT-mental model represents cause-effect relationships, linking mutual DT ontological concepts probabilistic through the analyses of DT-event history and logical trough input to the human knowledge model as provided by caregivers. The human knowledge model is a collection of interpretable logical statements that can be evaluated mentally in real time without additional resources.

The models are hierarchically ordered where the configuration is delegated in a top-down fashion. The human knowledge model is used in the configuration of the DT-mental model which in its term is used in the configuration of the DT-event and sampling model. Configuring thus selects the low-level monitoring tasks based on high-level input. Model calibration is directly performed trough caregiver's feedback and knowledge such as historical personal information.

The human knowledge model provides a structured approach for interpreting data, assessing situations, and making informed decisions based on domain understanding and cognitive constraints. The task for this model in our context is to improve interpretation of DT-events, states and alarms, as caregivers actively need to correct (calibrate) any mistakes in alarming. Dudyrev et al. (2022) [37] distilled constraints for these types of models, based on psychological and cognitive research on the human ability to memorize and compute. The constraints include the use of up to four Boolean variables, operators, and thresholds that convert non-Boolean variables into Boolean. With this rule-based human knowledge model, caregivers control the configuration of the system.

The DT-mental model bridges expert knowledge and data-driven insights. It represents probabilistic relationships between DT properties values based on available DT event history and incorporates additional expert knowledge on biological, psychological and social mechanisms. With this Bayesian network modelling approach, uncertainty and variability can be accounted for. The influence on behaviour of property values can be determined by learning conditional probabilities and uncovering both direct and indirect dependencies between DT property values through annotated logic. This strategy is useful as believes can be updated with new evidence either retrieved as information from the DT event history or as expert input.

The DT-event models take in streams of time series data to recognize DT states. These can take in heterogeneous data from different sensor modalities. Recognition can then be based on a time or condition-based approach. With the time-based approach, a fixed time interval of data is considered in pattern recognition. With the condition-based approach, if criteria such as thresholds are override, an event is recognized.

The sampling model performs the act of data acquisition on the sensor equipped devices. There will be situations in which only certain sensors need to be activated or certain sensors to acquire higher level of detail. This is the role of the sampling model. The sensitivity model describes the physical constrains of the sensing system in terms of its capabilities to capture physical phenomena. This represents the physical sensing system that creates transparency and virtualization of the physical processes.

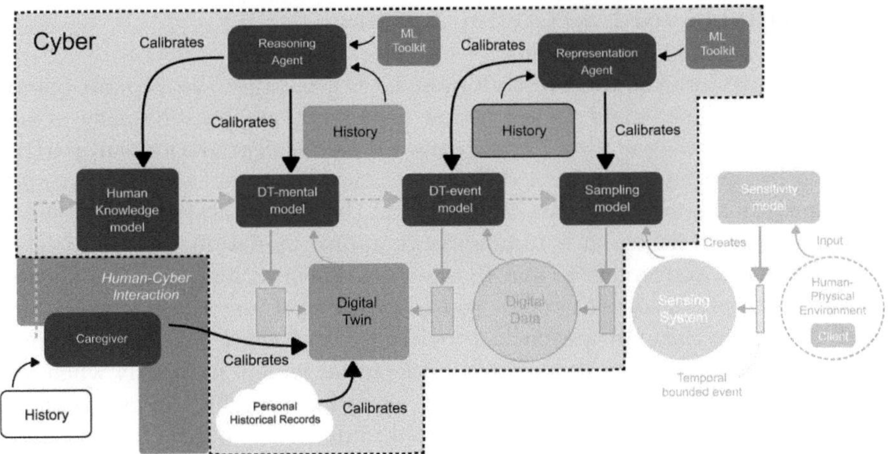

Fig. 4. The different agents (in purple) calibrating specific models by examining and comparing the model with historical information, updating these models using machine learning tools when the models have degraded. (Color figure online)

Table 1. Functions of the different agents with their respective goals, perception, actions, and behaviour in the proposed CPHS.

Agents	Goals	Perception	Actions	Behaviour
Caregiver	Provide personalized care	Digital Twin, personal memory, Human knowledge model	Configure Human Knowledge model, Interaction with Digital Twin	person-focused
Reasoning	Detect and explain mental state	Digital Twin Mental Model, Human Knowledge model, DT-Memory, DT-State	DT-Mental model Parameter estimation and calibration	Evidence-seeking
Representation	Personalize DT Event models	DT-event model, Sampling model, Digital Data memory, Digital Twin state, Digital Data state, sensing system state	DT-event model and Sampling model parameter estimation and calibration	Concept drift monitoring

5   Caregivers and Artificial Agents

Artificial agents are required to calibrate the DT because this process operates independently of caregivers. Calibration is crucial, as the reliability of models often diminishes over time. This temporal model degradation can partly be explained by underlying concept drift in measurable properties [38]. Within our CPHS design, there are two artificial agents: the representation agent and the reasoning agent. Their goal is to counter temporal model degradation that can occur at the DT concept level and in inter-relationships among DT concepts.

Caregivers are also considered agents in the system, as they guide situational awareness through feedback, providing a high-level calibration signal to the agents. Caregivers can provide feedback to the system implicitly when interacting in the person's environment or by accessing the DT. Accessing the DT or specific DT properties can be a valuable implicit signal for understanding the dynamic information demands of caregivers. They can also, as noted earlier, provide explicit configuration feedback within the human knowledge model. The representation and reasoning agents act in cyberspace and use digital data history and DT history, respectively, for calibration.

An example of concept drift is the variation in a person's resting heart rate over time, which depends on personal circumstances such as overall fitness. In this case, the reasoning agent can calibrate using contextual estimates of fitness. The representation agent aims to learn generalizable, feature-level representations that capture invariances across individuals. Personalization is achieved through parameter adjustment, enabling top-down calibration. In this way, learning establishes stable representations, while calibration adapts these representations to individual circumstances. Another example of drift is the change in relationships between concepts and CB over time. For instance, a person may alter their sensitivity to specific stimuli or develop new associations, either negative or positive. In both cases, drift must be detected, after which the agents calibrate the models accordingly. Figure 4 illustrates the relationship between the agents and the multi-layer transition model; their goals, perceptions, actions, and behaviour are elaborated in Table 1.

6   Current Implementation

This section describes the system architecture and its deployment during the second pilot study of the MOOD-Sense project. The architecture design was guided by our heuristics and constrained by available technology. The system enables data acquisition across environmental and personal contexts and supports digital behaviour assessment and registration (see Fig. 5). It comprises end-devices, routers, and a gateway. The gateway and routers provide processing capacity for edge computing, while the end-devices will support this capability in the near future.

The pilot was conducted in a closed ward of a Dutch nursing home. This pilot included 2 people with dementia, both meeting the inclusion criterion of a

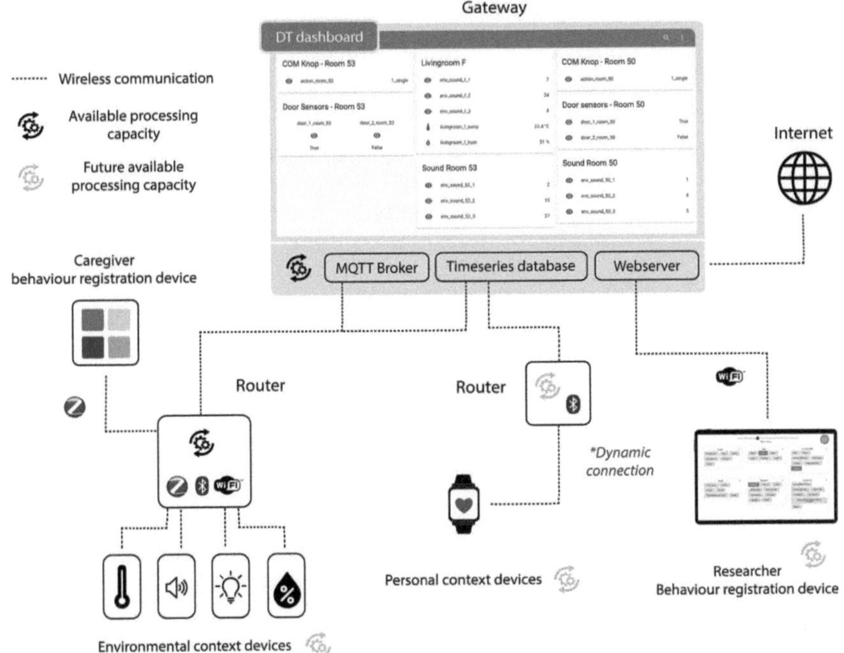

Fig. 5. The developed architecture for monitoring personal and environmental parameters with additional behaviour registration capability.

minimum Cohen-Mansfield Agitation Inventory score of 50. Each participant was provided with a wearable end-device, and additional end-devices were installed in their personal and communal living spaces. In the personal living area, caregivers used a colour-coded button for behavioural assessment, while in the communal area, researchers used a tablet running a behavioural registration application.

Per person, the following end-devices were deployed: one Garmin Vivoactive 4 smartwatch, three Arduino Nano 33 BLE Sense modules, two Aqara door sensors, one Xiaomi-Mi temperature and humidity sensor, one Raspberry Pi 4 (RPI4) with a cc2531 Zigbee dongle, one ESP32-WROOM, one Tuya Scene 4-button panel, and one Samsung Tab 2 tablet. The end-devices connected to the routers using either Zigbee or Bluetooth Low Energy (BLE). An ESP32-WROOM in a custom 3D-printed casing served as the BLE router, while a RPI4 functioned as the Zigbee router. Both routers relayed sensor data to the gateway over the local Wi-Fi network. The BLE router was configured with ESPHome software, and the Zigbee router with Zigbee2MQTT.

The gateway (Raspberry Pi 4), connected to the local network via Ethernet, operated with Home Assistant software and was configured to host an MQTT broker, an InfluxDB database, and the behavioural registration application. All MQTT messages, ESPHome events, and behavioural registration events were stored in InfluxDB with corresponding time labels.

The tablet-based behavioural registration application was developed following the recommendation to consider annotation an important component of pervasive healthcare applications [39]. It allowed synchronous labelling of sensor data while also functioning as a stand-alone assessment tool, replacing pen-and-paper annotation. Labels representing digital twin (DT) properties were displayed as interactive buttons that changed colour to indicate whether a property was currently observed. Each label included a structured database code and a language-specific representation (e.g., Dutch) for user interaction. To address space constraints, a speech button was included, enabling audio recordings of uncommon or context-specific information. Additionally, a slider with COM colour coding supported mental state assessment.

7 Path Forward

This paper presents the foundational framework of our studies. The initial phase in nursing homes enabled data acquisition, processing, and evaluation with persons with dementia and their caregivers. The results and challenges encountered during the iterative implementation phases with care institutes and professionals will be addressed in forthcoming publications. We foresee several extensions of the framework to fully achieve clinical validation. In particular, interoperability, Human–Computer–Agent interaction (HCAI), calibration methods (caregiver co-designed), and adaptive learning and reasoning capacities must be further developed. These advances enable situational awareness, reduce alarm burden [40], and support personalized recognition and communication of challenging behaviour.

From an interoperability perspective, existing ontologies and digital-twin frameworks are well formalized and should therefore be incorporated, tackling the overlapping domain representations within our project. Cognitive-building AAL digital twins prioritize environmental assets and scenarios but offer limited role and policy models for care teams [16]. Medical digital-twin ontologies emphasize entity-attribute modelling and governance rather than closed-loop control with caregiver override [17]. Cybonto provides a cognition-centric ontology for cybersecurity, not the multimodal sensing-to-intervention mappings in care [18]. The lack of some of these key constructs required by dementia-care workflows thus needs to be addressed by further constructing dementia-care specific concepts and relations and mediating our CPHS ontology to upper ontologies (e.g., BFO, SUMO, DOLCE).

Within the CPHS, HCAI should function as a continuous feedback cycle linking sensing and representation with reasoning, where each stage adapts in real time to both input data and caregiver feedback. Representation agents must translate multimodal signals into meaningful patterns with uncertainty levels, while reasoning agents adjust decisions based on explicit caregiver input and implicit responses to alarm. In digital twin communication, timing, modality, and urgency should align with caregiver preferences to keep information actionable without overload. To define requirements, upcoming pilot studies will use structured feedback loops in real care contexts, focusing on explicit inputs such as labelling and implicit measures such as reaction times. Computational demands related to stage interaction such as training and updating models must also be managed, with analyses of update windows and strategies such as predictive updates or pre-emptive calibration, system responsiveness, stability, and clinical reliability can be ensured.

Calibration methods that enhance the representation agent's effectiveness include self-supervised learning with adaptive encoding to capture events optimally [41,42]. Spiking neural networks (SNN) are suitable for encoding spatial-temporal information when systems face limits in memory, processing, and energy capacity [43]. Distributed SNN further improve bandwidth use in IoT architectures by utilizing idle computation resources and enhancing communication efficiency [44].

Federated learning provides another way to optimize calibration by enabling collaborative model training on edge devices without centralized data storage. These models can support early-stage calibration and reduce the need to learn patterns with low LOP. Incorporating SNN into federated strategies lowers both data traffic and energy consumption [45]. The complexity of implementing SNN remains a challenge, yet specialized processors such as the Speck chip are advancing these capabilities [46]. Future IoHT infrastructure should therefore include support for SNN-based calibration to achieve adaptive, energy-efficient, and clinically reliable systems.

The reasoning agent must also manage varying degrees of event certainty. Differences in event context, and duration introduce uncertainty, which makes purely logical reasoning insufficient. Fuzzy inference mechanisms can address this by improving monitoring efficiency and accuracy [47]. Reinforcement learning with experience replay can further support real-time alarm modelling, which will be essential in deployed systems [48]. As artificial agents become authorized in care, these developments will strengthen the management of CBs in dementia care.

8   Conclusion

In this paper, we introduced a CPHS designed to detect and communicate CBs in people with dementia living in nursing homes. The design focuses on creating a DT of the people with dementia and their environment and the integration of artificial agents to ensure a well calibrated system. Initial implementations of CPHS provided valuable insights into the practical challenges and considerations in deploying such a system in real-world settings. We observed that performing behavioural assessment by caregivers is possible with cyber enabled tools but that, to fully embed the system in their work process, functionalities needs to be established such as the possibility for caregivers to interact with the DT and the possibility for artificial agents to interact with the system and learn autonomously. During our pilot studies, we gathered valuable lessons, which we plan to discuss in subsequent publications. This future work will focus on the data collected in the pilot studies and propose a methodology for translational research in smart healthcare environments.

Appendix: CPHS Digital Twin Specification

Our CPHS ontology adopts SmartEnv's [49] event–situation pattern to support (i) atomic device events, (ii) aggregation into time-bounded situations, and (iii) contextual reasoning across human state, devices, and environment. We align with W3C vocabularies SOSA/SSN (sensing/actuation), OWL-Time (temporal extents), PROV-O (provenance) and FOAF (people). We create JSON-LD/RDF interfaces that can expose graph data to analytics and EHR/IoHT systems. Here we present a couple of core schema fragments.

People
- `cph:Person` ⊑ `foaf:Person` with disjoint `cph:Client` and `cph:Caregiver`. Person-centric states (`cph:MentalState`, `cph:BehaviouralState`, `cph:PhysicalState`, `cph:EmotionalState`) are qualities observed/assessed over time via `sosa:Observation`, each with explicit method provenance (`AssessedByCaregiver` vs. `InferredByAgent`) or . `MeasuredByDevice`) and OWL-Time instants/intervals (e.g., *sad this morning*).

Social/physical environment - Facility hierarchy (`cph:FacilityLocation` →Room/Bathroom/Corridor) and `cph:locatedIn` links persons/devices. `cph:SocialEnvironment` ⊑ `foaf:Group` with `cph:hasParticipant`, enabling queries such as *behavioural change while with visitors in the lounge.*

Devices/observations - Devices are `ssn:System/sosa:Platform`, wearable or environmentally hosting sensors/actuators. Observations cover raw and derived properties (heart rate, zone-presence, door state, audio bands, light), each linked to device, feature of interest, and time, bridging multimodal payloads to situations.

Events/situations/alarms - `cph:AtomicEvent` and `cph:Situation` are `time:TemporalEntity`; situations carry `time:hasBeginning/time:hasEnd` and optional certainty. Alarms are `prov:Entity` about a situation (`cph:aboutSituation`). severity, creation time, acknowledger, and free-text notes are recorded and linked via PROV to agents, interventions, and devices.

Caregiver interventions - Interventions are `prov:Activity` (e.g., `AssistToToilet`, `DeliverMedication`, `EnableNightLight`) targeting a person/location. They can be asserted from free text or inferred (e.g., alarm→door open→lights on→door close).

References

1. Bijak, J., et al.: Population and labour force projections for 27 European countries, 2002–2052: impact of international migration on population ageing. Eur. J. Popul. **23**(1), 1–31 (2007). https://doi.org/10.1007/s10680-006-9110-6
2. OECD: Health at a glance: Europe 2018: state of health in the EU cycle. OECD Publishing, Paris (2018). https://doi.org/10.1787/health_glance_eur-2018-en

3. Canadian Institute for Health Information (CIHI): Dementia in long-term care. https://www.cihi.ca/en/dementia-in-canada/dementia-care-across-the-health-system/dementia-in-long-term-care. Accessed 19 Aug 2025

4. Alzheimer's Association: Alzheimer's disease facts and figures. https://www.alz.org/alzheimers-dementia/facts-figures. Accessed 19 Aug 2025

5. National Council of Certified Dementia Practitioners (NCCDP): Understanding person-centered dementia care. https://www.nccdp.org/understanding-person-centered-dementia-care/. Accessed 19 Aug 2025

6. Alzheimer's Association: Dementia care practice recommendations for assisted living residences and nursing homes. Campaign for Quality Residential Care. Chicago, IL: Alzheimer's Association (2009). Accessed 19 Aug 2025

7. Wendling, P.: New report shows staggering costs of Alzheimer's disease (2024). https://www.medcentral.com/neurology/dementia/new-report-shows-staggering-costs-of-alzheimers-disease. Accessed 19 Aug 2025

8. Maleki Varnosfaderani, S., Forouzanfar, M.: The role of AI in hospitals and clinics: transforming healthcare in the 21st century. Bioengineering **11**(4), 337 (2024). https://doi.org/10.3390/bioengineering11040337

9. Rodrigues, J.J.P.C., et al.: Enabling technologies for the internet of health things. IEEE Access **6** (2018). https://doi.org/10.1109/ACCESS.2017.2789329

10. Annaswamy, A.M., et al. (eds.) Cyber-Physical-Human Systems: Fundamentals and Applications. Wiley, Hoboken (2023). https://doi.org/10.1002/9781119857433

11. Matthies, D.J., Gabrecht, M., Hellbrück, H.: Cyber-Physical & Human Systems (CPHS)—a review and outlook. In: Proceedings of Mensch und Computer 2023. New York, NY, USA: Association for Computing Machinery, pp. 364–369 (2023). https://doi.org/10.1145/3603555.3608527

12. Grieves, M., Vickers, J.: Digital twin: mitigating unpredictable, undesirable emergent behavior in complex systems. In: Kahlen, F.-J., Flumerfelt, S., Alves, A. (eds.) Transdisciplinary Perspectives on Complex Systems, pp. 85–113. Springer, Cham (2017). https://doi.org/10.1007/978-3-319-38756-7_4

13. Josifovska, K., Yigitbas, E., Engels, G.: Reference framework for digital twins within cyber-physical systems. In: Proceedings of the 2019 IEEE/ACM 5th International Workshop on Software Engineering for Smart Cyber-Physical Systems (SEsCPS) (2019). https://doi.org/10.1109/SESCPS.2019.00012

14. Lauer-Schmaltz, M.W., et al.: Towards the human digital twin: definition and design—a survey (2024). https://doi.org/10.48550/arXiv.2402.07922. arXiv: 2402.07922

15. Lin, Y., et al.: Human digital twin: a survey. J. Cloud Comput. **13**(1), 131 (2024). https://doi.org/10.1186/s13677-024-00691-z

16. Corneli, A., et al.: Digital twin models supporting cognitive buildings for ambient assisted living. In: Technological Imagination in the Green and Digital Transition. The Urban Book Series, pp. 167–178. Springer International Publishing, Cham (2023). https://doi.org/10.1007/978-3-031-29515-7_16

17. Mammadova, M.H., Ahmadova, A.A.: Development of digital twin ecosystem and ontology in medicine. Technol. Transfer: Fundamental Princip. Innov. Tech. Solutions, 21–23 (2023). https://doi.org/10.21303/2585-6847.2023.003203

18. Nguyen, T.N.: Cybonto: towards human cognitive digital twins for cybersecurity (2021). https://doi.org/10.48550/arXiv.2108.00551. arXiv: 2108.00551

19. Deters, J.K., et al.: Sensor-based agitation prediction in institutionalized people with dementia: a systematic review. Pervasive Mob. Comput. **98**, 101876 (2024). https://doi.org/10.1016/j.pmcj.2024.101876

20. Stokes, G.: Challenging behaviour in dementia: a person-centred approach. Routledge, London (2017). ISBN: 9780863883972. https://doi.org/10.4324/9781315168715

21. Banerjee, S., et al.: Quality of life in dementia: more than just cognition. An analysis of associations with quality of life in dementia. J. Neurol. Neurosurg. Psychiatry **77**(2), 146–148 (2006). https://doi.org/10.1136/jnnp.2005.072983

22. Jayakody, S., Arambepola, C.: Determinants of quality of life among people with dementia: evidence from a south asian population. BMC Geriatrics **22**(1) (2022). https://doi.org/10.1186/s12877-022-03443-3

23. Engel, G.L.: The need for a new medical model: a challenge for biomedicine. Science **196**(4286) (1977). https://doi.org/10.1126/science.847460

24. Schacter, D.L., Gilbert, D.T., Wegner, D.M.: Psychology. 2nd edn. New York, Worth (2011). ISBN: 9781429237192

25. Husebo, B.S., et al.: Sensing technology to facilitate behavioral and psychological symptoms and to monitor treatment response in people with dementia: a systematic review. Front. Pharmacol. **10**, 1699. (2019). https://doi.org/10.3389/fphar.2019.01699

26. Khan, S.S., et al.: DAAD: a framework for detecting agitation and aggression in people living with dementia using a novel multi-modal sensor network. In: IEEE International Conference on Data Mining Workshops (ICDMW), pp. 703–710 (2017). https://doi.org/10.1109/ICDMW.2017.98

27. Teipel, S., et al.: Multidimensional assessment of challenging behaviors in advanced stages of dementia in nursing homes-the inside DEM framework. Alzheimer's & Dementia: Diag. Assess. Dis. Monit. **8**, 36–44 (2017). https://doi.org/10.1016/j.dadm.2017.03.006

28. Kaye, J., et al.: Methodology for establishing a community-wide life laboratory for capturing unobtrusive and continuous remote activity and health data. J. Visual. Exp. **137**, e56942 (2018). https://doi.org/10.3791/56942

29. Davidoff, H., et al.: Toward quantification of agitation in people with dementia using multimodal sensing. Innov. Aging **6**(7) (2022). https://doi.org/10.1093/geroni/igac064

30. Goerss, D., et al.: Automated sensor-based detection of challenging behaviors in advanced stages of dementia in nursing homes. Alzheimer's Dementia **16**(4), 672–680 (2020). https://doi.org/10.1016/j.jalz.2019.08.193

31. Iaboni, A., et al.: Wearable multimodal sensors for the detection of behavioral and psychological symptoms of dementia using personalized machine learning models. Alzheimer's Dementia: Diagnosis, Assess. Disease Monit. **14**(1), e12305 (2022). https://doi.org/10.1002/dad2.12305

32. AuYeung, W.T.M., et al.: Sensing a problem: proof of concept for characterizing and predicting agitation. Alzheimer's Dementia: Transl. Res. Clin. Intervent. **6**(1), e12079 (2020). https://doi.org/10.1002/trc2.12079

33. Verbeek-Oudijk, D., Koper, I.: Life in a nursing home. The Hague (2021). 10.48592/56. https://www.scp.nl/binaries/scp/documenten/publicaties/2021/02/19/het-leven-in-een-verpleeghuis/Het%2Bleven%2Bin%2Been%2Bverpleeghuis_Summary.pdf

34. Rijksoverheid: Kwaliteitseisen zorgaanbieders (2025). https://www.rijksoverheid.nl/onderwerpen/kwaliteit-van-de-zorg/kwaliteitseisen-zorginstellingen

35. Elgazzar, K., et al.: Revisiting the internet of things: new trends, opportunities and grand challenges. Front. Internet Things 1, 1073780 (2022). https://doi.org/10.3389/friot.2022.1073780

36. en Veiligheid, M.V.J.: Richtlijnen voor het toepassen van algoritmen door overheden en publieksvoorlichting over data-analyses (2021). https://www.rijksoverheid.nl/documenten/richtlijnen/2021/09/24/richtlijnen-voor-het-toepassen-van-algoritmen-door-overheden-en-publieksvoorlichting-over-data-analyses. Accessed 31 Jan 2025
37. Dudyrev, E., et al.: Human knowledge models: learning applied knowledge from the data. PLoS ONE **17**(10), e0275814 (2022). https://doi.org/10.1371/journal.pone.0275814
38. Vela, D., et al.: Temporal quality degradation in AI models. Sci. Rep. **12**(1) (2022). https://doi.org/10.1038/s41598-022-15245-z
39. Yordanova, K.: Challenges providing ground truth for pervasive healthcare systems. IEEE Pervasive Comput. **18**(2), 100–104 (2019). https://doi.org/10.1109/MPRV.2019.2912261
40. Niemeijer, A.R. et al.: CE: Original research: the use of surveillance technology in residential facilities for people with dementia or intellectual disabilities: a study among nurses and support staff. AJN Am. J. Nurs. **114**(12), 28–37 (2014). https://doi.org/10.1097/01.NAJ.0000457408.38222.d0. https://journals.lww.com/ajnonline/Fulltext/2014/12000/CE_Original_Research__The_Use_of_Surveillance.14.aspx
41. Khan, S.S., et al.: Unsupervised deep learning to detect agitation from videos in people with dementia. IEEE Access **10**, 10349–10358 (2022). https://doi.org/10.1109/ACCESS.2022.3143990
42. Aridor, G., Grechi, F., Woodford, M.: Adaptive efficient coding: a variational autoencoder approach. bioRziv, p. 2020.05.29.124453 (2020). https://doi.org/10.1101/2020.05.29.124453
43. Lobo, J.L., et al.: Spiking neural networks and online learning: an overview and perspectives. Neural Netw. **121**, 88–100 (2020). https://doi.org/10.1016/j.neunet.2019.09.004
44. Liu, Y., Qin, Z., Li, G.Y.: Energy-efficient distributed spiking neural network for wireless edge intelligence. IEEE Trans. Wirel. Commun. **23**(9) (2024). https://doi.org/10.1109/TWC.2024.3374549
45. Yang, H., et al.: Lead federated neuromorphic learning for wireless edge artificial intelligence. Nat. Commun. **13**(1), 4269 (2022). https://doi.org/10.1038/s41467-022-32020-w
46. Yao, M., et al.: Spike-based dynamic computing with asynchronous sensing-computing neuromorphic chip. Nat. Commun. **15**, 4464 (2024). https://doi.org/10.1038/s41467-024-47811-6
47. Liu, S., et al.: Human inertial thinking strategy: a novel fuzzy reasoning mechanism for IoT-assisted visual monitoring. IEEE Internet Things J. **10**(5), 3735–3748 (2023). https://doi.org/10.1109/JIOT.2022.3142115
48. Adam, S., Busoniu, L., Babuska, R.: Experience replay for real-time reinforcement learning control. IEEE Trans. Syst. Man Cybern. Part C (Appl. Rev.) **42**(2), 201–212 (2012). https://doi.org/10.1109/TSMCC.2011.2106494
49. Alirezaie, M., et al.: SmartEnv ontology in E-care@home. In: Lefrançois, M., et al. (eds.) Proceedings of the 9th International Semantic Sensor Networks Workshop (SSN 2018), vol. 2213, pp. 72–79. CEUR Workshop Proceedings. Monterey, CA, USA: CEUR-WS.org (2018). https://ceur-ws.org/Vol-2213/paper7.pdf

DenseVoxelNet3D: A Compact 3D CNN Architecture for Human Activity Recognition Using LiDAR Point Clouds

Noel D'Avis$^{(\boxtimes)}$ ⓘ, Hendrik Hartmann ⓘ, Lars Grothe ⓘ, and Silvia Faquiri ⓘ

Hochschule RheinMain, Wiesbaden, Germany
`noel.davis@hs-rm.de`

Abstract. LiDAR-based point cloud analysis for Human Activity Recognition (HAR) is increasingly relevant in assistive technologies, particularly for supporting elderly and care-dependent individuals through applications such as fall detection. In this work, we present DenseVoxelNet3D, a compact and efficient 3D convolutional neural network designed for voxelized LiDAR input. The architecture combines a voxelization-based preprocessing pipeline with densely connected layers to improve feature propagation and mitigate vanishing gradient issues. By integrating global average pooling and dropout-based regularization, the model achieves strong generalization with minimal overfitting. On the HmPEAR dataset [14], DenseVoxelNet3D outperforms conventional architectures such as AlexNet and ResNet in terms of classification accuracy and computational efficiency. Our code is available at https://github.com/eckabeg/DenseVoxelNet3D.git.

Keywords: Human Activity Recognition · LiDAR · Point Cloud · 3D Convolutional Neural Network · DenseVoxelNet3D · Voxelization · Elderly Care · Fall Detection · Deep Learning · Spatiotemporal Analysis

1 Introduction

HAR and motion detection are essential components of modern assistive technologies in healthcare, smart home systems, and elderly care. In particular, the ability to accurately detect and classify daily movements such as walking, sitting, or falling can significantly enhance the autonomy and safety of elderly and care-dependent individuals. Early and robust fall detection, for instance, remains a critical requirement for enabling timely interventions and reducing the risk of injury [10]. Traditional HAR methods, based primarily on RGB video, are highly sensitive to environmental conditions such as poor illumination, shadows, or occlusions, rendering them unreliable in real-world, uncontrolled environments [18,20] (Fig. 1).

O. Durmaz Incel et al. (Eds.): iWOAR 2025, LNCS 16292, pp. 116–134, 2026.
https://doi.org/10.1007/978-3-032-13312-0_7

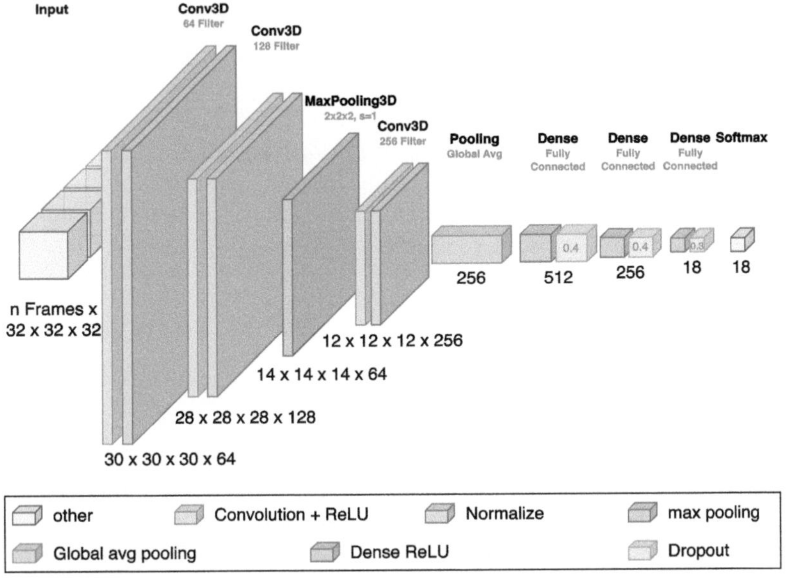

Fig. 1. Graphical Structure of DenseVoxelNet3D.

To address these shortcomings, LiDAR-based sensing has emerged as a robust alternative. LiDAR sensors capture high-resolution 3D point cloud data that is inherently invariant to lighting conditions and offers rich spatial information [16]. This makes them particularly well-suited for motion monitoring in private homes, hospitals, or care facilities. However, the effective use of LiDAR data for HAR poses its own set of challenges. Point clouds are sparse, irregularly sampled, and unordered, which limits the direct applicability of traditional Convulational Neural Network (CNN) designed for dense, grid-like inputs such as images [22]. Moreover, their high dimensionality increases the risk of overfitting, particularly when working with limited labeled data typical in healthcare domains.

In this work, we introduce DenseVoxelNet3D, a lightweight yet powerful 3D convolutional neural network tailored specifically for voxelized LiDAR input. The network is built upon a structured preprocessing pipeline that transforms raw point cloud sequences into dense voxel grids. This voxelization step discretizes the spatial domain while preserving temporal dynamics across successive frames, yielding a uniform input structure that can be efficiently processed by 3D convolutional layers [5]. The use of fixed-size voxel representations also facilitates batch processing and hardware acceleration, making the model suitable for deployment in real-time or resource-constrained environments.

At the core of our model are densely connected 3D convolutional layers. These connections encourage feature reuse and improve information flow throughout the network, effectively addressing the vanishing gradient problem often encountered in deeper architectures. The design further incorporates global average pooling and dropout-based regularization, combined with L2 weight penalties, to mitigate overfitting and ensure robust generalization from sparse input data.

We evaluate our model on the HmPEAR dataset [14], which comprises over 300,000 point cloud frames across 40 human activity classes recorded in various indoor settings. Using a relevant subset of 18 daily activities (Table 1), chosen for their applicability in medical and caregiving contexts, DenseVoxelNet3D achieves higher classification accuracy and computational efficiency than conventional architectures such as AlexNet and ResNet [6, 12].

2   Related Work

Human pose and activity recognition have been extensively researched, primarily on 2D videos and images, using heatmap-based approaches and regression methods [3,8]. They generally employ CNNs and Recurrent Neural Networks (RNNs) and have proved quite efficient in a controlled setup but are generally plagued by environmental factors like changes in light and occlusions [2,4].

Conversely, Inertial Measurement Unit (IMU)-based methods have emerged, which have overcome some of these limitations by measuring the body movements directly through wearable sensors. However, IMU-based methods tend to lose accuracy when compared to external accelerations and sensor drift over long spans of time [17].

In recent years, LiDAR sensors have been of especially interest, particularly for autonomous driving tasks, due to their inherent lack of sensitivity to external changes such as illumination and occlusion issues caused by fog or airborne particles. [11]. Though highly researched in pedestrian tracking and object detection, LiDAR-based human pose estimation has been fairly underrepresented due to the computational cost of operating with large sets of data and the real-time processing requirements prevalent in such procedures.

Some early methods borrowed from 2D image processing, including Histogram of Oriented Gradient (HOG) and limb segmentation, have been promising for 3D data [1,19]. Although HOG is effective in describing temporal motion patterns in visual data and typically generates heatmaps from frame pairs, it lacks sufficient performance in our tests when applied to 3D LiDAR data. Similarly, limb segmentation decomposes input data into body segments to estimate poses but requires enormous data labeling and skeletal representations, which are computationally expensive.

Direct regression techniques that do not involve intermediate representation creation such as heatmaps have been explored to simplify data pipelines. The techniques tend to suffer from severe overfitting issues when applied to high-dimensional point cloud data [15].

Recent approaches in motion detection rely on preprocessing sensor data through voxelization and densification techniques to extract information from consecutive frames. Various studies have reported achieving accuracies exceeding 86% [26].

Recent deep learning architectural developments consist of the integration of attention modules such as Squeeze-and-Excitation (SE) blocks [7] and Convolutional Block Attention Modules (CBAM) [25] that have strongly increased model performance with improved ability to extract spatial and channel-wise features. The methodologies have proved helpful in several vision recognition tasks with adaptively re-calibrated feature responses [25,27].

Additionally, transformer-based methods like LidPose utilize attention mechanisms in order to handle sparse and irregular LiDAR data efficiently [11]. Such methods provide information about ideal pose estimation using dense, sparse LiDAR scans based on the implementation of self-attention methods, indicating the preferability of attention-based structures with regards to processing 3D data.

AlexNet [12] was originally developed for large-scale image classification tasks. In our experiments, an adapted version using 3D convolutions achieved a final training accuracy of 76% and a validation accuracy of approximately 41%. While volumetric adaptations are possible [13], its shallow structure and lack of mechanisms for sparse input handling limit its effectiveness for voxelized LiDAR sequences.

ResNet [6] introduced residual connections to improve the training of deep networks. In our evaluation, the adapted ResNet10 variant reached a training accuracy of 99% but suffered from significant overfitting, with a final validation accuracy of only 36%. Although residual architectures facilitate the learning of complex representations, their high capacity and parameter count increase the risk of overfitting on sparse and small-scale datasets [21] typical for human activity recognition using LiDAR data.

While other recent architectures such as PointNet++, KPConv, MinkowskiNet, or transformer-based models (e.g., LidPose, VoxelSet) currently represent the state of the art in 3D point cloud analysis, these approaches typically entail significantly increased computational complexity, memory consumption, and hardware requirements [11,23,24]. As the goal of this work was to design a compact and efficient model suitable for real-time deployment on resource-constrained hardware, we deliberately limited our selection of baseline models to lightweight, practically deployable architectures. Furthermore, the available computational resources constituted a natural boundary for the extent of our empirical evaluation. Training and fine-tuning modern large-scale 3D transformer or point-based models on the HmPEAR dataset was not feasible within the scope and timeline of this project. Therefore, we focused our comparative analysis on adapted, resource-efficient 3D CNN architectures such as AlexNet and ResNet10, which continue to serve as relevant references for the development of edge-ready solutions. A comprehensive benchmarking study including current state-of-the-art models is planned for future work as soon as suitable computational resources and implementations are available.

In addition to existing approaches that adapt conventional convolutional architectures to 3D data, we propose DenseVoxelNet3D, a lightweight and regularized 3D convolutional network specifically designed for sparse voxelized

LiDAR sequences. By combining dense connectivity, global average pooling, and dropout-based regularization, our model improves feature propagation, mitigates overfitting, and offers a compact solution suitable for human activity recognition in resource-constrained environments.

The remainder of this paper is organized as follows: Sect. 3 details the pre-processing pipeline used to transform raw point cloud data into dense voxel representations suitable for 3D CNN processing. Section 4 presents the proposed DenseVoxelNet3D architecture, outlining its design choices and layer configurations. Section 5 describes the experimental validation, including a comparative evaluation against adapted baseline models. Section 6 discusses the implications of the findings, and Sect. 7 concludes the paper with a summary and outlines directions for future research.

3   Data Processing Pipeline

This chapter first describes the dataset used, followed by a detailed presentation of the processing pipeline developed for the preparation of the point cloud data.

For the purpose of training and validating the DenseVoxelNet3D model, the HmPEAR dataset [14] was used. This dataset consists of 300,000 point cloud frames, representing 40 unique human activity categories. The data was collected in various indoor environments and includes diverse movements ranging from simple postures to complex motion sequences.

Given the focus on daily activity recognition, a specific subset of 18 activity classes was utilized. Table 1 shows the classes used for training the model. The subset was chosen for its relevance to human movement recognition, particularly in the context of medical applications, where understanding daily activity patterns can aid in monitoring and diagnosing various health conditions. HmPEAR contains predefined training and test splits, which were used to ensure consistent evaluation.

Table 1. Classes used for training

bend over	carry sth	drink sth	hand waving
jump forward	jump up	pick up	running
sit down	sitting	squat down	stand up
standing	stretch onself	turn around	walking
	wave left hand	wave right hand	

Due to the inherent variability in the number of points within LiDAR Point Clouds, a preprocessing stage is essential. To address this, a point cloud sequence of an action is compressed into a space explicitly defined to ensure no temporal information is lost. This reduces the number of points needed to capture the relevant information and ensures that all processed frames possess a consistent spatial extent while preserving the relative positional information within each frame.

Given a sequence of point cloud frames $A = \{P^{(t)}\}_{t=1}^{T}$, where each frame is a set of 3D points $P^{(t)} = \{p_n^{(t)} \in \mathbb{R}^3\}_{n=1}^{N_t}$, the data is converted into a dense voxel map using the following steps:

1. Compute Global Bounds

$$\mathbf{p}_{\min} = \min_{t,n} \left(p_n^{(t)} \right), \quad \mathbf{p}_{\max} = \max_{t,n} \left(p_n^{(t)} \right) \tag{1}$$

2. Compute Uniform Scale Let $\mathbf{D} = (D_x, D_y, D_z)$ denote the target resolution of the dense voxel map along each spatial axis. For example, if $\mathbf{D} = (32, 32, 32)$, each point cloud frame is voxelized into a grid of $32 \times 32 \times 32$ binary cells. To ensure isotropic voxelization, compute a uniform scaling factor based on the target voxel grid shape $\mathbf{D} = (D_x, D_y, D_z)$ and the global bounds:

$$\mathbf{s} = \frac{\mathbf{D}}{\mathbf{p}_{\max} - \mathbf{p}_{\min}}, \quad s = \min(s_x, s_y, s_z) \tag{2}$$

3. Normalize and Translate Points To ensure the sequence uses the entire space, each point is normalized with the global minimum, and afterwards, the scale factor is applied.

$$\hat{p}_n^{(t)} = (p_n^{(t)} - \mathbf{p}_{\min}) \cdot s \tag{3}$$

4. Convert Map to Voxel Indices Each normalized point is converted to discrete voxel coordinates by rounding down:

$$(i, j, k) = \left\lfloor \hat{p}_n^{(t)} \right\rfloor \tag{4}$$

To ensure the voxel indices do not exceed the grid dimensions in any case, the values are set to the max bounding values:

$$(i, j, k) \leftarrow \min\left((i, j, k), (D_x - 1, D_y - 1, D_z - 1)\right) \tag{5}$$

5. Create the dense voxel map A 4D binary occupancy tensor $V \in \{0, 1\}^{T \times D_x \times D_y \times D_z}$ is created based on the voxel indices such that:

$$V(t, i, j, k) = \begin{cases} 1, & \text{if } \exists\, p_n^{(t)} \in P^{(t)} \\ 0, & \text{otherwise} \end{cases} \tag{6}$$

Figures 2 and 3 presents both a temporal sequence, consisting of 24 individual frames and an individual frame of a running subject, visualized in their raw LiDAR point cloud form as well as in their standardized representations. The previously described standardization is achieved via a dense voxel mapping process applied to both the full sequence and the individual frame. Notably, the

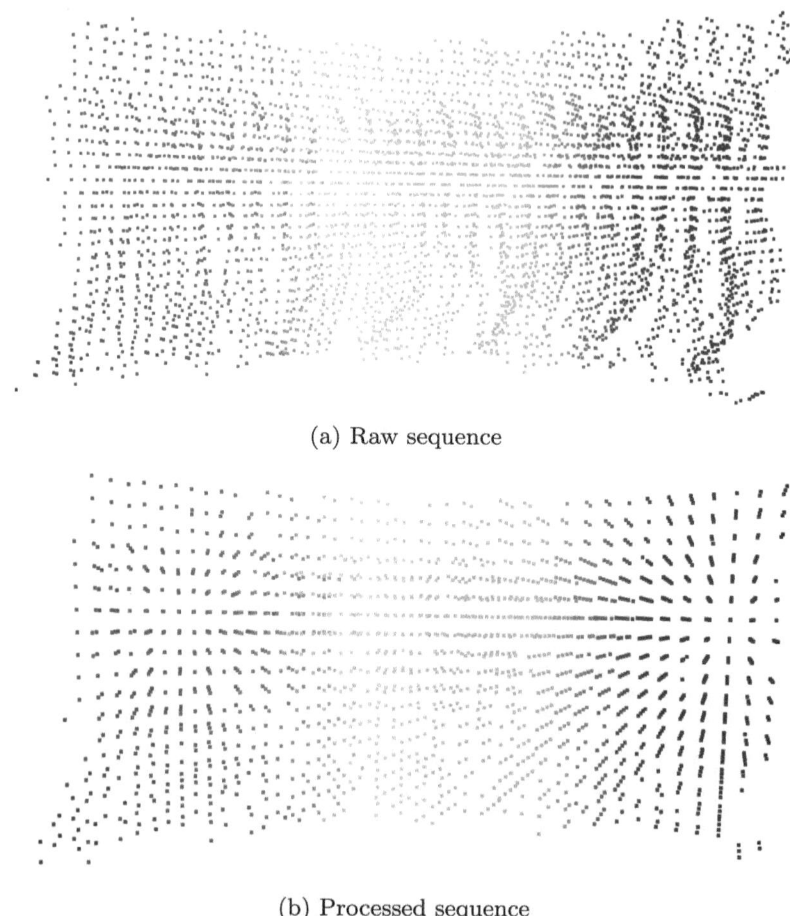

(a) Raw sequence

(b) Processed sequence

Fig. 2. Comparison of raw and processed movement sequences.

individual frame is extracted from the temporal sequence and serves as a representative example. Figure 2a depicts the unprocessed LiDAR point cloud data corresponding to the entire motion sequence of a running individual. In contrast, Fig. 2b illustrates the voxelized and standardized version of this sequence, which serves as input data for subsequent model training. Figure 3a shows a single unprocessed LiDAR frame—extracted from the sequence—while Fig. 3b displays the same frame after transformation using the dense voxel map, yielding a spatially normalized representation.

As a final step, an temporal grouping is applied to each activity sequence to account for variations in sequence length, as not all sequences contained the same number of frames. This grouping enables controlled manipulation of the number of consecutive frames used in the subsequent decision-making process. Additionally, by segmenting longer sequences into multiple overlapping or non-overlapping groups, more training samples could be generated, thereby increas-

(a) Raw frame   (b) Processed frame

Fig. 3. Comparison of raw and processed frames.

ing both the quantity and diversity of data available for model training. This approach also introduced greater flexibility in sequence representation, allowing the data processing pipeline to be better aligned with the requirements of the intended application.

4   DenseVoxelNet3D

The proposed model, DenseVoxelNet3D, accepts as input a sequence of densely voxelized LiDAR frames, where each frame is represented as a $32{\times}32{\times}32$ voxel grid. These frames are grouped together along the temporal dimension to form the model input. The first 3D convolutional layer applies 64 filters of size $3{\times}3{\times}3$ with a stride of 1. This layer is designed to learn spatiotemporal features by integrating information across multiple consecutive frames. The resulting feature map dimension is $30{\times}30{\times}30{\times}64$.

Table 2. DenseVoxelNet3D architecture

type	patch/stride	output shape	params
input	-	$32 \times 32 \times 32 \times 5$	-
convolution 3d	$3 \times 3 \times 3/1$	$30 \times 30 \times 30 \times 64$	8,704
batch normalization	-	-	256
convolution 3d	$3 \times 3 \times 3/1$	$28 \times 28 \times 28 \times 128$	221,312
batch normalize	-	-	512
max pooling	$2 \times 2 \times 2/1$	$14 \times 14 \times 14 \times 64$	-
convolution 3d	$3 \times 3 \times 3/1$	$12 \times 12 \times 12 \times 256$	884,992
batch normalize	-	-	1,024
gloabl avg. pooling	-	256	-
dense	-	512	131,584
dropout (0.4)	-	-	-
dense	-	256	131,328
dropout (0.4)	-	-	-
dense	-	18	4,626
dropout (0.3)	-	-	-
softmax	-	-	-

As this initial layer effectively captures the temporal dependencies across frames, no pooling is applied immediately afterwards. This design choice preserves spatial resolution and enables the model to extract more detailed local features in subsequent layers. The second convolutional layer uses the same kernel size and stride but increases the number of filters to 128, enabling the extraction of more complex and abstract representations. Following this, a max pooling layer with a kernel size of $2 \times 2 \times 2$ and a stride of 1 is employed to reduce the spatial dimensions of the feature map, thereby decreasing computational cost while retaining essential feature information.

The third convolutional layer, also using $3 \times 3 \times 3$ kernels and a stride of 1, increases the filter count to 256, producing a feature map of $12 \times 12 \times 12 \times 256$. Prior to the transition to fully connected layers, various pooling strategies were explored, including max pooling and flattening. However, these approaches resulted in a high number of parameters and increased the risk of overfitting. To mitigate this, a global average pooling operation is applied, which significantly reduces the number of trainable parameters and produces a compact 256-dimensional feature vector.

The final classification head is composed of three fully connected (dense) layers. The first dense layer contains 512 neurons, followed by a second layer with 256 neurons, and finally a third layer with 18 neurons, each corresponding to one of the activity classes. This specific configuration was chosen to strike a balance between model complexity and computational efficiency. By progressively reducing the number of neurons, the network is encouraged to learn compact and abstract feature representations, which helps in generalizing well to unseen data. The chosen sizes are small enough to keep the overall model lightweight, which is an important consideration for real-time or resource-constrained environments, and still large enough to retain the capacity for learning complex decision boundaries. To produce class probabilities, a softmax activation function is applied to the final layer. All convolutional and dense layers throughout the network employ the Rectified linear unit (ReLu) activation function, which introduces nonlinearity and helps mitigate issues such as vanishing gradients during training [9].

To enhance the model's generalization capabilities and reduce the risk of overfitting, a combination of regularization techniques was incorporated throughout the network. L2 regularization is applied to all convolutional layers to penalize large weights, promoting simpler and more robust feature representations. This is particularly important given that the model consists of approximately 1.38 million trainable parameters in total, making it relatively compact yet expressive enough for the complexity of activity recognition from voxelized LiDAR data. Batch normalization is applied after each convolutional layer to normalize feature distributions, which helps stabilize training dynamics, accelerate convergence, and reduce internal covariate shift.

In addition to these techniques, dropout is utilized after each fully connected layer to further prevent coadaptation of neurons. Dropout rates of 40%, 30%, and 30% are applied after the first, second, and third dense layers, respectively. These values were chosen empirically to strike a balance between regularization strength and model capacity, ensuring that the model remains expressive while improving its ability to generalize to unseen data.

The complete architectural configuration, including layer types, output shapes, and parameter counts, is summarized in Table 2.

5   Validation

To evaluate the effectiveness of the proposed DenseVoxelNet3D architecture, extensive training and validation experiments were conducted, comparing its performance against modified versions of AlexNet and ResNet. These baseline architectures were adapted to process 3D data by extending their convolutional and pooling layers to three dimensions. Furthermore, their overall scale and complexity were reduced to match the smaller input dimensions of the voxelized LiDAR point clouds and to accommodate the size of the available training dataset. Figures 4, 5, 6 and 7 present the training and validation performance of the models. The DenseVoxelNet3D-model was trained with a batch size of 32 for 50 epochs using the Adam optimizer (learning rate 0.001) and categorical crossentropy loss. A fixed random seed (42) was used for reproducibility, and training data was shuffled at the start of each epoch. L2 regularization (1e−4) was applied to all convolutional layers, with dropout rates of 0.4, 0.4, and 0.3 after the dense layers. No data augmentation or early stopping was used. The model input consisted of sequences of five frames, each voxelized to 32 × 32 ×

32, with 18 activity classes. A temporal grouping of five frames was selected as a trade-off between computational efficiency and recognition performance.

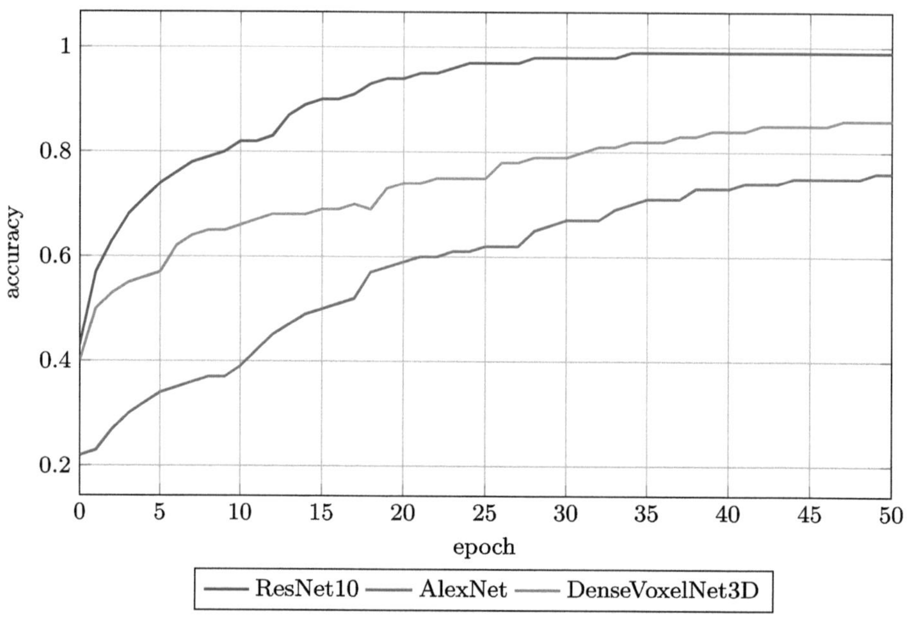

Fig. 4. Training Accuracy of ResNet10, AlexNet and DenseVoxelNet3D.

Figure 4 illustrates the evolution of the training accuracy for ResNet10, AlexNet, and DenseVoxelNet3D over the course of 50 epochs. ResNet10 demonstrates rapid improvement during the first 20 epochs, reaching an accuracy of 90%. From epoch 34 onward, it achieves a near-perfect accuracy of 99%, with little further improvement in the subsequent epochs.

AlexNet exhibits a slower but steady increase in accuracy. Initially, its accuracy is exceptionally low at 22%. Due to continuous growth, it reaches 73% by epoch 38. However, its growth rate significantly declines thereafter, culminating in a final training accuracy of 76%. Despite ongoing progress, AlexNet's overall performance remains lower compared to the other two models.

DenseVoxelNet3D begins training at an accuracy comparable to ResNet10 but does not match its rapid growth rate. Nevertheless, it demonstrates a consistent and smooth learning curve, surpassing AlexNet throughout the training process and ultimately achieving a final accuracy of 86%. These results indicate that DenseVoxelNet3D is capable of learning complex patterns effectively while maintaining stable optimization behavior throughout training.

The training loss curves, depicted in Fig. 5, mirror the trends observed in the accuracy results. ResNet10 exhibits the steepest decline in loss across all stages of training, dropping below 0.5 by epoch 20 and stabilizing at approximately 0.07 from epoch 34 onward.

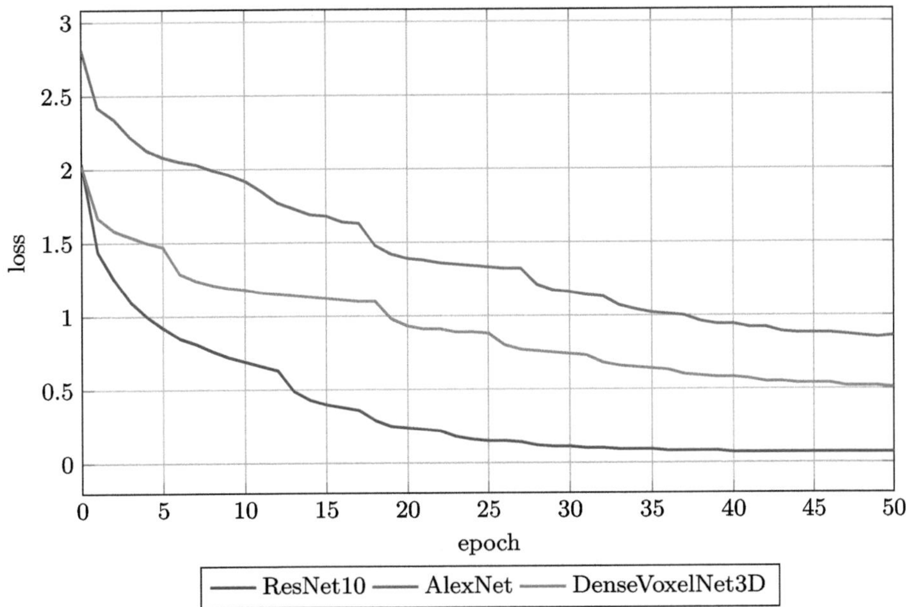

Fig. 5. Training Loss of ResNet10, AlexNet and DenseVoxelNet3D.

AlexNet shows a rapid reduction in loss during the first 20 epochs, followed by a more gradual decrease, reaching a final training loss of 0.86 by epoch 50. This behavior is consistent with its lower initial accuracy and slower convergence compared to the other models.

DenseVoxelNet3D achieves a steady and continuous reduction in training loss, culminating in a final loss of 0.51. Although the overall trend of loss reduction is comparable to that of AlexNet, DenseVoxelNet3D consistently maintains significantly lower absolute loss values throughout the training process. The smooth and stable downward progression of the DenseVoxelNet3D loss curve reflects more robust learning dynamics and more effective convergence behavior.

Figure 6 presents the validation accuracy trajectories of the three models across 50 epochs.

ResNet10 exhibits steady but limited improvement, increasing from an initial validation accuracy of around 11% to approximately 36% by epoch 50. After epoch 20, progress slows noticeably, and the validation accuracy stabilizes with minor fluctuations. Given the significant gap between its high training accuracy (99%) and relatively low validation accuracy, ResNet10 likely suffers from substantial overfitting.

AlexNet starts with a higher initial validation accuracy of approximately 25% but experiences considerable fluctuations in the early stages of training. Nevertheless, it improves steadily, reaching a maximum validation accuracy of around 41% by the end of training. Compared to ResNet10, AlexNet demon-

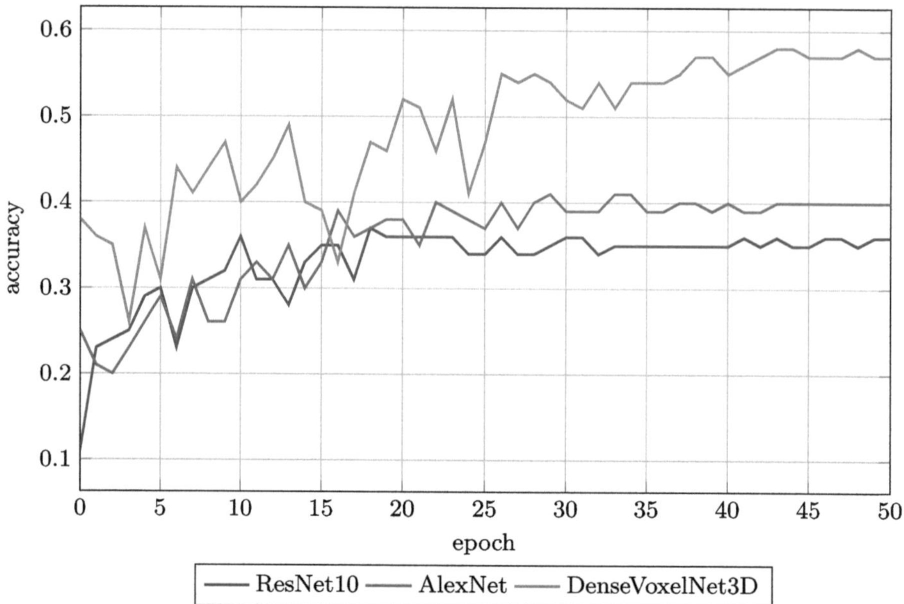

Fig. 6. Validation Accuracy of ResNet10, AlexNet and DenseVoxelNet3D.

strates stronger learning dynamics and better generalization, although with some instability.

In contrast, DenseVoxelNet3D consistently outperforms both baseline models across all epochs. It starts with an initial validation accuracy of approximately 38%, shows minor variability in the early training phase, and then steadily improves. After epoch 20, DenseVoxelNet3D stabilizes, ultimately achieving a peak validation accuracy of 58%. This superior performance highlights its enhanced learning capability and generalization ability compared to the other models. Additionally, it managed to reach a weighted F1 score of 0.56 and an F1 score of 0.50, clearly outperforming the other models, plateauing between 0.37 and 0.40.

The validation loss curves for the three models are shown in Fig. 7.

ResNet10 initially exhibits a high validation loss of approximately 5.2, which briefly decreases but then steadily increases after epoch 10, surpassing 8.5 by the end of training. This trend reinforces the observation that ResNet10 heavily overfits the training data despite achieving excellent training accuracy.

In comparison, AlexNet begins with a lower validation loss of approximately 2.5 and maintains a relatively stable trajectory throughout training. Although minor fluctuations are observed, the loss consistently remains below 3.0, with a final validation loss of 2.85 at epoch 50, indicating better generalization compared to ResNet10.

DenseVoxelNet3D achieves the best overall performance, starting with a low initial validation loss of approximately 2.1 and exhibiting a continuous downward

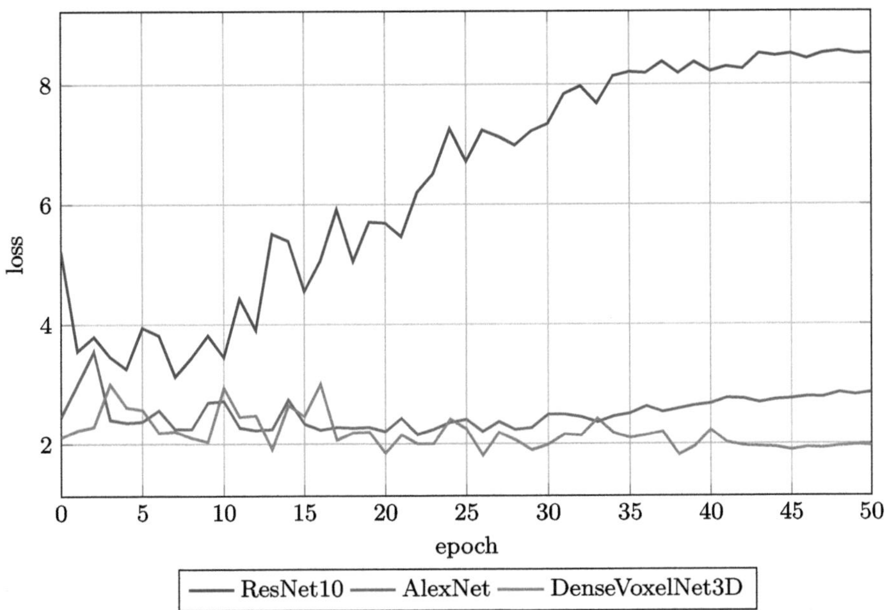

Fig. 7. Validation Loss of DenseVoxelNet3D.

trend. It maintains the lowest final loss among the three models, reaching values consistently below 2.0, with a minimum of 1.8. This stable and sustained loss reduction demonstrates the model's superior generalization ability and robustness on the validation set.

Figure 8 presents the confusion matrix of DenseVoxelNet3D evaluated on the validation dataset. The model achieves its highest accuracies for running (93%) and walking (79%). In contrast, the bending over activity is not recognized at all (0% accuracy), which is likely attributable to the small number of training samples (111 instances). The overall class distribution is shown in Fig. 9. All waving gestures exhibit poor recognition performance, indicating that the model has difficulty capturing subtle hand movements. Interestingly, the stretch oneself activity achieves an accuracy of 71% despite having only 1,224 training samples, considerably below the mean class size of 4,336 samples. Misclassifications also reveal semantically and visually similar activities: for instance, sitting is correctly classified in 57% of cases but frequently confused with sitting down (35%). This behaviour can be explained by the temporal limitation of the model, which processes only five consecutive frames, making activities with gradual transitions difficult to distinguish.

Overall, the results demonstrate that DenseVoxelNet3D achieves superior training and validation performance compared to the adapted versions of ResNet10 and AlexNet. While ResNet10 exhibits signs of overfitting and AlexNet shows limited learning capacity, DenseVoxelNet3D maintains stable learning dynamics, effective convergence, and strong generalization capabilities through-

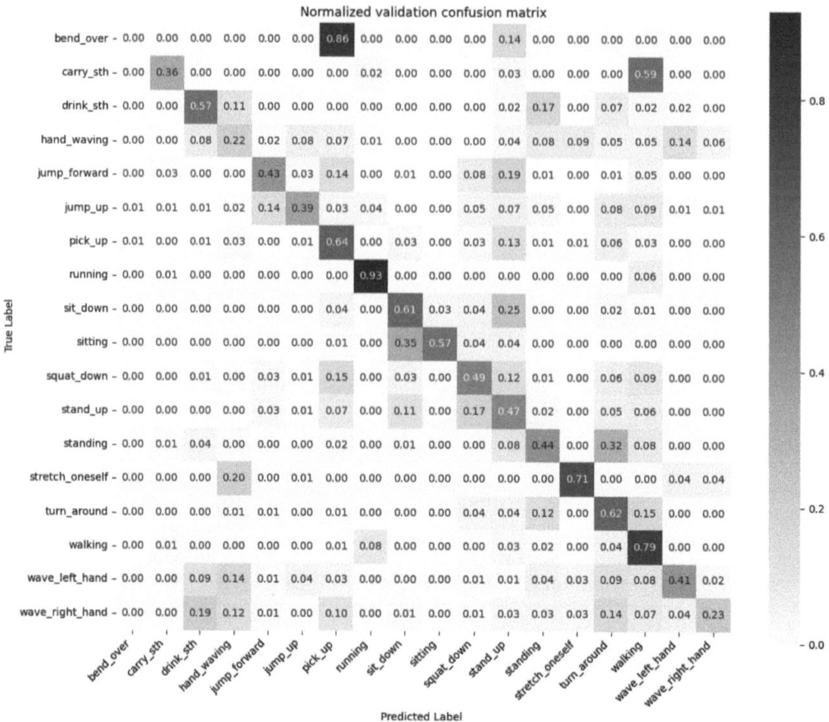

Fig. 8. Normalized validation confusion matrix of DenseVoxelNet3D

out training. These findings validate the effectiveness of the proposed architecture in handling voxelized LiDAR point cloud data and highlight its potential for further application in real-world 3D perception tasks.

6   Discussion

The work presented in this paper confirms the effectiveness of DenseVoxelNet3D, a tailored 3D convolutional neural network specifically developed for human activity recognition (HAR) utilizing LiDAR-derived point cloud data. DenseVoxelNet3D outperformed established architectures such as adapted AlexNet and ResNet10, achieving superior validation accuracy and stability while effectively addressing challenges posed by the sparsity and irregular structure inherent in LiDAR data. The densely connected convolutional architecture plays a crucial role in the model's robust performance. This design effectively mitigates the vanishing gradient issue common in deeper networks, promoting efficient information flow and enabling enhanced feature learning from voxelized inputs. Such structural advantages directly translate into improved model robustness and adaptability to the spatiotemporal dynamics characteristic of human movements. Furthermore, the inclusion of global average pooling significantly reduced model

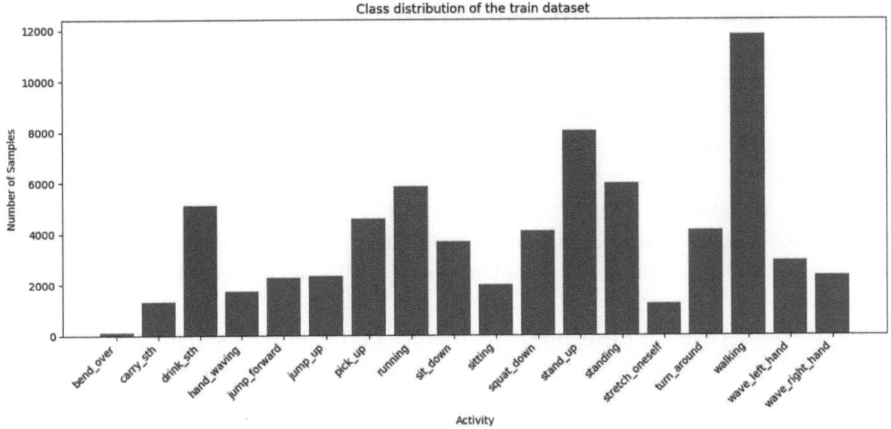

Fig. 9. Class distribution of the train dataset

complexity by limiting parameter counts without compromising the expressiveness required for accurate activity recognition. Complementing this, the use of dropout regularization alongside L2 penalties provided a balanced approach to model complexity and regularization, thus substantially improving generalization capability. This strategic regularization was essential in achieving the observed resilience against overfitting, particularly beneficial in real-world applications with limited data availability. Evaluation results on the HmPEAR dataset substantiate the strengths of DenseVoxelNet3D. Whereas AlexNet and ResNet10 exhibited significant discrepancies between training and validation performance—indicative of overfitting, DenseVoxelNet3D consistently demonstrated alignment between these metrics. This alignment underscores the model's ability to generalize effectively to unseen data, a critical requirement in practical scenarios such as medical monitoring and elderly care systems. The preprocessing pipeline, notably voxelization, significantly contributed to the overall performance by providing standardized and spatially consistent input. This approach facilitated computational efficiency, enabling efficient training and inference, and is vital for practical deployment in resource-constrained environments. Collectively, these insights demonstrate that tailored network designs specifically adapted to LiDAR data outperform traditional architectures adapted from other domains. Such tailored approaches provide a foundation for further exploration into robust, real-time capable HAR systems, beneficial in healthcare, safety, and assistive technologies. Rather than an exhaustive ablation analysis, this study focused on demonstrating robust real-world performance with carefully selected, empirically validated hyperparameters. We consider a dedicated ablation of individual architectural choices an interesting next step, complementing our practical findings.

7   Conclusion and Future Work

Throughout this work, we investigated the effectiveness of various 3D convolutional neural network architectures for HAR applied on LiDAR point cloud data. While established models such as AlexNet and ResNet demonstrated strong performance on the training set, achieving training accuracies of up to 98%, they suffer from substantial overfitting, with validation accuracies remaining below 30% and 50% respectively. This underlines the inherent challenge of generalizing from sparse 3D data using architectures originally designed for dense 2D image inputs.

To address these limitations, we introduced DenseVoxelNet3D, a custom-tailored 3D CNN architecture optimized for temporal voxelized input. By leveraging a compact design, carefully placed dropout layers, and kernel regularization, DenseVoxelNet3D is able to significantly improve generalization performance. The final model achieves a stable validation accuracy of 58–60% while maintaining high training accuracy, marking a substantial improvement of about 20% over the baseline architectures.

These results highlight the importance of designing architectures and preprocessing pipelines specifically for the characteristics of 3D LiDAR data. Our findings demonstrate that compact, specialized models can outperform deeper, generic ones in complex spatiotemporal tasks. We believe that this approach paves the way for more robust and efficient motion recognition systems in real-world applications, particularly in scenarios where data sparsity and overfitting pose significant obstacles.

Rather than introducing new architectural elements, this work demonstrates that careful adaptation and empirical tuning of existing 3D CNN techniques can yield practical, robust results for LiDAR-based HAR, especially on edge devices. We identify systematic benchmarking against recent SOTA methods and further exploration of advanced architectures as important directions for future research.

Looking ahead, future work should focus on further reducing overfitting and increasing the model's ability to generalize. This could be achieved by applying advanced data augmentation techniques such as random spatial transformations or temporal jittering. Expanding the training dataset, both in size and diversity, would also likely contribute to improved performance. Furthermore, we see strong potential in the selective use of frame sequences. By identifying and focusing on temporally informative segments with high motion saliency, the model could learn more discriminative features and achieve higher classification accuracy. Additional architectural enhancements, such as attention mechanisms or temporal encoding modules, may further improve the model's capability to capture complex spatiotemporal patterns and lead to more robust activity recognition.

References

1. Dhiman, C., Vishwakarma, D.K.: High dimensional abnormal human activity recognition using histogram oriented gradients and Zernike moments. In: 2017 IEEE International Conference on Computational Intelligence and Computing Research (ICCIC), pp. 1–4 (2017). https://doi.org/10.1109/ICCIC.2017.8524372
2. Dhiman, C., Vishwakarma, D.K.: A review of state-of-the-art techniques for abnormal human activity recognition. Eng. Appl. Artif. Intell. **77**, 21–45 (2019)
3. Fioranelli, F., Zhu, S., Roldan, I.: Benchmarking classification algorithms for radar-based human activity recognition. IEEE Aerosp. Electron. Syst. Mag. **37**(12), 37–40 (2022). https://doi.org/10.1109/MAES.2022.3216262
4. Franco, A., Magnani, A., Maio, D.: A multimodal approach for human activity recognition based on skeleton and RGB data. Pattern Recogn. Lett. **131**, 293–299 (2020)
5. Guo, Y., Wang, H., Hu, Q., Liu, H., Liu, L., Bennamoun, M.: Deep learning for 3D point clouds: a survey. IEEE Trans. Pattern Anal. Mach. Intell. **43**(12), 4338–4364 (2021). https://doi.org/10.1109/TPAMI.2020.3005434
6. He, K., Zhang, X., Ren, S., Sun, J.: Deep residual learning for image recognition (2015). https://arxiv.org/abs/1512.03385
7. Hu, J., Shen, L., Sun, G.: Squeeze-and-excitation networks. In: 2018 IEEE/CVF Conference on Computer Vision and Pattern Recognition, pp. 7132–7141 (2018). https://doi.org/10.1109/CVPR.2018.00745
8. Huang, F., Zeng, A., Liu, M., Lai, Q., Xu, Q.: DeepFuse: an IMU-aware network for real-time 3D human pose estimation from multi-view image (2019). https://arxiv.org/abs/1912.04071
9. Huang, G., Liu, Z., Van Der Maaten, L., Weinberger, K.Q.: Densely connected convolutional networks. In: 2017 IEEE Conference on Computer Vision and Pattern Recognition (CVPR), pp. 2261–2269 (2017). https://doi.org/10.1109/CVPR.2017.243
10. Karar, M.E., Shehata, H.I., Reyad, O.: A survey of IoT-based fall detection for aiding elderly care: Sensors, methods, challenges and future trends. Appl. Sci. **12**(7) (2022). https://doi.org/10.3390/app12073276, https://www.mdpi.com/2076-3417/12/7/3276
11. Kovács, L., Bódis, B.M., Benedek, C.: LidPose: real-time 3D human pose estimation in sparse lidar point clouds with non-repetitive circular scanning pattern. Sensors (Basel, Switzerland) **24**(11) (2024). https://doi.org/10.3390/s24113427, https://www.mdpi.com/1424-8220/24/11/3427
12. Krizhevsky, A., Sutskever, I., Hinton, G.E.: ImageNet classification with deep convolutional neural networks. In: Pereira, F., Burges, C., Bottou, L., Weinberger, K. (eds.) Advances in Neural Information Processing Systems, vol. 25. Curran Associates, Inc. (2012)
13. Labiadh, I., Boubchir, L., Seddik, H.: Optimization of 2D and 3D facial recognition through the fusion of CBAM ALEXNET and RESNEXT models. Vis. Comput. (2024). https://doi.org/10.1007/s00371-024-03718-3
14. Lin, Y., et al.: HMPEAR: a dataset for human pose estimation and action recognition. In: Proceedings of the 32nd ACM International Conference on Multimedia, pp. 2069–2078. MM 2024, Association for Computing Machinery, New York, NY, USA (2024). https://doi.org/10.1145/3664647.3681055
15. Martinez, J., Hossain, R., Romero, J., Little, J.J.: A simple yet effective baseline for 3D human pose estimation. In: 2017 IEEE International Conference on Computer Vision (ICCV), pp. 2659–2668 (2017). https://doi.org/10.1109/ICCV.2017.288

16. Park, J., et al.: All-solid-state spatial light modulator with independent phase and amplitude control for three-dimensional lidar applications. Nat. Nanotechnol. **16**(1), 69–76 (2021). https://doi.org/10.1038/s41565-020-00787-y
17. Patil, A.K., Balasubramanyam, A., Ryu, J.Y., Chakravarthi, B., Chai, Y.H.: An open-source platform for human pose estimation and tracking using a heterogeneous multi-sensor system. Sensors (Basel, Switzerland) **21**(7) (2021). https://doi.org/10.3390/s21072340
18. Pourdarbani, R., et al.: Comparison of 2D and 3D convolutional neural networks in hyperspectral image analysis of fruits applied to orange bruise detection. J. Food Sci. **88**(12), 5149–5163 (2023). https://doi.org/10.1111/1750-3841.16801
19. Rinchi, O., Nisbett, N., Alsharoa, A.: Patients arms segmentation and gesture identification using standalone 3-D lidar sensors. IEEE Sens. Lett. **7**(9), 1–4 (2023). https://doi.org/10.1109/LSENS.2023.3303081
20. Roche, J., De-Silva, V., Hook, J., Moencks, M., Kondoz, A.: A multimodal data processing system for lidar-based human activity recognition. IEEE Trans. Cybern. **52**(10), 10027–10040 (2022). https://doi.org/10.1109/TCYB.2021.3085489
21. Santos, C.F.G.D., Papa, J.a.P.: Avoiding overfitting: a survey on regularization methods for convolutional neural networks. ACM Comput. Surv. **54**(10s) (2022). https://doi.org/10.1145/3510413
22. Sarker, S., et al.: A comprehensive overview of deep learning techniques for 3D point cloud classification and semantic segmentation. Mach. Vis. Appl. **35**(4), 67 (2024). https://doi.org/10.1007/s00138-024-01543-1
23. Siarohin, A., Lathuilière, S., Tulyakov, S., Ricci, E., Sebe, N.: Animating arbitrary objects via deep motion transfer. In: 2019 IEEE/CVF Conference on Computer Vision and Pattern Recognition (CVPR), pp. 2372–2381 (2019). https://doi.org/10.1109/CVPR.2019.00248
24. Thomas, H., Qi, C.R., Deschaud, J.E., Marcotegui, B., Goulette, F., Guibas, L.J.: KPCONV: flexible and deformable convolution for point clouds (2019). https://arxiv.org/abs/1904.08889
25. Zakariah, M., Alnuaim, A.: Recognizing human activities with the use of convolutional block attention module. Egypt. Inf. J. **27**, 100536 (2024)
26. Zhang, J., Wang, D., An, X., Lv, M., Chen, D., Sun, A.: A voxel-based 3D reconstruction and action recognition method for construction workers. Adv. Eng. Inform. **65**, 103203 (2025)
27. Zhang, Y., et al.: DNN-CBAM: an enhanced DNN model for facial emotion recognition. J. Intell. Fuzzy Syst. **43**(5), 5673–5683 (2022). https://doi.org/10.3233/JIFS-212846

InSSeqTra: Inter Data Selective Sequential Transfer Learning for Domain Adaptation in CSI-Based HAR

Nikita Sharma$^{(\boxtimes)}$ iD, Minh Son Nguyen, and Le Viet Duc

University of Twente, Enschede, The Netherlands
`n.sharma@utwente.nl`

Abstract. Due to the dynamic nature of Wi-Fi channel state information (CSI), the traditional transfer learning (TL) approaches in CSI-based human activity recognition (HAR) are largely impacted by the issue of data mismatch. Data mismatch occurs when the training and testing data represent different distributions, causing pre-trained models to struggle to adapt to target CSI datasets. This issue is particularly evident when a single CSI dataset, often limited in size and diversity, is used to obtain a pre-trained model, which is subsequently utilized for TL on a CSI dataset representing another domain. Moreover, even when extended to multiple datasets, traditional TL methods are susceptible to the forgetting problem, where learning from the initial pre-trained dataset gradually diminishes. To address these challenges, a novel framework called Inter CSI-data Selective Sequential Transfer Learning (InSSeqTra) is proposed. This framework pre-trains a base model by leveraging multiple existing CSI datasets in a selective sequential pre-training scheme guided by divergence scores obtained from GAN-learned distributions of the pre-training datasets relative to the target dataset. InSSeqTra was evaluated by using four existing CSI-based HAR datasets, where three datasets (SignFi, WiAR, and UT-HAR) were used for the selective sequential pre-training, and the Wi-Gitation dataset served as a target dataset. The proposed framework shows promising results over traditional TL approaches, particularly achieving 11.3% improvement in person-wise and 6.5% in receiver-wise domain adaptation.

Keywords: Wi-Fi CSI · Transfer learning · Domain Adaptation · Data Mismatch

1 Introduction

Device-free sensing utilizing the Wi-Fi Channel State Information (CSI) technique has gained significant interest in developing Human activity recognition (HAR) systems due to its convenience and effectiveness compared to other sensing technologies like vision-based and tactile sensors [1,2]. Available research

© The Author(s), under exclusive license to Springer Nature Switzerland AG 2026
Ö. Durmaz Incel et al. (Eds.): iWOAR 2025, LNCS 16292, pp. 135–155, 2026.
https://doi.org/10.1007/978-3-032-13312-0_8

works have used Wi-Fi CSI to capture a wide range of *physical human activities* namely full-body activities (falling), fine-grained activities (hand gestures), physiological activities, and *subtle behaviors* (sleep patterns) [3,4].

Despite the successful demonstration of Wi-Fi CSI in HAR, its applications have not yet been fully commercialized. A realistic rationale for, as yet, the embryonic form of these CSI-based HAR systems is their inability to easily adapt to new domains [5]. The term "domain" here refers to the environment, context, persons, or conditions in which CSI-based HAR systems are desired to perform. CSI-based HAR systems exploit the phenomena of multipath propagation, in which any moving subject in the monitoring environment has the potential to impact the signal properties, e.g., signal strength, phase, and propagation delays [1]. While this precept of CSI is useful for HAR, it also appears to have a major drawback since any undesired objects in the given surroundings can also impact the CSI signals. Such that, along with the useful reflections due to the intended activities performed by monitored persons, the obtained CSI signals are more likely to contain some surrounding noise from the monitoring environment (i.e., reflections from moving furniture, persons, etc.). These undesired reflections exacerbate the data mismatch inherent in CSI datasets, making the adaptation of the CSI-based HAR systems to new domains challenging [6]. Specifically, in the cases where CSI-based HAR algorithms were purely trained on a set of activities of one person at specific locations (as illustrated in Fig. 1), often degraded performance can be expected when tested on different persons and locations for the same activities, attributing to person-wise domain mismatch (i.e., different persons inducing disparate levels of multipath propagation), and the location-wise domain mismatch (i.e., different locations where activities are performed or where the receiver is placed also induce disparate levels of multipath propagation) [6].

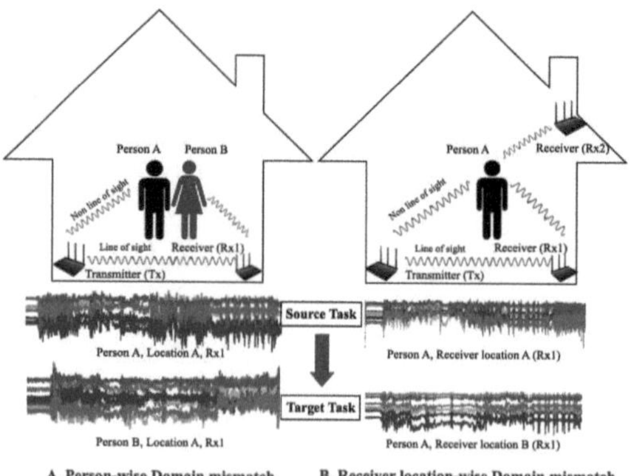

Fig. 1. Data Mismatch in the obtained CSI signals due to A) different person (A and B) and, B) different receiver locations (Rx1 and Rx2) while performing the same activities.

Domain adaptation-based methods, such as training the model on data distributions encompassing as many factors impacting CSI as possible, are being explored to mitigate the data mismatch issue. But dataset collection and analyses in such an extensive manner are time-, cost-, and resource-consuming processes [5,7]. To overcome this challenge, the transfer learning (TL) paradigm has been put forward [8], which reuses the knowledge learned from the source tasks and transfers it to a given target task.

Similar to computer vision, TL in the context of Wi-Fi CSI also involves a two-step process: pre-training a model on a large heterogeneous dataset, followed by fine-tuning it with a smaller, task-specific dataset [9,10]. However, unlike in computer vision, where pre-trained models from extensive datasets like ImageNet [11] or COCO [12] excel at new tasks, pre-trained models in CSI-based HAR often exhibit limited effectiveness and significant bias due to the scarcity of comprehensive pre-training datasets.

Considering this, the current study aims to design an efficient TL framework named Inter CSI-data Selective Sequential Transfer Learning (InSSeqTra) for domain adaptation. It utilizes knowledge from multiple existing small CSI-based HAR datasets to address to the issue of limited datasets. Moreover, a selective sequential approach was proposed because pre-training on multiple CSI datasets in random order might lead to the forgetting problem where previously learned relevant information for the target task gradually diminishes over the course of pre-training [13]. To sequence pre-training datasets, divergence scores were calculated using probabilistic distributions obtained through a Generative Adversarial Network (GAN) and ranked with the Jensen-Shannon Divergence (JDS) algorithm. This approach orders datasets by descending dissimilarity to the target dataset, positioning more dissimilar datasets farther in the pre-training sequence. This strategic ordering helps the model effectively align and transfer relevant CSI properties from pre-training datasets to the target dataset. Subsequently, akin to the traditional or intra-data TL, the resulting pre-trained model undergoes an additional TL process on a small subset of intra-data to fine-tune itself for diverse domains within the target dataset.

The InSSeqTra framework was evaluated for person-wise and receiver location-wise domain adaptation using four available CSI-based HAR datasets. Three datasets—SignFi [14], WiAR [15], and UT-HAR [16] were used as pre-training datasets, while Wi-Gitation [4] served as the target dataset. The classification performance of InSSeqTra was compared with various sequential TL variants. Additionally, to optimize the fine-tuning step in InSSeqTra, the impact of various fine-tuning schemes was also investigated.

2 Related Work

TL paradigm is a machine learning approach inspired by human cognition that leverages knowledge from source tasks (T_s) to enhance accuracy in target tasks (T_t). It is frequently used in CSI-based HAR for domain adaptation in two specific ways: *the model adoption*, and *the model customization*. In the model adoption, off-the-shelf pre-trained models related to the target task are reused as a starting point for the adaptation to the target task. For example, [17,18] adopted ImageNet pre-trained networks (e.g., VGG16, VGG19, ResNet18, etc.) to directly allow the process of fine-tuning on the images of CSI amplitudes in activity and gesture recognition.

The model customization approach necessitates pre-training a model on a large amount of CSI-specific source task data before fine-tuning. It allows the pre-trained model to become more acquainted with CSI properties, thereby increasing the chances of better performance when fine-tuned with a small target task dataset. In work by [19], the TL approach was used to recognize human activities like clapping, walking, and jumping, independent of participants. Similarly, WiTransfer employed TL to achieve cross-scene activity recognition, resulting in higher accuracy [20]. The work by [21] employs TL on CSI data for temporal indoor localization, in which three features (CSI amplitudes, wavelet transformations, and shape correlation) characterizing fine-grained information in CSI data were extracted to minimize the distances between CSI readings using transfer component analysis followed by a modified bayesian model to estimate a person's positions. The approach shows state-of-the-art results in the testing setup of sixteen different locations over different time slots.

The work conducted by [7] involves transferring a pre-trained model from the HAR dataset to the Human-ID dataset using various deep neural network models, including CNN-5, MLP, RNN, BiLSTM, and a series of ResNets, with CNN-5 and ResNet-18 demonstrating superior performance. Research by [22] addresses inadequate CSI dataset availability by combining CNN-LSTM for feature estimation with a metric learning-based HAR method to transfer pre-trained models across different locations with limited data. The work by [23], introduced the dynamic associate domain adaptation (DADA-AD) scheme, a semi-supervised transfer learning approach that enhances generalization, maximizes domain confusion, and minimizes classification loss for source and target domains.

2.1   Gap in Research

Despite advances in TL for domain adaptation in CSI-based HAR, several limitations persist. First, relying on ImageNet pre-trained models, designed for image data, is suboptimal for modalities like CSI. Transforming CSI signals into images risks losing critical contextual and structural information, potentially compromising model effectiveness. Second, customizing models by pre-training on CSI-based HAR requires substantial time and collaborative effort to create suitable datasets. This approach is also prone to the forgetting problem when sequentially trained on multiple datasets. Finally, most research is validated in controlled settings, limiting its applicability to dynamic real-world environments. To address these gaps, the InSSeqTra framework is proposed and evaluated.

3   Proposed Framework: InSSeqTra

The InSSeqTra framework (Fig. 2) consists of three main modules: *Data Acquisition, Selective Sequential Pre-training,* and *Intra-data Transfer Learning.*

3.1   Module 1: Data Acquisition

In this module (Fig. 2), we propose acquiring various publicly available CSI-based HAR datasets that include diverse factors affecting CSI-based HAR, such as variations in environments, persons, devices, and experimental protocols. These datasets will be used to develop a pre-trained model, and one of them (the target dataset) will be used for fine-tuning and evaluating domain adaptation. This intuition parallels image classification, where base models are pre-trained using multiple or large datasets (e.g., GoogleNet, ResNet), thereby achieving high accuracy upon fine-tuning with target datasets [24]. This leads us to our first hypothesis,

Pre-training a base model on multiple small CSI-based HAR datasets can help in exploiting more generic transferable CSI properties, thereby improving domain adaptation to the target dataset (Hypothesis 1).

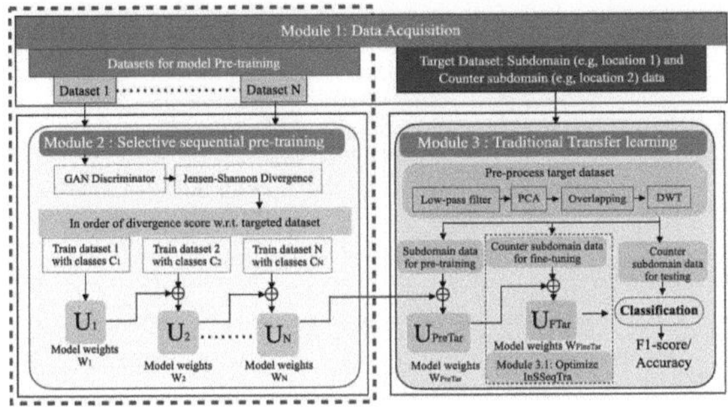

Fig. 2. Modules of InSSeqTra Framework: dataset acquisition, selective sequential pre-training, and traditional TL.

3.2   Module 2: Selective Sequential Pre-training

CSI datasets often come in varying input sizes, making simultaneous training on all datasets challenging. Moreover, sequential pre-training on multiple datasets can intensify the forgetting problem, where crucial cues relevant to the target dataset are overshadowed by irrelevant or dataset-specific information [25], thereby hindering domain adaptation performance. To address this, we propose to use selective sequential pre-training where the divergence scores were calculated using the *JDS* ranking algorithm on the discriminator distributions obtained from GANs to ensure a smooth transition among pre-training datasets and accommodate abrupt changes along the way (Fig. 3)

The divergence scores logically establish the descending affinity among pre-training datasets to the target, in which the least and the most related datasets to the target are, in turn, the first and the last in the sequence, respectively. Note that computing divergence scores directly on the datasets is challenging due to the absence of a pre-established distribution and the time-consuming, resource-intensive nature of iterative calculations. GAN-based architectures that can be well-trained on such datasets to indirectly approximate respective distributions were utilized to reduce this complexity.

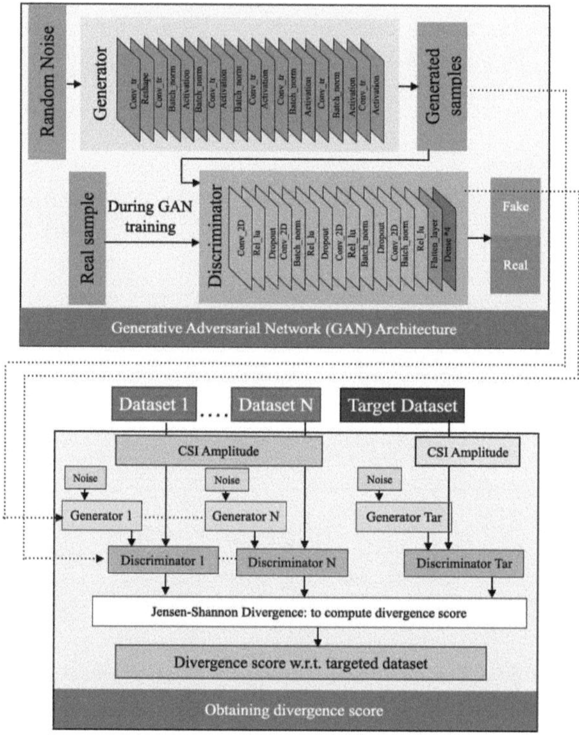

Fig. 3. Calculating divergence score for selective sequential transfer learning by using discriminator distributions obtained from GAN and JDS ranking algorithm.

Let $\hat{X}$ and X be the Generator G-generated data from noise variable $Z \in \mathbb{R}^{1 \times n}$ and the original data, respectively. According to Eq. 1, G attempts to perplex Discriminator D by differentiating between X and $\hat{X}$ by improving its modeling quality, while D always stays conscious of any new updates. The process is successfully completed at equilibrium, indicated by a reduction in D's accuracy and G's generative loss.

$$\min_{G} \max_{D} V(D, G) = \mathrm{E}_{x \sim P(X)}\left[\log D(x)\right] + \mathrm{E}_{z \sim P(Z)}\left[\log\left(1 - D\left(G\left(z\right)\right)\right)\right] \quad (1)$$

We assume that the GAN components are approximately well-trained (based on their diverging losses), then D can be described as $P(y = 1|\hat{X}) \propto P(y = 1 \cap \hat{X})$. It implies that at an equilibrium during adversarial training between G and D, $P(y = 1|\hat{X})$ implies the probability that $\hat{X}$ would occur in the original distribution $P(X)$ should be proportional to the joint probability $P(y = 1 \cap \hat{X})$ where $\hat{X}$ and its estimated labels are jointly considered. By reaching an equilibrium in two diametrically opposed tasks, the generated data $\hat{X}$ is compared with the original X in qualitative and quantitative aspects, which suggests $P(y = 1 \cap \hat{X}) \sim P(X)$. Based on that, $P(y = 1|\hat{X})$ can be used to approximately model $P(X)$ under Eq. 2. To this end, Algorithm 1 is formulated to compute divergent scores and their ranking among the pre-training datasets with reference to the target dataset.

$$JSD(P\|Q) = \frac{1}{2}\sum_{x \in X} P(x)\ln\left(M(x)\right) + \frac{1}{2}\sum_{x \in X} Q(x)\ln\left(M(x)\right) \quad (2)$$

$$where, M(x) = \frac{1}{2}\left(P(x) + Q(x)\right) \quad (3)$$

Overall, this module ensures that the pre-trained model has undergone training firmly, such that it can incrementally learn and largely retain highly relevant cues, especially in the final round, whilst still being able to abstain from irrelevant ones from the long pre-training process. Considering this, it is further hypothesized that,

If Hypothesis 1 holds, a novel pre-training process guided by divergence scores arranged in descending order with respect to the target dataset can facilitate the retention of learned relevant clues during sequential pre-training (Hypothesis 2).

Algorithm 1: Ranking algorithm

Generator $G_1 \& G_2$, Discriminators $D_1 \& D_2$, and random variable $Z \in \mathbb{R}^{1 \times n}$ Ranking result O

2 /* Computing $P_1 \& P_2$ with ζ and σ denoting softmax and sigmoid functions,

1   respectively.   */

3 $P_1 = \zeta\left(\sigma\left(D_1\left(G_1\left(Z\right)\right)\right)\right)$

   $P_2 = \zeta\left(\sigma\left(D_2\left(G_2\left(Z\right)\right)\right)\right)$

   $O = JDS\left(P_1 \| P_2\right)$

   return O

3.3　Module 3: Intra-data Transfer Learning

The intra-data TL applied in this work consists of four key steps - pre-processing, pre-training, fine-tuning, and testing (Fig. 2).

Pre-processing Targeted CSI Dataset: Pre-processing steps before the intra-data TL were applied to remove noise and accentuate the features corresponding to the intended activities. The nearest interpolation method can be utilized to address differences in the number of packets transmitted by the transmitter (Tx) and received by the receiver (Rx) caused by transmission delays. Further, for every CSI matrix, a low-pass filter is applied to remove high-frequency signals that might have been introduced by the electromagnetic effect.

Moreover, different antenna pairs and sub-carriers can exhibit varying levels of sensitivity towards the same activity, owing to the presence of frequency-selective fading [15]. Consequently, sub-carriers with low sensitivities may not be useful for HAR and might introduce noise to the system, thus can be removed by using principal component analysis (PCA) [26] technique. In addition to that, the first principal component, despite exhibiting the highest variance, is often discarded in CSI-based HAR. This component tends to capture burst noise and information associated with transient internal states in transmitter-receiver pairs, such as fluctuations in transmission power, adjustments in transmission rates, and changes in internal CSI reference levels [26,27]. Even after removing the first principal component, information related to dynamic reflections from activities is preserved, as it is captured in other principal components [26–28].

Moreover, CSI data is usually recorded perpetually for multiple iterations of the activities. However, to extract individual instances of these activities as input to a CNN, the obtained PCA component matrix can be segmented by applying a sliding window with a 50% overlap. This segmentation process is crucial in identifying signals representing specific activity, thereby improving the accuracy of CSI-based HAR systems. Lastly, HAR algorithms typically involve recognizing full-body or fine-grained activities that exhibit high variances in signal frequency. Fine-grained activities tend to produce small variations in signals (low-frequency), while full-body activities produce large variations in the signals (high-frequency), thus making it difficult to compare and identify signals corresponding to different activities. To address this, wavelet transform which offers a spectrum of resolutions that can highlight the signal characteristics at different frequencies can be employed. It can provide high-frequency resolution for low-frequency signals and low-frequency resolution for high-frequency signals [29]. This ensures uniformity across signals from different activities adding to the improvement of the classification of HAR algorithms based on CSI data [26,27,30]. Figure 4 presents and compares the random samples of raw (200×1) and pre-processed (100×1) data for disturbed walking, sitting-standing, kicking, and tapping activity. After pre-processing, a difference in signals corresponding to activities can be noticed more evidently.

Note that, none of the aforementioned pre-processing steps were applied to the pre-training datasets. This intentionally allows for a wider exploration space

Table 1. Overview of used datasets (R = Room, LOS = line of sight, NLOS = non-line of sight, BHK = bedroom, hall, kitchen, P = protocolised, SP = semi-protocolised)

Dataset	Participants	Environment	Device used	Activities
WiAR	10P (5M, 5F)	Empty R (6 m×8 m), Meeting R (6 m×10 m), Office R (6 m×10 m)	1 Tx (1 At)-Rx (3 At); Intel 5300 wireless NIC	P: Horizontal/high arm wave, two hands wave, high throw, draw X/tick, toss paper, forward/side kick, bend, hand clap, walk, phone call, drink water, sit down, squat
SignFi	5P	Lab (13 m×12 m)	1 Tx (3 At)- 1Rx (1 At); Intel 5300 wireless NIC	P: 276 sign gestures
UT-HAR	9P	Living R (3.79 m×3.45 m)	1 Tx-Rx; Intel 5300 wireless NIC	P: Sitting, clapping, waving, jumping, falling, walking
Wi-Gitation	16P (8M, 8F)	Simulated 1BHK apartment (8 m× 11 m)	1Tx (3 At), 4 Rx (3 At); Intel 5300 wireless NIC	SP: Disturbed walking (DW), Sitting-standing (SS), Tapping on the table (Tap), Kicking on furniture (Kick)

of multi-level representations that the pre-trained model can learn, but without exaggerating unnecessary differences among the datasets.

Pre-training, Fine-Tuning, and Testing Phases: Here, the target dataset can be partitioned into pre-training, fine-tuning, and testing proportions, depending on the domain adaptation scenarios in the target dataset (person-wise or location-wise). For example, the location-wise domain adaptation is designed for the case where a model trained on one location can be fine-tuned on a small amount of data from new locations, and its performance can be tested with the corresponding testing data. As depicted in Fig. 2, after the selective sequential pre-training scheme, the resulting model U_N is further pre-trained on the subdomain of the targeted dataset to obtain the updated model U_{PreTar}, which is then fine-tuned on the counter subdomain. Finally, the performance of the fine-tuned model U_{FTar} is assessed on the testing dataset.

Optimizing InSSeqTra: Fine-tuning is a crucial step in TL, optimized based on the relationship between pre-training and fine-tuning datasets [31]. If the fine-tuning dataset is highly similar to the pre-training data, the pre-trained model can serve as a feature extractor, requiring only a new classifier to be trained. For dissimilar and limited fine-tuning data, initial layers are frozen to leverage general-purpose features, while the rest are fine-tuned. When fine-tuning data is dissimilar but sufficiently large, the entire model is fine-tuned for effective knowledge transfer. In cases where the fine-tuning data is both large and similar, only the fully connected layers are fine-tuned, while the rest of the model remains frozen.

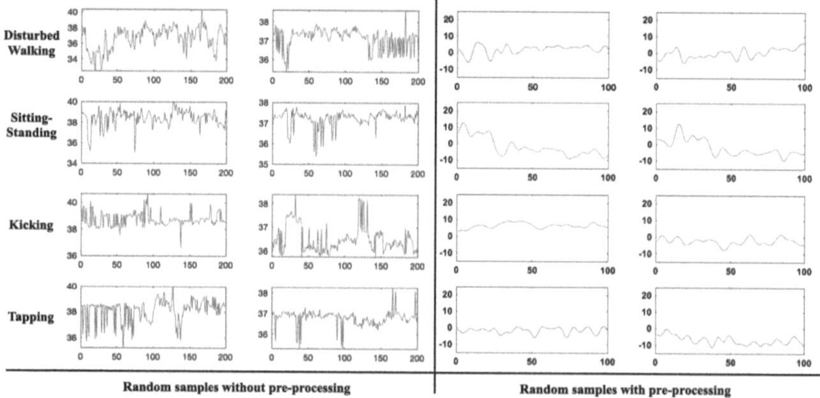

Fig. 4. Comparing raw and pre-processed signals of disturbed walking, sitting-standing, kicking, and tapping activity.

4   Implementation: InSSeqTra

An untrained version of ResNet-18 was acquired from Matlab 2021a. The hyper-parameters included a batch size of 32, Adam optimizer, scheduled learning rate starting from 0.0001 with a reduction of 0.2 every 5 epochs, and the maximum epochs were set to 50, with early stopping if validation accuracy not improving after fifteen iterations.

4.1   Data Acquired and Analysis Scheme

Data Acquired: Aligned with Hypothesis 1, we established a selective sequential pre-training scheme using three existing CSI-based HAR datasets namely WiAR [15], SignFi [14], and UT-HAR [16]. The Wi-Gitation dataset [4] is deemed the target dataset for this work, as it encompasses various domains such as different persons, two activity locations, and four receivers (three antennas each and operating at 5.32 GHz) in a simulated one-bedroom apartment. The data from sixteen participants (8 Males and 8 Females) performing four activities for 120 s each, including two full-body activities disturbed walking (DW) and sitting-standing (SS) repeatedly from a chair and two fine-grained activities tapping on a table (tap) and kicking (kick) a table were utilized. Table 1 details these CSI datasets.

Analysis Scheme: A scheme was defined to split the Wi-Gitation dataset into model pre-training, fine-tuning, and testing sets to evaluate InSSeqTra for person-wise and receiver location-wise domain adaptations.

For ease of reference, in this work, these domains are termed as 'Main domains'. Within each main domain, data are divided into a 'Sub-domain' that is used for pre-training, and a 'Counter sub-domain' that is used for fine-tuning and testing. Note that, both sub-domain and counter sub-domain contain data from different participants or locations or receivers, depending on the intended domain adaptation. Table 2 provides an overview of these schemes used in the performance evaluation of InSSeqTra.

Table 2. Data analyses schemes for person-wise, receiver location-wise domain adaptation in Wi-Gitation dataset (P = participant, Rx = Receiver, Loc = location)

Main Domain	Overall dataset used	Sub-domain pre-training data ($U1_D1WG$)	Counter sub-domain fine-tuning and testing data ($U1_D2WG$)	K-Fold cross validation
Person-wise	Data from 16 P, Rx0, and Location2	Randomly selected 13P (10P-tr, 3P-val)	Remaining 3P's data mixed and used for fine-tuning (2P) and testing (1P)	5 fold
Receiver location-wise	Data from all Rx (Rx0,Rx1,Rx3,Rx4), Location2, and 16P	Randomly selected Rx (2Rx-tr and 1Rx-val)	Remaining 1 Rx data mixed and used for fine-tuning and testing (14P-fine-tune, 2P-test)	3 fold

For *person-wise domain adaptation*, data from location 2, Rx0, and sixteen participants were utilized. Data from thirteen participants were allocated for pre-training (10 for training and 3 for validation) to create the $U1_{D1WG}$ model. The remaining three participant's data was used for fine-tuning $U1_{D1WG}$ to obtain $U1_{D2WG}$ model as well as testing it (Fig. 5). To ensure unbiased results, training, fine-tuning, and testing datasets were randomly selected with five-fold validation. This approach has practical applications in older adult care, where data scarcity is common. Algorithms trained on limited data from older adults or healthy subjects can be fine-tuned with a small dataset and a few epochs during deployment to adapt effectively to new older adults.

Receiver location-wise domain adaptation demonstrates the model's capacity to adjust to new receiver placements. Data from all receivers (Rx0, Rx1, Rx3, Rx4) at location 2 and sixteen participants were used. Two receivers' data were randomly selected for pre-training with three-fold validation, while the remaining receivers' data were reserved for validation, resulting in the $U1_{D1WG}$ model. This model was fine-tuned using data from the remaining receiver to create the $U1_{D2WG}$ model for testing (Fig. 5). In household setups, CSI-based HAR systems are prone to performance declines due to receiver placement changes, often necessitating re-training. Through this approach, we propose to fine-tune the pre-trained model for the new receiver placement.

Analyses were conducted to verify Hypotheses 1 and 2 defined for selective sequential pre-training (Table 3). To verify Hypothesis 1, intra-data TL was conducted where the Wi-Gitation dataset was divided into pre-training, fine-tuning, and testing data by considering the data analysis scheme. This analysis, when compared with InSSeqTra, can provide insights into the significance of using sequential pre-training with other CSI datasets. Furthermore, to verify Hypothesis 2, random and ascending sequential TL is conducted and compared with InSSeqTra. Random sequential TL presents the case where other acquired CSI

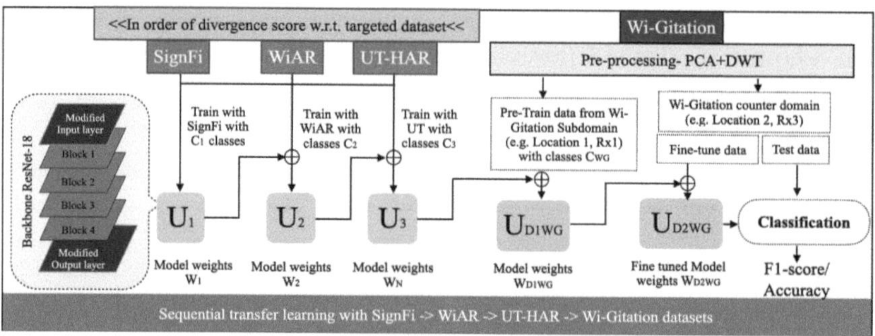

Fig. 5. Performing selective sequential TL by using three datasets (SignFi, WiAR, UT-HAR) for pre-training and Wi-Gitation dataset for target domain adaptions.

Table 3. Overview of the used TL paradigms.

To verify	TL Paradigm	Explanation
Hypothesis 1	Intra-data TL	It can be treated as a baseline, depicting the traditional TL paradigm i.e., the target dataset is divided into pre-training, fine-tuning, and testing sets.
Hypothesis 2	Ascending order TL	The pre-trained model is obtained by training with CSI datasets in ascending order of divergence score (UT-HAR − > WiAR − > SignFi) followed by traditional TL on Wi-Gitation.
Hypothesis 2	Random order TL	The pre-trained model is obtained by training with CSI datasets in random order of divergence score followed by traditional TL on Wi-Gitation.
Hypothesis 2	Pre-train 1	The pre-trained model is obtained by training with only one CSI dataset in descending order of divergence score (UT-HAR) followed by traditional TL on Wi-Gitation.
Hypothesis 2	Pre-train 2	The pre-trained model is obtained by training with the top two CSI datasets in descending order of divergence score (WiAR − > UT-HAR) followed by traditional TL on Wi-Gitation.
Proposed framework	**InSSeqTra**	The pre-trained model is obtained by training with all three CSI datasets in descending order of divergence score (SignFi − > WiAR − >UT-HAR) followed by traditional TL on Wi-Gitation.

datasets were used in random order for obtaining the pre-train model whereas ascending order sequential TL refers to the case when the dataset with the distribution distant (SignFi) to the target dataset (Wi-Gitation) is used for training the base model at the end. Additionally, the contribution made by each dataset in InSSeqTra is also evaluated in a step-by-step manner. At first, the closest distribution dataset (UT-HAR) is used to obtain the pre-train base model, followed by TL with Wi-Gitation (Pre-train 1). Second, the top two datasets (UT-HAR and WiAR) in sequence were used to obtain a base model, followed by TL on Wi-

Gitation (Pre-train 2). Note that, all the analyses followed the same intra-data TL scheme as mentioned in Table 2.

4.2   Intra-data TL on Wi-Gitation Dataset

Pre-processing: At first, the nearest interpolation was applied to ensure a consistent number of samples across the dataset i.e., 12000 samples ($120sec \times 100packets$) for each activity at each location and from each Rx were obtained followed by a low-pass filter to remove high-frequency signals (noise). With the help of PCA, the first principal component and lower components associated with noise were removed, reducing 270 channels ($3Txantenna \times 3Rxantenna \times 30sub-carriers$) to 20 channels (from the 2nd to 21st component). Furthermore, the obtained 12000×20 CSI data matrix is segmented by using a 50% sliding window to obtain individual activity instances from the whole set. Lastly, DWT with haar wavelet was applied to each activity instant for obtaining both temporal and spectral information. It resulted in a total of 119 CSI matrices of size 100×40 for each activity.

Pre-training, Fine-Tuning, and Testing on Wi-Gitation Dataset: InSSeqTra framework (Fig. 5) is implemented to show person-wise and receiver-location-wise domain adaptions. The selective sequential pre-trained model obtained by training on three datasets was used as a starting base model. U_3 model is retrained with intended sub-domain $D1_{WG}$ in the Wi-Gitation dataset to obtain the pre-trained model $U1_{D1WG}$ having four classification classes (disturbed walking, sitting-standing, tapping, and kicking) C_{WG} whereas counter sub-domain is used for obtaining the fine-tuned model U_{D2WG}. For example, if aiming for location-wise domain adaption, the data from location 1 is used to re-train the U_3 model to obtain the $U1_{D1WG}$ model whereas the data from location 2 is used for fine-tuning $U1_{D1WG}$ to get U_{D2WG} and test it.

   Optimizing TL: Six TL strategies for fine-tuning were evaluated (Fig. 6).

- Case A: No blocks in ResNet-18 were frozen and pre-trained weights were fine-tuned to obtain U_{D2WG}.
- Case B: 2a-2b blocks in ResNet-18 were frozen and pre-trained weights for the remaining blocks were retained and fine-tuned to obtain U_{D2WG}.
- Case C: 2a to 3b blocks in ResNet-18 were frozen and pre-trained weights for the remaining blocks were retained and fine-tuned to obtain U_{D2WG}.
- Case D: 2a to 4b blocks in ResNet-18 were frozen and pre-trained weights for 5a-5b blocks were retained and fine-tuned to obtain U_{D2WG}.
- Case E: 2a to 5b blocks in ResNet-18 were frozen and pre-trained weights for fully connected (fc) layer were retained and fine-tuned to obtain U_{D2WG}.
- Case F: 2a to 5b blocks in ResNet-18 were frozen and random weights were assigned to fully connected (fc) layer which was further fine-tuned to obtain U_{D2WG}.

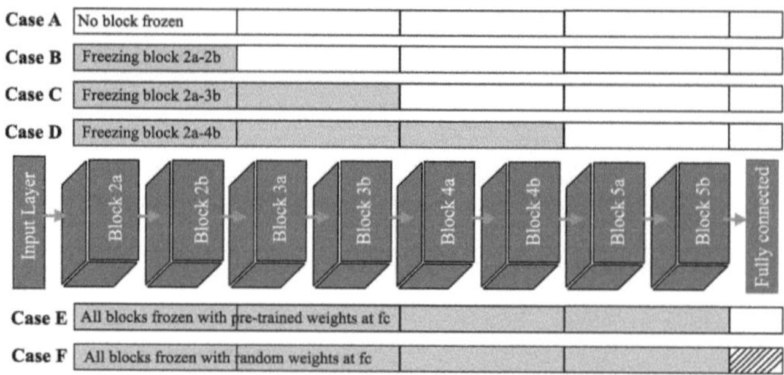

Fig. 6. Fine-tuning strategies for ResNet-50 for InSSqTra

5   Results

5.1   Impact of Pre-processing

From Table 4 and Fig. 7 the significant impact of used pre-processing steps can be observed in the comparison with raw generic data analysis i.e., when trained and tested on different participants and receiver locations in the Wi-Gitation dataset. Specifically, for person-wise generic data analysis, using pre-processed data improved the average $F1-scores$ by 0.205 (20.5%) and for receiver location-wise generic data analysis by 0.261 (26.1%). Also, for individual activities, significant improvements in $F1-scores$ were observed, with the highest improvement in sitting-standing (from 0.294 to 0.603 in person-wise and 0.20 to 0.62 in receiver location-wise) and tapping activity (from 0.128 to 0.413 in person-wise and 0.095 to 0.462 in receiver location-wise).

5.2   InSSeqTra Evaluation

Table 5 and Fig. 7, presents and compares the $F1-scores$ of ascending order sequential TL, random sequential TL, step-by-step (Pre-train 1 and Pre-train

Table 4. Impact of pre-processing steps: $F1-scores$ corresponding to person-wise (PW) and receiver location-wise (RW) generic data analysis (GDA) on raw and pre-processed data.

Activities	PW GDA		RW GDA	
	Raw data	Processed	Raw data	Processed
DW	0.444	0.545	0.412	0.515
SS	0.294	**0.603**	0.202	**0.620**
Kick	0.301	0.429	0.232	0.387
Tap	0.128	0.413	0.095	0.462
Avg	0.292	0.497	0.235	0.496

2) sequential TL, and InSSeqTra (case A: no blocks were frozen and fine-tuning whole model) with intra-data TL (baseline) for person-wise and receiver location-wise domain adaption.

In *person-wise domain adaptation*, when comparing with intra-data TL, $F1 - scores$ improved in random sequential TL, pre-train 2 TL and InSSeq-Tra paradigm, with the InSSeqTra framework yielding the best results (average $F1 - scores$: 0.864). It shows that using sequential TL with multiple datasets even though in random order increases the performance of the model by 4% in comparison to intra-data TL, ascending sequential TL, and pre-train 1. Conducting TL in sequential order by using the top two datasets (Pre-train 2) and all three datasets (InSSeqTra) (in the order of divergence score) further boosted the performance by 8.5% and 11% respectively in comparison to intra-data TL.

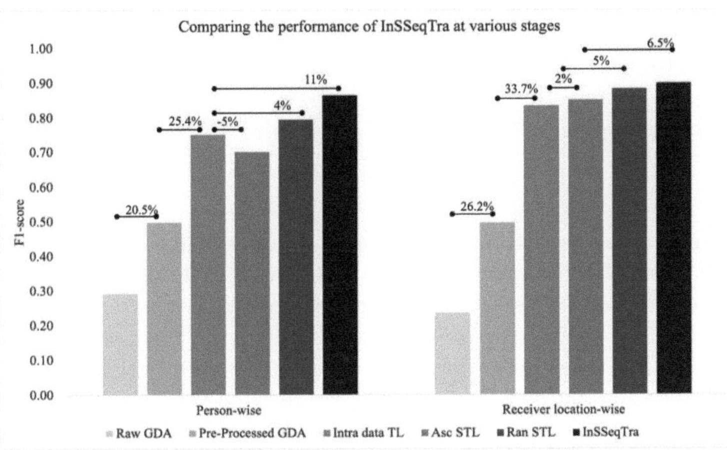

Fig. 7. Comparing the performance of raw data generic analysis (GDA), pre-processed data GDA, Intra data TL, Ascending sequential TL (Asc STL), Random sequential TL (Ran STL), and InSSeqTra.

In *Rx location-wise domain adaptation*, a slight increase in average $F1 - scores$ is observed in ascending STL (0.85) compared to Intra-data TL (0.83). However, it is comparable to Pre-train 1 (0.84) i.e., the base model pre-trained with only the UT-HAR dataset. Moreover, the average $F1 - scores$ increased when using random STL (0.88), with pre-train 2 and InSSeqTra framework yielding the best and similar performances ($F1 - scores$ 0.89). Overall, with the InSSeqTra approach, the performance of receiver location-wise domain adaptations increased by 6.5%.

5.3   Optimizing InSSeqTra

Table 5 (case A) and 6 provides the $F1 - scores$ of the defined optimization cases. The decline in $F1 - scores$ appears to be directly proportional to the

Table 5. Evaluating and comparing $F1-scores$ obtained from Intra data TL, Ascending sequential TL, Random order sequential TL, Pre-train 1 and Pre-train 2 with InSSeqTra for person-wise and receiver location-wise domain adaptation.

Act	Person-wise Domain Adaption					
	Intra	Ascending STL	Random STL	Pre-train1	Pre-train2	InSSeqTra
DW	0.806	0.700	0.821	0.792	0.893	0.911
SS	0.751	0.754	0.850	0.799	0.889	0.885
Kick	0.701	0.640	0.725	0.699	0.768	0.830
Tap	0.746	0.723	0.779	0.747	0.795	0.831
Avg	0.751	0.704	0.794	0.759	0.836	**0.864**
Act	Receiver location-wise Domain Adaption					
DW	0.848	0.878	0.886	0.876	0.897	0.913
SS	0.881	0.884	0.907	0.883	0.914	0.909
Kick	0.774	0.801	0.848	0.791	0.878	0.866
Tap	0.831	0.853	0.888	0.835	0.901	0.903
Avg	0.833	0.854	0.882	0.846	**0.898**	**0.898**

number of frozen ResNet-18 blocks. A decline in average $F1-scores$ from 0.85 to 0.83 to 0.79 and from 0.89 to 0.87 to 0.80 was found when 2a-2b, 2a-3b, 2a-4b blocks were frozen in person- and receiver location-wise domain adaptation (Table 6), with fine-tuning the whole model resulted in best performance. Note that, the differences were not significant when fine-tuning the whole model and fine-tuning the model after freezing block 2a-2b. However, the difference in performance decreased (by 7.2% for person-wise and 9.4% for receiver location-wise InSSeqTra) as we froze the blocks from 2a-4b. It could be because freezing the top blocks keeps the general CSI properties intact whereas freezing lower layers hinders the fine-tuning of the layers representing features of the target dataset.

In Case E and Case F, all the blocks (2a-5b) were frozen and the impact of using pre-trained and random weights on fine-tuning the fully connected layer was observed. From Table 6, it can be noted that using pre-trained weights in the fully connected layer always gave better performances than using random weights for both domain adaptations. However, the impact of using pre-trained weights instead of random weights was higher in person-wise domain adaptation, improving the classification performances by 19% (0.54 to 0.35).

Table 6. Evaluating and comparing $F1 - scores$ obtained from Case B, Case C, Case D, Case E, and Case F (Abb: PW: Person-wise, RW: Receiver location-wise.

Cases	DW	SS	Kick	Tap	Avg
PW InSSeqTra Optimization					
Case B	0.89	0.886	0.811	0.83	**0.854**
Case C	0.879	0.868	0.798	0.807	0.838
Case D	0.847	0.841	0.735	0.744	0.792
Case E	0.592	0.618	0.509	0.441	0.540
Case F	0.423	0.402	0.295	0.291	0.353
RW InSSeqTra Optimization					
Case B	0.908	0.919	0.859	0.887	**0.893**
Case C	0.897	0.906	0.844	0.869	0.879
Case D	0.836	0.853	0.743	0.787	0.804
Case E	0.716	0.730	0.556	0.60	0.651
Case F	0.678	0.703	0.528	0.562	0.618

6 Discussions

By considering the need to find a pertinent solution for domain adaption in CSI-based HAR, the present work proposed and evaluated the InSSeqTra framework. The applied pre-processing steps, particularly the combination of PCA and DWT, appeared advantageous in both noise reduction and feature extraction for both full-body and fine-grained activities but especially for location-bound activities like tapping and sitting-standing. This aligns with the findings reported in previous studies in CSI-based HAR [26]. It is also worth highlighting that in the literature, various pre-processing steps are proposed for the CSI-dataset as different datasets respond to different techniques differently, as they were collected using different experimental setups (transmission rate, frequency, environmental settings, etc.,). While we recommend the combination of PCA and DWT, other methods to determine the pre-processing steps can also be explored according to the target dataset to achieve better performance.

The novel contribution of the InSSeqTra framework lies in its selective sequential pre-training module, which enables the base model to progressively explore and exploit general CSI properties based on their divergence with respect to the target dataset to mitigate the forgetting problem in sequential TL. As observed in random or ascending sequential TL, the forgetting issue was found more pronounced in the person-wise domain adaptation compared to location-wise domain adaption. However, it could become more significant as the number of datasets in the pre-training set increases. By applying the InSSeqTra framework, notable improvements were achieved in person-wise (11%) and receiver location-wise (6.5%) domain adaptations. These obtained results also indicate that both Hypothesis 1 and Hypothesis 2 hold true but in tandem.

It could be noted that the improvements were comparatively higher in person-wise compared to receiver location-wise domain adaptation. This might be because CSI signals are largely impacted by new persons [6] and sequential TL might have acquired features that are more generic and less person-dependent. Furthermore, these findings can be juxtaposed with state-of-the-art studies in the domain adaptation of CSI-based HAR. For instance, in the research conducted by [7], CSI data from human activities were utilized to pre-train a model, subsequently fine-tuned on human identification data, achieving an accuracy of 85.95%. Another recent study by [5] introduced a domain-independent generative adversarial network for CSI-based HAR, resulting in accuracies of 76% for person-wise domain adaptation and 73% for activity-location-wise domain adaptation on the WiDAR 3.0 dataset.

This work implemented InSSeqTra with four existing CSI datasets, using the Wi-Gitation dataset [4] as the target dataset for fine-tuning and evaluations. Since Wi-Gitation contains various factors impacting CSI, evaluating InSSeqTra with it provided insights into its real-world implementation. For example, while the forgetting problem was significant in person-wise domain adaption the improvements were also higher in person-wise domain adaption compared to receiver-location domain adaption. Along with that, in real-world implementation of CSI-based HAR, a model should perform well with only a few training samples, requiring less computational power and shorter learning time [32]. In that regard, the optimization step was deemed useful. From the comparison of different optimization cases, it can be understood that, while fine-tuning the whole model is desirable, freezing top blocks representing in-general features will not hamper the overall model classifications but can reduce the time required for training [32]. However, the optimization step can be tailored according to the pre-train and target datasets.

Overall, InSSeqTra can be seen as a generic learning framework, with the potential for improved performance by incorporating additional pre-training datasets. Future research can validate InSSeqTra using datasets from various sensing modalities, such as wearables and camera-based systems. Similar to CSI-based HAR, areas like biodiversity monitoring, rare disease diagnosis, and speech recognition, also face dataset scarcity and are impacted by subject-specific or environmental factors. Therefore, it would also be worth applying the InSSeq-Tra framework in these use cases. Additionally, future research could also explore novel approaches for calculating the divergence score, beyond the suggested GAN-based method. Lastly, the optimization step was deemed useful, as real-world CSI-based HAR implementation requires a model that performs well with few training samples, requiring less computational power and shorter learning time.

7   Conclusion

A novel framework, InSSeqTra, employing a selective sequential TL approach guided by divergence scores to address the problem of forgetting while developing a pre-trained base model using multiple CSI-based HAR datasets, was presented and evaluated in this work. The findings indicate that developing a pretrained base model using multiple CSI datasets in descending order of divergence scores with respect to the target dataset yielded significant improvements in person-wise (11%) and receiver location-wise (6.5%) domain adaptations. Additionally, different fine-tuning schemes showed that fine-tuning the entire model was beneficial, while freezing initial layers had minimal impact on classification performance. Lastly, the use of a realistic dataset (Wi-Gitation) for evaluating InSSeqTra suggests that the obtained findings can be closely associated with real-world implementations.

Acknowledgments. The authors would like to thank Prof. Dr. Paul Havinga for providing valuable feedback during the conceptualization and review phase. This research was funded by the European Union's Horizon 2020 research and innovation program under the Marie Skłodowska-Curie grant agreement number 814072 for the 4-year innovative training network ENTWINE informal care.

Disclosure of Interests. None

References

1. Ma, Y., Zhou, G., Wang, S.: Wifi sensing with channel state information: a survey. ACM Comput. Surv. (CSUR) **52**(3), 1–36 (2019)
2. Sharma, N., Brinke, J.K., Van Gemert-Pijnen, J.E.W.C., Braakman-Jansen, L.M.A., et al.: Implementation of unobtrusive sensing systems for older adult care: Scoping review. JMIR Aging **4**(4), e27862 (2021)
3. Wang, Z., et al.: A survey on human behavior recognition using channel state information. IEEE Access **7**, 155986–156024 (2019)
4. Sharma, N., Klein Brinke, J., Braakman Jansen, L.A., Havinga, P.J., Le, D.V.: Wi-gitation: Replica Wi-fi CSI dataset for physical agitation activity recognition. *Data*, 9(1), 9 (2023)
5. Zinys, A., van Berlo, B., Meratnia, N.: A domain-independent generative adversarial network for activity recognition using WiFi CSI data. Sensors **21**(23), 7852 (2021)
6. Sharma, N., Le, D.V., Havinga, P.J.M.: Exploring the impact of locations and activities in person-wise data mismatch in CSI-based HAR. In: 2023 19th International Conference on Distributed Computing in Smart Systems and the Internet of Things (DCOSS-IoT), pp. 232–239. IEEE (2023)
7. Yang, J.: SenseFi: a library and benchmark on deep-learning-empowered Wifi human sensing. Patterns **4**(3), 100703 (2023)
8. Arshad, S., Feng, C., Yu, R., Liu, Y.: Leveraging transfer learning in multiple human activity recognition using Wifi signal. In: 2019 IEEE 20th International Symposium on "A World of Wireless, Mobile and Multimedia Networks" (WoW-MoM), pp. 1–10. IEEE (2019)
9. Xue, G.-R., Dai, W., Yang, Q., Yu, Y.: Topic-bridged PLSA for cross-domain text classification. In: Proceedings of the 31st Annual International ACM SIGIR Conference on Research and Development in Information Retrieval, pp. 627–634 (2008)

10. Pan, S.J., Zheng, V.W., Yang, Q., Hu, D.H.: Transfer learning for Wifi-based indoor localization. In: Association for the Advancement of Artificial Intelligence (AAAI) Workshop, vol. 6. The Association for the Advancement of Artificial Intelligence Palo Alto (2008)

11. Russakovsky, O., et al.: ImageNet large scale visual recognition challenge. Int. J. Comput. Vis. **115**, 211–252 (2015)

12. Lin, T.-Y., et al.: Microsoft COCO: common objects in context. In: Fleet, D., Pajdla, T., Schiele, B., Tuytelaars, T. (eds.) ECCV 2014. LNCS, vol. 8693, pp. 740–755. Springer, Cham (2014). https://doi.org/10.1007/978-3-319-10602-1_48

13. Wang, Z., Yang, E., Shen, L., Huang, H.: A comprehensive survey of forgetting in deep learning beyond continual learning. arXiv preprint arXiv:2307.09218 (2023)

14. Ma, Y., Zhou, G., Wang, S., Zhao, H., Jung, W.: SignFi: sign language recognition using WIFI. Proc. ACM Interact. Mob. Wearable Ubiquitous Technol. **2**(1), 1–21 (2018)

15. Guo, S., Guo, L., et al.: WIAR: a public dataset for WIFI-based activity recognition. IEEE Access **7**, 154935–154945 (2019)

16. Brinke, J.K., Meratnia, N.: Dataset: channel state information for different activities, participants and days. In: Proceedings of the 2nd Workshop on Data Acquisition to Analysis, pp. 61–64 (2019)

17. Bu, Q., Yang, G., Feng, J., Ming, X.: Wi-fi based gesture recognition using deep transfer learning. In: 2018 IEEE SmartWorld, Ubiquitous Intelligence & Computing, Advanced & Trusted Computing, Scalable Computing & Communications, Cloud & Big Data Computing, Internet of People and Smart City Innovation (SmartWorld/SCALCOM/UIC/ATC/CBDCom/IOP/SCI), pp. 590–595. IEEE (2018)

18. Ding, M., Wang, Q., Wang, C.: Deep transfer learning for actions recognition with Wifi signals. In: 2022 IEEE 10th International Conference on Information, Communication and Networks (ICICN), pp. 406–411. IEEE (2022)

19. Brinke, J.K., Meratnia, N.: Scaling activity recognition using channel state information through convolutional neural networks and transfer learning. In: Proceedings of the First International Workshop on Challenges in Artificial Intelligence and Machine Learning for Internet of Things, pp. 56–62 (2019)

20. Fang, Y., Sheng, B., Wang, H., Xiao, F.: Witransfer: a cross-scene transfer activity recognition system using WiFi. In: Proceedings of the ACM Turing Celebration Conference-China, pp. 59–63 (2020)

21. Yuqing Yin, X., Yang, P.L., Zhang, K., Chen, P., Niu, Q.: Localization with transfer learning based on fine-grained subcarrier information for dynamic indoor environments. Sensors **21**(3), 1015 (2021)

22. Ding, X., Jiang, T., Zhong, Y., Huang, Y., Li, Z.: Wi-fi-based location-independent human activity recognition via meta learning. Sensors **21**(8), 2654 (2021)

23. Chen, Y.-S., Chang, Y.-C., Li, C.-Y.: A semi-supervised transfer learning with dynamic associate domain adaptation for human activity recognition using wifi signals. Sensors **21**(24), 8475 (2021)

24. Sinno Jialin Pan and Qiang Yang: A survey on transfer learning. IEEE Trans. Knowl. Data Eng. **22**(10), 1345–1359 (2010)

25. Li, Z., Hoiem, D.: Learning without forgetting. IEEE Trans. Pattern Anal. Mach. Intell. **40**(12), 2935–2947 (2017)

26. Showmik, I.A., Sanam, T.F., Imtiaz, H.: Human activity recognition from Wi-Fi CSI data using principal component-based wavelet CNN. arXiv preprint arXiv:2212.13161 (2022)

27. Wang, W., Liu, A.X., Shahzad, M., Ling, K., Lu, S.: Understanding and modeling of WIFI signal based human activity recognition. In: Proceedings of the 21st Annual International Conference on Mobile Computing and Networking, pp. 65–76 (2015)
28. Yousefi, S., Narui, H., Dayal, S., Ermon, S., Valaee, S.: A survey on behavior recognition using WIFI channel state information. IEEE Commun. Mag. **55**(10), 98–104 (2017)
29. Tzanetakis, G., Essl, G., Cook, P.: Audio analysis using the discrete wavelet transform. In: Proceedings of the Conference in Acoustics and Music Theory Applications, vol. 66. Citeseer (2001)
30. Al-Rahbi, M.: Human activity recognition using channel state information (2019)
31. Jeong, J.-C., et al.: Selective layer tuning and performance study of pre-trained models using genetic algorithm. Electronics **11**(19), 2985 (2022)
32. Wang, Y., Sun, D., Chen, K., Lai, F., Chowdhury, M.: Egeria: efficient DNN training with knowledge-guided layer freezing. In: Proceedings of the Eighteenth European Conference on Computer Systems, pp. 851–866 (2023)

Topological Versus Spatiotemporal Gait Parameters for Fall Risk Detection with IMU Sensors

Redona Brahimetaj[1,2]([✉]) [iD], Elena Botti[1] [iD], Ivan Bautmans[3] [iD], Eva Swinnen[4] [iD], and Bart Jansen[1,2] [iD]

[1] Department of Electronics and Informatics (ETRO), Vrije Universiteit Brussel (VUB), Pleinlaan 2, 1050 Brussels, Belgium
{redona.brahimetaj,elena.botti,bart.jansen}@vub.be
[2] IMEC, Kapeldreef 75, 3001 Leuven, Belgium
[3] Frailty and Resilience in Ageing Research Unit (FRIA), Vitality Research Group, and Gerontology Department, Vrije Universiteit Brussel, Brussels, Belgium
ivan.bautmans@vub.be
[4] Rehabilitation Research Group, Vrije Universiteit Brussel, Brussels, Belgium
eva.swinnen@vub.be

Abstract. Spatiotemporal gait parameters (SGP) derived from inertial measurement units (IMUs) are well-established in gait analysis and fall risk assessment. These interpretable features (such as step time, symmetry, double support, etc.) require accurate gait event (GE) detection and are commonly used in clinical and research settings. In contrast, topological data analysis (TDA) is an emerging approach that captures the global geometric and temporal structure of time series without requiring step segmentation. TDA maps signals into higher-dimensional phase spaces via time-delay embedding and quantifies their topological structure using persistent homology.

In this study, we directly compare SGP and TDA features for classifying fall risk in a cohort of 78 older adults (41 non-fallers, 37 fallers) recruited at the University Hospital (UZ) Brussels. Each participant completed six IMU-recorded walking trials. SGP features were computed from GE using wavelet-based detection, while TDA features were extracted from vertical-axis acceleration. We also evaluate the impact of the time-delay embedding parameter (τ) on TDA classification performance.

Our results show that both TDA features and SGP achieved comparable classification performance, with an AUC of 0.81. While the overall performance remained stable across different τ values, subject-level analysis revealed that fallers are more affected by τ variations.

These results show that TDA can equal the discriminative power of handcrafted SGP features. To our knowledge, this is the very first direct comparison of SGP and TDA features in gait analysis - across any population - not just in elderly fall-risk assessment. This positions TDA as a promising alternative for future research in wearable sensors and human activity recognition tasks.

Ö. Durmaz Incel et al. (Eds.): iWOAR 2025, LNCS 16292, pp. 156–171, 2026.
https://doi.org/10.1007/978-3-032-13312-0_9

Keywords: Gait Analysis · Spatiotemporal Gait Parameters · Topological Data Analysis · Inertial Measurement Units · Fall Risk Assessment · Wearable Sensors

1   Introduction

Falls are a leading cause of injury, hospitalization and loss of independence among older adults. Timely and accurate fall risk assessment is therefore critical for guiding early intervention strategies and preventing serious health outcomes [1]. In clinical practice, fall risk is most commonly assessed using (subjective) screening tools (e.g.: the Timed Up and Go test, gait speed or balance scales) and self-reported fall history. While these approaches are simple and scalable, they are limited in sensitivity and often miss subtle impairments in gait or balance that precede a fall [2].

Advanced motion capture systems can provide detailed and accurate assessments of gait, but their use is largely confined to research or specialized rehabilitation labs due to high costs, setup complexity and limited accessibility. As a result, inertial measurement units (IMUs) have emerged as a practical alternative - enabling objective monitoring of human movement in both clinical and real-world settings. Worn on the lower back, foot, or other body segments, IMUs can capture gait-related signals that support the assessments of fall risk [3].

A widely used set of features extracted from IMU data are spatiotemporal gait parameters (SGP), which quantify clinically relevant metrics such as step time, step (a)symmetry, stride duration, double support etc. These parameters have been shown to discriminate fallers from non-fallers in elderly populations with moderate to high accuracy [4], and are commonly used in studies evaluating wearable-based fall risk prediction. However, the computation of some SGP relies on the accurate detection of gait events (GE), which can be challenging in individuals with atypical or irregular gait patterns.

In contrast to these (interpretable) biomechanical features, topological data analysis (TDA) offers a more abstract and emerging approach for analyzing time series data. TDA captures the underlying geometric and temporal structure of a signal using tools from algebraic topology. A common technique is persistent homology, which tracks topological features - such as connected components (H_0) and loops (H_1) - as the data is analyzed across multiple spatial and/or temporal scales. When applied to time series, the signal is first transformed into a time-delay embedding, producing a trajectory in a higher-dimensional space that reflects its dynamical structure. Persistent homology is then used to compute persistence diagrams, which are further summarized using descriptors such as landscapes, silhouettes, and Betti curves. These features are often considered robust to noise, capture global dynamics, and despite not used a lot, have shown promising results in various biomedical applications. For instance, persistent entropy and Betti curves have been used to classify Parkinson's disease severity from gait signals [5]. Topological motion analysis has successfully discriminated also between multiple neurodegenerative diseases based on subtle gait fluctuations [6]. Mishra et al. [7] introduced a comprehensive topological framework for analyzing human gait and demonstrated that persistent homology descriptors could capture biomechanical variability. Similarly, Phinyomark et al. [8] highlighted the potential of topological and nonlinear features for handling large-scale biomechanical datasets. Karan et al. [9] applied TDA to physiological time series for stress classification where they introduced a sub-windowing approach to efficiently extract stable features from the time delay embeddings. Their method demonstrated improved classification results using fewer features compared to traditional approaches. In [10], the authors explored the integration of topological descriptors to improve model performance in human activity recognition tasks, even under signal corruptions and across varied datasets. They proposed incorporating topological features within knowledge distillation frameworks and recommended this approach as a promising direction for future research. More recently, Zia et al. [11] discussed the broader role of topology in deep learning (DL), reinforcing the versatility of TDA across biomedical signal processing tasks.

Given the promising results of TDA in biomedical applications, a natural question arises: how does the TDA discriminative power compare to that of classical SGP features in gait analysis? Are TDA-derived features better, worse, or equally effective for specific classification tasks? We sought prior works addressing this question but, to the best of our knowledge, no study has directly compared TDA-derived features with classical SGP - neither for fall-risk assessment nor for any other gait analysis contexts. In this study, we aim to fill this gap by directly comparing the classification performance when using SGP and TDA features. We use wearable sensor data collected from 78 older adults (41 non-fallers and 37 fallers), each completing six walking trials while wearing a single IMU on the sacrum. We extracted GE from the accelerometer signals to compute SGP features, while TDA features were derived from the raw acceleration time series via delay embeddings and topological summaries.

Our study includes four main contributions: (1) a head-to-head performance comparison between SGP and TDA-based models using identical pipelines; (2) a systematic evaluation of the impact of the time-delay embedding parameter (τ) on TDA classification performance; (3) an analysis of subject-level variation in model sensitivity to τ; and (4) an evaluation of subject-level classification by aggregating trial predictions. Although our focus is not on traditional activity recognition, our approach - extracting discriminative features from wearable sensor data to classify functional status - is closely aligned with the broader goal of sensor-based analysis. Because TDA offers a flexible, data-driven framework for any time series, these results could inspire new methods for recognizing subtle or complex movements across a wide range of wearable-sensor applications or complex movement patterns.

2   Materials and Methods

2.1   Participants

The dataset used is obtained from [13] and consists of a total of 81 older adults. Elderly participants were recruited from the geriatrics department of University Hospital (UZ) Brussels, from the research department's database of elderly volunteers and from seniors' organizations. Exclusion criteria included cognitive impairment, inability to walk 20 m unaided, diagnosed Parkinson's disease or cerebrovascular accident with locomotor disability, and any acute or uncontrolled medical conditions. Participants were categorized as having an increased fall risk if they met at least one of the following clinical criteria: (1) a self-reported fall within the past six months, (2) a Timed Up and Go (TUG) test duration greater than 15 s, or (3) a Tinetti Performance-Oriented Mobility Assessment (POMA) score below 24/28. These criteria span self-reported, single-task, and multi-task performance assessments, and a fall was defined as unintentionally coming to rest on the ground or a lower surface, not caused by a major intrinsic or extrinsic factor. All participants provided written informed consent, and the study was approved by the ethics committee of UZ Brussels.

2.2   Gait Data Acquisition

Each participant completed three gait assessments, with each trial consisting of two consecutive 18-meter straight-line walks (referred to as walk-1 and walk-2). The walking path was marked on the floor with visible tape at both ends. Participants were instructed to begin standing still just before the first mark, walk at a comfortable, self-selected pace to the end of the marked path, and stop just after crossing the second mark. The total walking distance was measured precisely, to the nearest 0.01 m, including the final foot placement after the stop.

A tri-axial accelerometer (DynaPort MiniMod, McRoberts, The Hague Netherlands, ±2g range, 100 Hz) was attached to the sacrum of each participant using a strap. Between each of the three trials, the accelerometer was removed and repositioned by one of three trained research staff. Each participant was assessed by two different staff members in randomized order: one staff member conducted two of the three trials (intra-rater), and another conducted the remaining trial (inter-rater). The design in the original study [13] enabled the analysis of both intra and inter-rater variability in sensor positioning, reflecting realistic clinical or at-home monitoring scenarios. After each trial, raw accelerometer data were downloaded to a local computer using DynaPort GaitTest acquisition software (MiRA version 1.9.4.b2, McRoberts). Only raw accelerometer signals were used in this study; gyroscope data were not collected/analyzed. The current study does not use SGP as computed by the McRoberts software at the time of data collection. Rather we use more contemporary methods described in the section below.

2.3   Feature Extraction

Spatiotemporal Gait Parameters: Prior to feature extraction, all accelerometer signals were reoriented using a custom rotation-based method to standardize sensor orientation and compensate for individual sensor tilt across participants. Accurate detection of GE - specifically, initial contact and final contact - is essential for computing SGP. To compute GE, we used an adaptive wavelet-based algorithm applied to the vertical acceleration signal, following the Scikit-Digital-Health implementation [14]. Unlike fixed-scale wavelet approaches, the implemented method adapts the wavelet scale dynamically to improve robustness across subjects. Following event detection, SGP features were computed using the SensorMotion Python library. Extracted features include: step count, cadence, mean step time, step time standard deviation (std), coefficient of variation of step time, step regularity, stride regularity, and step symmetry. Double support time was calculated using a custom method in Python. Features were computed separately for each walking trial, and all trials were retained individually in the final dataset (no averaging across trials was performed).

Topological Features: TDA features were extracted directly from the raw vertical accelerometer signal using a multi-step pipeline designed to characterize the shape and temporal dynamics of gait. Preprocessing steps, including signal re-orientation as previously described and low-pass filtering (cutoff $= 10\,\mathrm{Hz}$), were performed. Although features were initially extracted from all three axes, ablation testing revealed that using only the vertical signal yielded a slightly superior classification performance. This is likely due to the vertical axis capturing the most salient gait-related dynamics in our controlled dataset, with reduced influence from lateral or anteroposterior noise. Nonetheless, in free-living environments, where instability and balance deficits may manifest more strongly in lateral or anteroposterior directions, these axes could provide additional discriminative value for fall-risk assessment.

Time-delay embedding (TDE) was used to reconstruct a 3D phase space from each 1D signal. This technique embeds temporal information into a spatial representation, enabling topological patterns in gait dynamics to be captured geometrically. TDE is parameterized by the delay parameter (τ), which affects the geometry of the resulting point cloud. To explore its impact, we systematically evaluated a wide range of τ values: 1, 3, 5, 10, 20, 30, 40, 50, 70, 90, 100, 150, 200, 250, 300, 350, 400, 500.

Persistent homology was then computed using Vietoris–Rips filtrations in homology dimensions 0 and 1, capturing topological structures such as H_0 and H_1 in the embedded signal. The resulting persistence diagrams were then transformed into fixed-length feature vectors using four classes of descriptors:

- Persistence statistics: numerical summaries of the diagrams, including the number of features, mean and std of lifetimes, maximum and minimum lifetimes, total persistence etc.
- Betti curves: counts of the number of topological features alive at each filtration threshold, capturing the evolution of H_0 and H_1.
- Silhouettes: weighted averages of lifetimes over the filtration range, emphasizing dominant topological features.
- Persistence landscapes: a multi-layered function representation of topological features that captures their prominence across filtrations.

Each descriptor was computed with 50 filtration bins, chosen as a practical trade-off between resolution and stability. The extracted TDA features per each descriptor class (excluding the persistence statistics, which we also computed ourselves) are continuous-valued and capture rich topological structure. With each descriptor providing multiple values per homology dimension (H_0 and H_1) and per filtration bin (and with additional values across layers specifically for the persistence statistics) the final TDA feature vector consisted of approximately 790 dimensions per walking trial. All extracted TDA features were included in the models, and no feature selection was applied, as their continuous nature across filtration levels makes selective pruning less meaningful and potentially inconsistent across subjects.

Classification Strategy: To evaluate the discriminative power of the extracted gait (both SGP and TDA) features, we implemented a subject-level Leave-One-Group-Out (LOGO) cross-validation scheme, where each fold holds out all gait trials from a single participant as the test set. From the remaining participants, a subject-level validation set was sampled by randomly selecting five fallers and five non-fallers for hyperparameter optimization. The remaining subjects were used for the training set. This approach ensures subject-level independence across train, validation, and test partitions, avoiding data leakage.

Three classification algorithms were assessed across both SGP and TDA feature sets: Support Vector Machine (SVM), Extreme Gradient Boosting (XGBoost), and a Multi Layer Perceptron (MLP) network. Each classifier was evaluated under a grid of hyperparameters, and the same parameter grid was applied consistently across all configurations to ensure comparability (12 configurations for XGBoost, 6 for SVM, and 13 for MLP). For the neural network, we used a 2-layer architecture with varying layer sizes and learning rates, trained using binary cross-entropy loss and Adam optimizer with early stopping based on validation loss.

In addition to these classical classifiers, we further explored the performance of sequential neural models - Long Short-Term Memory (LSTM), Bidirectional LSTM (BiLSTM), and Gated Recurrent Unit (GRU) - for classifying only TDA-derived features. Although topological descriptors are not raw time series, they contain quasi-continuous structure due to the way Betti curves, persistence landscapes, and silhouette curves are generated. These descriptors provide a vectorized 'signal' that unfolds over increasing filtration values/space, presumably making them suitable for modeling with recurrent models. Each network consisted of a single recurrent layer with the number of units selected from $16, 32, 64, 128, 256$ as part of hyperparameter optimization. A dropout layer was applied after the recurrent layers to reduce overfitting (dropout rates: 0.2–0.5), followed by a fully connected dense layer (units: 8–128). All models used binary cross-entropy loss and the Adam optimizer, with learning rates ranging from 1×10^{-5} to 1×10^{-3}. Training was performed using a batch size of 512 for up to 2000 epochs, and for each fold, the model checkpoint with the lowest validation loss was selected for test evaluation. Hyperparameters were tuned independently for each model type using the subject-level validation set. Our DL experiments were deliberately restricted to TDA features to ensure a fair and consistent comparison with SGP, both of which are computed on the full accelerometer signal.

All classical classifiers (SVM, MLP, and XGBoost) were trained using the original, unstandardized feature values of both SGP and TDA features. This choice was based on empirical comparisons, where applying z-score standardization consistently resulted in (slightly) lower performance. Most TDA features are inherently normalized within the filtration space, and standardizing them may disrupt their geometric interpretation or compress informative variation. Similarly, the SGP features are primarily derived from normalized metrics and further normalization was therefore unnecessary. In contrast, feature standardization was applied prior to training all LSTM, BiLSTM, and GRU models, as omitting this step led to unstable loss behavior and poor convergence.

3   Results

In this section we present the performance of models trained on SGP and TDA features. We first examine the effect of the time-delay parameter τ used in TDA. Then, we compare classification performance of TDA vs SGP across traditional ML and DL models. Finally, we report subject-level classification performance by aggregating predictions across multiple trials from each individual.

3.1   Effect of the Time Delay Parameter (τ) on TDA Performance

We investigated the impact of the time-delay parameter (τ) on classification performance using topological features derived from vertical-axis acceleration. As shown in Table 1, the AUC on the test set remains stable across a wide range of τ values (from 1 to 500), with slight fluctuations. The highest test AUC of 0.81 was achieved for both $\tau = 3$ and $\tau = 30$, with comparable F1-scores as well. These results suggest that while small values of τ may capture fine-grained gait dynamics, slightly larger values still retain enough temporal structure to produce topologically rich embeddings. However, as τ increases beyond 100, performance tends to decline slightly, likely due to temporal de-correlation and less informative embeddings. Based on the results summarized in Table 1, the delay parameter $\tau = 3$ is considered as an optimal choice for our study. This choice was motivated by its consistent performance across both validation and test sets, achieving one of the highest AUC scores (0.84 and 0.81, respectively), along with balanced sensitivity and specificity. Accordingly, the classification models evaluated in the next experiments (both ML and DL models) using TDA features were all trained with topological descriptors extracted from time-delay embeddings generated using $\tau = 3$.

Table 1. Validation and test performance of TDA-based models across different delay parameters τ. The highest metrics values are shown in bold. ('Acc' - Accuracy; 'AUC' - Area Under the Curve; 'F1' - F1 score; 'Sens' - Sensitivity; 'Spec' - Specificity)

Delay	Validation Set					Test Set				
	Acc	AUC	F1	Sens	Spec	Acc	AUC	F1	Sens	Spec
$\tau = 1$	0.77	0.83	0.74	0.66	0.88	0.76	0.80	0.71	0.63	0.87
$\tau = 3$	**0.77**	**0.84**	**0.75**	**0.68**	**0.86**	**0.76**	**0.81**	**0.72**	**0.64**	**0.87**
$\tau = 5$	0.77	0.84	0.74	0.66	0.87	0.76	0.80	0.71	0.63	0.87
$\tau = 10$	0.75	0.83	0.72	0.63	0.87	0.74	0.79	0.69	0.60	0.87
$\tau = 20$	0.76	0.83	0.73	0.64	0.88	0.75	0.79	0.70	0.61	0.88
$\tau = 30$	**0.76**	**0.84**	**0.73**	**0.65**	**0.87**	**0.75**	**0.81**	**0.71**	**0.62**	**0.87**
$\tau = 40$	0.76	0.83	0.72	0.62	0.89	0.75	0.80	0.69	0.59	0.89
$\tau = 50$	0.76	0.82	0.73	0.63	0.89	0.76	0.78	0.71	0.62	0.89
$\tau = 70$	0.76	0.83	0.73	0.64	0.88	0.76	0.80	0.71	0.61	0.89
$\tau = 90$	0.75	0.83	0.72	0.63	0.88	0.74	0.79	0.68	0.59	0.87
$\tau = 100$	0.75	0.83	0.71	0.62	0.88	0.75	0.79	0.69	0.59	0.89
$\tau = 150$	0.74	0.82	0.70	0.61	0.88	0.72	0.79	0.65	0.55	0.87
$\tau = 200$	0.75	0.83	0.69	0.56	0.94	0.73	0.79	0.65	0.52	0.93
$\tau = 250$	0.76	0.83	0.72	0.63	0.89	0.75	0.80	0.70	0.59	0.90
$\tau = 300$	0.75	0.82	0.71	0.62	0.88	0.75	0.79	0.70	0.60	0.89
$\tau = 350$	0.76	0.83	0.71	0.60	0.92	0.74	0.80	0.67	0.55	0.91
$\tau = 400$	0.75	0.82	0.72	0.63	0.88	0.74	0.78	0.68	0.59	0.87
$\tau = 500$	0.75	0.81	0.72	0.63	0.87	0.75	0.77	0.70	0.60	0.88

3.2   Comparison of SGP and TDA-Based Models

To evaluate and compare the performance of models trained on SGP and TDA features, we report accuracy, Area Under the Curve (AUC), F1-score, sensitivity, and specificity on both validation and test sets. While validation performance provides insight into generalization during training, the test set serves as the final benchmark for our conclusions (with AUC as our primary evaluation metric).

As shown in Table 2, both the SGP-based and TDA-based models achieved the same test AUC of 0.81, indicating equivalent discriminative power when using optimized traditional ML pipelines. These findings were also consistent across validation and test results, further reinforcing the stability of these models. For SGP, the best results were obtained using an MLP classifier, and for TDA, using SVM. In contrast, recurrent DL models such as LSTM, BiLSTM, and GRU - though evaluated on the same TDA feature set - consistently underperformed, with test AUC values around 0.71–0.74. Figure 1 shows the ROC curves for all test set predictions. The curves visually confirm the equivalent performance of

Table 2. Validation and test performance of models using SGP or TDA-based features. The highest metrics values are shown in bold.

Model	Validation					Test				
	Acc	AUC	F1	Sens	Spec	Acc	AUC	F1	Sens	Spec
SGP (ML)	**0.75**	**0.83**	**0.74**	**0.70**	**0.80**	**0.76**	**0.81**	**0.72**	**0.67**	**0.84**
TDA (ML)	**0.77**	**0.84**	**0.75**	**0.68**	**0.86**	**0.76**	**0.81**	**0.72**	**0.64**	**0.87**
TDA (LSTM)	0.70	0.73	0.69	0.65	0.76	0.71	0.71	0.68	0.63	0.79
TDA (BiLSTM)	0.71	0.76	0.69	0.66	0.78	0.72	0.74	0.68	0.65	0.78
TDA (GRU)	0.71	0.74	0.69	0.66	0.75	0.71	0.71	0.69	0.66	0.79

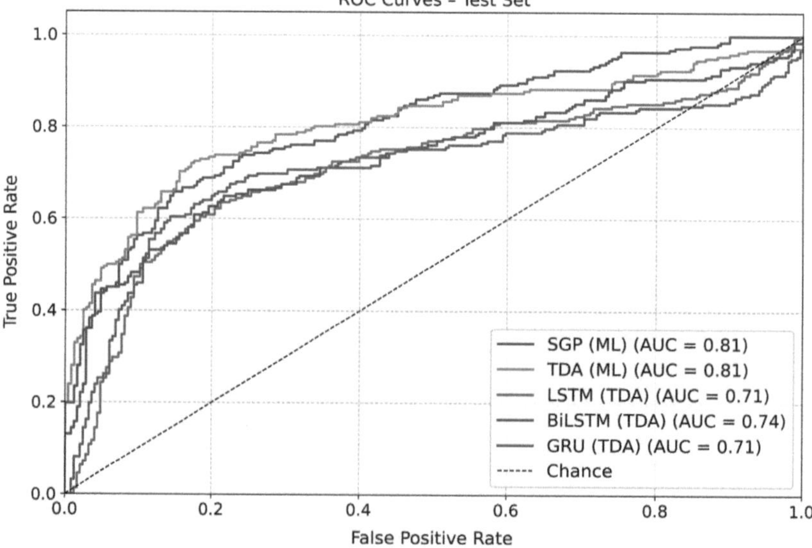

Fig. 1. ROC curves on the test set for models trained using either SGP or TDA-based features. Both SGP and TDA (ML) models reach an AUC of 0.81, while DL models (LSTM, BiLSTM, GRU) underperform with AUC values in the range 0.71–0.74.

the SGP and TDA (ML) models and the superior performance of ML compared to the DL ones.

Subject-Level Variation in Optimal τ: To assess how sensitive the classifier's predictions are to the choice of the delay parameter τ, we conducted a subject-level analysis, with results illustrated in Fig. 2. For each participant, we computed the mean and std of the test-set accuracy across all τ values. A high mean with a low std indicates that the participant was classified correctly and consistently across the entire τ range. In contrast, a large std suggests that the prediction varies considerably with τ, reflecting potential over- or under-embedding for that subject.

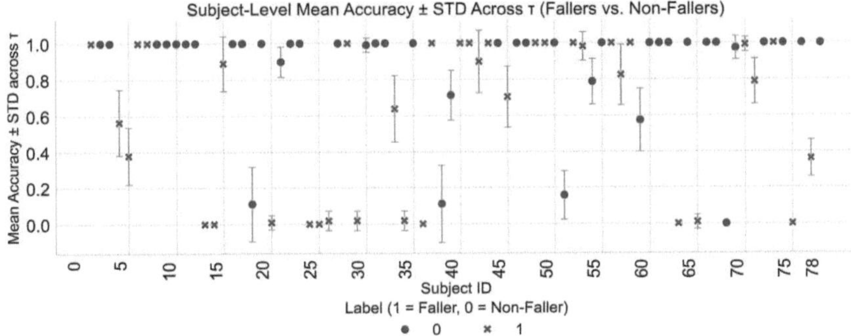

Fig. 2. Subject-level mean accuracy ($\pm$ std) over all τ values, test set. Red = non-fallers, blue = fallers. Fallers show lower accuracy and larger variance, indicating greater sensitivity to the choice of τ. (Color figure online)

Two patterns emerge. (i) Non-fallers (red dots) near the top of the plot with almost zero/minimal std, suggesting that their more regular, periodic gait is robustly captured by the TDA pipeline regardless of τ. (ii) Fallers (blue crosses) show markedly lower means and larger error bars, confirming that pathological or irregular gait reduces periodicity and makes the embedding (sometimes highly) τ-dependent. These findings highlight that the assumption of 'same-τ-value-fits-all' delay is questionable: a fixed τ can over-embed some gait cycles while under-embedding others. Nevertheless, because subject-specific tuning would require re-training or a nested optimization scheme that is impractical in real-world deployment, we adopted the pragmatic compromise and fixed $\tau = 3$ for all subsequent experiments as also mentioned in Sect. 3.1.

Subject-Level Classification Accuracy: While all performance metrics reported in previous sections are based on individual walking trials, each participant performed six trials in total. Section 3.1 examined classifier sensitivity to different τ values at the subject level, but those results were aggregated across all τ values. In this section, we focus on subject-level classification using a single, fixed τ value - specifically, the best-performing value of $\tau = 3$ identified earlier.

To better reflect the clinical goal of identifying individuals at risk of falling, we evaluated subject-level classification accuracy by aggregating trial-level predictions. Since each participant performed six trials, we classified a subject as a faller if a minimum number of their trials were predicted as faller. Specifically, we tested thresholds requiring at least 1, 2, 3, 4, 5 or 6 out of 6 trials predicted as faller. For each threshold, subject-level accuracy, sensitivity and specificity were computed, allowing a clear view of the sensitivity-specificity trade-off as the classification criterion is varied.

For both SGP- and TDA-based models, aggregating predictions across trials led to a slightly improved overall subject-level accuracy. The trial-level accuracy of the SGP model was 76%, which increased to 77% when using the subject-level aggregation strategy. Similarly, the TDA model improved from 76% to 78%. Note that AUC could not be reported for this analysis, as subject-level predictions were obtained by aggregating binary trial-level labels using our thresholding scheme (we have no probability scores).

Table 3. Subject-level performance for each aggregation threshold. SGP and TDA results are shown per each threshold. Thresholds represent the minimum number of trials predicted as faller to classify a subject as a faller.

Threshold	SGP - Test				TDA - Test			
	Acc	F1	Sens	Spec	Acc	F1	Sens	Spec
1	0.74	0.74	0.70	0.78	0.78	0.78	0.78	0.78
2	0.77	0.77	0.70	0.83	0.78	0.78	0.68	0.88
3	0.77	0.77	0.70	0.83	0.78	0.78	0.68	0.88
4	0.77	0.77	0.68	0.86	0.76	0.76	0.62	0.88
5	0.74	0.74	0.62	0.85	0.73	0.73	0.54	0.90
6	0.74	0.74	0.60	0.88	0.73	0.73	0.51	0.93

4   Discussion

This work presents the very first systematic comparison between two fundamentally different classes of wearable-sensor features for fall-risk assessment in older adults: traditional SGP, which rely on explicit GE detection, and TDA descriptors, which capture the global geometry of the accelerometer signals without requiring GE detection. It is also the first study to conduct a comprehensive sweep of the time-delay embedding parameter τ, analyzing its influence on TDA-based classification performance. Both feature types were evaluated using identical traditional ML models, and - exclusively for TDA - also tested with recurrent DL architectures including LSTM, BiLSTM, and GRU.

Performance Comparison: Across all traditional ML pipelines (SVM, XGBoost, MLP), the best SGP model and the best TDA model reached the same test-set AUC of 0.81. In other words, TDA can match the discriminative power of handcrafted gait metrics. This parity is striking: SGP require accurate initial contact and final contact detection, whereas the TDA model needs no event detection at all, yet extracts equivalent discriminative signal directly from raw acceleration. Practically, this means TDA can potentially serve as an alternative when accurate step-finding or accurate GE detections fails (for example, in noisy free-living recordings or in subjects with highly irregular gait). While this may seem surprising at first, it likely reflects two complementary perspectives: SGP extract interpretable gait parameters from event-detected steps and strides, whereas TDA bypasses event detection and instead captures the global geometry of the signal. The comparable accuracy of both approaches suggests that the essential discriminative information for fall-risk assessment can be preserved through either representation. At the same time, we acknowledge that TDA descriptors are more abstract; however, ongoing research in topological machine learning is beginning to develop visualization and feature-attribution methods aimed at improving their interpretability [11]. It is worth noting that this comparable performance was achieved with a much larger TDA feature space (790 features) compared to only 9 SGP features. From a computational perspective, this makes SGP clearly more compact and efficient. However, TDA features are generated directly from the raw signal without requiring GE detection, which can be error-prone in subjects with noisy or irregular gait. Moreover, dimensionality alone is not prohibitive for ML pipelines, which can handle hundreds of descriptors reliably. We therefore view TDA not as a replacement for SGP, but as a complementary representation that may prove advantageous in scenarios where global signal geometry carries discriminative value.

Meanwhile recurrent neural networks - LSTM, BiLSTM and GRU - consistently under-performed (AUC: [0.71–0.74]). Two factors can explain the shortfall. (1) The chosen architectures, despite relevant to consider, normally exploit long temporal dependencies, yet the TDA vectors used here are short and low-dimensional sequences, and quasi temporal. For instance, there may be/is some continuity within certain descriptors (e.g., Betti curves), but the feature vector jumps from one descriptor type to another (e.g., from Betti curves to Silhouettes) with limited temporal or semantic continuity between them. This disrupts the sequential structure that RNNs are designed to exploit. (2) Our modest dataset size (78 subjects × six trials) is insufficient for deep sequential models to effectively learn class-discriminative patterns - these architectures typically require much larger datasets to reach their full potential. Given the current sample size and feature structure, classical ML models remain the most suitable choice for classifying our TDA descriptors. Deep RNNs, by contrast, will likely require either substantially larger cohorts (and longer IMU recordings) or a denser, more semantically coherent topological representation to bridge the performance gap.

Prior work has shown that with sufficiently large datasets, DL can match or surpass the performance of SGP by discovering discriminative patterns directly from data [12]. This broader context illustrates a noteworthy distinction: traditional SGP encode decades of biomechanical knowledge, DL leverages data-driven representation learning to achieve comparable performance at scale, and TDA provides yet another route - extracting signal geometry without hand-crafted priors or large datasets. That such distinct paradigms can converge on similar discriminative power is intriguing and merits further exploration.

Role of the Delay Parameter τ: Because TDA descriptors are computed on time-delay embeddings, we assessed the choice of the delay parameter τ in the classification performance. Results show that classification performance is relatively robust across a wide range of τ values. Test-set AUC varied by less than 0.3 across the entire sweep ($\tau = 1$ to 500), with optimal performance at $\tau = 3$ and $\tau = 30$. A clear pattern emerges in Table 3: once τ grows beyond the very small values, test AUC slips from 0.81 (at $\tau = 3$) down to 0.77 (at $\tau = 500$). In other words, the farther apart we space the points in the delay-embedding, the less accurately the model classifies fall risk. The reason is intuitive. Our IMU delivers one sample every 10 ms; when τ is small (e.g.: 1–10), the delay embedding links points that are 10–100 ms apart, meaning they fall within a single gait cycle (typically around 1 s). Notably, this may also explain why classification performance remains relatively stable across this range of τ: embeddings constructed from closely spaced points within the same gait event (e.g., a single step) are likely to preserve similar geometric patterns. In other words, different small τ values might yield similarly structured embeddings because they all reflect the same underlying periodic gait activity - just sampled at slightly different offsets. However, once τ becomes too large, the embedding joins samples that are hundreds of ms apart, mixing different phases of the step. The topological signal might simply become less distinct, and classification performance gradually degrades.

The delay parameter τ is a critical component of time-delay embedding, yet we found little guidance in the literature regarding how to choose an appropriate value for gait signals. In practice, the optimal τ may be both task-specific and gait-specific, varying substantially between individuals depending on the regularity or complexity of their movement. To analyze whether a 'same-τ-value-fits-all' assumption is valid, we analyzed the variance in per-subject classification accuracy across all τ values. Non-fallers consistently showed high accuracy with minimal variance, indicating that their regular gait is captured equally well by any reasonable τ. Fallers, however, exhibited both lower mean accuracy and markedly higher std, confirming that pathological or irregular gait disturbs the periodicity on which the embedding relies (see Fig. 2). A fixed τ can therefore over-embed some fallers and under-embed others. These findings require careful interpretation as we are testing the very assumption we imposed. In other words, when we report that '$\tau = 3$ works better', that conclusion is drawn from a model trained on all subjects at $\tau = 3$, not from finding each individual's true optimal delay. This circular dependency undermines our claim that any single τ is universally valid. To face this limitation, future work must allow τ to vary per subject - either by training separate models for multiple delays and inference on features computed on multiple delays too, or by building multi-τ ensembles, or by developing adaptive embedding schemes that select the most informative scale for each individual. Only then can we properly assess the true embedding delay that best captures each person's unique gait. In addition, Fig. 2 should be interpreted with caution, as our definition of 'faller' is broad [13] - combining self-reported falls with clinical test scores (e.g., Tinetti and TUG). This inclusive labeling strategy may classify individuals as fallers based on minor or uncertain self-reported events, introducing heterogeneity into the ground truth. Such noise can affect model training and interpretation; for example, several fallers in Fig. 2 are consistently misclassified: it can possibly be because their gait patterns are not too different from those of non-fallers. It should also be noted that τ is expressed in samples, so its temporal meaning depends on both the sensor's sampling rate and the subject's walking speed. In our setup (100 Hz IMU, with a gait cycle of approximately 1 s), $\tau = 3$ corresponds to a delay of about 30 ms, which represents a small fraction of a typical gait cycle. Different sensor frequencies or markedly slower/faster gait patterns would shift the effective temporal span of each τ, potentially altering the range of values that preserve discriminative signal. This dependency highlights the importance of considering sensor characteristics and cadence when generalizing delay choices across studies.

Subject Level Performance: We also evaluated performance at the subject level by aggregating predictions across each participant's six gait trials. While all primary results were reported at the trial level, the clinical reality is that fall risk is determined per person and not only per trial. For this analysis, we focused on subject-level classification using a single, fixed τ value - specifically, the best-performing value of $\tau = 3$ identified earlier. Aggregating predictions slightly improved overall accuracy: SGP model performance increased from 76% to 77%, and TDA model accuracy rose from 76% to 78%. More importantly, subject-level aggregation consistently boosted sensitivity, which is a more critical metric in clinical screening for fall prevention. These results show that trial-level variability can be smoothed out by simple threshold-based voting, enhancing the model's ability to identify individuals at risk.

Relevance to Human Action Recognition (HAR) and Other Research: Taken together, our study has clear implications for the wearable sensing communities, HAR community, and AI-based modeling. We demonstrated that TDA - a relatively underexplored method - can match the discriminative power of conventional gait metrics. As such, we encourage researchers working on similar/related tasks, to consider exploring it as well. One key advantage of TDA is that it operates directly on raw acceleration signals, without requiring explicit step/event segmentation (i.e.: detecting initial/final contacts or gait cycles). Given that its classification performance matches that of SGP, it may be particularly useful in free-living settings or among populations with irregular movement patterns, where traditional methods often struggle. At the same time, we acknowledge that free-living settings may amplify the challenges associated with selecting an appropriate τ, highlighting the importance of developing adaptive or subject-specific embedding strategies in future work. Nevertheless, we believe this study opens promising directions for HAR and AI research by encouraging the exploration of topological representations in activity classification pipelines.

5   Limitations and Future Work

This study has several limitations. (1) We extracted TDA features from entire walking trials; testing windowed segments could generate more samples and may particularly benefit DL models. (2) Some TDA parameters (e.g., number of bins) were fixed and not fully optimized, future work should explore their effect on performance. (3) Although TDA and SGP features were evaluated separately, combining them through fusion strategies may improve robustness. (4) Finally, some recent DL models such as PersLay, DeepSet, and TopoNet can take persistence diagrams or their vectorized forms (e.g., persistence images, landscapes, or graphs) directly as input (allowing end-to-end learning from topological features). Exploring these approaches is interesting and may lead to improved performance.

6 Conclusion

This study presents the first comparison of two different IMU feature classes for fall-risk assessment: classical SGP and TDA descriptors.

Using a leave-one-group-out protocol and identical traditional ML pipelines, we showed that the TDA-based performance matches the best SGP model, achieving both an AUC = 0.81. A systematic sweep of the time-delay embedding parameter τ revealed that while τ-level performance remained relatively stable across different values, subject-level analysis showed greater sensitivity among fallers. This highlights the limitations of a same-τ-value-fits-all approach to τ selection.

Taken together, these results position TDA as possible alternative to classical SGP - offering comparable performance with fewer domain-specific assumptions.

Acknowledgments. We thank all researchers working in this field for their contributions to the advancement of gait analysis and fall-risk assessment.

References

1. Center for Disease Control and Prevention (CDC), Older Adult Fall Prevention. https://www.cdc.gov/falls/data-research/facts-stats/index.html. Accessed 10 July 2025
2. Jepsen, B., et al.: Predicting falls in older adults: an umbrella review of instruments assessing gait, balance, and functional mobility. BMC Geriatr. **22**, 731 (2022). https://doi.org/10.1186/s12877-022-03271-5
3. Hulleck, A., et al.: Present and future of gait assessment in clinical practice: towards the application of novel trends and technologies. Front. Med. Technol. **14**, 815124 (2022). https://doi.org/10.3389/fmedt.2022.901331
4. Mortaza, N., et al.: Are the spatio-temporal parameters of gait capable of distinguishing a faller from a non-faller elderly? Eur. J. Phys. Rehabil. Med. **39**(1), 118–122 (2014)
5. Tong, J., et al.: Severity classification of Parkinson's disease based on permutation-variable importance and persistent entropy. Appl. Sci. **11**(4), 1531 (2021). https://doi.org/10.3390/app11041834
6. Yan, Y., et al.: Classification of neurodegenerative diseases via topological motion analysis - a comparison study for multiple gait fluctuations. IEEE Access **8**, 100278–100288 (2020)
7. Mishra, C., et al.: Topological gait analysis: a new framework and its application to the study of human gait. IEEE J. Biomed. Health Inform. **28**(1), 123–134 (2024). https://doi.org/10.1109/JBHI.2024.3427700

8. Phinyomark, A., Petri, G., Ibáñez-Marcelo, E., Osis, S.T., Ferber, R.: Analysis of big data in gait biomechanics: current trends and future directions. J. Med. Biol. Eng. **38**(2), 244–260 (2017). https://doi.org/10.1007/s40846-017-0297-2

9. Karan, A., et al.: Time series classification via topological data analysis. Expert Syst. Appl. (2021). https://arxiv.org/pdf/2102.01956

10. Jeon, E., et al.: Robustness of topological persistence in knowledge distillation for wearable sensor data. EPJ Data Sci. (2024). https://doi.org/10.1140/epjds/s13688-024-00512-y

11. Zia, A., et al.: Topological deep learning: a review of an emerging paradigm. Artif. Intell. Rev. (2024). https://doi.org/10.48550/arXiv.2302.03836

12. Alharthi, A.S., et al.: Deep learning for monitoring of human gait: a review. IEEE Sens. J. **19**(21), 9575–9591 (2019). https://doi.org/10.1109/JSEN.2019.2928777

13. Bautmans, I., et al.: Reliability and clinical correlates of 3D-accelerometry based gait analysis outcomes according to age and fall-risk. Gait Posture (2011). https://doi.org/10.1016/j.gaitpost.2010.12.003

14. Adamowicz, L., et al.: SciKit digital health: python package for streamlined wearable inertial sensor data processing. JMIR mHealth uHealth e36762 (2022). https://doi.org/10.2196/36762

Towards Efficient Wearable Monitoring of Cognitive Fatigue in Human-Robot Interaction: A Comparative Study of ECG and EDA Signals

Krishna Kodur[(✉)] , Manizheh Zand , and Maria Kyrarini

Department of Electrical and Computer Engineering, Santa Clara University, Santa Clara, CA 95053, USA
{kkodur,mzand,mkyrarini}@scu.edu

Abstract. Wearable sensing technologies offer promising solutions for unobtrusive, continuous monitoring of cognitive fatigue (CF) during human–robot interaction (HRI). This paper presents a novel dataset collected from wearable electrocardiography (ECG) and electrodermal activity (EDA) sensors during collaborative HRI tasks and evaluates their effectiveness for low, medium, and high CF classification. Physiological features were extracted from both modalities and used to train supervised machine learning models. The best-performing model, a Gradient Boosting Machine (GBM), achieved a mean accuracy of 95.86% and an F1 score of 95.75%, demonstrating strong sensitivity across all fatigue levels. ECG-based features were particularly discriminative, while combining ECG with EDA offered slight gains in robustness, especially for medium fatigue detection. These results highlight the feasibility of using lightweight wearable sensors for accurate CF assessment and support their integration into fatigue-aware, adaptive support systems for assistive robotics. This work contributes to the growing field of wearable cognitive state monitoring.

Keywords: Cognitive Fatigue · Human–Robot Interaction · Wearable Computing · Physiological Sensing · Gradient Boosting · Machine Learning · Activity Recognition

List of Abbreviations

ADL	Activities of Daily Living
CF	Cognitive Fatigue
ECG	Electrocardiography
EDA	Electrodermal Activity
GBM	Gradient Boosting Machine Classifier
GSR	Galvanic Skin Response
HF	High Frequency

Ö. Durmaz Incel et al. (Eds.): iWOAR 2025, LNCS 16292, pp. 172–184, 2026.
https://doi.org/10.1007/978-3-032-13312-0_10

HR	Heart Rate
HRI	Human-Robot Interaction
HRV	Heart Rate Variability
IRB	Institutional Review Board
LF	Low Frequency
LF/HF	Ratio of (Low Frequency) to (High Frequency)
NASA-TLX	NASA Task Load Index
pNN50	Number of adjacent NN intervals which differ by more than 50 ms
QT	Interval time between the Q wave and the T wave on an electrocardiogram (ECG)
RF	Random Forest Classifier
rMSSD	Root Mean Square of the Successive Differences between RR intervals, where an RR interval is the time between two consecutive R-wave peaks on the ECG
SCL	Skin Conductance Level
SCR	Skin Conductance Response
SD	Standard Deviation
SD1	Standard deviation of the short-term instantaneous beat-to-beat RR interval variability, measured perpendicular to the line-of-identity in a Poincaré plot of RR intervals.
SD2	Standard deviation of the long-term continuous RR interval variability, measured along the line-of-identity in the Poincaré plot.
SDNN	Standard Deviation of NN Intervals where NN intervals is the time between normal-to-normal R-wave peaks
SVM	Support Vector Machine Classifier
T wave	Repolarization of the heart's ventricles
VAS-F	Visual Analogue Scale for Fatigue

1 Introduction

Cognitive Fatigue (CF) is a dynamic neurophysiological state marked by reduced attentional capacity, slowed thinking, and increased error susceptibility [1]. In human–robot interaction (HRI), particularly in assistive and collaborative settings, unaddressed CF can impair performance and compromise user safety [2,3]. Continuous CF estimation is therefore essential for enabling adaptive robotic systems that respond intelligently to users' cognitive states.

While questionnaires like the Visual Analogue Scale for Fatigue (VAS-F) [4] and NASA Task Load Index (NASA-TLX) [5] offer validated insights, they rely on self-reporting and are unsuitable for real-time applications [1]. In contrast, physiological signals offer an objective and scalable alternative. Wearable sensors, such as Electrocardiography (ECG) and Galvanic Skin Response (GSR), also known as Electrodermal Activity (EDA), are non-invasive and capture autonomic nervous system activity with high temporal resolution. ECG-derived Heart Rate Variability (HRV) reflects parasympathetic and sympathetic modulation, while EDA quantifies sympathetic arousal through skin conductance responses [6,7].

Previous work on physiological CF detection has largely focused on binary classification (fatigued vs. non-fatigued) [2,8]. However, CF exists on a spectrum, and coarse binary models often miss intermediate states that are critical for adaptive Human-Robot Interaction (HRI) systems [1]. This work presents a supervised learning framework to classify CF into three levels: low, medium, and high using wearable ECG and EDA data collected during collaborative Activities of Daily Living (ADL)s. We extract time, frequency, and event based domain features and evaluate model performance across standard classification metrics. Our aim is to identify effective sensing and modeling strategies for continuous CF monitoring in HRI environments.

2   Related Work

Wearable biosensors have become integral to CF monitoring, offering real-time, objective insights into user state during task execution [1,6]. ECG and EDA are particularly popular due to their non-invasiveness and responsiveness to cognitive and affective load [9,10]. HRV features derived from ECG reflect autonomic nervous system regulation [7], while EDA measures sympathetic arousal [6]. These modalities have demonstrated strong performance in CF detection, especially in binary classification settings [2].

However, CF is not binary; it fluctuates continuously. Binary models, while common, limit the resolution necessary for adaptive systems [1]. Multiclass approaches provide a more granular view of CF states. Cos *et al.* achieved over 95% F1-score using a three-class (No Fatigue, Fatigue, Severe Fatigue) model with ECG, EDA, and respiration [6], while Tjolleng *et al.* used ECG-derived features to classify workload levels in driving tasks [8]. However, these studies were not conducted in the context of HRI and instead took place in controlled lab environments using short, static tasks visible on the screen (e.g., the Stroop test, arithmetic), which limits their applicability to real-world interaction scenarios.

Despite recent advances, physiological CF detection in HRI remains under-explored. Most prior work uses simulated or constrained tasks [1]. For example, Rajavenkatanarayanan *et al.* used ECG and EDA to classify cognitive load during collaborative assembly [2], while Kanal *et al.* studied fatigue in rehabilitation robotics, with a focus on physical fatigue [3].

In contrast to prior work, which has largely focused on controlled laboratory settings with brief, artificial tasks (e.g., the Stroop test, arithmetic), our study investigates CF in HRI environments. Previous studies, though effective in demonstrating high classification performance, such as Cos *et al.* achieving over 95% F1-score using ECG, EDA, and respiration [6], and Tjolleng *et al.* classifying workload levels in driving tasks using ECG-derived features [8], do not generalize well to HRI environments.

Our work addresses this gap by evaluating CF during ADL with a robot across multiple sessions, introducing greater physiological and behavioral variability. This setup enables a more realistic assessment of fatigue in assistive HRI.

Additionally, we compare three signal configurations: ECG-only, EDA-only, and combined ECG+EDA, to assess the effectiveness of each modality for real-time CF monitoring. Through multiclass classification, longitudinal data collection, and real-life task scenarios, our study contributes toward developing fatigue-aware robotic systems capable of detecting cognitive states.

3   Experimental Setup

This study builds upon the protocol established in our earlier work [11], which involved a multimodal cognitive fatigue assessment framework in semi-naturalistic HRI contexts. The workspace where the participants will be interacting with the robot is shown in Fig. 1.

Fig. 1. Workspace Setup

Sixteen participants completed assistive ADL scenarios across multiple visits, including cooking and getting ready for work scenarios and involving a 2-back cognitive task. The study duration was up to 2 h. To induce varying levels of CF, depending on the session, N-back tasks were included in the session to induce CF. Fatigue ground truth was assigned based on the VAS-F scale, administered both before and after the activity.

Wearable physiological data were collected using the Biosignalsplux platform [12], capturing synchronized ECG and EDA signals via chest and wrist sensors, respectively. Data streams were recorded continuously and later segmented into analysis windows annotated with CF class labels: *low* (VAS-F < 35), *medium* ($35 \leq$ VAS-F ≤ 70), and *high* (VAS-F > 70). All sessions were conducted in a home-like laboratory environment, with ethical approval and informed consent obtained from all participants, Institutional Review Board (IRB): 2022-0549.1.

4   Data Processing

Throughout the entire study duration, ECG and EDA signals are collected continuously, and VAS-F scores are collected intermittently. The physiological signals are sampled at a frequency of 1000 Hz. Since VAS-F scores are collected intermittently, linear interpolation is applied to align them temporally, ensuring that each ECG and EDA reading is associated with a corresponding VAS-F score.

To prepare the data for analysis, the raw ECG and EDA signals undergo preprocessing to remove noise and artifacts, as detailed in [11]. Once the signals are cleaned, features are extracted using a sliding window approach. Specifically, a 45-second segment of ECG and EDA data is analyzed, and the window is advanced by 5.625 s to generate the next segment. Within each 45-second window, the average of all VAS-F scores is computed and used to represent the fatigue level corresponding to that segment.

From each 45-second segment, a set of features is extracted from the ECG signals. These include Root Mean Square of the Successive Differences between RR intervals, where an RR interval is the time between two consecutive R-wave peaks on the ECG (rMSSD), Standard Deviation of NN Intervals where NN intervals is the time between normal-to-normal R-wave peaks (SDNN), Number of adjacent NN intervals which differ by more than 50 ms (pNN50), HRV, Heart Rate (HR) min, mean, and max, as well as the time between the Q wave and the T wave on an electrocardiogram (ECG) (QT Interval), Repolarization of the heart's ventricles (T wave) amplitude, Standard deviation of the short-term instantaneous beat-to-beat RR interval variability, measured perpendicular to the line-of-identity in a Poincaré plot of RR intervals. (SD1), Standard deviation of the long-term continuous RR interval variability, measured along the line-of-identity in the Poincaré plot. (SD2), SD1/SD2, Low Frequency (LF), High Frequency (HF), and Ratio of (Low Frequency) to (High Frequency) (LF/HF). These features capture various aspects of heart rate variability and cardiac dynamics.

In parallel, a comprehensive set of features is also extracted from the EDA signals. These include the Number of Skin Conductance Response (SCR) peaks, Mean amplitude of SCR peaks, and SCR min, mean, and max height. Additional features are derived from the Skin Conductance Level (SCL) Tonic component, including its standard deviation (Standard Deviation (SD)), the standard deviation of its first derivative, as well as the skewness and kurtosis of this derivative.

Furthermore, the area under the SCL Tonic curve and the minimum, mean, and maximum of its second derivative are computed. Other features include the mean of EDA autocorrelation, the mean number of zero crossings in the SCR Phasic signal, and their standard deviation. A detailed description of all extracted features can be found in [11].

Using the ECG and EDA features extracted from each 45-second segment, machine learning models are then trained to classify the corresponding segment into one of three fatigue levels: low, medium, or high. The methodology and results of this classification task are elaborated in the next section.

5 Classification Model and Evaluation

To evaluate the feasibility of wearable physiological monitoring for real-time cognitive fatigue (CF) detection, we developed a multiclass classification model using features extracted from ECG and EDA signals. Fatigue levels were categorized into three classes—low, medium, and high—based on participants' self-reported scores from the VAS-F. Three machine learning models were trained to classify the fatigue level: Random Forest Classifier (RF), Support Vector Machine Classifier (SVM), Gradient Boosting Machine Classifier (GBM). To train the machine learning models used in this study, Scikit-Learn [13] version 1.7.1 was employed. A random seed of 42 was used throughout to ensure reproducibility. The following subsections provide details on any non-default parameters used during model training. Unless explicitly stated, all parameters should be assumed to retain their default values as defined in the specified version of the library. The RF Classifier was configured with the hyperparameters "n_estimators" set to 500 and criterion set to "log_loss". Similarly, the GBM Classifier was trained using the hyperparameters "n_estimators" set to 500, "learning_rate" set to 0.01, and "max_depth" set to 10.

Additionally, we employed stratified 3-fold cross-validation [14] to maintain class balance across splits, and model performance was assessed using standard classification metrics: accuracy, precision, recall, and F1 score as shown in Table 1. To examine the contribution of different physiological signals, models were trained under three configurations: using combined ECG and EDA features, ECG-only features, and EDA-only features.

Table 1. Average K-Fold Classification Metrics for RF, SVM, and GBM Models Using Combined ECG+EDA, ECG-Only, and EDA-Only Features

	ECG + EDA				ECG only				EDA Only			
	Accuracy (%)	Precision (%)	Recall (%)	F1 (%)	Accuracy (%)	Precision (%)	Recall (%)	F1 (%)	Accuracy (%)	Precision (%)	Recall (%)	F1 (%)
Random Forest Classifier	86.07	91.24	86.07	85.52	**94.46**	94.51	**94.46**	**94.02**	82.54	89.38	82.54	81.20
Support Vector Machine Classifier	85.71	88.01	85.71	85.41	93.35	93.87	93.35	93.23	79.74	79.72	79.74	78.27
Gradient Boosting Machine Classifier	**95.86**	**96.09**	**95.86**	**95.75**	93.65	**95.28**	93.65	93.35	**89.30**	**91.67**	**89.30**	**88.44**

5.1 Combined ECG and EDA Features

Among the combined ECG–EDA models, the GBM classifier consistently delivered the best performance. In particular, GBM achieved the highest overall accuracy (95.86%) and F1-score across all three fatigue levels, with very few instances of any class being misclassified (see Table 2). The SVM model also performed competitively, correctly classifying the vast majority of medium-fatigue samples and a substantial fraction of high-fatigue samples, resulting in strong sensitivity for these levels (as shown in Table 2). RF model, while its overall accuracy was slightly lower (86.07%), strongly predicted low and medium fatigue. Its consistency, interpretability, and computational efficiency make GBM an attractive choice for continuous wearable deployment.

Table 2. K-Fold Averaged Confusion Matrix for RF, SVM, GBM models when trained on ECG+EDA features

	RF			SVM			GBM		
Actual ↓/Predicted →	Low	Medium	High	Low	Medium	High	Low	Medium	High
Low	3335.33	85	0	3342.33	78	0	3390.67	27.67	2
Medium	119	2718	0	135	2506	196	138.33	2698.33	0.33
High	20.67	730.67	732.67	1.33	916.33	566.33	23.33	70.67	1390

5.2 ECG-Only Features

Further evaluations were conducted using ECG-only data across the three classifiers (RF, SVM, GBM). The K-Fold averaged confusion matrices are presented in Table 3. The RF classifier achieved the highest overall accuracy (94.46%), recall (94.46%), and F1-score (94.02%), driven by its strong recall across all fatigue levels. Notably, it correctly identified all high-fatigue cases and showed minimal confusion between medium and low classes. GBM slightly outperformed RF in precision (95.28% vs. 94.51%), as reflected in its lower false-positive rates for medium and high classes. This aligns with GBM 's strengths in error correction but also its tendency to overfit. SVM, while slightly less accurate, it maintained a balanced classification profile, with reasonable sensitivity across fatigue states. Overall, RF's robustness, interpretability, and efficiency make it well-suited for continuous ECG-based fatigue monitoring, while GBM's precision may be preferred in applications where false alarms are costlier.

Table 3. K-Fold Averaged Confusion Matrix for RF, SVM, GBM models when trained on ECG features

Actual ↓/Predicted →	RF			SVM			GBM		
	Low	Medium	High	Low	Medium	High	Low	Medium	High
Low	3341	79.33	0	3396.67	23.67	0	3411.33	9	0
Medium	280.33	2556.67	0	261.67	2460.33	115	288	2547.67	1.33
High	94	0	1390	60.33	35.33	1388.33	92.67	2	1389.33

5.3 EDA-Only Features

To assess the effectiveness of unimodal EDA signals for CF detection, models were evaluated under consistent preprocessing and partitioning conditions. The K-Fold averaged confusion matrices are shown in Table 4. Among the three classifiers, GBM achieved the highest overall accuracy (89.30%), precision (91.64%), recall (89.30%), and F1-score (88.44%), with particularly strong performance in detecting high-fatigue states, correctly classifying over 1000 high-fatigue samples and minimizing confusion with medium fatigue. RF model performed competitively in detecting low and medium fatigue. SVM exhibited higher recall for the medium-fatigue category but showed increased misclassification of high-fatigue samples as medium, indicating reduced specificity at higher arousal levels. These results suggest that while EDA alone is a viable input modality, its predictive power is enhanced when used with a robust classifier such as GBM, which is better suited to handling noisy and overlapping physiological signal patterns.

Table 4. K-Fold Averaged Confusion Matrix for RF, SVM, GBM models when trained on EDA features

Actual ↓/Predicted →	RF			SVM			GBM		
	Low	Medium	High	Low	Medium	High	Low	Medium	High
Low	3368	89	0	3371	86	0	3398.67	58.33	0
Medium	183	2743.67	1	247.67	2410	270	220.33	2707.33	0
High	25.67	926.33	593.33	1	1260.67	283.67	35.33	493.33	1016.67

5.4 Results

As shown in Table 1, GBM consistently outperformed the RF across all metrics: accuracy, precision, recall, and F1-score, when using the combined ECG+EDA features and with EDA-only input. In contrast, for ECG-only input, RF achieved higher accuracy and recall, while GBM yielded superior precision and F1-score.

This performance pattern is consistent with known differences in how these ensemble methods handle data complexity and noise. GBM's sequential learning process enables it to capture complex, nonlinear interactions across multimodal features, making it particularly effective in fusing complementary signals such as ECG and EDA [15,16]. Its focus on iteratively correcting classification errors allows it to emphasize subtle physiological variations, thereby improving overall classification quality [17].

In contrast, ECG signals are typically more susceptible to noise and variability, and RF's bagging strategy provides a natural resistance to overfitting in such settings [18]. RF's ensemble of decorrelated trees stabilizes predictions and enhances generalization when only ECG data are available. This explains its higher recall and accuracy in the ECG-only condition.

However, GBM's targeted focus on misclassified instances allows it to minimize false positives, which leads to higher precision and F1-score even when its recall is slightly lower. This balance is especially valuable in clinical or assistive settings, where false positives can be costly. Thus, while RF benefits from its robustness in unimodal noisy conditions, GBM offers superior discrimination in both multimodal and precision-sensitive contexts.

6   Discussion

The classification results (Table 1) reveal clear patterns in model performance that carry important implications for sensor and model selection in wearable HRI applications. In the multimodal setting (combined ECG+EDA), the GBM classifier achieved the highest accuracy, precision, recall, and F1-score, outperforming both the RF and SVM across all metrics. A similar advantage for GBM is observed with EDA-only input, where its ability to handle the noisier, lower-discriminative EDA features enabled superior performance compared to the other models. These findings highlight GBM's strength in multimodal scenarios, suggesting that boosting-based models can effectively fuse complementary physiological signals and extract subtle patterns that might be missed by other classifiers. In contrast, for the unimodal ECG-only input, the RF slightly surpassed GBM in overall accuracy and recall (both around 93.65%), indicating that RF may generalize better from a single sensing modality. This can be attributed to RF's bagging ensemble mechanism, which effectively averages out noise and prevents overfitting when modeling the inherently variable ECG signals. By aggregating predictions from many decorrelated trees, the RF provides a stable decision boundary, thereby achieving higher sensitivity (recall) and overall accuracy in the ECG-only condition.

Notably, the GBM still maintained a slight edge in precision for ECG-only data, achieving a higher precision (95.28%) than RF (94.56%) in our experiments. This outcome aligns with GBM's focus on iteratively correcting misclassifications, a strategy that tends to reduce false positives. In practice, GBM's targeted error-correction minimizes spurious fatigue detections, yielding a higher precision (and consequently a strong F1-score) even if its recall is marginally lower than RF's. This precision-oriented advantage is valuable in wearable HRI contexts where false alarms (false positive fatigue alerts) could lead to unnecessary or disruptive interventions. In such assistive settings, a classifier that errs on the side of precision can enhance user trust and system efficiency by triggering responses (e.g., adaptive support or alerts) only when the confidence in fatigue detection is high. On the other hand, RF's higher recall with ECG-only input means it is slightly more sensitive to detecting fatigue cases, which might be preferable if missing a true high-fatigue event is deemed more critical than a false alarm. Thus, the choice between GBM and RF may be guided by the specific balance between precision and recall desired in the application, though both ensembles demonstrated robust performance with physiological data. Importantly, the consistently superior metrics of GBM in multimodal and EDA-only scenarios, combined with its competitive ECG-only performance, suggest that boosting methods are well-suited for capturing complex nonlinear relationships in multimodal wearable data, whereas bagging methods like RF excel in single-modality scenarios by capitalizing on their noise-averaging effect.

From a sensing perspective, our results underscore that ECG is a more informative modality for cognitive fatigue classification than EDA alone, as evidenced by higher baseline accuracy and F1 scores with ECG-based features. This is consistent with the known sensitivity of heart rate variability measures to changes in cognitive fatigue. Nevertheless, the modest gains observed by combining ECG and EDA (especially in improving the detection of medium fatigue levels) indicate that there are complementary physiological signatures in EDA that can bolster overall robustness. For designers of wearable fatigue-monitoring systems, this finding suggests that, if hardware and ergonomics permit, a multimodal setup (including both cardiac and electrodermal sensors) paired with a powerful classifier, such as GBM, will provide the most reliable performance. Such a configuration leverages the strength of GBM to integrate multi-sensor data, yielding high accuracy and robustness to varying fatigue levels. On the other hand, if system constraints limit the sensing to a single modality, an ECG-based solution would be the priority given its superior discriminative power; in this case, an ensemble model such as RF could be advantageous to ensure generalization under ECG's noisier conditions.

Additionally, our experiments found that the SVM consistently underperformed across all feature configurations (ECG+EDA, ECG-only, and EDA-only), with substantially lower metrics compared to both RF and GBM. This result can be explained by the inherent limitations of SVMs on high-dimensional, nonlinear physiological data: the physiological feature space is rife with artifacts, inter-subject variability, and overlapping class distributions, which challenge the assumptions of margin-based classifiers. Without extensive tuning of kernel functions and regularization, the SVM struggled to separate the three fatigue classes, especially in a noisy multi-class setting. In contrast, the tree-based ensembles demonstrated a resilience to noise and variability, owing to their structural averaging and error-correcting properties. The superior performance of RF and GBM across our experiments thus reinforces the suitability of ensemble learning for wearable sensor data, echoing ensemble theory that combining multiple learners can model complex patterns while smoothing out idiosyncratic noise.

In summary, the updated classification results highlight that *(i)* leveraging multiple physiological signals with an advanced ensemble model (GBM) yields the best overall accuracy and reliability for fatigue detection, and *(ii)* even with a single modality, careful model selection (favoring noise-resistant ensembles like RF or GBM) can achieve high performance. These insights are significant for the development of fatigue-aware intelligent systems in HRI. They suggest a clear path forward: integrate multimodal wearables when possible and employ ensemble classifiers to robustly interpret the data. By doing so, future cognitive fatigue monitoring systems can more accurately and promptly gauge user states, enabling adaptive robotic behaviors that enhance safety and efficacy in long-term human–robot collaboration.

7   Conclusion and Future Work

Our experimental results demonstrate that physiological signal-based classifiers can effectively detect cognitive fatigue (CF) in a continuous manner. For both combined ECG+EDA inputs and EDA-only inputs, the GBM classifier achieved the highest performance across all evaluated metrics (accuracy, precision, recall, and F1-score), outperforming the other models. With ECG-only data, RF slightly outperformed GBM in terms of accuracy, recall, and F1-score, whereas GBM maintained a marginally higher precision. In contrast, the support vector machine (SVM) consistently underperformed across all configurations, yielding the lowest accuracy and F1-scores. These findings confirm the viability of leveraging physiological signals (ECG and EDA) for CF monitoring. In particular, the superior results obtained by combining ECG and EDA modalities highlight the benefit of multimodal sensing: fusing complementary physiological signals produced more robust fatigue detection than any single modality alone. This multimodal approach is especially relevant for adaptive human-robot interaction (HRI), where a reliable, continuous assessment of the user's CF level can enable a robotic system to adjust its assistance or behavior dynamically, improving both safety and performance.

In future work, we aim to further enhance the system's accuracy and adaptability. First, we will explore ensemble modeling techniques (e.g., combining GBM, RF, and other classifiers) to exploit the complementary strengths of different algorithms and potentially boost overall performance. Second, we plan to incorporate temporal dynamics into the fatigue detection model: since CF evolves over time, utilizing time-series features or sequential models (such as recurrent neural networks) could allow the system to capture trends and changes in fatigue levels more effectively. Third, we intend to integrate context-aware adaptation into the monitoring framework. By accounting for situational factors (such as task difficulty or environment) and individual baseline differences, the system can adjust its predictions or decision thresholds to maintain accuracy across varying conditions. We anticipate that these enhancements will further improve the robustness and practical applicability of physiological signal-based CF monitoring in real-world, adaptive HRI scenarios.

Acknowledgements. This material is based upon work supported by the National Science Foundation under Grant 2226165. Any opinions, findings, conclusions, or recommendations expressed in this material are those of the author(s) and do not necessarily reflect the views of the National Science Foundation.

The authors would like to thank the user study participants for their time and feedback.

References

1. Kakhi, K., Jagatheesaperumal, S.K., Khosravi, A., Alizadehsani, R., Acharya, U.R.: Fatigue monitoring using wearables and AI: trends, challenges, and future opportunities. Comput. Biol. Med. **195**, 110461 (2025)
2. Rajavenkatanarayanan, A., Nambiappan, H.R., Kyrarini, M., Makedon, F.: Towards a real-time cognitive load assessment system for industrial human-robot cooperation. In: 29th IEEE International Conference on Robot and Human Interactive Communication, RO-MAN 2020, pp. 698–705 (2020)
3. Kanal, V., Brady, J., Nambiappan, H., Kyrarini, M., Wylie, G., Makedon, F.: Towards a serious game based human-robot framework for fatigue assessment. In: ACM International Conference Proceeding Series, pp. 527–532 (2020)
4. Shahid, A., Wilkinson, K., Marcu, S., Shapiro, C.M.: Visual analogue scale to evaluate fatigue severity (VAS-F). In: STOP, THAT and One Hundred Other Sleep Scales, pp. 399–402 (2011)
5. Hart, S.G., Staveland, L.E.: Development of NASA-TLX (task load index): results of empirical and theoretical research. Adv. Psychol. **52**, 139–183 (1988)
6. Cos, C. A., Lambert, A., Soni, A., Jeridi, H., Thieulin, C., Jaouadi, A.: Enhancing mental fatigue detection through physiological signals and machine learning using contextual insights and efficient modelling. J. Sens. Actuator Netw. **12**, 77 (2023)
7. Butkevičiūtė, E., Michalkovič, A., Bikulčienė, L.: ECG signal features classification for the mental fatigue recognition. Mathematics **10**, 3395 (2022)
8. Tjolleng, A., et al.: Classification of a driver's cognitive workload levels using artificial neural network on ECG signals. Appl. Ergon. **59**, 326–332 (2017)
9. Shi, Y., Ruiz, N., Taib, R., Choi, E., Chen, F.: Galvanic skin response (GSR) as an index of cognitive load. In: Conference on Human Factors in Computing Systems - Proceedings, pp. 2651–2656 (2007)
10. Cinaz, B., Arnrich, B., Marca, R.L., Tröster, G.: Monitoring of mental workload levels during an everyday life office-work scenario. Pers. Ubiquitous Comput. **17**, 229–239 (2013)
11. Zand, M., Wylie, G.R., Wolfe, A., Kyrarini, M.: Automatic cognitive fatigue assessment using physiological sensors during human-robot interaction for activities of daily living. Authorea Preprints (2025)
12. Biosignals, P.: Plux biosignals. https://www.pluxbiosignals.com/. Accessed 06 Dec 2023
13. Buitinck, L., et al.: API design for machine learning software: experiences from the scikit-learn project. In: ECML PKDD Workshop: Languages for Data Mining and Machine Learning, pp. 108–122 (2013)
14. Nti, I.K., Nyarko-Boateng, O., Aning, J.: Performance of machine learning algorithms with different k values in k-fold crossvalidation. Int. J. Inf. Technol. Comput. Sci. **13**, 61–71 (2021)

15. Ke, G., et al.: Lightgbm: a highly efficient gradient boosting decision tree. In: Advances in Neural Information Processing Systems, vol. 30 (2017)
16. Chen, T., Guestrin, C.: Xgboost: a scalable tree boosting system. In: Proceedings of the ACM SIGKDD International Conference on Knowledge Discovery and Data Mining, vol. 13-17-August-2016, pp. 785–794 (2016)
17. Friedman, J.H.: Greedy function approximation: a gradient boosting machine. Ann. Stat. 1189–1232 (2001)
18. Breiman, L.: Random forests. Mach. Learn. **45**, 5–32 (2001)

Radar Placement Effects on Multi-patient Heart and Respiration Monitoring, SiViS Dataset Validation

Karla Miriam Reyes Leiva$^{(\boxtimes)}$, Ankit Gupta , and Martin Cerny

Faculty of electrical engineering and computer science, VSB Technical University of Ostrava, Ostrava, Czech Republic
{rey0014,ankit.gupta,martin.cerny}@vsb.cz

Abstract. Noncontact radar sensing offers a compelling solution for estimation and continuous monitoring of vital signs. Despite significant progress in single patient vital sign detection, estimations for multi patient scenarios using a single radar sensor remains challenging due to the need of disentangling the overlapping physiological signals from a single radar data cube. To address this challenge, this paper presents a technical validation of the SiViS dataset. Specifically, we validate the influence of radar placement on vital sign estimation and benchmark a reference two-stage signal processing pipeline (adaptive Minimum Variance Distortionless Response, MVDR, beamforming followed by phase-based estimation). The focus of this work is on dataset validation and characterization of placement effects, rather than proposing a novel algorithm for heart and respiration rate estimation. Our preliminary evaluations test the optimal radar position for estimation and demonstrated the feasibility of concurrently estimating these vital signs in a multi patient scenario, benchmarking our basic pipeline. In conclusion, this work advances the capability of single sensor radar systems from single patient to multi patient noncontact monitoring, thereby highlighting future directions for robust multi patient monitoring.

Keywords: multi patient radar sensing · MVDR beamforming · Heart rate · Respiration Rate

1 Introduction

Noncontact radar sensing has rapidly advanced from basic CW Doppler prototypes to sophisticated MIMO FMCW millimeter-wave systems capable of accurately measuring human cardiopulmonary activity across multiple patients, achieving simultaneous monitoring with up to four individuals [1]. Advanced configurations further estimate heart rate variability metrics with mean absolute errors below 2 bpm (beats per minute) in controlled conditions [2]. Ultrawideband radar surveys highlight continued innovations in array architectures and deep learning-based demodulation for robust vital sign detection across

Ö. Durmaz Incel et al. (Eds.): iWOAR 2025, LNCS 16292, pp. 185–195, 2026.
https://doi.org/10.1007/978-3-032-13312-0_11

diverse environments [3]. Recent reviews document machine learning pipelines that optimize signal processing and classification architectures, demonstrating median errors below 3% for heart rate (HR) and respiratory rate (RR) in single-patient benchmarks [4]. Benchmark datasets such as the Six Port radar heart sounds collection and newer multi-patient FMCW radar repositories provide raw IQ traces synchronized with ECG and respiratory belts, fostering algorithm development but remain limited in patient count or validation scope [5,6].

Despite these advances, most validated systems still assume one stationary patient, and their performance degrades when reflections from multiple targets overlap [7]. A few approaches address multi-patient scenarios employing sparsity-enhanced separation or fusion with optical imaging to achieve sub-5% error rates, yet they lack publicly available, standardized benchmarks and rigorous technical validation [8]. Moreover, a critical but often overlooked factor is the placement of the radar sensor itself. Distance, angle, and orientation strongly affect the received signal quality: oblique angles reduce Doppler sensitivity, near-field setups introduce coupling and multipath effects, and increased target distance reduces the effective radar cross section. While beamforming techniques, particularly Capon's Minimum Variance Distortionless Response (MVDR), can theoretically isolate angular arrivals under interference, experimental quantification of how placement influences multi-patient vital sign extraction remains scarce [9]. Thus, understanding the impact of radar location is essential for translating these systems into reliable clinical or home-monitoring deployments.

To bridge these gaps, we introduce the **Sivis Dataset Technical Validation**, which explicitly evaluates the influence of radar placement on multi-patient vital sign monitoring [15]. The contributions of this work are:

- A public, synchronized radar and reference dataset for up to three patients under varied spacing, postures, and sensor positions.
- A baseline two-stage signal processing pipeline consisting of adaptive MVDR beamforming and phase-based HR and RR extraction, serving as a reproducible benchmark rather than a novel algorithm.
- A systematic validation of how radar placement affects estimation accuracy, using correlation analyses and clinical error limit assessments.

2   Methodology

This work focuses on the technical validation of the SiVis Dataset for multiple reasons, such as testing the suitability of multi patient vital signs estimations from a single radar sensors for different clinical conditions; establishing benchmark standards; assessing signal fidelity; and identifying dataset limitations from the perspective of algorithm development. This section first provides an overview of the SiViS dataset, followed by proposing a signal processing pipeline for phase based vital sign estimations in different configurations (distance and angle based variations) of the multi patient settings.

2.1 SiViS DataSet

The SiViS dataset was developed in collaboration with Ostrava University Training Hospital to provide a comprehensive, reproducible benchmark for multi patient radar vital sign estimation. It comprises simultaneous recordings from two to three high fidelity SimMan® 3G PLUS mannequins, each programmed to exhibit one of twelve physiological states ranging from healthy resting (Respiration Rate (RR) = 14 rpm respiration per minute, Heart Rate (HR) = 80 bpm) to acute emergencies such as apnea (RR = 0 rpm), asthma attack (RR = 33 rpm, HR = 130 bpm), and cardiac arrest (HR = 160 bpm). The data was collected using two radar modalities: 1) TI IWR6843AOP FMCW mmWave radar (77–81 GHz, 3 TX × 4 RX) interfaced via DCA1000EVM, producing 16 bit complex samples at up to 1 Msps, and 2) Infineon XENSIV BGT60LTR11AIP Doppler radar (60 GHz, 1 TX × 1 RX) with 12 bit I/Q outputs at 2 kHz per frame. The raw IWR6843AOP outputs were stored as non interleaved .bin files (decoded to per antenna *CSV* for FAIR compliance), while BGT60LTR11AIP data were saved in header tagged *.txt* format. This organization ensures easy parsing of sensor parameters and ground truth synchronization for each multi patient scenario.

The data collection process involved simulating three experimental setups. The first set up (Area Set up) involved placing radar sensors in three different positions (top, frontal, lateral views; distances of 1–4 m; 0°/45° angles) with respect to the mannequins. Two mannequins were placed sideways in this setup, to assess the effect of spatial configurations on the accuracy of the estimations. The second setup involves the placement of two/three mannequins in TopFront positions (2 m and 4 m heights) under different clinical states A–L, to assess the impact of distances, and overlap of the physiological information (characterised by the presence of two or three patients) on the estimation accuracy. The third set up involved varying sensor parameters, such as varying chirp parameters on the IWR6843AOP (ADC samples: 64/128/256; chirps per loop: 32/64/128; frame periodicity: 24/40/60 ms; ramp times: 60/80 µs; gains: 30/40 dB; frequency slopes: 30/60 MHz/µs), for algorithms development and generalization.

2.2 Signal Processing

The SiViS dataset's raw radar recordings were first converted from interleaved binary to a four dimensional complex array (frames × receivers × chirps × samples) using a custom decoder based on TI's DCA1000 data format using Algorithm 1.

Algorithm 1. Decoding IWR6843 Raw Data (nonInterleaved Complex Format)

1: **Input:** binary file path P; receivers N_r; chirps per frame N_c; ADC samples per chirp N_a
2: **Output:** $\mathbf{X} \in \mathbb{C}^{N_f \times N_r \times N_c \times N_a}$
3: Read binary file P as int16 array $\mathbf{d}$
4: Reshape $\mathbf{d}$ to $[1, 2]$ and form complex samples: $\mathbf{c} \leftarrow \mathbf{d}[:, 0] + j\,\mathbf{d}[:, 1]$
5: $S \leftarrow N_r \times N_c \times N_a$
6: $N_f \leftarrow \mathrm{len}(\mathbf{c})/S$
7: Initialize $\mathbf{X}$ as complex array of shape $N_f \times N_r \times N_c \times N_a$
8: **for** $f = 0$ **to** $N_f 1$ **do**
9:     **for** $r = 0$ **to** $N_r 1$ **do**
10:         $s \leftarrow fS + r\,N_c N_a$
11:         $e \leftarrow s + N_c N_a$
12:         $\mathbf{y} \leftarrow \mathbf{c}[s : e]$
13:         Reshape $\mathbf{y}$ to $[N_c, N_a]$
14:         $\mathbf{X}[f, r, :, :] \leftarrow \mathbf{y}$
15:     **end for**
16: **end for**
17: **return** $\mathbf{X}$

Next, a fast time Fast Fourier Transform (FFT) is applied to each frame to generate range profiles, which are then transformed via. a spatial FFT into range–angle maps. Peaks in these maps patients to minimum physical separations in range and angle, are selected as candidate targets. For each detected reflector, an adaptive MVDR beamformer computes spatial filtering weights from the sample covariance matrix and a steering vector at the detected angles. Applying these weights yields one complex slow time series per target, effectively isolating each mannequin's chest movement signal from interference and clutter.

Once separated, the instantaneous phase of each slow time signal is unwrapped. Two band limited filters then extract physiological oscillations: Cardiac (0.8–3.0 Hz), and Respiratory (0.1–0.6 Hz) bands. From the cardiac band, the dominant spectral peak in this range gives the heart rate. On the other hand from the respiratory band (0.1–0.6 Hz), breathing cycles are identified via peak detection to compute the respiratory rate. Conclusively, the pipeline comprising the conjencture of adaptive beamforming and phase based demodulation, minimizes cross contamination between patients and reliably recovers heart and respiratory rates under realistic multi patient conditions. This pipeline is not intended as a novel algorithm but as a standardized, reproducible reference baseline to benchmark radar placement effects on vital sign estimation.

2.3   Data Evaluation

The validation of the dataset is analysed by computing mean quantitative metrics for different configurations mentioned in Sect. 2.1. The metrics used for performance analysis are root-mean-square error (RMSE), mean absolute error (MAE), bias, standard deviation of the error, and Lin's concordance correlation coefficient (CCC).

3   Results

As mentioned earlier, the SiViS dataset was collected using different configurations such as different distances, angles affecting subject positions. This section deals with presenting a quantitative analysis to assess the effect of sensor positioning on HR and RR estimations. The sensor position is defined in terms of sensor placement, sensor subject distances and angles. We assess the effect of radar sensors placed sideways at different distances and angles (Fig. 1), followed by presenting the similar analysis for frontal position of the radar sensors Fig. 2.

3.1   Side Position

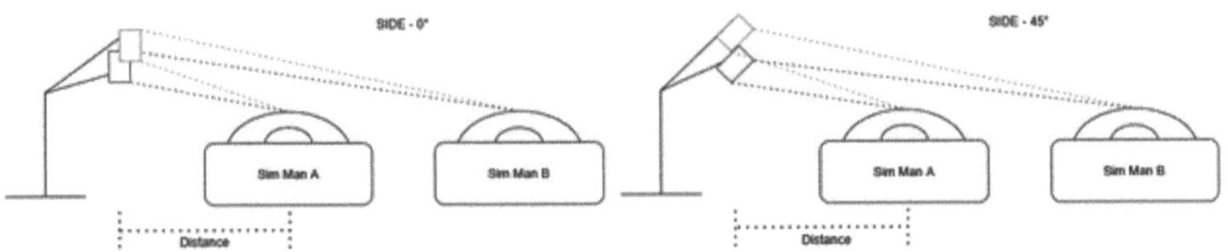

Fig. 1. Schematics of Side position

Table 1. Performance metrics for HR and RR estimation at different distances and angles in Side position.

Distance	Angle	Type	MAE (bpm/rpm)	RMSE (bpm/rpm)	Bias (bpm/rpm)	SD of Error
3 m	0°	HR	14.00	17.21	+14.00	14.14
		RR	0.56	0.70	+0.47	0.73
	45°	HR	38.00	46.05	−38.00	30.03
		RR	1.54	2.01	−1.52	1.53
2 m	0°	HR	29.00	3.50	−21.00	34.48
		RR	2.14	2.43	−1.79	1.91
	45°	HR	33.00	34.50	−33.00	11.50
		RR	4.21	5.30	−3.88	4.17
1 m	0°	HR	32.00	36.06	−32.00	23.78
		RR	1.81	2.01	−1.81	1.06
	45°	HR	12.00	14.14	+8.00	13.47
		RR	1.60	1.89	+1.60	1.16

HR estimation proved most accurate at the side 3 m position, where it exhibited a positive bias of 14 bpm (MAE = 14.0 bpm) but only moderate variability (CCC ≈ 0). In contrast, HR was severely underestimated at both 3 m/45° (−38bpm bias) and 1 m/0° (−32bpm bias), each with very wide limits of agreement and essentially no concordance. The smallest HR bias occurred at 1 m/45° (+8bpm), but scatter remained high (MAE = 12 bpm; CCC ≈ 0). Measurements at 2 m also performed poorly, with biases of −21 bpm (9°) and −33 bpm (45°) and poor agreement throughout. By comparison, RR estimation was far more robust: at 3 m/0° it achieved a negligible bias (+0.47 rpm) and strong concordance (CCC = 0.89), and only moderate underestimation (bias −1.5 to −1.8 rpm; CCC ≈ 0.2–0.3) at 3 m/45° and 1 m/0°. The greatest RR errors appeared at 2 m/45° (bias −3.9 rpm, RMSE = 5.3 rpm; CCC ≈ 0), indicating that, unlike HR, RR estimation is relatively insensitive to angle and distance except under the most extreme conditions (Table 1).

3.2 Frontal Position

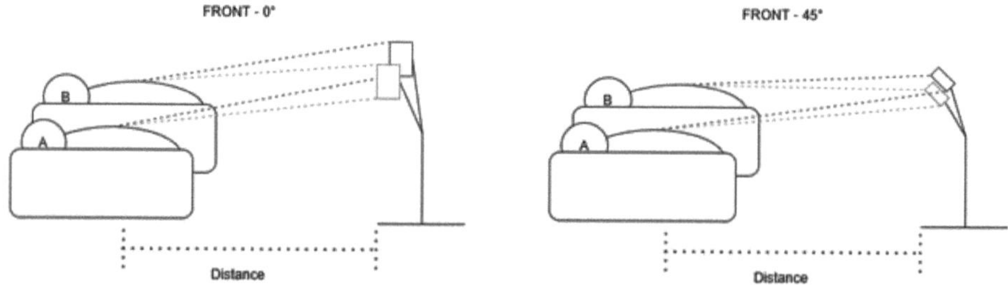

Fig. 2. Schematics of Frontal position

At the 3 m, 0° side position, HR estimates exhibited a MAE of 18.0 bpm and an RMSE of 21.0 bpm, with a systematic underestimation bias of −14.0 bpm and an SD of 18.0 bpm (CCC = 0.00). RR for the same geometry showed much smaller errors (MAE = 1.93 rpm, RMSE = 2.35 rpm), a modest bias of −0.98 rpm, and SD of 2.47 rpm (CCC = 0.00). Rotating to 45° at 3 m had negligible impact on HR accuracy (identical MAE/RMSE/bias/SD), whereas RR performance degraded slightly (MAE = 3.52 rpm, RMSE = 4.39 rpm, bias = −2.86 rpm, SD = 3.84 rpm; CCC = 0.00). This is an interesting finding, as RR errors are insensitive to the change of angles in the sideway positioning of radar sensors. This change in behavior is attributed to the smaller cross sectional area due to frontal placement of the radar, unlike sideways, where the radar sensor was fully aligned with the area near the diaphragm, offering relatively larger cross sectional area.

Moving closer to 1 m at 0°, HR underestimation intensified (MAE = 44.0 bpm, RMSE = 54.2 bpm; bias = −44.0 bpm; SD = 36.5 bpm), while RR error remained moderate (MAE =2.59 rpm, RMSE = 3.20 rpm; bias = −2.59 rpm; SD = 2.17 rpm). At 1 m/45°, HR bias flipped to +8.0 bpm (MAE = 12.0 bpm, RMSE = 14.1 bpm; SD = 13.5 bpm), and RR showed a small underestimation (MAE = 1.74 rpm, RMSE = 2.34 rpm; bias = −1.72 rpm; SD = 1.84 rpm).

Finally, at 2 m the pattern recurred: at 0° HR still suffered large underestimation (MAE = 35.0 bpm, RMSE = 44.8 bpm; bias = −27.0 bpm; SD = 41.2 bpm), whereas RR errors were small (MAE = 1.21 rpm, RMSE = 1.30 rpm; bias = −0.86 rpm; SD = 1.14 rpm). At 2 m/45°, HR bias lessened (MAE = 13.0 bpm, RMSE = 13.4 bpm; bias = −9.0 bpm; SD =11.5 bpm), but RR again showed moderate dispersion (MAE = 2.68 rpm, RMSE = 3.16 rpm; bias = −2.00 rpm; SD = 2.59 rpm).

Overall, while RR estimation remains within a few rpm error across all side-position configurations, HR estimation is highly sensitive to both distance and angle—exhibiting large systematic biases and wide variability except at 3 m directly in front. Higher sensitivity of HR estimations is due to higher variability of HR distributions, i.e. 50 180 bpm, unlike RR, where values range between 6 and 33 rpm for later. Additionally, periodic displacements caused by the RR have significantly higher magnitude than those caused by HR. Tracking chest displacement variations ranging between 0.2 and 0.5 mm caused by cardiac activity is comparatively challenging compared to variations (4 to 12 mm) caused by respiratory activity (Tables 2 and 3).

Table 2. Performance metrics for HR and RR estimation at different distances and angles in Frontal position

Distance	Angle	Type	MAE (bpm/rpm)	RMSE (bpm/rpm)	Bias (bpm/rpm)	SD of Error
3 m	0°	HR	18.00	20.98	−14.00	18.04
		RR	1.93	2.35	−0.98	2.47
	45°	HR	18.00	20.98	−14.00	18.04
		RR	3.52	4.39	−2.86	3.84
2 m	0°	HR	35.00	44.78	−27.00	41.23
		RR	1.21	1.30	−0.86	1.14
	45°	HR	13.00	13.42	−9.00	11.49
		RR	2.68	3.16	−2.00	2.59
1 m	0°	HR	44.00	54.20	−44.00	36.51
		RR	2.59	3.20	−2.59	2.17
	45°	HR	32.00	34.06	+8.00	13.45
		RR	1.74	2.34	−1.72	1.84

3.3 Top Position

Under the top-side and top-front views at 2 m/45°, HR estimations showed moderate underestimation (bias ≈ −20 bpm and −4 bpm, respectively) with MAE in the range 20–23 bpm and higher SD of > 22 bpm. RR estimates remained close to ground truth (MAE ≈ 4 rpm) with small biases (<1 rpm) but moderate variability (SD ≈ 5–6 rpm).

Table 3. Performance metrics for HR and RR estimation at different distances and angles in Top position.

Viewpoint	Distance	Angle	Type	MAE (bpm/rpm)	RMSE (bpm/rpm)	Bias (bpm/rpm)	SD of Error
Top-Side	2 m	45°	HR	23.15	29.54	−19.96	22.18
			RR	3.99	5.63	0.69	5.69
Top-Front	2 m	45°	HR	20.46	24.16	− 3.96	24.27
			RR	4.08	5.61	0.47	5.69
Top	4 m	0°	HR	28.89	36.17	−7.29	35.83
			RR	7.26	9.46	−1.07	9.50

For the case of three mannequins placed 4 m away from radar sensor, HR bias was −7.3 bpm (MAE ≈ 28.9 bpm, SD ≈ 35.8 bpm), while RR bias was −1.07 rpm (MAE ≈ 7.26 rpm, SD ≈ 9.50 rpm), indicating that increasing target count and distance modestly degrades accuracy and precision for both vital-sign estimations. The potential reason for this is that as the distance increases, the area of cross section decreases, which makes it challenging to capture all displacement variations, caused by cardiopulmonary activity. On the otherhand, increasing the number of subjects in the multi patient environment results in higher order of overlapping between the physiological signals of multiple subjects (Fig. 3).

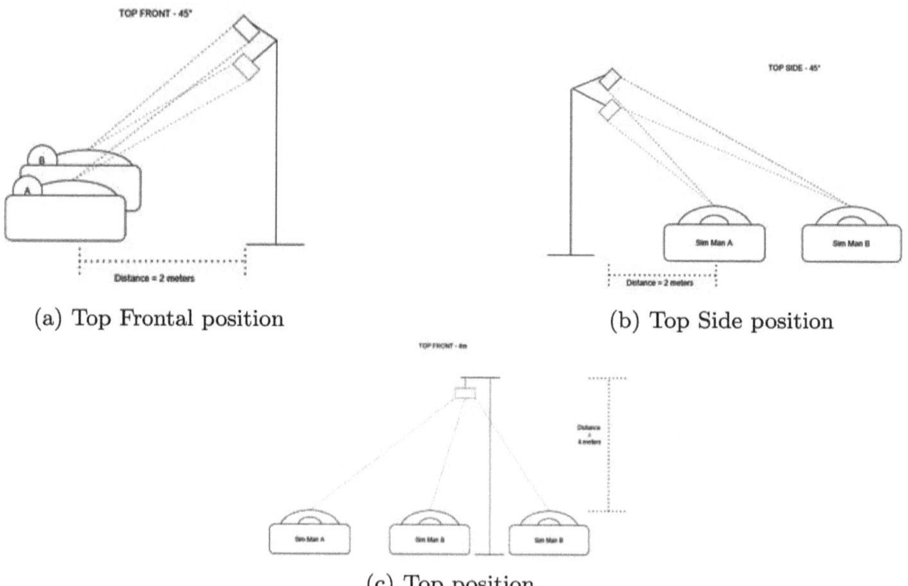

(a) Top Frontal position   (b) Top Side position

(c) Top position

Fig. 3. Schematics of radar placements from different viewpoints.

4 Discussion

The radar-based vital-sign estimation is highly sensitive to sensor placement, distance, and orientation. HR estimates were most accurate at a frontal 3 m, 0° position (MAE = 14 bpm), but exhibited large systematic errors and variability at nearer distances (1 m) or off-axis angles (45°), with MAE rising to 38 bpm and bias exceeding −38 bpm. At near field distances or oblique angles, the antenna beam covers a wider area and side lobes introduce additional reflections. These non ideal beam patterns reduce signal-to-noise ratio and create interference from non-target directions, degrading HR estimation [4]. Moreover, oblique angles introduce phase shifts and lower Doppler sensitivity, further impairing HR extraction [10].

In contrast, RR estimation remained comparatively robust across geometries, with MAE < 2 rpm at 3 m and CCC > 0.8 under frontal viewing. The slower periodic motion of the chest wall produces stronger, lower-frequency Doppler signatures that are less sensitive to beam misalignment [11]. However, RR errors grew under extreme angles or increased target count (e.g., top-side 2-mannequin at 2 m/45°, MAE ≈ 4 rpm), reflecting inter-target interference and overlapping micro-Doppler spectra [12]. Our overhead experiments further revealed that vertical views (top, top-side, top-front) can mitigate multipath clutter but introduce new blind spots depending on antenna elevation and mannequin arrangement [13]. In three-mannequin scenarios, HR MAE rose to 29 bpm at 4 m, 0°, while RR MAE reached 7 rpm, underscoring how target multiplicity degrades both signal separation and parameter estimation [14].

Radar placement must be optimized for the intended vital-sign: frontal, moderate-distance (2–3 m) installation yields acceptable HR and RR accuracy, whereas near-field or oblique mounting calls for advanced beamforming and interference-mitigation techniques. Our findings inform practical deployment in clinical and home settings, highlighting the trade-offs between coverage area and estimation fidelity.

Finally, a Lin's Concordance Correlation Coefficient (CCC) above 0.80 is generally considered to indicate strong agreement, with values below 0.40 regarded as weak or clinically unacceptable. In this study, while certain radar placements—particularly at 0° and 3 m—yield RR estimates within clinically acceptable MAE and CCC ranges, the HR estimation often deviates significantly in other rdar placements, with MAE exceeding 20 bpm and CCC values frequently approaching zero. In our study, RR estimates reached CCC = 0.89 in the optimal placement, but HR estimates often had CCC ≈ 0, indicating poor agreement despite seemingly low mean errors in some cases. This underscores the limitation of HR monitoring with current configurations.

5 Conclusion

In this work, we have presented the first comprehensive technical validation of the SiViS dataset for non contact, multi-patient vital sign monitoring using mmWave radars. By combining adaptive MVDR beamforming with phase based demodulation in a two stage pipeline, we have demonstrated that HR and RR estimates can be recovered even under challenging multi mannequin conditions. The study revealed that frontal, moderate-distance deployments (2–3 m, $0°$) achieve the best HR accuracy (MAE $\approx$ 14 bpm, CCC $\approx$ 0) and RR precision (MAE $<$ 0.6 rpm, CCC $\approx$ 0.9), while near field and oblique angles markedly degrade HR performance due to reduced beamforming gain and increased clutter. Our results demonstrate that respiration rate can be estimated within clinically acceptable error bounds in multi-patient scenarios under certain radar placements. However, heart rate estimation remains challenging: errors $>$20 bpm and CCC $\approx$ 0 in many conditions indicate that clinically viable HR monitoring requires improved beamforming, denoising, or sensor fusion. Thus, the SiViS dataset should primarily be considered a resource for developing and validating such advanced methods.

Acknowledgment. The author(s) declare that financial support was received for the research, authorship, and/or publication of this article. This article has been produced with the financial support of the European Union under the LERCO CZ.10.03.01/00/22_003/0000003 project via the Operational Programme Just Transition. The work and the contributions were supported by the project SP2025/032 Biomedical Engineering systems XXI.

References

1. Xue, S., Xu, Z., Wang, Y., Shi, J., Yucel, A.C.: Simultaneous multi person vital signs monitoring using multiple input multiple output FMCW millimeter wave radar. AEU Int. J. Electron. Commun. **2024**, 155578 (2024). https://doi.org/10.1016/j.aeue.2024.155578
2. Vignoli, E., Guerzoni, G., Vitetta, G.M.: A novel method for estimating heart rate variability through a multiple input multiple output FMCW radar. IEEE Access **12**, 178062–178079 (2024). https://doi.org/10.1109/ACCESS.2024.3507365
3. Cheraghinia, M., Luchie, S., Shahid, A., De Poorter, E.: UWB Radar Survey. arXiv preprint arXiv:2402.05649v3 [eess.SP], 26 Apr 2025. License: CC BY NC ND 4.0. https://arxiv.org/abs/2402.05649
4. Shirazi, M.H., Yongchareon, S., Singh, A., Ma, J.: A survey on machine learning approaches for vital sign monitoring using radar. Measurement **253**, Part D, 117707 (2025). https://doi.org/10.1016/j.measurement.2025.117707
5. Shi, K., Schellenberger, S., Will, C., et al.: A dataset of radar recorded heart sounds and vital signs including synchronised reference sensor signals. Sci. Data **7**, 50 (2020). https://doi.org/10.1038/s4159702003901
6. Lei, G., Cheng, W., Yin, X., Wu, Y.: The dataset of multi target vital signs monitored by FMCW radar. Data Brief **57**, 111027 (2024). https://doi.org/10.1016/j.dib.2024.111027. PMID: 39498155; PMCID: PMC11532813
7. Eder, Y., Eldar, Y.C.: Sparsity Based Non-Contact Vital Signs Monitoring of Multiple People Via FMCW Radar. arXiv preprint arXiv:2205.05152 [eess.SP] (2022). https://doi.org/10.48550/arXiv.2205.05152

8. Wang, C., Hu, X., Yang, X., Chang, W., Cao, G.: Multi-target vital signs detection by fusing radar and optical images. In: Proceedings of the Third International Conference on Algorithms, Microchips, and Network Applications (AMNA 2024), Proc. SPIE **13171**, 131710X (2024). https://doi.org/10.1117/12.3032020

9. Ahmed, S., Park, J., Cho, S.H.: Effects of receiver beamforming for vital sign measurements using FMCW radar at various distances and angles. Sensors **22**(18), 6877 (2022). https://doi.org/10.3390/s22186877

10. Ishrak, M.S., Cai, F., Islam, S.M.M., Borić-Lubecke, O., Wu, T., Lubecke, V.M.: Doppler radar remote sensing of respiratory function. Front. Physiol. **14**, 1130478 (2023). https://doi.org/10.3389/fphys.2023.1130478. PMID: 37179837; PMCID: PMC10172641

11. Hao, Z., Wang, Y., Li, F., Ding, G., Gao, Y.: mmWave-RM: a respiration monitoring and pattern classification system based on mmWave radar. Sensors **24**, 4315 (2024). https://doi.org/10.3390/s24134315

12. Yu, J., Zhang, J., Li, Z., Zhou, Y., Geng, Y.: Multi-person micro-doppler signal decomposition based on millimeter wave radar. In: Proceedings of the Fifteenth International Conference on Signal Processing Systems (ICSPS 2023), Proc. SPIE **13091**, 130910W (2024). https://doi.org/10.1117/12.3023198

13. Yin, M., et al.: Unobtrusive sleep health assessment using impulse radar: a pilot study in older people. IEEE Trans. Biomed. Eng. (2025). https://doi.org/10.1109/TBME.2025.3548780. Epub ahead of print. PMID: 40048348

14. Parajuli, H.N., Bakhtiyarov, G., Nakarmi, B., Ukaegbu, I.A.: Interference mitigation in multi-radar environment using LSTM-based recurrent neural network. In: Proceedings of the International Conference on Intelligent Human Computer Interaction (IHCI 2023). Lecture Notes in Computer Science (LNCS), vol. 14532, pp. 151–161. Springer, Cham (2024). https://doi.org/10.1007/978-3-031-55529-8_13

15. Reyes Leiva, K.M., Gupta, A., Grosmaire, A., Cerny, M.: SiViS - simulated multi-patient physiological clinical states. Harvard Dataverse (2025). https://doi.org/10.7910/DVN/S9SNAK

Scenario-Controlled Synthetic Data Augmentation: In Application of Agitation Monitoring

Ali Najem[1,2], Jan Kleine Deters[2(✉)], Mehdi Sedighi[2],
and Heinrich Wörtche[2]

[1] Master: Smart Systems Engineering, Hanze University of Applied Sciences, 9747
AS Groningen, The Netherlands
[2] Sensors and Smart Systems Group, Institute of Engineering, Hanze University of
Applied Sciences, 9747 AS Groningen, The Netherlands
{ja.kleine.deters,m.sedighi,h.j.wortche}@pl.hanze.nl

Abstract. Reinforcement learning offers a promising approach for personalized, early-stage detection of behavioral events such as agitation in individuals with dementia, particularly when contextual insights from care staff are integrated. Given the scarcity and the ethical constraints of real-world agitation data, training an early-stage detection model in such an approach can be done using synthetic data, by training models with variational simulated scenarios. Therefore, we propose a proof-of-concept scenario-controlled synthetic data augmentation pipeline. The pipeline is designed to translate textual scenario descriptions into synthetic sensor data, using text to structure translations, activity classification, features extraction, and generative models. The system is trained with multi-modal sensor data including accelerometer, blood volume pulse, electrodermal activity, and skin temperature. The system makes use of an activity classification model, trained with the Capture-24 dataset by making use of the accelerometer data, to define the scenario conditions for the generative models. The system effectively generated synthetic data for accelerometer signals, while the remaining three sensors require further improvement. Future work will explore sensor-semantic and human-semantic representation alignment, sensor specific temporal modeling, causal feature learning and improved high-level control. This will enable training models with human feedback to achieve early-stage detection of agitation.

Keywords: Dementia · Agitation · Simulation · Synthetic Data · Conditional Generative Modeling

1 Introduction

Worldwide, more than 55 million people are living with dementia [1], and projections exceed 130 million by 2050 [2]. As prevalence rises, overall care needs

O. Durmaz Incel et al. (Eds.): iWOAR 2025, LNCS 16292, pp. 196–221, 2026.
https://doi.org/10.1007/978-3-032-13312-0_12

increase while available clinical time per person declines. This imbalance contributes to further worsening delayed and reactive dementia care management, which is partly driven by time constraints [3]. Behavioural issues are prevalent in people with dementia, of which agitation is one of the most common symptoms [4,5]. Agitation can function as nonverbal communication [6] and contributes to caregiver burden and depression [7], particularly when it manifests as resistiveness to care [8]. Therefore, it can potentially become a negative feedback loop, and thus early-stage detection will benefit both the person with dementia and their caregiver. Detection is complicated as behavioural patterns vary across individuals [9] in type, frequency, and severity. However, agitation is well suited for sensor-based monitoring due to its observable and measurable nature [10].

Existing behavioural assessment tools can be time-consuming [11] and are not optimised for detecting agitation [12]. This motivates sensor-based approaches that reduce time and burden on caregivers. Pilot studies now deploy IoT sensors in nursing homes, and recent models can detect agitation from sensor data [13–16].

Recent research has explored the integration of human Digital Twins (DTs) in healthcare to address diverse needs, including personalized health monitoring, athletic performance tracking, and elderly care [17–21]. Human-related data have been categorized into external, physiological, behavioral, social, and environmental domains to guide effective modeling and analysis [19,20]. In the context of dementia care, Kleine Deters et al. [22] designed a DT framework to monitor challenging behaviors in people with dementia using parameters such as location, social setting, mental state, behavioral state, and physical condition. Deploying human DTs as an integral part of Cyber-Physical-Human Systems (CPHS) requires sensor data collection to train models. However, data collection in nursing homes is sensitive and complex. Furthermore, caregiver feedback on sensor data can enrich situational descriptions, support adaptation to new contexts, and advance CPHS development [21]. These constraints, combined with the need for large, diverse, privacy-compliant datasets and caregiver knowledge integration, motivate our investigation of scenario-controlled synthetic data augmentation.

Training a personalized early-stage detection model with reinforcement learning (RL) in a controlled simulation is advantageous, as simulations can generate features that sensors cannot directly capture [23]. Synthetic data support training models prior to deployment and enable the modeling of rare or critical scenarios while preserving privacy [24]. Prior studies indicate the utility of synthetic datasets in health policy analysis [25,26] and medical imaging [26,27]. Agent-based simulations also demonstrate realistic human and clinical interactions for advancing medical AI [28,29]. However, challenges remain in synthetic data fidelity, scenario diversity, and validation rigor [30].

Methods for generating synthetic data rely on self-supervised learning strategies such as autoencoders and generative adversarial networks (GANs). Autoencoders compress inputs to a latent space and reconstruct the input from this representation [31]. For time-series data, LSTM-based autoencoders are useful as they are able to capture temporal dependencies [31]. GANs learn to produce

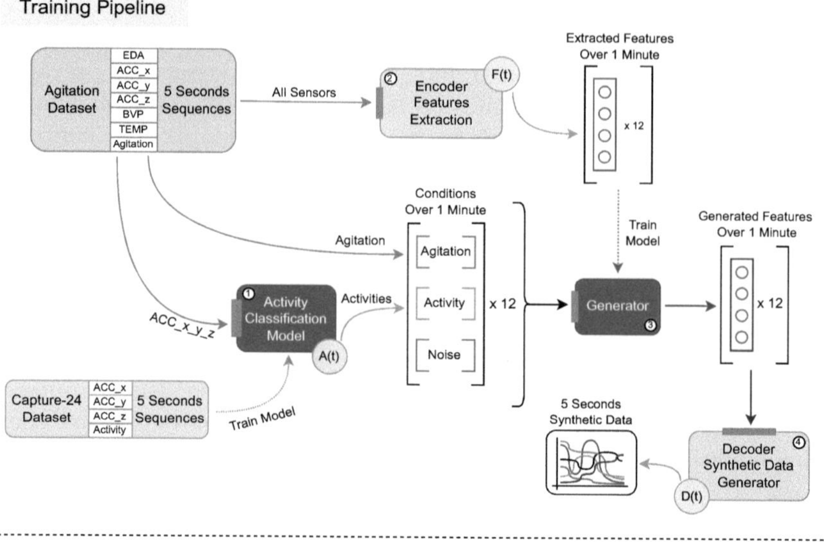

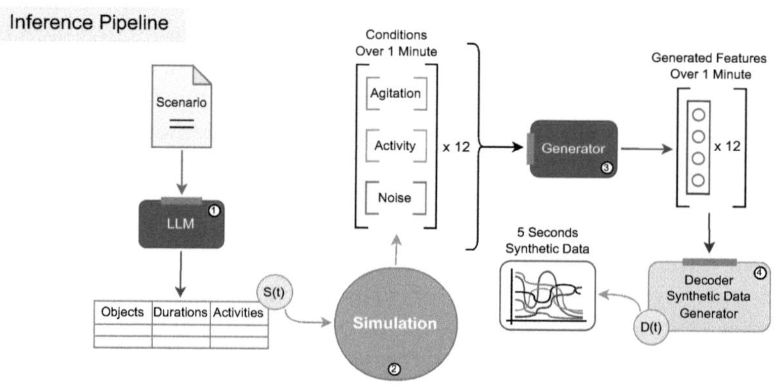

Fig. 1. Proposed training and inference pipelines of the scenario-controlled data augmentation system. The training pipeline learns the features representations from conditions to generate synthetic data. The inference pipeline translates a textual scenario to simulation conditions, which are then used to generate synthetic data.

realistic samples but can be unstable to train [24,32]. Conditional and time-series variants, including CGAN [33], RCGAN [34], TimeGAN [35], and TTS-GAN with conditional extensions [36–38], improve control and temporal realism through conditioning, recurrence, and attention. With temporal modelling and conditional control, the required level of detail (LOD), level of context (LOC), and level of personalisation (LOP) for human DTs can be established.

The MOOD-Sense research project of Hanze and UMCG [39], in collaboration with healthcare professionals, investigates CPHS in dementia care for early detection of challenging behaviour. The CPHS builds on a DT of the person with dementia and their environment, an Internet of Health Things infrastructure, and artificial agents. The DT provides metrics relevant to caregiver intervention in dementia care. To address DT initialisation for deployment in CPHS, we propose a scenario-controlled synthetic data augmentation system, shown in Fig. 1. It includes a training and inference pipeline (see Sect. 2). The system generates synthetic sensor data from simulations that can be instructed with textual scenarios by caregiver. The system uses a multi-stage data-generation process that increases LOD and LOC at each stage (See Fig. 2). The first stage is defining a textual scenario description, which is then used to simulate activities and trajectories in the simulation environment. The resulting state table is used to generate feature vector sequences and, consequently, sensor data sequences.

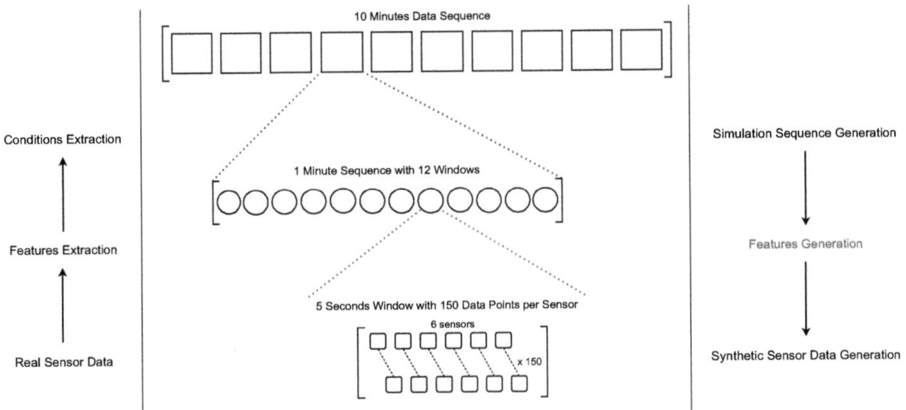

Fig. 2. Illustration of the LOC of the multi-layer transition model with its extractive part (left) and generative part (right) with their different levels of temporal context.

The paper is organized as follows: Sect. 2 details the proposed system design, Sect. 3 details the methods used, Sect. 4 presents the obtained results, and finally, the discussion and conclusions are presented in Sect. 5 and Sect. 6 respectively.

2   System Design

The data augmentation system, shown in Fig. 1, consisted of two main components: the training pipeline and the inference pipeline. The training pipeline is responsible for learning features representations from conditions to generate synthetic data. The inference pipeline translates textual scenario into state-windows using LLM. These states serve as an input for the simulation to simulate the scenario and provide conditions as DT parameters. These conditions serve as input for the trained models to generate features and synthetic data relative to the scenario.

2.1   Training Pipeline

The training pipeline utilized three models: an Activity Classification Model (ACM), a Features Generation Model, and a Synthetic Sensor Data Generation Model. The ACM was used to classify the possible activities in the Agitation Dataset, which determine the scenarios to be simulated. This model was trained using the Capture-24 Dataset. Further, the important features from the Agitation Dataset were extracted in the form of a compressed latent vectors along one-minute window. A one-minute window was chosen because research found it more effective for classifying agitation than larger windows [14,21]. These extracted features were used to train the Features Generation Model that generates scenario features based on conditions along one minute windows. These generated features were then used by the Synthetic Sensor Data Generation Model to generate synthetic data of 5 s windows.

2.2   Inference Pipeline

Based on the work of Civitarese et al. (2024) [40], we propose in the inference pipeline a Text-to-Simulation approach to make a scenario generation model, as shown in Fig. 3. The LLM, with some system instructions, got an input of a textual scenario with a set of activities that was processed to create a temporal window of states. The states include objects to interact with, the duration of the interaction, and the type of interaction (activity). An example of this is given in Appendix C.

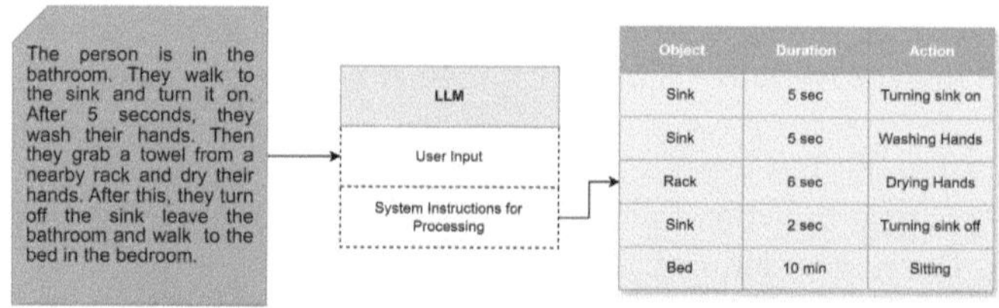

Object	Duration	Action
Sink	5 sec	Turning sink on
Sink	5 sec	Washing Hands
Rack	6 sec	Drying Hands
Sink	2 sec	Turning sink off
Bed	10 min	Sitting

Fig. 3. An example of generating states' window from textual scenario using LLM.

These states were then transformed into positions and were simulated in the simulation by making use of A* automated pathfinding technique based on a tutorial in a GitHub repository[1]. This Text-to-Simulation method provided the ability to quickly simulate many variational scenarios. Based on that, the simulation can provide the conditions that can be used to generate the scenario features and use these features as an input for the trained LSTM-decoder to generate synthetic data.

---

[1] https://github.com/SebLague/Pathfinding.

The simulation environment[2], shown in Fig. 4, was developed in Unity and was improved by modeling dynamic interactions between the simulated person with dementia and the objects added to each room in the environment.

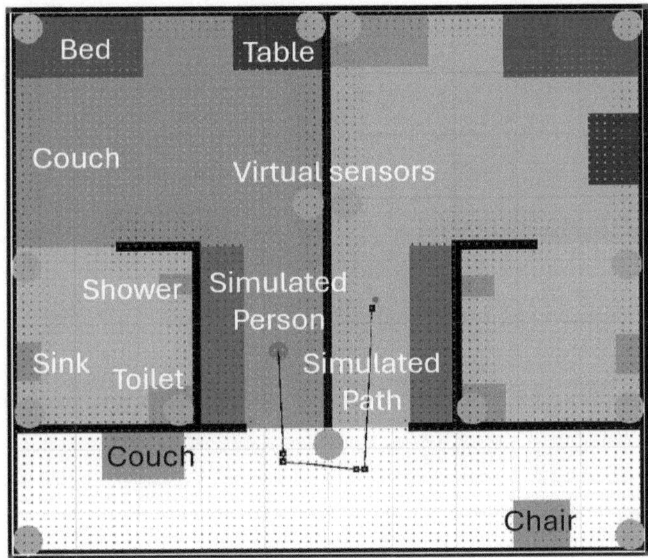

Fig. 4. Simulation environment showing objects and simulated individual walking towards a target position (red point) in the environment using A* algorithm. (Color figure online)

Dynamic interaction within the simulation was managed using a Simulation Control System (SCS) developed in Python. This system communicated with Unity using MQTT protocol. Its functions included scenario execution and object configuration.

For scenario execution, the SCS parsed the LLM-generated states and translated them into actionable commands. These commands were published to Unity to guide the simulated person with dementia by updating target positions and managing transitions between scenario states. The SCS also monitored scenario progress by subscribing to completion signals from Unity, to ensure sequential execution of states.

As for object configuration, the SCS adjusted the positions and properties of objects based on user-defined parameters, enabling varied and customizable simulated scenarios. Updated configurations were published via MQTT, and Unity adjusted the simulation accordingly.

A virtual target point was added to Unity to serve as a navigation goal for the simulated person with dementia. The virtual point received the target positions

---

[2] https://youtu.be/MKD3TZ1fl98.

from the SCS, allowing the simulated agent to move toward it while avoiding obstacles.

The objects and the simulated person with dementia continuously communicated their real-time (x, y) positions via MQTT. The simulation subscribed to incoming data such as target positions, interaction durations, and object configurations, and dynamically adjusted the scene layout based on these inputs. Upon successful execution of each state, the simulation published a state completion signal, allowing the SCS to proceed to the next state.

3   Methods

This section explains the detailed process of the implementation regarding the data pre-processing and models training. This research was carried out on a Windows 11 desktop equipped with an Intel(R) Core(TM) i7-9700K CPU with a speed of 3.60 GHz, an NVIDIA GeForce RTX 2080 Super GPU of 8 GB, and an installed RAM of 16 GB with a speed of 2666 MT/s. The Python version running on the desktop was 3.10.7 and the simulation was running on Unity version 2021.3.22f1.

3.1   Data Characteristics

For this research, two datasets were used. The Capture-24 dataset, which was used to train the ACM, and the Agitation dataset, which was used with the simulation to create a synthetic data augmentation system. The Agitation dataset, made by Khan et al. (2024) [41], was acquired from 20 participants with dementia. It consisted of data measured from three-dimensional accelerometer (ACC; mean = [-2.98e-01, 5.65e-02, 3.56e-01], std = [0.58, 0.48, 0.46]), electrodermal activity (EDA; mean = 3.99e-01, std = 1.18), blood volume pulse (BVP; mean = 1.00e-03, std = 123.98), and skin temperature (TEMP; mean = 3.33e+01, std = 12.46) sensors in an Empatica E4 wearable device, with the time of the day and an agitation label as a boolean. The heart rate and the inter beat interval can be derived from the BVP sensor that uses photoplethysmography [42]. The duration of agitation events varied, ranging from 1 min to 3 h. The data contains 231 normal days, 140 fully labeled agitation days, and 64 partially labelled/unlabeled agitation days. The sensors' data except the BVP were resampled to 64 Hz to match the sample rate of the BVP sensor. For this research, participant 13 was chosen as this participant had the most days of agitation and most number of agitation events. The data were securely handled and analyzed exclusively on the research group's computer.

The Capture-24 dataset [43] was acquired from 151 participants in a free-living setting, where participants carried out their normal daily activities, that provided a diverse and wide range of 206 unique activity annotations. The dataset consisted of data measured from a three-dimensional accelerometer sensor in a wrist-worn Axivity AX3 with a sample rate of 100 Hz.

3.2   Data Pre-processing

In order to train and apply the ACM, both the Capture-24 and Agitation datasets required preprocessing to match the model input's requirement. First, both datasets were divided into sequences of 5 s because the shorter the time window, the more insights are available about the activities that were performed, to form the shape (number of sequences, number of channels, number of samples), where the number of channels is the number of sensors. For the ACM, only the accelerometer sensors from the Agitation dataset were used. As for the autoencoder model, all the data from all sensors were used. Both datasets were resampled to 30 Hz, as the ACM required an input of 30 Hz to classify activities. For the ACM, the data of both datasets were resampled using resample function from SciPy library. To generate synthetic data from the Agitation dataset, a fractional resampling approach was applied for the autoencoder to preserve the original data. With this approach, an evenly spaced fractional indices were generated across the original data range. These indices were then rounded to the nearest integers to determine which data points to keep. Using the selected indices, the corresponding data points from the original dataset were extracted along the (number of samples) axis. This process kept the overall structure of the data, while reducing its temporal resolution.

3.3   Activity Classification Model

In a study made by Yuan et al. (2024) [44], they proposed a pretrained model for features extraction from accelerometer data, which can be used to train an activity classification model using transfer learning. The pre-trained model together with the trained classification model was applied on the accelerometer data from the Capture-24 dataset to classify the activity. The pretrained model took an input of a 5-second sequence with a data rate of 30 Hz. The classification model consisted of 1 hidden layer of 512 neurons, and an output layer which is set to a specified number of classes.

In literature, different studies had used the Capture-24 dataset in a way that they grouped the 206 labels into smaller sets of labels based on their study objectives [45–47]. For instance, Willetts et al. [45] made two smaller labels sets from the Capture-24 for the objective of activity recognition. One label set contained 10 specific activity labels and the other contained eight broader activity labels. The labels' mappings are given in appendix B. However, assuming that the grouping of labels was done based on the labels itself and not on the data, the grouped set of labels might not be suitable from the perspective of the data characteristics.

So, the data was split randomly into 80% training and 20% test sets. Then, the model was trained to classify 206 classes as the total number of labels in the Capture-24 dataset. The hyperparameters of the ACM are provided in Table 2 in Appendix A.1. After training, a confusion matrix was made and used to cluster the 206 labels into a number of meta-labels.

The meta-label creation process, shown in Fig. 5, used an evolutionary algorithm that tries to find the best way to cluster the 206 classes into meta-clusters, by trying to maximize the macro f1 score, which is the average of f1 scores across all meta-classes. Based on the algorithm's prediction, the number of meta-labels was set to 10 and the meta-labels were mapped to the original 206 labels as numbers. In order to convert these numbers into text labels, ChatGPT was used to provide a label name to each meta-class, based on the activities and MET scores in the original labels correlated with that meta-class. These meta-labels were then mapped to the data.

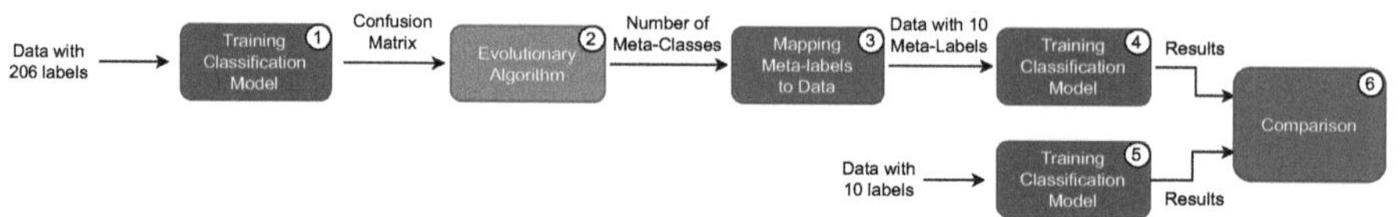

Fig. 5. The creation process of meta-labels from a confusion matrix using an evolutionary algorithm.

Then, the same ACM was trained with the same hyperparameters used before to classify the meta-labels and the 10 specific labels from Willetts et al. [45] as a baseline. This is done to test and compare the model's performance in classifying activities with different label sets. For further evaluation, confusion matrices and Receiver Operating Characteristic (ROC) curves with Area Under the Curve (AUC) were used as well. To better understand the relationships between the original Capture-24 label set and both label sets (Willetts-specific and meta-labels), a graph database using Neo4j was used, to help visualize and analyze overlaps and similarities between the original label set and both mappings.

3.4   Sensor Data Generator

The Synthetic Sensor Data Generator used an LSTM autoencoder model, where the model's encoder was used to extract features and the model's decoder was used to generate synthetic data. In order to extract features from the Agitation dataset, the resampled dataset with sequences of 5 s was used. Then, all channels (sensors) were normalized using a standard scaler function. As the sensors measure different things and have different distributions, each sensor was normalized separately; except the ACC sensors, they were normalized together as they measure the same thing. The data was split into 80% training and 20% test sets, not randomly, as the data was sequential.

The LSTM autoencoder was trained using PyTorch and its hyperparameters were tuned using Optuna [48]. After tuning the hyperparameters, the model consisted of 2 layers and a hidden size of 64 for both encoder and decoder, a latent space of 10 as a bottleneck vector in between, and an output fully connected layer with a linear activation function to reconstruct the original sequence. In order to make the autoencoder stateful, the model was made in such a way that it passes the hidden-states from one batch to the next, to preserve meaningful information across batches. The hyperparameters of the LSTM autoencoder are provided in Table 3 in Appendix A.2.

After training, the encoder was used to extract features from the real data and the decoder was used to reconstruct the data. The features of each sequence were saved to train the scenario features generator model later. The model's performance was assessed using visual plots of real and synthetic data, Mean Squared Error (MSE) reconstruction loss, and R^2 score, which calculates the coefficient of determination.

3.5   Scenario Features Generator

To train the scenario features generator, feature vectors sequences generated by the sensor data generator encoder were used as ground truth. These sequences were split into 80% training and 20% test sets sequentially. The labels were one-hot encoded to facilitate multi-class classification of both the activity and agitation.

Initially a TTS-CGAN architecture was implemented, but given its instability during training, an LSTM seq2seq encoder-decoder structure was used instead. The encoder received the vector of one-hot encoded conditions and normal distribution noise. The decoder used a 0.5 teacher forcing ratio in both training and testing, which means that it used the ground truth features to help converge. The model was trained with hyperparameters provided in Table 4 in Appendix A.3. After training, the model was used to generate feature vector sequences based on conditions. The features were saved to be used by the autoencoder's decoder to generate synthetic data. The model's performance was assessed using visual plots of generated and autoencoder's features, MSE reconstruction loss, and R^2 score.

4   Results

This section provides the results of the research implementation regarding the ACM, the feature extraction model, and the scenario features generator model with a discussion that describes the strengths and limitations of the designed system related to the objective of this research.

4.1   Activity Classification

As mentioned in Sect. 3.3, the same model was trained with three different label sets for comparison. Table 1 presents the model's classification performance with the three label sets. To get a clear idea of which model performed better, and because there is imbalance in the dataset, accuracy can be misleading, as it captures the general accuracy across all classes. Therefore, the macro-f1 score was chosen as the primary evaluation metric, as it provides a balanced measure of performance across each class. As given in Table 1, the model trained with the Capture-24 label set achieved a macro-f1 score of 0.03, indicating difficulty in classifying 206 activities. On the other hand, the model trained with Meta-labels achieved a macro-f1 score of 0.46, outperforming the model trained with Willetts-specific label set, which achieved 0.37. This indicates that the model trained with Meta-labels achieved a higher macro-f1 score while maintaining a better balance between precision and recall across all classes.

Table 1. Comparison of classification performance of the model across three different label sets; Original Capture-24 labels, Willetts-specific labels, and the proposed Meta-labels.

Label-set	Macro Precision	Macro Recall	Macro F1	Accuracy
Capture-24 labels	0.06	0.03	0.03	0.46
Willetts-specific [45]	0.61	0.34	0.37	0.69
Meta-labels	**0.73**	**0.39**	**0.46**	**0.69**

Figure 10a and Fig. 10b in Appendix A.1 shows the ROC curves with its AUCs for the model trained with Willetts-specific label set and Meta-labels, respectively, illustrating their performance in distinguishing between classes. The AUC reflects the model's ability to differentiate between positive and negative instances. The model trained with meta-labels achieved a higher Macro-AUC value of 0.92, indicating better classification performance while treating classes equally, compared to the model trained with Willetts-specific label set which had a Macro-AUC of 0.83. Also, the ROC curves of the model trained with Meta-labels show steeper curves of all classes, indicating higher true positive rates with fewer false positives.

To get a better understanding about the relationships between the Capture-24 labels and both label sets (Willetts-specific and meta-labels), a graph is shown in Fig. 13 in Appendix B, illustrating the most overlap of the Capture-24 labels (the small nodes) connected to both labels' sets (Meta-labels in blue and Willetts-specific in different colors). As illustrated, the Capture-24 labels mapped to Willetts-specific label set were divided between 2 or 3 meta labels. For instance, Capture-24 labels mapped to label 7 from Willetts-specific label set, were split across Meta-labels 2, 3, 4, and 8. This indicates that the meta-labels distinguish overlapping labels that were treated as a single entity in Willetts-specific label set. This means the meta-labels offered a more detailed segmentation, that improved the model in classifying the activities.

After applying the classifier on the Agitation dataset the following activities were present: Rest & Sedentary (197522 windows), Light Sedentary and Care (147960 windows), High-Intensity and Transport (72192 windows), Walking Activities Across Contexts (129 windows), Household & Light Manual (31 windows), and Hiking & Walking (6 windows).

4.2   Sensor Data Generation

The LSTM autoencoder was able to extract features and generate synthetic data. During the training of the model, the training and validation losses were monitored over epochs to assess the model convergence and generalization. Figure 11a in Appendix A.2 shows the training loss gradually decreasing, indicating that the model minimized the reconstruction loss. Also, the validation loss followed a similar trend, indicating good generalization. However, the validation loss indicates that the validation dataset is easily recognized by the model. In this case, the validation set should have used complex data to better test the model's generation, while considering the statefulness of the model and the order of the time series data.

For further evaluation of the performance of the LSTM autoencoder, the R^2 score was calculated at each epoch. R^2 score provides insight into how well the real data fit the synthetic data. A high R^2 score suggests that the model captures underlying data patterns well, whereas a lower score would indicate insufficient learning. The R^2 curve, shown in Fig. 11b, gradually increased until it stabilized as training progressed to 0.75 and validation progressed to 0.77. This indicates a well-performing LSTM-autoencoder in reconstructing time-series patterns, especially as the real data was noisy.

To evaluate the quality of the generated data, a comparison was made between the synthetic and real data, as shown in Fig. 6a and 6b. The plots reveal that the synthetic data, by accelerometer (x, y, z) sensors, follow the real-data distribution, while keeping the temporal structures and trends. However, the plots also show a difficulty in generating data for BVP, TEMP, and EDA sensors.

Additionally, periodic spikes occurring every 150 data points were observed in the synthetic data. Figure 7, shows the averaged root mean squared error (RMSE) of each data point of the 150 samples over all sequences between real and synthetic data. The RMSE by all sensors is noticeably higher at the beginning of the sequences, indicating the occurring spikes. The accelerometer sensors exhibit low standard deviations in their real data, and low RMSE values in the segments between 30 and 120. This indicates that the generative model is performing well on low variance signals and is capable of generating better data in these segments. In contrast, the BVP sensor has a high standard deviation over 123 with a high RMSE values that only drops at the end of the sequence, which indicates less accurate generation of the data. TEMP sensor has a standard deviation over 12 with a fluctuating RMSE, indicating difficulty in generating this data. This reflects that the high variability of the real data poses a challenge for reconstruction and might require more advanced generative models capable of capturing and modeling complex temporal dynamics. The difficulty in generating the data for BVP and TEMP might have contributed to the inability of generating data for the EDA sensor, as its standard deviation is relatively low when compared to BVP and TEMP.

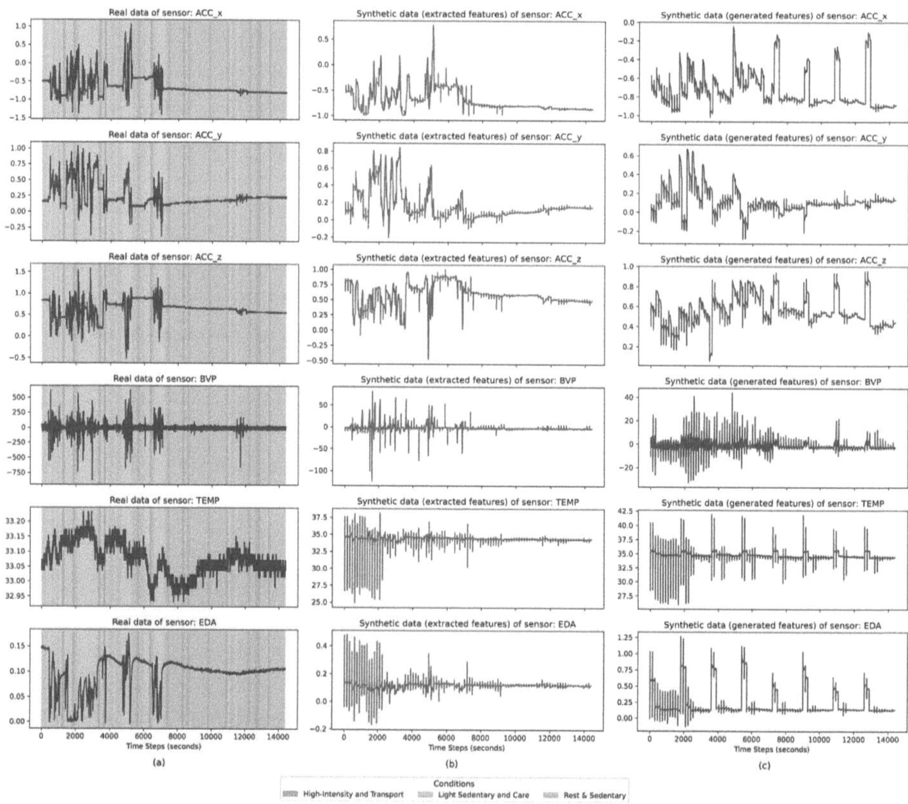

Fig. 6. A comparison between real data, synthetic data generated with extracted features, and synthetic data generated with generated features for about 8 min.

4.3   Scenario Features Generation

The performance of the alternative seq2seq LSTM encoder-decoder model had better performance in generating conditional features in comparison with TTS-CGAN. The training behavior exhibited stable behavior as the loss curves dropped smoothly with more stable validation loss, as shown in Fig. 12a in Appendix A.3. On the other hand, the R^2 score increased gradually until it had reached 0.84 by training and 0.89 by validation, as shown in Fig. 12b. The generated features followed a similar pattern to the encoder's features, as shown in Fig. 8, showing four features out of the total ten features.

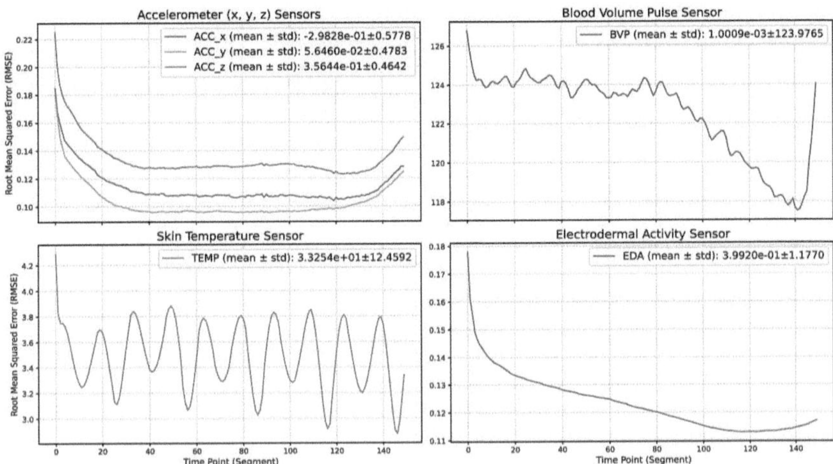

Fig. 7. Averaged RMSE of each data point of the 150 samples over all sequences for each sensor. The mean and standard deviation of the real data for each sensor are included in the legend to understand the magnitude of the RMSE.

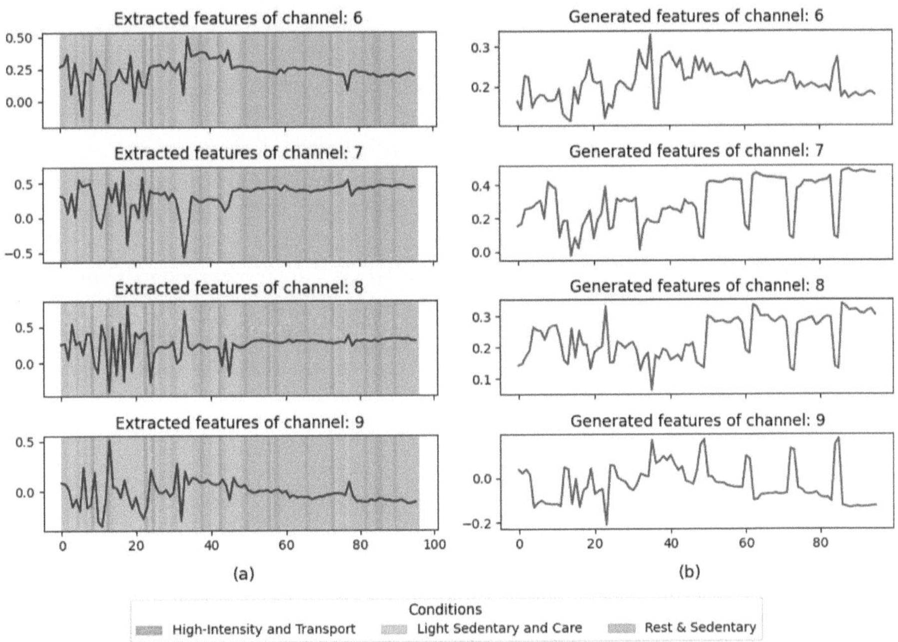

Fig. 8. Extracted features by the autoencoder model in comparison with generated features by the seq2seq LSTM encoder-decoder model for about 8 min.

4.4   Inference Pipeline

The final evaluation aimed to assess the pipeline in generating synthetic data from conditional features generated by the scenario features generator. The goal for this evaluation was to use the text to simulation to provide the conditions, however it was not applied in this way because of the limitation of the seq2seq LSTM encoder-decoder model that used 0.5 teacher forcing ratio on the features generated by the autoencoder. This caused the inability to evaluate the full pipeline, and instead the conditions from the dataset were used. The generated data from the pipeline are shown in Fig. 6c alongside the real and autoencoder data. By comparing the data, it is clear that the accelerometer sensors' data were well generated, considering the R^2 scores of both the autoencoder and seq2seq LSTM encoder-decoder models and their limitations in generating data for the other sensors.

5   Discussion and Future Work

Monitoring agitation in dementia demands models that generalize across people and settings, and that can adapt rapidly on site. We addressed this with a scenario-controlled synthetic data augmentation pipeline in which LLM-driven text-to-simulation parameterizes persons, contexts, and environments to generate multimodal sensor data sequences with scenario tags. The synthetic data serves pretraining transferable representations and enables few-shot personalization at deployment to increase minority-state recall while limiting labelling burden. This aligns with recommendations on actively managing alarm fatigue from wearables that capture agitation-related changes [49,50]. For downstream demonstration of few-shot personalization and deployment we see several future improvements, namely: (i) Sensor-semantic and human-semantic representation alignment, (ii) accurate temporal modeling of signals, (iii) causal feature learning and (iv) improved high-level control.

Empirically, our custom meta-labels improved activity recognition (macro-$F_1 = 0.46$) relative to Willetts labels. However, the improvement coincided with reduced alignment between sensor semantics (ACC patterns) and human semantics (clinician-facing descriptors). Overlapping classes within the meta-labels do remain aligned. However, for non-overlapping classes, additional context is required to disambiguate the sensor signal (e.g., scene tags or co-occurring events).

The generative model produced realistic accelerometer (ACC; x, y, z) sequences ($R^2 = 0.77$) but underperformed for BVP, TEMP, and EDA. High short-term variability in BVP and low variance/slow dynamics in TEMP/EDA likely contributed. Start-of-sequence spikes in generated data indicate boundary uncertainty and limited temporal memory. Initializing channel-wise decoders with frame buffers and sensor-specific windows is expected to mitigate this effect. Mean-squared-error loss promoted over-smoothed samples, therefore conditional adversarial objectives may improve accuracy.

Creating channel-wise autoencoders with sensor-specific windows can shift correlation and causal learning to the feature space, facilitate cross-person transfer, and support few-shot personalization without retraining sensor data encoders. Learning feature causality can be framed via Causal Feature Learning (CFL), which induces macro-variables, yielding context-invariant, interpretable factors for counterfactual simulation and stable prediction [51].

More structured prompting, through the use of templates and scenario schemas, would strengthen control over the level of detail, context, and personalization in synthetic data generation. Templates constrain the model to produce information with consistent granularity, while schemas define relevant dimensions such as personal profile, environment, and activity. This added structure not only improves reproducibility but also allows rare yet clinically important states to be systematically represented. Recent work shows that enforcing schema compliance in LLMs increases the fidelity and reliability of structured outputs [52,53].

Collectively, resolving semantic alignment, temporal modeling, causal feature learning and advancing high-level control will enable reliable pretraining and few-shot personalization. Expanding the participant pool and introducing a simulated healthcare-worker could further support reinforcement learning based on our synthetic data augmentation system. With this, early detection of agitation without burdening caregivers with excessive situation labelling and alarm interaction can be realized.

Key Results

- **Pipeline:** A Proof-of-concept in scenario-controlled synthetic data generation was developed.
- **Meta-labelling:** Activity meta-labels achieved macro-$F_1 = 0.46$, outperforming Willetts labels on activity recognition.
- **Synthetic data:** Synthetic ACC generation reached $R^2 = 0.77$.

Limitations

- **Semantic alignment:** Sensor-discriminative meta-labels conflict with human-semantic conditioning.
- **Cross-dataset scaling:** Possible ACC scale mismatch (Capture-24 $\pm 8g$ vs. unspecified).
- **Temporal context:** Start-of-sequence spikes present in decoded signals indicate lack of memory.
- **Sensor heterogeneity:** BVP (high variance) vs. TEMP/EDA (low variance) require sensor-specific temporal windows and encoders.
- **Teacher forcing:** Generative quality dropped at teacher forcing $= 0$.

6 Conclusion

The number of people with dementia is rising, stressing the need for dynamic CPHS capable of detecting agitation. Current systems are limited by scarce data, high labelling burden, and lack of adaptability. RL offers a way to continuously adapt decision policies based on human feedback, but requires reliable training data, which scenario-controlled synthetic data augmentation supports.

Our proposed pipeline applies LLM-driven text-to-simulation to parameterize persons, contexts, and environments, enabling the generation of multimodal sensor data with scenario tags. This synthetic data allows pretraining of transferable representations and supports few-shot personalization at deployment, thereby improving minority-state recall while mitigating alarm fatigue. Future work should focus on enhancing semantic alignment, temporal modeling, and causal feature learning, while expanding scenario diversity through structured prompting and simulated healthcare-worker agents. Together, these developments will enable robust CPHS that integrate human feedback, reinforcement learning, and synthetic data to support early detection and management of agitation in dementia.

Acknowledgments. We would like to express our sincere gratitude to the Knowledge Centre Biobased Economy (KCBBE) of Hanze University of Applied Sciences for their support and resources provided throughout this research.

Disclosure of Interests. The authors have no competing interests.

A   Appendix: Models

Hyperparameters and results of the models used in this research are given in this appendix.

A.1   Activity Classification Model

Hyperparameters of the Activity Classification Model in Table 2.

Table 2. Hyperparameters of Activity Classification Model.

Optimizer	Adam
Loss Function	Cross Entropy
Learning Rate	0.001
Weight-decay	1e-5
Batch-size	16
Epochs	20
Hidden Layer	512
Output Size	10 and 206

The confusion matrices of the models trained with Willetts-specific label set and Meta-labels are shown in Fig. 9a and 9b respectively. The confusion matrix provides insight into the misclassifications made by each model, which highlights the strengths and weaknesses in distinguishing between different classes. The diagonal elements indicate correctly classified activities, while off-diagonal elements represent misclassifications.

The confusion matrix for Willetts-specific label set shows high correct classification accuracy for sitting and sleeping, indicating that sedentary activities were well recognized. However, the model also shows misclassification among activities, where some misclassified activities have similar motion patterns. Most of the activities were confused with sitting. For instance, bicycling activity was correctly classified 38.67%, but it was 45.36% confused with sitting activity. Standing activity had the highest misclassification of 74.14%, where it was also confused with sitting.

The confusion matrix for the meta-labels shows better correctly classified activities when looking at the diagonal elements, which indicates better model convergence across classes. For instance, Rest & Sedentary activity was correctly classified 93.31% and walking activities across contexts was correctly classified 61.92%. Also, fewer activities were misclassified and confused with rest & seden-

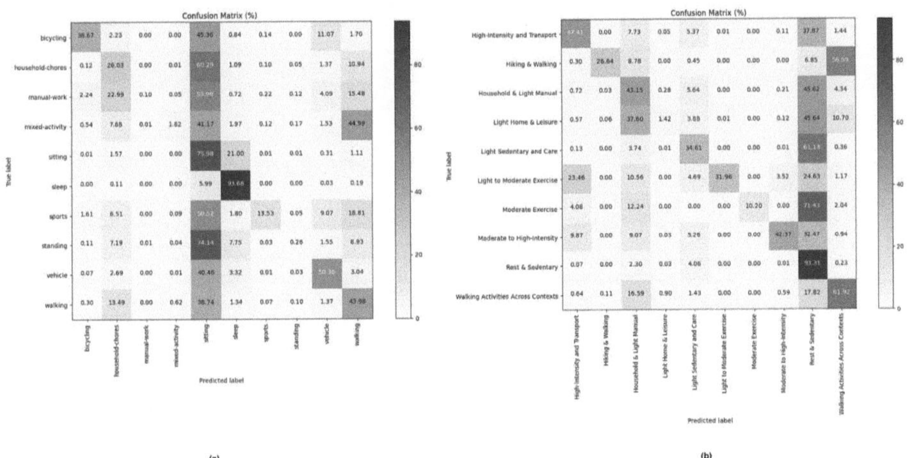

Fig. 9. Confusion Matrix of the model trained with Willetts-specific labels (a) and Meta-labels (b) sets.

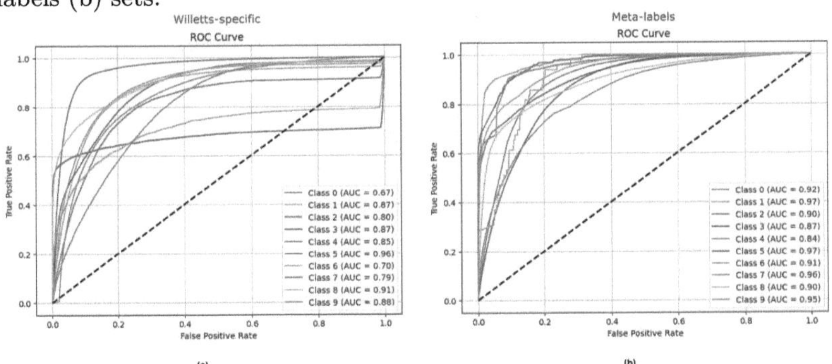

Fig. 10. ROC-curves of the model trained with Willetts-specific labels (a) and Meta-labels (b) sets.

tary. Some activities had overlap, like household & light manual with light home & leisure and hiking & walking with walking activities across contexts.

A.2 Sensor Data Generator: LSTM Autoencoder

Hyperparameters of the LSTM Autoencoder model in Table 3.

Table 3. Hyperparameters of LSTM Autoencoder Model.

Optimizer	Adam
Loss Function	MSE Loss
Learning Rate	0.0002305394710098038
Batch-size	16
Epochs	37
Teather forcing ratio	0.5
Dropout	0.2
LSTM layers	2
LSTM Hidden-Size	64
Input-size	6
Feature-dimension	10
Output-size	150
Sensors order	[Acc-X, Acc-y, Acc-z, BvP, TEMP, EDA]

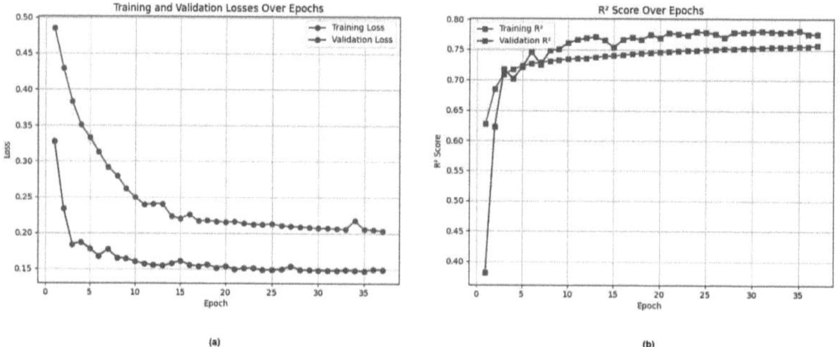

Fig. 11. Training and validation losses of the autoencoder model (a) and the training and validation R^2 scores (b) over epochs.

A.3   Seq2seq LSTM Encoder-Decoder

Hyperparameters of the Seq2seq LSTM encoder-decoder model in Table 4.

Table 4. Hyperparameters of Seq2seq LSTM encoder-decoder Model.

Optimizer	Adam
Loss Function	MSE Loss
Learning Rate	0.0002305394710098038
Batch-size	16
Epochs	50
Teather forcing ratio	0.5
Dropout	0.2
LSTM layers	2
LSTM Hidden-Size	64
Input-size	8
Output-size	10

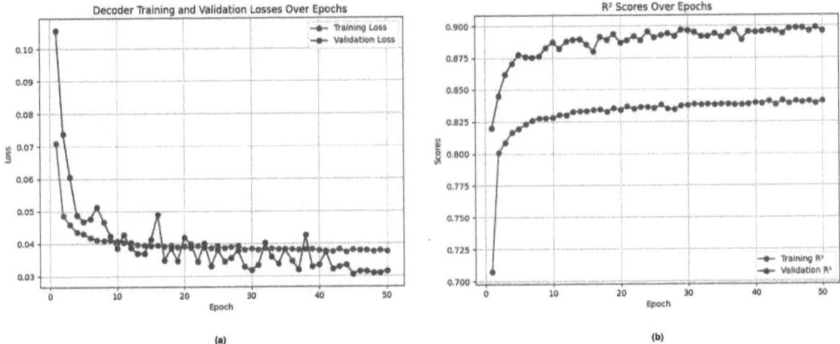

Fig. 12. The training and validation losses of the seq2seq LSTM encoder-decoder model (a) and the training and validation R^2 scores (b) over epochs.

B   Appendix: Labels Mappings

The full graph is shown in Fig. 13.

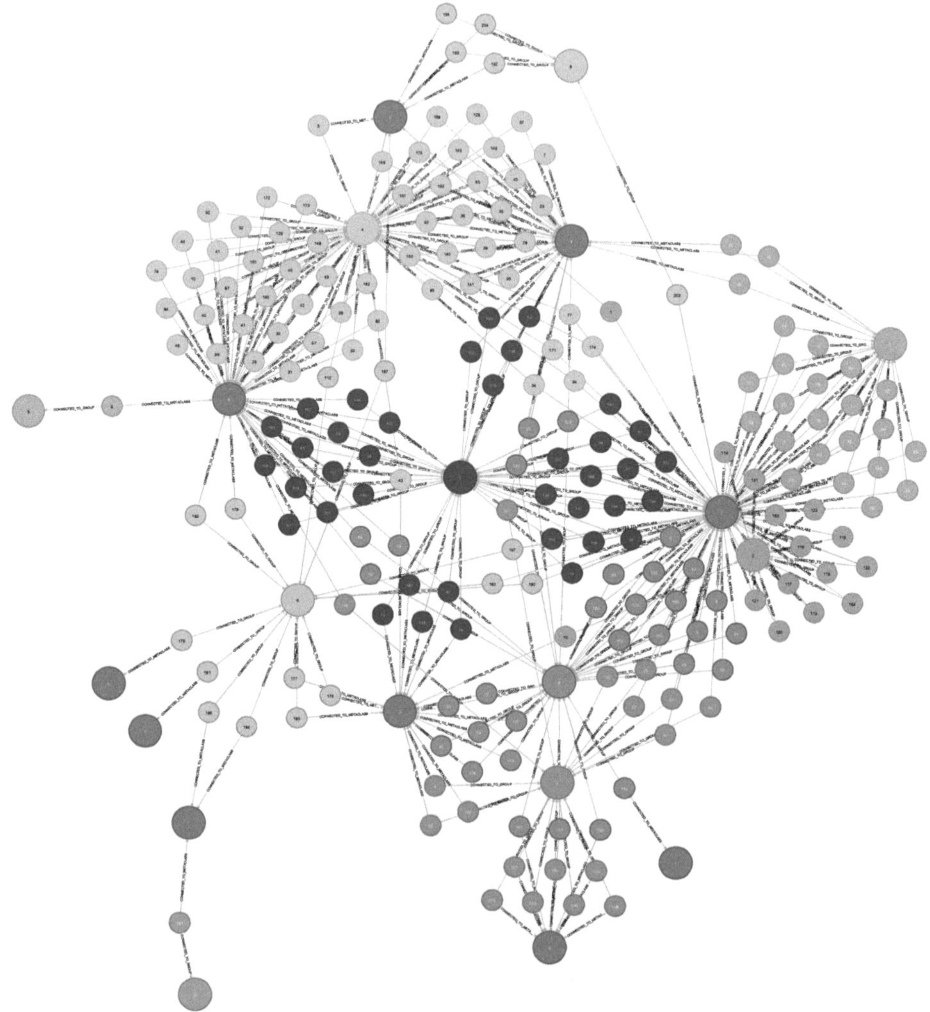

Fig. 13. The full graph showing all connections between the Capture-24 labels and the Willetts-specific labels and meta-labels sets.

The mappings of the labels are provided in the paper [43].

C   Appendix: Text-to-Simulation

System Prompt: '*You are a task planner that generates a structured list of tuples for states and durations from a given scenario. Each scenario will involve* *a subject interacting with various rooms and objects. For each scenario: Create a list containing tuples, each tuple representing a distinct action or position of the subject as (object, action, duration). Each interaction should be listed as a separate state in chronological order. For example: ("Sink", "Turn On Faucet", 2). In each tuple: The first element should be the name of the object the subject is interacting with (e.g., "Sink" or "Towel"). The second element should be a brief description of the action (e.g., "Turn On Faucet" or "Pick Up Towel"). The third element should be the estimated duration in seconds for the action. If no duration is provided, use reasonable estimates based on typical timing for each action. Rooms and objects that the subject can interact with include: Bathroom: bathsink, faucet, towel, towel rack, soap dispenser, mirror, toilet, shower. Bedroom: bed, nightstand, lamp, closet. Kitchen: stove, refrigerator, kitchen-sink, cabinet, countertop. Living Room: sofa, coffee table, TV, bookshelf. The states should reflect only interactions with objects. Output only the list of tuples and nothing else.'*

User Prompt 1 (Scenario 1): *'The subject is in the bathroom. They walk to the sink and turn it on. After 5 s, they wash their hands. Then they grab a towel from a nearby rack and dry their hands. After this, they turn off the sink, leave the bathroom, and walk to the bed in the bedroom. Please generate a table of states and durations based on this scenario.'*

LLM States of Scenario 1:
("Bath Sink", "Turn On Faucet", 5),
("Bath Sink", "Wash Hands", 15),
("Towel Rack", "Grab Towel", 2),
("Bath Sink", "Turn Off Faucet", 2),
("Bathroom", "Leave Bathroom", 2),
("Bed", "Walk To Bed", 10)

User Prompt 2 (Scenario 2): *'The subject is in the kitchen. They open the cabinet and take out a box of cereal. After 5 s, they place the box on the countertop and move toward the fridge. After opening the fridge, they wait for 8 s before retrieving a carton of milk. They close the fridge, walk back to the countertop, and prepare a bowl of cereal.'*

LLM States of Scenario 2:
("Cabinet", "Open", 1),
("Cabinet", "Take Out Cereal", 1),
("Countertop", "Place Cereal", 5),
("Fridge", "Open", 8),
("Fridge", "Retrieve Milk", 2),
("Fridge", "Close", 1),
("Countertop", "Move Toward Fridge", 1),
("Countertop", "Prepare Bowl", 3)

References

1. World Health Organization. Fact sheet Dementia (2023). https://www.who.int/news-room/fact-sheets/detail/dementia
2. Ijaopo, E.: Dementia-related agitation: a review of non-pharmacological interventions and analysis of risks and benefits of pharmacotherapy. Transl. Psychiatry **7**(10), e1250 (2017). https://doi.org/10.1038/tp.2017.199
3. Hinton, L., Franz, C.E., Reddy, G., Flores, Y., Kravitz, R.L., Barker, J.C.: Practice constraints, behavioral problems, and dementia care: Primary care physicians' perspectives. J. Gen. Internal Med. **22**(11), 1487–1492 (2007). https://doi.org/10.1007/s11606-007-0317-y
4. Cerejeira, J., Lagarto, L., Mukaetova-Ladinska, E.B.: Behavioral and psychological symptoms of dementia. Front. Neurol. **3** (2012). https://doi.org/10.3389/fneur.2012.00073
5. Hendriks, S.A., Smalbrugge, M., Galindo-Garre, F., Hertogh, C.M., Van Der Steen, J.T.: From admission to death: prevalence and course of pain, agitation, and shortness of breath, and treatment of these symptoms in nursing home residents with dementia. J. Am. Med. Directors Assoc. **16**(6), 475–481 (2015). https://doi.org/10.1016/j.jamda.2014.12.016
6. Mulkey, M.A., Munro, C.L.: Calming the agitated patient: providing strategies to support clinicians. Medsurg Nursing: Off. J. Acad. Med.-Surg. Nurses **30**(1), 9 (2021)
7. Cheng, S.-T.: Dementia caregiver burden: a research update and critical analysis. Curr. Psychiatry Rep. **19**(9), 1–8 (2017). https://doi.org/10.1007/s11920-017-0818-2
8. Volicer, L., Van Der Steen, J.T., Frijters, D.H.: Modifiable factors related to abusive behaviors in nursing home residents with dementia. J. Am. Med. Directors Assoc. **10**(9), 617–622 (2009). https://doi.org/10.1016/j.jamda.2009.06.004
9. Fernández-Llatas, C., et al.: Behaviour patterns detection for persuasive design in nursing homes to help dementia patients. In: 2011 Annual International Conference of the IEEE Engineering in Medicine and Biology Society, pp. 6413–6417 (2011). https://doi.org/10.1109/IEMBS.2011.6091583
10. Ooi, C., Yoon, P., How, C., Poon, N.: Managing challenging behaviours in dementia. Singapore Med. J. **59**(10), 514–518 (2018). https://doi.org/10.11622/smedj.2018125
11. Neville, C.C., Byrne, G.J.A.: Behaviour rating scales for older people with dementia: which is the best for use by nurses? Australas. J. Ageing **20**(4), 166–172 (2001). https://doi.org/10.1111/j.1741-6612.2001.tb00381.x
12. Ye, B., et al.: Challenges in collecting big data in a clinical environment with vulnerable population: lessons learned from a study using a multi-modal sensors platform. Sci. Eng. Ethics **25**(5), 1447–1466 (2018). https://doi.org/10.1007/s11948-018-0072-y
13. Sefcik, J.S., Ersek, M., Libonati, J.R., Hartnett, S.C., Hodgson, N.A., Cacchione, P.Z.: Heart rate of nursing home residents with advanced dementia and persistent vocalizations. Heal. Technol. **10**(3), 827–831 (2019). https://doi.org/10.1007/s12553-019-00397-2
14. Khan, S.S., et al.: Agitation detection in people living with dementia using multimodal sensors. In: 2019 41st Annual International Conference of the IEEE Engineering in Medicine and Biology Society (EMBC), pp. 3588–3591 (2019). https://doi.org/10.1109/EMBC.2019.8857781

15. Spasojevic, S., et al.: A pilot study to detect agitation in people living with dementia using multi-modal sensors. J. Healthc. Inform. Res. **5**(3), 342–358 (2021)
16. Iaboni, A., et al.: Wearable multimodal sensors for the detection of behavioral and psychological symptoms of dementia using personalized machine learning models. Alzheimer's Dementia Diagn. Assess. Dis. Monit. **14**(1), e12305 (2022)
17. Barricelli, B.R., Casiraghi, E., Gliozzo, J., Petrini, A., Valtolina, S.: Human digital twin for fitness management. IEEE Access **8**, 26637–26664 (2020). https://doi.org/10.1109/ACCESS.2020.2971576
18. Liu, Y., et al.: A novel cloud-based framework for the elderly healthcare services using digital twin. IEEE Access **7**, 49088–49101 (2019). https://doi.org/10.1109/ACCESS.2019.2909828
19. Miller, M.E., Spatz, E.: A unified view of a human digital twin. Hum.-Intell. Syst. Integr. **4**(1-2), 23–33 (2022). https://doi.org/10.1007/s42454-022-00041-x
20. Lin, Y., et al.: Human digital twin: a survey. J. Cloud Comput. Adv. Syst. Appl. **13**(1) (2024). https://doi.org/10.1186/s13677-024-00691-z
21. Kleine Deters, J., Janus, S., Lima Silva, J.A., Wörtche, H.J., Zuidema, S.U.: Sensor-based agitation prediction in institutionalized people with dementia A systematic review. Pervasive Mob. Comput. **98**, 101876 (2024). https://doi.org/10.1016/j.pmcj.2024.101876
22. Kleine Deters, J., et al.: A cyber-physical-human system design for challenging behaviour monitoring in people with dementia. In: Sensor-Based Activity Recognition and Artificial Intelligence: 10th International Workshop, iWOAR 2025, Enschede, The Netherlands, 18–19 September 2025. Springer (2026)
23. Saadallah, A., Finkeldey, F., Buß, J., Morik, K., Wiederkehr, P., Rhode, W.: Simulation and sensor data fusion for machine learning application. Adv. Eng. Inform. **52**, 101600 (2022). https://doi.org/10.1016/j.aei.2022.101600
24. Pezoulas, V.C., et al.: Synthetic data generation methods in healthcare: a review on open-source tools and methods. Comput. Struct. Biotechnol. J. **23**, 2892–2910 (2024). https://doi.org/10.1016/j.csbj.2024.07.005
25. Davis, P., Lay-Yee, R., Pearson, J.: Using micro-simulation to create a synthesised data set and test policy options: the case of health service effects under demographic ageing. Health Policy **97**(2), 267–274 (2010). https://doi.org/10.1016/j.healthpol.2010.05.014
26. Giuffrè, M., Shung, D.L.: Harnessing the power of synthetic data in healthcare: innovation, application, and privacy. NPJ Digit. Med. **6**(1) (2023). https://doi.org/10.1038/s41746-023-00927-3
27. Das, H.P., et al.: Conditional Synthetic Data Generation for Robust Machine Learning Applications with Limited Pandemic Data. arXiv (Cornell University) (2021). https://doi.org/10.48550/arxiv.2109.06486
28. Park, J.S., O'Brien, J.C., Cai, C.J., Morris, M.R., Liang, P., Bernstein, M.S.: Generative Agents: interactive simulacra of Human Behavior. arXiv (Cornell University) (2023). https://doi.org/10.48550/arxiv.2304.03442
29. Li, J., et al.: Agent Hospital: A Simulacrum of Hospital with Evolvable Medical Agents. arXiv (Cornell University) (2024). https://doi.org/10.48550/arxiv.2405.02957
30. Goyal, M., Mahmoud, Q.H.: A systematic review of synthetic data generation techniques using generative AI. Electronics **13**(17) (2024). https://doi.org/10.3390/electronics13173509
31. Xu, W., et al.: Long-short-term-memory-based deep stacked sequence-to-sequence autoencoder for health prediction of industrial workers in closed environments

based on wearable devices. Sensors **23**(18) (2023). https://doi.org/10.3390/s23187874

32. Figueira, A., Vaz, B.: Survey on synthetic data generation, evaluation methods and GANs. Mathematics **10**(15) (2022). https://doi.org/10.3390/math10152733

33. Mirza, M., Osindero, S.: Conditional generative adversarial Nets. arXiv (Cornell University) (2014). https://doi.org/10.48550/arxiv.1411.1784

34. Esteban, C., Hyland, S.L., Rätsch, G.: Real-valued (Medical) Time Series Generation with Recurrent Conditional GANs. arXiv (Cornell University) (2017). https://doi.org/10.48550/arxiv.1706.02633

35. Yoon, J., Jarrett, D., van der Schaar, M.: Time-series generative adversarial networks. In: Wallach, H., Larochelle, H., Beygelzimer, A., d'Alché-Buc, F., Fox, E., Garnett, R. (eds.) Advances in Neural Information Processing Systems, vol. 32. Curran Associates, Inc. (2019). https://proceedings.neurips.cc/paper_files/paper/2019/file/c9efe5f26cd17ba6216bbe2a7d26d490-Paper.pdf

36. Li, X., Metsis, V., Wang, H., Ngu, A.H.H.: TTS-GAN: a transformer-based Time-Series Generative adversarial network. arXiv (Cornell University) (2022). https://doi.org/10.48550/arxiv.2202.02691

37. Li, X., Ngu, A.H.H., Metsis, V.: TTS-CGAN: a transformer Time-Series conditional GAN for biosignal data augmentation. arXiv (Cornell University) (2022). https://doi.org/10.48550/arxiv.2206.13676

38. Liu, Z.G., Ji, T.Y., Chen, J.W., Zhang, L.J., Zhang, L.L., Wu, Q.H.: Conditional-timegan for realistic and high-quality appliance trajectories generation and data augmentation in nonintrusive load monitoring. IEEE Trans. Instrum. Meas. **73**, 1–15 (2024). https://doi.org/10.1109/TIM.2024.3381263

39. Hanze: MOOD-Sense — Hanze UAS (2021). https://www.hanze.nl/en/research/centres/research-centre-biobased-economy/projects/mood-sense-en

40. Civitarese, G., Fiori, M., Choudhary, P., Bettini, C.: Large Language Models are Zero-Shot Recognizers for Activities of Daily Living. arXiv (Cornell University) (2024). https://doi.org/10.48550/arxiv.2407.01238

41. Khan, S.S., et al.: A novel multi-modal sensor dataset and benchmark to detect agitation in people living with dementia in a residential care setting. ACM Trans. Comput. Healthcare **6**(3) (2025). https://doi.org/10.1145/3720550

42. Schuurmans, A.A.T., et al.: Validity of the empatica E4 wristband to measure heart rate variability (HRV) parameters: a comparison to electrocardiography (ECG). J. Med. Syst. **44**(11), 1–11 (2020). https://doi.org/10.1007/s10916-020-01648-w

43. Chan, S., et al.: CAPTURE-24: a large dataset of wrist-worn activity tracker data collected in the wild for human activity recognition. Sci. Data **11**(1) (2024). https://doi.org/10.1038/s41597-024-03960-3

44. Yuan, H., et al.: Self-supervised learning for human activity recognition using 700,000 person-days of wearable data. NPJ Digit. Med. **7**(1) (2024). https://doi.org/10.1038/s41746-024-01062-3

45. Willetts, M., Hollowell, S., Aslett, L., Holmes, C., Doherty, A.: Statistical machine learning of sleep and physical activity phenotypes from sensor data in 96,220 UK Biobank participants. Sci. Rep. **8**(1) (2018). https://doi.org/10.1038/s41598-018-26174-1

46. Doherty, A., et al.: GWAS identifies 14 loci for device-measured physical activity and sleep duration. Nat. Commun. **9**(1) (2018). https://doi.org/10.1038/s41467-018-07743-4

47. Walmsley, R., et al.: Reallocating time from machine-learned sleep, sedentary behaviour or light physical activity to moderate-to-vigorous physical activity is

associated with lower cardiovascular disease risk. medRxiv (2020). https://doi.org/10.1101/2020.11.10.20227769

48. Akiba, T., Sano, S., Yanase, T., Ohta, T., Koyama, M.: Optuna: a next-generation hyperparameter optimization framework. In: Proceedings of the 25th ACM SIGKDD International Conference on Knowledge Discovery and Data Mining (2019)

49. Cvach, M.: Monitor alarm fatigue: an integrative review. Biomed. Instrum. Technol. **46**(4), 268–277 (2012). https://doi.org/10.2345/0899-8205-46.4.268

50. Cheung, J.C.W., So, B.P.H., Ho, K.H.M., Wong, D.W.C., Lam, A.H.F., Cheung, D.S.K.: Wrist accelerometry for monitoring dementia agitation behaviour in clinical settings: a scoping review. Front. Psych. **13**, 913213 (2022). https://doi.org/10.3389/fpsyt.2022.913213

51. Chalupka, K., Eberhardt, F., Perona, P.: Causal feature learning: an overview. Behaviormetrika **44**(1), 137–164 (2016). https://doi.org/10.1007/s41237-016-0008-2

52. Wang, D.Y.B., Shen, Z., Mishra, S.S., Xu, Z., Teng, Y., Ding, H.: Slot: structuring the output of large language models. arXiv preprint arXiv:2505.04016, May 2025

53. Geng, S., et al.: Generating structured outputs from language models: benchmark and studies. arXiv preprint arXiv:2501.10868, January 2025

Illusion of Precision: How Averaging Undermines Pulse Measurement Accuracy

Gerald Bieber[1]($\boxtimes$) (iD), Erik Endlicher[1]($\boxtimes$) (iD), Timo Forstner[2]($\boxtimes$) (iD), and Milad Geravand[2]($\boxtimes$) (iD)

[1] Fraunhofer-Institut fuer Graphische Datenverarbeitung IGD, Rostock, Germany
`{gerald.bieber,erik.endlicher}@igd-r.fraunhofer.de`
[2] Deep Care GmbH, Ludwigsburg, Germany
`{timo.forstner,milad.geravand}@deep-care.de`

Abstract. Accurate heart rate measurement is a fundamental requirement in many fields, including medicine, veterinary science, sports performance, and health monitoring. Devices designed to monitor pulse rate are widely used in both human and animal applications, and their reliability is often taken for granted.

However, a curious and counterintuitive effect can occur: some devices consistently report a minor changing value—such as 72 beats per minute for heart beat detection—regardless of the actual physiological state of the subject. At first glance, this appears to be a minor flaw, especially since the reported value may align with the average resting heart rate in humans. From a statistical standpoint, the device could even appear reasonably accurate when evaluated over a large group of individuals.

Yet this illusion of accuracy masks a critical flaw: individual deviations are ignored, and potentially important physiological variations go undetected. This paper explores how averaging can give rise to the appearance of precision, while in reality, the measurement fails to reflect real-time or individualized heart rate data. We argue that devices with such behavior introduce systematic bias, which poses significant risks in both clinical and practical applications.

Keywords: vital data recognition · sensor technologies · pulse · respiration detection · risk of systematic bias

1 Introduction

The continuous monitoring of vital signs has become increasingly important in healthcare, sports, and everyday wellness applications. Among the most widespread tools are smartwatches and fitness trackers equipped with photoplethysmography (PPG) sensors, which allow for non-invasive heart rate detection. These devices generally perform well under resting conditions, providing accurate and stable readings.

Ö. Durmaz Incel et al. (Eds.): iWOAR 2025, LNCS 16292, pp. 222–233, 2026.
https://doi.org/10.1007/978-3-032-13312-0_13

However, during movement or physical activity, PPG-based measurements become highly susceptible to motion artifacts. In such cases, the data collected may become so noisy that the device is no longer able to measure the actual pulse accurately. Instead, it appears to estimate or approximate the heart rate—often converging toward the average resting value. This creates an illusion of stability and accuracy while masking real physiological fluctuations.

Interestingly, this phenomenon is not limited to heart rate monitoring. Newer vital data monitoring technologies that track respiration rate, core body temperature, or even blood oxygen levels sometimes exhibit similar behavior: when faced with unreliable or inconsistent data, the systems tend to revert to average values. Paradoxically, these "guessed" values can statistically align more closely with group-level averages than the moment-to-moment true measurements.

This raises an important question: Can a device be considered accurate if it consistently reports the correct population mean, even while failing to reflect individual variation? This paper examines this paradox and argues that the averaging behavior of certain monitoring systems introduces systematic errors that can undermine their reliability and safety. We explore the implications of such behavior in both human and animal monitoring contexts and highlight the need for more robust validation strategies that go beyond mean error metrics.

2   Description of the Effect

In ideal conditions, wearable sensors aim to track physiological signals such as heart rate in real time. Photoplethysmography (PPG) sensors, for example, detect blood volume changes in the microvascular bed of tissue using light absorption. When a person remains still, the signal-to-noise ratio is high, and accurate readings can be obtained. However, during movement—such as walking, running, or even slight wrist rotations—motion artifacts introduce substantial noise into the signal, often overwhelming the pulse waveforms.

Faced with such distortion, some devices resort to internal estimation algorithms. These algorithms may interpolate, smooth, or average values over time or across similar contexts. In certain cases, when the signal is deemed too unreliable, the device may default to a statistically derived average—typically close to the human resting heart rate (e.g., 60–80 bpm). As a result, the displayed value remains within a plausible range, even though it no longer reflects the user's true heart rate.

This effect can be misleading. From the user's perspective, the measurement appears stable and trustworthy. In reality, however, it has become a generic estimate. When aggregated across a large number of users or time points, this behavior may paradoxically improve the device's statistical accuracy in terms of mean error—despite being incorrect at the individual level.

A similar pattern is observed in other biometric sensors, such as those measuring respiration rate, core temperature, or blood oxygen saturation. In the face of noisy input, systems sometimes converge toward normative values rather than reporting data that reflect momentary physiological states. This behavior highlights a fundamental trade-off in real-time vital sign monitoring: the choice between reporting uncertain, possibly erratic real data, or delivering stable but generalized values that may be misleading in critical situations.

3   Theoretical Background

To understand the implications of devices reverting to average values during noisy measurements, it is essential to distinguish between key measurement concepts: accuracy, precision, bias, and validity.

"Accuracy" refers to how close a measured value is to the true value. "Precision" describes the consistency or repeatability of measurements. A system can be precise without being accurate if it consistently reports the wrong value [3]. "Systematic bias" occurs when a measurement consistently deviates from the true value in a particular direction. In the case of fixed or averaged outputs during sensor failure, the device introduces a bias toward the population mean [11].

This leads to a critical distinction between "group-level accuracy" and "individual-level validity". A device may perform well in large-scale evaluations by producing low average error across many users. However, this statistical performance can mask poor individual performance. When a system consistently outputs "average" values, it may minimize total error over a dataset, but at the cost of clinical or practical relevance for individual cases.

In psychometrics and clinical diagnostics, this issue is well known: an instrument must not only produce accurate average results but must also be sensitive to individual variability and capable of capturing extreme or atypical cases [9]. In the context of wearable vital sign monitors, this requirement is often neglected in favor of smooth, artifact-free outputs that feel reliable to users.

Moreover, "algorithmic compensation strategies", such as filtering, smoothing, or replacing uncertain data with averages, reflect design choices that prioritize perceived stability over real-time accuracy. These trade-offs raise concerns about the "validity" of such systems—whether they truly measure what they claim to measure, especially under dynamic, real-world conditions (Table 1).

This theoretical framework underpins the need for more nuanced evaluation methods for vital sign monitoring technologies, especially those deployed in uncontrolled, everyday environments.

4   Related Work

Several studies have shown that wearable photoplethysmography (PPG) devices often demonstrate good performance at the group level, while significantly underperforming at the individual level. This discrepancy arises particularly under conditions with motion artifacts, where measurements become unreliable and are often replaced or smoothed by algorithms that default to statistical averages.

Table 1. Key Measurement Concepts in Vital Sign Monitoring

Term	Definition	Example in Pulse Measurement
Accuracy	Closeness of a measurement to the true (actual) value.	A reading of 75 bpm when the actual heart rate is 76 bpm is highly accurate.
Precision	Consistency of repeated measurements under unchanged conditions.	Device reports 72 bpm five times in a row during rest.
Bias	Systematic deviation from the true value in one direction.	Device always shows 72 bpm, even when actual heart rate is much higher or lower.
Validity	Extent to which a device measures what it claims to measure, especially in context.	A device may show stable numbers, but fails to track real-time pulse under movement.

Often, some algorithm provide a plausible but not always true signal. A very commonly used technique for dealing with noisy physiological signals is the application of bandpass filters, such as the Butterworth filter. These filters are often configured to pass only frequencies within a biologically plausible range—for example, 0.7 to 3 Hz for human heart rates (corresponding to 42–180 bpm). While effective at suppressing high-frequency noise and baseline drift, such filters can also introduce a critical problem: they will always yield a dominant frequency component within the defined passband, even if no valid heart rate signal exists in the input.

In scenarios where the signal is heavily corrupted, e.g. due to motion, sensor detachment, or poor contact, the filter output may still appear clean and stable, giving the illusion of a valid heart rate. This creates a risk of falsely interpreting filtered noise as a real physiological measurement (Fig. 1). The widespread use of Butterworth filters in commercial and research-grade wearable systems is therefore a double-edged sword: they improve apparent signal quality but may obscure the true absence of measurable data. This phenomenon reinforces the challenge discussed in this paper, in which systems prioritize plausibility and stability over ground-truth accuracy under uncertain conditions.

Dunn et al. [4] tested multiple commercial wearable devices on a diverse group of participants. They found that while the mean absolute error (MAE) across the entire cohort remained within acceptable limits, the individual error rates increased significantly during movement, with some devices showing up to 30% higher error compared to resting conditions.

Frye et al. [5] evaluated devices such as the Apple Watch and Fitbit and reported that although 71% of the readings fell within a 3% margin of error at rest, this level of accuracy was not sustained during physical activity. Instead, large individual deviations were masked by averaging across time or users.

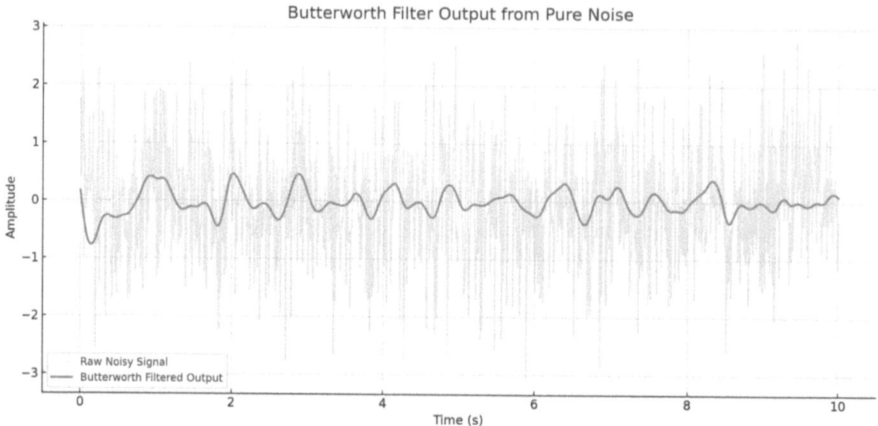

Fig. 1. Butterworth filter applied to pure noise. Although no actual heart rate is present, the filter generates a smooth, plausible waveform within the defined frequency band (0.7–3 Hz). This demonstrates the risk of falsely interpreting filtered noise as valid physiological data.

Other studies [6, 7] investigating motion artifact removal techniques such as independent component analysis (ICA), adaptive filtering, or multi-channel PPG fusion found that while these methods improve average group-level accuracy (often reducing error to less than 2 bpm), they frequently rely on discarding unreliable segments or interpolating values. As a result, the final output is often biased toward average physiological values.

Furthermore, reviews such as in [1] noted systematic bias introduced by smoothing algorithms and sensor limitations, especially across different skin tones and activity types. These findings suggest that some wearables are designed to maintain a perception of stability, potentially at the cost of reporting incorrect values for outliers or individuals with atypical physiology.

While these works acknowledge the statistical discrepancy between group-level and individual-level performance, few address the deeper issue: that certain monitoring systems systematically revert to population averages when confronted with uncertainty. This behavior can create a misleading sense of precision. Moreover, most of the existing literature focuses the accuracy in general, related to many users, and not to the individual in value areas that are special. To date, no comprehensive work has evaluated whether similar bias exists in newer wearable metrics, such as respiratory rate or core body temperature, particularly in contexts beyond healthy adult populations, such as in veterinary monitoring.

5   Method Comparison

The average resting heart rate in healthy adults typically ranges from 60 to 100 beats per minute (bpm), with population-level studies reporting mean values around 70–75 bpm [2,8]. Devices that consistently report values near this range may appear accurate in a statistical sense, even when they fail to reflect true physiological states in individual users.

To illustrate the illusion of accuracy caused by averaging, we compare hypothetical device outputs with actual physiological values. For example, a person with a true heart rate of 110 bpm during physical exertion may receive a reading of 75 bpm from a smartwatch affected by motion artifacts. Likewise, an individual with bradycardia and a true pulse of 50 bpm might receive a similarly averaged value. In both cases, the reported value falls closer to the population mean than to the actual physiological state.

This phenomenon can appear statistically valid when performance is assessed across a large sample. If a device consistently reports values near the mean heart rate of the population (e.g., 70–75 bpm), it will exhibit low overall error in group-level analysis. However, such behavior systematically hides true variability and distorts individual data.

The critical insight here is that **measurement is not the same as meaningful information**. A pulse reading of 72 bpm may appear plausible in nearly any situation, but if it does not reflect the subject's actual condition, it fails in its core purpose. This trade-off between statistical error minimization and real-world validity is especially problematic in settings where accurate, individualized data are essential.

Figures 2 and 3 illustrate the relative error between measured and true heart rate values as a function of the reported heart rate. In Fig. 2, the errors of two measurement systems—a commercial smartwatch and a remote photoplethysmography (rPPG) system—are shown. Figure 3 presents the corresponding error when the device outputs a fixed, non-measured value of 72 bpm regardless of the actual heart rate. The real data were acquired through a study involving 22 subjects (10 men and 12 women, aged 31 ± 10.9 years). A study in respiration rate monitoring provided respiration rate cycles (breath per minute) with the same effect. Hereby we were using 69 subjects (gender was equally distributed). In general, the margin of error for the respiration rate when measured by a true measuring unit is smaller than for a device that provides a fixed value. Interestingly, a fixed value provides a smaller error in the area close to the average (or fixed value), see Fig. 5.

The error is calculated using the formula:

$$\text{Error} = \left| \frac{\text{Measured Value}}{\text{True Value}} - 1 \right|$$

Interestingly, within the range of approximately 40–80 bpm—i.e., in the lower physiological band, the error from the real measurement devices is in many cases *greater* than that of the non-measuring device that always outputs 72 bpm. Even in the upper heart rate range (above 100 bpm), the error introduced by the fixed-value device remains only moderately higher (approximately 35%) compared to the actual sensors. This result highlights how averaging or default behaviors can statistically outperform noisy real-world measurements in terms of mean relative error, despite lacking any real-time physiological sensing.

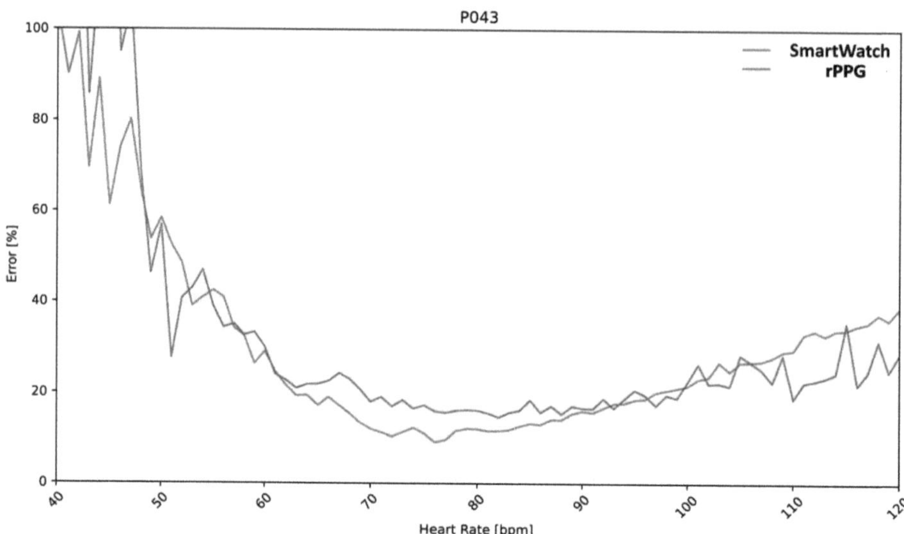

Fig. 2. Error in relation to the heart rate, recorded by a smartwatch and a rPPG heart rate monitor, groundtruth by ECG data.

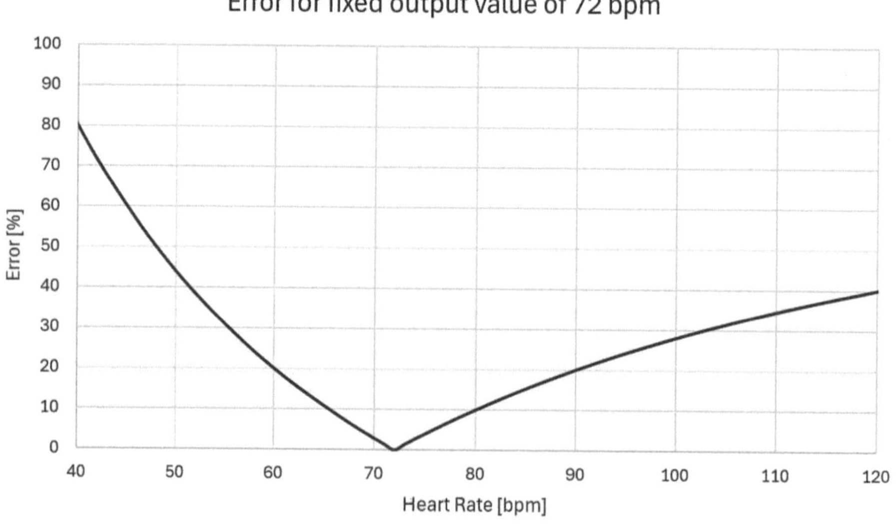

Fig. 3. True PPG signal with artifacts

Fig. 4. Error in relation to the heart rate by a device that provides a fixed value of 72 bpm. In the range of 40–80 bpm, the error of the fixed output is lower than the measuring devices.

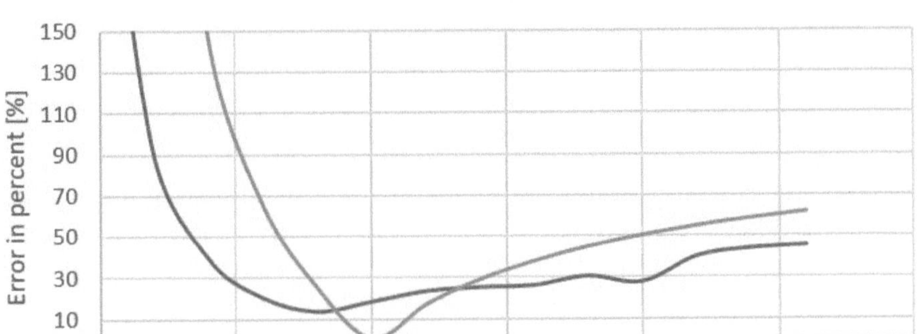

Fig. 5. Respiration rate detection, error of the measurement in relation to the respiration rate, recorded by a time-of-flight camera (blue line), in comparison to a fixed respiration detection of 10 rpm (red line), groundtruth by a breast band. (Color figure online)

6   Consequences for Application

The implications of this averaging behavior vary depending on the application context.

In human medicine, devices that underreport or mask physiological extremes can delay or prevent critical diagnoses. For instance, undetected tachycardia in a patient with cardiovascular risk may remain unnoticed if the device outputs stable but false "normal" values. Similarly, signs of bradycardia, arrhythmia, or stress responses may go unrecognized due to averaging or fallback algorithms.

In animal monitoring, such as livestock or wildlife observation, wearable sensors are increasingly used to detect stress, illness, or deviations from baseline behavior. If these systems default to population norms when signals are unclear, signs of suffering or disease may be missed. In cases such as precision farming, this could lead to the failure of early warning systems and inappropriate treatment decisions.

Across domains, decisions based on average-leaning data may falsely suggest a subject is in a healthy or normal state, leading to missed alarms, incorrect feedback loops, or even legal and ethical complications. Apparent numerical stability must not be confused with diagnostic certainty.

7 Discussion

An examination of the error curves clearly shows that, within certain target ranges, a fixed output value can result in lower average errors than actual physiological measurements. This effect is particularly pronounced when the true value lies close to the fixed output—for example, when the real heart rate fluctuates around 72 bpm.

Statistically, values near the population mean (such as heart rate, respiratory rate, or body temperature) occur more frequently. Therefore, evaluating accuracy solely based on aggregated group data is misleading. Such an approach favors devices that exploit population-level distributions without truly measuring individual physiological states.

To obtain a meaningful assessment of measurement accuracy, error must be analyzed on an individual basis and, depending on the use case, with attention to uniformity across the measurement range. Only then can the performance of a monitoring system be reliably evaluated and compared.

Despite their limitations, devices that rely on averaging or default values are widely used. Several factors contribute to their popularity:

- **User expectations**: Consumers prefer smooth, stable values over fluctuating or uncertain readings, even if this comes at the cost of accuracy.
- **Regulatory thresholds**: Some devices are not classified as medical equipment and thus are subject to less stringent validation requirements.
- **Technical constraints**: In real-world environments, especially during movement, perfect signal quality is often unattainable. Designers opt for algorithms that ensure robustness rather than physiological fidelity.

However, this raises a crucial point: **statistical accuracy is not equivalent to practical relevance**. A system that shows low mean error across 1000 users may still mislead in every individual case. For applications that rely on correct real-time interpretation—such as clinical decision-making, athlete monitoring, or animal welfare—devices must be calibrated not only to the population but to the individual context.

This suggests a need for improved system design:

- Incorporating uncertainty quantification,
- Offering transparent error reporting,
- Adapting to individual baselines and physiological profiles.

8 Conclusion

The accuracy of heart rate monitoring devices is typically assessed by how closely the measured values approximate the true heart rate across a large population. The larger the number of individuals included in such evaluations, the more the overall error tends to converge toward the population mean. Consequently, a device that simply outputs a fixed average heart rate may appear accurate when viewed across many users, even though it produces significant errors for any given individual.

This phenomenon creates the *illusion of precision*, a false sense of accuracy that does not hold true at the individual level. In this paper, we demonstrated that a device outputting a constant, non-adaptive heart rate (e.g., 72 bpm) can, in certain frequency ranges, exhibit lower relative error than actual sensing systems. Specifically, in the lower heart rate range (below 80 bpm), the fixed-value output was mathematically closer to the true values than those reported by real measurement devices under noise and artifact conditions.

Even at higher heart rates, where the discrepancy between the fixed output and true values is naturally larger, the relative error remains moderate. This effect can easily be transferred to other vital signs such as respiratory rate detection. This further reinforces the misleading appearance of accuracy in systems that prioritize statistical consistency over physiological fidelity.

This paper highlights a critical but often overlooked flaw in wearable monitoring systems: the tendency to favor statistical consistency over individualized accuracy. While group-level averaging may reduce overall error metrics, it creates a false sense of reliability when the measured values do not reflect the subject's actual condition.

Averaging Can Deceive. Systems that always return plausible numbers, regardless of real input quality, fail in their most important function: to inform, detect, and alert. Devices must not only be precise in controlled evaluations but must also deliver individually valid, context-aware measurements in real-world conditions.

Addressing this challenge requires a shift from error minimization across populations toward personalized, transparent, and adaptive monitoring solutions.

9   Outlook

Future development of wearable vital sign monitoring systems must address the limitations described in this work. Several promising directions exist to reduce reliance on statistical averaging and improve individualized measurement validity:

- **Adaptive Algorithms**: Future devices should use adaptive signal processing or machine learning models that account for user-specific baselines, skin characteristics, activity levels, or species-specific parameters in animal applications.
- **Uncertainty Reporting**: Rather than silently smoothing or replacing data, systems should explicitly flag uncertain measurements or degraded signal quality. Providing confidence intervals or signal quality indices could improve transparency and user trust.

- **Multi-Modal Integration**: Combining multiple physiological signals—such as PPG, accelerometry, temperature, and respiration—may allow for better cross-validation and artifact detection. Fusion-based systems can use one modality to verify or challenge another.
- **Context-Aware Monitoring**: Integrating contextual information (e.g., time of day, user activity, known conditions) could help tailor interpretations and avoid inappropriate generalizations.
- **Standardized Evaluation Metrics**: The development of new benchmark protocols that assess not only average error but also individual deviation and real-time validity will be critical for fair comparison between systems.

Additionally, research into ethical implications—particularly in medical and animal welfare applications—will be essential. Systems that appear accurate but systematically mislead may have far-reaching consequences that current validation frameworks fail to capture.

The challenge for the next generation of wearable technology is to bridge the gap between statistical correctness and real-world truth. Only by embracing variability and context can monitoring systems achieve the individual relevance that users increasingly demand.

On the other hand, the described phenomenon of the illusion of high precision should be used to optimize current algorithms and focus on application-balanced datasets for evaluation and optimization.

Acknowledgments. This paper was funded by Fraunhofer Society and by the German Federal Ministry for Economic Affairs and Energy (Project KK5547001GR3). We also thank the AI tool FHGenie [10] for linguistic support to improve expression, spelling and clarity in this work.

Disclosure of Interests. The authors have no competing interests to declare that are relevant to the content of this article.

References

1. Alenezi, M., Pino, E., Cho, H.: Skin tone bias in heart rate monitoring devices: an evaluation across diverse participants. IEEE Access **8**, 160850–160860 (2020). https://doi.org/10.1109/ACCESS.2020.3021120
2. Alsulami, T., Abulaban, A., Alharbi, A., et al.: Resting heart rate in a sample of healthy adult saudi population. J. Family Commun. Med. **19**(1), 20–25 (2012). https://applications.emro.who.int/imemrf/J_Fam_Community_Med/J_Fam_Community_Med_2012_19_1_20_25.pdf
3. Cohen, E.R.: An introduction to error analysis: the study of uncertainties in physical measurements. Meas. Sci. Technol. **9**(6), 022 (1998). https://doi.org/10.1088/0957-0233/9/6/022
4. Dunn, J., Runge, R., Snyder, M.: Wearable sensors for monitoring physical activity and health metrics in clinical populations: a review. NPJ Digit. Med. **3**, 1–8 (2020). https://doi.org/10.1038/s41746-020-0226-6

5. Frye, A., Hickey, K., Nelson, L.: Accuracy of consumer wearable heart rate measurement during exercise. JMIR Mhealth Uhealth **8**(9), e18694 (2020). https://doi.org/10.2196/18694

6. Ismail, I., Shabana, W., Zahra, A.: Motion artifact removal techniques in wearable PPG-based heart rate monitoring systems: a review. Sens. Actuators A **345**, 114663 (2023). https://doi.org/10.1016/j.sna.2022.114663

7. Matsumura, K., Yamakoshi, T.: Comparison of the wearable green light PPG sensor with conventional sensors in daily activities. PLoS ONE **9**(1), e87117 (2014). https://doi.org/10.1371/journal.pone.0087117

8. What your heart rate is telling you (2021). https://www.health.harvard.edu/heart-health/what-your-heart-rate-is-telling-you. Accessed July 2025

9. Stuart, A., Ord, K.: Kendall's Advanced Theory of Statistics, Distribution Theory. Wiley (2010)

10. Weber, I., Linka, H., Mertens, D., Muryshkin, T., Opgenoorth, H., Langer, S.: Fhgenie: a custom, confidentiality-preserving chat AI for corporate and scientific use. In: 2024 IEEE 21st International Conference on Software Architecture Companion (ICSA-C), pp. 26–31. IEEE (2024). https://doi.org/10.1109/icsa-c63560.2024.00011

11. Zhang, F., Knoll, A.: Systematic error modeling and bias estimation. Sensors **16**(5), 729 (2016). https://doi.org/10.3390/s16050729

Synthetic Data Generation Using a Smart Floor Digital Twin for Fall Detection

Milan Milivojčević[1]([✉]) [ID], Niki Hrovatin[1,3] [ID], Jernej Vičič[1,2,4] [ID],
and Aleksandar Tošić[1,2,3] [ID]

[1] Faculty of Mathematics, Natural Sciences and Information Technologies, University
of Primorska, Glagoljaška 8, 6000 Koper, Slovenia
{milan.milivojcevic,niki.hrovatin,jernej.vicic,aleksandar.tosic}@famnit.upr.si
[2] Institute Andrej Marušič (IAM), University of Primorska,
Muzejski trg 2, 6000 Koper, Slovenia
[3] InnoRenew CoE, Livade 6a, 6310 Izola, Slovenia
[4] Research Centre of the Slovenian Academy of Sciences and Arts, The Fran Ramovš
Institute, Novi Trg 2, 1000 Ljubljana, Slovenia

Abstract. The creation of reliable fall detection systems requires access
to large quantities of labeled sensor data. Collecting such data in real
world settings, especially for critical events such as falls, poses practical,
ethical, and safety challenges. In this work, we propose a digital twin of a
pressure-sensor-based floor system designed to simulate realistic human-
floor interactions in a virtual environment. Our virtual replica mirrors
the physical floor structure, composed of tightly networked sensor tiles,
enabling the simulation of various fall scenarios using rigid-body ragdoll
models. Synthetic sensor data is generated through virtual collisions,
providing time-series pressure patterns analogous to real-world recordings. This method enables scalable data generation for training machine
learning models focused on binary fall detection, with future expansion to multi-class activity recognition. Our approach aims to bridge
the gap between the physical constraints of data collection and the need
for extensive training data-sets in ambient assisted living systems.

Keywords: Digital twin · Fall detection · Synthetic data · Smart
floor · Human activity recognition · Artificial Intelligence

1 Introduction

Falls are a leading cause of injury, hospitalization, and loss of independence
among older adults [24]. Early detection of fall events and the ability to monitor
daily movement patterns play a key role in preventing long-term consequences
and improving quality of life. Although a range of sensing solutions have been
explored, including wearable devices [4], vision-based systems [1], and radar or
WiFi-based sensing [23], each carries limitations related to user compliance, privacy, or environmental constraints. Research indicates that older adults often
favor non-wearable sensing technologies for in-home monitoring [9].

Ö. Durmaz Incel et al. (Eds.): iWOAR 2025, LNCS 16292, pp. 234–249, 2026.
https://doi.org/10.1007/978-3-032-13312-0_14

In this context, floor-embedded pressure sensor systems offer a compelling alternative. These systems operate passively, require no user intervention, and can be seamlessly integrated into everyday environments such as homes, hospitals, and assisted living facilities. By capturing spatial pressure distributions and temporal activity patterns, they can potentially detect falls, assess gait irregularities, and support broader applications in ambient healthcare [5, 6, 14].

Despite this promise, intelligent floor systems remain relatively underexplored, particularly in the context of machine learning for activity recognition. A major bottleneck is the scarcity of large-scale labeled data-sets, especially for rare events like falls, which are ethically and practically difficult to collect [8, 22]. This makes model training, benchmarking, and generalization across users or environments challenging.

To address these issues, recent trends have turned towards *synthetic data generation* and *digital twin frameworks*. These methods simulate physical systems and human movement virtually, allowing scalable and ethically safe data-set creation [10, 16, 19]. However, current work in this area has largely focused on other sensing modalities (e.g., camera-based or inertial simulations) [18, 21], leaving pressure-based simulation models relatively untouched.

In this paper, we present a digital twin framework for an intelligent pressure-sensor-based floor system designed to simulate realistic fall events and generate synthetic pressure data. By simulating fall dynamics within a controllable virtual environment, it becomes possible to create large-scale, labeled datasets for training and evaluating machine learning models. To evaluate the plausibility of our generated data, we compare the output of our simulation with real-world recordings from an existing pressure-floor dataset. This comparison highlights key similarities and differences, offering insights into how synthetic environments can approximate real-world dynamics. Our results show that, despite simplifications, the core structure of fall events is preserved, making this a promising approach for scalable fall detection development and the broader deployment of intelligent flooring systems in ambient healthcare.

2 Related Work

2.1 Pressure-Sensor Network Architectures

Early demonstrations of pressure-sensor–based floors showed their promise for non-intrusive activity detection. Tošić et al. [20] introduced a wired grid of 16 force-sensing resistors in a 1.2×1.2 m panel, interfaced to microcontrollers and custom logging software, and collected 420 fall and activity trials from 60 participants [20].

Subsequent systems have introduced additional hardware and networking features. Cocconcelli *et al.* built a smart floor with piezoresistive tiles and LED feedback, all coordinated via MQTT for IoT integration [7]. Zompanti *et al.* designed energy-harvesting tiles using piezoelectric stacks to power human–machine interfaces [25]. Murphy *et al.* presented a wireless tactile sensing framework (WiReSens) supporting arrayed pressure sensors with calibration and real-time visualization [15]. These systems highlight the evolving capabilities of sensor networks, from data collection and edge processing to energy autonomy and connectivity.

2.2 Digital Twins and Synthetic Data Generation

Generating large, labeled data-sets for rare events like falls remains challenging. Digital twin and simulation-based approaches have been adopted in various domains to overcome data scarcity. Kim *et al.* created a 3D digital twin of an indoor environment and ran particle-based fire simulations to generate synthetic RGB-D flame images for early-warning model training [12]. Jang *et al.* developed a driving simulator digital twin to produce vast quantities of road scene images, improving traffic-signal recognition when combined with limited real data [11]. In manufacturing, Lopes *et al.* modeled production lines in simulation to synthesize event logs and sensor readings for process analytics [13].

Game engines such as Unity have become popular platforms for these tasks. The Unity Perception package enables automated scene variation and annotation for computer vision data-sets [2]. Cauli and Recupero demonstrated that action-classification models benefit from Unity-generated video augmentations [3]. Sabir *et al.* compared Unity and Unreal Engine for construction-hazard scenario simulations, underlining the ability of both engines to create complex, labeled training data [17].

In this work, Unity is likewise used to build a digital twin of the pressure-sensor floor, enabling controlled generation of synthetic fall events for downstream model development and evaluation.

3 System Overview

3.1 Real-World Pressure-Sensor Network

The physical pressure-sensor network underlying this study represents an evolution of the prototype introduced in [20]. The updated system adopts a modular tile-based architecture designed for high scalability, currently composed of 30 independent MCUs—each responsible for a single tile and managing 8 Force Sensing Resistor (FSR) sensors. While the present implementation covers an area of 16 square meters, the architecture supports further expansion with minimal configuration effort. Significant enhancements have been made to the communication protocol, allowing for autonomous topology reconstruction. This enables flexible deployment in varying environments and supports hot-swapping of tiles without requiring manual reconfiguration. Each tile is constructed from a cork-based lower layer, on top of which 8 FSR sensors (identical to those used in [20]) are fixed (see Fig. 1). An ESP32-based MCU is embedded within each tile to process sensor data and handle communication. The surface layer above the sensors is interchangeable, allowing adaptation to different use cases or design requirements.

Fig. 1. Prototype tile with cork base and 8 mounted FSR sensors.

3.2 Digital Twin Architecture and Design Goals

The primary goal of the proposed digital twin is to enable realistic simulation, scalable data generation, and compatibility with real-world pressure sensor datasets, particularly for applications in fall detection and ambient assisted living. By offering a virtual replica of a sensor-equipped floor system, the digital twin addresses a key challenge in this research area: the limited availability of ethically and practically feasible fall data for training machine learning models.

To support modular development and extensibility, the digital twin is structured into three conceptual layers:

Sensor Grid Layer. This layer represents the foundation of the simulation: a network of pressure-sensitive tiles arranged in a grid layout. Each virtual tile emulates a real-world sensor that responds to dynamic pressure inputs generated during human-floor interactions. Forces from ragdoll body parts are projected onto this grid through collision detection in the simulation engine, producing time-series outputs that closely resemble actual sensor readings. The granularity of the grid, temporal resolution, and sensor response characteristics can be adjusted to match different physical prototypes.

Surface Layer. While surface materials such as parquet, vinyl, or carpeting can influence pressure distribution and damping, this component is not explicitly modeled in the current version of the virtual environment. Instead, we approximate its presence by applying a constant additive offset across all sensor outputs during data generation. This allows us to "bake in" surface effects as a configurable parameter, without complicating the simulation physics. This abstraction enables the current focus to remain on dynamic interaction and fall modeling, while also leaving room for future exploration of material-specific behavior.

Above-Floor Layer. This top layer contains a ragdoll agent composed of rigid-body segments connected via physical joints. No animation scripts are applied, hence movements result entirely from gravity and physics-based interactions within the environment. The ragdoll's body mass distribution approximates a typical adult human and enables realistic fall dynamics in various scenarios. This configuration ensures that fall events emerge naturally from the simulation rather than being manually choreographed, improving data realism and diversity.

By separating the system into these three layers, the digital twin framework promotes modular experimentation, easier debugging, and clearer reasoning about each component's contribution to the final data-set. This structure also supports incremental expansion toward more complex simulations, such as multi-agent environments or adaptive flooring materials.

4 Virtual Environment and Implementation

4.1 Simulation Platform

The virtual environment was developed using the Unity Engine Editor, version 6000.0.28f1. Unity was chosen not for its novelty but for its well-established physics engine, support for rigidbody dynamics, and ease of integration with common game development workflows. In this work, we leverage Unity's existing and widely used functionalities, such as rigidbodies, colliders, joints, and physics-based interactions, to build a practical and reproducible digital twin of a pressure-sensor-based floor system. The goal is not to introduce new mechanics at the engine level, but rather to use Unity's built-in tools in a structured way that enables realistic fall simulation and synthetic data generation. This approach ensures accessibility for others in the field and prioritizes simulation logic and sensor modeling over low-level engine customization.

4.2 Ragdoll and Sensor Interaction

The human figure in the simulation is implemented as a ragdoll agent, created from a skinned mesh character rigged with a full bone hierarchy in a 3D modeling environment. This structure enables physics-based fall dynamics without relying on predefined animations, ensuring that movement and posture changes arise naturally from gravitational and collisional forces.

Each major body part, such as the hips, spine, upper and lower extremities, shoulders, and head, is represented by a rigid body component in Unity. These rigidbodies define physical properties such as mass and enable the agent to respond to forces and torques. Importantly, each rigidbody's previous position and velocity (initialized to zero) are stored during every time interval. This allows acceleration to be calculated in the next interval, a key quantity in pressure estimation during collisions, while also updating the stored previous position and velocity values.

The rigidbodies are connected using Character Joints, which constrain the motion between connected parts while allowing a limited range of rotation. This setup maintains human-like articulation and prevents unrealistic limb detachment or collapse during motion.

Colliders are assigned to each body part to handle physical interactions. These are invisible shapes that approximate the body part's volume for collision detection. To balance realism with computational efficiency, we employ a simplified setup:

- Capsule colliders for arms and legs (two per limb);
- Box colliders for the hips and spine;
- A sphere collider for the head.

This structure offers a reasonable trade-off between physical accuracy and simulation performance. A more detailed collider configuration could yield more realistic pressure distribution but would significantly increase computational cost.

On the other side of the interaction, the floor system is modeled as a 6×5 tile grid with no gaps between tiles. Each tile contains a rigid upper surface and hosts eight virtual sensors. Both the tile surface and individual sensors are assigned box colliders to detect contact with ragdoll body parts.

During the simulation, every sensor calculates the applied pressure at each time step. This value includes two components:

1. Direct collisions with ragdoll parts (when the sensor collider is triggered), and
2. Indirect pressure transferred from the overlying tile surface.

The tile surface detects collisions with ragdoll body parts but does not store pressure values itself. Instead, it distributes the detected pressure among the tile sensors using Inverse Distance Weighting (IDW). This means that sensors physically closer to the point of impact receive a greater proportion of the pressure.

The pressure computation depends on the contact state:

- When a new collision occurs, the pressure is estimated using the mass of the colliding rigid body, its acceleration, and the contact area A:

$$P = \frac{m \cdot a}{A} \tag{1}$$

- For ongoing contact (in frames following initial collision), the pressure is calculated as the weight of the rigid body distributed over the contact area:

$$P = \frac{m \cdot g}{A} \tag{2}$$

Importantly, in both cases, the mass is not limited to the contacting part of the body. Instead, a percentage of the total ragdoll mass—representing the influence of non-contacting parts—is distributed among currently active sensors, again using IDW centered on the ragdoll's spine object, which serves as an approximate center of mass. This approach mimics how body weight is redistributed during partial support, improving realism in pressure estimation, and simulating the way body segments collectively contribute to the floor reaction forces.

4.3 Sampling and Time Resolution

The simulation operates at a fixed sampling interval of 30 milliseconds, corresponding to an effective update rate of approximately 30 Hz. In our setup, this was the lowest practical sampling rate chosen due to the computational complexity of simulating physics-based interactions, multiple colliders, and sensor pressure calculations in real time. Running the system at finer temporal resolutions (e.g., below 30 ms) significantly increases processing demands without offering proportionate gains for the target application of fall detection.

That said, the system is designed to support flexible sampling rates, allowing researchers to adjust the update interval based on experimental needs or hardware capabilities. At each time step, the system updates:

- The positions and velocities of all ragdoll body parts;
- Collision states between the ragdoll and floor components;
- The calculated pressure values for each sensor;
- And the metadata associated with the simulation frame (e.g., whether a fall event is ongoing).

All sensor readings are stored in structured time-series format, making the output directly compatible with standard pipelines used in activity recognition and fall detection tasks.

5 Synthetic Data Generation and Evaluation

5.1 Simulated Fall Scenarios

Simulating realistic fall events is a non-trivial task, particularly when relying only on physics-based interactions rather than scripted animations. Although there may appear to be many ways to simulate a fall, most rely on predefined animations, obstacle triggers, or hybrid systems that involve motion control. In contrast, achieving naturalistic falls from a fully physics-driven character, without any walking behavior or injection of external force, is far from straight-forward. Simulating even basic upright posture under gravity requires specialized setups, such as active ragdolls, which blend physics with motion targets to maintain balance and locomotion. In this work, we deliberately avoid this complexity to focus on the raw dynamics of uncontrolled falls. We use a passive ragdoll, initialized without any animation or movement logic, such that it immediately begins to fall as soon as the simulation starts.

To introduce variability across fall events while remaining within this passive setup, we randomize the initial conditions of the ragdoll across several dimensions:

- Spatial placement: whether the ragdoll is spawned directly on the floor or slightly elevated;
- Orientation and lean direction: including forward, backward, or lateral tilts to influence fall direction;
- Joint constraints: varying the degrees of freedom on select joints (e.g., stiffening knees or arms) to simulate stiffness, injury, or age-related limitations.

These randomized factors allow us to generate a diverse set of fall trajectories and outcomes, all driven entirely by the underlying physics engine. See Fig. 2 for illustrations of several final ragdoll positions after falling under different conditions.

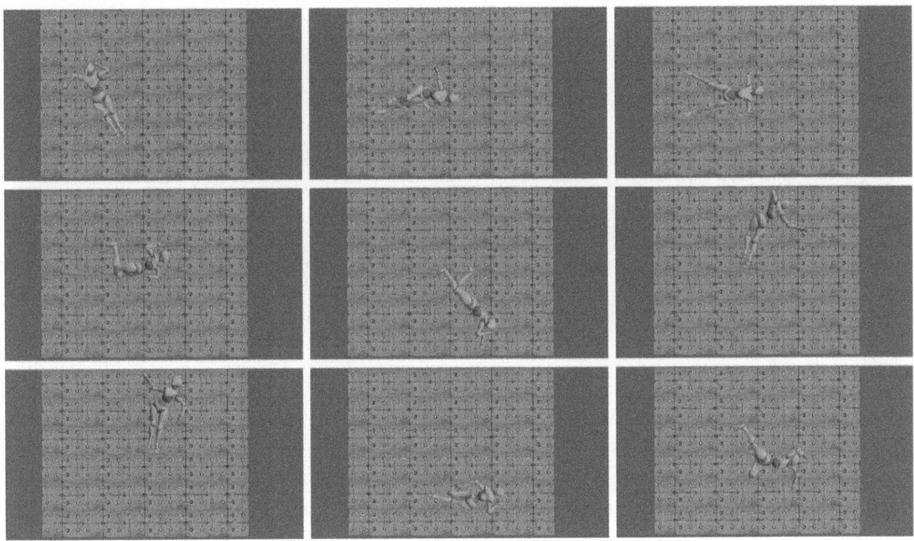

Fig. 2. Examples of final ragdoll positions after various simulated falls. Different outcomes are achieved by randomizing joint constraints, initial orientation and spatial placement.

5.2   Sensor Data Output and Labeling Format

The output of each fall simulation is stored as a CSV-formatted time series, where each row corresponds to a single time step (30 ms by default). Each row contains:

- Pressure values from all individual sensors (flattened into columns);
- Timestamp of the frame;
- Experiment duration (time intervals between calculations, constant across simulation);
- Total ragdoll mass (constant across simulation);
- A fall detection label (binary: fall or no fall).

Fall detection is inferred based on which part of the ragdoll makes contact with the floor. Specifically, when the collision between the ragdoll and the floor occurs via any body part other than the left or right lower leg, the system marks it as a fall event. This distinction allows for differentiation between intentional standing or walking postures (typically involving feet) and unintended collapses involving the upper body, hips, or head.

This structure ensures that the generated data can be directly fed into machine learning pipelines for training classification models or analyzing temporal fall signatures. An example visualization of raw pressure data over time from 16 sensors is shown in Fig. 3.

5.3   Comparison with Real-World Data

To validate the potential of our simulation setup, we performed a comparative test using data from the publicly available data-set by Tošić, Hrovatin, and Vičič [20], which contains fall event recordings collected via a pressure-sensor-based smart floor. Their experimental setup shares structural similarities with our simulated sensor grid, making it a suitable reference for initial evaluation.

For this comparison, we configured our virtual agent with physical attributes matching those of subject ID 39 from the data-set—specifically, a height of 183 cm and a mass of 70 kg. We selected a fall scenario from both data-sets corresponding to test category 3, described in [20] as a "forward fall ending laying flat". This specific category was chosen intentionally, as other recorded fall types involved motion interruptions such as stopping on the knees, arm protection during descent, or postfall recovery movements - all of which are currently not replicable with our setup due to the use of a passive ragdoll. In contrast, category 3 represents a direct, unassisted fall, which better aligns with the capabilities and behavior of our physics-driven agent.

To approximate this fall type within our simulation, we pre-conditioned the ragdoll with a slight forward tilt of 2°, and restricted the knee joint ranges to promote a forward fall rather than a collapse into a kneeling position. Similarly, shoulder joint constraints were applied to limit arm movement and prevent mid-air rotation, increasing the likelihood that the ragdoll would fall directly forward

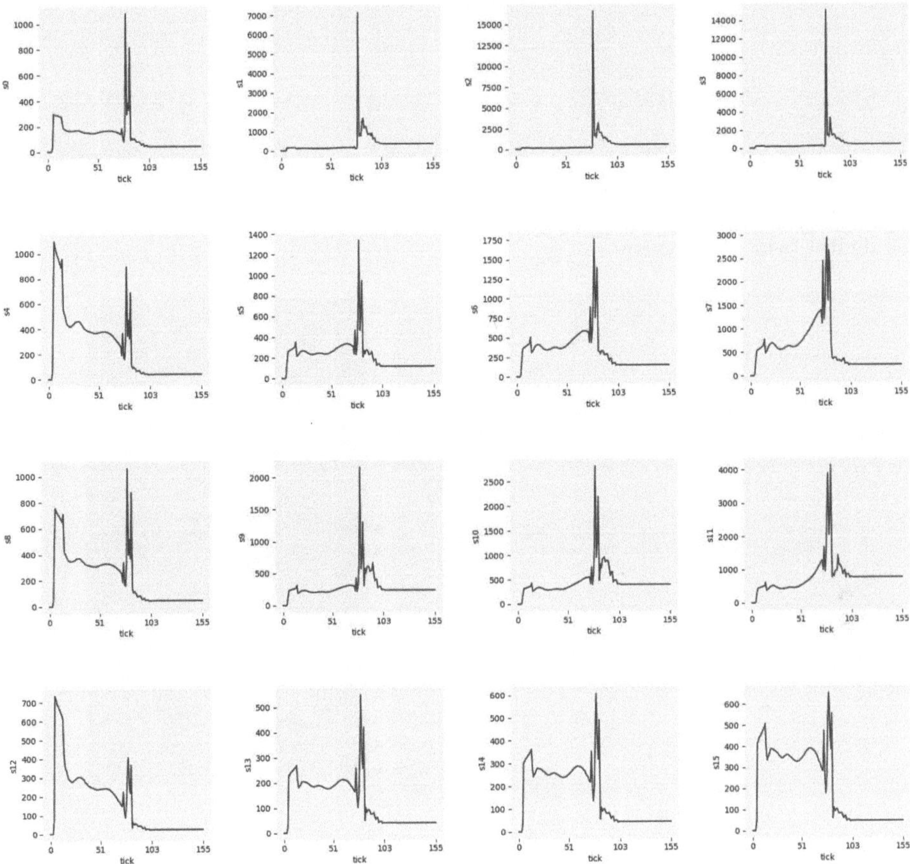

Fig. 3. An example of raw data from 16 pressure sensors, with pressure force shown on the y axis and the sample index on the x axis.

and land in a flat prone posture. These adjustments imitation a more realistic emulation of the fall pattern recorded in the real-world data-set.

The fall trajectory of the virtual agent in our simulation is illustrated in Fig. 4 as a sequence of snapshots taken over time, and its final posture is shown along with the generated pressure heatmap in Fig. 5. For comparison, we extracted raw sensor data from both systems and focused on the total pressure measured across all sensors over time.

To align the sampling resolution between data-sets, we downsampled the original 10 ms resolution data from Tošić et al. [20] by selecting every third reading, matching our 30 ms simulation timestep. The resulting normalized total pressure time series for both the real and simulated fall events are presented in Fig. 6, where each point represents the total pressure detected across all sensors

Fig. 4. Sequence of frames showing the simulated forward fall of the virtual agent in the digital twin environment.

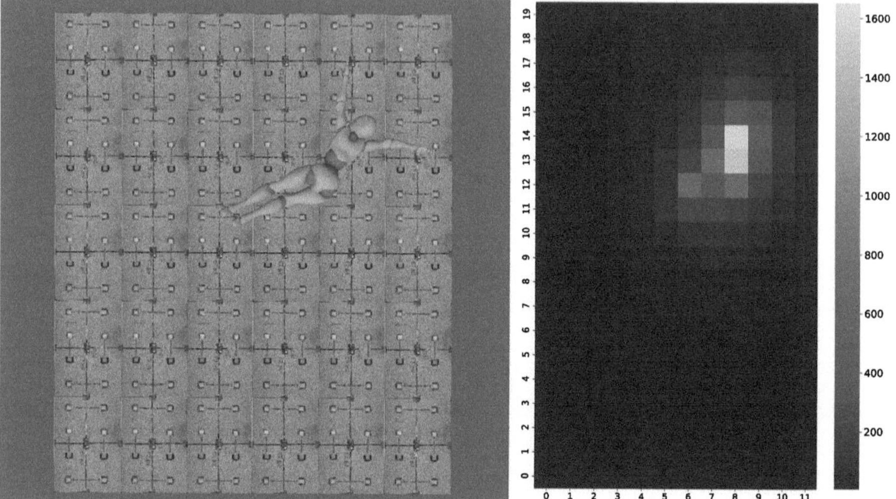

Fig. 5. Final position of the simulated fall, on the left and the corresponding pressure heat map generated by the sensorized floor on the right.

in a given time interval, normalized as a percentage of peak pressure for that fall.

The interpretation of the comparison is further elaborated in the Discussion section.

6   Discussion

To evaluate the fidelity of the synthetic fall data generated in our digital twin environment, we compared it against real-world data from Tošić et al. [20], focusing on a forward fall ending flat (category 3). The comparison, illustrated in Fig. 6, reveals both promising similarities and areas where further refinement is needed.

At a glance, both data-sets show a distinct peak representing the moment of initial body impact with the floor, followed by a sequence of smaller pressure fluctuations and a final stabilization phase. This consistency suggests that our

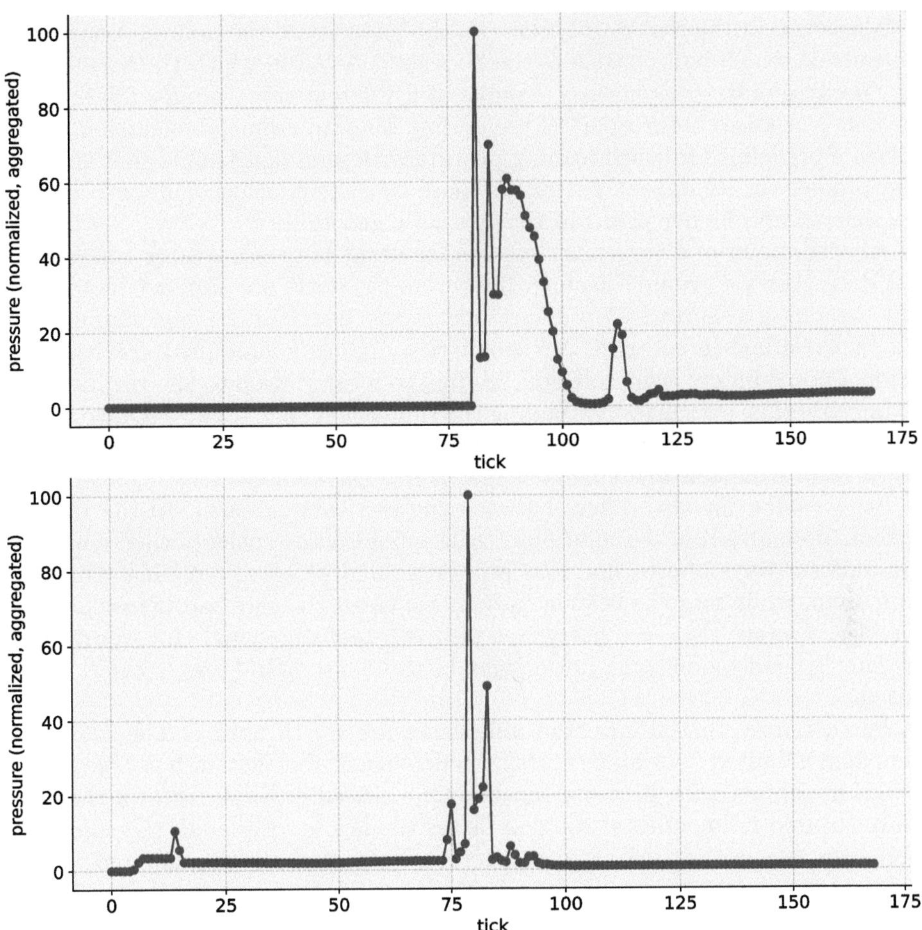

Fig. 6. Comparison of normalized raw pressure sensor data during a forward fall. The top graph shows real-world data from participant 39 in fall category 3 (forward fall ending flat) from Tošić et al. [20], while the bottom graph shows corresponding synthetic data generated using our simulation environment.

simulation framework can successfully replicate the overall dynamics of a forward fall. However, several differences remain that highlight the complexity of simulating such events.

One of the key differences lies in the shape and distribution of the pressure peaks. In real-world data, multiple distinguishable local maxima appear after the initial peak. This likely reflects the sequential contact of different body parts (e.g., torso, limbs) with the floor, a behavior inherently variable in human motion. In contrast, our synthetic data exhibit a simpler post-impact signature, partly due to the limited number of colliders (only 11), which reduces the granularity of physical interaction captured during the fall.

Moreover, in the real-world scenario, the intensity of the main pressure peak depends on which body part hits the floor first. A fall in which the torso is first hit - because of its greater mass - results in a different signal than a fall in which the hands or knees absorb part of the energy. Since our simulated ragdoll always falls in a predefined forward-leaning posture with joint constraints that suppress arm protection, its impact pattern is more consistent, which may also explain the sharper and higher peaks in the synthetic graph.

Another point of divergence concerns the decay of pressure after impact. The real data shows a gradual decline, likely due to subtle post-impact movements and the physical spread of pressure across the floor surface and through the soft mat overlay. In contrast, our simulation applies a simplified gravity-based formula immediately after collision, leading to a rapid drop to the resting state. To improve this, we suggest extending the simulation logic to incorporate a short transitional phase with smoothed deceleration or applying a pressure decay curve rather than a discrete switch.

Sensor behavior also differs between the two environments. In the physical system, pressure from a single point can spread across neighboring sensors in non-uniform ways due to material properties and physical coupling. Our digital system, while more consistent, assumes a cleaner separation between sensor readings, leading to a less noisy but also less realistic signal. Incorporating a pressure spread model or a noise layer in the Sensor Grid Layer could bridge this gap.

Furthermore, spatial coverage differences are worth noting. The real-world setup had a limited floor area $(1, 2m^2)$, which meant that not all body parts were always in contact with pressure sensors. Our virtual environment, on the other hand, ensured full contact through a larger tile layout. Although this allows for more complete data, it may also exaggerate pressure readings compared to their real-world counterparts.

From the perspective of our three-layer architecture, the differences can be interpreted as follows:

- Above-Floor Layer: Variability in fall mechanics and contact dynamics is critical and could be enriched with more randomized fall behaviors or by modeling non-ideal poses;
- Sensor Grid Layer: The pressure propagation could benefit from a diffusion model or physically-inspired blur kernel to simulate how pressure spreads through real materials;
- Surface Layer: Adding random noise, simulating sensor calibration errors, or mimicking the influence of floor padding could improve realism and replicate the imperfections seen in the real-world data.

Despite these differences, the core structure of the fall is still clearly detectable in both data-sets, especially the main impact moment. This indicates that our simulation approach can serve as a useful and viable proof of concept for generating synthetic fall data in a controlled environment. As the field of fall detection continues to grow, refining such simulations can provide a cost-effective and scalable way to train and validate models where real-world data is limited, sensitive, or difficult to obtain.

7   Conclusion and Future Work

In this work, we presented a proof-of-concept digital twin environment for pressure-sensor-based floor systems, aimed at generating synthetic data for fall detection. Through a comparative analysis between our synthetically generated data and real-world recordings from Tošić et al. [20], we demonstrated that our simulation setup can reproduce key structural patterns of fall events, most notably the primary impact peak. This supports the utility of our approach for initial development, testing, and validation of fall detection models in scenarios where real data is limited, sensitive, or difficult to collect.

However, several simplifications in our current system contribute to observable differences between real and synthetic signals. These differences provide meaningful opportunities for improvement. Future work may focus on:

- Adding surface layer noise to better mimic the variability and imperfections of real-world sensor installations;
- Exploring alternative models for pressure spread, possibly incorporating physical deformation or dynamic redistribution across neighboring sensors;
- Increasing the number of colliders on the virtual agent to enable finer spatial detail and more distinguishable pressure peaks;
- Integrating active ragdoll physics to better reflect muscular control, joint stiffness, and non-passive body responses during a fall.

These enhancements will not only improve realism but also increase the representational diversity of the generated data-set, which is essential for training robust machine learning models. Ultimately, our goal is to evolve this simulation framework into a flexible and scalable tool for supporting fall detection research across a range of scenarios and user profiles.

Disclosure of Interests. The authors declare no competing interests.

References

1. Anderson, D., Keller, J.M., Skubic, M., Chen, X., He, Z.: Recognizing falls from silhouettes. In: 2006 International Conference of the IEEE Engineering in Medicine and Biology Society, pp. 6388–6391. IEEE (2006)
2. Borkman, S., et al.: Unity perception: generate synthetic data for computer vision. arXiv preprint: arXiv:2107.04259 (2021)
3. Cauli, N., Recupero, D.R.: Synthetic data augmentation for video action classification using unity. IEEE Access (2024)
4. Chen, J., Kwong, K., Chang, D., Luk, J., Bajcsy, R.: Wearable sensors for reliable fall detection. In: 2005 IEEE Engineering in Medicine and Biology 27th Annual Conference, pp. 3551–3554. IEEE (2006)

5. Chen, Y.J., et al.: Pressure-sensor-based gait analysis for disabled people. Sensors Mater. **34** (2022)
6. Cheng, J., Sundholm, M., Zhou, B., Hirsch, M., Lukowicz, P.: Smart-surface: large scale textile pressure sensors arrays for activity recognition. Pervasive Mob. Comput. **30**, 97–112 (2016)
7. Cocconcelli, F., Matrella, G., Mora, N., Casu, I., Vargas Godoy, D.A., Ciampolini, P.: IoT smart flooring supporting active and healthy lifestyles. Sensors **23**(6), 3162 (2023)
8. Delahoz, Y.S., Labrador, M.A.: Survey on fall detection and fall prevention using wearable and external sensors. Sensors **14**(10), 19806–19842 (2014)
9. Demiris, G., et al.: Older adults' attitudes towards and perceptions of 'smart home' technologies: a pilot study. Med. Inform. Internet Med. **29**(2), 87–94 (2004)
10. Grieves, M., Vickers, J.: Digital twin: mitigating unpredictable, undesirable emergent behavior in complex systems. In: Transdisciplinary Perspectives on Complex Systems: New Findings and Approaches, pp. 85–113. Springer (2016)
11. Jang, I.S., Li, K.J., Joo, E.O., Kim, M.S.: Synthetic training dataset generation using a digital twin-based autonomous driving simulator. Sensors Mater. **36** (2024)
12. Kim, H.C., Lam, H.K., Lee, S.H., Ok, S.Y.: Early fire detection system by using automatic synthetic dataset generation model based on digital twins. Appl. Sci. **14**(5), 1801 (2024)
13. Lopes, P.V., Silveira, L., Guimaraes Aquino, R.D., Ribeiro, C.H., Skoogh, A., Verri, F.A.N.: Synthetic data generation for digital twins: enabling production systems analysis in the absence of data. Int. J. Comput. Integr. Manuf. **37**(10-11), 1252–1269 (2024)
14. Muheidat, F., Lo'Ai, A.T.: In-home floor based sensor system-smart carpet-to facilitate healthy aging in place (AIP). IEEE Access **8**, 178627–178638 (2020)
15. Murphy, D., Zhu, J., Liang, P.P., Matusik, W., Luo, Y.: WiReSens toolkit: an open-source platform towards accessible wireless tactile sensing. arXiv preprint: arXiv:2412.00247 (2024)
16. Murtaza, H., Ahmed, M., Khan, N.F., Murtaza, G., Zafar, S., Bano, A.: Synthetic data generation: state of the art in health care domain. Comput. Sci. Rev. **48**, 100546 (2023)
17. Sabir, A., et al.: Synthetic data generation with unity 3D and unreal engine for construction hazard scenarios: a comparative analysis. In: International Conference on Construction Engineering and Project Management, pp. 1286–1288. Korea Institute of Construction Engineering and Management (2024)
18. Shi, Y., Zhang, Y., Li, Z., Yuan, S., Zhu, S.: IMU/UWB fusion method using a complementary filter and a Kalman filter for hybrid upper limb motion estimation. Sensors **23**(15), 6700 (2023)
19. Sun, T., He, X., Li, Z.: Digital twin in healthcare: recent updates and challenges. Digital Health **9**, 20552076221149652 (2023)
20. Tošić, A., Hrovatin, N., Vičič, J.: Data about fall events and ordinary daily activities from a sensorized smart floor. Data Brief **37**, 107253 (2021)
21. Uhlenberg, L., Haeusler, L.O., Amft, O.: SynHAR: augmenting human activity recognition with synthetic inertial sensor data generated from human surface models. IEEE Access (2024)
22. Usmani, S., Saboor, A., Haris, M., Khan, M.A., Park, H.: Latest research trends in fall detection and prevention using machine learning: a systematic review. Sensors **21**(15), 5134 (2021)

23. Wang, W., Liu, A.X., Shahzad, M., Ling, K., Lu, S.: Device-free human activity recognition using commercial WiFi devices. IEEE J. Sel. Areas Commun. **35**(5), 1118–1131 (2017)
24. World Health Organization: Falls (2021). https://www.who.int/news-room/fact-sheets/detail/falls
25. Zompanti, A., Romeo, P., Sabatini, A., Vollero, L., Santonico, M., Pennazza, G.: Energy-harvesting smart tiles for human–machine interface applications. In: Proceedings, vol. 97, p. 35. MDPI (2024)

Real-Time ECG and HRV Monitoring in Handball Using a Low-Cost Wearable Sensor

Jonas Pöhler[(✉)] [iD], Dimitri Laumann, and Kristof Van Laerhoven [iD]

University of Siegen, Siegen, Germany
`jonas.poehler@uni-siegen.de`

Abstract. The proliferation of wearable technology has revolutionized sports science, providing detailed insights into athlete performance and physical condition. However, the use of ECG in dynamic, high-contact sports like handball presents significant challenges. This paper introduces HeartTrack, an open-source wearable electrocardiogram (ECG) monitoring system designed specifically for monitoring athlete exertion in real-world sporting conditions. The system employs a distributed architecture based on the Message Queuing Telemetry Transport (MQTT) protocol for robust and decoupled data handling. Firstly, the system provides a real-time dashboard for the immediate visualization of the incoming ECG waveform alongside the calculated physiological parameters. Secondly, we report on a system validation study conducted during a handball training session, demonstrating the system's capability to quantify significant changes in cardiovascular metrics corresponding to player exertion. The key findings confirmed that the system could effectively track significant changes in heart rate and heart rate variability that correspond directly to varying levels of physical exertional activity. The system design and software is shared at: hearttrack.cloud.

Keywords: Wearable Sensors · Athlete Monitoring · Handball

1 Introduction

The proliferation of wearable technology has significantly advanced sports science, enabling more accessible insights into athlete performance and physical condition. While metrics like speed and distance, commonly tracked by GPS and accelerometers, offer valuable information about an athlete's external load, they often fail to capture the internal physiological load, which is the physiological response to the exercise performed. This internal load is critical for optimizing training, preventing overtraining, and reducing injury risk. Electrocardiography (ECG), which measures the heart's electrical activity, offers a direct measurement of the cardiovascular system's response to physical stress, making it a gold standard for assessing player exertion.

O. Durmaz Incel et al. (Eds.): iWOAR 2025, LNCS 16292, pp. 250–260, 2026.
https://doi.org/10.1007/978-3-032-13312-0_15

However, the use of ECG in dynamic, high-contact sports such as handball poses significant challenges. Commercial systems are often expensive and function as proprietary "black boxes," limiting both data access and customization for researchers. In this work, we use the term dynamic sports to describe activities with irregular, high-intensity movement patterns and frequent body contact, for example handball, basketball, or rugby. These conditions generate far more severe motion artifacts than those typically observed in endurance sports like running or cycling. This distinction underlines why developing robust, low-cost ECG monitoring systems for these contexts is particularly challenging and necessary.

There is a clear need for accessible, open-source tools that allow researchers and practitioners to not only collect physiological data in these challenging environments but also to study and address these fundamental signal quality issues.

This paper introduces HeartTrack, an open-source wearable ECG system designed specifically for monitoring athlete exertion in real-world sporting conditions. Our contribution is threefold. First, we present the complete hardware and software design of the HeartTrack system, which is fully open-source to encourage adaptation and further development by the community. Second, we report on a system validation study conducted during a handball training session, demonstrating the system's capability to track meaningful trends in player exertion through heart rate monitoring. Third, we provide a crucial characterization of the primary limitation we encountered: the significant impact of motion artifacts on signal quality during high-intensity athletic movements.

By validating our system in a practical setting and transparently reporting on its limitations, we provide a realistic baseline for on-body ECG sensing in dynamic sports. This work serves as both a practical tool for sports scientists and a foundational study for future research aimed at developing robust algorithms to mitigate motion artifacts. This paper is structured as follows: We first review related work on wearable ECG systems and motion artifact challenges. We then detail the HeartTrack system architecture, followed by the methodology of our validation study. Subsequently, we present the results, focusing on both successful exertion tracking and the analysis of signal artifacts. Finally, we discuss the implications of our findings and outline future work to enhance the system's reliability.

2   Related Work

The foundation of this research rests on three key areas: the landscape of wearable ECG devices, the persistent challenge of motion artifacts in physiological sensing, and the specific application of monitoring player exertion in handball.

Wearable ECG devices are becoming increasingly prevalent for monitoring the cardiac activity of athletes and health-conscious individuals. Their potential for detecting arrhythmias and other cardiac events in real-world settings is significant [22,23]. Research has shown that these devices can be non-inferior to standard care for arrhythmia detection [10]. A variety of form factors exist, from user-friendly smartwatches and handheld devices to patches and mobile telemetry systems designed for continuous monitoring [4].

However, the scientific community acknowledges key limitations. Sanchis-Gomar et al. [23] highlight a scarcity of large-scale trials focused on identifying exercise-related arrhythmias with wearables. While popular devices like the Apple Watch and Fitbit have demonstrated acceptable heart rate accuracy in everyday conditions [17], recent studies confirm their accuracy declines significantly during intense exercise [14], especially for sensitive metrics like Heart Rate Variability (HRV) [3,8]. This gap underscores a critical need for standardized validation protocols to ensure the reliability of these devices in athletic contexts [21], a need that our present validation study of the HeartTrack system aims to address.

Our work is positioned within a landscape of diverse wearable sensors, each with distinct trade-offs for athletic monitoring. Commercial chest-strap systems, such as the Polar H10, are well-regarded for providing high-quality ECG data but function as proprietary "black boxes" that limit raw data access and customization for researchers. Consumer smartwatches, including the Apple Watch, offer user-friendly interfaces but primarily rely on photoplethysmography (PPG) for continuous heart rate monitoring, a method susceptible to motion artifacts during intense exercise. While they offer on-demand single-lead ECGs, they do not support continuous raw ECG streaming suitable for in-depth analysis. On the other end of the spectrum, open-source research platforms like BITalino [13,24] offer high flexibility and data access but at a substantially higher cost, with kits starting at over $149. The Heart Track system was specifically designed to fill a gap between these options, offering a unique combination of continuous 250 Hz ECG data streaming in a fully open-source framework at a hardware cost of approximately €18 per unit. This makes it a financially accessible and customizable tool for sports science researchers who require raw, high-resolution physiological data. The single greatest challenge to obtaining ECG data during physical activity is the presence of motion artifacts. These artifacts, caused by electrode movement and muscle contractions, can mask the underlying cardiac signal and make clinical interpretation or automated analysis unreliable. A significant body of research is dedicated to mitigating this noise.

Two primary approaches exist: wavelet-based methods and adaptive filtering. While wavelet transforms can be useful for improving signal correlation, they often introduce phase variability and are less suited for real-time applications [5,25]. In contrast, adaptive filtering algorithms have consistently shown superior performance. Studies have demonstrated that adaptive filters, particularly those utilizing the Least Mean Squares (LMS) algorithm and its variants (IPNLMS, PNLMS, BLMS), significantly outperform wavelet-based and traditional methods in reducing motion artifacts [2,7]. The use of a secondary sensor, such as an accelerometer, to provide a reference signal for the motion noise can further enhance the clarity of the filtered ECG signal [9]. Overall, adaptive filtering remains the state-of-the-art and preferred approach for motion artifact reduction in wearable ECG monitoring [1,18,20].

In dynamic team sports like handball, understanding player exertion is crucial for optimizing performance and training regimens. Research has consistently shown that physiological markers, particularly heart rate, are strongly linked to performance outcomes and vary significantly by playing position. For instance, studies have found that wing players often exhibit higher heart rates and superior aerobic capacity compared to backcourt players and pivots [11,16]. Conversely, backcourt players tend to cover more distance during matches, also resulting in high average heart rates [19].

Furthermore, research highlights the importance of repeated sprint and jumping ability, especially for wing players [12], and the negative correlation between body fat and running speed across all positions [6]. The consensus in the literature is that aerobic capacity is a key differentiator of performance among players [15]. This body of work underscores the clear need for position-specific training and validates the use of heart rate as a primary metric for assessing internal training load. Our study leverages these findings by validating an ECG-based system specifically within the demanding context of a handball training session.

3   The HeartTrack System

3.1   Hardware Design

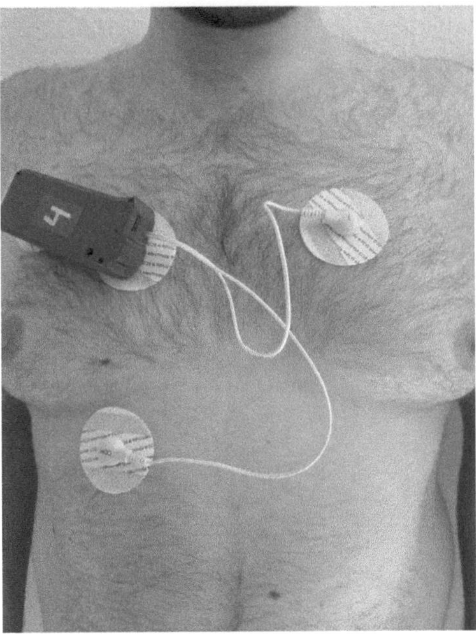

Fig. 1. The HeartTrack wearable sensor unit with electrode placement on a participant

A low-cost, wearable electrocardiogram (ECG) monitoring system was developed to capture, transmit, and analyze cardiac biopotentials. The data acquisition hardware is housed within a custom 3D-printed enclosure worn on the chest. It comprises an AD8232 analog front-end for ECG signal conditioning, which is subsequently digitized by a 16-bit ADS1115 analog-to-digital converter to ensure high-resolution signal capture. The sensor data is captured with a resolution of 250 Hz. An ESP32-based microcontroller (Lolin32 Lite) orchestrates device operations, including sensor interfacing and wireless communication. The firmware, developed in C++, is responsible for acquiring the digital ECG signal, checking sensor-body contact, monitoring battery levels, and synchronizing time with an NTP server to guarantee accurate timestamping for all data points.

3.2 System Architecture and Data Transmission

The system employs a distributed architecture based on the Message Queuing Telemetry Transport (MQTT) protocol for robust and decoupled data handling. The wearable device connects to the network via Wi-Fi and publishes the raw, timestamped ECG data, formatted as a JSON object, to a central MQTT broker. This broker disseminates the information to two independent client applications. The first client is a Python script that subscribes to the raw data feed. This script utilizes the Neurokit2 library to perform real-time signal processing, including signal cleaning, R-peak detection, and the subsequent calculation of heart rate (BPM) and heart rate variability (HRV) metrics. These computed features are then published back to the MQTT broker on a separate topic.

3.3 Real-Time Processing and Visualization

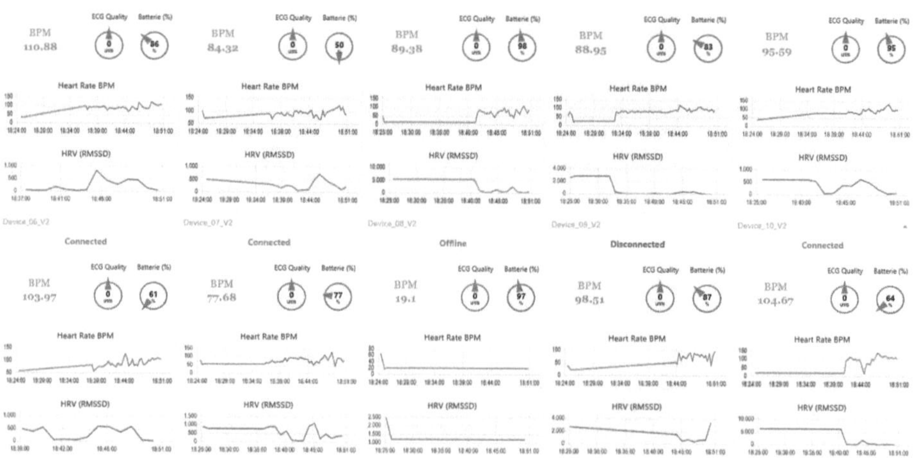

Fig. 2. The real-time monitoring dashboard built in Node-RED, displaying data from nine concurrent participants (Color figure online)

Concurrently, a second client, built on the Node-RED platform, subscribes to both the raw data and the processed-data topics from the MQTT broker. This component serves a dual purpose. Firstly, it provides a real-time dashboard (see 2) for the immediate visualization of the incoming ECG waveform alongside the calculated physiological parameters. Secondly, it ensures data persistence by systematically logging the raw, timestamped ECG signal to a comma-separated values (CSV) file, making the complete dataset available for comprehensive offline analysis.

4   Results

The developed wearable ECG system was deployed to monitor cardiovascular dynamics during a 75-minute training session with a female handball team. Data collection was attempted for 10 athletes, with nine of the ten sensor units functioning correctly throughout the entire session, resulting in a 90% success rate for data acquisition. One unit failed to maintain a stable connection mid-session and its data was excluded from further analysis. The nine complete datasets were successfully correlated with a concurrent video recording of the training, which enabled the annotation of distinct activity phases: a running warm-up, static stretching, specific handball drills, and scrimmage play.

Analysis of the acquired data revealed distinct physiological responses corresponding to the annotated training phases. During the initial low-intensity stretching period, baseline heart rate (BPM) values were stable. The subsequent running warm-up elicited a steady, progressive increase in heart rate across all participants. For example, the average BPM rose from a baseline of approximately 75 BPM to 140 BPM by the conclusion of the warm-up. This was accompanied by a statistically significant decrease in Heart Rate Variability (RMSSD), from a mean of 45 ± 10 ms during stretching to 12 ± 5 ms during scrimmage play ($p < .001$).

The most dynamic cardiovascular responses were observed during the high-intensity drills and scrimmage play. During these periods, the system recorded rapid fluctuations in heart rate, with peak values for some athletes exceeding 180 BPM during intense, game-like situations. The real-time dashboard provided immediate visualization of these rapid fluctuations in heart rate. Concurrently, HRV metrics were significantly suppressed throughout these high-exertion phases, reflecting the high physiological stress of the sport. Despite the vigorous, high-impact movements inherent to handball, the nine functional units consistently captured ECG waveforms, and the complete, timestamped raw data was reliably logged to CSV files for each athlete, providing a comprehensive dataset for detailed post-session analysis.

4.1   Motion Artifact Characterization

In line with the third contribution of this work, this section provides a characterization of the impact of motion artifacts on signal quality. Figure 3 (top) displays

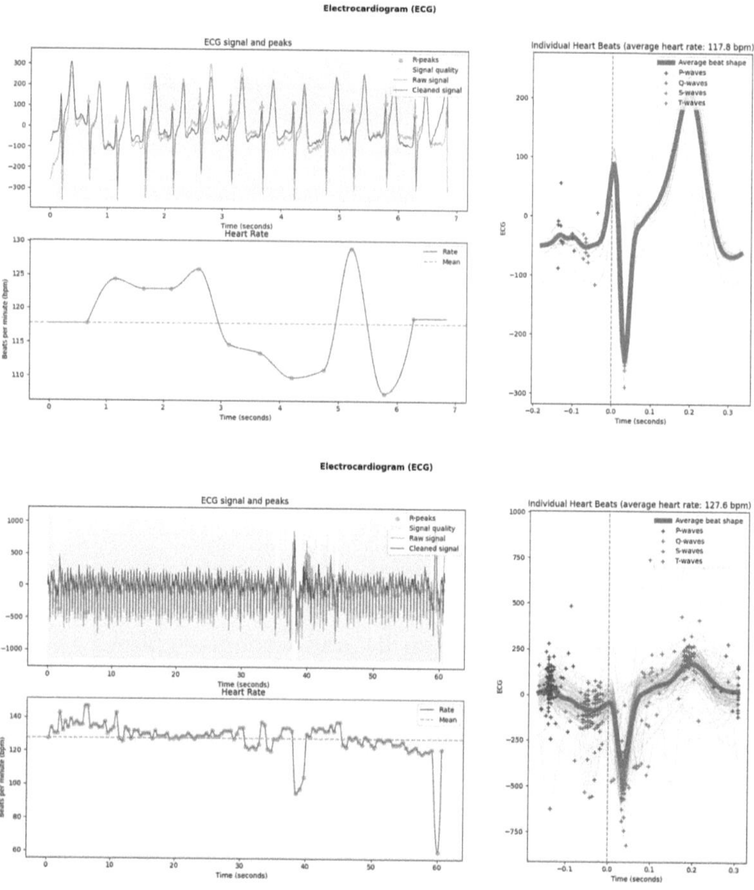

Fig. 3. Representative ECG data segments. (Top) A 7-second recording during a warm-up, showing a clean signal and stable heart rate (around 118 BPM). (Bottom) A 60-second recording during a high-intensity game scene, showing significant motion artifacts and an erratic, higher heart rate (around 127.6 BPM)

a 7-second segment from a participant during the running warm-up, illustrating a period of high signal quality. The data is characterized by high signal quality and a clean, consistent ECG morphology, with clearly discernible P, QRS, and T waves. The corresponding heart rate is elevated but stable at approximately 118 BPM, which is indicative of steady-state aerobic exercise. The overlay of individual heartbeats shows minimal variation, confirming the high fidelity of the signal captured during controlled movement. This is contrasted with Fig. 3 (bottom), which shows a segment heavily affected by motion artifacts during high-intensity gameplay. This recording reflects the challenges of data acquisition in a dynamic sporting environment. The signal exhibits significant motion artifacts, leading to periods of degraded quality, particularly around the 40-second mark. The heart rate is not only higher on average (127.6 BPM) but also highly erratic, fluctuating rapidly in response to the unpredictable demands of the game. The wide scatter of the overlaid individual heartbeats is a result of both this physiological variability and the residual noise in the signal. These figures visually confirm that while the system can capture the high-intensity cardiovascular response to gameplay, data quality is inherently more variable compared to more controlled exercise conditions.

5 Discussion

The primary goal of this project was to develop and validate a low-cost, wearable ECG system in a demanding, real-world athletic environment. The results confirm that the system successfully captured physiological data with enough fidelity to differentiate between training phases. The successful acquisition of nine complete datasets over 75 min, despite the high-impact and dynamic nature of the sport, underscores the viability of using inexpensive, custom-built hardware for field-based research.

The quantitatively distinct cardiovascular responses across various training phases, from the stable, elevated heart rate during the warm-up to the erratic, peak responses during scrimmage play, highlights the system's sensitivity to changing metabolic demands. The statistically significant decrease in RMSSD between low- and high-intensity phases, quantitatively confirms the expected swing in autonomic nervous system balance. This demonstrates that the captured data aligns with established physiological principles (e.g., an increase in heart rate and a decrease in heart rate variability with rising exercise intensity), which allows for valid physiological interpretation. The accompanying video annotations proved invaluable, providing the necessary context to move beyond simple data logging toward a quantitative analysis of athlete physiology in response to specific stimuli.

However, the study also revealed important limitations. The failure of one of the ten sensor units serves as a crucial reminder of the reliability challenges inherent in low-cost electronics compared to medical-grade equipment. Furthermore, the motion artifacts observed in the data during high-intensity gameplay, as illustrated in the results, are a significant consideration. While the cleaning algorithms from the Neurokit2 library were effective, periods of severe noise can obscure the underlying signal, potentially affecting the accuracy of beat detection and subsequent HRV calculations. This highlights a critical trade-off between cost, wearability, and signal fidelity in extreme motion contexts. While this study focused on validating the physiological data capture, a quantitative evaluation of the MQTT data transmission characteristics (e.g., latency, packet loss) or a direct comparison of different signal filtering algorithms was outside the scope of this initial validation. These remain important areas for future technical evaluation. We acknowledge that this study was conducted with an all-female cohort. Future work should include male athletes to investigate potential differences in signal quality related to chest anatomy and electrode placement.

Furthermore, the current prototype shown in Fig. 1, while functional for a single session, requires further refinement to improve long-term comfort and robustness for longitudinal studies. Future work should focus on addressing these limitations. Improvements to the hardware, such as a more robust enclosure design and the use of advanced motion-cancellation electrodes, could mitigate artifacts. On the software side, implementing more sophisticated, real-time artifact detection and signal reconstruction algorithms could further enhance data quality. Additionally, future studies could leverage this system to investigate more complex research questions, such as quantifying training load, monitoring athlete fatigue over a season, or providing real-time biofeedback to coaches and players. Taken together, these findings map directly to the three contributions outlined in the introduction. First, the open-source nature of HeartTrack makes it a reusable platform for both applied sports monitoring and methodological research, filling a gap left by closed commercial systems. Second, our validation study during a real-world handball training session demonstrated that despite the challenges of high-intensity motion, the system reliably tracked meaningful trends in heart rate and HRV, confirming its practical usability for exertion monitoring. Third, our analysis of motion artifacts provides a transparent characterization of the system's primary limitation, offering a realistic baseline for future algorithmic improvements.

6   Conclusion

This study successfully demonstrated the design, implementation, and validation of a wearable, low-cost ECG monitoring system. The system proved capable of capturing and analyzing cardiovascular data from athletes during a live handball training session. The key findings confirmed that the device could effectively track significant changes in heart rate and heart rate variability that correspond directly to varying levels of physical exertion. Despite challenges related to motion artifacts and hardware reliability, the project establishes a framework for applying affordable, custom-built sensor technology in applied sports science. This work provides a foundation for future research into accessible, field-based physiological monitoring, potentially enabling more widespread and frequent analysis of athlete performance and well-being.

References

1. Al-Sheikh, B.: Adaptive algorithm for motion artifacts removal in wearable biomedical sensors during physical exercise. IEEE Sens. J. **23**(9), 9491–9499 (2023). https://doi.org/10.1109/jsen.2023.3256959
2. An, X., K. Stylios, G.: Comparison of motion artefact reduction methods and the implementation of adaptive motion artefact reduction in wearable electrocardiogram monitoring. Sensors **20**(5), 1468 (2020). https://doi.org/10.3390/s20051468
3. Choi, H.I., et al.: Efficacy of wearable single-lead ECG monitoring during exercise stress testing: a comparative study. Sensors **24**(19), 6394 (2024). https://doi.org/10.3390/s24196394

4. Davis, A.J., Driscoll, T., Orchard, J.W., Raju, H., Gray, B., Orchard, J.J.: Relative utility of portable ECG devices in capturing arrhythmias in athletes. Expert Rev. Med. Devices **21**(12), 1179–1188 (2024). https://doi.org/10.1080/17434440.2024.2438313

5. Foo, J.Y.A.: Comparison of wavelet transformation and adaptive filtering in restoring artefact-induced time-related measurement. Biomed. Signal Process. Control **1**(1), 93–98 (2006). https://doi.org/10.1016/j.bspc.2006.01.001

6. Sporis, G., Vuleta, D., Vuleta Jr, D., Milanovic, D.: Fitness profiling in handball: physical and physiological characteristics of elite players. Collegium Antropologicum (2010)

7. Galdos, J., Lopez Colque, N., Medina Rodirguez, A., Huarca Quispe, J., Rendulich, J., Sulla Espinoza, E.: Comparison and evaluation of LMS-derived algorithms applied on ECG signals contaminated with motion artifact during physical activities. Appl. Comput. Sci. **20**(1), 157–172 (2024). https://doi.org/10.35784/acs-2024-10

8. Georgiou, K., Larentzakis, A.V., Khamis, N.N., Alsuhaibani, G.I., Alaska, Y.A., Giallafos, E.J.: Can wearable devices accurately measure heart rate variability? A systematic review. Folia Medica **60**(1) (2018). https://doi.org/10.2478/folmed-2018-0012

9. Huang, M., Chen, D., Xiong, F.: An effective adaptive filter to reduce motion artifacts from ECG signals using accelerometer. In: Proceedings of the 2019 9th International Conference on Biomedical Engineering and Technology, pp. 83–88. ACM (2019). https://doi.org/10.1145/3326172.3326214

10. Kamga, P., Mostafa, R., Zafar, S.: The use of wearable ECG devices in the clinical setting: a review. Curr. Emerg. Hosp. Med. Rep. **10**(3), 67–72 (2022). https://doi.org/10.1007/s40138-022-00248-x

11. Krüger, K., Pilat, C., Ückert, K., Frech, T., Mooren, F.C.: Physical performance profile of handball players is related to playing position and playing class. J. Strength Conditioning Res. **28**(1), 117–125 (2014). https://doi.org/10.1519/jsc.0b013e318291b713

12. Michalsik, L.B., Madsen, K., Aagaard, P.: Physiological capacity and physical testing in male elite team handball. J. Sports Med. Phys. Fitness (2015)

13. Lazaretti, G., Teixeira, J., Kuhn, E., Borghi, P.: Android-based ECG monitoring system for atrial fibrillation detection using a BITalino® ECG sensor:. In: Proceedings of the 15th International Joint Conference on Biomedical Engineering Systems and Technologies, pp. 177–184. SCITEPRESS - Science and Technology Publications, Online Streaming, — Select a Country — (2022). https://doi.org/10.5220/0010905400003123

14. Martín-Escudero, P., et al.: Are activity wrist-worn devices accurate for determining heart rate during intense exercise? Bioengineering **10**(2), 254 (2023). https://doi.org/10.3390/bioengineering10020254

15. Massuca, L., Branco, B., Miarka, B., Fragoso, I.: Physical fitness attributes of team-handball players are related to playing position and performance level. Asian J. Sports Med. **6**(1) (2015). https://doi.org/10.5812/asjsm.24712

16. Mohorič, U., Šibila, M., Štrumbelj, B.: Positional differences in some physiological parameters obtained by the incremental field endurance test among elite handball players. Kinesiology **53**(1), 3–11 (2021). https://doi.org/10.26582/k.53.1.1

17. Nelson, B.W., Allen, N.B.: Accuracy of consumer wearable heart rate measurement during an ecologically valid 24-hour period: intraindividual validation study. JMIR mHealth uHealth **7**(3), e10828 (2019). https://doi.org/10.2196/10828

18. Poungponsri, S., Yu, X.H.: An adaptive filtering approach for electrocardiogram (ECG) signal noise reduction using neural networks. Neurocomputing **117**, 206–213 (2013). https://doi.org/10.1016/j.neucom.2013.02.010
19. Póvoas, S.C.A., et al.: Physiological demands of elite team handball with special reference to playing position. J. Strength Conditioning Res. **28**(2), 430–442 (2014). https://doi.org/10.1519/jsc.0b013e3182a953b1
20. Raya, M., Sison, L.: Adaptive noise cancelling of motion artifact in stress ECG signals using accelerometer. In: Proceedings of the Second Joint 24th Annual Conference and the Annual Fall Meeting of the Biomedical Engineering Society] [Engineering in Medicine and Biology. IEEE (2002). https://doi.org/10.1109/iembs.2002.1106637
21. Romagnoli, S., Ripanti, F., Morettini, M., Burattini, L., Sbrollini, A.: Wearable and portable devices for acquisition of cardiac signals while practicing sport: a scoping review. Sensors **23**(6), 3350 (2023). https://doi.org/10.3390/s23063350
22. Sana, F., Isselbacher, E.M., Singh, J.P., Heist, E.K., Pathik, B., Armoundas, A.A.: Wearable devices for ambulatory cardiac monitoring. J. Am. Coll. Cardiol. **75**(13), 1582–1592 (2020). https://doi.org/10.1016/j.jacc.2020.01.046
23. Sanchis-Gomar, F., Lavie, C.J., Perez, M.V.: Consumer wearable technologies to identify and monitor exercise-related arrhythmias in athletes. Curr. Opin. Cardiol. **36**(1), 10–16 (2020). https://doi.org/10.1097/hco.0000000000000817
24. da Silva, H.P., Guerreiro, J., Lourenço, A., Fred, A., Martins, R.: BITalino: a novel hardware framework for physiological computing. In: Proceedings of the International Conference on Physiological Computing Systems - Volume 1: PhyCS, pp. 246–253. INSTICC, SciTePress (2014). https://doi.org/10.5220/0004727802460253
25. Xiong, F., Chen, D., Huang, M.: A wavelet adaptive cancellation algorithm based on multi-inertial sensors for the reduction of motion artifacts in ambulatory ECGs. Sensors **20**(4), 970 (2020). https://doi.org/10.3390/s20040970

Robust and Efficient Writer-Independent IMU-Based Handwriting Recognition

Jindong Li[1]([✉])[iD], Tim Hamann[2][iD], Jens Barth[2][iD], Peter Kämpf[2], Dario Zanca[1][iD], and Björn Eskofier[1,3][iD]

[1] Machine Learning and Data Analytics Lab, Friedrich-Alexander-Universität Erlangen-Nürnberg, Erlangen, Germany
`jindong.li@fau.de`
[2] STABILO International GmbH, Heroldsberg, Germany
[3] Translational Digital Health Group, Institute of AI for Health, Helmholtz Zentrum München - German Research Center for Environmental Health, Neuherberg, Germany

Abstract. Handwriting recognition (HWR) using inertial measurement unit (IMU) data remains challenging due to variations in writing styles and the limited availability of datasets. Previous approaches often struggle with handwriting from unseen writers, making writer-independent (WI) recognition a crucial yet difficult problem. This paper presents a model designed to improve WI HWR on IMU data, using a CNN encoder and BiLSTM-based decoder. Our approach demonstrates strong robustness to unseen handwriting styles, outperforming existing methods on the WI splits of both the public OnHW dataset and our word-based dataset, achieving character error rates (CERs) of 7.37% and 9.44%, and word error rates (WERs) of 15.12% and 32.17%, respectively. Robustness evaluation shows that our model maintains superior performance across different age groups, with knowledge learned from one group generalizing better to another compared to other approaches. Evaluation on our sentence-based dataset further demonstrates the potential for recognizing full sentences. Through comprehensive ablation studies, we show that our design choices achieve a strong balance between performance and efficiency. These findings support the development of more adaptable and scalable HWR systems for real-world applications. The code is available at: https://github.com/jindongli24/REWI.

Keywords: Online Handwriting Recognition · Time-Series Analysis · Inertial Measurement Unit

1 Introduction

Handwriting has served as a primary means of recording and sharing information throughout human history. As technology has advanced, the demand for digitizing handwritten content has grown significantly. HWR, which converts handwritten symbols into computer-readable text, has consequently emerged as an important area of research.

Offline HWR, as one of the main types of HWR, has been widely used in various fields [6,17]. However, it is limited to recognizing static images of handwritten text. In contrast, online HWR processes time-series data in real-time, capturing dynamic handwriting features such as stroke trajectories, tip positions, writing directions, and velocities as they occur. This data is typically collected using touchscreens and styluses on mobile devices [2], which limits the available writing surface for users. Another approach to online HWR uses pens equipped with IMUs [1,14,22]. These sensors capture pen movements without requiring precise tip positioning, enabling the pen to operate independently of external devices and demonstrating strong potential for broader online HWR applications.

However, IMU-based HWR faces several challenges that affect recognition performance. First, similar to other HWR approaches, handwritten text varies vastly across different writers in terms of style, including slant angle, letter connections, and spacing between letters and words, making WI recognition particularly challenging [9]. Additionally, noise from rough surfaces, signal drift caused by heat accumulation inside the device, and artifacts during signal communication or transmission present additional technical difficulties [15]. Moreover, as an online task, latency must also be considered, which poses another challenge for efficiency.

This paper presents a sequence-to-sequence model for IMU-based online HWR, designed to address efficiency challenges and those arising from handwriting style variations and noise. The model adopts an encoder-decoder architecture that combines a convolutional neural network (CNN) with a bidirectional long short-term memory (BiLSTM) network. We evaluate the proposed model by benchmarking it against several existing IMU-based HWR methods, as well as adapted mainstream models that have achieved strong performance in various deep learning tasks. Evaluation is performed on the public OnHW dataset and our custom IMU-based handwriting datasets, where our datasets each address different aspects of the problem space. Experimental results demonstrate that our model outperforms others in terms of efficiency, robustness, and flexibility for WI HWR.

2 Related Works

2.1 IMU-Based HWR

IMU-based HWR has been an active area of research for decades. Early studies, such as [3,8], employed dynamic time warping algorithms to recognize digit data collected with IMU-based pens, achieving recognition rates above 90%. Later works, including [13,14], explored LSTM-based models for recognizing individual English characters, reporting recognition accuracies of up to 99.68% and 79.01% on their respective datasets. Although these methods achieved excellent performance, they rely on isolated character recognition, processing entire input sequences to classify single characters. This character-by-character approach disrupts the natural writing flow, making it impractical for real-world applications where writing typically occurs word by word.

To address more complex tasks, [15,23] employed CNN-BiLSTM models with connectionist temporal classification (CTC) [5] to recognize sequences of English and German characters. Additionally, [15] explored the potential of various architectures for IMU-based HWR. These models were evaluated on datasets collected using the IMU-based pen developed by STABILO, achieving CERs of 27.8% and 17.97%, respectively. These results marked an important step toward recognizing full words and sentences, bringing the field closer to practical applications.

2.2 Advancements in Deep Learning Architectures

In recent years, the introduction of ResNet [7] and Transformer [21] has significantly advanced deep learning model development. ResNet addressed the vanishing gradient problem through skip connections, enabling effective training of very deep neural networks. Transformers introduced self-attention mechanisms, which improved parallelization and enhanced the modeling of long-range dependencies compared to CNNs or recurrent neural networks.

Building on these innovations, several new approaches have emerged. MLP-Mixer [19] demonstrated that strong performance in vision tasks can be achieved without convolutions or self-attention, relying solely on multi-layer perceptrons to mix spatial and channel information. Swin Transformers [10,11] introduced a hierarchical architecture with shifted window-based self-attention, enabling efficient multi-scale modeling for various vision tasks. Vision Transformer (ViT) [4] treats images as sequences of patch embeddings fed into a Transformer encoder, showing that pure self-attention can rival CNNs on large-scale vision tasks. ConvNeXt [12] integrated concepts from both CNNs and Transformers, achieving state-of-the-art performance while preserving the simplicity and efficiency of traditional CNNs.

Although these models were originally designed for different tasks, their core principles, such as self-attention and hierarchical structures, are potentially well-suited for time-series data. Applying these techniques to IMU-based HWR could enhance performance and open new research opportunities in the field.

3 Methods

3.1 Datasets

Private Dataset. Our datasets were collected using the IMU-based pen developed by STABILO. Data collection followed pseudo-anonymous procedures where voluntary participants' names appeared only on consent agreements, while all data were stored anonymously on the server, ensuring that only minimal and necessary personal information was collected. For commercial reasons, our private dataset will not be made publicly available.

The pen generates 13 output channels at a selectable sampling rate of 100 Hz, 200 Hz, or 400 Hz, using two accelerometers (one at each end), a gyroscope, a magnetometer, and a force sensor, as shown in Fig. 1. Each sensor provides three channels of data, except the force sensor, which provides a single channel.

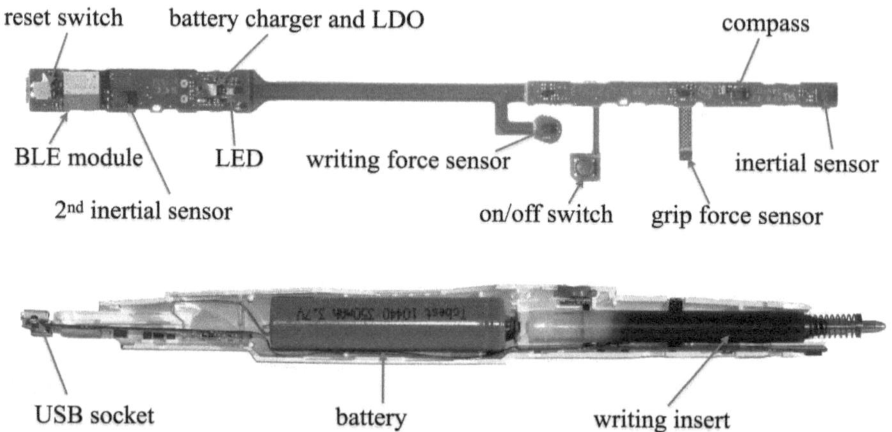

Fig. 1. Digipen Architecture. The pen includes two IMUs (one with an accelerometer and gyroscope, the other with only an accelerometer) located at both ends, a magnetometer (compass), a writing force sensor, and a grip force sensor (not used in the experiments).

We conducted 1,547 recording sessions with 520 participants of various ages and handedness, collecting both English and German words and sentences. All samples were converted to a 100 Hz sampling rate and divided into two subsets: a word-based dataset and a sentence-based dataset.

The word-based dataset contains 24,163 samples of English and German words, covering 59 character categories, including both uppercase and lowercase letters from both languages. The sentence-based dataset includes 20,639 samples of English and German sentences, spanning 84 character categories, including letters, numbers, symbols, and spaces. Given the distribution of sample lengths, only samples shorter than 1,024 time steps for word signals and 4,096 time steps for sentence signals are retained. Visualizations of character category distributions and sample lengths are provided in Appendix A.

After preprocessing, the data samples are split into training (80%) and validation (20%) sets using 5-fold cross-validation. The data are divided at the writer level to ensure that no writer appears in both training and validation sets. To maintain balanced representation between the sets, stratification based on participants' handedness and age is applied.

To evaluate the robustness of the system, we also analyze subsets of our dataset based on participants' ages. Since children are still developing their handwriting skills, their handwriting patterns differ significantly from those of adults, particularly in writing speed and discontinuity due to high cognitive load, with these patterns typically stabilizing around 14 years old [16,18]. This finding is further supported by Fig. 2 and Appendix A, which demonstrate that writers under 14 years old write significantly more slowly than their older counterparts.

Based on the distinct writing characteristics of writers at different ages, we classify participants aged 12 and under as children to ensure that most writers represent typical children handwriting patterns, and those aged 18 and older as adults. Data from participants aged 13 to 17 are excluded from these subsets because some have already developed mature and fluent handwriting, making them less representative of either the children or adult groups. Notably, the adult subset (13,899 samples) is approximately twice the size of the children subset (7,762 samples).

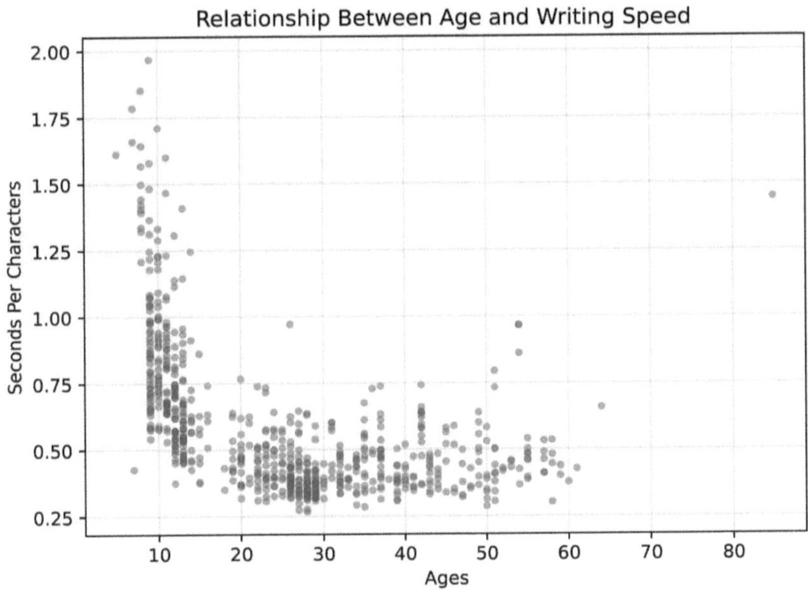

Fig. 2. Relationship Between Age and Writing Speed. This visualization shows the average writing time per character for writers in our word-based dataset, illustrating how writing speed varies across different ages.

OnHW Dataset. We also use the WI split from the right-handed subset of the public OnHW-words500 dataset [15], which contains 13-channel handwriting data for 500 words written by 53 writers. The left-handed subset, which includes only 1,000 samples and offers only a single train-validation split, is excluded from our experiments due to its limited size and configuration.

3.2 Model Architecture

Although [15,23] have presented promising CNN-BiLSTM-based approaches to HWR of words and delivered strong performance, both works still leave considerable room for improvement. In terms of robustness, neither approach targets unseen handwriting styles, and both struggle with WI HWR. Regarding efficiency, both employ simple and regular CNN designs that cannot effectively utilize the limited number of parameters. To design a robust and efficient IMU-based HWR baseline, building upon CLDNN [23], we designed our model by incorporating various delicated modifications in the CNN architecture to improve both efficiency and robustness, as illustrated in Fig. 3.

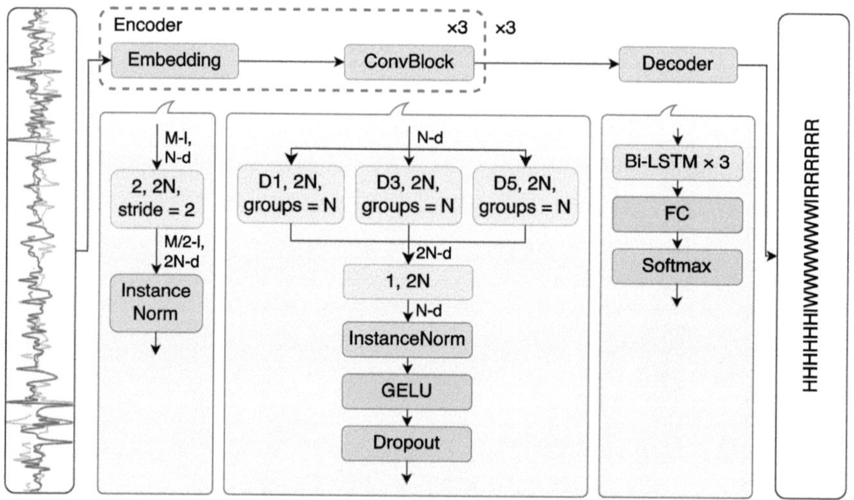

Fig. 3. Model architecture. The model consists of a three-stage CNN encoder and a BiLSTM-based decoder. The convolutional blocks use separable depthwise convolutional layers with inverted bottleneck and multi-scale designs to improve efficiency.

Encoder. The encoder consists of three stages, each containing an embedding layer followed by three convolutional blocks. Each embedding layer uses a convolutional layer with kernel size 2 and stride 2 to downsample the input sequences, followed by an instance normalization layer [20] to reduce representation variance between samples with different handwriting styles. Except for the first stage, which processes inputs with 13 channels, each convolutional layer doubles the number of output channels relative to the input channels.

To reduce computational cost, we used an inverted bottleneck design. This starts with a grouped convolutional layer (kernel size 5) that doubles the channel count using one group per input channel. A pointwise convolutional layer then restores the original channel dimensions. This approach creates a larger hidden space for better feature representation while using fewer computational resources than conventional convolutional layers. It also offers advantages over standard depthwise separable convolutions.

Additionally, we introduce a multi-scale design that adds two more grouped convolutional layers with kernel sizes of 1 and 3 during training, in addition to the existing layer with kernel size 5. The input sequence is processed in parallel by all three convolutional layers, and their outputs are summed before passing to the pointwise convolutional layer. After training, we merge the weights from the smaller-kernel layers into the kernel size 5 layer, resulting in the same number of parameters as the original variant of the depthwise separable convolution. This approach enables multi-scale feature learning during training without adding extra parameters or computational cost during inference.

Decoder. The decoder consists of three BiLSTM layers, each with a hidden size of 128 and a dropout rate of 0.2. These are followed by a fully connected layer and a softmax layer for pointwise classification, omitting the intermediate hidden layers used in CLDNN to improve efficiency. The softmax outputs are then processed by a greedy CTC decoder to generate the final text predictions.

Edge Optimization. To better support edge computing, we also introduce a small version of the model that uses only one convolutional block per stage and reduces the embedded channel sizes from 128, 256, and 512 to 64, 128, and 256. The BiLSTM decoder is also reduced in size, with the hidden size decreased to 64 and the number of layers reduced to 2.

3.3   Data Augmentation

To enhance robustness against noise and diverse handwriting styles, we applied four data augmentation schemes: AddNoise, Drift, Dropout, and TimeWarp. Each scheme has a 25% probability of being applied to a given signal. TimeWarp affects only the time dimension, while the other methods are applied multiplicatively to ensure their contributions are not overshadowed by the magnitude of the original signals. Visualizations of all data augmentation methods are provided in Appendix B.

AddNoise adds Gaussian noise to the original signals, simulating noise from rough writing surfaces and other sources. **Drift** divides the signals into segments and applies random drift within each segment, simulating drift caused by heat accumulation inside the pen. **Dropout** randomly replaces small segments of the signal with the last value preceding each segment, simulating communication imperfections. **TimeWarp** randomly adjusts the speed of segments within the original signal, simulating variations in writing speed.

After augmentation, each signal sample is individually normalized at the channel level, rather than globally, to minimize the influence of writer-specific characteristics such as pen pressure and pen angle. This approach encourages the model to focus on the actual writing content rather than individual writing habits.

4   Experiments

The experiments consist of four parts: evaluation on word-based datasets, robustness evaluation, evaluation on our sentence-based dataset, and an ablation study. In each part, models are trained using 5-fold cross-validation, and the best result from validation set of each fold is used to calculate the average across all five folds, which is reported as the final result.

We first include two previous works: CNN+BiLSTM [15] and CLDNN [23]. Since their code is not publicly available, we re-implemented both models in PyTorch based on the original papers. For CLDNN, we followed the described training and preprocessing pipeline. However, training details for CNN+BiLSTM were not clearly specified, so we trained it using our own pipeline to ensure fair comparison. These two models are compared with the small version of our model, given their similar sizes.

For broader comparison, we implemented ResNet, MLP-Mixer, ViT, ConvNeXt, and Swin Transformer V2 (SwinV2) backbones as encoders, replacing the CNN encoder in the base version of our model. Since these backbones were not originally designed for time-series inputs, we made minimal but necessary modifications to them. Due to architectural limitations, MLP-Mixer, ViT, and SwinV2 require fixed-size inputs. Therefore, input sequences are zero-padded to a length of 1,024 for word samples and 4,096 for sentence samples when using these models. Additionally, encoders and decoders are configured with hyperparameters to ensure comparable parameter counts when input sequences are of the same length. Given their sizes, these approaches are compared against the base version of our model.

Except for CLDNN [23], which is trained as described in its original paper, all other models are trained using the same procedure. We use the AdamW optimizer with a learning rate of 0.001 for 300 epochs. To improve training stability and convergence, linear learning rate warm-up is applied, starting at 0.0001 for the first 30 epochs, followed by a cosine annealing schedule for the remaining epochs. The training process uses the CTC loss function and a batch size of 64. Models are evaluated every 5 epochs during training.

To measure model performance, we use two metrics: CER and WER. CER reflects errors at the character level, while WER reflects errors at the word level. These metrics measure how many errors appear in the predictions, including substitutions, deletions, and insertions, compared to the total number of characters or words in the ground truth text. We also evaluate memory usage and computational cost by reporting the number of parameters (#Params) and the number of multiply-accumulate operations (MACs). These are calculated using a random input sequence with 13 channels and 1,024 timesteps for word-based datasets, and 4,096 timesteps for the sentence-based dataset.

4.1 Evaluation on Word-Based Datasets

In this section, we compare our models with other approaches using the WI splits of our word-based dataset and the right-handed subset of the OnHW dataset. For reference, we also include the published results for CNN+BiLSTM on the OnHW-words500 dataset [15].

Table 1. Results on Our Word-Based Dataset and the Right-Handed Subset of the OnHW Dataset. We compare our models with other approaches on the WI splits of our dataset and the right-handed subset of the OnHW-words500 dataset. Metrics include CER, WER, #Params, and MACs. Error rates are reported as percentages. The best results are shown in **bold**.

Models	Ours		OnHW		#Params	MACs
	CER	WER	CER	WER		
CLDNN	19.05	60.20	15.62	36.71	0.75 M	291 M
CNN+BiLSTM (orig.)	—	—	27.80	60.91	—	—
CNN+BiLSTM	21.32	64.83	17.66	43.45	**0.40 M**	152 M
Ours-Small	**15.29**	**50.70**	**10.55**	**24.94**	0.53 M	**79 M**
ResNet (enc.)	10.89	36.71	8.22	18.35	3.97 M	591 M
MLP-Mixer (enc.)	13.37	43.25	9.74	21.87	3.90 M	802 M
ViT (enc.)	13.89	45.24	10.49	22.71	**3.71 M**	**477 M**
ConvNeXt (enc.)	12.25	42.16	8.23	18.46	3.86 M	600 M
SwinV2 (enc.)	11.70	40.69	8.62	19.60	3.88 M	601 M
Ours-Base	**9.44**	**32.17**	**7.37**	**15.12**	3.89 M	600 M

As shown in Table 1, the small version of our model outperforms other IMU-based HWR approaches in both CER and WER on our dataset (15.29% and 50.70%) and the OnHW dataset (10.55% and 24.94%), while maintaining the lowest computational cost. The second-best approach, CLDNN, performs 24.6% and 18.7% worse on our dataset, and 48.1% and 47.2% worse on the OnHW dataset, respectively. Furthermore, CLDNN has 43.4% more parameters and 268% higher computational cost. When comparing the CER and WER of CNN+BiLSTM from the original paper with those from our re-implementation, our training pipeline and data augmentation strategies clearly lead to significant performance improvements, reducing CER and WER by 36.5% and 28.7%, respectively.

Compared to other competitors, the base version of our model achieves the lowest CER and WER on our dataset (9.44% and 32.17%) and the OnHW dataset (7.37% and 15.12%). Notably, unlike backbones designed for local attention, such as CNNs and SwinV2, backbones that focus on global information, like ViT and MLP-Mixer, perform poorly across all metrics. This reveals that IMU-based HWR prioritizes local information over global information.

Additionally, we investigate the errors made by our base-version model on our word-based dataset. As shown in Appendix C, substitution is the primary error type. Most substitution errors result from confusion between uppercase and lowercase letters with similar patterns, such as "c"/"C" and "w"/"W". Similarly, there are also instances of confusion between different letters with similar shapes, such as "q" and "g".

4.2   Robustness Evaluation

In this section, we assess the robustness of the models by evaluating them on the WI splits of the adult and children subsets of our word-based dataset. Additionally, we test the performance of models trained on the adult subset against the validation sets of the children subset (Adult2Child), and vice versa (Child2Adult). Trained models from each fold are tested on all validation sets of the other subset, and the mean of all 25 evaluation results is reported as the final result.

Table 2. Results on the Adult and Children Subsets of Our Word-Based Dataset. We compare our models with other approaches on the WI splits of the adult and children subsets of our word-based dataset, categorized by age group (Adults: $\geqslant 18$ years old; Children: $\leqslant 12$ years old). Models trained on one subset are also evaluated on the other (Adult2Child/Child2Adult).

Models	Adults		Children		Adult2Child		Child2Adult	
	CER	WER	CER	WER	CER	WER	CER	WER
CLDNN	21.62	63.79	28.78	74.06	44.67	86.74	52.32	94.62
CNN+BiLSTM	22.99	67.31	32.11	78.48	45.97	87.25	47.08	92.61
Ours-Small	**16.22**	**52.40**	**22.97**	**65.47**	**41.28**	**81.48**	**40.69**	**87.96**
ResNet (enc.)	13.74	42.96	18.07	53.64	37.94	78.59	37.89	85.43
MLP-Mixer (enc.)	16.30	50.89	75.29	98.35	41.33	81.94	79.98	99.74
ViT (enc.)	16.42	51.32	32.71	74.88	39.73	81.02	49.74	93.35
ConvNeXt (enc.)	14.63	47.07	24.85	63.85	37.11	79.17	44.48	90.23
SwinV2 (enc.)	14.49	47.48	24.93	66.13	35.97	78.63	42.43	89.53
Ours-Base	**10.98**	**36.16**	**15.00**	**46.11**	**35.86**	**74.86**	**36.22**	**82.88**

As shown in Table 2, on the adult subset, our small-version model achieves CER and WER that are 25.0% and 17.9% better than the second-best model, CLDNN. Our base-version model outperforms its closest competitor, ResNet, by 20.1% and 15.8% in CER and WER, respectively. On the children subset, CLDNN and ResNet remain the strongest among the competing models. However, CLDNN is still 25.3% and 13.1% worse than our small-version model in CER and WER, while ResNet is 20.5% and 16.3% worse than our base-version model.

For cross-subset evaluation, our models consistently achieve the best performance across all evaluations. When trained on the larger adult subset and evaluated on the children subset, our small-version model performs 7.6% and 6.1%

better than its best-performing competitor, CLDNN, in CER and WER, while our base-version model performs 17.0% and 14.0% better than ResNet. Conversely, when trained on the children subset and evaluated on the adult subset, our small-version model performs 13.6% and 5.0% better than CNN+BiLSTM, while our base-version model performs 4.4% and 3.0% better than ResNet.

Notably, the MLP-Mixer failed to converge when trained on the children subset, resulting in poor performance across both evaluation subsets.

We also compare the error patterns made by our base-version model on the adult and children subsets when trained on their respective datasets. As shown in Appendix C, the children subset presents significantly more challenging conditions. While the adult subset exhibits sparse, predictable errors primarily between visually similar characters or rare characters, the children subset shows dense, widespread confusion patterns across multiple character classes that extend beyond shape similarity. This degraded performance may be attributed partly to the children subset being smaller than the adult subset, but also to the additional recognition complexities inherent in children handwriting.

4.3   Evaluation on Our Sentence-Based Dataset

In this section, we compare our models with other approaches using the WI split of our sentence-based dataset.

Table 3. Results on Our Sentence-Based Dataset. We compare our models with other approaches on the WI split of our sentence-based dataset.

Models	CER	WER	#Params	MACs
CLDNN	17.47	59.17	0.75 M	1.17 B
CNN+BiLSTM	18.94	66.25	**0.41 M**	0.61 B
Ours-Small	**13.22**	**48.75**	0.54 M	**0.32 B**
ResNet (enc.)	8.20	28.74	3.97 M	2.37 B
MLP-Mixer (enc.)	75.14	100.00	15.71 M	8.04 B
ViT (enc.)	10.57	37.35	**3.72 M**	**1.93 B**
ConvNeXt (enc.)	9.48	34.72	3.87 M	2.40 B
SwinV2 (enc.)	9.06	33.44	3.89 M	2.41 B
Ours-Base	**6.78**	**24.63**	3.90 M	2.40 B

As shown in Table 3, our models achieve the lowest error rates. The small version reaches a CER of 13.22% and a WER of 48.75%, which are 24.3% and 17.6% better than the second-best model, CLDNN, while also consuming the least computational resources. The base version achieves a CER of 6.78% and a WER of 24.63%, outperforming the second-best model, ResNet, by 20.9% and 16.7%, respectively.

Notably, the MLP-Mixer again failed to converge, resulting in a WER of 100% on this dataset, despite having a significantly larger number of parameters and higher computational cost than other approaches. ViT, another global attention-based model, performs second worst, with a CER of 10.57% and a WER of 37.35%, although it has the smallest model size and lowest computational cost.

Furthermore, we analyze the errors made by the base version of our model on the WI split of our sentence-based dataset. As shown in Appendix C, substitution remains the primary error type, although deletions occur more frequently than in the word-based dataset. In addition to confusion between uppercase and lowercase versions of the same letter, errors caused by extreme data imbalance are more prominent, especially for "Q". Some characters are also frequently misrecognized as "Q" due to its low frequency of occurrence, as illustrated in Appendix A.

4.4 Ablation Study

In this section, we conduct an ablation study on our word-based dataset. Since our method builds upon CLDNN, we evaluate the performance improvements achieved through a series of incremental changes, including an optimized training procedure, data augmentation, architectural enhancements, and model size scaling.

The CLDNN architecture consists of three convolutional layers with 512, 256, and 128 output channels and kernel sizes of 5, 3, and 3 respectively, each followed by batch normalization, ReLU activation, max pooling, and dropout. These convolutional features are then processed through two BiLSTM layers with hidden size of 64, which connect to a final dense layer with ReLU activation. The model is trained using CTC loss and the Adam optimizer with an initial learning rate of 0.01, while a learning rate scheduler monitors validation loss and reduces the learning rate by a factor of 0.8 with patience of 10 epochs. Data preprocessing uses z-score normalization to standardize the input features.

Table 4. Ablation Study Results. We evaluate the performance of our model on the WI split of our dataset, incorporating incremental modifications based on CLDNN.

Modifications	CER	WER	#Params	MACs
CLDNN	19.05	60.20	0.75 M	291 M
+ Improved training	17.81	56.54	0.75 M	291 M
+ Data augmentation	17.22	55.60	0.75 M	291 M
+ Reverse dimension order	16.09	53.62	0.92 M	214 M
+ Embedding layer	19.04	58.52	0.64 M	99 M
+ Separable convolution	18.00	56.59	0.55 M	81 M
+ Multi-scale convolution	18.15	56.56	0.55 M	81 M
+ Instance normalization	15.60	51.31	0.55 M	81 M
+ GELU	15.34	50.88	0.55M	81 M
− Hidden layer (Ours-Small)	15.29	50.70	0.53 M	79 M
+ Scale up (Ours-Base)	9.44	32.17	3.89 M	600 M

As shown in Table 4, we first employ an improved training pipeline and data augmentation, which together improve performance by 9.6% and 7.6% in CER and WER, respectively, without any modifications to the model architecture. Reversing the dimension order of each stage from 512, 256, 128 to 128, 256, 512 slightly increases model size but reduces both error rates and computational cost. Using embedding layers with smaller dimensions of 64, 128, and 256 increases the CER from 16.09% to 19.04% and the WER from 53.62% to 58.52%, but reduces the number of parameters and MACs by 30.4% and 53.7%, respectively.

A combination of micro modifications to the convolutional blocks, including inverted-bottleneck separable depthwise convolution, multi-scale convolution, instance normalization, and GELU, significantly improves performance to 15.34% CER and 50.88% WER, representing gains of 19.4% and 13.1%, respectively. Among these changes, instance normalization provides additional improvements of 14.0% in CER and 9.3% in WER, building on the gains already achieved by depthwise-dilated separable convolution and multi-scale convolution. This highlights the effectiveness of normalization in projecting representations from different handwriting styles into a shared space, enhancing the model ability to adapt to diverse handwriting patterns.

In addition to modifications to the convolutional encoder, we removed the hidden layers from CLDNN, resulting in the small version of our model. It achieves 15.29% CER and 50.70% WER, which are 19.7% and 15.8% better than CLDNN, while using only 0.53M parameters and 79M MACs, representing reductions of 29.3% and 72.9% compared to CLDNN. We then scale up the model by using three convolutional blocks per stage, encoder dimensions of 128, 256, and 512, a BiLSTM with 128 hidden size, and three BiLSTM layers. This results in the base version of our model, which achieves 9.44% CER and 32.17% WER, representing 50.4% and 46.6% improvements over CLDNN, using 3.89M parameters and 600M MACs, which are 5.2× and 2.1× those of CLDNN.

5   Discussion

5.1   Efficiency

Across all evaluations, we demonstrate the strong efficiency of our models, particularly the small version, which is designed for deployment on edge devices. It achieves significantly lower error rates compared to other IMU-based HWR approaches while using only 53.3% of the parameters and 27.1% of the computational cost of CLDNN. This efficiency can greatly enhance the user experience on capable edge devices by providing better recognition without incurring communication latency from remote servers.

The base version, in contrast, is designed for server-side deployment, prioritizing higher recognition accuracy by processing raw signals with more parameters. Our base-version model achieves the best performance on the WI splits while maintaining comparable model size and computational cost, demonstrating a strong balance between efficiency and performance.

5.2   Robustness

Handwriting styles vary greatly among individuals, posing significant challenges for HWR. Since it is unrealistic to train a model on data that captures every possible handwriting style, evaluating models on WI datasets provides a more practical and meaningful measure of performance. WI evaluation ensures that handwriting styles in the training and test sets do not overlap, more accurately reflecting real-world scenarios where a model must generalize to unseen writers. Our models outperform all competitors across all WI splits, demonstrating a strong ability to extract robust handwriting features that generalize effectively across diverse writing styles.

Children are beginners in handwriting, and their writing styles differ significantly from those of adults, making HWR more challenging. However, children are also an important user group for HWR systems, given the frequent handwriting activities in educational settings. Therefore, developing a solution that performs well for both adults and children is essential for the success of an HWR system. Our robustness evaluation shows that our models outperform all competitors on both adult and children subsets. Moreover, the results from the cross-subset evaluation suggest that our models learn more generalizable representations, as they maintain better performance even when trained and validated on different age groups.

Additionally, noise caused by various properties of the writing surface, such as hardness and roughness, and sensor imperfections is common in HWR systems and can potentially degrade performance, limiting the environments in which these systems can be used. In our ablation study, we demonstrate that using data augmentations such as AddNoise, Drift, and Dropout can significantly improve the performance of our HWR system. This shows that data augmentation can be an effective solution for handling noise and improving the system robustness.

5.3   Flexibility

Due to the nature of handwriting, handwriting signals always vary in length. Models like ViT and Swin Transformers, constrained by positional embeddings or shifting mechanisms, require suboptimal compromises such as padding or truncating to process inputs of different sizes. However, padding increases meaningless computational overhead, while truncating can lead to the loss of important information. In contrast, the CNN-BiLSTM design processes inputs of any size without resizing, enabling efficient computation and adaptability. Thus, approaches that can process inputs of varying sizes are essential for IMU-based HWR.

6   Conclusion and Outlook

In conclusion, our experiments demonstrate that the proposed models consistently outperform competitors on WI datasets, showcasing strong robustness, efficiency, and flexibility in HWR.

However, we have not yet investigated the error patterns in the data. By identifying and addressing semantic errors such as typographical errors or misalignments between sensor signals and text labels, we could curate the datasets to improve their quality. This refinement could enhance HWR system performance, produce more reliable results, and offer deeper insights into the remaining challenges in HWR.

Additionally, although the models show strong performance on our sentence-based dataset, character-level recognition remains a suboptimal approach for leveraging contextual information. It results in a pattern-matching solution that lacks understanding of language semantics from the sensor signals. This limitation could potentially be addressed by incorporating natural language processing techniques into HWR systems.

A   Visualization of Character and Length Distribution

The character distributions show consistent patterns across our datasets. Both word-based (Fig. 4) and sentence-based (Fig. 5) datasets are dominated by lower-case letters, with "e", "n", and "r" appearing most frequently. This matches the typical letter frequencies in English and German. In the sentence-based dataset, the space character ranks as the second most frequent character, which makes sense given its essential role in sentence structure.

The word-based dataset reveals clear differences between age groups. Adult (Fig. 6) and children (Fig. 7) handwriting samples show distinct distribution patterns, with children samples having longer average lengths than adult samples.

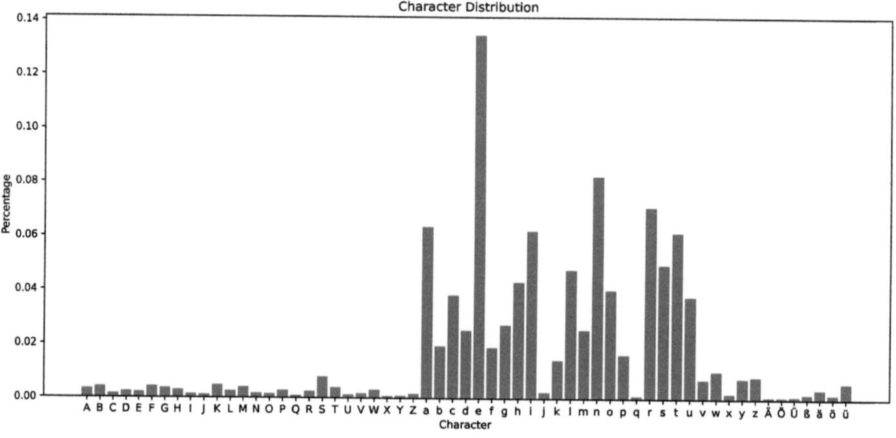

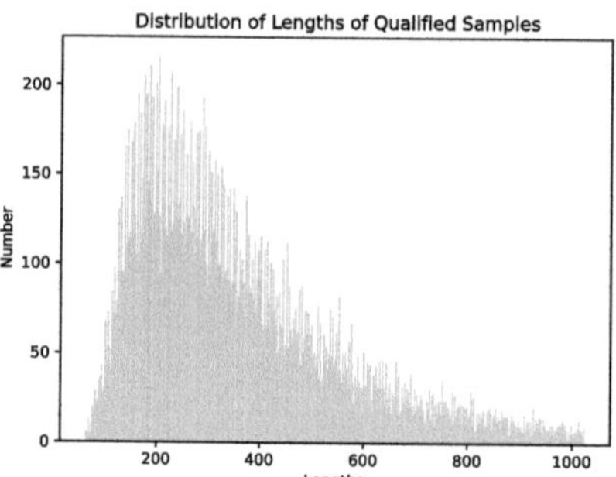

Fig. 4. Character and sequence length distributions in the word-based dataset. The top plot shows the frequency of each character, while the bottom plot shows the distribution of sequence lengths.

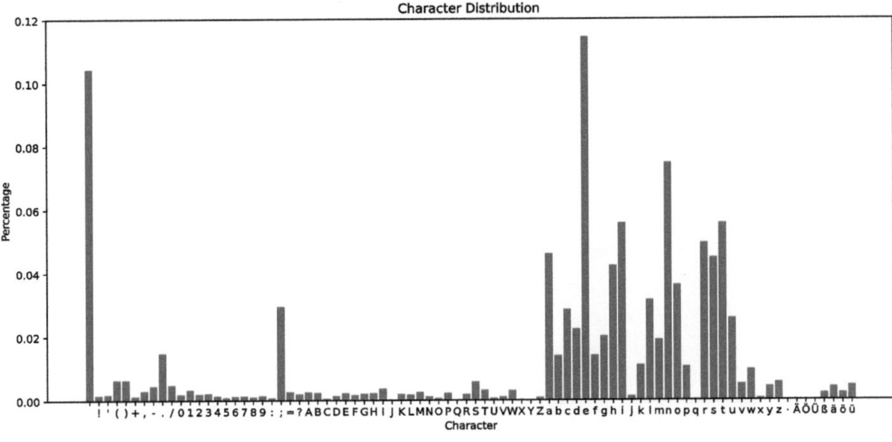

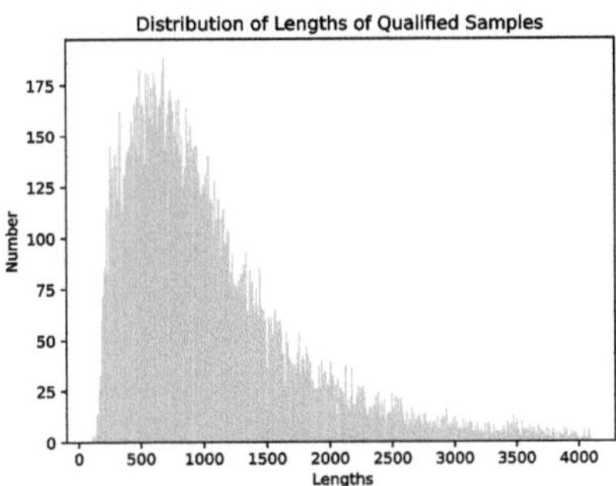

Fig. 5. Character and sequence length distributions in the sentence-based dataset. The top plot shows the frequency of each character, while the bottom plot shows the distribution of sequence lengths.

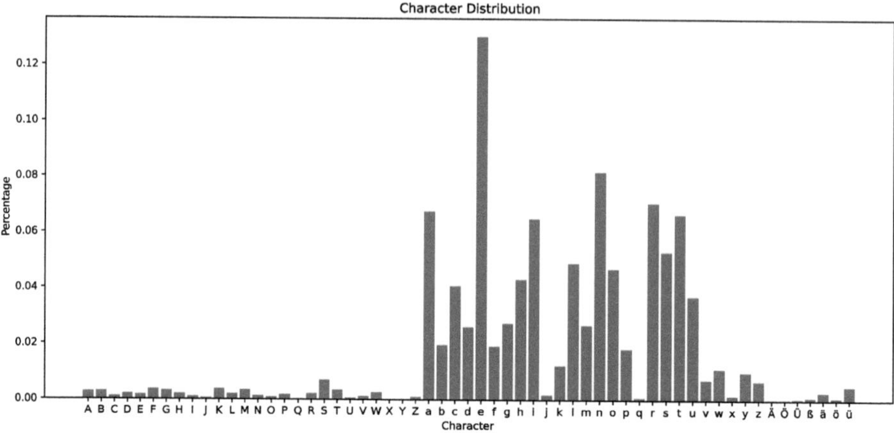

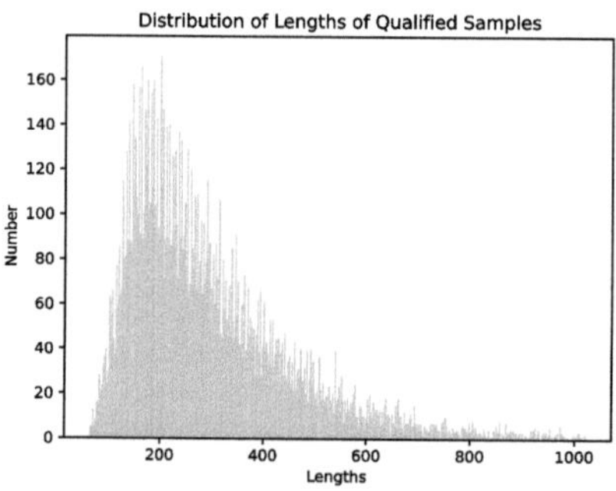

Fig. 6. Character and sequence length distributions in the adult subset of the word-based dataset. The top plot shows the frequency of each character, while the bottom plot shows the distribution of sequence lengths.

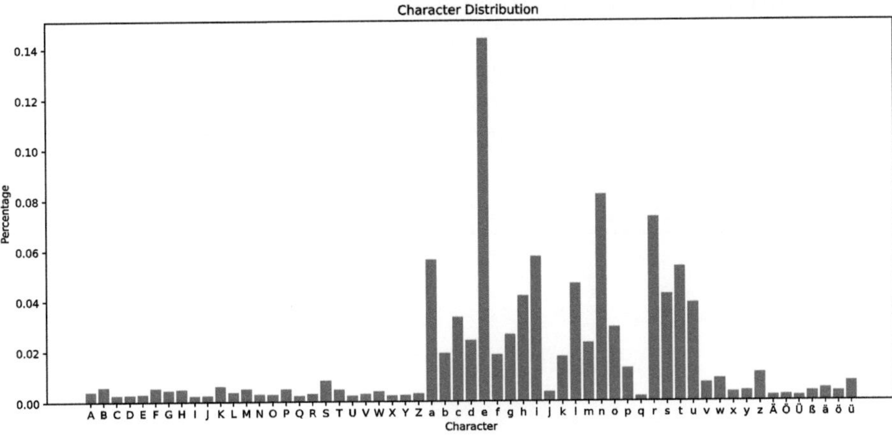

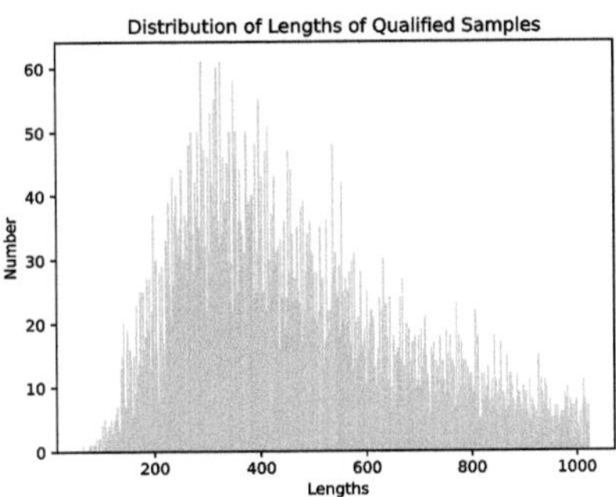

Fig. 7. Character and sequence length distributions in the children subset of the word-based dataset. The top plot shows the frequency of each character, while the bottom plot shows the distribution of sequence lengths.

B   Visualization of Data Augmentation

As shown in the visualization of data augmentations in Fig. 8, AddNoise, Drift, and Dropout are applied in a multiplicative manner to ensure that the augmentation magnitude neither overshadows the original signal nor dominates it.

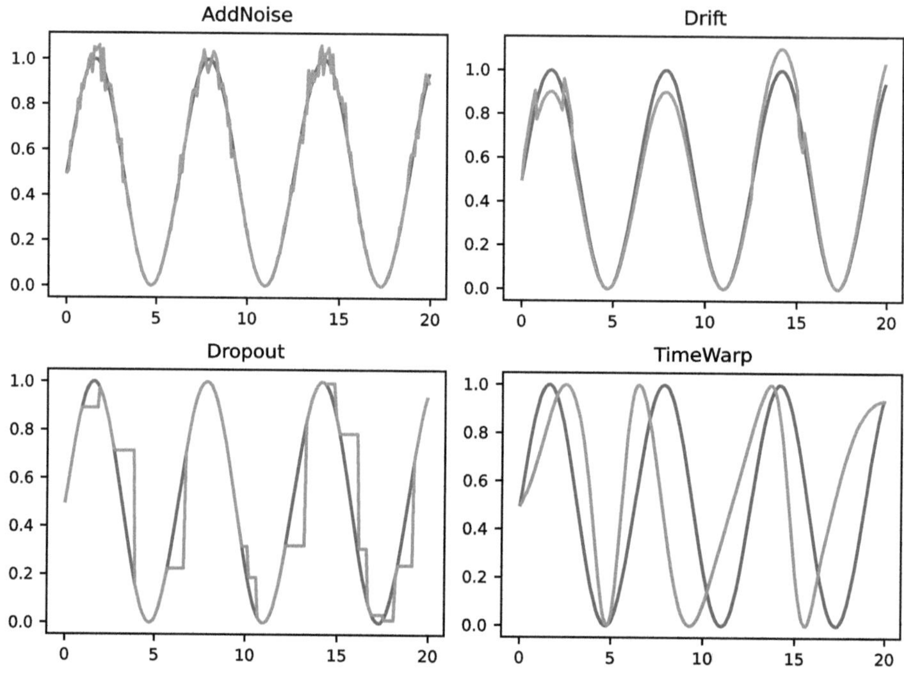

Fig. 8. Data augmentation. Examples of sine signals with different data augmentation techniques applied. The blue curve represents the original sine signal and the orange curve represents the augmented signal.

C   Visualization of Substitution Error Rates

Figure 9 shows the substitution error matrix of our base-version model on the first fold of the WI split of our word-based dataset. Figure 10 shows the substitution error matrix of our base-version model on the first fold of the WI split of the adult subset of our word-based dataset. Figure 11 shows the substitution error matrix of our base-version model on the first fold of the WI split of the children subset of our word-based dataset. Figure 12 presents the substitution error matrix of the same model on the first fold of the WI split of our sentence-based dataset.

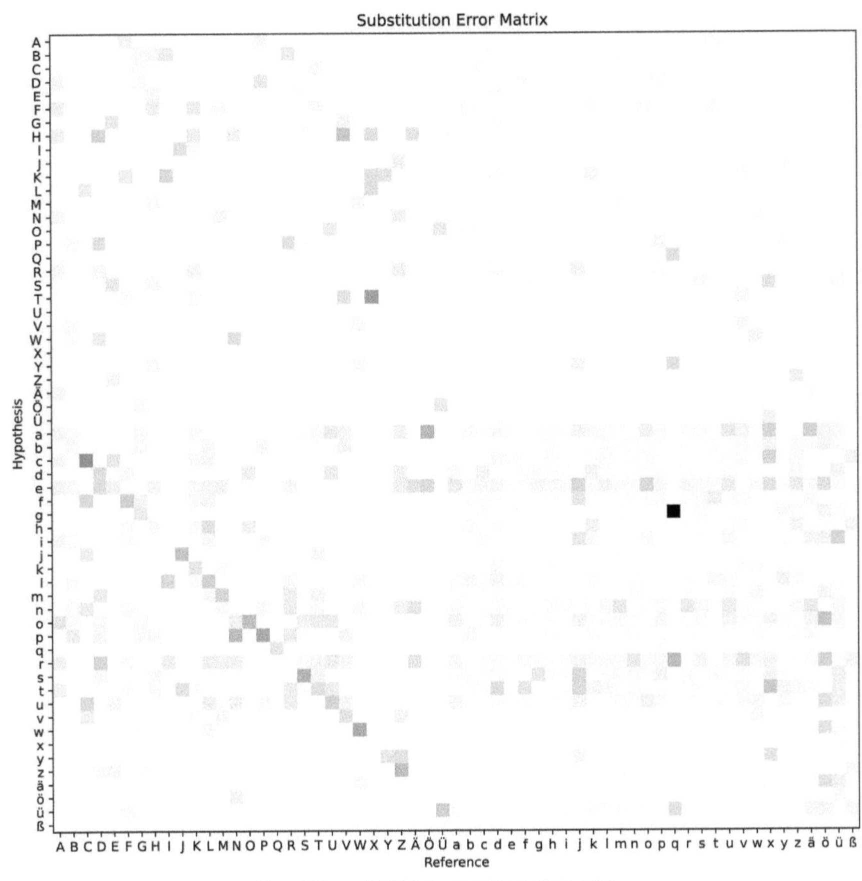

Fig. 9. Substitution Errors on Word-Based Dataset. Substitution errors made by the base version of our model on the first fold of the WI split of our word-based dataset are visualized. Darker shades indicate higher error rates.

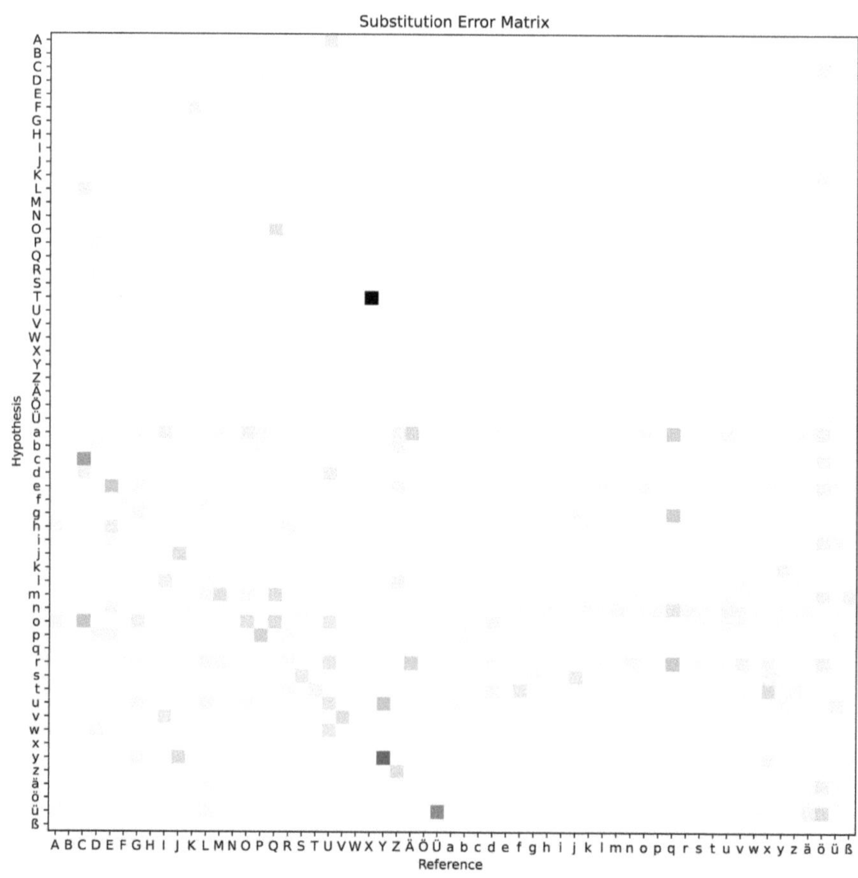

Fig. 10. Substitution Errors on the Adult Subset. Substitution errors made by the base version of our model on the first fold of the WI split of the adult subset of our word-based dataset are visualized. Darker shades indicate higher error rates.

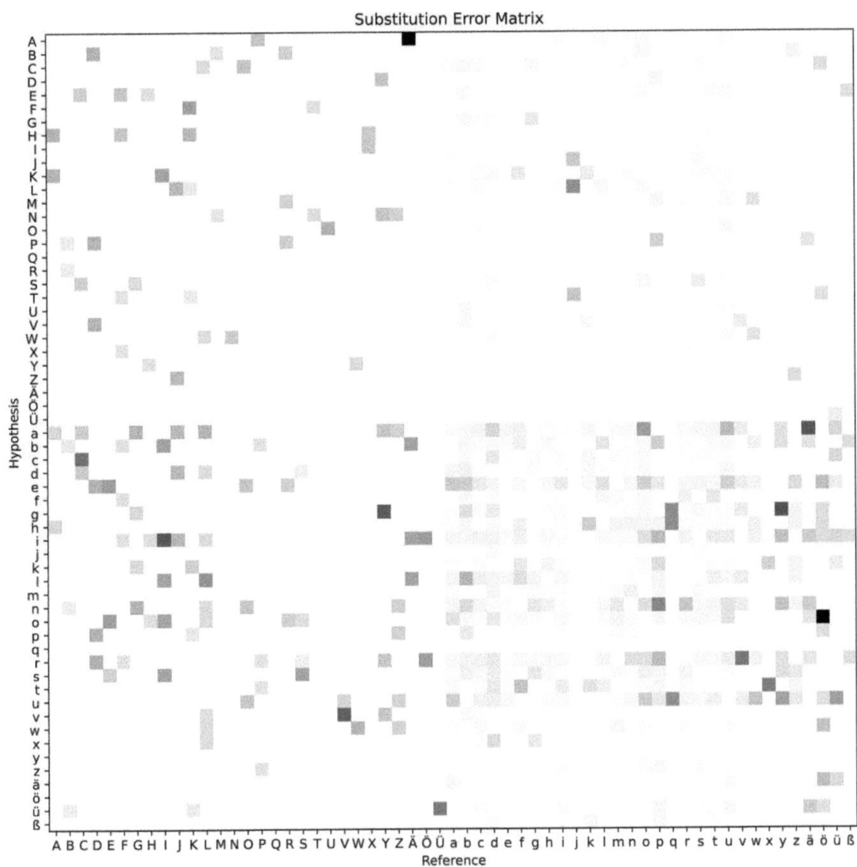

Fig. 11. Substitution Errors on the Children Subset. Substitution errors made by the base version of our model on the first fold of the WI split of the children subset of our word-based dataset are visualized. Darker shades indicate higher error rates.

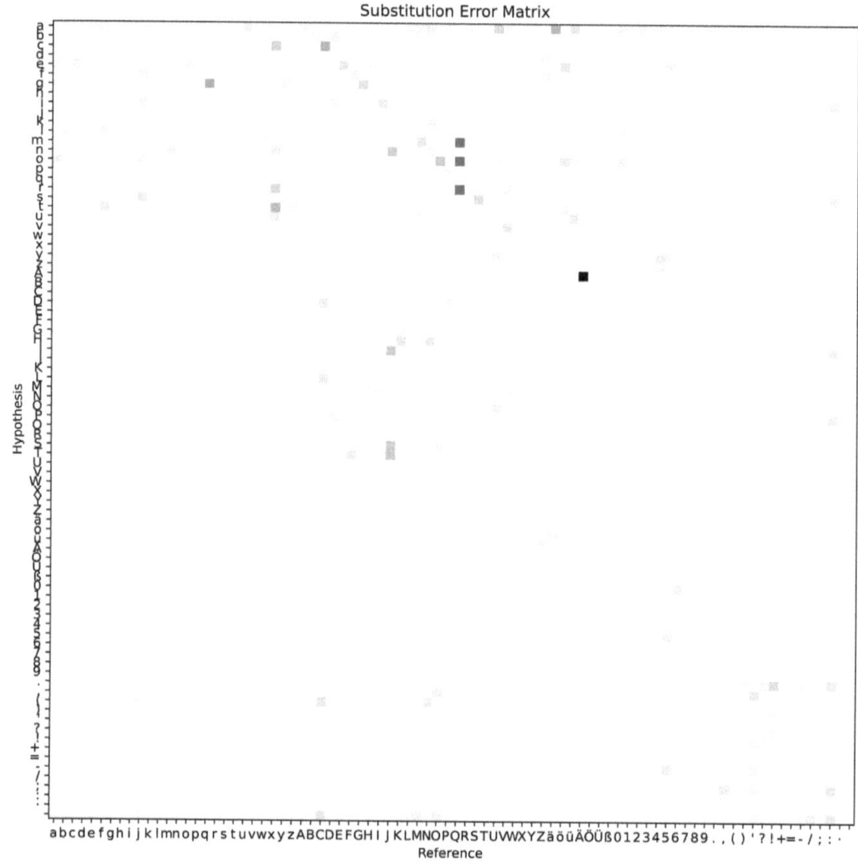

Fig. 12. Substitution Errors on Sentence-Based Dataset. Substitution errors made by the base version of our model on the first fold of the WI split of our sentence-based dataset are visualized.

References

1. Alemayoh, T.T., Shintani, M., Lee, J.H., Okamoto, S.: Deep-learning-based character recognition from handwriting motion data captured using IMU and force sensors. Sensors **22**(20) (2022). https://doi.org/10.3390/s22207840
2. Carbune, V., et al.: Fast multi-language LSTM-based online handwriting recognition. Int. J. Doc. Anal. Recogn. (IJDAR) **23**(2), 89–102 (2020). https://doi.org/10.1007/s10032-020-00350-4
3. Choi, S.D., Lee, A.S., Lee, S.Y.: On-line handwritten character recognition with 3D accelerometer. In: 2006 IEEE International Conference on Information Acquisition, pp. 845–850 (2006). https://doi.org/10.1109/ICIA.2006.305842
4. Dosovitskiy, A., et al.: An image is worth 16x16 words: transformers for image recognition at scale. In: International Conference on Learning Representations (2021). https://openreview.net/forum?id=YicbFdNTTy

5. Graves, A., Fernández, S., Gomez, F., Schmidhuber, J.: Connectionist temporal classification: labelling unsegmented sequence data with recurrent neural networks. In: Proceedings of the 23rd International Conference on Machine Learning, ICML '06, pp. 369–376. Association for Computing Machinery, New York (2006). https:// doi.org/10.1145/1143844.1143891

6. Hassan, E., Tarek, H., Hazem, M., Bahnacy, S., Shaheen, L., Elashmwai, W.H.: Medical prescription recognition using machine learning. In: 2021 IEEE 11th Annual Computing and Communication Workshop and Conference (CCWC), pp. 0973–0979 (2021). https://doi.org/10.1109/CCWC51732.2021.9376141

7. He, K., Zhang, X., Ren, S., Sun, J.: Deep residual learning for image recognition. In: Proceedings of the IEEE Conference on Computer Vision and Pattern Recognition (CVPR) (2016). https://doi.org/10.1109/CVPR.2016.90

8. Jeen-Shing, W., Yu-Liang, H., Cheng-Ling, C.: Online handwriting recognition using an accelerometer-based pen device. In: Proceedings of the 2nd International Conference on Advances in Computer Science and Engineering (CSE 2013), pp. 231–234. Atlantis Press (2013). https://doi.org/10.2991/cse.2013.52

9. Kohút, J., Hradiš, M., Kišš, M.: Towards writing style adaptation in handwriting recognition. In: Fink, G.A., Jain, R., Kise, K., Zanibbi, R. (eds.) Document Analysis and Recognition - ICDAR 2023, pp. 377–394. Springer Nature Switzerland, Cham (2023). https://doi.org/10.1007/978-3-031-41685-9_24

10. Liu, Z., et al.: Swin transformer V2: scaling up capacity and resolution. In: International Conference on Computer Vision and Pattern Recognition (CVPR) (2022). https://doi.org/10.1109/CVPR52688.2022.01170

11. Liu, Z., et al.: Swin transformer: hierarchical vision transformer using shifted windows. In: Proceedings of the IEEE/CVF International Conference on Computer Vision (ICCV) (2021). https://doi.org/10.1109/ICCV48922.2021.00986

12. Liu, Z., Mao, H., Wu, C.Y., Feichtenhofer, C., Darrell, T., Xie, S.: A convnet for the 2020s. Proceedings of the IEEE/CVF Conference on Computer Vision and Pattern Recognition (CVPR) (2022). https://doi.org/10.1109/CVPR52688.2022.01167

13. Lopez-Rodriguez, P., Avina-Cervantes, J.G., Contreras-Hernandez, J.L., Correa, R., Ruiz-Pinales, J.: Handwriting recognition based on 3D accelerometer data by deep learning. Appl. Sci. **12**(13) (2022). https://doi.org/10.3390/app12136707

14. Meißl, F., Eibensteiner, F., Petz, P., Langer, J.: Online handwriting recognition using LSTM on microcontroller and IMU sensors. In: 2022 21st IEEE International Conference on Machine Learning and Applications (ICMLA), pp. 999–1004 (2022). https://doi.org/10.1109/ICMLA55696.2022.00167

15. Ott, F., et al.: Benchmarking online sequence-to-sequence and character-based handwriting recognition from IMU-enhanced pens. Int. J. Doc. Anal. Recognit. **25**(4), 385–414 (2022). https://doi.org/10.1007/s10032-022-00415-6

16. Pontart, V., Bidet-Ildei, C., Lambert, E., Morisset, P., Flouret, L., ALAMARGOT, D.: Influence of handwriting skills during spelling in primary and lower secondary grades. Front. Psychol. **4** (2013). https://doi.org/10.3389/fpsyg.2013.00818

17. Seuret, M., et al.: Combining OCR models for reading early modern books. In: Fink, G.A., Jain, R., Kise, K., Zanibbi, R. (eds.) Document Analysis and Recognition - ICDAR 2023, pp. 342–357. Springer Nature Switzerland, Cham (2023). https://doi.org/10.1007/978-3-031-41734-4_21

18. Skar, G.B., Lei, P.-W., Graham, S., Aasen, A.J., Johansen, M.B., Kvistad, A.H.: Handwriting fluency and the quality of primary grade students' writing. Read. Writ. (2), 1–30 (2021). https://doi.org/10.1007/s11145-021-10185-y

19. Tolstikhin, I.O., et al.: MLP-mixer: an all-MLP architecture for vision. In: Ranzato, M., Beygelzimer, A., Dauphin, Y., Liang, P., Vaughan, J.W. (eds.) Advances in Neural Information Processing Systems, vol. 34, pp. 24261–24272. Curran Associates, Inc. (2021)
20. Ulyanov, D., Vedaldi, A., Lempitsky, V.: Instance normalization: the missing ingredient for fast stylization (2017). https://arxiv.org/abs/1607.08022
21. Vaswani, A., et al.: Attention is all you need. In: Guyon, I., Luxburg, U.V., Bengio, S., Wallach, H., Fergus, R., Vishwanathan, S., Garnett, R. (eds.) Advances in Neural Information Processing Systems, vol. 30. Curran Associates, Inc. (2017)
22. Wehbi, M., Hamann, T., Barth, J., Eskofier, B.: Digitizing handwriting with a sensor pen: a writer-independent recognizer. In: 2020 17th International Conference on Frontiers in Handwriting Recognition (ICFHR), pp. 295–300 (2020). https://doi.org/10.1109/ICFHR2020.2020.00061
23. Wehbi, M., Hamann, T., Barth, J., Kaempf, P., Zanca, D., Eskofier, B.: Towards an IMU-based pen online handwriting recognizer. In: Lladós, J., Lopresti, D., Uchida, S. (eds.) ICDAR 2021. LNCS, vol. 12823, pp. 289–303. Springer, Cham (2021). https://doi.org/10.1007/978-3-030-86334-0_19

Help the Machine to Help You:
an Evaluation in the Wild of Egocentric
Data Cleaning via Skeptical Learning

Andrea Bontempelli$^{(\boxtimes)}$, Matteo Busso , Leonardo Javier Malcotti ,
and Fausto Giunchiglia

University of Trento, Trento, Italy
`andrea.bontempelli@unitn.it`

Abstract. Any digital personal assistant, whether used to support task performance, answer questions, or manage work and daily life—including fitness schedules—requires high-quality annotations to function properly. However, user annotations, whether actively produced or inferred from context (e.g., data from smartphone sensors), are often subject to errors and noise. Previous research on Skeptical Learning (SKEL) addressed the issue of noisy labels by comparing offline active annotations with passive data, allowing for an evaluation of annotation accuracy. However, this evaluation did not include confirmation from end-users, the best judges of their own context. In this study, we evaluate SKEL's performance in real-world conditions with actual users who can refine the input labels based on their current perspectives and needs. The study involves university students using the iLog mobile application on their devices over a period of four weeks. The results highlight the challenges of finding the right balance between user effort and data quality, as well as the potential benefits of using SKEL, which include reduced annotation effort and improved quality of collected data.

Keywords: data quality · longitudinal studies · interactive machine learning

1   Introduction

Any personal assistant requires knowledge of the user's context to operate effectively. For instance, a navigation app needs to know the user's current location and their intended destination to provide the best route. Similarly, a smart home assistant must recognize the user's voice and identify the connected smart devices, and even a simple calendar application requires information about upcoming events to send notifications. This contextual information can often be inferred without direct user interaction, such as through a smartphone's GPS signal indicating location. However, it frequently necessitates direct input from the user, who possesses the most comprehensive understanding of their own context [4]. Thus, personal context can be defined as a *"theory of the world*

Ö. Durmaz Incel et al. (Eds.): iWOAR 2025, LNCS 16292, pp. 287–307, 2026.
https://doi.org/10.1007/978-3-032-13312-0_17

which encodes an individual's subjective perspective about it" [17]. Following the approaches identified by [18], context can be modeled across four dimensions: *location* (where the person is), *activity* (what they are doing), *social context* (who the person is with), and *object context* (which objects are with the person). This information, which may come as feedback, vocal or written notes from the user, enhances the assistant's comprehension of both context and the goals it aims to achieve.

Past experiences in AI [7] and in social science in general, particularly through methods like Experience Sampling Method (ESM) [12,24] or Ecological Momentary Assessment (EMA), demonstrate how this type of information can be collected continuously and frequently over extended periods. This collection process can combine user annotations with data from sensors, thus allowing for the analysis of habits, routines, and social practices. Frequent context questions lead to granular data, enabling the observation of more detailed behaviors. However, this approach is susceptible to errors that can compromise data quality (see, e.g., [1,24,32]), both from user annotations and sensor information, which may end up in producing noisy labels. To tackle the problem of noisy labels, Skeptical Learning detects potentially suspicious responses and prompts the user to revise them when necessary [5,35]. Prior studies have evaluated SKEL using both synthetic and real-world datasets, where an oracle simulates user responses to assess the algorithm's performance. The oracle reflects an objective point of view, relying on methods such as deriving location from GPS coordinates. These evaluations often made assumptions about users and data to lessen the impact of external factors. For instance, they typically require that examples arrive in a specific order, and assume that users respond immediately. However, these assumptions overlook the complexities of real life; users may leave the experiment, or sensor data may be unavailable if the user disables the sensor (like GPS) or if it is not present on their device.

In this work, we evaluate SKEL with real users in the wild. We do this, as proposed in [5], in a longitudinal study based on the use of the participants' smartphones. In longitudinal studies, the benefit of SKEL is twofold. First, the ML model recognizes the participant's context from the sensor data to automatically answer questions about their context, thus reducing the effort required for answering. Second, SKEL improves the answer quality, therefore allowing to learn a model with higher predictive performance and improving the accuracy of the answers. The model is trained on a per-user basis, using only the user data, ensuring an egocentric recognition bound to the point of view of a single person, as done in the computer vision domain [14]. This is because the context is user-specific and captures the subjective perspective. For instance, both the student and the professor are in the same room, but they are performing different activities, i.e., listening and speaking, respectively. The user is thus empowered to clean his/her own contextual annotation. We designed and ran a study with university students from the University of Trento, aiming to identify their locations using SKEL.[1] The ultimate goal of SKEL is to reduce the number of questions sent to the user by asking the model to answer the questions about the user's position. Our main contributions are as follows:

- We leverage SKEL as a solution to annotation errors in longitudinal studies;
- We design a study and operationalize SKEL inside an existing data collection platform to evaluate it in the wild with real users and report preliminary results.

The structure of the paper is as follows. Section 2 presents how data quality is addressed in machine learning and in longitudinal studies, and Sect. 3 briefly introduce SKEL. Then, we detail the experiment design in Sect. 4 and the results in Sect. 5. Section 6 reports final remarks.

2   Related Work

2.1   Data Quality in Machine Learning

In data-driven disciplines such as machine learning, the quality of data is fundamental for reliable model performance. Data may fail to capture the diversity of users and contexts in which a model will operate, while classification labels are often noisy due to annotation errors, leading to performance degradation. Several strategies exist to mitigate these issues, such as developing robust models, cleaning the data [16], or collecting additional datasets. However, large-scale data acquisition is frequently infeasible due to cost and logistical constraints, creating a trade-off between dataset size and data quality, as well as between the use of large and small models [30].

To address these challenges, data-centric AI has emerged as a paradigm that prioritizes iterative improvement of data quality over simply scaling models [22]. Within this paradigm, our work emphasizes the *human-in-control* principle, where users themselves are empowered to actively clean and refine their data.

2.2   Data Collection in the Social Sciences

In the social sciences, researchers often collect data on human behavior using participants' personal mobile devices. This approach integrates the experience sampling method (ESM) [12,24]—a longitudinal design in which participants repeatedly report on feelings, contexts, and behaviors—with passive sensor data [29]. Questionnaires are typically delivered via smartphones and smartwatches, allowing high-frequency data collection while simultaneously capturing sensor-based contextual information such as location, activity, and social interactions [7]. This combination enables fine-grained insights into daily routines and practices.

Extensive literature highlights how the quality of measurements and the dynamics of participant–researcher interaction influences the reliability of collected data [11,32].

---

[1] This experiment involves human subjects and has been approved by the Research Ethics Committee of the University of Trento (protocol n. 2023-006).

2.3   Reliability Issues in Collected Data

Self-reported data, while widely used, are prone to several biases. The asymmetric relationship between researcher and participant can give rise to phenomena such as the *Hawthorne effect* [20,23], where participants alter their behavior due to awareness of observation. Similarly, *social desirability* bias leads respondents to provide answers perceived as favorable [11], while *non-attitudes* occur when participants respond at random due to lack of knowledge or understanding of the question. Another critical issue is *respondent burden* [27], which reflects the perceived effort of participation, including time investment, difficulty, and emotional cost. In intensive longitudinal studies, this burden can reduce data quality through missing or careless responses. Several works have focused on the reasons linked to the respondent burden [13] and ways to reduce its impact, such as through more immediate and short interactions, also called μEMA [26].

Although less studied, sensor-based data collection also raises reliability concerns [6]. Sensing technologies, such as smartphone-based measurements, are often seen as more "objective" alternatives to self-reports, yet they introduce specific challenges. Participants may disable notifications, turn off devices, or deactivate sensors (e.g., GPS, Bluetooth) for privacy or convenience, while technical issues—such as server crashes, notification failures, operating system incompatibilities, or missing hardware—can further compromise data quality. Thus, both annotations and sensors data are vulnerable to reliability issues, though through different mechanisms. Addressing these challenges is essential to balance participant burden, data quality, and technological feasibility.

3   Skeptical Learning

The benefit of SKEL in the scenario described above is twofold. First, the machine learning model can precompile or autonomously answer these questions when certain about its prediction, reducing the effort of the participants and maintaining a higher level of granularity in the answer compared to μEMA. Second, the quality of the answers can be improved both to obtain better data for the researchers and to train a more accurate model. We first introduce the main algorithm and then describe how we have applied it in the study described in this paper.

3.1   SKEL

We tackle interactive classification in the wild, namely under label noise. The machine receives a sequence of examples $\mathbf{x}_t$, for $t = 1, 2, \ldots$, where $\mathbf{x}_t \in \mathbb{R}^d$, i.e., the vector of sensor readings, and outputs $\hat{y}_t \in \mathbb{Y}$, i.e., the user's location. The machine can query the user to report the ground-truth label $y_t \in \mathbb{Y}$. The goal is to learn a model that performs well on future examples while keeping the number of queries at minimum to avoid the burden of the user. Label noise occurs when the user provides a label $\tilde{y}$ that is wrong, i.e., $\tilde{y} \neq y_t$. This may be caused by inattention, failing to understand the question or reporting a socially desirable label. Label noise affects the model performance [16]. To acquire a clean dataset and a high-quality model, Skeptical Learning (SKEL) was introduced by [35] and revised in [5].

Algorithm 1 outlines the pseudo-code of SKEL. In brief, SKEL sequentially learns from incoming examples. In each iteration, the machine receives an example $\mathbf{x}_t$ for which predicts y_t. If the machine is not sufficiently confident about the prediction, it requests the user to label the uncertain example, as it is more likely to impact the model. Once the label is received, SKEL has to

---

Algorithm 1 Pseudo-code of SKEL.

1: **for** $t = 1, 2, \ldots$ **do**
2:     receive $\mathbf{x}_t$
3:     predict $\hat{y}_t$ for $\mathbf{x}_t$
4:     **if** uncertain about $\hat{y}_t$ **then**
5:         request label, receive $\tilde{y}_t$
6:         **if** skeptical about $\tilde{y}$ **then**
7:             challenge user with $\hat{y}_t$, receive y'_t
8:             add $(\mathbf{x}_t, y'_t)$ to data set
9:             update classifier

---

decide whether to challenge the user's label. A label is suspicious if the model is confident that the model prediction is right and the user's annotation is wrong. Thus, the model estimates on its own prediction and on the user's annotation. Then, the user is asked to revise his/her annotation if the prediction has higher confidence than the annotation. The confidence computation depends on the actual implementation. [35] empirically estimates the accuracy of the machine based on training set size and confidence reported by the model. The confidence in the user is derived from the number of past spotted mistakes. [5] estimates the difference between the model's uncertainty on both the annotator label and predicted label. In this user study, we focus on the latter.

The first formulation of SKEL has been implemented on top of random forests (RF) [35]. While RF is robust to noise, this method tends to be over-confident, thus avoiding querying the user on new and informative examples or continuously contradicting the user regardless of his/her past performance. Another limitation is the difficulty of fine-tuning its parameters in the interactive setting. To overcome these limitations in interactive classification in the wild, a redesign of SKEL based on Gaussian Processes (GPs), non-parametric distributions over functions, has been proposed [5]. GPs are defined by a mean and covariance function, where the latter encodes the assumptions about the modeled functions. The uncertainty is estimated by the prior assumption about the function and the observed data. In a nutshell, uncertainty decreases close to the observed training examples. SKEL leverages the explicit model uncertainty estimation of GPs to decide when to query, overcoming the pathological cases of the previous SKEL formulation and better allocating the labeling and contradiction queries. Moreover, it supports efficient incremental learning model updates, making it suitable for the settings of this work. Thus, for this study, we used SKEL on GPs and operationalized it as described in the next section.

3.2 SKEL in the Wild

The goal is to use SKEL to assist users in answering the contextual questions and to improve answer quality. For each user, the SKEL model is trained on the sensor data and annotations that arrive as a stream of data. The annotations are given by the user and capture his/her subjective view. If SKEL is suspicious about the provided annotation, then the user can revise it if necessary. Acquiring correct annotations is crucial to learn an effective model that can assist the user. The algorithm, as described in the previous section, has been slightly adapted and organised into two phases, as follows.

There is an initial bootstrap phase in which the algorithm collects annotations and trusts them regardless of the machine suspicion. The duration of this phase is fixed and addresses the problem of the cold start, which occurs when there is not enough data for a specific user. The drawback of not being suspicious about any annotations is that the model may start learning from noisy examples. This can be addressed by reporting the past examples as an explanation supporting the machine's suspicion [28]. In this work, we want to stress that the user is in control of the data cleaning, namely, he/she is asked by the machine to revise his/her own data by providing the annotation reflecting her/his personal point of view.

Hence, in the second phase, the user collects his/her data and makes it fit the purpose of the data collection. The previous formulation of SKEL asked to revise previous labels as soon as the machine receives the example and decides to be skeptical. This implies that skeptical questions can continuously interrupt the user, increasing the number of interruptions. To avoid this, the skeptical questions generated during the day are sent all together at once. Potentially, this approach could allow the user to answer them in an aggregate manner, for instance, by selecting on a map the location where they spent the morning, without having to annotate all the examples collected during that period.

4 Study Design

This section presents the research protocol of the SKEL evaluation study, which involved a multi-disciplinary team composed of a sociologist and software engineers. We employ SKEL to recognize the location of the participants. The experiment focuses only on the spatial dimension for three main reasons. First, the location dimension is easier to recognize by the machine with respect to the other dimensions, like activity recognition or social context. Second, taking into account all context dimensions would require the user to answer more questions, one for each dimension, increasing the user effort and making it more difficult to evaluate SKEL. Finally, it is possible to compute the ground-truth position from the GPS coordinates of the University of Trento and of the main home. The ground-truth labels can then be compared with the labels provided by the

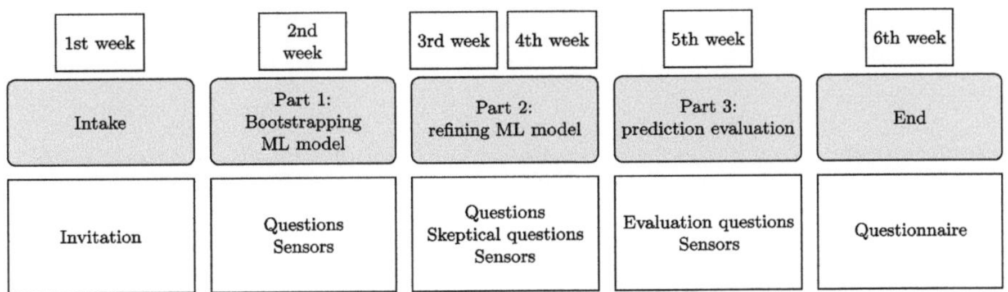

Fig. 1. Research protocol. Blue boxes report the study phase and the white boxes the instruments. (Color figure online)

user. To run the study, we integrated SKEL in an existing data collection platform [21].[2]

4.1   Research Protocol

Fig. 1 outlines the phases of the research protocol. The overall length of the experiment is six weeks, and four of them are allocated to the data collection.

Intake. We contacted the students of the University of Trento via email to present the research project and to provide instructions on how to join the study by installing the iLog app [21,34] on Android devices. The installation on the personal device allows the collection of data that faithfully describes their daily life and does not alter their daily routines. Participating students must read and accept the privacy information through the app and authorize data collection for each sensor individually. The incentive strategy includes bonuses as follows: €30 to all participants with at least 75% completed questions, prizes of €100 to three randomly selected most active participants.

Part 1. During this first data collection phase, the app collects data from the sensors for one week. Moreover, every 30 min, the app asks the participant's location, which is the context dimension we investigate (Fig. 2a shows a screenshot of the question page in the app). Table 2 lists all answer options. SKEL algorithm bootstraps the learning on this data before transitioning to the next phase.

Part 2. For two weeks, the participant continues to answer the time diaries, and in addition, the model challenges the participant on suspicious labels. A label is suspicious if it is different from the predicted labels and the model is sufficiently confident that its label is correct [5]. The participant can confirm the predicted labels, and in this case, the model correctly detected that the label provided

---

[2] We refer the reader to [3, Section 7.3] for a detailed overview of the architecture implementing this integration.

(a) Time diary answer options (Q1)

(b) List of skeptical questions to revise (Q2)

(c) List of annotations to evaluate (Q4)

Fig. 2. The three types of questions shown on the iLog app.

as the answer to the time diary was not correct. If this is not the case, a new answer is provided. The model is then refined by considering this participant feedback. The model sends the contradictions every evening at 7 pm, all at once, to concentrate the answering effort in single and specific periods of time, and reduce interruptions. Figure 2b shows an example of the contradiction question.

Part 3. The goal of the last week of the data collection is to evaluate the model predictions and, thus, the machine-participant alignment. The participant selects the incorrect prediction location labels from a list (e.g., Fig. 2c). This question is the only interaction with the participant in this phase, and it occurs at 7 pm.

Conclusion. In the last phase, the participant is expected to fill out a questionnaire to collect socio-demographic information.

4.2   Study Setup

Sensors. The sensor readings are continuously collected during the four weeks of data collection. The full list of the collected sensors is presented in Table 3, which also reports their collection frequency. In this experiment, we use a subset

Table 1. Structure of the questions. Q1 is the time diary, Q2 and Q3 are the skeptical questions, and Q4 is the evaluation question.

	Timing/Condition	Question	Answer options
Q1	1st week: every 30 min	Where are you now?	see Table 2
Q2	2nd and 3rd week at 7:00 pm	Is <time> <predicted label> correct?	1. Yes 2. No
Q3	if Q2 = No	Where are you at <time>?	go to Q1
Q4	4th week at 7:00 pm	Select the labels that are incorrect	1. <time> <predicted label> 2. <time> <predicted label> 3. ... 4. All correct

of the 30 sensors supported by the application to avoid draining the battery excessively. We selected the sensors that are more informative in predicting the location. The data streams are temporarily stored on the device and updated on the server periodically. The raw sensor data are aggregated in time windows of 30 min, which is the time between two consecutive annotations. The generated feature vectors, described in Table 4, are the input of the model.

Questions. Table 1 lists the questions. Time diaries are sent every 30 min, and the user is asked to indicate his or her location. The list of location options (see Table 2) is derived from the guidelines for time use surveys [15]. To reduce the user effort, the options are aggregated into main categories. Skeptical questions are sent once a day, one for each suspicious answer. One evaluation question is sent daily in the final phase, listing the predicted labels, from which the user must select the incorrect ones. If time diaries and questions are not answered within 8 and 12 h, respectively, then they expire and cannot be answered.

Hyperparamters. We employ the SKEL version proposed by [5]. This learner leverages Gaussian Process (GP) and we modified it as described in Sect. 3.2. All GP-methods use a combination of constant (with a constant value of 1), rational quadratic (with a length scale of 0.2 and a scale mixture parameter of 1), squared exponential (length scale of 1) and white noise kernels, and $\rho = 10^{-8}$, without any optimization.

5   Results

This section presents the main results and statistics about the sensor data, interaction with the participants and performance of SKEL. The number of participants that downloaded and installed the iLog application on their devices is

Table 2. List of answer options to the time diary question *Where are you now?*.

Main category	Subcategory
University	1. My faculty 2. Other faculty (UniTn) 3. Other
Home	1. Main home 2. Weekend home or holiday apartment 3. Other people's home
Travelling	1. Foot 2. Bicycle 3. Moped, motorcycle or motor-boat 4. Passenger car 5. Other private transport mode 6. Public transport
Other	1. Restaurant, cafe, or pub 2. Shopping centers, malls, market, other shops 3. Hotel, guesthouse, camping site 4. Street, square, city park 5. Sports center 6. Other

77, 58 uploaded sensor data and answers. During the data collection, we sent a questionnaire to collect demographic information. We obtained the data from 42 participants, of which 90% consider themselves male and 10% female. All the participants belong to the Department of Information Engineering and Computer Science of the University of Trento. Most of the participants are pursuing a bachelor's degree (74%), and the remaining a master's degree (26%).

5.1 Sensor Data

The attrition effects are clearly visible in Fig. 3 and led to participants leaving the study. During the first week, the server received sensor data from 48 participants, whereas it decreased to 37 in the last week. A second common problem in real-world datasets is the missing values. In this experiment, the percentage of missing values for every numeric feature varies considerably, as shown in Fig. 10. The reasons for missing values can be unsupported mobile devices or participants actively disabling one or more sensors. For instance, the incompatibility of some Android versions resulted in a large number of missing values for features derived from Bluetooth.

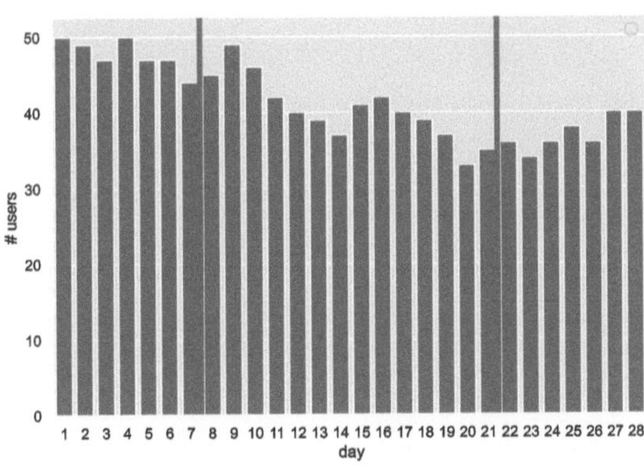

Fig. 3. Number of users who uploaded sensor data by day of the experiment. Red lines divide the three data collection phases. (Color figure online)

5.2   Time Diaries

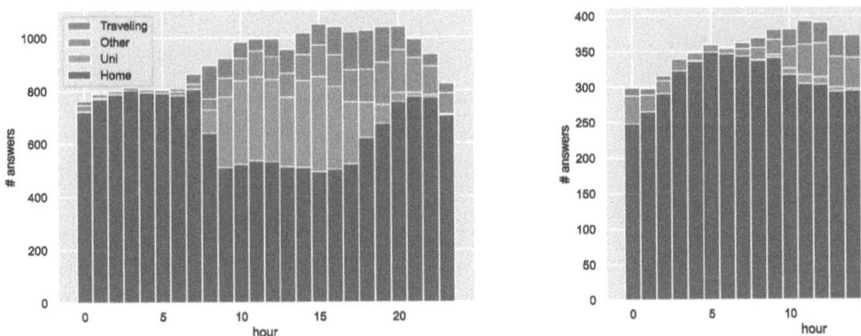

Fig. 4. Number of time diary answers by hour of the day, divided by weekdays (left) and weekends (right). The answers are aggregated by main categories.

The mobile application sends time diaries every 30 min. Figure 4 shows the distribution of the answer over hours of the day and compares weekdays and weekend days. As expected, the dataset is highly unbalanced given the high number of labels related to home (main home, weekend home, or others' home). The labels related to university are the ones that vary the most between weekdays and weekends. The dataset is highly unbalanced, and the data distribution shifts between weekdays and weekends, thus making the recognition task more challenging.

Figure 5 shows the time diary answers for each user over the first three weeks. Each cell of the heatmap is an interval of 30 min, and the color denotes the main category of the answer, i.e., university, home, traveling and other. Blue cells are unanswered questions. Note how the answering pattern varies across users. The top rows represent users who regularly provide answers, whereas the bottom rows represent less active users, who left the experiment at a certain

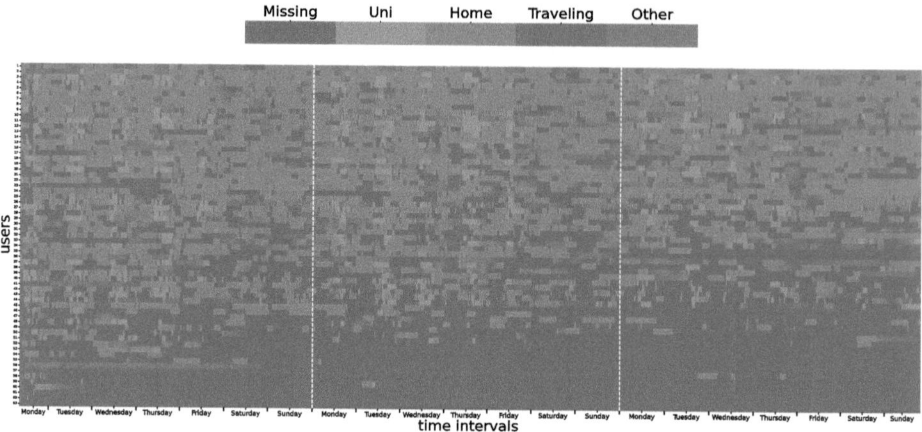

Fig. 5. The main category of the time diary answers over the first three weeks of the experiment. Rows: all users of the experiment. Columns: time interval of 30 min (i.e., annotation). White vertical lines denote each week.

point. Users in the central part alternate days with answers and periods where the question expires. Thus, SKEL is not helpful for all types of users, as discussed in the following sections.

5.3 Skeptical Questions

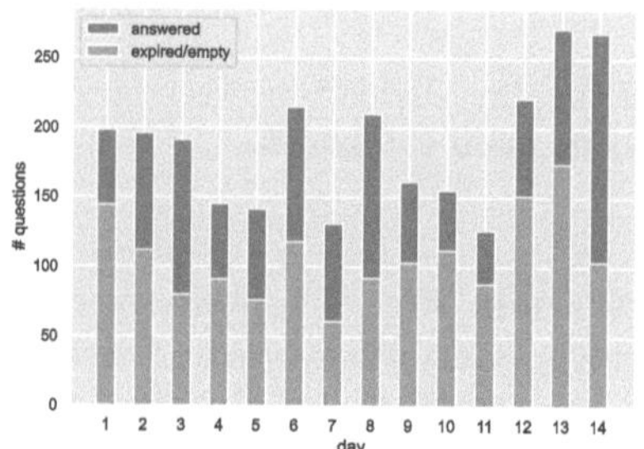

(a) Number of questions with (blue) and without (orange) an answer.

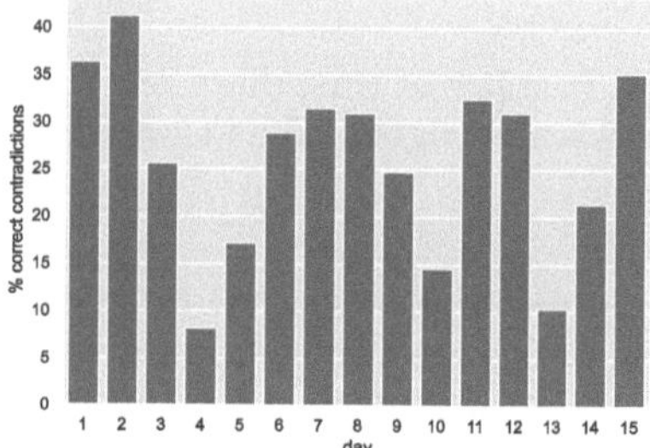

(b) Percentage of skeptical contradiction in which the machine label is confirmed as correct by the user.

Fig. 6. Statistics about skeptical questions during the two weeks of Part 2 of the study.

The time diary answers are used to train the SKEL model, one model for each user. The model learns the mapping between sensor data and location labels.

As described in [5], mistaken labels badly affect the machine's performance. In phase two of the experiment (the second and third week of the study), the machine sends skeptical questions to contradict the user whenever it is suspicious about the label. The goal is to give the participant the opportunity to fix wrong labels. Figure 6a shows the total number of contradictions sent to the users, split between answered and not answered. The fraction of missing answers is high, namely more than 50% for most of the days. The main causes are that the question is not delivered because the phone was not connected to the Internet, or users did not respond in time. In 25% of the answers, the machine prediction was selected as correct, whereas in the rest of the answers, the user provided a different label. When rejecting the predicted label, in 80% of cases, the participants confirmed the label they provided the first time. Figure 6b plots the number of times the machine was right. Therefore, when contradicted, the participants considered their answers correct most of the time, and revised their previous answers in one-fourth of the cases.

5.4   Evaluation Questions

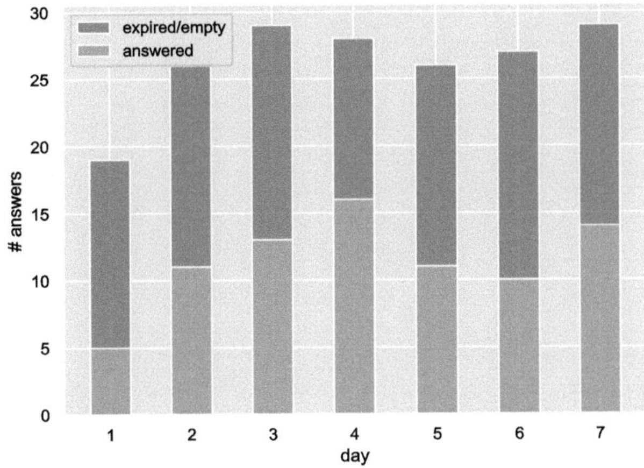

Fig. 7. Total number of evaluation questions sent to the user for each day of the last week of the experiment. Orange: number of received answers. Blue: number of questions without answer. (Color figure online)

In the third and last phase, each day, the participant is asked to evaluate the predictions of the machine. The questions, sent at 7 pm, list the location labels predicted in the last 24 h. Then, the user selects those labels that she/he considers wrong. Figure 7 shows the number of questions sent to the user for each day of the last week of the experiment. The fraction of unanswered questions is more than 50% (blue bar). In 25% of the received answers, the participants evaluated the prediction of that day as all correct. Each day, participants have to evaluate

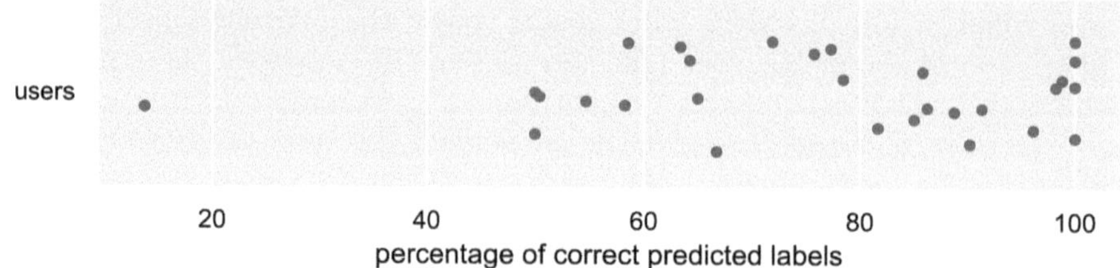

Fig. 8. Percentage of predicted labels that are evaluated as correct by the user. Each point is a user.

30 predicted labels on average (out of 48 possible prediction in the last 24 h). Figure 8 details, for each user, the percentage of the correct labels. The average percentage is 76%, showing that the participants rated as correct the majority of the predicted locations, thus highlighting the potential of SKEL to reduce the answering effort.

5.5   SKEL Performance

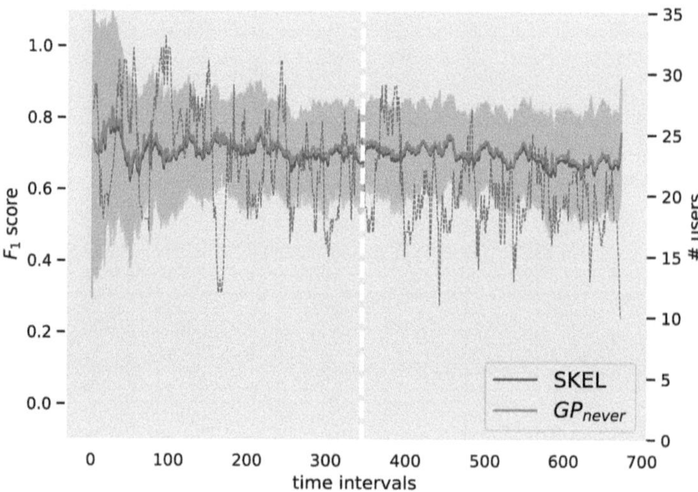

Fig. 9. Progressive $F1$-score averaged over all users. Time intervals are the 30-minute windows of two weeks. Shaded area is the standard deviation. Violet dashed line represents the number of users. Blue line is the SKEL, as presented in [5]. Orange line: SKEL variant in which the user is never contradicted.(Color figure online)

We compare the effectiveness of SKEL with a variant that never contradicts the user (denoted with GP_{never}). Figure 9 reports the experimental results on these two methods averaged over all users. The plot shows the progressive F_1 over the third and fourth week for every 30-minute timeslot. Since the user label, which is used as ground truth, or the input data are not always available, the number of users varies over the time intervals (violet dashed line). The performance of SKEL and GP_{never} are overlapping, which shows that, on average, there was no advantage in being skeptical. Indeed, in only 25% of the contradictions, the machine was correctly skeptical about the participant supervision (see Fig. 6b). The motivations are that the participants were consistent in providing the annotation even after being contradicted. As shown in [35] and discussed in the next section, the performance of SKEL depends on the user behaviors. Another cause is the high fraction of missing values that impacts the predictive power of the model and thus reduces the benefits of SKEL.

5.6   Discussion

The results show that in this study, the participants were mostly consistent with the provided supervision. This might be explained by the limited respondent burden due to the short experiment period and the focus on only one context question, i.e., the participant's location. Additionally, [35] identified four different prototypical users and showed how the performance of the SKEL is affected by the user behaviors. Inattentive and predictable users are cases in which SKEL generates substantial benefits. For the reliable user, SKEL does not provide improvements, but at the same time, it is not harmful. The last type is the tricky user, for whom SKEL fails to learn. However, the positive result is that the participants rated as correct the majority of the labels predicted in the evaluation week, confirming the benefits of employing the model in longitudinal studies. The benefits of skeptical learning become more visible when running longer data collections with multiple questions. Additionally, the low response rate to the questions and the missing sensor readings impacted the performance of SKEL. Thus, this result highlights the difficulties of running studies in the wild with real users.

This work, however, has some limitations. The number of participants is small and consists of only students from one university department. With respect to the SKEL version presented in [5], we removed the active queries because the examples were not available in real-time to the machine learning model to decide when to query, and thus, during the first three weeks, labels were asked on all incoming examples regardless of the machine prediction confidence. The evaluation questions were sent in the last week of the experiment and are designed to allow the user to select wrongly predicted labels. Participants may have selected only a subset of the mistakes to avoid going through the full list of predictions. Regarding skeptical questions, participants may have felt frustrated by the contradiction and thus consistently rejected the machine label. Future work should investigate the psychological and behavioral implications that arise from interacting with a machine that learns about your routines and contradicts your answers.

Furthermore, future experiments should consider other factors that impact the quality of the answers, such as user reaction time and completion time, time of the day, mood and situational context of the participant [2]. A better question scheduling to improve response rate and answer quality [36]. Additionally, the usability and effectiveness of the iLog app need to be assessed to evaluate the impact on the label quality. One possible enhancement is the visualization of recognized locations on an interactive timeline, which can help users identify errors more intuitively. The model performance can be improved by implementing per-user hyperparameter tuning, which adapts the model to the specific user. To this end, recent works proposed solutions for hyperparameter tuning on data streams [9,31] and AutoML for online learning [10]. Future evaluations should also explore the emotional responses of participants when interacting with the machine learning model, especially when being challenged by the machine. The future work includes applying SKEL to other domains than context recognition and extending it to multi-modal inputs.

6   Conclusion

We designed and executed a study with real users in the wild to evaluate SKEL. The study focused on a social science use case, specifically, longitudinal studies in which participants provide information about their daily lives multiple times per day. In this context, the results show the potential of SKEL to reduce respondent burden by allowing the system to automatically answer questions when it is sufficiently confident in its predictions. The number of questions can thus be reduced, allowing the researcher to increase the duration of data collection and mitigating the drop-out problem. Moreover, SKEL ensures the quality of the collected labels by involving the users in fixing their answers.

Acknowledgments. The research leading to these results has received funding from the European Union's Horizon 2020 Research and Innovation Programme, through the TRUMAN project, under Grant Agreement No. 101214000. Views and opinions expressed are, however, those of author(s) only and do not necessarily reflect those of the European Union or European Health and Digital Executive Agency (HADEA). Neither the European Union nor the granting authority can be held responsible for them. The content in Sects. 4 and 5 is based on Chap. 7 of AB's PhD thesis [3]. We acknowledge the use of Grammarly as a tool for grammar refinement.

Disclosure of Interests. The authors have no competing interests.

A   Appendix

Table 3 provides an overview of the sensor data collected in the study, and Table 4 details the engineered features utilized as inputs to the model. The distribution of missing values is illustrated in Fig. 10.

Table 3. List of iLog sensors collected during the four weeks of experiment.

Sensor	Description
Connectivity	
Bluetooth normal, Bluetooth low energy	Returns the discovered Bluetooth normal or low energy devices
WiFi Event	Returns information related to the WIFI network to which the phone is connected; if connected, it also reports the WIFI network ID
WiFi Networks Event	Returns all WIFI networks detected by the smartphone
ACTIVITY	
Accelerometer	Returns the acceleration of the device along the three coordinate axes
Activities	Return the user's activity recognized by the Google Activity Recognition API. The recognized activities are *in vehicle, on bicycle, on foot, running, still, tilting, walking* and *unknown*. The sensor reports a confidence score between 0 and 100, which represents the likelihood that the user is performing the activity
Step detector	An event is triggered each time the user takes a step
Orientation	Returns the position of the device relative to the earth's magnetic north pole
LOCATION	
Location event	GPS coordinates (latitude, longitude and altitude)
Magnetic field	Reports the ambient magnetic field along the three sensor axes
Proximity Event	Measures the distance between the user's head and the phone. Depending on the phone, it may be measured in centimetres (i.e., the absolute distance) or as labels (e.g., 'near', 'far')
SOFTWARE	
Battery Charge Event	Returns whether the phone is on charge and the type of charger
Battery Monitoring Log	Returns the phone's battery level

Table 4. List of features generated by aggregating raw sensor data in windows of 30 min.

Feature name	Type	Description
TIME		
time_is_workday	boolean	True for the days from Monday to Friday
time_is_morning	boolean	True for the hours between 6 am and 9 am
time_is_noon	boolean	True for the hours between 10 am and 1 pm
time_is_afternoon	boolean	True for the hours between 2 pm and 5 pm
time_is_evening	boolean	True for the hours between 6 pm and 9 pm
time_is_night	boolean	True for the hours between 10 pm and 5 am
time_sin_hour, time_cos_hour	float	Sine and cosine transformations of the hour to encode a stronger connection between two nearby hours
CONNECTIVITY		
bluetoothdevices_rssi_ {mean,var}	float	Mean and variance of the Received Signal Strength Indicator (RSSI) of the detected Bluetooth devices
bluetoothdevices_nunique	integer	Number of unique Bluetooth normal and low energy devices
wifi_connection_count	integer	number of times the device connected to a WiFi network
wifi_is_connected	boolean	True if the devices connected to a WiFi network at least once
wifinetworks_nunique	integer	Number of unique networks detected
ACTIVITY		
step_detection_count	integer	Number of step detection events
activity_ {invehicle,onbycicle,onfoot, running,still,unknown, walking}	boolean	True if the Google activity recognition API has recognized the activity
accelerometer_avg_{x,y,z}	float	Mean of all accelerometer values for each axes separately
accelerometer_magnitude_ {avg,var}	float	Mean and variance of the magnitude of each sensor reading
orientation_avg{x,y,z}	float	Mean of all orientation values for each axes separately
orientation_magnitude_ {avg,var}	float	Mean and variance of the magnitude of each sensor reading
LOCATION		
location_ {altitude,longitude,latitude}	float	Averaged GPS coordinates
location_direct_distance	float	Distance between the first and last location point
location_total_distance	float	Total distance covered [8]
location_radius_of_gyration	float	Deviation from the centroid of the GPS points [19, 25, 33]
magneticfield_avg{x,y,z}	float	Mean of all magnetic field values for each axis separately
magneticfield_magnitude_ {avg,var}	float	Mean and variance of the magnitude of each sensor reading
proximity_{mean,var}	float	Mean and variance of the proximity values
SOFTWARE		
battery_deltashift	float	Battery level difference between the beginning and the end of the interval
battery_charge_count	integer	Number of times the phone has been connected to a charging source during the interval

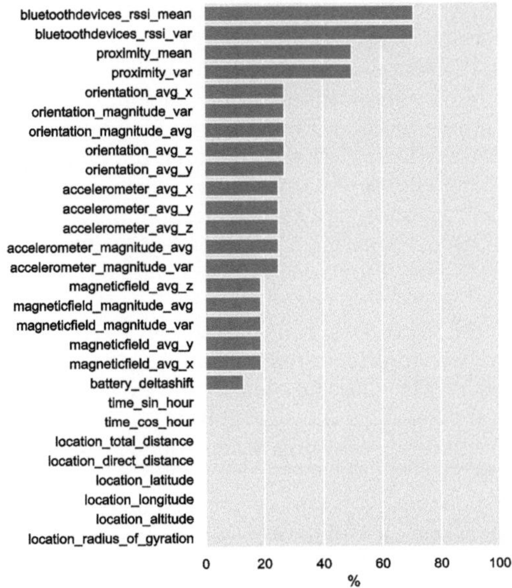

Fig. 10. Percentage of missing values for each numeric feature.

References

1. Biemer, P.P., et al.: Total Survey Error in Practice. John Wiley & Sons (2017)
2. Bison, I., Zhao, H., Giunchiglia, F.: What impacts the quality of the user answers when asked about the current context? (2024). https://arxiv.org/abs/2405.04054
3. Bontempelli, A.: Human-machine alignment for context recognition in the wild (2024)
4. Bontempelli, A., et al.: Lifelong personal context recognition. arXiv preprint: arXiv:2205.10123 (2022)
5. Bontempelli, A., Teso, S., Giunchiglia, F., Passerini, A.: Learning in the wild with incremental skeptical Gaussian processes. In: Proceedings of the Twenty-Ninth International Joint Conference on Artificial Intelligence, IJCAI'20, Yokohama, Yokohama, Japan, pp. 2886–2892 (2021)
6. Busso, M.: The iLog methodology for fostering valid and reliable Big Thick Data. Ph.D. thesis (2024)
7. Busso, M., et al.: DiversityOne: a multi-country smartphone sensor dataset for everyday life behavior modeling. Proc. ACM Interact. Mob. Wearable Ubiquitous Technol. **9**(1) (2025). https://doi.org/10.1145/3712289
8. Canzian, L., Musolesi, M.: Trajectories of depression: unobtrusive monitoring of depressive states by means of smartphone mobility traces analysis. In: Proceedings of the 2015 ACM International Joint Conference on Pervasive and Ubiquitous Computing (2015)
9. Carnein, M., Trautmann, H., Bifet, A., Pfahringer, B.: confStream: automated algorithm selection and configuration of stream clustering algorithms. In: Kotsireas, I.S., Pardalos, P.M. (eds.) LION 2020. LNCS, vol. 12096, pp. 80–95. Springer, Cham (2020). https://doi.org/10.1007/978-3-030-53552-0_10

10. Celik, B., Singh, P., Vanschoren, J.: Online AutoML: an adaptive AutoML framework for online learning. Mach. Learn. (2023)
11. Corbetta, P.: Social Research: Theory, Methods and Techniques. Sage (2003)
12. Csikszentmihalyi, M., Csikszentmihalyi, M., Larson, R.: Validity and reliability of the experience-sampling method. Flow and the foundations of positive psychology: the collected works of Mihaly Csikszentmihalyi, pp. 35–54 (2014)
13. Eisele, G., et al.: The effects of sampling frequency and questionnaire length on perceived burden, compliance, and careless responding in experience sampling data in a student population. Assessment **29**(2), 136–151 (2022)
14. Erculiani, L., Giunchiglia, F., Passerini, A.: Continual egocentric object recognition. In: ECAI 2020. IOS Press (2020)
15. Eurostat: harmonised European time use surveys (HETUS) (2018). https://ec.europa.eu/eurostat/web/products-manuals-and-guidelines/-/ks-gq-20-011
16. Frénay, B., Verleysen, M.: Classification in the presence of label noise: a survey. IEEE Trans. Neural Netw. Learn., Syst. (2014)
17. Giunchiglia, F.: Contextual reasoning. Epistemologia, special issue on 'I Linguaggi e le Macchine' (1993)
18. Giunchiglia, F., Bignotti, E., Zeni, M.: Personal context modelling and annotation. In: 2017 IEEE International Conference on Pervasive Computing and Communications Workshops (PerCom Workshops), pp. 117–122. IEEE (2017)
19. Gonzalez, M.C., Hidalgo, C.A., Barabasi, A.L.: Understanding individual human mobility patterns. Nature (2008)
20. Hart, C.: The Hawthorne experiments. Can. J. Econ. Polit. Sci./Revue canadienne de economiques et Sci. politique **9**(2), 150–163 (1943)
21. Kayongo, I., Malcotti, L., Zhao, H., Giunchiglia, F.: A methodology and a platform for high-quality rich personal data. https://doi.org/10.48550/arXiv.2501.16864
22. Liang, W., et al.: Advances, challenges and opportunities in creating data for trustworthy AI **4**(8), 669–677. https://doi.org/10.1038/s42256-022-00516-1
23. McCarney, R., Warner, J., Iliffe, S., Van Haselen, R., Griffin, M., Fisher, P.: The Hawthorne effect: a randomised, controlled trial. BMC Med. Res. Methodol. (2007)
24. Myin-Germeys, I., Kuppens, P.: The Open Handbook of Experience Sampling Methodology: A Step-by-step Guide to Designing, Conducting, and Analyzing ESM Studies (2nd ed.). Center for Research on Experience Sampling and Ambulatory Methods Leuven (2022)
25. Pappalardo, L., Rinzivillo, S., Qu, Z., Pedreschi, D., Giannotti, F.: Understanding the patterns of car travel. Eur. Phys. J. Spec. Top. (2013)
26. Ponnada, A., Wang, S.D., Li, J., Wang, W.L., Dunton, G.F., Hedeker, D., Intille, S.S.: Longitudinal user engagement with microinteraction ecological momentary assessment (μema). Proc. ACM Interact. Mob. Wearable Ubiquitous Technol. **9**(3) (2025). https://doi.org/10.1145/3749541
27. Rolstad, S., Adler, J., Rydén, A.: Response burden and questionnaire length: is shorter better? a review and meta-analysis. Value Health **14**(8), 1101–1108 (2011)
28. Teso, S., Bontempelli, A., Giunchiglia, F., Passerini, A.: Interactive label cleaning with example-based explanations. In: Advances in Neural Information Processing Systems, vol. 34, pp. 12966–12977. Curran Associates, Inc., https://proceedings.neurips.cc/paper/2021/hash/6c349155b122aa8ad5c877007e05f24f-Abstract.html
29. Van Berkel, N., Ferreira, D., Kostakos, V.: The experience sampling method on mobile devices. ACM Comput. Surv. (CSUR) (2017)
30. Varoquaux, G., Luccioni, A.S., Whittaker, M.: Hype, sustainability, and the price of the bigger-is-better paradigm in AI (2024). https://doi.org/10.48550/arXiv.2409.14160

31. Veloso, B., Gama, J., Malheiro, B., Vinagre, J.: Hyperparameter self-tuning for data streams. Inf. Fusion (2021)
32. Weisberg, H.F.: The Total Survey Error Approach. University of Chicago Press (2009)
33. Yue, Y., Lan, T., Yeh, A.G., Li, Q.Q.: Zooming into individuals to understand the collective: a review of trajectory-based travel behaviour studies. Travel Behav. Soc. (2014)
34. Zeni, M., Zaihrayeu, I., Giunchiglia, F.: Multi-device activity logging. In: UbiComp (2014)
35. Zeni, M., Zhang, W., Bignotti, E., Passerini, A., Giunchiglia, F.: Fixing mislabeling by human annotators leveraging conflict resolution and prior knowledge. IMWUT (2019)
36. Zhao, H., Giunchiglia, F.: Scheduling real-time acquisition of context information (2023)

Improved Strategies for Multi-modal Atmospheric Sensing to Augment Wearable IMU-Based Hand Washing Detection

Robin Burchard[✉] [ID], Hurriat Ali [ID], and Kristof Van Laerhoven [ID]

University of Siegen, 57076 Siegen, Germany
`robin.burchard@uni-siegen.de`

Abstract. Previous work in the area of hand washing detection has hinted at the usefulness of atmospheric sensors for hand washing detection. Specifically, a humidity sensor can be used to measure nearby tap water flow using wearable devices. For this work, we expand on previous findings and a pre-existing dataset by recording 10 additional participants with a self-made open-source prototype recording device. We introduce an updated dataset with 20 participants instead of 10 participants, for which we make available IMU, humidity, temperature, and pressure measurements. The newly recorded participants conducted more complex background activities, which increased our dataset's real-world relevance. Additionally, we show how to train an optimized deep-learning-based classifier on different parts of the combined dataset, improving on the previous study's results, achieving significantly better F1 scores (82% instead of 70%) on the pre-existing dataset. Furthermore, by leveraging a BIO-BANK semi-supervised pretrained model, we show that, unlike in previous work, the addition of humidity sensors to IMU data has a positive impact on the classification performance on the old and the new dataset, improving the F1-score on the combined dataset from 60% to 68%. All code and data are publicly available on GitHub.

Keywords: Multi-Modal · Hand Washing Detection · Atmospheric Sensing · Human Activity Recognition · Humidity Sensor · Data Recording · Open Source

1 Introduction

The detection of hand washing is related to multiple applications in our everyday lives. A system that can automatically detect and analyze hand washing frequency, duration, and performance would be useful and could act as a personal hygiene assistant. Additionally, a similar system could be employed in professional environments, especially in the food industry and in the medical

R. Burchard and H. Ali—Contributed equally to this research.

O. Durmaz Incel et al. (Eds.): iWOAR 2025, LNCS 16292, pp. 308–323, 2026.
https://doi.org/10.1007/978-3-032-13312-0_18

domain. Properly washing one's hands has been shown to dramatically reduce the spread of pathogens in the population [7]. Therefore, a system that detects hand washing over the day could help its user to maintain a high level of hand hygiene, protecting the user and their surroundings.

Hand washing detection can also be employed in the context of obsessive-compulsive disorder, where overly frequent hand washing has a negative impact [5,21,22]. There, a system could help by logging hand washing occurrences over the day, by helping the user understand how often and how long they wash their hands or by providing valuable insights to treatment experts.

Both RGB-camera-based and wearable sensor-based methods exist to detect hand washing. However, the use of cameras comes paired with privacy concerns, and IMU sensor-based detection suffers from the ambiguity of rapid movement patterns [5]. Some devices, like the Apple Watch [12] have built-in proprietary hand washing detectors, but there exists no data on their reliability. While traditional sensor-based human activity recognition systems often rely on IMU data only, this work focuses on making use of the contextual information, which can be provided by additional modalities. One example would be Bluetooth beacons placed in a users home, which provide a clue about the location, but come with the downside of being constrained to environments where beacons can be placed [19]. We therefore opt for a modality that we can easily measure on-device, everywhere, with affordable, highly accurate sensors: Humidity. Our previous, preliminary study, for which we investigated multiple environmental sensors (humidity, pressure, temperature), had shown promising results, as we could find a clear pattern in the humidity signal when a participant was washing their hands [6]. Thus, for this work, we recorded 10 additional participants while they were conducting different everyday activities and while they were washing their hands. Whereas our previous study was solely a feasibility study, in which the additional modalities could not be shown to improve the classification performance, we were able to outperform the previous study's preliminary results substantially by including additional participants, more diverse background activities, and applying a more sophisticated deep learning pipeline.

1.1 Goals and Contributions

The goal of this work was to improve on the previous study's preliminary results and further evaluate the usefulness of the addition of a humidity sensor.

Our contributions are threefold:

1. Recording, labeling, comparing, and making available data from 10 more participants with more diverse background activities.
2. In-depth evaluation of the usefulness of the humidity sensor in hand washing detection, on previously available and newly recorded data, significantly improving on the previous study's results
3. Employing and evaluating more complex network architectures, including the application of a pre-trained model, to achieve significantly improved classification results.

2 Related Work

While some works on hand washing detection only using IMUs exist, they are mostly in-lab studies or constrain the user to hand washing patterns recommended by the WHO, which does not cohere well with real-world hand washing without artificial constraints [19, 23]. For other studies that also focus on unstructured hand washing recognition and achieve high classification accuracies [13], other limitations apply, such as small sample sizes or the absence of leave-one-out validation patterns. Thus, we will focus on multi-modal approaches for unconstrained hand washing detection in this work.

2.1 Sensors for Multi-modal Activity Recognition

While human activity recognition (HAR) can be approached with a single sensor modality, such as the commonly used RGB(D)-cameras or IMUs, previous work in multi-modal HAR exists and employs a multitude of sensor modalities. Combining multiple sensing modalities leads to higher classification performance due to the usually provided additional context, but introduces additional complexity [10]. The most commonly fused sensors include IMU and RGB(D)-cameras, or other visual systems in various positions (e.g., body worn or stationary in a task-specific location). Additional modalities include audio, environmental sensors such as temperature, humidity, barometer, or light, and physiological sensors such as measuring oxygen saturation, heart rate, or electrocardiography [9, 10, 16]. However, not all sensing modalities can be applied for all applications and in all environments. Especially, cameras and microphones are ethically difficult, as they record data of their surroundings, including, e.g., private conversations. For our research interest in general-purpose omnicontextual hand washing detection, cameras are hardly feasible, due to their inappropriateness in bathrooms and many public spaces. We thus conclude that in hand washing detection, the needed additional context should be provided by privacy-preserving modalities. E.g., microphone data, as used in a preliminary lab study by Zhuang et al. [26], would need to be processed on-device and then discarded. A good basis for microphone-aided hand washing detection could be offline tap water audio detection [4]. Unlike cameras and microphones, the atmospheric data we utilized for this work is anonymous by default, and therefore does not pose a challenge to the users' privacy.

2.2 Humidity Sensing for Activity Recognition

Any activity detection problem related to changes in ambient humidity could likely profit from humidity sensors. Oftentimes, humidity sensors are paired with other atmospheric sensors such as barometers and temperature sensors to enhance the classification of activities of daily living [2, 8, 20]. In these works, the atmospheric sensors are applied together with other modalities such as IMU recordings. The atmospheric sensors aid the classification by providing additional context to the otherwise ungrounded IMU recordings.

Picking up on this idea, in a recent work, we proposed WearPuck, a wearable sensing platform that synchronously records accelerometer, gyroscope, humidity, temperature, and barometric pressure [6]. We applied the novel fully open-source data collection device to the task of hand washing detection, in an experiment with 10 participants and a total of 40 hand washes. Although it was shown that especially the recorded humidity changes measurably during hand washing instances, the prediction performance of simple machine learning classifiers did not improve consistently with added humidity features. Therefore, we concluded that additional efforts in data recording, data processing, and machine learning were the logical next step. To the best of the authors' knowledge, no other work utilizing humidity sensors and IMUs for hand washing detection has been published.

2.3   Machine Learning for Multi-modal Activity Recognition

Fusion Strategies. In multi-modal activity recognition, one of the main problems is the question of when and how to fuse the different modalities' signals. In early fusion, the input modalities are fused before passing them into the machine learning models. Early fusion enables the models to learn the different sensors' co-dependencies jointly. In late fusion, the modalities are processed separately and are only fused at the decision stage [10], so that the models initially learn independent features for all modalities, before fusing these representations and classification. Münzner et al. showed that for the PAMAP2 dataset, late fusion performs better than early fusion [15], but the performance difference was small, and the best method must likely be determined for each dataset and modality combination separately.

Learning Strategies. In HAR tasks, labeled data has to be obtained with great effort and is therefore scarce, leading to small labeled datasets. As deep-learning models require extensive amounts of data to be trained, these small datasets are suboptimal. One solution can be sought in semi-supervisedly pre-trained models, which were trained on large amounts of unlabeled data and which are able to either provide good embeddings of the modality for downstream tasks or can be fine-tuned for a specific task and dataset. Their performance is usually significantly higher than for models trained only on the downstream dataset [25]. Thanks to the scientific community, many such models are freely available. One example of such a self-supervised pre-trained model is the HARNet model by Yuan et al. [24], which we also employed for this publication. The HARNet model is based on ResNet and was trained on 700,000 person-days of accelerometer data taken from the UK Biobank accelerometer dataset.

3   Dataset Expansion: Recording and Validation

3.1   Collection of New Data

The previously collected data from 10 participants served as a good baseline for the initial proof-of-concept. While the inclusion of additional modalities did not improve the preliminary machine learning performance, we were able to highlight a distinct response pattern of the humidity sensor to hand washing.

To create a better model and train more efficiently, additional data was required. Hence, we collected data from 10 additional participants, who had not partaken in the first experiment. All participants were volunteers and signed an informed consent form. The previous data collection included a lot of sitting and desk work in its recording procedure, interrupted by short walks, hand washing, and stair walking, as well as a few other activities. To increase the variability of the dataset, we also enforced additional background activities during the recording. By doing so, we increased the difficulty of classification, as there are more movement patterns, and the new dataset contains more active behaviour. The background activities include:

- going up and down the stairs (as in previous work)
- playing the guitar (new)
- playing with a ball (new)
- playing video games (new)
- washing dishes (new)
- other natural movements that involve active hand use (new)

As a result of this increased diversity, the classification task became more challenging. However, this also enhanced the ecological validity of the dataset, as the recorded movements better reflect real-world behavior.

The data was collected using our own, open-source wearable device, WearPuck[1]. The technical aspect of the data recording and labeling procedure was identical to the one described in our previous publication [6]. Thus, we refer the interested reader to this publication for a more detailed description of the recording, labeling, and post-processing steps.

3.2   Validation and Comparison to Existing Dataset

The newly recorded n = 10 participants (7f, 3 m, aged between 20 and 30 years) performed a total of 39 hand washing instances. Thus, the newly recorded dataset contains roughly the same amount of data as we recorded for the same duration with the same number of participants. However, as explained in Sect. 3.1, the background activities were much more diverse. Additionally, the durations of the hand washes were different, with a mean duration of 45 s.

Figure 1 shows the response of the recorded humidity values to the hand washing. Both the pre-existing dataset and the newly collected data show a similar behaviour, with a peak of around +8%-points between 20 to 50 s after the beginning of a hand washing instance. As previously reported, the humidity starts to increase immediately when hand washing starts. After peaking, the humidity signal starts to decline again. We expect that the hand washing mostly ends a short time ahead of the peak, which is better visible in the subplot (a) of Fig. 1. For the newly collected data, the trend is still visible, but slightly less

---

[1] https://github.com/kristofvl/WearPuck.

pronounced, due to the higher diversity in hand washing duration, which spreads out the end of hand washing instances more.

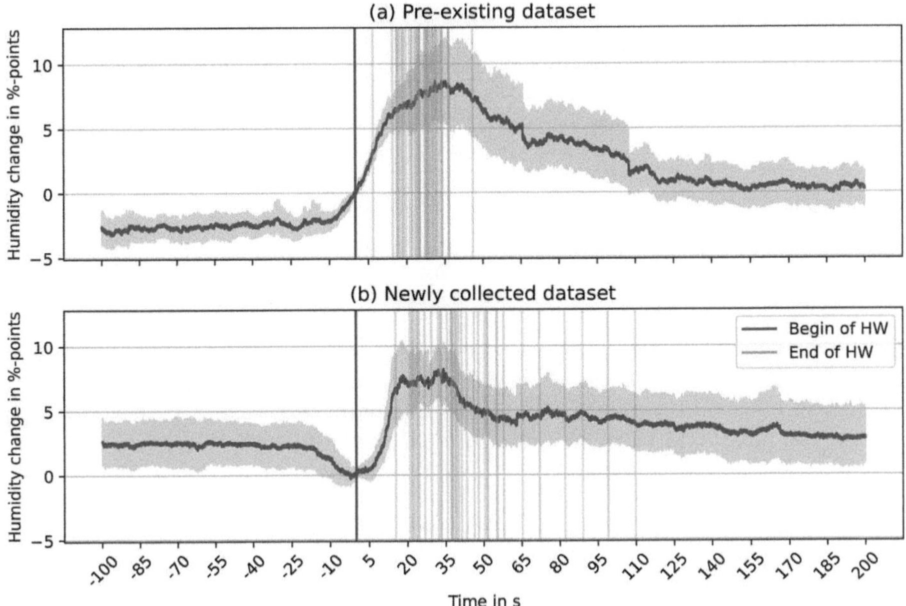

Fig. 1. Response of the humidity sensors to hand washing, averaged (in dark blue) over all recorded hand washes of (a) the pre-existing dataset and (b) the newly collected dataset, with bootstrapped 95% confidence interval (in light blue). The start of the hand washing is marked with a green vertical line. The yellow vertical lines mark the respective ends of all the handwashing instances. (Color figure online)

Figure 2 displays the distribution of hand washing durations across the pre-existing, the newly recorded, and the combined datasets. The hand washing durations differ, with the newly collected participants washing for 45 s on average, compared to 25 s in the previous data collection. The new data collection also includes some outlier durations of up to 109 s. This comparatively long duration was not enforced or encouraged by the conducting experiment supervisors, as participants were asked to wash their hands as they normally would, if they felt "dirty". After combining the datasets, we ended up with a mean hand washing duration of 35 s (median: 30 s). The minimum hand washing duration of 6.5 s was not undercut by the newly recorded participants. The maximum hand washing duration in the combined dataset is 109 s.

As shown in Table 1, the newly recorded dataset contains more hand washing than the pre-existing dataset, thanks to the participants washing for longer durations. The number of instances of hand washing is similar, but the newly recorded participants contribute more washing data to the combined dataset.

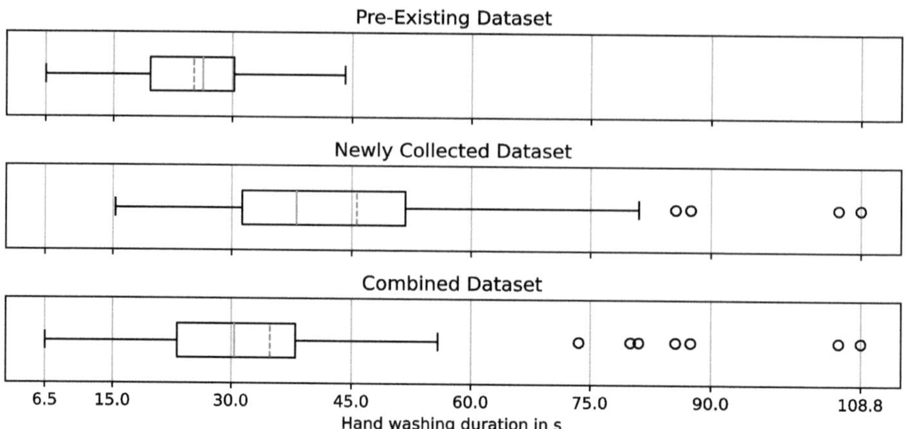

Fig. 2. Statistics for the duration in seconds of all existing and newly recorded hand washes. The box plot shows the median (orange solid line), mean (green dashed line), quartiles (box extents), outliers (circles), and minimum and maximum durations inside 1.5 times the inter-quartile range (whiskers). (Color figure online)

Table 1. Recorded minutes of activities and ratio of hand washing for the pre-existing and the newly recorded dataset. The new dataset contains 1.64 times as many minutes of hand washing as the pre-existing dataset. The combined dataset contains 47.7 min of hand washing, which makes up for around 4% of the recorded 1240 min.

Dataset	Recording duration (min)	Hand washing duration (min)	Ratio (%)
Pre-existing	612.18	18.05	2.95
Newly recorded	627.99	29.65	4.72
Combined	1240.17	47.71	3.85

The combined dataset now has a total length of 1240 min (almost 21 h), and contains 48 min (4%) of hand washing. Altogether, this means that the total hand washing duration in the combined dataset has now become 2.64 times as large as in the pre-existing dataset only. The dataset remains highly imbalanced, with 96% of it belonging to the class of background activities. However, hand washing is still over-represented in comparison to what could be expected in-the-wild.

Overall, the newly recorded data significantly enlarges our database and contains more variety in the durations of handwashing. Meanwhile, the effect of the humidity rising while washing the hands is equally present in the new data as in the previously collected. Thus, we conclude that the measured effect seems to generalize well to diverse other environments and participants.

4   Methods

For this publication, we revisited the previously recorded dataset and applied a better deep learning model to the hand washing classification with and without the added humidity modality. Afterward, we combined the data of the newly collected 10 additional participants with the existing dataset and developed an additional optimal model for this combined dataset. All code and data are publicly available in our GitHub repository[2].

4.1   CNN-GRU Model and Training Procedure

Due to the usually high performance of previous combinations of CNNs with recurrent network parts like DeepConvLSTM [3,18], we opted for a CNN model with a gated recurrent unit (GRU). The model with the GRU slightly outperformed DeepConvLSTM in preliminary testing. The full network consisted of two one-dimensional convolutional layers, followed by max-pooling, the GRU, a 4-headed attention mechanism, layer norm, global average pooling, and two dense layers with dropout ($p = 0.5$) as the classification head. We trained it on the IMU data (accelerometer, gyroscope) with and without the added modality of humidity, on sliding windows (5 s, 50% overlap).

To make use of the humidity data, we extracted six types of features from the sliding windows of sensor readings that capture both the statistical structure and temporal dynamics of the signal. The mean and standard deviation quantify the overall humidity level and local variability, to capture and identify the characteristic rise and fluctuation patterns we associate with hand washing. We use frequency-domain features derived from the Fourier transform to encode periodic components introduced by repetitive patterns, which the humidity sensor might pick up. Higher-order statistics such as skewness and kurtosis capture asymmetric distributions and heavy tails, as likely caused by sharp humidity spikes. We also calculated the mean of first-order differences, i.e., the mean steepness between two consecutive sensor values, which reflects the rate of change over time, to detect the rapid increase and the decrease while and after washing the hands (c.f. Fig. 1). While this worked well on the pre-existing dataset, we developed a more elaborate set of features for the combined dataset, which we describe below.

The previous dataset contained 10 controlled office-setting recordings where the participants performed handwashing mostly followed by returning to a seated position. This means that the motion patterns that were outside the hand washing segments had limited variation. The sensor modalities recorded in the previous dataset were the same as for our new recording, including a 3-axis accelerometer and gyroscope sampled at 52 Hz, as well as a humidity, temperature, and atmospheric pressure sensor sampled at 1 Hz.

While the previous publication relied on random forest classifiers (RF) and hand-crafted features, we used a deep neural network trained with focal loss and

---

SMOTETomek [1] resampling to handle class imbalance. We focused on the previously best-performing 5 s sliding window approach to segment the time-series data. The classification was performed using the same leave-one-participant-out method to ensure full comparability and the most realistic approximation of real-world performance on unseen users.

To assess the generalizability of the model and to validate the newly recorded data, we also evaluated the handwashing detection on a combined dataset of the new and the previously collected dataset. As opposed to the previous dataset, the newly collected dataset contains a wider range of real-world activities, so we expected the performance to differ.

4.2 Applying Semi-supervised Embeddings and Better Modality Fusion

To improve generalization across subjects and address the limitations of hand-crafted features, as well as to tackle the problem of the still small dataset size, we employed a semi-supervised learning approach using a pretrained model to generate IMU embeddings. Specifically, we leveraged HARNet, a ResNet-based model from the BioBank SSL repository [24]. This model was pre-trained on large-scale (>700.000 person days) wearable sensor data in a self-supervised manner. For each 5-second window of accelerometer data, a 1024-dimensional embedding can be extracted from HARNet to capture rich motion representations.

In parallel, we included 11 statistical and temporal features from the humidity signal, including the measures mean, standard deviation, minimum, median, maximum, count of high values, range between 10%-, and 90%-percentile, peak count, mean and sd of first order derivative, and difference between last and first value of each window. We redesigned the humidity features compared to previous work, in order to make better use of the humidity response discussed in Sect. 3.2.

The humidity features were concatenated with the 1024-dimensional IMU embeddings to form a unified input vector for classification.

The concatenation of humidity features and the IMU embeddings was then jointly used to train a classification head. We trained a three-layer fully connected neural network (layers: 128->64->1 neuron(s)) with dropout, batch normalization, and Gaussian noise layers on this feature set. We applied a focal loss to handle class imbalance and further used SMOTE-Tomek resampling to improve minority class representation. Additionally, data augmentation was performed on samples belonging to the positive class using Gaussian noise injection and amplitude scaling. All features were standardized using z-score normalization. The predictions were smoothed using a median filter to reduce jitter. All evaluations in this publication followed a leave-one-participant-out (LOSO) protocol, allowing us to evaluate performance on completely unseen subjects, thus ensuring the best approximation of real-world performance. The results for each subject were then averaged to form the final F1 scores and accuracies.

As shown in Sect. 3.2, the class distribution is imbalanced and therefore high F1 scores are difficult to achieve, while extremely high accuracy values are easier to achieve but less meaningful.

5 Machine Learning Results

Although we performed multiple separate experiments on different subsets of the available data, the main results are jointly shown in Table 2. This table shows the mean results, averaged over all participants.

Table 2. F1 score and accuracy score result comparison of different methods (newly contributed methods in bold font). While previous work could not make use of the humidity features well, our CNN-GRU model was able to outperform the reported F1-score by 13% points. The accuracy was not reported for the Random Forest baseline. On the combined dataset, including humidity values boosts the performance for the HARNet-embedding based network (SSL Emb.). This model, based on the semi-supervised BioBank IMU embeddings, performs best on the larger and more complicated dataset (F1 = 0.68).

Dataset & Model	F1 Score		Accuracy	
	IMU+H	IMU	IMU+H	IMU
Pre-ex. Dataset (Baseline, RF, [6])	0.69	0.70	-	-
Pre-ex. Dataset (CNN-GRU)	**0.82**	0.74	**0.99**	0.98
Combined Dataset (CNN-GRU)	0.54	0.58	0.93	0.94
Combined Dataset (SSL Emb.)	**0.68**	0.60	**0.96**	0.94

We evaluated the CNN-GRU model's performance with and without humidity features on the pre-existing dataset using LOSO cross-validation. In the previous study, including humidity as a sensing modality did not have a positive impact on the classification performance (0.69 with humidity features vs. 0.70 without humidity features). However, as also shown in Table 2, when we applied our CNN-GRU model to the pre-existing dataset, the models that included humidity data achieved an average F1 score of 0.82, compared to 0.74 when humidity characteristics were excluded. Only a single percentage-point of accuracy could be gained when including humidity features (99% vs 98%). However, as explained above, accuracy is a less meaningful metric on highly imbalanced data. In general, adding humidity now significantly contributed to the higher performance of the model, in combination with the deep learning architecture outperforming the RF classifier.

Building on the analysis of the previous dataset, we next examined the model's performance on the combined dataset. As shown in Table 2, when applying the same CNN-GRU model, only relatively low F1-scores (0.54 with humidity features, 0.58 without humidity features) were reached, and including humidity values slightly worsened the performance. This led us to the conclusion, that the newly recorded data's additional background activities made it harder to train a general model, as certain background activities (such as playing the guitar) were only conducted by some subjects, and never in the pre-existing dataset.

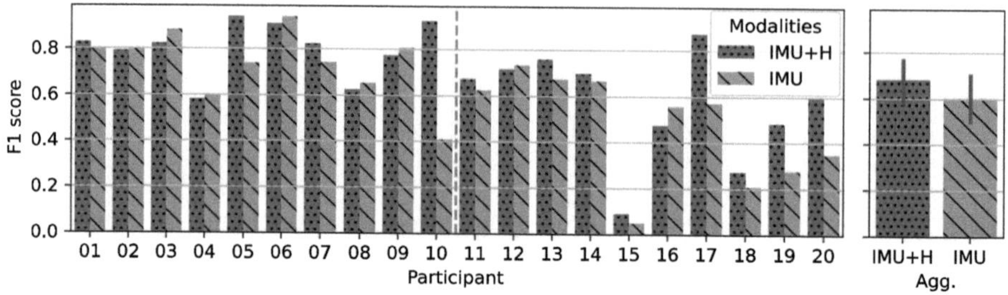

Fig. 3. Combined dataset results for the embedding-based model. Left: Per participant F1 scores of the LOSO-evaluation, with and without added humidity (IMU+H/IMU). Participants 1 to 10 belong to the pre-existing dataset, and 11 to 20 belong to the newly recorded dataset (separated by the dashed gray vertical line). Right: Aggregated F1 scores for both modality sets.

Our solution of applying the pre-trained BioBank "harnet" model, together with better manually engineered humidity features yielded much stronger performance on the combined dataset. When including humidity, an F1 score of 0.68 was reached (+0.14 compared to CNN-GRU), while without humidity features, the F1 score was lower with only 0.60 (+0.02 to CNN-GRU). The accuracy values of 96% vs 94% followed suit. Per participant results for this best model are shown in Fig. 3. Generally, the performance for participants belonging to the pre-existing dataset is stronger, with a mean F1 score of 0.8 for this subset (IMU+H). Notably, the results with and without the added humidity sensor are similar for most subjects. For some distinct participants, namely 05, 10, 17, 19, and 20, adding the humidity sensor boosts performance more significantly.

Another special participant is participant 15, for whom the system failed to detect hand washing reliably, with an F1 score below 0.1. We investigated this failure by visualizing hand washing procedures of participant 15 and comparing them to other participants. One such example is displayed in Fig. 4, where we compare the accelerometer data and humidity values for one entire hand washing procedure. We found the usual high frequency pattern (visible for participant 13 in subplot (b) of Fig. 4, 8–22 s) to be completely missing from participant 15's hand washing procedures, which explains the model's difficulties in detecting the washes. This finding highlights the uniqueness in hand washing patterns, which can differ strongly from person to person. Added to that, it shows that humidity changes alone are also not suitable for reliable detection, as humidity changes can occur for different reasons and during different activities, such as "washing dishes", which is included in the newly recorded dataset. Excluding participant 15 from only the evaluation step or from both the training and evaluation step

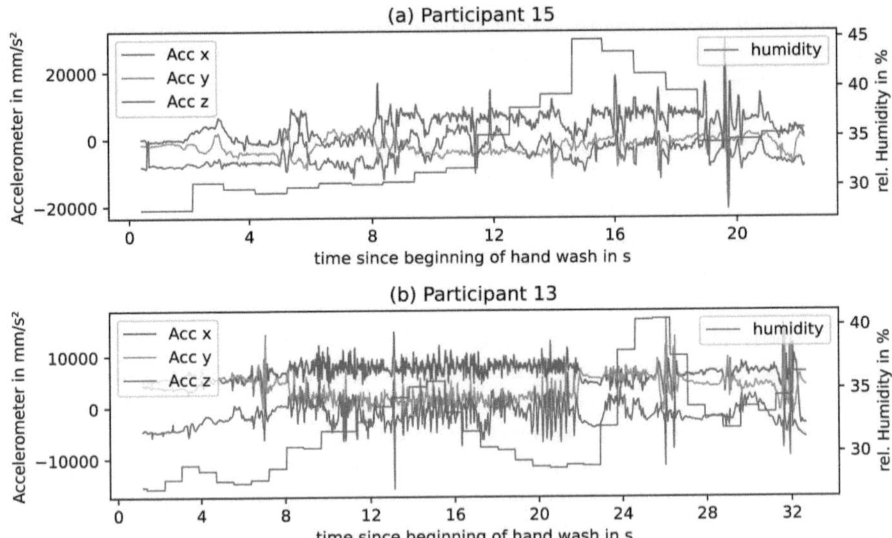

Fig. 4. Two hand washing procedures, with accelerometer and humidity values plotted. (a) For participant 15, (b) for participant 13. While the humidity rises for both subjects with a small delay, the IMU shows that, in comparison, participant 15 (a) moves more slowly, as the distinctive high-frequency hand washing pattern exists only for participant 13 (b).

increased the mean LOSO F1 score to 0.71 and 0.72, respectively, showing that this participant's peculiar hand washing patterns slightly confounded the model.

6   Discussion and Future Work

From the machine learning results on all collected data, we can derive that humidity is a valuable modality for hand washing detection. While previous work failed to reliably make use of the clearly visible humidity pattern around hand washes, our new results show that adding humidity to the IMU data provides context and thus improves the performance. This statement does not hold true, when the complexity of the activities and the small amount of available training data diminish the model's generalization capabilities, as was the case with our CNN-GRU model on the combined dataset. Humidity alone can also not solve the problem, as the results for participant 15 highlighted, for whom the movement patterns were too unique to be recognized well.

The variance of achieved F1 scores between different subjects is high, due to the highly personal hand washing styles. Especially participant 15 displayed a unique hand washing pattern. Although the model performed better when it could make use of humidity, the performance remained weak for this specific participant. In a previous study [6], we showed that personalized re-training with only a small amount of data can boost the performance further, even for participants for which a generalized model struggles. A "user calibration step", i.e., personalized retraining, therefore makes sense for the real-world deployment of such hand washing detection systems. This finding is fully in line with the literature, where real-world hand washing is also described as "unstructured" [13]. Even with the differences between subjects, the comparison of modalities showed that the model with humidity as an additional modality was never significantly outperformed. However, for some participants, adding humidity significantly improved the performance. Therefore, we conclude that its inclusion is justified, and we urge researchers to continue to include it in future data recordings.

As in many other domains in which labeled training data is scarce, utilizing a model that was pre-trained semi-supervisedly on a large unlabeled dataset yielded the best performance. We did not try finetuning the parameters of the pre-trained model, and only trained the classification head. Finetuning all layers could lead to even better performance in the future, as it has been shown to sometimes perform better than just training a fully-connected classification head [14,17]. With the significantly higher F1 scores achieved on both the previous dataset and the combined dataset, we came one step closer to a reliable, environment-independent, in-the-wild hand washing detection model, thanks to the inclusion of a pre-trained model in the pipeline and to adding more sophisticated, yet handcrafted, humidity features.

The newly recorded data is more diverse in its activities, and thus it is harder to predict the included hand washing instances. However, a large portion of the performance that was lost when compared to the simpler pre-existing dataset could be made up using the semi-supervised embedding model. The dataset is now twice as large, which, in theory, makes training models easier and enables better generalization capabilities. We freely offer the combined dataset for downloading in our GitHub repository[3].

The WearPuck recording device was also re-validated with this research, as we used it to record another 10 participants. It worked reliably and made it fairly easy to collect data from the participants, as all sensors are attached to one device and no further synchronization is needed.

In the future, even more complex models can be tested for offline classification. Our collected data can serve as a starting point for model training, likely of a pre-trained established model and architecture. For online classification, lightweight models, which can be run directly on wearable devices, could be trained with it.

An additional modality, which could probably be employed well to detect hand washing events would be sound. Microphone recordings could help, as the sound of tap water is usually audible, and tap water datasets already exist [11], just not in conjunction with hand washing [4]. A combined wearable system of IMU, humidity sensor, and microphone could be the solution to the most reliable system for the environment-agnostic detection of hand washing.

---

[3] https://github.com/AliHurriat/HandwashingDetection-WearPuck.

7   Conclusion

In this work, we extended our previous publication on hand washing detection using multi-modal sensing. We deepened our understanding of the usefulness of the inclusion of humidity sensors by analyzing it on a per-participant level, and, unlike related work, we were able to show that the humidity sensor boosts performance when added to IMU recordings for the hand washing detection task. To do so, we leveraged a model that was pre-trained on large amounts of unlabeled IMU data. We expect that humidity sensors can be useful in handwashing-related tasks and other water- or humidity-related HAR tasks as well, which remains underexplored.

We analyzed the weak outlier performance of one participant due to their unique hand washing style and propose to use small amounts of data for personalization in future work.

Additionally, we presented and evaluated the recordings of 10 new participants, increasing the size of the dataset to 20 participants and more than 20 h. The newer recordings contain significantly more unlabeled background activities, less idleness, and are fully compatible with the previous recordings. Our dataset can be used to train even more sophisticated models for the task of hand washing detection.

Possible future work includes combining even more wearable sensors into one multi-modal detection system, which in turn also requires additional data collection and method development.

Disclosure of Interests. The authors have no competing interests to declare that are relevant to the content of this article.

References

1. Batista, G.E.A.P.A., Prati, R.C., Monard, M.C.: A study of the behavior of several methods for balancing machine learning training data. ACM SIGKDD Explor. Newsl. **6**(1), 20–29 (2004). https://doi.org/10.1145/1007730.1007735
2. Bharti, P., De, D., Chellappan, S., Das, S.K.: HuMAn: complex activity recognition with multi-modal multi-positional body sensing. IEEE Trans. Mob. Comput. **18**(4), 857–870 (2019). https://doi.org/10.1109/TMC.2018.2841905
3. Bock, M., Hölzemann, A., Moeller, M., Van Laerhoven, K.: Improving deep learning for HAR with shallow LSTMs. In: Proceedings of the 2021 ACM International Symposium on Wearable Computers, ISWC 2021, pp. 7–12. Association for Computing Machinery, New York (2021). https://doi.org/10.1145/3460421.3480419
4. Burchard, R., Laerhoven, K.V.: Enhancing Wearable Tap Water Audio Detection through Subclass Annotation in the HD-Epic Dataset (2025). https://doi.org/10.48550/arXiv.2505.20788
5. Burchard, R., Scholl, P.M., Lieb, R., Van Laerhoven, K., Wahl, K.: WashSpot: real-time spotting and detection of enacted compulsive hand washing with wearable devices. In: Proceedings of the 2022 ACM International Joint Conference on Pervasive and Ubiquitous Computing, pp. 483–487. ACM, Cambridge United Kingdom (2022). https://doi.org/10.1145/3544793.3563428

6. Burchard, R., Van Laerhoven, K.: Multi-modal atmospheric sensing to augment wearable IMU-based hand washing detection. In: Konak, O., Arnrich, B., Bieber, G., Kuijper, A., Fudickar, S. (eds.) Sensor-Based Activity Recognition and Artificial Intelligence, pp. 55–68. Springer, Cham (2025). https://doi.org/10.1007/978-3-031-80856-2_4

7. Burton, M., Cobb, E., Donachie, P., Judah, G., Curtis, V., Schmidt, W.P.: The effect of handwashing with water or soap on bacterial contamination of hands. Int. J. Environ. Res. Public Health **8**(1), 97–104 (2011). https://doi.org/10.3390/ijerph8010097

8. De, D., Bharti, P., Das, S.K., Chellappan, S.: Multimodal wearable sensing for fine-grained activity recognition in healthcare. IEEE Internet Comput. **19**(5), 26–35 (2015). https://doi.org/10.1109/MIC.2015.72

9. Demrozi, F., Pravadelli, G., Bihorac, A., Rashidi, P.: Human activity recognition using inertial, physiological and environmental sensors: a comprehensive survey. IEEE Access **8**, 210816–210836 (2020). https://doi.org/10.1109/ACCESS.2020.3037715

10. Ezzeldin, M., Ghoneim, A., Abdelhamid, L., Atia, A.: Survey on multimodal complex human activity recognition. FCI-H Inform. Bull. **7**(1) (2025)

11. Gemmeke, J.F., et al.: Audio set: an ontology and human-labeled dataset for audio events. In: 2017 IEEE International Conference on Acoustics, Speech and Signal Processing (ICASSP), pp. 776–780 (2017). https://doi.org/10.1109/ICASSP.2017.7952261

12. Set up Handwashing on Apple Watch (2024). https://support.apple.com/en-my/guide/watch/apdc9b9f04a8/watchos

13. Lattanzi, E., Calisti, L., Freschi, V.: Unstructured handwashing recognition using smartwatch to reduce contact transmission of pathogens. IEEE Access **10**, 83111–83124 (2022). https://doi.org/10.1109/ACCESS.2022.3197279

14. Logacjov, A., Herland, S., Ustad, A., Bach, K.: SelfPAB: large-scale pre-training on accelerometer data for human activity recognition. Appl. Intell. **54**(6), 4545–4563 (2024). https://doi.org/10.1007/s10489-024-05322-3

15. Münzner, S., Schmidt, P., Reiss, A., Hanselmann, M., Stiefelhagen, R., Dürichen, R.: CNN-based sensor fusion techniques for multimodal human activity recognition. In: Proceedings of the 2017 ACM International Symposium on Wearable Computers, pp. 158–165. ACM, Maui Hawaii (2017). https://doi.org/10.1145/3123021.3123046

16. Ni, J., Tang, H., Haque, S.T., Yan, Y., Ngu, A.H.H.: A Survey on Multimodal Wearable Sensor-based Human Action Recognition (2024). https://doi.org/10.48550/arXiv.2404.15349

17. Nshimyimana, D., Rey, V.F., Suh, S., Zhou, B., Lukowicz, P.: PIM: Physics-Informed Multi-task Pre-training for Improving Inertial Sensor-Based Human Activity Recognition (2025). https://doi.org/10.48550/arXiv.2503.17978

18. Ordóñez, F., Roggen, D.: Deep convolutional and LSTM recurrent neural networks for multimodal wearable activity recognition. Sensors **16**(1), 115 (2016). https://doi.org/10.3390/s16010115

19. Samyoun, S., Shubha, S.S., Sayeed Mondol, M.A., Stankovic, J.A.: iWash: a smartwatch handwashing quality assessment and reminder system with real-time feedback in the context of infectious disease. Smart Health **19**, 100171 (2021). https://doi.org/10.1016/j.smhl.2020.100171

20. Vepakomma, P., De, D., Das, S.K., Bhansali, S.: A-Wristocracy: deep learning on wrist-worn sensing for recognition of user complex activities. In: 2015 IEEE

12th International Conference on Wearable and Implantable Body Sensor Networks (BSN), pp. 1–6. IEEE, Cambridge, MA, USA (2015). https://doi.org/10.1109/BSN.2015.7299406

21. Wahl, K., Scholl, P.M., Miché, M., Wirth, S., Burchard, R., Lieb, R.: Real-time detection of obsessive-compulsive hand washing with wearables: research procedure, usefulness and discriminative performance. J. Obsessive-Compulsive Related Disord. **39**, 100845 (2023). https://doi.org/10.1016/j.jocrd.2023.100845

22. Wahl, K., et al.: On the automatic detection of enacted compulsive hand washing using commercially available wearable devices. Comput. Biol. Med. **143**, 105280 (2022). https://doi.org/10.1016/j.compbiomed.2022.105280

23. Wang, C., Sarsenbayeva, Z., Chen, X., Dingler, T., Goncalves, J., Kostakos, V.: Accurate measurement of handwash quality using sensor armbands: instrument validation study. JMIR Mhealth Uhealth **8**(3), e17001 (2020). https://doi.org/10.2196/17001

24. Yuan, H., et al.: Self-supervised learning for human activity recognition using 700,000 person-days of wearable data. NPJ Digit. Med. **7**(1), 91 (2024). https://doi.org/10.1038/s41746-024-01062-3

25. Zeng, M., Yu, T., Wang, X., Nguyen, L.T., Mengshoel, O.J., Lane, I.: Semi-supervised convolutional neural networks for human activity recognition. In: 2017 IEEE International Conference on Big Data (Big Data), pp. 522–529 (2017). https://doi.org/10.1109/BigData.2017.8257967

26. Zhuang, H., Xu, L., Nishiyama, Y., Sezaki, K.: Detecting hand hygienic behaviors in-the-wild using a microphone and motion sensor on a smartwatch. In: Streitz, N.A., Konomi, S. (eds.) Distributed, Ambient and Pervasive Interactions. LNCS, pp. 470–483. Springer, Cham (2023). https://doi.org/10.1007/978-3-031-34609-5_34

No Cloud, No Problem: A Real-Time HAR Insole with On-Device Inference

Ruben Schlonsak[1,3]($\boxtimes$), Jiabao Yu[1,2], Hans-Christian Jetter[4],
and Denys J. C. Matthies[1,3]

[1] Technical University of Applied Sciences Lübeck, Lübeck, Germany
ruben.schlonsak@th-luebeck.de
[2] East China University of Science and Technology, Shanghai, China
[3] Fraunhofer IMTE, Lübeck, Germany
[4] University of Lübeck, Lübeck, Germany

Abstract. We present an ankle-mounted insole artifact enabling real-time recognition of seven daily activities. Classification is performed on-chip on a dual-core ESP32-S3 microcontroller without requiring any cloud or smartphone connection. Our proposed program design allows for multi-threading, treating sensing (SensorTask), inference (ModelTask), and wireless output (BLETask) as three periodic tasks within FreeRTOS. The SensorTask acquires six pressure channels and a six-axis IMU sampling at 20 Hz. The ModelTask dequeues the sample and executes a post-training-quantized one-dimensional convolutional network in 54 ms. The BLETask transmits the predicted class on change, keeping the radio duty cycle below 7%. Across eight subjects, the system reaches 92.8% leave-one-subject-out accuracy with a worst-case end-to-end latency of up to 555 ms. The mean current increases by 2.24 mA above a 100 mA sensor baseline, allowing for nearly 5 h of operation on a 500 mAh cell. Stability is underpinned by a zero-loss of sensor frames during two hours of continuous streaming with a minimal task jitter below 2 ms. To our knowledge, this is the first insole that reports a complete timing–energy–accuracy triad for entirely local inference on an ESP32-class microcontroller. The results demonstrate that careful task scheduling, rather than network compression alone, is sufficient for achieving reliable edge intelligence in resource-constrained wearables.

Keywords: Human Activity Recognition · Edge AI · Smart Insole · Real-Time Inference · FreeRTOS · TinyML

1 Introduction

In human activity recognition (HAR), foot interfaces, such as insoles, have migrated from research labs to commercial gait analysis and rehabilitation products [21]. Most systems still offload sensor streams to a smartphone or cloud service, incurring 200 ms to 400 ms network latency, high radio power, and

© The Author(s), under exclusive license to Springer Nature Switzerland AG 2026
O. Durmaz Incel et al. (Eds.): iWOAR 2025, LNCS 16292, pp. 324–342, 2026.
https://doi.org/10.1007/978-3-032-13312-0_19

possible privacy leakage [18,31]. Recent studies have demonstrated that convolutional and recurrent networks can be efficiently compressed using post-training quantization and executed in real-time on microcontrollers, such as the ESP32 [2,11,29]. Nevertheless, firmware design remains an under-examined bottleneck. Inference is often placed inside a single polling loop. When Bluetooth advertising or Wi-Fi interrupts occur, periodic sensing deadlines slip, queues overflow, and the reported accuracy cannot be reproduced in the field. Very few published wearables quantify task jitter or verify that their schedulers remain deterministic when radio traffic is present (Fig. 1).

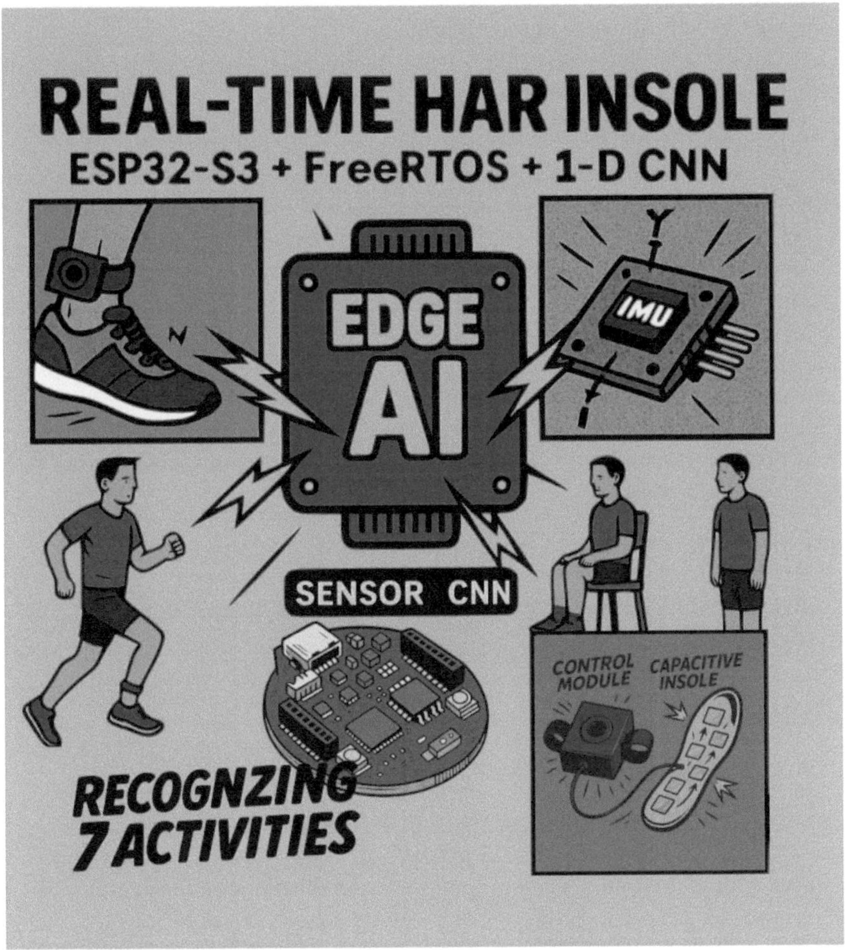

Fig. 1. Our sensor prototype: The ESP32 S3 module with the 6-axis IMU and the battery placed in a 3D-printed case that is strapped around the ankle, while six capacitive sensors are embedded in the connected insole, which was part of former work [29].

A real-time operating system (RTOS) provides a principled remedy. FreeRTOS version 11.1 extends symmetric multiprocessing and memory-protection features to commodity microcontrollers [15], yet prior insole projects that report timing figures usually rely on more powerful system-on-chip or external co-processors [8,14]. To the best of our knowledge, no earlier work combines timing, energy, and accuracy for a FreeRTOS-based insole that performs all inference on an ESP32-class device [24]. Symmetric multiprocessing allows one kernel instance to balance work across both cores; however, published examples discuss how tasks are pinned or how per-core utilization is measured. Earlier studies also omit worst-case execution time budgets and do not show that queue depths are sufficient to prevent frame loss during continuous walking [16]. These gaps obscure reproducibility and cloud reliability.

This paper addresses that gap by treating edge inference as just another periodic task in a real-time schedule:

1. Deterministic FreeRTOS schedule. We design a three-task pipeline that includes sensor acquisition, 1-D CNN inference, and Bluetooth Low Energy (BLE) reporting, all of which are pinned to the two cores of an ESP32-S3. Worst-case execution times (WCET) and semaphore-protected queues guarantee no sample loss at 20 Hz.
2. Compact edge model. A post-training-quantized 1-D CNN (304 kB flash, 86 kB RAM) classifies seven daily activities in 54 ms on the device while maintaining 92.8% leave-one-subject-out accuracy.
3. Comprehensive evaluation. We publish end-to-end latency, per-task jitter distributions, energy overhead ($+2.24$ mA on a 500 mAh Li-Po), and memory footprint, offering the first timing-energy-accuracy triad for a FreeRTOS HAR insole on the ESP32-S3.

By demonstrating that strict task-level scheduling can deliver deterministic sensing alongside neural inference without compromising battery life or accuracy, this work advances the design of privacy-preserving, low-power wearables that rely solely on local intelligence.

2   Related Work

2.1   Smart Insoles for Activity Recognition

Wearable sensor-equipped insoles have been developed that collect foot sensor data and usually transmit it for expensive data processing to external devices with higher computational power, such as to a smartphone [28], smart glass [5], tablet computer [17], PC [7] etc. Early smart-insole systems focused primarily on sensing and wireless streaming, leaving feature extraction and classification to off-body devices. These systems typically stream plantar pressure or motion data via Bluetooth or similar wireless links to a smartphone or cloud, where algorithms analyze gait metrics or detect specific events. Early examples include CapSoles [17], a battery-powered insole prototype that submits 6 CapSense values to a computer, where the data is processed with machine learning, such as to identify the wearer and six different terrains. Another recent example is presented by Wang et al.; a self-powered insole equipped with 22 pressure sensors and solar energy harvesting, which sends real-time gait data via Bluetooth to a smartphone for analysis [28]. Their system uses a machine-learning model on the phone to recognize eight motion states (sitting, standing, running, etc.) from the transmitted pressure patterns. This approach improves user posture and provides early warnings for foot or neurological conditions by offloading the computational inference to the phone. Martini et al. developed a wireless insole with 16 optoelectronic force sensors, focusing on real-time gait event detection [16]. The insole's onboard microcontroller samples the sensors at a rate of 100 Hz. It transmits the raw data via an ultra-wideband link to a remote processor (National Instruments SOM), which calculates gait phase variables and center of pressure in real-time.

Typical HAR capabilities with insole- or shoe-placed sensors include body posture, ambulation activity, gait abnormalities, and terrain [12]. Prior research projects have shown rich detection capabilities with smart footwear prototypes, while the data is usually wirelessly streamed to an external device that has richer computational power. This laid the groundwork for our approach, which aims to integrate the entire HAR pipeline directly into the insole prototype itself.

2.2 Edge-AI Inference on MCUs

Deep learning algorithms have proven high performance in HAR, while light models are now fit to work "on the edge" [1]. This trend in "TinyML" has enabled running neural network inference directly on resource-constrained microcontrollers, such as the ARM Cortex-M series (e.g., STM32, ESP32, nRF52). Key techniques include model compression (quantization, pruning), efficient architecture design, and optimized inference runtimes that contend with tight memory (tens of kB RAM) and limited CPU speed [13,25]. Likewise, optimized models for sensor data have been demonstrated to run in real-time on microcontroller-class wearables. Shakerian et al. present a chest-mounted IMU sensor with an integrated CNN that performs HAR inference locally on a low-cost MCU, removing the need for any external phone or computer during operation [25]. The 1D convolutional network in their device classifies activities from accelerometer signals on board with high accuracy and low latency. The idea of using CNN on accelerometer data is not new, but has already been proposed at iWOAR 2018 [19]. Meanwhile, researchers have successfully deployed similar architectures, such as recurrent neural networks on microcontrollers. Di Leo et al. implemented an LSTM-based gesture recognition on an STM32L4 MCU, achieving >90% accuracy while maintaining real-time performance [3]. These examples illustrate the growing capability for on-device HAR in wearables, thanks to TinyML toolkits (e.g. TensorFlow Lite Micro) and efficient model design. Running inference at the edge brings well-known benefits: it avoids wireless latency, reduces battery drain from constant radio use, and preserves user privacy by keeping personal sensor data local [31]. Very recent work is even pushing toward on-device learning – for instance, Zuo et al. propose an edge AI platform that can incrementally train or adapt an activity model on a device (a smartphone in their case) without cloud interaction [31]. Shalby et al. likewise introduce a TinyML method for on-device learning of new human activities on a resource-constrained MCU (STM32), highlighting the trend toward personalization on the edge [26]. Recently, Peretti et al. [22] investigated energy efficiency of feature selection for HAR running on MCU. The study effectively shows that with around two dozen thoughtfully selected features, energy consumption during feature extraction on a typical low-power smartwatch platform can be minimized without significantly sacrificing HAR accuracy. This makes a strong case for adopting energy-aware feature selection in resource-constrained wearable ML applications. All literature in its entirety show that contemporary wearable devices can perform non-trivial HAR inference locally on microcontroller hardware, provided the features and models are carefully optimized. Our work builds on this foundation by not only deploying a quantized CNN in a foot-worn MCU but also by architecting the firmware to meet real-time scheduling demands in a multi-task wearable system.

2.3   RTOS Scheduling in Wearables

Resource-constrained wearables often rely on a real-time operating system (RTOS), such as FreeRTOS or Zephyr, to schedule concurrent tasks (including sensor sampling, wireless communication, and inference) under timing and energy constraints [23]. An RTOS provides preemptive multitasking, priority-based scheduling, and inter-task synchronization, which are crucial for reliable performance in wearables, medical devices, and other latency-sensitive embedded systems [10]. FreeRTOS, a widely used open-source RTOS, facilitates the allocation of high priority to critical tasks, such as sensor reading, ensuring their execution on schedule. Concurrently, lower-priority tasks, such as data transmission over Bluetooth, are subject to delay or preemption as needed [30]. This design prevents slow peripherals or network interrupts from blocking the main sensor loop. Zhang et al. illustrate this in a multi-sensor wearable for Parkinson's disease monitoring, where they adopted FreeRTOS to ensure that data acquisition at 100 Hz would not be disrupted by other processes, such as writing to an SD card or handling Wi-Fi communication [30]. As a result, the device maintains stable sampling and avoids missing data frames, even when network traffic is present.

Another example by Luna-Perejón et al. is an ankle-worn device for recording a fall detection dataset. They report using FreeRTOS in the firmware to "correctly process the information and transmit it without losing data" at 50 Hz from a 3-axis accelerometer [14]. Recent surveys of wearable systems emphasize the need for rigorous scheduling to ensure reproducible performance in real-world deployments [10]. While an RTOS greatly enhances reliability, it also adds overhead and complexity. To address this, some work has explored lightweight scheduling alternatives. Kos et al. (2025) argued that complete RTOS solutions (FreeRTOS, ChibiOS, NuttX, etc.), with their rich features (preemptive multitasking, IPC, etc.), can introduce unnecessary overhead in simple wearable biofeedback applications [10]. To address this issue, they developed a custom cooperative scheduler that executes tasks in a fixed cyclic order within a timer interrupt, eliminating the need for context switching except at predetermined points. Their minimalist scheduler achieved a context-switch overhead of only 3 µs, compared to 5–15 µs for FreeRTOS on the same Cortex-M microcontroller [10].

3 System Design

This section details the design and implementation of the edge AI insole, covering the hardware platform, model architecture, firmware design, and the end-to-end deployment pipeline. The system is designed to meet the stringent requirements of low power and low latency operation on a resource-constrained microcontroller.

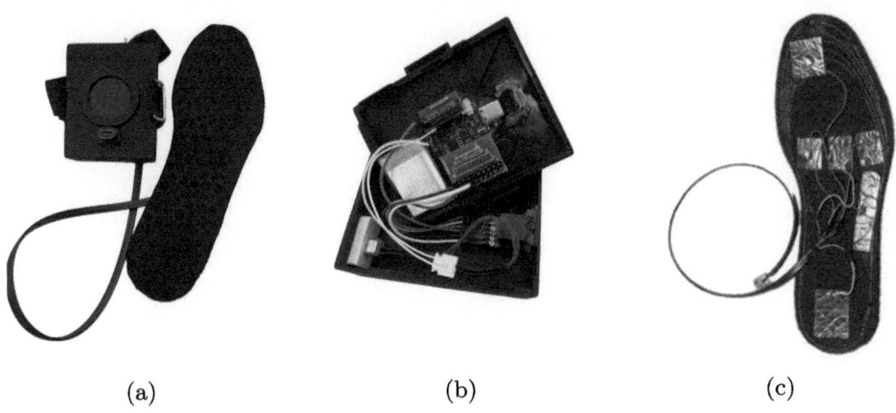

(a)   (b)   (c)

Fig. 2. Hardware prototype of the smart insole system. (a) Wearable unit showing the external enclosure and attachment to the insole. (b) Internal view of the electronics, including microcontroller, IMU, battery, and connectors. (c) Internal view of the insole with embedded capacitive pressure sensors and wiring.

3.1 Hardware Platform

The system is built upon the Waveshare ESP32-S3-LCD-1.28, a compact development board featuring a dual-core Xtensa® LX7 processor operating at 240 MHz. The board is equipped with 2 MB of PSRAM, 16 MB of flash memory, and integrated 2.4 GHz Wi-Fi and Bluetooth 5 (LE) connectivity. For sensor data acquisition, the platform features an onboard QMI8658 6-axis Inertial Measurement Unit (IMU), which provides data from a 3-axis accelerometer and a 3-axis gyroscope. This is augmented by six external capacitive sensors connected to GPIO pins strategically placed to capture pressure distribution across the insole. The developed prototype is shown in Fig. 2.

3.2 Data Acquisition and Pre-processing

A dataset was collected from eight adult participants performing seven everyday activities: running, walking, climbing stairs, descending stairs, sitting, standing, and lying (weight: 60–100 kg, height: 170–190 cm). The 12-dimensional sensor data (6-axis IMU and six pressure channels). We sample at 20 Hz because plantar–pressure and foot-IMU spectra contain negligible energy above 10 Hz; Elstub et al. report <3% peak-force error when decimating to 20 Hz [4]. For segmentation size, we used a 0.5 s window (10 frames) that spans a full stance or swing sub-phase of the 1 s gait cycle, providing sufficient context while capping worst-case latency below 0.6 s; Nazari et al. found 0.5 s to be the optimum for CNN-based gait HAR (99.95% F1) [20]. To mitigate the risk of overfitting [27], a leave-one-subject-out split was employed during the training process. To prepare the data for the neural network, a sliding window technique was employed. A window size of 0.5 s (10 consecutive samples) was chosen to ensure low system latency. The window moves with a stride of one sample, creating overlapping frames that enhance the temporal resolution of the input data, resulting in more robust classification.

3.3 Model Architecture and Training

Model Selection. Considering the resource constraints of the target MCU, a one-dimensional convolutional neural network (1D-CNN) was selected. This architecture offers a strong balance between classification performance and computational efficiency for time-series data, making it more suitable for embedded deployment than more complex models such as LSTMs or hybrid networks, which typically have higher memory and computational demands. The 1D-CNN architecture was implemented using the Keras API in TensorFlow and consists of the architecture described in Fig. 3. The model was trained on a desktop PC using the Adam optimizer and the sparse categorical cross-entropy loss function.

Model Optimization and Deployment. To deploy the model on the ESP32-S3, an end-to-end pipeline was established:

- **Quantization:** The trained Keras model was converted to the TensorFlow Lite (TFLite) format. Post-training quantization was applied, converting the model's 32-bit floating-point weights to 8-bit integers. This reduced the model's storage footprint by approximately 65% while the input and output layers were kept as float32 to maintain precision.
- **Conversion to C Array:** The quantized TFLite model file was converted into a C header file using the xxd tool. This transforms the model into a static unsigned char array that can be directly compiled into the firmware.
- **Firmware Integration:** The model was integrated into the firmware using the TensorFlow Lite for Microcontrollers (TFLM) library. A MicroInterpreter was instantiated, and a tensor arena, a statically allocated memory region for

model operations, was defined. To minimize binary size, only the TFLM operations required by the model (e.g., Conv1D, Dense, Softmax) were registered using a MicroMutableOpResolver.

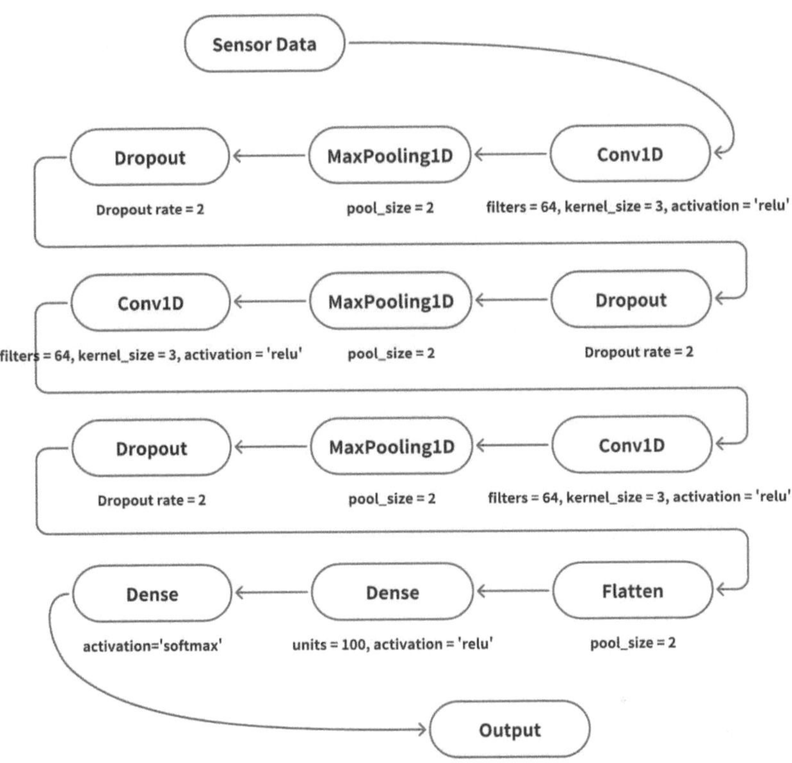

Fig. 3. One-dimensional convolutional neural network (1D-CNN) architecture for human-activity recognition from smart-insole sensor data. The model ingests a frame of 10 time steps $\times$ 12 sensor channels, processes it through three identical convolutional blocks each consisting of a 64-filter Conv1D layer (kernel = 3, ReLU), a MaxPooling1D layer (pool = 2), and dropout (rate = 0.2), and then flattens the feature maps. A fully connected layer with 100 ReLU units precedes a seven-unit softmax layer that outputs the class-probability distribution.

3.4   Real-Time Task Scheduling with FreeRTOS

To manage concurrent operations and prevent task interference, a multi-tasking architecture was implemented using FreeRTOS, leveraging the ESP32-S3's dual-core capabilities. The three-task scheduler is summarized in Algorithm 1.

Algorithm 1 Minimal RTOS Task Layout

    Shared: `dataQueue, modelReady, modelResult`

1: **procedure** SensorTask(every 50 ms)
2:     frame ← ReadSensors()   ▷ ADC+IMU+touch
3:     Enqueue(`dataQueue`, frame)
4: **end procedure**
5: **procedure** ModelTask
6:     **while** true **do**
7:         window ← DequeueN(`dataQueue`, W)
8:         `modelResult` ← Infer(window)
9:         Give(`modelReady`)
10:     **end while**
11: **end procedure**
12: **procedure** BleTask
13:     **while** true **do**
14:         Take(`modelReady`)
15:         **if** connected **then**
16:             NotifyBLE(`modelResult`)
17:         **end if**
18:     **end while**
19: **end procedure**

Task Design. The following three primary tasks were implemented: 1) the acquisition of sensor data, 2) the utilization of the developed model for predictions, and 3) the transmission of the latest classification results via Bluetooth Low Energy, as described in Table 1.

Table 1. FreeRTOS task breakdown.

Task	Core	Priority	Avg. rate	Function
`sensorTask`	0	2	20 Hz	Acquire IMU & pressure data
`modelTask`	1	1	≈ 20 Hz	Assemble 0.5 s windows & invoke CNN
`bleTask`	1	1	on demand	Advertise latest prediction

A FreeRTOS queue is used to safely pass data from the high-frequency sensorTask to the lower-frequency modelTask, preventing data loss and ensuring FIFO processing. A binary semaphore synchronizes the modelTask and bleTask, ensuring that BLE transmissions occur only when a new prediction is available, thereby preventing redundant transmissions and conserving energy. This partitioned, priority-based scheduling strategy isolates time-critical sensing from computationally intensive inference and non-deterministic BLE communication, ensuring system stability and real-time performance (Fig. 4).

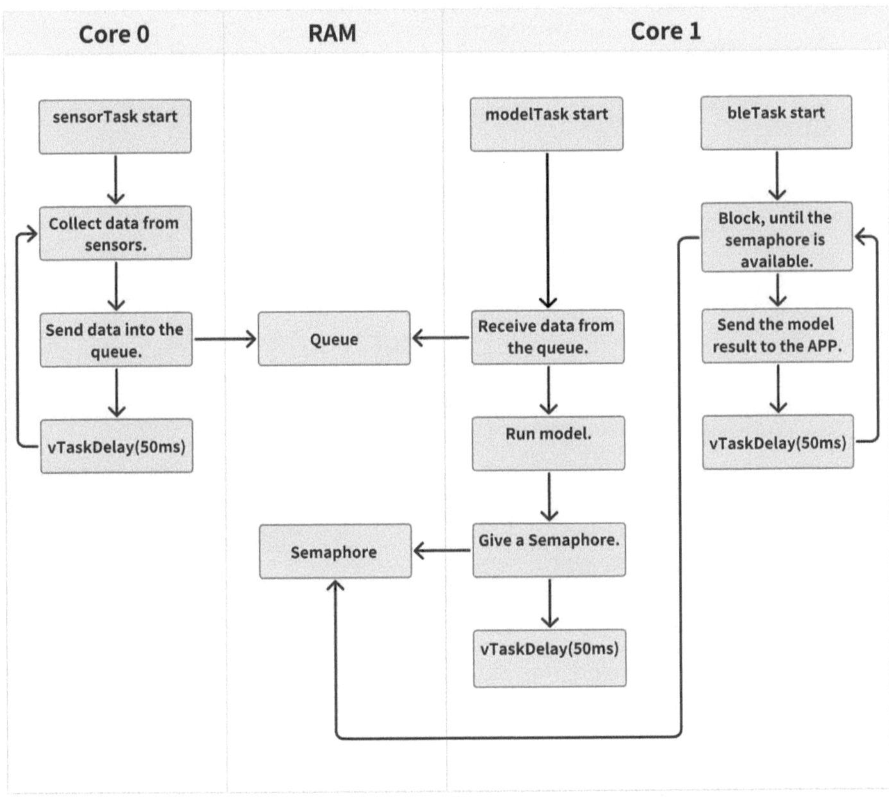

Fig. 4. Task-level schedule on the dual-core ESP32-S3.

4   Evaluation

The system was evaluated using a structured framework that assessed classification performance, task scheduling behavior, and resource consumption (including latency, energy, and memory) on both a PC and the target embedded device.

Person-Independent Accuracy (Leave-One-Subject-Out Cross-Validation)

To assess generalization, a Leave-One-Subject-Out Cross-Validation (LOSOCV) was performed. The model achieved an average accuracy of 92.8%. The corresponding confusion matrix is presented in Fig. 5 While performance was strong for most activities, some confusion was observed between 'sitting' and 'standing'. This is attributable to the similarity in foot pressure and orientation in these static states, making it difficult to distinguish them without more diverse training data that covers a range of body weights and postures.

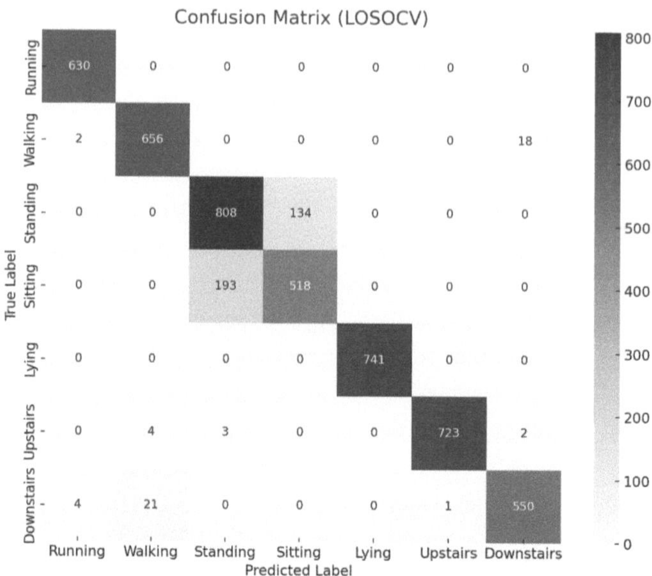

Fig. 5. Normalised confusion matrix for leave-one-subject-out cross-validation (LOSOCV).

On-Device Performance

After deploying the quantized model to the ESP32-S3, the model's real-world performance was tested with new participants not included in the training set. The system achieved an average accuracy of 92.76%, demonstrating that the post-training quantization and on-device execution had a negligible impact on classification performance. The misclassification patterns (e.g., 'sitting' vs. 'standing') were consistent with the PC-based evaluation.

4.1 System Performance Metrics

The FreeRTOS task scheduling was verified by monitoring serial output logs. The logs confirmed that the sensorTask executed consistently at 20 Hz without being disrupted by other tasks. The modelTask was triggered correctly after 10 sensor readings, and the bleTask was only activated after the modelTask completed inference, validating the effectiveness of the queue and semaphore synchronization mechanisms.

Inference Latency. The time taken for a single inference cycle on the ESP32-S3 was measured by logging timestamps before and after the *interpreter->Invoke()* call.

- Inference Latency: The average time to run the 1D-CNN model was 54 ms.
- End-to-End Latency: The total time from the start of data collection for a window to the final classification is approximately 554 ms (500 ms for data acquisition + 55 ms for inference). This is well within the acceptable range for real-time HAR applications.

As shown in Fig. 6, our Edge-AI smart-insole solution achieves an end-to-end inference latency of 55 ms, outperforming typical cloud-based inference (up to 300 ms) [6]. Due to higher computation power, modern smartphone-based inference can surpass this latency.

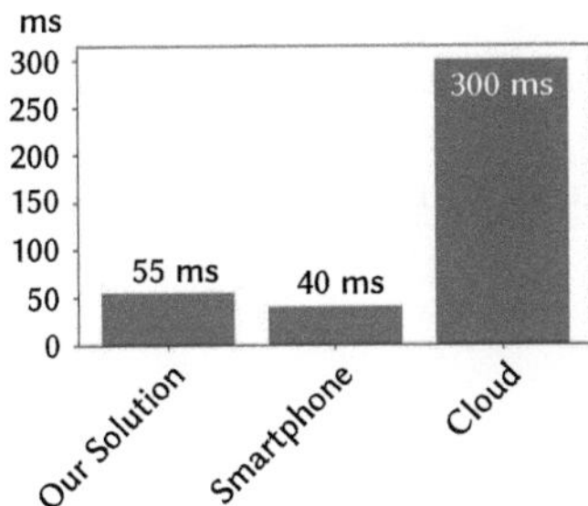

Fig. 6. End-to-end inference latency for our Edge-AI smart-insole solution (55ms), typical smartphone inference (up to 40ms), and cloud server inference (up to 300ms)

Energy Consumption. Energy consumption was measured using a Nordic Power Profiler Kit II (PPK2). The power consumption measurements are as follows: Baseline (Sensors + BLE, no scheduling) at 159.06 mA; with FreeR-TOS Scheduling (no inference) at 150.24 mA, reducing consumption by preventing redundant BLE transmissions; and Full System (Scheduling + Inference) at 152.48 mA. By disconnecting the display from the microcontroller, we can save an additional 50 mA of power, resulting in a total of 102.48 mA. The results are presented in Figs. 9 and 10.

As illustrated in Fig. 7, disabling the display yields the most energy savings, reducing the average current consumption by 35.6% compared to the baseline. In contrast, integrating FreeRTOS task scheduling and ML inference introduces only minor variations of less than 6%.

Memory Usage. The impact of quantization and deployment on memory was analyzed using PlatformIO. Post-training quantization reduced the model's C header file size from 866 KB to 304 KB (a 64.9% reduction). Deploying the model and TFLM engine increased the firmware's total resource usage. Static RAM usage increased by 86.36 KB, and Flash usage increased by 1213.77 KB compared to the baseline firmware (only sensing). The final firmware (sensing + model) occupied 93.3% of the available Flash and 44.7% of the RAM, confirming that the system fits within the microcontroller's constraints (Fig. 8).

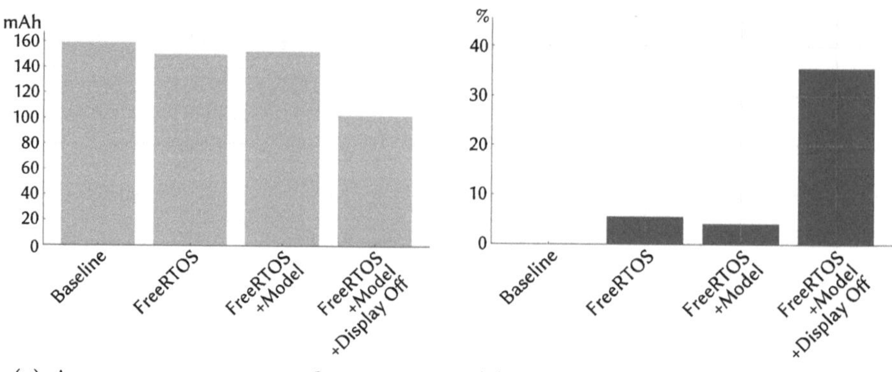

(a) Average current per configuration.   (b) Percentage reduction vs. baseline.

Fig. 7. Comparison of absolute and relative energy impact for each firmware version.

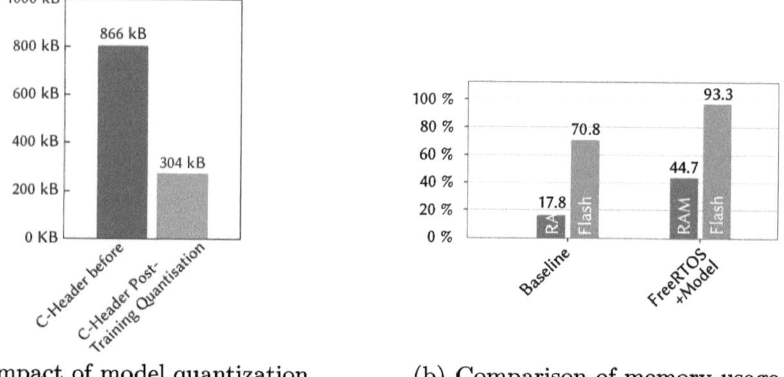

(a) Impact of model quantization.   (b) Comparison of memory usage

Fig. 8. Comparison of absolute and relative energy impact for each firmware version.

5   Discussion and Limitations

The three-task FreeRTOS schedule delivered the deterministic behavior that real-time sensing demands. Across two hours of continuous operation, the insole did not miss a single twenty-hertz sample, and the measured sensor-loop jitter stayed within two milliseconds. Fixing each task to a specific core and moving data only through queues proved sufficient to isolate radio interrupts and other asynchronous events.

The end-to-end delay combines the half-second sensor window, a 54 ms inference pass, and trivial queue overhead, yielding a worst-case latency of approximately 555 milliseconds. For rehabilitation feedback, this margin sits well below the one-second threshold that therapists consider acceptable. It would, however, be tight for applications such as powered exoskeleton control, which require sub-half-second responses.

Energy measurements indicate that the convolutional network contributes only 2.24 mA to a sensor-only baseline of 100 mA, maintaining an average draw of below 110 mA. A 500 mAh lithium-polymer cell, therefore, supports more than 4 h of operation. Radio bursts reach 150 mA, yet the class-change filter keeps the Bluetooth transmitter active less than seven percent of the time, so the impact on mean current is modest.

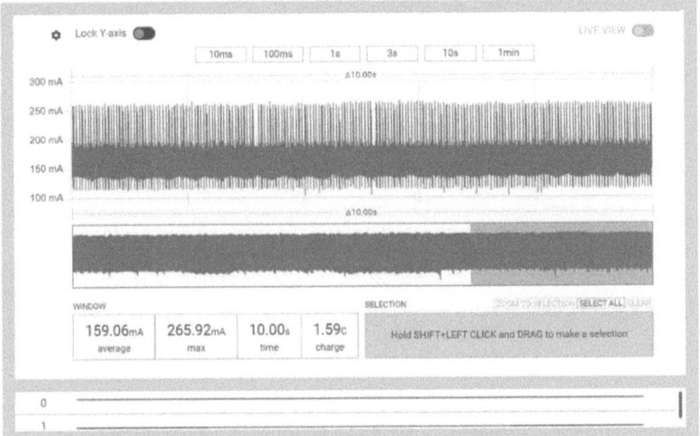

(a) Baseline: BLE @ 20 Hz, no RTOS or ML.

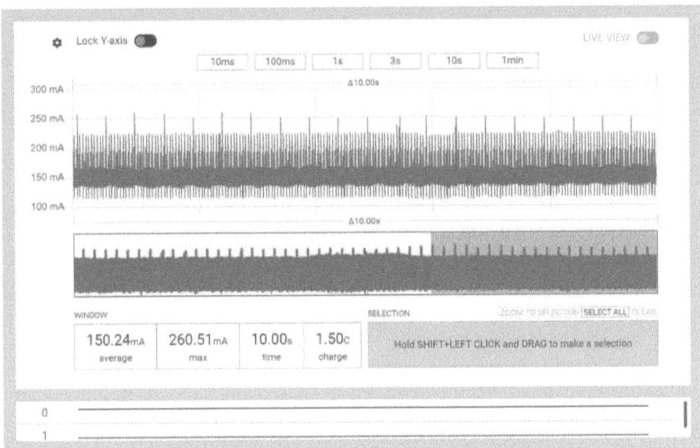

(b) FreeRTOS scheduler, BLE only.

Fig. 9. Current profiles for the baseline and FreeRTOS-only configurations.

Memory headroom is generous. The quantized network consumes 304 kB of flash and allocates 86 kB of RAM, leaving ample space for firmware updates or additional models. Static allocation and the absence of dynamic memory calls eliminate the risk of fragmentation during long runs.

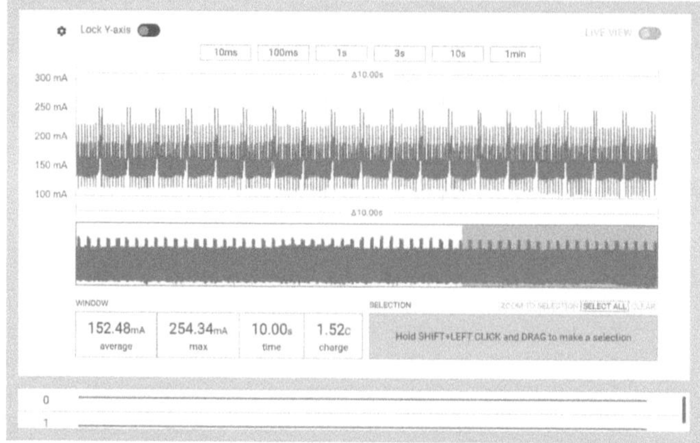

(c) FreeRTOS + CNN inference (0.5 s windows).

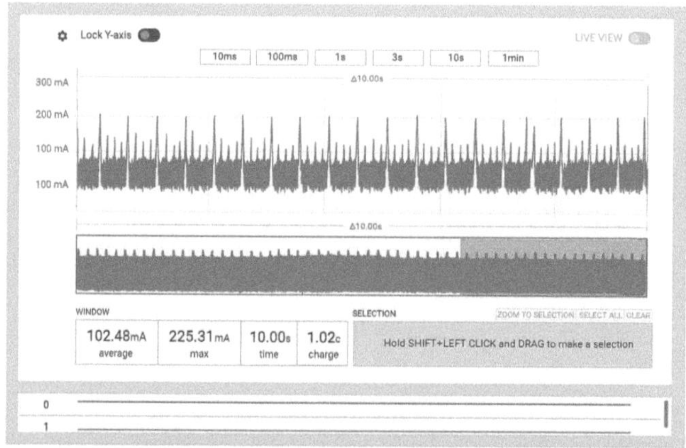

(d) Same as (c) with LCD turned off.

Fig. 10. Current profiles for configurations including CNN inference. Disabling the display saves about 50 mA.

Together, these results confirm the central premise of the work: edge inference performs well when treated as a periodic real-time task with a clearly defined worst-case execution time. The scheduler, not the network, is the primary lever for reliable field performance.

Several weaknesses remain. The dataset contains recordings from only eight healthy volunteers wearing similar shoes, so the model may not generalize to atypical footwear, pathological gait, or significant variations in body mass. The network recognizes seven broad activities and cannot yet distinguish fine-grained states such as stair climbing or uneven terrain. The inference rate is fixed at one window every 500 ms, regardless of walking speed; an adaptive window tied to step cadence could reduce latency and energy consumption. Baseline consumption is dominated by sensors and an always-on microcontroller, indicating that deeper sleep modes and duty-cycled sensing are necessary for prolonged outdoor wear. Finally, the design stores fixed weights; any personalization must occur off-device, followed by a firmware update, which undercuts the goal of complete privacy and autonomy. Future work should enlarge the dataset, test adaptive timing and low-power modes, and explore on-device continual learning that fits inside the existing memory budget.

6 Conclusion and Outlook

This work demonstrates that real-time human-activity recognition can be performed entirely within a shoe when inference is treated as an ordinary periodic task. A simple three-task FreeRTOS schedule on an ESP32-S3 meets every 20 Hz sampling deadline, while a post-training, quantized, one-dimensional convolutional network delivers 92.8% leave-one-subject-out accuracy in 54 milliseconds. The total latency from the first sample to the class label remains below 555 milliseconds, and the complete pipeline draws only 2.4 milliamps more than sensor-only operation, allowing for nearly 5 h of uptime on a modest 500mAh cell. The fundamental lesson that emerges is that the design of the scheduler, rather than the architecture of the model, often proves to be the predominant factor in achieving reliable edge intelligence. By assigning tasks to cores, determining worst-case execution times, and utilizing queues for all hand-offs, the insole circumvents the missed samples and jitter that often afflict bare-metal solutions. As memory and energy remain available, future research may investigate adaptive window sizes, deeper sleep modes, and on-device continual learning. These enhancements would propel the platform from a robust laboratory prototype to a practical, privacy-preserving instrument for routine gait monitoring and rehabilitation support.

Edge-AI, as proposed, enables power-efficient, real-time, and privacy-preserving HAR. It can also address challenges [9] like data handling and reducing annotation effort by processing sensor data directly on-device. To advance the state-of-the-art, one would explore adaptive sampling and inference rates tied to gait dynamics to further reduce latency and power consumption. In future, integrating on-device continual learning would allow the system to personalize models locally, enhancing privacy and performance. Finally, deploying deeper sleep modes and duty-cycled sensing could significantly extend battery life, paving the way for all-day wearable use in rehabilitation and gait monitoring scenarios.

Acknowledgments. This publication is a result of the research funded by the Federal Ministry for Economic Affairs and Climate Protection of Germany (KK5646401RH4) and by the Federal Ministry of Research, Technology and Space of Germany (03DPC0711A).

References

1. Agarwal, P., Alam, M.: A lightweight deep learning model for human activity recognition on edge devices. Procedia Comput. Sci. **167**, 2364–2373 (2020). https://doi.org/10.1016/j.procs.2020.03.289

2. Daghero, F., et al.: Human activity recognition on microcontrollers with quantized and adaptive deep neural networks. ACM Trans. Embed. Comput. Syst. **21**(4) (2022). https://doi.org/10.1145/3542819

3. Di Leo, K., Biagetti, G., Falaschetti, L., Crippa, P.: Microcontroller implementation of LSTM neural networks for dynamic hand gesture recognition. Sensors **25**(12) (2025). https://doi.org/10.3390/s25123831. https://www.mdpi.com/1424-8220/25/12/3831

4. Elstub, L., Grohowski, L., Wolf, D., Owen, M., Noehren, B., Zelik, K.: Effect of pressure insole sampling frequency on peak force accuracy during running. bioRxiv (2022). https://doi.org/10.1101/2022.05.18.492523

5. Elvitigala, D.S., Matthies, D.J.C., Weerasinghe, C., Nanayakkara, S.: Gymsoles++: combining google glass with smart insoles to improve body posture when performing squats. In: Proceedings of the 14th PErvasive Technologies Related to Assistive Environments Conference, pp. 48–54 (2021). https://doi.org/10.1145/3453892.3453898

6. Ferrari, P., Sisinni, E., Brandão, D., Rocha, M.: Evaluation of communication latency in industrial IoT applications. In: 2017 IEEE International Workshop on Measurement and Networking (M&N), pp. 1–6 (2017). https://doi.org/10.1109/IWMN.2017.8078359

7. Gabrecht, M.T., Wang, H., Matthies, D.J.C.: Pneushoe: a pneumatic smart shoe for activity recognition, terrain identification, and weight estimation. In: Proceedings of the 8th International Workshop on Sensor-Based Activity Recognition and Artificial Intelligence (iWOAR), pp. 1–5 (2023). https://doi.org/10.1145/3615834.3615853

8. Khandakar, A., et al.: Design and implementation of a complete wearable smart insole solution to measure plantar pressure and temperature (2022). https://arxiv.org/abs/2206.07779

9. Kirsten, K., et al.: The supervised learning dilemma: Lessons learned from a study in-the-wild. In: International Workshop on Sensor-Based Activity Recognition and Artificial Intelligence, pp. 181–195. Springer (2024). https://doi.org/10.1007/978-3-031-80856-2_12

10. Kos, A., et al.: Lightweight periodic scheduler in wearable devices for real-time biofeedback systems in sports and physical rehabilitation. Appl. Sci. **15**(12) (2025). https://doi.org/10.3390/app15126405. https://www.mdpi.com/2076-3417/15/12/6405

11. Lattanzi, E., Calisti, L., Contoli, C.: Are transformers a useful tool for tiny devices in human activity recognition? In: Proceedings of the 2024 8th International Conference on Advances in Artificial Intelligence, ICAAI 2024, pp. 339–344. Association for Computing Machinery, New York (2025). https://doi.org/10.1145/3704137.3704171

12. Li, X., Matthies, D.J.C.: Shoetect: detecting body posture, ambulation activity, gait abnormalities, and terrain with multisensory smart footwear. In: Proceedings of the 7th International Workshop on Sensor-based Activity Recognition and Artificial Intelligence (iWOAR), pp. 1–10 (2022). https://doi.org/10.1145/3558884.3558904

13. Lin, J., Chen, W.M., Lin, Y., Cohn, J., Gan, C., Han, S.: Mcunet: tiny deep learning on IoT devices (2020). https://arxiv.org/abs/2007.10319
14. Luna-Perejón, F., Salvador-Domínguez, B., Perez-Pe.ña, F., Rodríguez Corral, J.M., Escobar-Linero, E., Morgado-Estévez, A.: Correction: Luna-perejón et al. smart shoe insole based on polydimethylsiloxane composite capacitive sensors. sensors 2023, 23, 1298. Sensors **25**(11) (2025). https://doi.org/10.3390/s25113560. https://www.mdpi.com/1424-8220/25/11/3560
15. Maintainers, F.: Symmetric multiprocessing support in freertos kernel v11.1.0 (2024). https://www.freertos.org/symmetric-multiprocessing-introduction.html. Accessed 15 July 2025
16. Martini, E., et al.: Pressure-sensitive insoles for real-time gait-related applications. Sensors **20**(5) (2020). https://doi.org/10.3390/s20051448. https://www.mdpi.com/1424-8220/20/5/1448
17. Matthies, D.J.C., Roumen, T., Kuijper, A., Urban, B.: Capsoles: who is walking on what kind of floor? In: Proceedings of the 19th International Conference on Human-Computer Interaction with Mobile Devices and Services, pp. 1–14 (2017). https://doi.org/10.1145/3098279.3098545
18. Mazilu, S., et al.: Online detection of freezing of gait with smartphones and machine learning techniques. In: 2012 6th International Conference on Pervasive Computing Technologies for Healthcare (PervasiveHealth) and Workshops, pp. 123–130 (2012). https://doi.org/10.4108/icst.pervasivehealth.2012.248680
19. Nair, N., Thomas, C., Jayagopi, D.B.: Human activity recognition using temporal convolutional network. In: Proceedings of the 5th international Workshop on Sensor-based Activity Recognition and Interaction, pp. 1–8 (2018). https://doi.org/10.1145/3266157.3266221
20. Nazari, F., Shajari, A., Nahavandi, D., Mohajer, N.: Optimum signal duration for human activity recognition based on deep convolutional neural networks (2024). https://arxiv.org/abs/2406.11164
21. Park, B., Kim, M., Jung, D., Kim, J., Mun, K.R.: Smart insole-based abnormal gait identification: deep sequential networks and feature ablation study. Digit Health **11**, 20552076251333000 (2025)
22. Peretti, S., Contoli, C., Lattanzi, E.: An experimental study on the energy efficiency of feature selection for human activity recognition with wrist-worn devices. In: International Workshop on Sensor-Based Activity Recognition and Artificial Intelligence (iWOAR), pp. 40–54. Springer (2024). https://doi.org/10.1007/978-3-031-80856-2_3
23. Promwad Team: Choosing an rtos: Freertos vs. zephyr vs. threadx vs. mbed os (2025). https://promwad.com/news/choosing-rtos-freertos-zephyr-threadx-comparison. Accessed 15 July 2025
24. Santos, V.M., Gomes, B.B., Neto, M.A., Amaro, A.M.: A systematic review of insole sensor technology: recent studies and future directions. Appl. Sci. **14**(14) (2024). https://doi.org/10.3390/app14146085. https://www.mdpi.com/2076-3417/14/14/6085
25. Shakerian, A., Douet, V., Shoaraye Nejati, A., Landry, R.: Real-time sensor-embedded neural network for human activity recognition. Sensors **23**(19) (2023). https://doi.org/10.3390/s23198127. https://www.mdpi.com/1424-8220/23/19/8127
26. Shalby, H.H.Y., Roveri, M.: Dendron: enhancing human activity recognition with on-device tinyml learning. In: 2025 IEEE Symposium on Computational Intelligence on Engineering/Cyber Physical Systems (CIES), pp. 1–8. IEEE (2025). https://doi.org/10.1109/cies64955.2025.11007628

27. Tello, A., Degeler, V., Lazovik, A.: Too good to be true: accuracy overestimation in (re)current practices for human activity recognition. In: 2024 IEEE International Conference on Pervasive Computing and Communications Workshops and other Affiliated Events (PerCom Workshops), pp. 511–517. IEEE (2024). https://doi.org/10.1109/percomworkshops59983.2024.10503465
28. Wang, Q., et al.: A wireless, self-powered smart insole for gait monitoring and recognition via nonlinear synergistic pressure sensing. Sci. Adv. **11**(16), eadu1598 (2025). https://doi.org/10.1126/sciadv.adu1598
29. Willnow, P., Sternitzke, M., Schlonsak, R., Gabrecht, M., Matthies, D.J.C.: Surfsole: demonstrating real-time surface identification via capacitive sensing with neural networks. In: International Workshop on Sensor-Based Activity Recognition and Artificial Intelligence (iWOAR), pp. 251–259. Springer (2024). https://doi.org/10.1007/978-3-031-80856-2_16
30. Zhang, H., Li, C., Liu, W., Wang, J., Zhou, J., Wang, S.: A multi-sensor wearable system for the quantitative assessment of Parkinson's disease. Sensors **20**(21) (2020). https://doi.org/10.3390/s20216146. https://www.mdpi.com/1424-8220/20/21/6146
31. Zuo, J., Arvanitakis, G., Ndhlovu, M., Hacid, H.: Magneto: edge AI for human activity recognition – privacy and personalization (2024). https://arxiv.org/abs/2402.07180

Pervasive Intelligent Diagnostics for High-Tech Systems

Rob Bemthuis[1]([✉])[iD], Thomas Nägele[2][iD], and Cor van der Struijf[2]

[1] Pervasive Systems, University of Twente,
Drienerlolaan 5, 7522NB Enschede, The Netherlands
`r.h.bemthuis@utwente.nl`
[2] TNO-ESI, High Tech Campus 25, 5656AE Eindhoven, The Netherlands
`{thomas.nagele,cor.vanderstruijf}@tno.nl`

Abstract. High-tech systems are growing more complex due to mass customization, integration of diverse technologies, and long lifecycle demands. Customers increasingly expect service contracts based on performance and availability, yet diagnostics remain largely reactive and reliant on human expertise. This position paper proposes a Pervasive Intelligent Diagnostics (PID) framework that integrates pervasive sensing, model-based digital twins, and hybrid AI for predictive diagnostics and sustainable lifecycle management. PID embeds collaborative sensing and reasoning within operational environments. We outline a research agenda for leveraging pervasive sensing and digital twins to advance intelligent diagnostics in high-tech systems. Key directions include: integrating heterogeneous sensor data with system models, automatically generating diagnostic models, and evaluating them in high-tech case studies. Expected benefits include reduced downtime, improved resource use, and stronger retention of expert knowledge. These outcomes align with industry roadmaps for sustainable, dependable systems.

Keywords: Intelligent Diagnostics · Pervasive Computing · Digital Lifecycle Management · Digital Twins

1 Introduction

High-tech systems, such as semiconductor manufacturing equipment and advanced production lines, are evolving into software-intensive cyber-physical systems that span multiple engineering disciplines [12,15,23]. Mass customization makes each system unique, while digitalization extends operational lifetimes and introduces AI-enabled capabilities. These shifts have prompted a broader agenda for human-centric, resilient, and sustainable industry, often framed as Industry 5.0 [6]. In this paper, we treat diagnostics as a practical lever for this agenda.

Traditional diagnostic approaches are typically manual, reactive, and service-oriented, making them ill-suited for large-scale, distributed, and evolving systems. As a result, industry roadmaps (e.g., [16,17,19]) call for new design

Ö. Durmaz Incel et al. (Eds.): iWOAR 2025, LNCS 16292, pp. 343–352, 2026.
https://doi.org/10.1007/978-3-032-13312-0_20

and maintenance approaches that address increasing complexity, sustainability demands, and workforce challenges. Meeting these demands requires overcoming several interrelated challenges that affect the development and deployment of intelligent diagnostics in high-tech environments:

- **Technical complexity and data heterogeneity.** High-tech systems generate large, multimodal data streams from distributed sensors, controllers, and software logs. Data may be incomplete or noisy [30]. Frequent configuration changes can disrupt diagnostic models [7]. At the system level, subsystem dependencies can magnify fault effects.
- **Knowledge loss and organizational constraints.** Much diagnostic expertise is tacit, residing in experienced engineers [2]. Workforce turnover risks permanent knowledge loss, slowing both maintenance and innovation [9].
- **Sustainability and regulatory pressures.** Maintenance consumes resources, while unplanned downtime increases waste and emissions. Regulatory frameworks now emphasize energy efficiency, circularity, and responsible lifecycle management. Diagnostics should therefore meet both reliability and environmental goals [14, 26].

Pervasive computing (also known as ubiquitous computing) research envisions environments where sensing, computation, and reasoning are seamlessly embedded, scalable, and adaptive [27]. Applying these principles to diagnostics could potentially integrate intelligence throughout a system's lifecycle rather than adding it after design.

This position paper therefore asks: *How can pervasive sensing and digital twins be combined to create intelligent diagnostic systems that improve reliability, sustainability, and knowledge retention in high-tech equipment?* We use "digital twin" in a pragmatic sense: a validated, executable system model, continuously synchronized with the asset's state and configuration via operational data and design artifacts, that provides reference behavior and what-if analyses to support diagnostics across the lifecycle.

The remainder of the paper is structured as follows. Section 2 discusses background and related work. Section 3 defines research objectives. Section 4 outlines the proposed framework. Section 5 summarizes expected contributions, and Sect. 6 discusses future directions.

2   Background and Related Work

This section situates our work within five strands of prior work: data-driven systems engineering, digital twin–based anomaly detection, model-based diagnostics and hybrid AI, performance monitoring and telemetry, and pervasive systems. We summarize what each strand contributes and where gaps persist, motivating the design choices and research questions developed later in the paper.

2.1 Data-Driven Systems Engineering

Growing volumes of operational data offer opportunities to improve lifecycle performance and enable service-oriented business models. However, increased system complexity and customization challenge traditional systems engineering, which often depends on undocumented human expertise. TNO-ESI proposes integrating data-driven insights with knowledge-driven models to support system-level reasoning [11]. Demonstrators indicate that combining knowledge engineering and data analysis can semi-automatically identify root causes of factory performance degradation.

2.2 Digital Twins and Anomaly Detection

Digital twins replicate system behavior by combining domain-specific models with operational data. Feeding sensor data into virtual prototypes and simulators can yield digital twins that generate reference actuator behavior. Comparing reference and operational data enables automatic detection of anomalies and their root causes. Surveys identify digital twins as key enablers of predictive maintenance across product lifecycles [28,31]. By collecting real-time data, running simulations, and detecting subtle faults, they can reduce downtime and maintenance costs [5]. Research increasingly advocates AI-enhanced digital twin systems engineering for Industry 5.0, coupling systems engineering principles with AI to address complex industrial scenarios [29]. Digital twin frameworks have also been proposed to train diagnostic models from system-level data, reducing reliance on labeled fault data [18].

2.3 Model-Based Diagnostics and Hybrid AI

TNO-ESI has developed a model-based diagnostic methodology that supports diagnostics across the system lifecycle, from design to operation [20]. Diagnostic models and a probabilistic reasoning framework are derived semi-automatically from design artifacts. During design, the method algorithmically computes failure observability and sensor placement; during operation, it recommends repair or measurement actions from logged data.

The models, integrate with Model-Based Systems Engineering (MBSE) approaches, whose functional and hardware decomposition can improve scalability. Nonetheless, creating diagnostic models for systems with thousands of components remains challenging, and requires more automated use of structured information. Hybrid diagnostic frameworks have the potential to address this; for example, the FLAGS methodology fuses expert knowledge with machine learning for adaptive anomaly detection and root-cause analysis on sensor streams [24].

2.4 Performance Monitoring and Telemetry

Modern large-scale distributed software systems generate rich, high-dimensional telemetry data that can facilitate fine-grained anomaly detection [3,21]. Telemetry can be used to construct software dependency graphs, identify architectural anti-patterns, and detect anomalies [3]. Combining distributed traces with profiling metrics has yielded high-precision anomaly detection in microservice systems [21]. Large-scale systems produce telemetry data with hundreds of thousands of dimensions; recent work [13] provides datasets and reference implementations for anomaly detection in such settings. Benchmarks like RCAEval [22] offer datasets and evaluation frameworks for root-cause analysis.

2.5   Pervasive Systems Research

The Pervasive Systems group at the University of Twente develops environments enriched with sensors, computing, and wireless communication to address both societal and industrial needs [25]. Its research emphasizes unobtrusive sensing, scalability, adaptivity, and trust, principles that are key to pervasive computing. This vision, first articulated by Weiser [27], describes technology seamlessly embedded in daily life, augmenting human activity while remaining unobtrusive. Seminal advances in context-aware computing [1] and scalable sensor networks [8] extended this foundation to real-time, distributed, in situ decision-making.

Recent work underscores the continued relevance of pervasive systems research. For example, Bimpas et al. [4] survey how pervasive computing now underpins ambient intelligence through distributed, adaptive systems in complex environments. In parallel, emerging edge-based architectures support AI services in pervasive, or "smart" spaces, enabling the shift toward scalable, modular platforms at the network edge [10].

These principles also guide the design of our PID framework. Modern high-tech equipment operates as cyber-physical environments with heterogeneous sensing and distributed control. Integrating diagnostic intelligence into these environments aligns with the pervasive computing paradigm, where sensing, data fusion, and reasoning occur continuously and adaptively. In PID, diagnostics are embedded into normal system operation rather than added as a separate function, supporting the development of maintainable and sustainable high-tech systems.

3   Research Objectives

As a position paper, we articulate and assess the feasibility of a PID framework that (i) semi-automatically derives diagnostic and prognostic models from heterogeneous sensor data and systems engineering artifacts, (ii) maintains a synchronized digital twin for health monitoring, root-cause analysis, and prognosis, and (iii) supports human experts with hybrid AI and explanation to improve reliability, sustainability, and knowledge retention.

This objective has been translated into several research questions:

1. **Data and knowledge integration**: How can real-time sensor streams, telemetry, and operational logs be fused with design artifacts (e.g., MBSE models) to build and update a digital twin?

2. **Model generation**: How can structured knowledge from MBSE models be used to semi-automatically derive scalable, actionable probabilistic diagnostic models?
3. **Hybrid reasoning**: How can reasoning formalisms and AI be combined with human expertise to provide interpretable diagnostic suggestions?
4. **Sustainability and lifecycle impact**: How does predictive diagnostics affect resource use, energy efficiency, and lifecycle performance compared with reactive maintenance?
5. **Human–model co-learning and UX**: How can engineer feedback update models while the system, through transparent and provenance-aware explanations, teaches engineers?

Notice that the third research question focuses on interpretable *inference mechanisms*, whereas the fifth one addresses the *learning loop* and two-way knowledge transfer between humans and the system.

4   Proposed Framework

This section presents the proposed PID framework. It first describes the conceptual system architecture, structured into four main layers and that reflect the functional blocks shown in Fig. 1. Next, it outlines candidate approaches for generating and updating diagnostic models. Finally, it proposes an evaluation plan.

4.1   System Architecture

The PID framework comprises four layers (see Fig. 1):

1. **Pervasive sensing:** Distributed sensors embedded in high-tech assets collect multimodal data, including vibration, temperature, current, and pressure. Agents on edge devices manage sampling, buffering, and data transfer via on-premises gateways or message buses.
2. **Digital twin:** MBSE artifacts define a baseline model of structural and behavioral characteristics. Live sensor streams update the twin to produce near-real-time reference behavior, supporting deviation detection. The physical system and its virtual counterpart remain continuously synchronized.
3. **Diagnostic reasoning:** Probabilistic models (e.g., Bayesian networks) and anomaly detection algorithms compare reference and observed behaviors, identify root causes, and recommend interventions. Reasoning addresses both hardware (mechanical components, sensors) and software (control logic, orchestration) faults. Models are maintained in a registry and updated via online, offline, and batch training/tuning.
4. **Human-centric interface:** Engineers access dashboards, KPIs, alerts, and provenance-aware explanations (e.g., "what-if" probes). An annotation tool records feedback, such as confirmed diagnoses and repair outcomes, and feeds it into subsequent model updates.

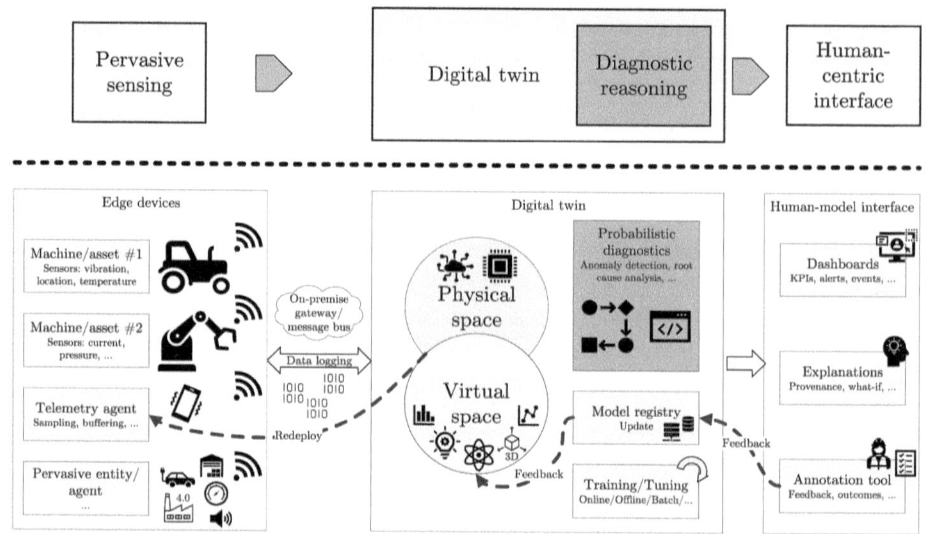

Fig. 1. PID framework based on pervasive sensing, digital twins, probabilistic diagnostics, and human–machine interaction.

These four layers define the conceptual architecture rather than a fixed implementation. They are intended as a starting point whose specific mechanisms will be refined and adapted to different domains, requirements, and insights gained from empirical evaluation.

4.2   Model Generation and Updating

The diagnostic network can be based on an ontology defining node types (e.g., functions, hardware, tests, observables) and their relationships. MBSE artifacts can be traversed to generate network components and link observables to specific sensors. During operation, models are updated incrementally with live data and engineer feedback. Annotation loops allow probability updates that combine statistical evidence with expert input, balancing adaptability and interpretability.

4.3   Evaluation Methodology

To validate the framework, we plan to implement prototypes in high-tech case studies with industrial partners. Each case will evaluate key performance indicators (KPIs):

1. **Diagnostic accuracy**: Agreement between system-generated diagnoses and expert assessments.
2. **Downtime reduction**: Reductions in mean time to repair (MTTR) and unplanned downtime.

3. **Sustainability impact**: Estimated resource savings (e.g., reduced energy use and fewer component replacements) enabled by predictive maintenance.
4. **Scalability**: Performance of model generation and reasoning as system size (components and sensors) increases.
5. **User feedback**: Engineer assessments of interpretability, contextual relevance, and practical value of recommendations.

Together, these indicators operationalize our three KPIs: reliability (accuracy, downtime), sustainability (impact, resource effects), and knowledge retention (user feedback and model reuse), with scalability enabling each at system level.

5 Expected Contributions and Benefits

This industrial research aims to demonstrate how pervasive sensing and digital twins can be combined to create intelligent diagnostic systems. Anticipated contributions include:

1. **Support operational availability**: Early fault detection and targeted diagnostic recommendations can shorten repair times and reduce unplanned downtime, contributing to more consistent system performance.
2. **Enhance sustainability**: Predictive diagnostics can inform maintenance strategies that reduce waste and energy consumption, supporting climate-neutral objectives.
3. **Preserve expert knowledge**: Capturing domain expertise in digital models and reasoning frameworks can help retain critical knowledge during workforce transitions.
4. **Advance MBSE practices**: Demonstrating the automatic generation of diagnostic models from MBSE artifacts may encourage closer integration of design and operational processes.
5. **Bridge research and industry**: Industrial case studies can provide evidence of the benefits of pervasive intelligence and support technology transfer.

6 Discussion and Outlook

We take the position that the growing complexity of high-tech systems can be addressed via four complementary verticals (i.e., pervasive sensing, model-based digital twins, hybrid diagnostic reasoning, and human-centric interaction), and oriented around cross-cutting system or organizational qualities (i.e., reliability, sustainability, and knowledge retention). In the view of this position paper, sensing provides observability; digital twins supply system context; diagnostic reasoning proposes actionable hypotheses; and the interface explains results and captures expert knowledge and feedback.

The proposed framework aligns with practices for managing complexity in high-tech systems and reducing unscheduled downtime through intelligent diagnostics. It also reflects the pervasive systems vision of ubiquitous sensing and embedded intelligence. Key challenges remain: data governance, privacy, and user trust in AI-driven recommendations. We must also address the scalability of model generation and user acceptance of AI-driven outputs. Sustainability metrics should be integrated explicitly so that diagnostic decisions balance operational performance and environmental impact.

Future work will explore federated learning and edge AI to enhance privacy and reduce communication overhead. We plan to integrate telemetry-based performance analysis with diagnostics to provide a more complete view of system health. Strengthening the human–machine interaction layer is key. Diagnostic insights should be presented in context and in interpretable, actionable forms to build operator trust and support effective decision-making. Aligned with systems engineering roadmaps and industrial collaboration, this research seeks to advance sustainable, dependable, and intelligent high-tech systems.

Acknowledgments. We gratefully acknowledge the support and collaboration of the TNO–UT Joint Innovation Centre for Digital Lifecycle Management (JIC DLM) and its partners. Some of the case studies presented were undertaken within these and other collaborative projects; the paper should be read with their applied industrial context in mind. We also thank Sabari Nathan Anbalagan for constructive feedback and helpful suggestions.

References

1. Abowd, G.D., Dey, A.K., Brown, P.J., Davies, N., Smith, M., Steggles, P.: Towards a better understanding of context and context-awareness. In: International Symposium on Handheld and Ubiquitous Computing, pp. 304–307. Springer (1999)
2. Aedo, I., Onorati, T., Tucci, C., Díaz, P., Montero, Á., Castro, J.: Bridging the gap between knowledge and human expertise: integrating explicit and tacit knowledge in maintenance operations. In: Proceedings of the 1st International Workshop on Human-Centered AI for Human-Machine Teams. CEUR Workshop Proceedings, vol. 3978. CEUR-WS.org (2024)
3. Al Maruf, A., Bakhtin, A., Cerny, T., Taibi, D.: Using microservice telemetry data for system dynamic analysis. In: 2022 IEEE International Conference on Service-Oriented System Engineering (SOSE), pp. 29–38. IEEE (2022)
4. Bimpas, A., Violos, J., Leivadeas, A., Varlamis, I.: Leveraging pervasive computing for ambient intelligence: a survey on recent advancements, applications and open challenges. Comput. Netw. **239**, 110156 (2024)
5. Bofill, J., Abisado, M., Villaverde, J., Sampedro, G.A.: Exploring digital twin-based fault monitoring: challenges and opportunities. Sensors **23**(16), 7087 (2023)
6. Breque, M., De Nul, L., Petridis, A.: Industry 5.0: towards a sustainable, human-centric and resilient European industry (2021). https://research-and-innovation.ec.europa.eu/knowledge-publications-tools-and-data/publications/all-publications/industry-50-towards-sustainable-human-centric-and-resilient-european-industry_en
7. Chapelin, J., et al.: Data-driven drift detection and diagnosis framework for predictive maintenance of heterogeneous production processes: application to a multiple tapping process. Eng. Appl. Artif. Intell. **139**, 109552 (2025)

8. Estrin, D., Govindan, R., Heidemann, J., Kumar, S.: Next century challenges: scalable coordination in sensor networks. In: Proceedings of the 5th Annual ACM/IEEE International Conference on Mobile Computing and Networking, pp. 263–270 (1999)

9. Galan, N.: Knowledge loss induced by organizational member turnover: a review of empirical literature, synthesis and future research directions (Part I). Learn. Organ. Int. J. **30**(2), 117–136 (2023)

10. Gill, S.S., et al.: Edge AI: a taxonomy, systematic review and future directions. Clust. Comput. **28**(1), 18 (2025)

11. Huijbrechts, B.: Empower system engineering with data insights. Technical report, TNO – ESI (Embedded Systems Innovation) (2019). https://downloads.esi.nl/leaflets/data_insights_2019c.pdf. Accessed 30 July 2025

12. Iqbal, R., Doctor, F., More, B., Mahmud, S., Yousuf, U.: Big data analytics and computational intelligence for cyber-physical systems: recent trends and state of the art applications. Futur. Gener. Comput. Syst. **105**, 766–778 (2020)

13. Islam, M.S., Rakha, M.S., Pourmajidi, W., Sivaloganathan, J., Steinbacher, J., Miranskyy, A.: Anomaly detection in large-scale cloud systems: an industry case and dataset. arXiv preprint arXiv:2411.09047 (2024)

14. Karuppiah, K., Sankaranarayanan, B., Ali, S.M.: On sustainable predictive maintenance: exploration of key barriers using an integrated approach. Sustain. Prod. Consum. **27**, 1537–1553 (2021)

15. Kim, J.H.: A review of cyber-physical system research relevant to the emerging IT trends: industry 4.0, IoT, big data, and cloud computing. J. Ind. Integr. Manag. **2**(03), 1750011 (2017)

16. Leibbrandt, W., Wesselius, J., Beenker, F.: TNO-ESI-Systems engineering methodologies for managing complexity in the high-tech equipment industry: our roadmap. Insight **25**(4), 15–21 (2022). https://doi.org/10.1002/inst.12406

17. List, F., Verberk, R., Janssen, V., Hulshof, E., van Ulsen, P., Stojanovic, I.: Roadmap for semiconductor manufacturing equipment 2024–2027. Technical report, Holland High Tech (2024). https://hollandhightech.nl/_asset/_public/Innovatie/Technologieen/z_pdf_roadmaps/240115-Roadmap-Semiconductor-Manufacturing-Equipment-2024-2027-V3.pdf. Accessed 30 July 2025

18. Mc Court, K., Mc Court, X., Du, S., Zeng, Z.: Use digital twins to support fault diagnosis from system-level condition-monitoring data. In: 2025 IEEE 22nd International Multi-Conference on Systems, Signals & Devices (SSD), pp. 1064–1069. IEEE (2025)

19. Meier, B., Skelin, M., Beenker, F., Leibbrandt, W.: HTSM systems engineering roadmap. Technical report, Holland High Tech (2020). https://hollandhightech.nl/_asset/_public/Innovatie/Technologieen/z_pdf_roadmaps/Roadmap-Systems-Engineering-update-2020-final-v20200724.pdf

20. Nägele, T., Barbini, L., van den Braak, G., Lipplaa, M., Piedrafita, A.: From knowledge graphs to probabilistic models for system-level diagnostics. In: 13th IMA International Conference on Modelling in Industrial Maintenance and Reliability - MIMAR2025 (2025)

21. Panahandeh, M., Hamou-Lhadj, A., Hamdaqa, M., Miller, J.: Serviceanomaly: an anomaly detection approach in microservices using distributed traces and profiling metrics. J. Syst. Softw. **209**, 111917 (2024)

22. Pham, L., Zhang, H., Ha, H., Salim, F., Zhang, X.: Rcaeval: a benchmark for root cause analysis of microservice systems with telemetry data. In: Companion Proceedings of the ACM on Web Conference 2025, pp. 777–780 (2025)

23. Sinha, D., Roy, R.: Reviewing cyber-physical system as a part of smart factory in industry 4.0. IEEE Eng. Manag. Rev. **48**(2), 103–117 (2020)
24. Steenwinckel, B., et al.: Flags: a methodology for adaptive anomaly detection and root cause analysis on sensor data streams by fusing expert knowledge with machine learning. Futur. Gener. Comput. Syst. **116**, 30–48 (2021)
25. University of Twente, EEMCS - PS Group: PS Group - Pervasive Systems (2025). https://www.utwente.nl/en/eemcs/ps/. Accessed 30 July 2025
26. Van Oudenhoven, B., Van de Calseyde, P., Basten, R., Demerouti, E.: Predictive maintenance for industry 5.0: behavioural inquiries from a work system perspective. Int. J. Prod. Res. **61**(22), 7846–7865 (2023)
27. Weiser, M.: The computer for the 21st century. ACM SIGMOBILE Mob. Comput. Commun. Rev. **3**(3), 3–11 (1999)
28. You, Y., Chen, C., Hu, F., Liu, Y., Ji, Z.: Advances of digital twins for predictive maintenance. Procedia Comput. Sci. **200**, 1471–1480 (2022)
29. Zhang, H., Li, Y., Zhang, S., Song, L., Tao, F.: Artificial intelligence-enhanced digital twin systems engineering towards the industrial metaverse in the era of Industry 5.0. Chin. J. Mech. Eng. **38**(1), 40 (2025)
30. Zhang, J., et al.: Multimodal data imputation and fusion for trustworthy fault diagnosis of mechanical systems. Eng. Appl. Artif. Intell. **150**, 110663 (2025)
31. Zhong, D., Xia, Z., Zhu, Y., Duan, J.: Overview of predictive maintenance based on digital twin technology. Heliyon **9**(4) (2023)

Toward Unobtrusive Monitoring of Everyday Activities Using Multimodal Wearable and Ambient Data: A Multiroom Living Lab Feasibility Study

Kristina Kirsten[1]([⊠])[iD], Tim Walz[2][iD], David Weese[2][iD], and Bert Arnrich[1][iD]

[1] Digital Health - Connected Healthcare, Hasso Plattner Institute,
University of Potsdam, Potsdam, Germany
{kristina.kirsten,bert.arnrich}@hpi.de
[2] D4L, data4life gGmbH, Potsdam, Germany
{tim.walz,david.weese}@hpi.de

Abstract. Developing unobtrusive systems for digital health monitoring requires addressing fundamental design challenges, such as understanding the role of spatial context, the detectability of repeated activities, and the impact of sensor placement. The SLICE study investigates these aspects in a feasibility setting. In a multiroom living lab, twelve participants performed routine and deliberately repetitive variants of everyday tasks, including handwashing, table cleaning, and checking if a door is closed. Using wearable motion sensors and Bluetooth beacons, we evaluated traditional and deep learning models across four tasks: activity recognition, execution pattern differentiation, spatial context, and sensor placement. In the multiclass activity recognition task, the Random Forest model reached F1 scores of 0.63 for handwashing, 0.68 for table cleaning, and 0.34 for door checking, resulting in a macro F1 of 0.55. The LSTM model performed less well overall, with F1 scores of 0.40, 0.42, and 0.17 (macro F1 = 0.47). Across tasks, distinguishing routine from repetitive execution remained inconsistent, suggesting that simulated repetition alone may not yield distinct sensor signals. Location features improved accuracy, and the right wrist provided stronger input for asymmetric activities. We also describe the modular data collection platform D4L Collect, which supported synchronized multimodal sensing, task annotation, and questionnaire delivery. The findings demonstrate the potential of combining wearable and location data for behavioral monitoring and illustrate how feasibility studies can inform the design of robust digital health systems for everyday use.

Keywords: HAR · IPS · Wearables · Digital Mental Health

1 Introduction

Wearable-based human activity recognition (HAR) has become a central approach in digital health, enabling continuous and unobtrusive monitoring of daily

Ö. Durmaz Incel et al. (Eds.): iWOAR 2025, LNCS 16292, pp. 353–363, 2026.
https://doi.org/10.1007/978-3-032-13312-0_21

life behavior. While established methods can accurately detect common physical activities, capturing more subtle aspects of behavior, such as variations in how activities are executed or when they are repeated, remains a complex and under-explored challenge. Understanding such nuances is essential for advancing digital phenotyping, as repetitive or altered execution of everyday actions may provide valuable insights into well-being, habit formation, or mental health symptoms. For example, compulsive behavior in conditions such as obsessive-compulsive disorder (OCD) often manifests through repeated actions, making it a potential application area for such monitoring systems.

Our long-term vision is to develop integrated tools that combine objective sensor data with subjective input, such as questionnaire responses, to support behavioral monitoring in everyday life. As a step toward this goal, we conducted the SLICE study (*Simulated Location-based Identification of Compulsive Events*), a feasibility study in a multiroom living lab under semi-structured conditions. Twelve participants performed both routine and deliberately repetitive variants of handwashing, table cleaning, and door checking – activities that are not only common in daily life but also relevant in clinical contexts. Participants wore motion sensors on both wrists, and their location was tracked using multiple ultra-wideband (UWB) beacons placed throughout the environment. In addition, we describe the mobile data collection platform *D4L Collect*, which was developed collaboratively and shaped by the SLICE use case to support multimodal sensing, annotation, and questionnaire delivery.

We evaluated classification performance across four tasks: activity recognition, execution pattern differentiation, spatial context, and sensor placement. Rather than optimizing models, the goal was to examine the feasibility of distinguishing routine and repetitive behaviors and to assess how location information and sensor configuration affect recognition. These findings provide insights that can guide the design of unobtrusive behavioral monitoring systems and lay the basis for future studies in clinical populations and real-world environments.

2   Related Work

The broad topic of HAR has been widely explored over the past two decades, with significant improvements in accuracy driven by the rapid development and widespread adoption of consumer-grade wearables, such as smartwatches and even smart rings [16]. Multimodal and personalized approaches have been frequently discussed in the literature. Although deep neural networks are commonly explored in this context, particularly on large-scale public datasets such as Opportunity [4] or WISDM [12], traditional supervised machine learning models, such as Random Forests (RFs), are still frequently used. This is especially true in scenarios involving smaller datasets, limited computational resources, or the need for interpretability. Recent benchmarking studies confirm that RF remain competitive with deep models, particularly for sensor-based HAR tasks using moderate-sized datasets [9].

In recent years, conducting HAR studies outside the laboratory, in daily life, has gained significant attention, particularly in the field of digital health, due to the growing interest in capturing a more holistic and realistic view of human behavior. Despite their enormous value, such studies come with specific requirements, from the need for an unobtrusive, low-cost, user-friendly sensor setup to addressing the unsupervised nature of the environment, while still extracting reliable information about activities from a continuous data stream [1,6,11]. While applications of HAR in digital health are becoming more common, their use for mental health monitoring is still limited [10]. In particular, studies targeting OCD have mostly focused on one specific behavior, namely handwashing [15], and are often conducted in controlled environments [8,14]. Prior work has demonstrated that simulated compulsive and routine handwashing can be distinguished using wearable sensor data and supervised learning models [3,15]. The SLICE study extends this research by exploring how such behaviors can be detected in realistic environments with more complex activity patterns.

3   Study Design: SLICE

The study presented in this paper, titled **SLICE** (*Simulated Location-based Identification of Compulsive Events*), is a semi-controlled feasibility study investigating the potential of wearable devices and indoor localization to detect routine and repetitive activity patterns. The study consisted of a one-hour session in which participants engaged in both naturalistic and protocol-driven activities within a semi-controlled multiroom residential lab environment.

3.1   Study Design and Procedure

The feasibility study was conducted at the Hasso Plattner Institute in Potsdam, Germany, designed to replicate everyday living conditions (Fig. 1). The environment included a kitchen, bathroom, main room, and hallways, and supported high-resolution, multimodal sensor data collection. The study was approved by the ethics commission of the University of Potsdam (Approval No. 38/2022). Each participant completed the recording session alone in the lab. They engaged in everyday activities (e.g., reading, preparing food, working on a laptop), which served as a baseline (NULL data), and additionally performed three target activities: handwashing, table cleaning, and door checking. Each was carried out in two variants, representing routine execution and repetitive execution patterns, where repetitive meant three consecutive repetitions for table cleaning and handwashing, and five consecutive repetitions for door checks.

3.2   Participants

Seventeen healthy adults were recruited; two were excluded because they did not meet the inclusion requirements. Of the fifteen eligible participants, valid data were obtained from twelve participants.

- **Age:** $M = 26.27$, $SD = 4.36$, range $= 18$–37
- **Gender:** 8 female, 7 male
- **Handedness:** 13 right-handed, 2 left-handed

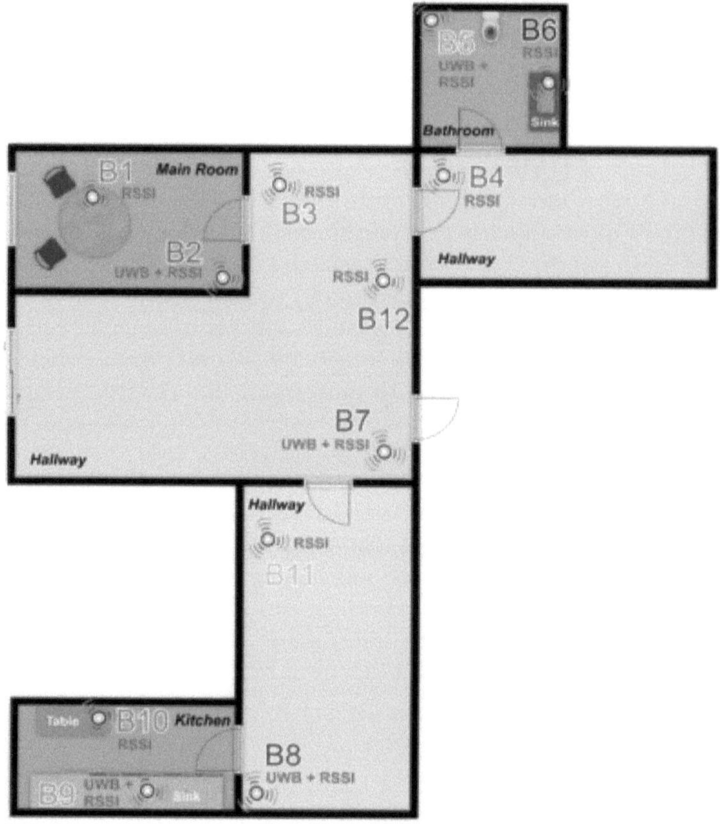

Fig. 1. Floor plan of the multiroom living lab with beacon locations.

3.3   Sensor Setup

Participants wore two wrist-mounted inertial measurement unit (IMU) devices recording tri-axial free acceleration, angular velocity, and Euler angles at 60 Hz. A head-mounted egocentric camera provided first-person video for annotation, which was deleted after processing. Indoor localization was supported by UWB beacons placed in key areas (kitchen, bathroom, hallway) to provide precise distance estimation.

3.4   Data Collection Platform: D4L Collect

Sensor data was collected using **D4L Collect**, a secure and GDPR compliant mobile research platform developed by Data4Life[1] in close collaboration with our academic team. The SLICE study played a key role in shaping the

---

[1] https://www.data4life.care/en/our-solutions/d4l-collect/.

platform's functionality, serving as a representative use case for digital health research focused on real-world behavior monitoring.

D4L Collect enables unified acquisition of multimodal data, including raw signals from wearable devices such as IMU sensors and fitness trackers, biosignals like electrocardiogram (ECG), derived physiological parameters such as heart rate, general health metrics, and blood glucose levels. It also supports location tracking through Bluetooth beacons using both Received Signal Strength Indicator (RSSI) and UWB signals. The platform allows for the collection of questionnaire-based data, including standardized instruments such as patient-reported outcome measurements (PROMs) and ecological momentary assessments (EMAs). It offers time-synchronized recording, flexible task annotation, and interoperable data formats, while maintaining full researcher control over study design and data storage. Studies can be set up and managed through an intuitive web interface that requires no programming expertise, and participants contribute data through a mobile app that facilitates device setup and user engagement. D4L Collect is well-suited for longitudinal studies, enabling researchers to monitor participants over extended periods to better understand health trajectories, behavioral patterns, and intervention effects in everyday settings. The platform is already in use across various studies, such as in [2].

3.5   Annotation and Behavioral Statistics

All recordings were manually annotated using the ELAN open-source annotation platform [13] based on the first-person video footage to establish ground truth for supervised learning. A total of 893 activity instances were labeled across the 12 complete datasets. The single activity counts and the mean execution duration in seconds are listed in Table 1. With these annotations, we created a reliable dataset for training and evaluating multimodal activity recognition models, with a particular focus on identifying behaviors that resemble compulsive-like routines in a setting that closely reflects everyday life.

Table 1. Annotated activities across participants (N = 12)

Activity	Count	Mean Duration (s)
Door Checks	351	1.72
Handwashing	282	18.41
Table Cleanings	260	8.43

4   Methodology

The following section describes the preprocessing pipeline, feature extraction methods, and machine learning approaches used to analyze the sensor and location data collected in the SLICE study. We describe the classification tasks, model configurations, and evaluation procedures applied to distinguish between activity types and execution patterns.

4.1 Data Preprocessing

Raw data from IMU sensors and UWB beacons was synchronized using relative timestamps, with gaps, duplicates, and missing entries corrected or imputed; temporal alignment was validated through video annotations. IMU signals were filtered with a low-pass Butterworth filter to remove high-frequency noise, while UWB distance estimates were smoothed using a Kalman filter. Activities were annotated from egocentric video using the ELAN annotation software [13], with labels specifying both activity type and execution variant (routine or repetitive).

4.2 Machine Learning

Statistical features (mean, standard deviation, skewness, kurtosis, signal energy) were extracted from IMU and UWB data using three-second sliding windows with tsfresh [7], computed per sensor axis. All experiments used leave-one-subject-out (LOSO) cross-validation with evaluation based on accuracy, precision, recall, F1 score, confusion matrices, and receiver operating characteristic (ROC)-area under the curve (AUC). For feature-based classification, an RF model was trained with class imbalance addressed using synthetic minority over-sampling technique (SMOTE) [5] and recursive feature elimination (RFE) applied for feature selection. In parallel, an Long Short-Term Memory (LSTM) network with a 128-unit hidden layer, dropout (0.5), and softmax output was trained directly on raw IMU and UWB sequences.

4.3 Overview of Classification Tasks

We explored four classification tasks reflecting both deployment scenarios and methodological considerations:

- **Task 1: Multiclass Activity Classification.** Segments were classified as `handwashing`, `table`, `door`, or `NULL`, independent of execution style. This task addresses general activity recognition.
- **Task 2: Routine vs. Repetitive Execution.** We tested whether models can distinguish between routine and repetitive variants of the same activity (e.g., washing hands once vs. three times). `NULL` windows were excluded, enabling evaluation of whether wearable and location data capture execution differences.
- **Task 3: Contribution of Location Features.** To assess spatial context, we compared model performance with/without UWB-based location features, testing whether positional information improves activity recognition.
- **Task 4: Sensor-Hand Relevance.** Models were trained with data from the left wrist, right wrist, or both. This setup explores the effect of sensor placement, particularly for asymmetric activities (door, table) versus symmetric ones (handwashing).

5   Results

Task 1 (Multiclass Activity Classification). The RF model classified segments as `handwashing`, `table`, or `door`, achieving F1 scores of 0.63, 0.68, and 0.34 respectively (macro F1 = 0.55). `Handwashing` and `table` were recognized reliably, while `door` was often confused with background activity (Appendix A.1). The LSTM performed weaker, with F1 scores of 0.40, 0.42, and 0.17 (macro F1 = 0.47), showing high confusion between classes, especially for `door` (Appendix A.2). Overall, the RF outperformed the LSTM, suggesting feature-based classification was more effective than sequence modeling with a basic LSTM.

Task 2 (Single vs. Repetitive Execution). Neither model reliably distinguished routine from repetitive behavior. Recall for repetition was high, but overall performance remained near chance. The RF was biased toward repetition, rarely detecting routine executions, while the LSTM showed similar trends with low specificity and poor class balance. These results highlight the limits of simulated repetition and the need for richer signals or real-world data.

Task 3 (Influence of Location). The RF showed only slight gains from adding location features, with small improvements for `handwashing` and `table`, while `door` remained challenging to classify. The LSTM showed smaller but consistent gains. These findings underline the added value of spatial context for distinguishing activities with overlapping movement patterns.

Task 4 (Sensor-Hand Relevance). For the RF, the left wrist gave an F1 of 0.63 for `handwashing`, but poor results for `table` (0.26) and `door` (0.13). The right wrist markedly improved `table` (0.68) and slightly improved `door` (0.18), but reduced `handwashing` (0.53). The overall ROC-AUC remained similar (0.87), suggesting that single-sensor setups remain viable. The LSTM showed a comparable trend, with stronger results on the right wrist for `table` (0.57 vs. 0.08) and failing to detect `door` activities, while `handwashing` was slightly better on the right (0.42 vs. 0.40). These patterns likely reflect right-hand dominance in most participants, underscoring the importance of sensor placement.

6   Discussion

The SLICE study examined the feasibility of using wearable IMU sensors and UWB beacons to classify daily activities and simulate compulsive-like behavior in a semi-controlled home environment. While general activity recognition showed promise, detecting subtle execution differences proved substantially harder.

In **Task 1**, both models classified target activities reasonably well, with the RF outperforming the LSTM. `Door` checking was the most difficult to detect, often misclassified as `NULL`, while `handwashing` and `table` cleaning were recognized more reliably. The weak performance on `door` checking likely reflects its brief, variable nature (avg. 1 s), which is poorly captured in 3 s windows, making it a challenging target for window-based models.

In **Task 2**, neither model distinguished routine from compulsive-like behavior reliably. Both overpredicted the compulsive class, yielding low specificity and near-chance balanced accuracy. This suggests that simulated repetitions did not provide enough signal variation, highlighting the limitations of scripted tasks with non-clinical participants as proxies for compulsivity.

Task 3 confirmed the value of spatial context: removing location features reduced performance, particularly for the RF. Room-level positioning thus offers useful contextual cues for indoor activity recognition.

Task 4 demonstrated the impact of sensor placement. The right wrist yielded stronger results for asymmetric tasks (`door`, `table`), while both wrists combined gave the best overall accuracy. As most participants were right-handed, this points to the role of hand dominance, which should be considered in future sensor setups.

Overall, the SLICE study highlights the potential of multimodal wearable and environmental sensing for unobtrusive monitoring, but also emphasizes the need for more naturalistic, clinically grounded data to effectively model mental health conditions such as obsessive-compulsive disorder.

7   Conclusion and Future Work

The SLICE study examined the feasibility of identifying routine and compulsive-like behavior using wearable IMU sensors and UWB-based indoor location data in a semi-controlled multiroom living lab. We evaluated several classification tasks with traditional and deep learning models, focusing on activity recognition, execution patterns, spatial context, and sensor placement.

Activity classification performed well, particularly for `handwashing` and `table` cleaning, but neither model reliably distinguished routine from repetitive behavior. This indicates that simulated compulsive-like executions lack the distinct sensor signatures needed for accurate classification, especially when performed by non-clinical participants. These results highlight both the potential and the current limitations of sensor-based approaches for monitoring behaviors relevant to obsessive-compulsive disorder. Beyond classification, this work contributes a scalable, modular setup for multimodal data collection, enabled by the D4L Collect platform, which supports reproducible digital health research in everyday contexts. Future work will focus on collecting data from clinical populations in natural settings to capture clinically meaningful behavioral variation. We also plan to integrate subjective measures such as EMAs, and to explore transfer learning and personalization strategies to improve generalizability and clinical relevance in OCD research.

Acknowledgements. We would like to thank all participants who took part in the study for their time and cooperation. We also gratefully acknowledge the development team at Data4Life for providing and maintaining the D4L Collect platform, and for their support with technical issues during data collection.

A   Additional Results

A.1   Task 1: Random Forest Performance

The RF model achieved strong results (macro F1 = 0.55), with reliable recognition of `handwashing` and `table`, but frequent confusion of `door` with `NULL` (Fig. 2).

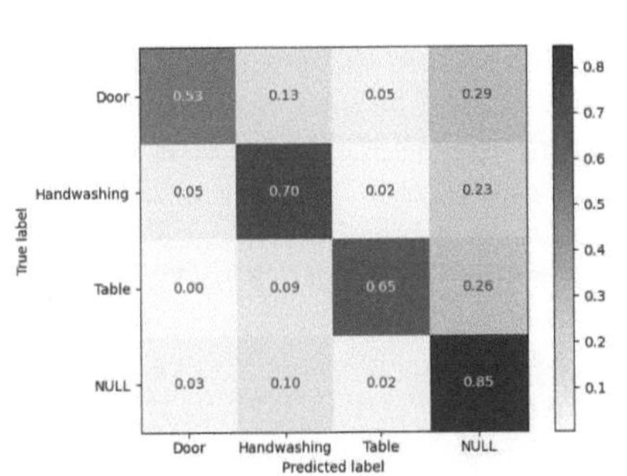

(a) Confusion matrix showing reduced performance for **door**.

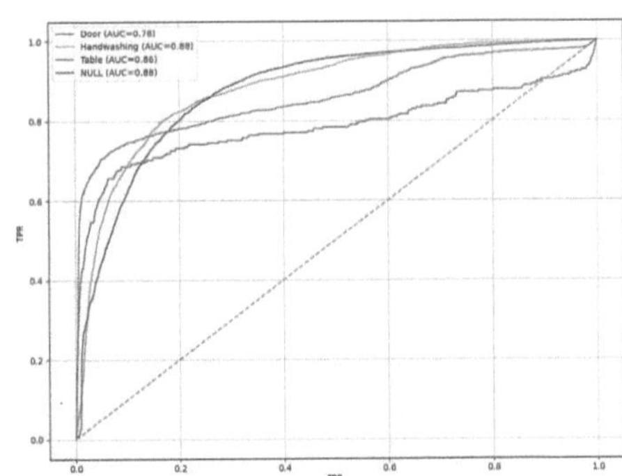

(b) ROC curves with highest AUC for **handwashing**.

Fig. 2. RF performance on Task 1.

A.2   Task 1: LSTM Performance

The LSTM model showed weaker performance (macro F1 = 0.47). Confusion matrices indicate substantial overlap between classes, especially `door` and `NULL`, and ROC curves show lower discriminability overall (Fig. 3).

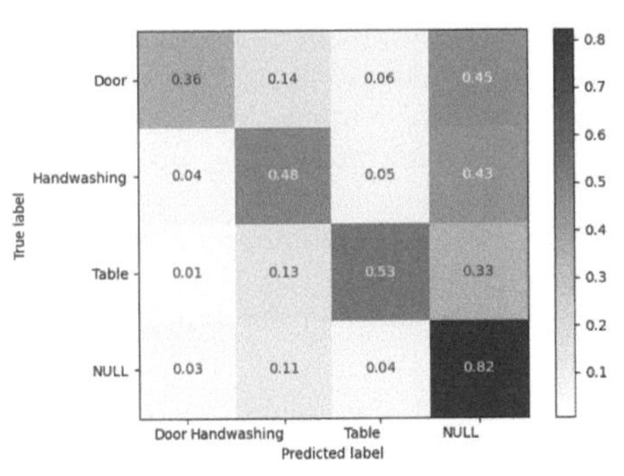

(a) Confusion matrix showing increased class confusion compared to the RF.

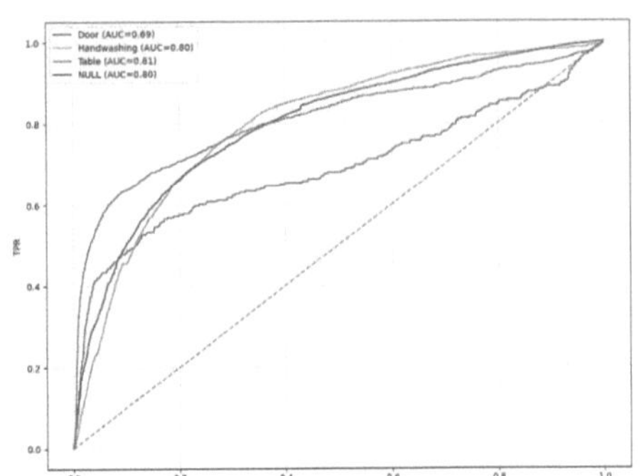

(b) ROC curves for the LSTM.

Fig. 3. LSTM performance on Task 1.

References

1. Al Machot, F., Ranasinghe, S., Plattner, J., Jnoub, N.: Human activity recognition based on real life scenarios. In: 2018 IEEE International Conference on Pervasive Computing and Communications Workshops (PerCom Workshops), pp. 3–8. IEEE (2018)
2. Albert, J., et al.: Using wearable sensors in stroke rehabilitation. In: Konak, O., Arnrich, B., Bieber, G., Kuijper, A., Fudickar, S. (eds.) Sensor-Based Activity Recognition and Artificial Intelligence, pp. 277–282. Springer, Cham (2025)
3. Burchard, R., Scholl, P.M., Lieb, R., Van Laerhoven, K., Wahl, K.: Washspot: real-time spotting and detection of enacted compulsive hand washing with wearable devices. In: Adjunct Proceedings of the 2022 ACM International Joint Conference on Pervasive and Ubiquitous Computing and the 2022 ACM International Symposium on Wearable Computers, pp. 483–487 (2022)
4. Chavarriaga, R., et al.: The opportunity challenge: a benchmark database for on-body sensor-based activity recognition. Pattern Recognit. Lett. **34**(15), 2033–2042 (2013)
5. Chawla, N.V., Bowyer, K.W., Hall, L.O., Kegelmeyer, W.P.: SMOTE: synthetic minority over-sampling technique. J. Artif. Intell. Res. **16**(1), 321–357 (2002)
6. Chen, K., Zhang, D., Yao, L., Guo, B., Yu, Z., Liu, Y.: Deep learning for sensor-based human activity recognition: overview, challenges, and opportunities. ACM Comput. Surv. (CSUR) **54**(4), 1–40 (2021)
7. Christ, M., Braun, N., Neuffer, J., Kempa-Liehr, A.W.: Time series FeatuRe extraction on basis of scalable hypothesis tests (tsfresh – a python package). Neurocomputing **307**, 72–77 (2018). https://doi.org/10.1016/j.neucom.2018.03.067. https://linkinghub.elsevier.com/retrieve/pii/S0925231218304843
8. Frank, A.C., Li, R., Peterson, B.S., Narayanan, S.S.: Wearable and mobile technologies for the evaluation and treatment of obsessive-compulsive disorder: scoping review. JMIR Mental Health **10**, e45572 (2023)
9. Hossain, M.M., Han, T.A., Ara, S.S., Shamszaman, Z.U.: Benchmarking classical, deep, and generative models for human activity recognition. arXiv preprint arXiv:2501.08471 (2025)
10. Kirsten, K., Arnrich, B.: Elements of a system for automatic monitoring of specific mental health characteristics at home. In: Proceedings of the 25th International Multiconference Information Society 2022, IS 2022, Ljubljana, Slovenia (2022)
11. Kirsten, K., et al.: The supervised learning dilemma: lessons learned from a study in-the-wild. In: Konak, O., Arnrich, B., Bieber, G., Kuijper, A., Fudickar, S. (eds.) Sensor-Based Activity Recognition and Artificial Intelligence, pp. 181–195. Springer (2025)
12. Kwapisz, J.R., Weiss, G.M., Moore, S.A.: Activity recognition using cell phone accelerometers. ACM SIGKDD Explor. Newsl. **12**(2), 74–82 (2011)
13. Max Planck Institute for Psycholinguistics, The Language Archive: Elan (2025). https://archive.mpi.nl/tla/elan. [Computer software]

14. Olesen, K.V., Lønfeldt, N.N., Das, S., Pagsberg, A.K., Clemmensen, L.K.H.: Predicting obsessive-compulsive disorder events in children and adolescents in the wild using a wearable biosensor (wrist angel): protocol for the analysis plan of a non-randomized pilot study. JMIR Res. Protoc. **12**(1), e48571 (2023)
15. Wahl, K., et al.: On the automatic detection of enacted compulsive hand washing using commercially available wearable devices. Comput. Biol. Med. **143**, 105280 (2022)
16. Wang, J., Chen, Y., Hao, S., Peng, X., Hu, L.: Deep learning for sensor-based activity recognition: a survey. Pattern Recogn. Lett. **119**, 3–11 (2019)

Evaluating LoRa Mesh Networks for Personal Dead Reckoning of Firefighters

Arnout Luinge[1] and Sabari Nathan Anbalagan[1,2]

[1] Pervasive Systems, EEMCS, University of Twente, Drienerlolaan 5, 7522 NB Enschede, The Netherlands
sabari@inertia-technology.com
[2] Inertia Technology B. V., Hengelosestraat 583, 7521 AG Enschede, The Netherlands
https://inertia-technology.com/

Abstract. Reliable localization of firefighters, especially in indoor and GPS-denied environments, remains a persistent challenge. Personal Dead Reckoning (PDR), powered by wearable inertial sensors, presents a viable solution but relies on resilient communication to transmit real-time position data to coordination centers. This paper examines the feasibility of using LoRa-based mesh networks as an infrastructure-free communication solution for wearable PDR systems in firefighting scenarios. We evaluate the performance of Meshtastic LoRa mesh nodes through controlled range tests and a live multi-floor residential firefighting exercise. Results indicate that LoRa mesh networks can meet the data needs of wearable PDR systems in most operational contexts, with minimal infrastructure and setup. We also propose practical deployment strategies, including firetruck-node integration and repeater placement, demonstrating that many building types can be covered with minimal effort. These findings support the development of robust, infrastructure-independent systems for on-body localization and mission-critical communication.

Keywords: LoRaMesh · Meshtastic · IMU · Firefighters

1 Introduction

Firefighters are frequently deployed in environments where standard GPS-based localization fails - deep inside buildings, underground, or in rapidly changing emergency contexts. Knowing the exact location of each responder is essential for safety, rescue coordination, and post-event analysis [5]. Personal Dead Reckoning (PDR) offers a promising wearable solution, estimating position based on inertial sensor data [1]. However, its effectiveness hinges on the ability to transmit these data reliably to commanders or central systems in real time.

In fire scenarios, the existing communication infrastructure can be compromised, unavailable, or impractical to use. Traditional methods like voice updates

© The Author(s), under exclusive license to Springer Nature Switzerland AG 2026
Ö. Durmaz Incel et al. (Eds.): iWOAR 2025, LNCS 16292, pp. 364–372, 2026.
https://doi.org/10.1007/978-3-032-13312-0_22

are unreliable under stress, and cellular or Wi-Fi-based systems depend on infrastructure that may not exist or remain functional. This study investigates whether LoRa-based mesh networks, specifically the open-source Meshtastic platform [3], can fill this communication gap. We focus on practical deployment requirements such as ease of setup, connectivity, and range, particularly when used to support PDR in real-world firefighter deployment contexts.

2   Background and Related Works

PDR systems use Inertial Measurement Units (IMUs) worn on the body to infer movement. These sensors capture accelerations, rotations, and magnetic headings to estimate position changes relative to a starting point. PDR works in GPS-denied spaces like stairwells, basements, and tunnels. Yet, without a robust wireless link, even the most accurate on-body localization cannot be utilized in real-time decision making.

Many indoor localization systems (e.g., Epic Blue's Shyn [2], NASA POINTER [4]) depend on BLE, Wi-Fi, or cellular LTE-M/NB-IoT networks. However, these require existing infrastructure or involve proprietary, bulky systems not suitable for dynamic, ad hoc deployment.

LoRa mesh networks overcome these constraints through peer-to-peer communication. Nodes can join dynamically and forward data across multiple hops, with no fixed infrastructure. Meshtastic offers encrypted multi-hop messaging on inexpensive hardware with minimal configuration [3]. These properties make it ideal for body-centric systems in firefighting.

3   Methodology

We used Heltec WiFi LoRa 32 V3 microcontrollers flashed with Meshtastic firmware to emulate wearable PDR nodes. Devices were mounted on poles (simulating body-worn elevation) or carried by firefighters.
In each test setup, the network included:

- One firetruck node: static, representing a command centre for fire-fighting operation (see Fig. 1a)
- One wearable node: mobile, representing a firefighter in action (see Figs. 1b and 1c)
- Optional static repeaters (for extended coverage)

Communication used Meshtastic's "LongFast" mode, supporting small PDR data packets. Although the PDR packets are usually 10–12 bytes sent every 10 s, during the experiments, the nodes were emulated to send only 5 bytes every 5 s due to software limitations. Throughput and delivery were monitored using onboard metrics and Meshtastic message acknowledgments. We organized the environments into four categories:

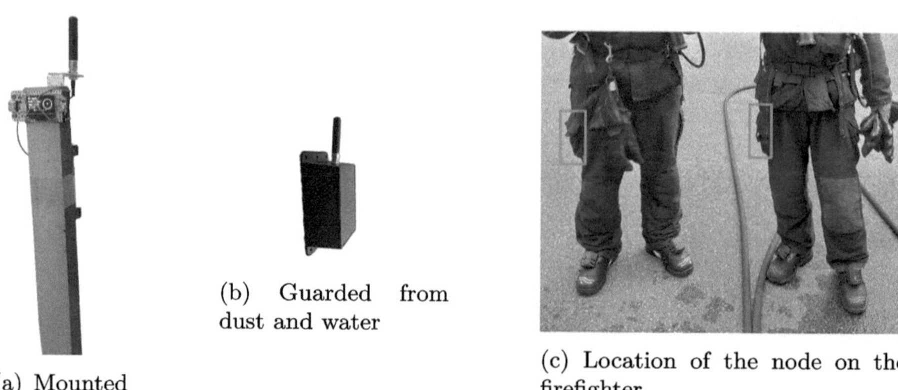

(a) Mounted
on a pole

(b)   Guarded   from
dust and water

(c) Location of the node on the
firefighter

Fig. 1. Nodes used in experiments

1. Outdoor Environments: forest path with gentle hills
2. Residential and Commercial Buildings: office, terraced house
3. Underground Structures: multi-level garage
4. Live Firefighting Scenario: multi-floor house with real firefighters, with and without fire

4   Results and Observations

4.1   Outdoor Environments

In forested paths (see Fig. 2) and gentle hillside terrain (see Fig. 3), we observed line-of-sight communication up to 2.2 km. Connection quality dropped when terrain or structures interrupted LOS. The mesh can maintain multi-hop stability across minor elevation/interruptions.

4.2   Residential and Commercial Buildings

In a 3-floor residential home (see Fig. 4), 5-floor narrow office building (see Fig. 5) and a 12-floor lean tower (see Fig. 6), a single-hop communication was sufficient. In the case of a 5-floor but wide office building (see Fig. 7), a repeater placed near stairwells improved delivery from deep interior rooms.

4.3   Underground Structures

Multi-level car parks and garages required one or two strategically placed repeaters. Stairwells and ramps offered effective relay points. One floor underground bicycle parking was sufficiently covered by single-hop. The results are presented in Fig. 8.

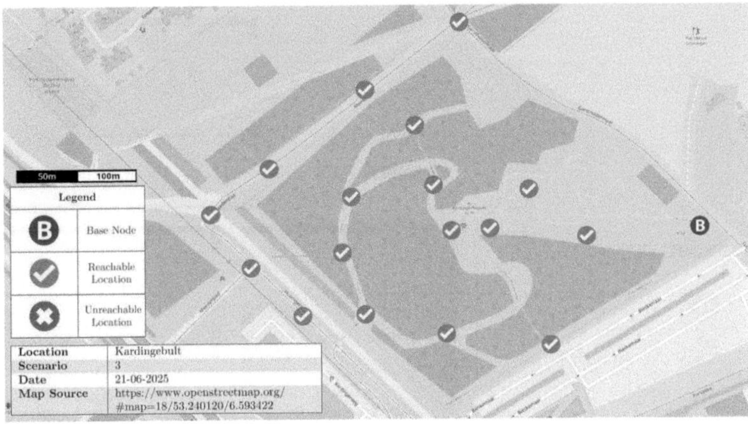

Fig. 2. Forest terrain coverage map

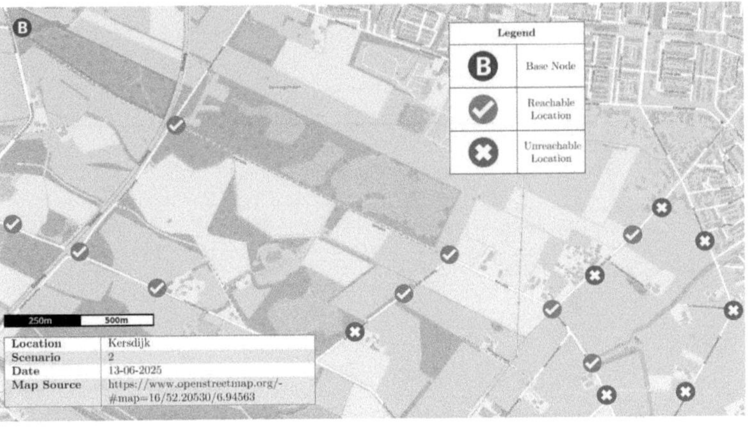

Fig. 3. Mild-hills terrain coverage map

4.4   Live Firefighting Scenario

We conducted two tests in a multi-floor training house with professional fire-fighters: 1) During navigation drills without fire; and 2) During live fire training with smoke, full gear, and hose deployment (Figs. 9 and 10).

The wearable node transmitted (simulated) PDR updates to the firetruck parked outside, which was integrated into the LoRa mesh. Despite interference and movement, communication was stable in both sessions. There were some packet losses ($< 5\%$) for one of the two firefighters, but the cause of it is yet unclear. This is an interesting future work to have more controlled setting and to pre-test the reliability of the nodes prior to testing.

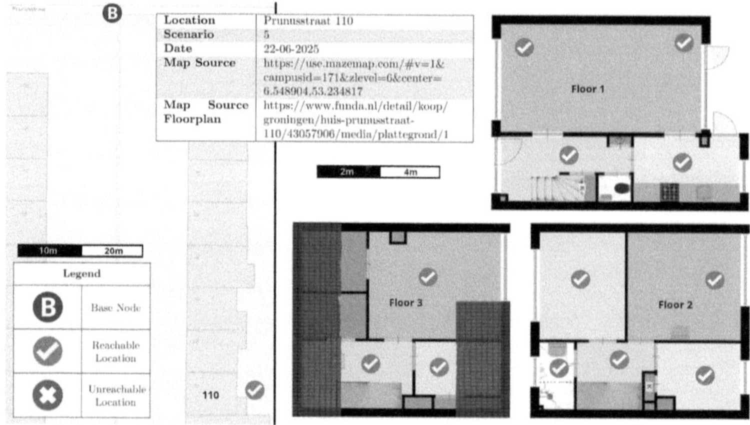

Fig. 4. 3-floor residential building with a front yard

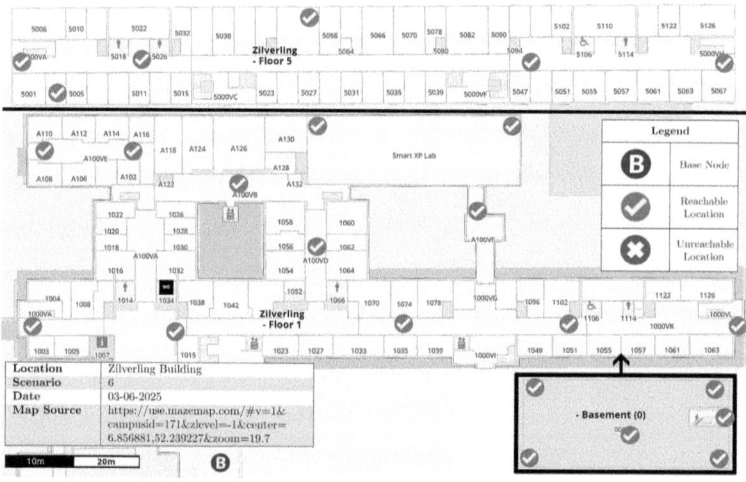

Fig. 5. 5-floor narrow office building

4.5 Summary

Our results support the feasibility of using LoRa mesh for wearable PDR communication in realistic firefighting environments. The consistent use of a firetruck node as a mobile relay simplified network setup. Strategic placement of repeaters in vertical or concrete-dense areas improved performance.

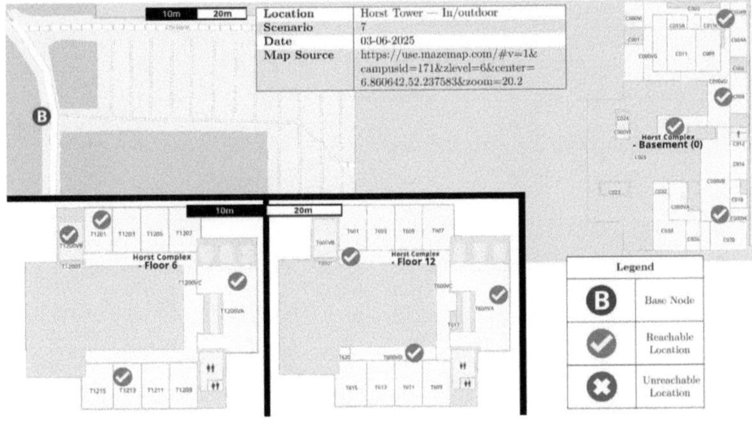

Fig. 6. 12-floor lean tower with lecture halls

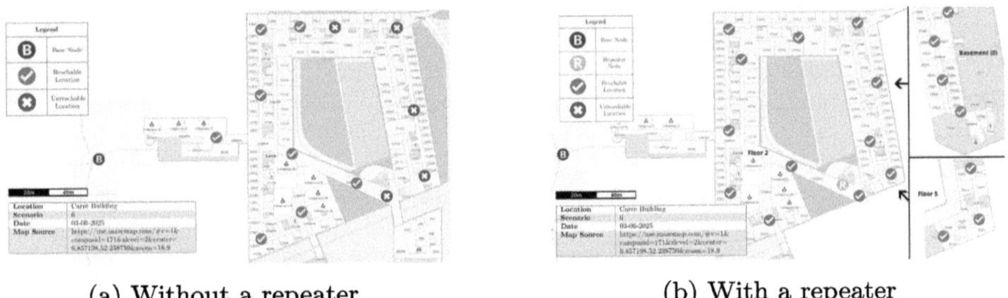

(a) Without a repeater   (b) With a repeater

Fig. 7. 5-floor wide office building with a long entrance hall

The live test validated that communication can remain stable even during active fire conditions. While throughput dropped in the most RF-hostile spots, positioning updates remained frequent enough for tracking. Limitations include lack of full throughput benchmarking and no multi-wearable load test.

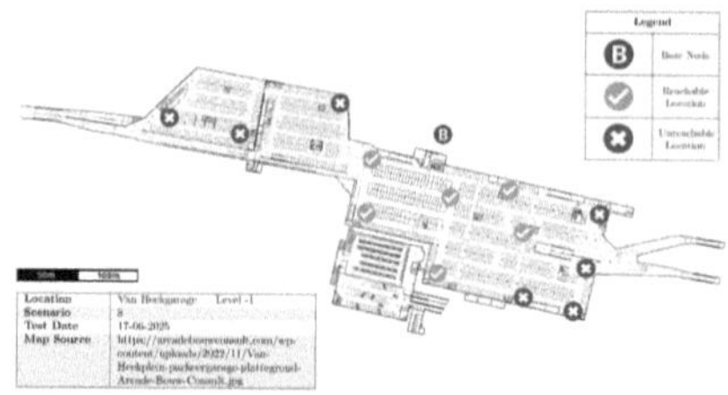

(a) Without a repeater, Level (minus)1

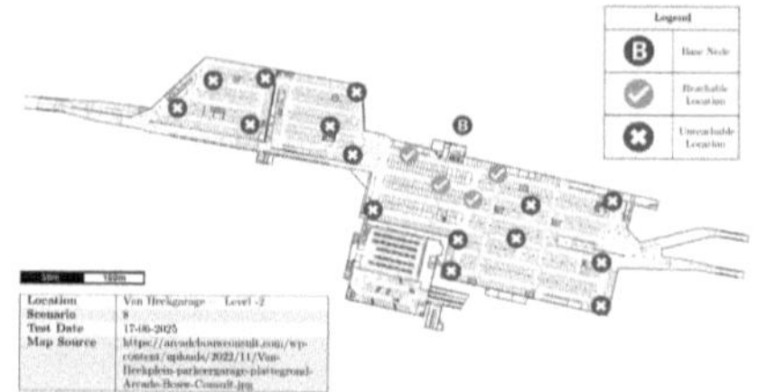

(b) Without a repeater, Level (minus)2

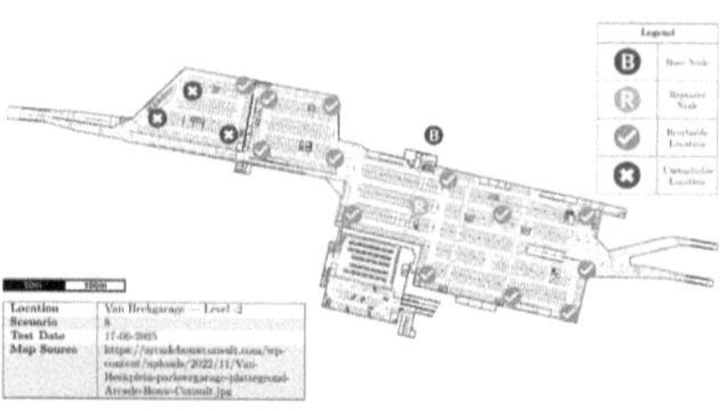

(c) With a repeater centrally positioned, Level (minus)2

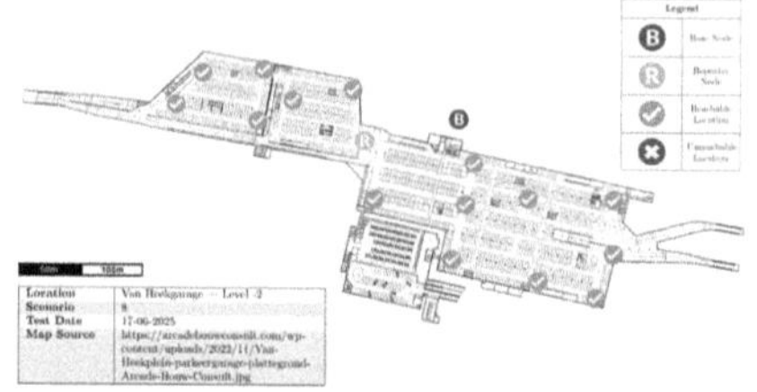

(d) With a repeater strategically placed, Level (minus)2

Fig. 8. Thick Underground car parking with 2 levels

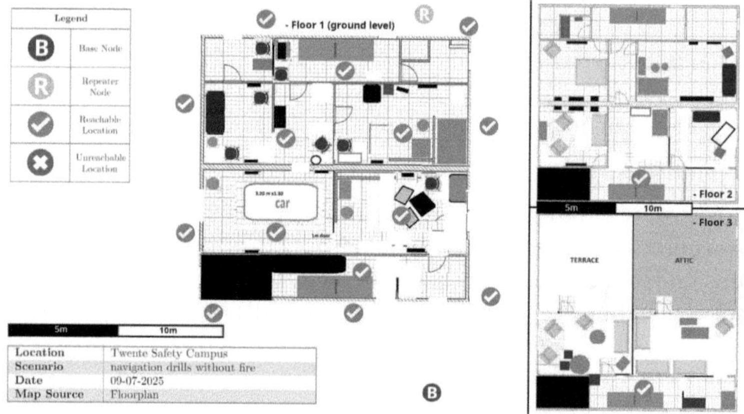

Fig. 9. Navigation drill in and around the house prior to fire test

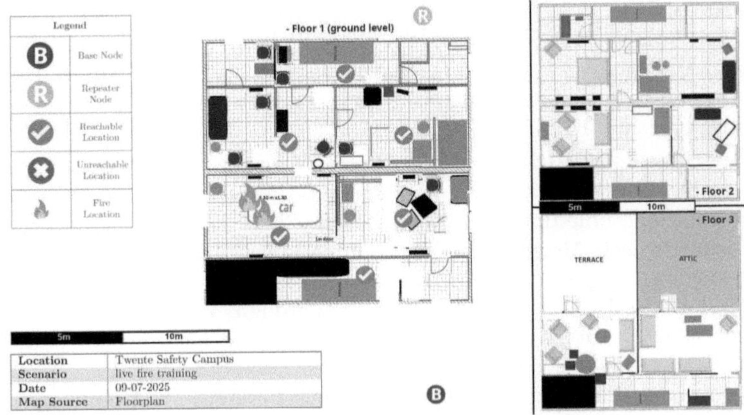

Location	Twente Safety Campus
Scenario	live fire training
Date	09-07-2025
Map Source	Floorplan

Fig. 10. Fire search and extinguishing drill inside the house

Table 1. Grouped Summary of Test Environments and Findings

Scenario	Environment	Fire	Notes	Repeater
Outdoor	Forest path	No	2.2 km LOS, drops near buildings	No
Outdoor	Hill terrain	No	Full wraparound coverage	No
Residential	3-floor house	No	Full indoor coverage	No
Commercial	Office buildings	No	Repeater improved deep coverage	Yes
Underground	Multi-level garage	No	Repeaters needed for full coverage	Yes
Fire scenario	Training house	Yes	Minor dropouts, stable overall	No

5   Conclusions

LoRa mesh networks offer a practical, low-cost, and deployable solution to the communication bottleneck in wearable personal dead reckoning systems for emergency responders. With minimal setup and repeaters, full building coverage was often achievable. Firetruck-based nodes proved effective as mobile infrastructure. Future work includes stress-testing under multiple-wearable setups and incorporating visual PDR tracking dashboards.

Acknowledgements. This research was supported in part by Inertia Technology, Enschede, within the Eurostars project 4145 iTrack, funded by Eureka and RVO. The authors also acknowledge the collaboration with the Twente Safety Centre, Enschede, The Netherlands, for providing the live fire scenarios.

References

1. Bosch, S.: Pushing the Limits of Inertial Motion Sensing. Ph.D. thesis, University of Twente, Enschede, The Netherlands, Ph.D. thesis (2022). https://doi.org/10.3990/1.9789036554350
2. Indiana University RedLab: Epic Blue: Wearable 3D Positioning for First Responders (2023). https://redlab.iu.edu/projects/frst-challenge/frst-challenge-competitors/epic-blue-dot.html. Accessed July 2025
3. Meshtastic Project: Meshtastic: Open Source LoRa Mesh Project (2024). https://meshtastic.org. Accessed July 2025
4. O'Neill, I.J., Verrico, J.: Pointer: Seeing Through Walls to Help Locate Firefighters (2021). https://www.nasa.gov/centers-and-facilities/jpl/pointer-seeing-through-walls-to-help-locate-firefighters/
5. van der Zwaag, B.J., Marin-Perianu, R., Marin-Perianu, M.: Deliverable D2.1 Scenarios and User Requirements. http://www.aiosat.eu/index.php/documents/

Grounded in Reality of Human-Computer Interaction: Robust Smartphone-Based Gesture Recognition

Fatemeh Naderi⬤, Judith S. Heinisch$^{(\boxtimes)}$⬤, Lars Mathuseck⬤, and Klaus David⬤

University of Kassel, Wilhelmshöher Allee 73, 34121 Kassel, Germany
`comtec@uni-kassel.de`

Abstract. Gesture recognition using smartphones is crucial for enabling intuitive human-computer interaction, particularly under real-world conditions. However, reliable gesture recognition across diverse users while performing physical activities, such as walking, remains challenging. Consequently, this paper presents a person-independent gesture recognition system that utilizes gravitational readings derived from the smartphone's IMU sensor for robust smartphone-based gesture recognition. The system was evaluated based on data from 13 participants who performed four different gestures while walking or standing. We have trained and evaluated a Support Vector Machine (SVM) and a Random Forest (RF) classifier to distinguish five classes and achieved an accuracy of 91.37% for Support Vector Machine, and 90.31% for Random Forest over all participants and gestures. Furthermore, we applied leave-one-subject-out to prove person independence (mean accuracy 88.25% SVM; 87.53% RF), in addition to robustness against walking (mean accuracy 83.64% SVM; 81.21% RF). The results indicate the system's suitability for real-world, smartphone-based gesture recognition.

Keywords: Gesture Recognition · Human-Activity Recognition · IMU

1 Introduction

Touch-based interfaces dominate smartphone interaction, but these interfaces are impractical in many real-world contexts, such as while walking or interacting with Smart City services. Gesture recognition offers an intuitive solution. In our previous work (Interact360) [11], we introduced a paradigm where smartphones can act as controllers for Smart City services, for example, triggering a pedestrian traffic light by pointing the smartphone in the direction of the traffic light and performing a gesture with the smartphone. Such interaction requires robust, low-energy [7] gesture recognition that works reliably across diverse users and during physical activities, such as walking [9].

In this paper, we take one step towards the vision of Interact360 by focusing on the recognition of four essential tilt gestures: vertical forward (scroll

Ö. Durmaz Incel et al. (Eds.): iWOAR 2025, LNCS 16292, pp. 373–381, 2026.
https://doi.org/10.1007/978-3-032-13312-0_23

down), vertical backward (scroll up), horizontal up (confirm), and horizontal down (dismiss). These gestures represent core interactions for everyday applications and form the basis of broader gesture vocabularies for Smart City applications [11]. We present a gravity-sensor-based gesture recognition model that is robust against the interference of walking and person-independent, demonstrating initial evidence of real-world feasibility.

2   Related Work

Gesture recognition has been widely explored using wearable and smartphone devices, leveraging multiple sensing modalities and machine learning models [5, 7,9,12]. Early work relied largely on accelerometer and gyroscope data, assuming the user was stationary. For example, Kong et al. [7] combined inertial sensors with gaze estimation to classify seven gestures, achieving a mean accuracy of 97.2% with ten participants. Although innovative, the evaluation was limited to the stationary condition, and it is unclear whether gestures can still be detected while the user is walking.

Research with wearable devices (e.g., smartwatches) has extended gesture recognition to dynamic conditions such as walking. Ling et al. [9] investigated 14 wrist and finger gestures using accelerometer and photoplethysmography signals across sitting, walking, jogging, and running. They employed Support Vector Machine (SVM), Long Short-Term Memory networks, and Convolutional Neural Networks (CNN), reporting classification accuracies above 90% in a user-dependent setting. Zhao et al. [12] proposed a CNN for 17 hand gestures using wrist-worn inertial sensors, achieving 94.0% precision and 91.2% recall with leave-one-subject-out (LOSO) validation on five participants. Kunwar et al. [8] integrated accelerometer, gyroscope, and gravity signals from a smartwatch to distinguish arm gestures in daily activities and a payment gesture, reaching over 95% accuracy in binary LOSO classification scenarios. Kang et al. [5] used accelerometer data and applied empirical mode decomposition to separate gesture patterns from walking-induced noise. They achieved above 90% accuracy across ten participants. These studies demonstrate the feasibility of gesture recognition during walking with wearables but rely on constrained device placement that may not transfer to smartphones, which exhibit a higher freedom of movement.

Compared to wearables, smartphone-based studies under walking conditions remain limited. Katsuma and Amiya [6] analyzed walking data and 13 hand gestures performed while standing. Using the accelerometer, they distinguished these 14 classes by training k-Nearest Neighbor, SVM, and Random Forest classifiers, reporting an average F1-score of 97.34% over all participants (person dependent). Ehrmann et al. [4] proposed a three-stage classifier for smartphone interaction activities (i.e., texting, recording voice messages) during walking or running. Using accelerometer and gyroscope data from 30 participants, their Random Forest model achieved 75% accuracy. The question remains whether interaction gestures, as proposed by [11], can be recognized person independent and if executed while walking.

Considering the aforementioned research gaps, this paper proposes a gesture recognition system that evaluates person independence and walking interferences while performing gestures, exclusively using the gravity sensor.

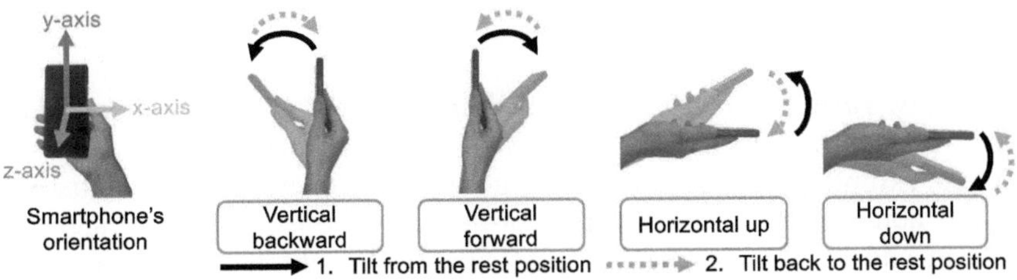

Fig. 1. Smartphone's orientation and four predefined tilt gestures with movement directions indicated by arrows.

3   Experimental Setup

In our experiment, 13 participants were asked to perform four predefined gestures with a smartphone while standing and walking.

Figure 1 illustrates the predefined gestures selected from [11]. Each gesture involves transitioning the smartphone from a neutral orientation (i.e., vertical or horizontal) to a target direction and returning to the original position.

The participants were recruited in a university context and were accustomed to using their smartphones while walking. All participants were right-handed. However, six participants were instructed to perform the gestures with their left hands to ensure balance. First, the participants were briefed on the experiment's objective and procedure and encouraged to ask questions to ensure complete understanding. Each participant was instructed to hold the smartphone (Motorola Moto G (5G) Plus).

We split our experiment into separate sessions. We started with the sessions under **walking** and continued under **standing conditions**. Before each session, participants were informed of the corresponding condition (i.e., walking or standing) and shown the target gesture (see Fig. 2, blue box). Within each session, the participants were then instructed to perform the shown gesture 30 times (i.e., **gesture phase**), with approximately five seconds between each repetition (i.e., **rest phase**) under the selected condition (i.e., either while walking or standing). The **gesture phase** consists of the single execution of the instructed gesture, which is one out of four predefined gestures (see Fig. 1). This execution was performed either while walking or standing, according to the selected condition. The **rest phase** captured idle periods (5 s) between gestures, during which the participant either kept the smartphone still in their hand or randomly moved it while maintaining the device's final orientation (i.e., vertical or horizontal).

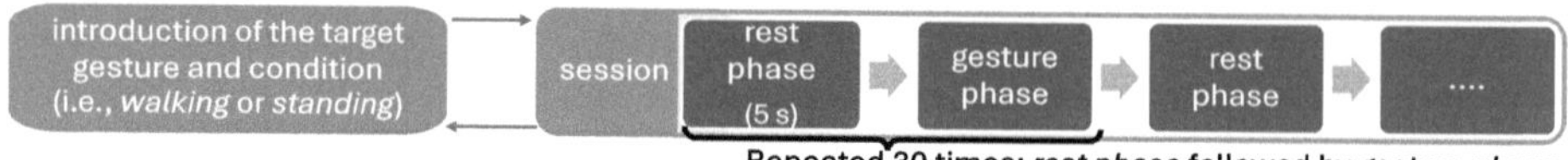

Fig. 2. Overview of the experimental procedure.

Accordingly, tilting or other hand/speaking gestures were not allowed. During the rest phase, the selected condition had to be continued.

These two phases ensured that intentional gesture execution was distinguishable and non-gesture periods were represented. The experimenter signaled the start and end of each session, so participants did not have to count the performed phases. The experimenter used a second smartphone to label each phase performed and manually adjusted using a time series annotation tool [10].

4   Evaluation

4.1   Data Analysis and Sensor Selection

We analyzed the gathered acceleration and gravity sensor data to prove which sensor and axis are most suited for gesture recognition. Our test device uses a software-based gravity sensor to isolate gravity from raw acceleration data using a low-pass filter [1,3]. We found that gestures can be identified using solely the y- and z-axes of the accelerometer and gravity sensor, which helps to reduce dimensionality and computational effort. Furthermore, we found more fluctuations and noise within the accelerometer data compared to the gravity sensor data, as this sensor is sensitive to factors such as hand tremors and slight body movements. These findings substantiate our choice of sensor and axis. Next, we compared the acceleration and gravity data while walking. Figure 3 shows an exemplary scene of one participant performing the *Horizontal up* gesture. Each step while walking was expected to be reflected in the sensor data. This assumption is confirmed for both sensors. Gravity is much less affected by these movements and shows less noise than the acceleration sensor (Fig. 3). In vertical orientation, walking mainly interferes with the z-axis; in horizontal orientation, it interferes with the y-axis. However, since participants often tilt the smartphone, interference is always present on both axes.

These observations support the exclusive use of gravity y- and z-axis readings for our gesture recognition, to reduce computational complexity and, therefore, energy usage.

4.2   Segmentation and Classification

We evaluated our gesture recognition with a scene-based evaluation method, like [2]. This method was used because it can be used for unbalanced datasets, as we have. Each scene consists of an initial rest phase, followed by a gesture phase, and concluding with a rest phase (see Fig. 4). Windows A1 and A2 are labeled as

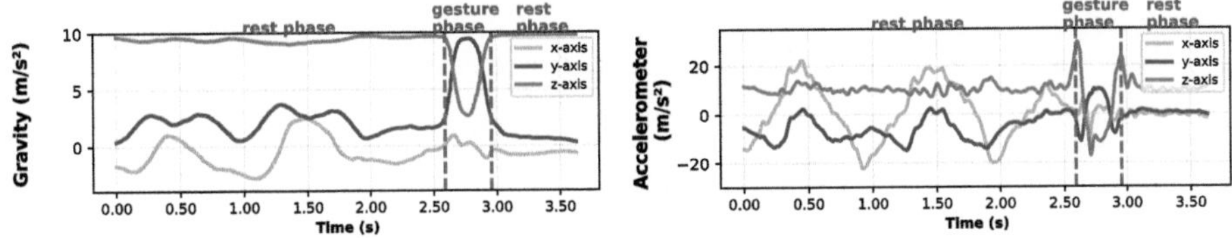

(a) Gravity signal of the *Horizontal up* gesture showing a clear gesture pattern with low noise and strong axis separation

(b) Accelerometer signal of the *Horizontal up* gesture showing high fluctuations and walking interference

Fig. 3. a) Gravity and b) accelerometer sensor data in a walking condition containing a *Horizontal up* gesture and rest phases performed by one participant.

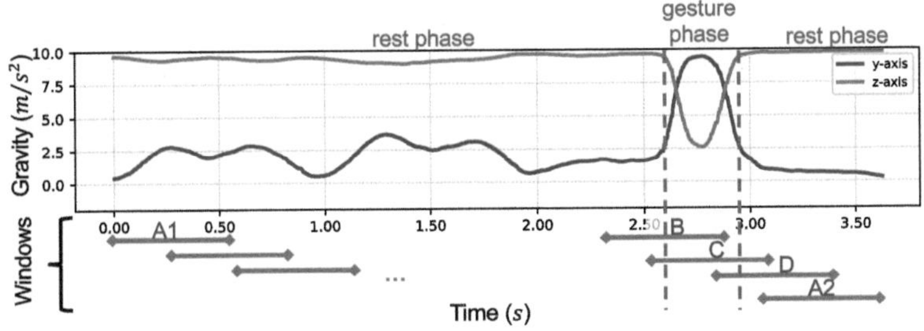

Fig. 4. Example of *Horizontal up* gravity sensor for one scene.

rest phase, while B, C, and D received the corresponding gesture performed in the gesture phase as labels. Later, the windows of each scene are consecutively classified until one window is recognized as a gesture. If this detected gesture matches the gesture actually performed, the whole scene is considered a True Positive (TP). The overall accuracy, across all scenes and, thus, all classes, is defined as Accuracy $= \frac{\text{True Positive}}{\text{Total number of scenes}}$. The gravity signal corresponding to each scene was segmented using sliding window. Similar to [7], we evaluated window sizes (ranging from 0.1 to 1.0s; 0.1s steps) and overlaps (ranging from 0% to 90%; 10% steps), to prove whether the window sizes and overlaps of the state of the art, examined on accelerometer and gyroscope data, fits for our gravity-based model as well. The window sizes proposed by Kong et al. [7] also matched the mean (and standard deviation) execution duration of the four gestures (see Table 1). Finally, we applied a 50%-random split on the data of all participants' scenes. We found the best results for RF with 0.3s and 80% overlap (90.31% accuracy) and SVM with 0.2s and 50% overlap (91.37% accuracy).

We trained a Random Forest (RF) [6] and a Support Vector Machine (SVM) [6,9] classifier to distinguish five classes: four gestures and rest phase. The classifiers were configured with the following hyperparameters, selected via randomized search. For the SVM, a Radial Basis Function kernel was used with

Table 1. Gestures' duration in seconds

Gesture	Mean (s)	Median (s)	Standard Deviation (s)
Horizontal down	0.43	0.39	0.33
Horizontal up	0.52	0.47	0.28
Vertical backward	0.46	0.41	0.25
Vertical forward	0.61	0.52	0.42

$C = 0.1, 1.0$ and $\gamma = 0.01, 0.001$. For the RF, the number of trees was set to 100, 200, 400, or 600, and the minimum samples per split were 2, 3, or 4.

On each window, five statistical features per axis were extracted, chosen as the most discriminative between gesture and rest phases. The minimum and maximum capture the device tilt extremes, highlighting gesture amplitude, particularly for vertical backward and vertical forward gestures. The range measures movement extent, while the mean provides a baseline orientation, distinguishing minimal-movement gestures from rest phases, during which the gravity y- and z-axis remain near 0 or $9.8\,\text{m/s}^2$. Variations in mean across windows indicate shifts in orientation, separating active gestures from rest. The slope quantifies the rate of change in gravity data, capturing gesture dynamics and differentiating gestures from mere orientation changes.

4.3 Gesture Similarity

We evaluated gesture confusion for each model using confusion matrices, with the best configuration we found for each classifier as discussed in the previous section.

Figure 5 shows the confusion of the SVM and the RF. For the SVM (left) and the RF (right), most confusion occurred between vertical forward and horizontal up, as well as between horizontal up and horizontal down. These models show nearly identical classification performance, differing only slightly in misclassification rates (e.g., vertical forward misclassified as horizontal up at 4.3% for SVM vs. 5.0% for RF). This suggests that the two models can struggle to disambiguate gestures with overlapping signal characteristics.

4.4 Person-Independent Evaluation

Next, we evaluate the generalization of our approach regarding person independence. For this evaluation, we used the leave-one-subject-out cross-validation with the configuration that showed the best results from the previous section (Sect. 4.2). The distribution of the results was positively skewed with a median accuracy across all participants and classes of 90.45% (mean $= 88.25\%$, SD $= 8.07\%$) and an interquartile range (IQR) of 10.65% for SVM and a median accuracy of 90.61% (mean $= 87.53\%$, SD $= 8.32\%$) and an IQR of 14.23% for RF, indicating a strong generalization of our models among our participants. Such

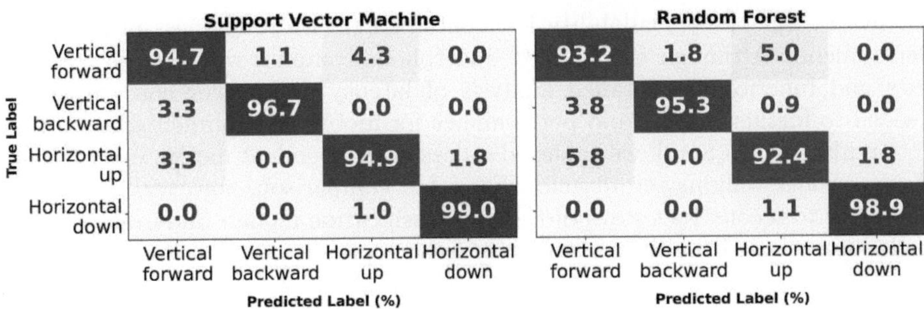

Fig. 5. Resulting confusion matrices for testing Support Vector Machine and Random Forest.

generalization capabilities are important for real-life feasibility, supporting the models' choice for real-life gesture recognition.

4.5 Walking Robustness Evaluation

Finally, we evaluated the robustness of our SVM with respect to the walking condition. We again used our optimal parameters (see Sect. 4.2) for classification. We applied a leave-one-subject-out cross-validation, but trained exclusively on gesture data collected while standing and evaluated with data recorded during walking conditions. We observe a positive skewness of the accuracies across all participants and all classes, with a median accuracy of 87.965% (mean = 83.64%, SD = 13.77%) and an IQR of 17.65% for SVM and a median accuracy of 85.18% (mean = 81.21%, SD = 13.04%) and an IQR of 14.15% for RF, showing a good robustness of our models with respect to walking scenarios.

5 Discussion

The drawn vision of gestures functioning as controllers for Smart City services has many requirements: low gesture complexity, flexibility in smartphone orientation, low power consumption, real-time processing, and person-independence, to name some [11]. Therefore, more intuitive gestures, as mentioned in [11], are envisioned in ongoing research. The current experiment focuses on walking as an interference. However, evaluating our approach under real-world conditions, considering the effects of additional physical human activities (e.g., different walking speeds, climbing stairs, jogging), remains an open challenge. Further, the experiment was conducted exclusively with right-handed, technically-minded participants, which restricts the robustness of our current model in terms of dominant hand and the manner of gesture execution. For example, no instruction regarding gesture execution speed was given, indicating that our model generalizes across our participants' execution speeds. However, a systematic evaluation of different execution speeds remains, as not all realistic speed ranges were represented. Evaluating the model's generalization across devices with varying sensor hardware and sensor availability is essential to ensure robustness in real-world deployments. Although the utilized smartphone complies with current capabilities and functions, a detailed analysis of latency and power consumption is needed to further understand performance for mobile environments.

Similar to [4,5,8,12], we achieved a person-independent model, even though, if we consider walking interference. For a fair comparison, however, it would be necessary to reconstruct state-of-the-art classification models and evaluate them under scene-based conditions with interference present.

6   Conclusion

This paper presents an approach for smartphone-based gesture recognition using gravitational readings from the smartphone's IMU sensor to address the challenge of gesture recognition while the user performs physical activities, such as walking. We show that gravity sensors are resistant to the influence of gait-induced noise. Two models, namely a Support Vector Machine (SVM) and a Random Forest (RF), were trained and evaluated to distinguish five classes (i.e., four predefined gestures and rest phase), achieving accuracies of 90.31% for RF, and 91.37% for SVM. Our evaluation, which includes 13 participants, shows the robustness with a mean classification accuracy of 83.64% (SD = 13.77%) for SVM and 81.21% (SD = 13.04%) for RF while walking and 88.25% (SD = 8.07%) for SVM and 87.53% (SD = 8.32%) for RF for the generalization across different participants. We plan to extend this work by incorporating more gestures and employing more complex machine learning models. Our results represent an initial step toward demonstrating the feasibility of accurate real-world gesture recognition using minimal sensor input, enabling future human-computer interaction applications in the smart city.

Acknowledgements. We thank Minh Chi Tai Le for his valuable support in the data acquisition process. This research was partly funded by the Hessian research funding program LOEWE – funding code LOEWE/2/17/519/03/10.001(0006)/112. This research was partly conducted within the PharmaXR project, funded by the German Federal Ministry of Education and Research (BMBF).

Disclosure of Interests. The authors have no competing interests to declare that are relevant to the content of this article.

References

1. Android Developers: Motion sensors (2025). https://developer.android.com/develop/sensors-and-location/sensors/sensors_motion. Accessed July 2025
2. Bieshaar, M., Depping, M., Schneegans, J., Sick, B.: Starting movement detection of cyclists using smart devices. In: 2018 IEEE 5th International Conference on Data Science and Advanced Analytics (DSAA), pp. 313–322. IEEE (2018). https://doi.org/10.1109/DSAA.2018.00042

3. DeviceSpecifications.com: Motorola moto g 5g plus specifications (2025). https://www.devicespecifications.com/en/model/663553f6. Accessed July 2025

4. Ehrmann, L., Stolle, M., Klieme, E., Tietz, C., Meinel, C.: Detecting interaction activities while walking using smartphone sensors. In: International Conference on Advanced Information Networking and Applications, pp. 382–393. Springer (2021). https://doi.org/10.1007/978-3-030-75075-6_31

5. Kang, P., Li, J., Fan, B., Jiang, S., Shull, P.B.: Wrist-worn hand gesture recognition while walking via transfer learning. IEEE J. Biomed. Health Inform. **26**(3), 952–961 (2022). https://doi.org/10.1109/JBHI.2021.3100099

6. Katsuma, R., Amiya, T.: High-F1-score recognition of input gestures while holding smartphone by reducing false detection due to walking noise. Sens. Mater. **34** (2022). https://doi.org/10.18494/SAM3938

7. Kong, A., Ahuja, K., Goel, M., Harrison, C.: Eyemu interactions: gaze + IMU gestures on mobile devices. In: Proceedings of the 2021 International Conference on Multimodal Interaction, ICMI 2021, pp. 577–585. Association for Computing Machinery, New York (2021). https://doi.org/10.1145/3462244.3479938

8. Kunwar, U., et al.: Robust and deployable gesture recognition for smartwatches. In: 27th International Conference on Intelligent User Interfaces, pp. 277–291. ACM (2022). https://doi.org/10.1145/3490099.3511125

9. Ling, Y., Chen, X., Ruan, Y., Zhang, X., Chen, X.: Comparative study of gesture recognition based on accelerometer and photoplethysmography sensor for gesture interactions in wearable devices. IEEE Sens. J. **21**(15), 17107–17117 (2021). https://doi.org/10.1109/JSEN.2021.3081714

10. Mathuseck, L., Fischer, D., Thelemann, D., David, K.: Time series annotation tool (2024). https://github.com/larsmathuseck/timeseries-annotation. Accessed Aug 2025

11. Mathuseck, L., Lange, S., David, K.: Interact360: a new paradigm for interacting with a future smart city. In: Datenbanksysteme für Business, Technologie und Web - Workshopband (BTW 2025). Lecture Notes in Informatics (LNI), vol. P-363, pp. 33–42. Gesellschaft für Informatik, Bonn (2025). https://doi.org/10.18420/BTW2025-102

12. Zhao, H., Ma, Y., Wang, S., Watson, A., Zhou, G.: Mobigesture: mobility-aware hand gesture recognition for healthcare. Smart Health **9**, 129–143 (2018). https://doi.org/10.1016/j.smhl.2018.07.010

Monitoring Harness Trotters in Diverse Cases Using an Online Platform to Collect Synchronised Physiology and Locomotion Data

Jeanne I. M. Parmentier[1,2,3]($\boxtimes$) , Rhana M. Aarts[2] , Zala Žgank[4,5] ,
Elin Hernlund[4] , Raluca Marin-Perianu[1], Mihai Marin-Perianu[1] ,
and Marie Rhodin[4]

[1] Inertia Technology B.V., Enschede, The Netherlands
`{jeanne,raluca,mihai}@inertia-technology.com`
[2] Department of Clinical Sciences, Faculty of Veterinary Medicine, Utrecht University, Utrecht, The Netherlands
`r.m.aarts@uu.nl`
[3] Pervasive Systems Group, EEMCS, University of Twente, Enschede, The Netherlands
[4] Department of Anatomy, Physiology and Biochemistry, Swedish University of Agricultural Sciences, Uppsala, Sweden
`{zala.zgank,elin.hernlund,marie.rhodin}@slu.se`
[5] Menhammar Stuteri, Ekerö, Sweden

Abstract. Monitoring horses during training sessions is important to ensure welfare. In most cases, monitoring is limited to the physiological response; however, the locomotory response also provides relevant and complementary information. In this work, we show that the newly developed online platform Varenne, which enables the synchronised collection of physiological and locomotion data, can be used for different circumstances in Standardbred trotters, and we discuss its limitations. The use of such training tools allows not only for performance improvement, health monitoring, and veterinary follow-ups, but also for extensive (research) data collection and thus new knowledge creation. The use of these training tools requires training and expert knowledge in certain domains, possibly limiting their everyday use. Ultimately, the objective quantification of equine physiology and locomotor parameters will enhance the assessment and assurance of welfare in horses.

Keywords: exercise physiology · gait analysis · longitudinal monitoring · welfare · horses

1 Introduction

Monitoring horses during training is essential for optimal performance and welfare assurance. A training response is essential to adapt to a training stimulus

Ö. Durmaz Incel et al. (Eds.): iWOAR 2025, LNCS 16292, pp. 382–392, 2026.
https://doi.org/10.1007/978-3-032-13312-0_24

and increase fitness in both humans and horses [1]. The required fitness is dependent on various factors, such as age, health status, and the discipline in which the horse needs to perform. In harness races, Standardbred trotters are trained for speed and stamina to cover distances as fast as possible whilst pulling a sulky.

2   Background and Related Works

During Standardbred trotter training sessions, heart rate (HR) is often monitored to evaluate fitness and cardiovascular health [2]. In addition to HR, locomotory parameters are of interest to evaluate movement strategies to increase speed, such as stride length and stride frequency [3]. Quantitative gait analysis also provides insights into possible movement asymmetries. The latter is especially relevant for Standardbred trotters due to the high prevalence of asymmetries [4], which can be related to pain and a clinical sign of lameness. By combining HR and locomotion parameters, a more complete view of the equine training response can be obtained, allowing for the early identification of changes in physiological and locomotor parameters. These changes can indicate the onset of underlying problems such as fatigue and/or pain [5,6], and allow for rapid interventions in terms of veterinary care or training adaptations. The use of an online platform to collect real-time data facilitates individual and group monitoring, but also comparison of horses over time.

Several tools have been developed to monitor equine physiology and locomotion [7]. Recently, the Varenne project took advantage of two already existing tools: the Polar® Equine[1] belt combined with the H10® sensor and the Equi-Pro®[2] gait analysis system. Using these tools, Varenne offers an online platform to monitor equine physiology and locomotion during training sessions [8]). Shortly, the platform provides near real-time HR and locomotion symmetry information to the driver and to the trainer, accessible from anywhere with an internet connection. Moreover, thorough analysis of the data can be conducted post-training, and the raw data can be exported to the Equi-Pro® platform for in-depth analysis of the locomotion parameters.

In this work, we present and discuss three case studies in which this new data collection platform was used to monitor individuals or groups of harness race horses. Each case is presented in the following section.

3   Materials and Methods

3.1   Ethical Aspect

All data used for this work were collected during normal training sessions or veterinary examinations of each horse; therefore are not subject to ethical review under either European legislation. Regardless, informed consent was obtained from the trainers regarding the use of the horses' data for future publications.

---

[1] https://www.polar.com/en/products/horse-heart-rate-monitors/polar-equine-heart-rate-monitor-for-trotters.

[2] https://inertia-technology.com/product/equi-pro/.

3.2   Data Collection

Horses were equipped with the complete Equi-Pro® inertial measurement units (IMUs) setup (head, withers, sacrum, left and right tuber coxae, lateral aspect of the lower limbs), and an additional sensor was placed on the girth at the sternum level. All sensors included a 3D gyroscope ($\pm$2000 deg/s), a 3D low-g accelerometer ($\pm$8 g for the body, $\pm$16 g for the limbs) and a 3D high-g accelerometer ($\pm$100 g for the body and $\pm$200 g for the limbs). All sensors were sampled at 200 Hz. One sensor per horse also included a Global Navigation Satellite System (GNSS) chip sampled at 10 Hz, placed either on the head, sacrum, or one of the tuber coxae. Sensors were either ProMove-mini[3] or ProMove-V[4], the newest version of the sensors, which are waterproof and, when relevant, include a higher quality GNSS chip. Additionally and when available, horses were equipped with a Polar® Equine belt to retrieve heart rate data (1 Hz). An example of a horse equipped with the full setup is shown in Fig. 4 (Appendix).

Horses were equipped with their own tack and sulky, and driven by their usual driver. They followed the training program set by the trainer for that day. For this paper, we focus on the following use cases:

– One example of a group training session of young horses
– One example of health monitoring with subsequent orthopaedic exam
– One example of a large-scale data collection

Each case is further described below.

Young Horse Group Training Session: In the harness horse industry, horses start to participate in training sessions around the age of 18 months. Their cardio-respiratory and locomotory systems undergo adaptations to sustain the training load and the competition demands. Regular monitoring can enable the detection of racing predispositions and early detection of health issues that could impair equine welfare. For this case study, data were collected for a group of three 2-year-old trotters during a "heat" training session. During a heat training, horses follow an interval schedule consisting of several bouts of alternating low and higher trotting speeds.

Health Monitoring: During training, drivers might notice (locomotor) abnormalities that require further investigation. Usually, this means that a veterinarian is contacted for orthopaedic examination. In this case, the horse exhibited signs of poor performance compared to its peers, together with an uneven trot. A driven veterinary gait analysis exam was performed to localize the potential source of pain, and the data was exported to the Equi-Pro® platform for further analysis.

---

[3] https://inertia-technology.com/product/motion-capture-promove-mini/.
[4] https://inertia-technology.com/product/inertial-sensor-promove-v/.

Large-Scale Data Collection: Data collection is an important part of research. The newly developed Varenne platform allows for efficient large-scale data collection. In the described case, we demonstrate the use of Varenne to collect data from five groups of three horses each (total: 15 individuals) during one morning. With these data, a simple evaluation of the influence of the track (straight track versus curved track) on diverse gait parameters is conducted.

4 Results and Discussion

In the following part of this paper, the main output per case is presented, and possible limitations are discussed.

4.1 Young Horse Group Training Session

A group of three horses started with a warm-up trot on a forest track, followed by three acceleration bouts and a recovery trot on the track on a straight line (Fig. 5, Appendix). For the high-speed segments and the subsequent recovery trot, the average heart rate, stride speed, stride frequency, and symmetry and regularity indices at the sternum level are presented in Fig. 1.

For high-speed bouts 1 and 3, H03 presented much lower average heart rates than H01 and H02. Although this could indicate a good physiological response to training, it is most likely due to an artifact in the Polar$^{®}$ belt. During high intensity, skin contact of the electrodes can be impaired due to movement artifacts, resulting in unreliable data output. This has been identified as a limitation of the Varenne system.

When comparing the average stride speed, H01 and H02 reached similar speeds in segments 2 and 3. However, different strategies were used: H01 systematically used a higher stride frequency and shorter stride length compared to H02. This is an interesting pattern that can be monitored in future training sessions [3].

In addition to comparisons between horses, follow-up measurements and comparisons over time (e.g., during a training season) may ensure proper training workload of these young horses to avoid overloading injuries [9].

4.2 Health Monitoring

All results are shown in Fig. 7 and Table 1 (Appendix). For the health monitoring, the horse was equipped with the full locomotion setup and driven on a straight line at a comfortable trotting speed. An initial baseline (without any treatment) measurement was conducted. Here, the horse presented a significant and consistent left hind (LH) limb asymmetry (sacrum and hips sensors), as well as right front (RF) limb asymmetry (head and withers sensors) [10] (Fig. 7a). After the baseline measurement, local analgesia was applied to remove potential pain sensation in the lower LH hoof (abaxial nerve block, Fig. 7b) and the measurement was repeated, but no asymmetry improvements were noted. A second

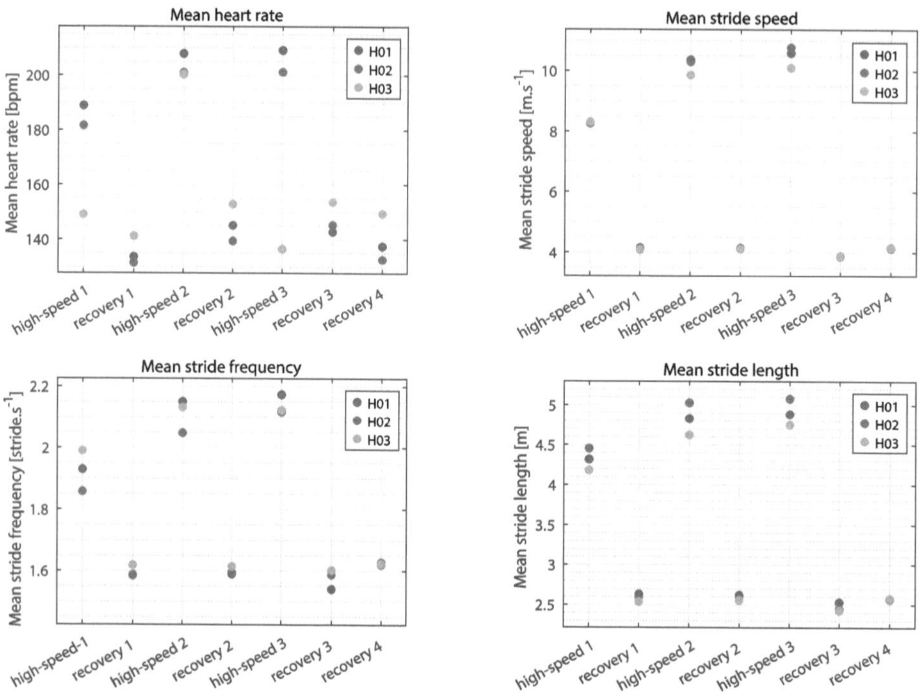

Fig. 1. Between-horses comparison of mean heart rate, mean stride speed, mean stride frequency, and mean stride length for the different bouts of high-speed and their subsequent recovery segments.

local analgesia was applied (low 4 point nerve block), which led to a decrease of the LH limb-related asymmetry, indicating that pain was removed in this area (Fig. 7c). However, the horse then presented right hind (RH) limb asymmetry, and the RF limb asymmetry remained, implying a multi-limb lameness.

The following day, the location of the pain in the LH limb was confirmed by repeating the baseline measurement and blocking the pain sensation in the fetlock joint. The baseline results were similar to the previous day (Fig. 7d), and the block removed the LH asymmetry (Fig. 7e). The horse presented a RH limb asymmetry again. Local analgesia was also applied at two locations on the RF limb (abaxial nerve block and low 4 point nerve block) to try and locate the source of pain. The RF asymmetry was more inconsistent, and seemed to somewhat improve with blocks, but it was not completely eliminated (Fig. 7f, 7g).

After this, it was decided to treat the primary source of pain (LH limb) and to give the horse a period of rest. Three weeks after treatment, the horse had progressively returned to training and was measured again, without any local analgesia. There were no asymmetry in the hind limbs any more and the RF asymmetry had decreased, indicating that the combination of treatment and a rest period contributed to the horse's improvement (Fig. 7h).

Locomotion quantification tools such as the Varenne platform, interoperable with the Equi-Pro® system, are valuable when trying to determine the cause of pain during veterinary lameness exams. However, they can be time-consuming and should be performed by trained practitioners only, as correct sensor placement is essential. Likewise, veterinary data interpretation requires expert knowledge. Education programs for veterinarians are provided where they can learn about interpretations of the results and practical implications, which are crucial for an efficient and correct use of the tool. These programs currently focus on leisure and sport horses. In the future, collecting datasets from different populations, such as harness trotters, will also benefit these programs, as new knowledge in how these horses move will be produced.

4.3   Large-Scale Data Collection

For this pilot study, the hypothesis was that horses would present larger locomotor instabilities on the curved tracks compared to the straight lines (Fig. 6, Appendix).

Average stride length, stride frequency, and stride speed are presented in Fig. 2. The results of the coefficient of variation (CV) for each segment and track type are presented in Fig. 3. The CV values for the stride frequency increased with speed on both the straight lines and the curved track, while the CV values of the stride length presented a systematic increase with speed on the curved path only. As the median speed among horses was similar between curve tracks 7 and 8 (Fig. 2), there might be an effect of either fatigue or the driver asking the horse to slow down to exit the oval track.

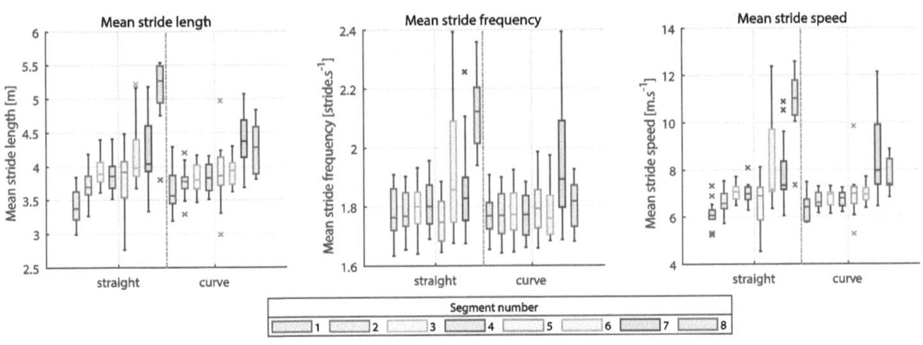

Fig. 2. Comparison of the mean values per segment for the stride length, stride frequency, and stride speed on the straight lines and curved tracks.

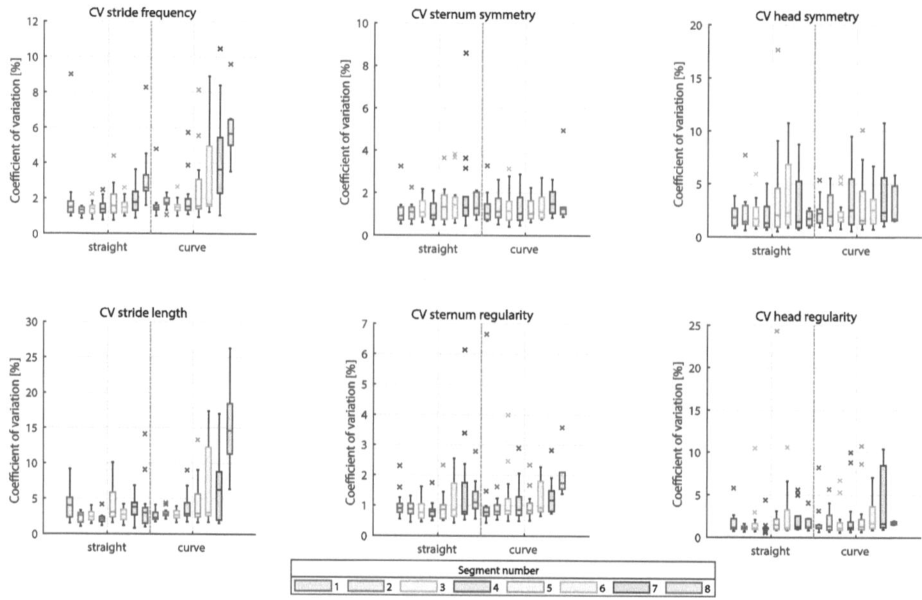

Fig. 3. Comparison of the mean coefficient of variations per segment for the stride frequency, stride length, sternum/head symmetry, and regularity indices on the straight lines and curved tracks.

Overall, CV values for the head symmetry and regularity indices were higher compared to the sternum. This result was to be expected as the head has more degrees of freedom, therefore more variation possibilities. Sternum regularity CV values seem to increase in the later segments, as well as the head symmetry and regularity CV values.

More in-depth and statistical analysis of these data is needed to conclude on the effect of curved tracks versus straight lines, together with an increased understanding of how horses move on curved tracks.

5   Conclusion and Future Considerations

In this paper, we presented different applications for harness race horse monitoring, made available through the newly developed Varenne platform. This system enables the synchronised data collection of different modalities (heart rate, multiple motion sensors, GNSS) but also of different horses training simultaneously. The interoperability between the Varenne system and the gait analysis system Equi-Pro® also offers the possibility of equine gait analysis for veterinary exams and longitudinal gait asymmetries monitoring. The availability of such tools enables the collection of large datasets from high-quality sensors. This enables a more fine-grained monitoring of equine performance and welfare, both at the individual and group levels, over time. In the future, more reliable heart rate monitoring tools should be integrated to also allow for electrocardiogram monitoring, in order to detect cardiovascular abnormalities [11]. Combined with already integrated high-quality motion sensors, the Varenne system can lead to further research on the physiology and locomotion of race horses in real-life conditions. Additionally, horses can be closely monitored for early detection of health issues, ultimately improving animal welfare.

Acknowledgements. The authors would like to thank the horses, trainers, and grooms involved in the tests of the Varenne platform during the different data collections. This work was funded by EUREKA Eurostars (project "Varenne" E!114697).

Disclosure of Interests. J.I.M.P., R.M.-P., and M.M.-P. are respectively part-time employee and co-founders of Inertia Technology B.V., the company that develops and sells the motion sensors used in this study, and that coordinated the Varenne project.

Appendix

Fig. 4. Example of a horse equipped with the Varenne system. Blue rectangle: head and sternum sensors (minimum setup); yellow rectangle full lines: limb sensors; yellow rectangle dotted lines: withers, sacrum, and tuber coxae (full setup), grey box: data acquisition unit; green oval: heart rate belt.

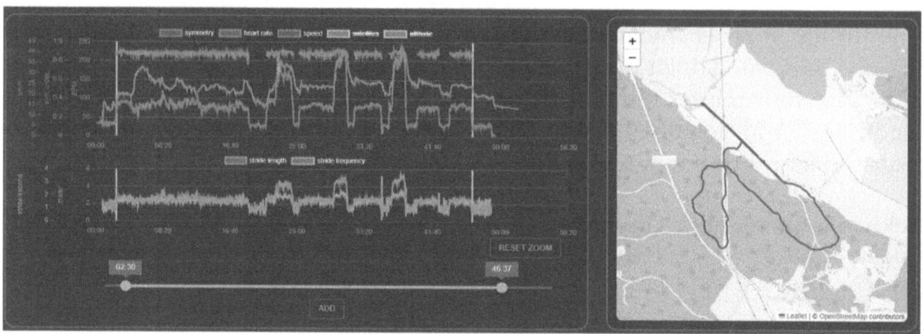

Fig. 5. Example of screenshot of the Varenne platform for a young horse's training session. The segments of interest were the three high-speed segments and their subsequent recovery trot, all on the straight track.

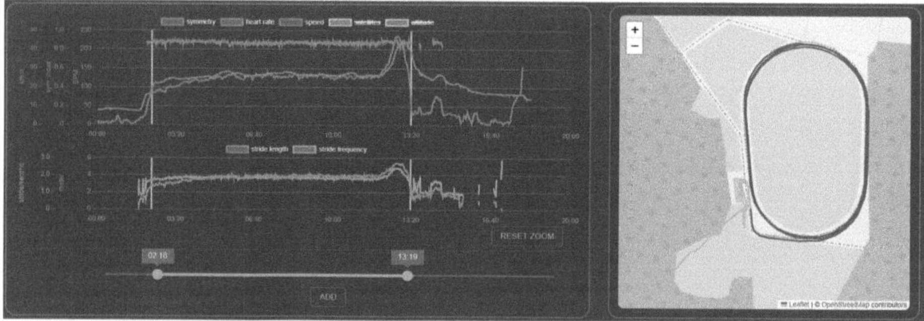

Fig. 6. Example of screenshot of the Varenne platform for one horse involved in the large-scale data collection. All straight lines and their subsequent curved tracks were identified for further data processing.

Table 1. Average ± standard deviation values for the different asymmetry parameters calculated in Equi-Pro®. Negative and positive values indicate left and right asymmetries, respectively. LH: left hind; RF: right front, mm: millimetre.

Day	Block/Limb	Head		Withers		Sacrum		Hips		
		MinDiff	MaxDiff	MinDiff	MaxDiff	MinDiff	MaxDiff	Swing	Stance	Speed
		mm	mm	mm	mm	mm	mm	mm	mm	$m.s^{-1}$
D1	Baseline	-20.0 ± 13.8	21.1 ± 20.5	16.8 ± 3.9	21.0 ± 4.5	-8.3 ± 12.0	-24.6 ± 9.1	-44.8 ± 12.0	-29.7 ± 14.4	5.6 ± 0.6
	Abaxial LH	-0.0 ± 10.1	34.6 ± 14.5	14.4 ± 5.0	20.3 ± 4.3	-11.7 ± 5.7	-15.9 ± 9.5	-37.6 ± 11.2	-22.9 ± 11.8	5.4 ± 0.7
	Low 4 point LH	7.6 ± 15.9	23.5 ± 21.0	4.9 ± 4.3	16.6 ± 4.6	6.3 ± 7.8	17.6 ± 7.6	30.1 ± 14.5	26.6 ± 13.5	5.3 ± 0.5
D2	Baseline	-8.9 ± 14.3	16.6 ± 19.1	20.6 ± 5.2	19.4 ± 5.7	-10.6 ± 4.4	-9.0 ± 9.0	-23.2 ± 12.6	-20.7 ± 9.5	4.9 ± 0.09
	Fetlock LH	0.2 ± 17.9	36.9 ± 22.1	4.2 ± 8.6	15.6 ± 5.0	14.6 ± 10.6	12.9 ± 8.2	43.6 ± 12.1	39.4 ± 11.4	5.1 ± 0.8
	Abaxial RF	-22.5 ± 11.8	7.5 ± 18.9	-4.0 ± 6.3	10.9 ± 5.8	3.1 ± 13.5	8.0 ± 10.9	46.0 ± 16.6	42.2 ± 16.4	5.8 ± 0.3
	Low 4 point RF	-17.0 ± 12.1	20.5 ± 16.6	-4.4 ± 4.7	13.9 ± 5.8	24.7 ± 6.6	21.8 ± 7.3	55.4 ± 14.0	55.3 ± 15.8	5.5 ± 0.7
Re-check		-12.0 ± 14.8	26.9 ± 18.6	10.9 ± 6.0	22.5 ± 3.6	-3.3 ± 5.4	5.0 ± 7.1	-8.8 ± 10.6	-3.2 ± 8.4	5.1 ± 0.3

For more information regarding the meaning of the parameters, refer to: https://inertia-technology.com/techarticle/upper-body-parameters/

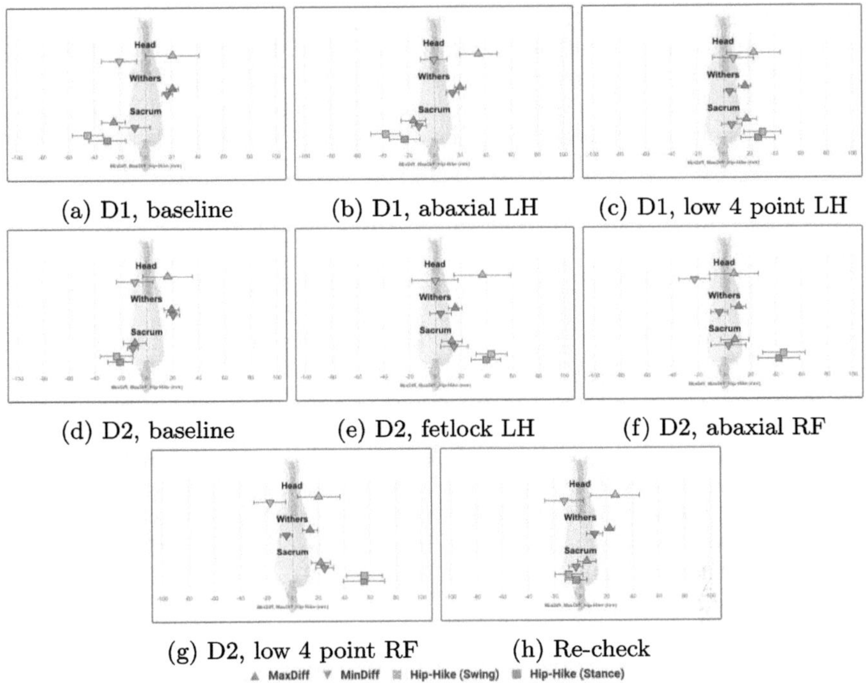

(a) D1, baseline   (b) D1, abaxial LH   (c) D1, low 4 point LH

(d) D2, baseline   (e) D2, fetlock LH   (f) D2, abaxial RF

(g) D2, low 4 point RF   (h) Re-check

Fig. 7. Asymmetry parameters visualisations in the Equi-Pro® software. Notice the switch from left to right sacrum asymmetry (green triangles and orange/brown rectangles) between (a-b) and (c) after low 4 point LH analgesia and between (d) and (e) after fetlock LH analgesia. (f) and (g) show attempts at block the RF asymmetry. Additionally, sacrum asymmetry is close to 0 (indices close to midline) in (h), 3 weeks after treatment and rest. Shapes indicate mean values and moustaches indicate standard deviation values.

References

1. Allen, K., Erck-Westergren, E., Franklin, S.: Exercise testing in the equine athlete. Equine Vet. Educ. **28**, 89–98 (2016). https://beva.onlinelibrary.wiley.com/doi/abs/10.1111/eve.12410
2. Allen, K., Young, L., Franklin, S.: Evaluation of heart rate and rhythm during exercise. Equine Vet. Educ. **28**, 99–112 (2016). https://beva.onlinelibrary.wiley.com/doi/abs/10.1111/eve.12405
3. Leleu, C., Cotrel, C., Barrey, E.: Relationships between biomechanical variables and race performance in French Standardbred trotters. Livestock Prod. Sci. **92**, 39–46 (2005). https://www.sciencedirect.com/science/article/pii/S0301622604001654
4. Kallerud, A., et al.: Objectively measured movement asymmetry in yearling Standardbred trotters. Equine Vet. J. **53**, 590–599 (2021). https://beva.onlinelibrary.wiley.com/doi/abs/10.1111/evj.13302
5. Jansson, A., Ringmark, S., Johansson, L., Roepstorff, L.: Locomotion asymmetry in young standardbred trotters in training and links to future racing career. Comp. Exerc. Physiol. **18**, 85–92 (2022). https://doi.org/10.3920/CEP210035

6. Darbandi, H., Munsters, C., Parmentier, J., Havinga, P.: Detecting fatigue of sport horses with biomechanical gait features using inertial sensors. PLOS ONE **18**(4), e0284554, 1–19 (2023). https://doi.org/10.1371/journal.pone.0284554

7. Aarts, R.M., Siegers, E.W., Serra Bragança, F.M., van Weeren, P.R.: Technologies for equine welfare and performance monitoring under field conditions – where do we stand? Equine Vet. J. https://beva.onlinelibrary.wiley.com/doi/abs/10.1111/evj.70092

8. Parmentier, J.I.M., et al.: Varenne: un outil de collection de données de haute qualité pour les chevaux de trot attelé. In: Proceedings of Equ'IA – Sciences Équines et Intelligence Artificielle: Applications, Innovations et Perspectives, Villejuif, France (2025)

9. Crawford, K., Ahern, B., Perkins, N., Phillips, C., Finnane, A.: The effect of combined training and racing high-speed exercise history on musculoskeletal injuries in thoroughbred racehorses: a systematic review and meta-analysis of the current literature. Animals **10** (2020). https://www.mdpi.com/2076-2615/10/11/2091

10. Persson-Sjödin, E., et al.: Withers vertical movement symmetry is useful for locating the primary lame limb in naturally occurring lameness. Equine Vet. J. **56**, 76–88 (2024). https://beva.onlinelibrary.wiley.com/doi/abs/10.1111/evj.13947

11. Slack, J., Boston, R., Soma, L., Reef, V.: Occurrence of cardiac arrhythmias in standardbred racehorses. Equine Vet. J. **47**, 398–404 (2015). https://beva.onlinelibrary.wiley.com/doi/abs/10.1111/evj.12299

GenIMU: Simulate Realistic IMU Data Using Video Generation Models

Nikolas Rieger[(✉)] , Bert Arnrich , and Orhan Konak

Hasso-Plattner-Institute, University of Potsdam, Potsdam, Germany
nikolas.rieger@student.hpi.de, {bert.arnrich,orhan.konak}@hpi.de

Abstract. This paper introduces a pipeline for generating synthetic Inertial Measurement Unit data to address data scarcity in Human Activity Recognition (HAR). The ability to differentiate between activities benefits fall detection, fitness tracking, and health analysis. However, limited availability and high cost of labeled training data hinders robust model development. While current synthetic data approaches remain cumbersome and require extensive domain expertise, this automated pipeline makes data generation more accessible, enabling researchers to develop more powerful HAR systems. The proposed methodological framework combines video generation models with pose estimation techniques and physics-based kinematic transformations to produce synthetic sensor data that effectively augments real-world measurements. Through evaluation across established benchmark datasets, results demonstrate that models trained on a combination of real and synthetic data achieve improved performance compared to baseline approaches, with F1-score improvements of up to 1.7% points. The proposed pipeline offers several advantages, including cost-efficiency, accessibility on standard computational infrastructure, and privacy preservation capabilities that address key limitations of traditional data collection protocols. The consistent improvements observed across multiple experimental configurations demonstrate the potential of synthetic data generation for HAR applications, particularly for enhancing model robustness and improving recognition of rare or underrepresented activities.

Keywords: Human Activity Recognition · Synthetic Data Generation · Inertial Measurement Unit · Sensor Data Synthesis · Wearable Sensors

1 Introduction

Inertial Measurement Units (IMUs) have become essential for Human Activity Recognition (HAR), enabling diverse applications in healthcare, sports science, and human-computer interaction [6,12]. However, a critical bottleneck persists: the scarcity of labeled training data. Collecting and annotating IMU datasets is labor-intensive and often lacks diversity across movements, participants, and environmental conditions [8].

Ö. Durmaz Incel et al. (Eds.): iWOAR 2025, LNCS 16292, pp. 393–403, 2026.
https://doi.org/10.1007/978-3-032-13312-0_25

We introduce a novel end-to-end pipeline that generates synthetic IMU data through text-to-video generation models. Our approach combines Large Language Models (LLMs) for movement description generation, state-of-the-art text-to-video synthesis, and pose-based IMU simulation with realistic noise characteristics [7,13,20].

Our contributions are threefold: (1) a prompt augmentation module using LLMs to generate diverse, semantically controlled activity descriptions, (2) integration of HunyuanVideo and SkyReels text-to-video models with MediaPipe and ViTPose pose estimation for accurate 3D joint trajectories, and (3) demonstration that supplementing real training data with 10% synthetic data achieves consistent F1-score improvements up to 1.7% points across RealWorld, OPPORTUNITY, and PAMAP2 datasets.

2 Related Work

Human Activity Recognition employs vision-based or sensor-based approaches [14]. While vision-based methods leverage cameras and deep learning, sensor-based approaches using wearable IMUs offer distinct advantages: continuous monitoring, privacy preservation, and robustness to environmental conditions [11].

Limited annotated data availability, particularly for special activities, remains a major HAR challenge [10] and motivated synthetic data generation research.

Recent advances in motion capture and generation have enhanced synthesis capabilities. Modern pose estimation employs transformer-based models like ViTPose for accuracy [23] and real-time frameworks like MediaPipe for efficient 3D keypoint tracking [13]. Video generation has progressed through diffusion models such as HunyuanVideo and SkyReels V1, achieving realistic human motion synthesis with strong text-video alignment [7,20].

Several frameworks convert human motion to virtual IMU data. Virtual IMU extracts skeletal models from video and transforms anatomical landmarks using mathematical formulations [4]. IMUTube combines 2D pose estimation from videos with depth estimation for 3D pose reconstruction and IMU synthesis [8]. IMUGPT generates activity descriptions via LLMs, converts them to 3D motion through a Text-to-Motion Generative Pretraining Transformer (GPT), then produces synthetic IMU data [9] (Table 1).

While these approaches demonstrate feasibility, they face limitations in data diversity, technical accessibility, or integration complexity. Our work addresses these challenges through a unified pipeline combining latest text-to-video generation advances with robust pose estimation and IMU simulation.

Table 1. Comparison of GenIMU versus existing synthetic IMU generation pipelines across domain expertise requirements, automation level, realism of sensor noise. GenIMU is the only approach that fully automates the end-to-end text-to-video-to-IMU workflow.

Approach	Domain Expertise	Automation	Noise Realism
IMUTube (Kwon et al.)	High	Partial	Medium
Video-to-IMU (Gavier et al.)	Medium	Partial	Low
IMUGPT (Leng et al.)	Medium - Low	Medium	Low
GenIMU (Ours)	Low	Full	Medium

3 Methodology

Our pipeline integrates three components: textual processing for prompt generation, video synthesis, and IMU data generation through pose estimation and kinematic modeling (Fig. 1).

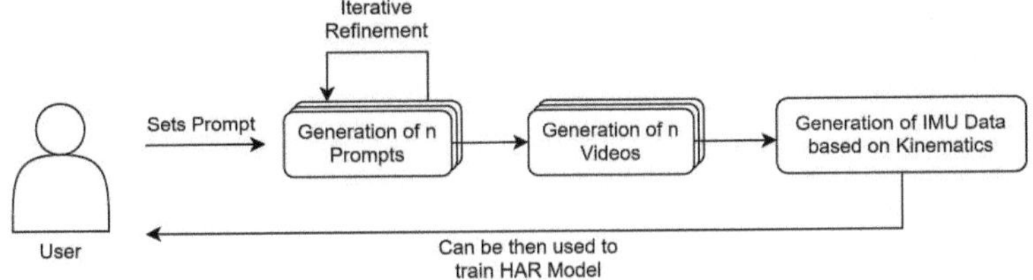

Fig. 1. End-to-end pipeline for synthetic IMU data generation: prompt augmentation via LLMs, text-to-video synthesis with SkyReels V1, pose estimation using MediaPipe or ViTPose, and conversion to IMU data through kinematic modeling.

3.1 Textual Processing and Video Generation

We employ LLMs for prompt augmentation, generating diverse activity description variations. For instance, "walking" expands to "slow walking," "rushed walking," or "walking while looking around." Prompts are optimized following Yang et al. [24], ensuring single-person visibility, full-body capture, and fixed camera positioning for reliable pose estimation.

The generated prompts feed SkyReels V1 [20], selected for fast inference and human-centric training data. Videos are generated at 960×544 resolution with guidance scale 6.0, balancing prompt alignment and computational efficiency on consumer GPUs.

3.2 IMU Data Generation

Generated videos undergo pose estimation using MediaPipe [13] for direct 3D landmarks and ViTPose [23] with depth estimation for enhanced accuracy. Following Gavier et al. [4], anatomical landmarks are mapped to BVH format and converted to IMU measurements.

Acceleration is computed as: $a(t) = R^T(t)\left(\frac{d^2}{dt^2}p(t) + g\right)$

Angular velocity follows: $\omega(t) = [\times]^{-1}\left(R^T(t)\frac{d}{dt}R(t)\right)$

where $p(t)$ represents landmark position, $R(t)$ rotation matrix, and g gravitational acceleration. Adaptive median filtering stabilizes outputs, and rank transformation aligns synthetic and real data distributions.

3.3 Evaluation Setup

We evaluate on three established HAR datasets: RealWorld [21] (15 subjects total, 7 subjects with all activities), OPPORTUNITY [17] (12 subjects, 2 subjects with all activities), and PAMAP2 [16] (9 subjects, 5 subjects with all activities). DeepConvLSTM [15] serves as our classifier, chosen for proven HAR performance combining convolutional feature extraction with LSTM temporal modeling.

Training configurations include: (1) real-only data, (2) mixed real-synthetic data (90% real, 10% synthetic), and (3) synthetic-only data. Subject-reduction experiments evaluate performance under limited training conditions.

Generation accuracy validation uses synchronized IMU-video recordings collected with five Movella Dot sensors at standardized body locations (shoulders and hips) for direct comparison between generated and recorded sensor data.

4 Results

We evaluate our pipeline by IMU data generation accuracy and classification performance when augmenting real HAR datasets with synthetic data.

4.1 IMU Data Generation Accuracy

Our synthetic IMU generation follows Gavier et al. [4], whose population model achieved NRMSE of 15.7% for acceleration and 16.3% for angular velocity in video-to-IMU conversion (Table 2). We evaluate orientation accuracy using geodesic error between quaternions, comparing MediaPipe and ViTPose pose estimation models.

Table 2. Reference literature performance metrics from Gavier et al. [4] for video-to-IMU conversion showing RMSE and NRMSE values for acceleration (a) and angular velocity (ω) from video inputs.

Input	Metric	Value
Video	a RMSE/NRMSE	$4.07\,\mathrm{m/s^2}/15.7\%$
	ω RMSE/NRMSE	$3.52°/\mathrm{s}/16.3\%$

Table 3. Orientation accuracy comparison for different pose estimation models using average geodesic error between predicted and ground truth quaternions from synchronized video-sensor recordings, both before and after applying the calibration procedure. ViTPose shows marginal improvement over MediaPipe.

Model	Average Geodesic Error (AGE) (degrees)	AGE after calibration (degrees)
MediaPipe	56.70	15.61
ViTPose	54.52	15.17

The geodesic error values for the orientation quaternions appear relatively high (see Table 3), which may initially raise concerns about the method's accuracy. However, this discrepancy can be primarily attributed to the inherent differences in the reference frames between the simulation and real-world measurements, as well as the simple calibration techniques used [25]. The initial orientation in our simulations contain systematic offsets compared to the ground truth orientations due to imperfect calibration and inherent limitations in establishing absolute reference frames. After applying calibration, which aligns the initial offset between sensor and camera angles, the average geodesic error decreases to approximately 15°, which shows that the residual error is mostly systematic and not a limitation of the proposed method itself.

4.2 Classification Performance Evaluation

DeepConvLSTM models [15] were trained on real-only, synthetic-only, and mixed data (90% real, 10% synthetic) configurations. Results averaged over 10 runs with outlier removal demonstrate consistent improvements when augmenting real data with synthetic samples (Table 4).

Table 4. F1-score comparison across datasets. Real: real data only; Virtual: synthetic data only; Mix: 90% real + 10% synthetic. Mixed outperforms real-only.

Dataset	Method	Mean F1-Score
OPPORTUNITY	Real	0.8165 ± 0.0178
	Virtual	0.2481 ± 0.0432
	Mix	$\mathbf{0.8193 \pm 0.0126}$
RealWorld	Real	0.6619 ± 0.0291
	Virtual	0.2355 ± 0.0248
	Mix	$\mathbf{0.6792 \pm 0.0275}$
PAMAP2	Real	0.7416 ± 0.0081
	Virtual	0.0351 ± 0.0119
	Mix	$\mathbf{0.7561 \pm 0.0175}$

Mixed training achieves F1-score improvements of 1.73% points (RealWorld), 1.45 points (PAMAP2), and 0.28 points (OPPORTUNITY). Maximum Mean Discrepancy (MMD) values between real and synthetic data distributions remain low (0.003–0.015), indicating good distributional alignment.

We ran one-tailed paired t-tests (H$_1$: mix $>$ real) with $\alpha = 0.05$ over $N = 10$ runs per dataset and computed Cohen's d. Results are summarized in Table 5.

Table 5. One-tailed paired t-test statistics and Cohen's d for mixed vs. real training. $p < 0.05$ indicates statistical significance at $\alpha = 0.05$.

Dataset	$t(9)$	p-value	Cohen's d
OPPORTUNITY	1.77	0.055	0.56
RealWorld	2.38	0.020	0.75
PAMAP2	3.23	0.009	1.22

Overall, this analysis shows a trend-level gain on OPPORTUNITY, and a statistically significant improvement on RealWorld and PAMAP2, confirming that mixed-data augmentation consistently enhances HAR performance.

Subject-reduction experiments reveal mixed training particularly benefits limited-data scenarios. Table 6 shows mixed datasets outperform real-only in 9 of 14 subject configurations.

Table 6. Subject-reduction experiments comparing mixed versus real-only training. Bold indicates superior performance. Mixed training shows strongest benefits with limited subjects, outperforming real-only in 9 of 14 configurations.

Dataset	Subjects	F1/Accuracy (mixed)	F1/Accuracy (real)
REALWORLD	1	**0.494 ± 0.031/0.514 ± 0.029**	0.427 ± 0.049/0.458 ± 0.044
	2	0.519 ± 0.031/0.541 ± 0.030	**0.568 ± 0.039/0.587 ± 0.039**
	3	**0.606 ± 0.029/0.615 ± 0.034**	0.575 ± 0.032/0.602 ± 0.025
	4	0.616 ± 0.043/0.633 ± 0.041	**0.640 ± 0.041/0.639 ± 0.037**
	5	**0.628 ± 0.039**/0.636 ± 0.040	0.627 ± 0.044/**0.652 ± 0.038**
	6	0.595 ± 0.061/0.617 ± 0.056	**0.648 ± 0.057/0.672 ± 0.042**
	7	**0.652 ± 0.085/0.656 ± 0.086**	0.644 ± 0.120/**0.671 ± 0.092**
OPPORTUNITY	1	**0.613 ± 0.014**/0.625 ± 0.019	0.608 ± 0.022/**0.630 ± 0.019**
	2	**0.673 ± 0.032/0.693 ± 0.018**	0.668 ± 0.033/0.682 ± 0.017
PAMAP2	1	0.457 ± 0.112/0.271 ± 0.125	**0.558 ± 0.054/0.577 ± 0.050**
	2	**0.568 ± 0.051/0.589 ± 0.052**	0.547 ± 0.048/0.580 ± 0.043
	3	0.548 ± 0.045/0.554 ± 0.072	**0.588 ± 0.065/0.614 ± 0.059**
	4	**0.616 ± 0.066/0.639 ± 0.061**	0.601 ± 0.063/0.627 ± 0.054
	5	**0.639 ± 0.064/0.656 ± 0.058**	0.620 ± 0.133/0.637 ± 0.122

These results demonstrate that modest synthetic data augmentation (10%) provides consistent performance gains, particularly valuable for data-scarce scenarios common in HAR applications.

5   Discussion

The comprehensive evaluation reveals significant insights regarding the efficiency, limitations, and applications of our synthetic IMU data generation pipeline. Results demonstrate a nuanced relationship between synthetic data quality and model performance with important implications for HAR systems.

5.1   Comparative Analysis

Our experiments show that combining real and synthetic IMU data consistently yields better performance than using real data alone. Across all three datasets (OPPORTUNITY, RealWorld, and PAMAP2), the mixed approach yielded higher F1-scores compared to using only real data. The consistent improvement across diverse datasets suggests that artificial IMU data, even with its limitations in absolute orientation representation, contributes valuable motion patterns that help the model generalize better to unseen data [18].

The improvement observed in the mixed approach can be attributed to several factors. First, the artificial data introduces controlled variations that might not be present in the original dataset, effectively expanding the model's exposure to different motion patterns while maintaining the semantic integrity of the activities. Second, the synthetic data may help mitigate biases present in the real dataset. Finally, combining real and synthetic data can act as a form of regularization, reducing overfitting to anomalies or spurious patterns in the real dataset.

Although mixed datasets yielded promising results overall, their inclusion did not consistently lead to performance improvements across all evaluation runs. One plausible explanation is the relatively small size of the virtual dataset compared to the entire real dataset. Additionally, the short duration of the video sequences used to simulate activities due to inherent limitations in the video generation model may have constrained the richness and completeness of the captured motion patterns. With the progression in the domain of video generation models, the models are now able to generate longer video sequences [1].

Despite high geodesic errors in quaternion representation without calibration (54.52° for ViTPose, 56.70° for MediaPipe, see Table 3), synthetic data positively impacts performance when combined with real data. This apparent contradiction reflects HAR models' reliance on relative motion patterns rather than absolute orientation. Dynamic components, such as acceleration and angular velocity derived from temporal changes, are captured with sufficient fidelity, consistent with previous research showing low NRMSE values for these quantities [4] (see Table 2).

Rank transformation for distribution mapping proved critical. MMD scores indicate strong statistical alignment between synthetic and real data distributions, validating this approach. While synthetic-only performance still lags real-only training, these findings highlight the potential of statistical alignment techniques.

5.2 Cost Analysis

The pipeline offers substantial cost advantages. Using a single NVIDIA A40 GPU, approximately 10 s of training data costs $0.40 and one hour to generate [2, 19]. This dramatically reduces costs compared to traditional collection involving participant compensation ($10–15/hour), researcher supervision ($30–50/hour), and equipment costs ($1,000–3,000 per sensor) [3,5,22].

5.3 Practical Applications

The ability to generate artificial IMU data on-demand also addresses the challenge of data scarcity in specialized domains or for rare activities that are difficult to capture in sufficient quantities through conventional means. Furthermore, the pipeline's reliance on commercially available video generation models and open-source pose estimation frameworks ensures that it remains accessible to a wide range of researchers and practitioners. Recent developments already demonstrate this trajectory of improvement, for example, the release of Skyreels-V2 has eliminated the previous 5-second duration constraint, enabling the generation of longer, more contextually coherent motion sequences [1].

Synthetic generation addresses privacy concerns by producing fictional human figures unlinked to specific individuals. It can enhance diversity and representation while mitigating human subjects research concerns, though biases from video generation training data remain a consideration.

5.4 Future Work

Demonstrated improvements enable applications in healthcare monitoring, sports science, industrial safety, and consumer electronics. Future work should focus on sophisticated physics models for IMU derivation, domain adaptation techniques, extension to complex activities, active learning integration, and transfer learning for new domains lacking real data. Key challenges requiring investigation include semantic ambiguities in activity descriptions ($<5\%$ of all generated videos), occasional generation of non-human subjects ($<1\%$ of all generated videos), and sensor value interpolation for occluded body locations (for failure cases see also Appendix A).

6 Conclusion

We presented a novel pipeline generating synthetic IMU data through video generation, pose estimation, and kinematic transformations. The approach addresses

HAR data scarcity through cost-effective, accessible, and privacy-preserving synthetic data generation.

Evaluation on OPPORTUNITY, RealWorld, and PAMAP2 datasets demonstrated that augmenting real data with 10% synthetic samples consistently improves performance, achieving F1-score gains up to 1.7% points. This highlights synthetic data's complementary value in enhancing model generalization.

While synthetic data cannot replace real measurements, our findings demonstrate clear value as a complementary resource. The pipeline enables scalable HAR data generation with measurable performance improvements and practical benefits in cost-efficiency, privacy, and adaptability.

Disclosure of Interests. The authors have no competing interests to declare that are relevant to the content of this article.

A   Appendix A: Qualitative Analysis of Video Generation Results Representative Examples of Success and Failure Cases

Fig. 2. Good video generation results. (a) Running, (b) standing, (c) walking. The model successfully captures motion dynamics, temporal consistency, and a full body view.

Fig. 3. Poor video generation results. (a) Preparing food (no full body view), (b) lying (semantic ambiguity with lying on a bed), (c) standing (action carried out by non-human actor/ human actor occluded)

References

1. Chen, G., et al.: Skyreels-v2: infinite-length film generative model (2025). https://arxiv.org/abs/2504.13074
2. CUDO Compute: Nvidia a40 cloud GPU (2025). https://www.cudocompute.com/products/gpu-cloud/nvidia-a40

3. Farnell: XSENS MTI-630 9-axis IMU module (2025). https://de.farnell.com/en-DE/c/sensors-transducers/sensors/motion-sensors-position-sensors/inertial-measurement-units-imu?brand=xsens
4. Gavier, I., Liu, Y., Lee, S.I.: Virtualimu: generating virtual wearable inertial data from video for deep learning applications. In: 2023 IEEE 19th International Conference on Body Sensor Networks (BSN), pp. 1–4 (2023). https://doi.org/10.1109/BSN58485.2023.10331242
5. Indeed: Researcher salary (2025). https://www.indeed.com/career/researcher/salaries
6. Jaramillo, I.E., et al.: Real-time human activity recognition with IMU and encoder sensors in wearable exoskeleton robot via deep learning networks. Sensors **22**(24) (2022). https://www.mdpi.com/1424-8220/22/24/9690
7. Kong, W., et al.: Hunyuanvideo: a systematic framework for large video generative models (2025). https://arxiv.org/abs/2412.03603
8. Kwon, H., et al.: Imutube: automatic extraction of virtual on-body accelerometry from video for human activity recognition (2020). https://arxiv.org/abs/2006.05675
9. Leng, Z., Kwon, H., Ploetz, T.: Generating virtual on-body accelerometer data from virtual textual descriptions for human activity recognition. In: Proceedings of the 2023 ACM International Symposium on Wearable Computers, ISWC 2023, pp. 39–43. Association for Computing Machinery, New York (2023). https://doi.org/10.1145/3594738.3611361
10. Leng, Z., Kwon, H., Plötz, T.: On the benefit of generative foundation models for human activity recognition (2023). https://arxiv.org/abs/2310.12085
11. Lopez-Nava, I.H., Muñoz-Meléndez, A.: Human action recognition based on low- and high-level data from wearable inertial sensors. Int. J. Distrib. Sensor Netw. **15**(12), 1550147719894532 (2019). https://doi.org/10.1177/1550147719894532
12. Loreti, D., et al.: Complex reactive event processing for assisted living: the habitat project case study. Expert Syst. Appl. **126**, 200–217 (2019)
13. Lugaresi, C., et al.: Mediapipe: a framework for building perception pipelines (2019). https://arxiv.org/abs/1906.08172
14. Martínez-Villaseñor, L., Ponce, H.: A concise review on sensor signal acquisition and transformation applied to human activity recognition and human–robot interaction. Int. J. Distrib. Sensor Netw. **15**(6), 1550147719853987 (2019). https://doi.org/10.1177/1550147719853987
15. Ordóñez, F.J., Roggen, D.: Deep convolutional and LSTM recurrent neural networks for multimodal wearable activity recognition. Sensors **16**(1) (2016). https://doi.org/10.3390/s16010115.
16. Reiss, A., Stricker, D.: Introducing a new benchmarked dataset for activity monitoring. In: 2012 16th International Symposium on Wearable Computers, pp. 108–109 (2012). https://api.semanticscholar.org/CorpusID:10337279
17. Roggen, D., et al.: Collecting complex activity datasets in highly rich networked sensor environments. In: 2010 Seventh International Conference on Networked Sensing Systems (INSS), pp. 233–240 (2010). https://api.semanticscholar.org/CorpusID:953131
18. Ruiz-Torrubiano, R., Kormann-Hainzl, G., Paudel, S.: Using synthetic data for improving robustness and resilience in ml-based smart services. In: West, S., Meierhofer, J., Buecheler, T. (eds.) Smart Services Summit, pp. 3–13. Springer, Cham (2024)
19. RunPod: Rent nvidia a40 GPUs on-demand. https://www.runpod.io/gpu/a40

20. SkyReels-AI: Skyreels v1: Human-centric video foundation model (2025). https://github.com/SkyworkAI/SkyReels-V1
21. Sztyler, T., Stuckenschmidt, H.: On-body localization of wearable devices: an investigation of position-aware activity recognition. In: 2016 IEEE International Conference on Pervasive Computing and Communications (PerCom), pp. 1–9 (2016). https://doi.org/10.1109/PERCOM.2016.7456521
22. University, C.M.: Post a study - center for behavioral and decision research (2025). https://www.cmu.edu/cbdr/information-for-researchers/post-a-study.html
23. Xu, Y., Zhang, J., Zhang, Q., Tao, D.: Vitpose: simple vision transformer baselines for human pose estimation (2022). https://arxiv.org/abs/2204.12484
24. Yang, Z., et al.: Cogvideox: text-to-video diffusion models with an expert transformer. arXiv preprint arXiv:2408.06072 (2024)
25. Zuo, C., et al.: Transformer IMU calibrator: dynamic on-body IMU calibration for inertial motion capture. In: SIGGRAPH 2025, vol. 44. ACM, Vancouver, Canada (2025). https://orca.cardiff.ac.uk/id/eprint/177840

A Technical Insight Into Sensor-S Study: Effect of Wearable Sensors on Patient Engagement and Motivation in Post-stroke Rehabilitation

Fatemeh Sardadvar[1]([⊠])(iD), Valentin Kennel[2](iD), Athina Tome[2],
Nurcennet Kaynak[2](iD), Alexa Straus[3], Rok Kos[3], Felix Schmidt[4],
Alexander Heinrich Nave[2](iD), and Bert Arnrich[1](iD)

[1] Digital Health – Connected Healthcare, Hasso Plattner Institute, University of
Potsdam, Potsdam, Brandenburg, Germany
{fatemeh.sardadvar,bert.arnrich}@hpi.de
[2] Department of Neurology, Charité – Universitätsmedizin Berlin Center for Stroke
Research Berlin, Berlin, Germany
[3] D4L, data4life gGmbH, Potsdam, Brandenburg, Germany
[4] Michels Brandenburgklinik, Berlin, Brandenbburg, Germany

Abstract. The Sensor-S study pioneers a novel integration of multimodal wearable sensors with standard care stroke rehabilitation through a randomized controlled trial design, representing a significant advancement in post-stroke care methodology. Our technical framework combines synchronized inertial measurement units, medical-grade smartwatches, and continuous glucose monitors to objectively quantify recovery biomarkers while maintaining gold-standard clinical protocols.

Initial results from 27 participants demonstrate the system's technical robustness. Clinically, we observe improvements in movement smoothness (15–22% reduction in normalized jerk scores) and gait symmetry (18% reduction in deviation indices), while simultaneously achieving a high patient compliance with daily wearable use. The adaptive trial design allows continuous refinement of technical components (e.g., reducing IMU packet loss).

As the study progresses toward full enrollment ($n = 156$), these interim results provide preliminary insights towards the potential of wearable systems to bridge the critical gap between objective measurement and therapeutic intervention in post-stroke recovery.

Keywords: Stroke Rehabilitation · Wearable Sensors · Inertial Measurement Units · Continuous Glucose Monitoring

1 Introduction

Stroke is a leading cause of disability worldwide, often resulting in sensory and motor impairments that significantly impact patients' quality of life [1]. Effective

Ö. Durmaz Incel et al. (Eds.): iWOAR 2025, LNCS 16292, pp. 404–412, 2026.
https://doi.org/10.1007/978-3-032-13312-0_26

rehabilitation is crucial for recovery, but its success depends on factors such as patient engagement, motivation, and the ability to monitor progress objectively [2].

Traditional rehabilitation methods face challenges in providing continuous, personalized feedback, which can limit their efficacy. The Sensor-S study addresses this gap by integrating wearable sensors into a controlled randomized trial design within standard clinical care protocols. This dual approach enables rigorous evaluation of whether wearable-generated biofeedback can influence patient motivation and engagement during stroke rehabilitation, an area lacking robust clinical evidence despite widespread technological adoption [3].

Wearable sensors offer a transformative solution by enabling real-time monitoring of physiological and behavioral data. Devices like inertial measurement units (IMUs), smartwatches, and continuous glucose monitors (CGMs) can track gait patterns, cardiovascular metrics, and metabolic trends, providing clinicians and patients with actionable insights [3,4]. Critically, they may improve outcomes through enhancing motivation via personalized feedback loops [4] and enabling early detection of complications (e.g., falls, mood disorders) [2].

Building on validated methods for sensor-based data analysis [3], the Sensor-S study represents a pioneering effort to merge multimodal wearable technologies with gold-standard rehabilitation. Our multicentric randomized controlled trial, conducted in collaboration with Charité Universitätsmedizin Berlin, D4L data4life gGmbH, and Brandenburgklinik Berlin-Brandenburg, has generated promising preliminary findings that warrant further investigation through continued data collection and analysis.

Preliminary results confirm our sensors capture clinically meaningful metrics (e.g., gait asymmetry) while revealing implementation challenges that are actively being addressed [5]. By bridging technological innovation and patient-centered care, this study aims to establish whether wearables can systematically improve rehabilitation trajectories, a critical step toward personalized, data-driven stroke recovery [6–8].

2 Data Collection Framework

The foundation of any robust data analysis lies in the systematic acquisition of reliable and clinically meaningful datasets. To this end, it is necessary to detail the technical architecture of the Sensor-S data collection framework. This framework addresses three critical requirements for rehabilitation research: high-fidelity signal acquisition through validated wearable devices, temporal synchronization across heterogeneous data streams, and real-world applicability in clinical and home settings [5,6]. This section details the specific wearable sensor technologies employed in our study and their respective data outputs.

2.1 Inertial Measurement Unit

Inertial Measurement Units (IMUs) are compact sensor systems that measure and report specific force (via accelerometers) and angular rate (via gyroscopes), providing precise quantification of movement kinematics [9,10]. In the Sensor-S study, we employ Movella Xsens DOT IMUs (see Fig. 1a) to capture triaxial acceleration (± 16 g range) and angular velocity ($\pm 2000°/$s range) at high temporal resolution.

In the Sensor-S study, five kinetic tasks have been designed to employ IMUs:

Gait Analysis (120 Hz Sampling) focuses on stride length, swing phase symmetry, and toe-off force.

Sit-to-Stand (60 Hz) focuses on lower-limb power and ascent/descent coordination.

Timed Up-and-Go (60 Hz) focuses on transitional mobility and turning kinematics.

Water Task (60 Hz) focuses on upper-limb coordination and movement smoothness.

Spasticity Assessment (60 Hz) focuses on joint angular velocity during passive stretching.

The elevated 120 Hz sampling for gait analysis enables precise detection of sub-movement events (e.g., heel strike timing within ± 8.3 ms [11]), while 60 Hz suffices for slower functional tasks.

2.2   Smartwatch

The Samsung Galaxy Watch 6 serves as the primary platform for continuous physiological monitoring, passively recording three key parameters: heart rate (sampled at 1 Hz via PPG optical sensor), step counts (derived from 10 Hz accelerometer data), and skin temperature (measured at 0.1 Hz intervals) [8].

This commercially available smartwatch was selected based on its validated clinical-grade sensors, demonstrating strong agreement with ECG for heart rate monitoring [12], and its widespread adoption among at-risk populations (25–30% usage rate) which enhances patient compliance [12,14]. In clinical validation, the watch showed 92% concordance with gold-standard actigraphy for step counting in stroke populations [12]. Designed for continuous wear, the system captures data for approximately 20 h daily (excluding charging periods), with all measurements encrypted locally before secure transmission to maintain patient privacy [8]. This combination of technical reliability, patient familiarity, and robust data security makes the smartwatch an ideal component of our multimodal monitoring system.

2.3   Continuous Glucose Monitor

For metabolic monitoring, continuous glucose monitors (Dexcom G7 CGMs) were selected (see Fig. 1b) due to their clinical validation and non-invasive interstitial fluid measurement [4,12]. While primarily used to investigate glycemic variability's impact on stroke outcomes [4], these sensors also serve as engagement tools by providing patients with retrospective daily glucose trends via the study app [8]. This dual purpose aligns with growing evidence that metabolic monitoring can motivate lifestyle modifications in rehabilitation [11,12].

2.4   Data4Life Platforms

The Sensor-S study leverages D4L's integrated platform ecosystem to create a seamless pipeline from patient data collection to researcher analysis, combining the patient-facing D4L Collect mobile application with the Research Studio web platform (Fig. 2). The D4L Collect mobile application serves as the central hub for wearable integration, managing Bluetooth Low Energy (BLE) connections to IMU sensors and smartwatches. For CGM, the system employs a distinct architecture to transmit data exclusively to the Dexcom mobile app, with glucose values subsequently retrieved by the D4L Collect app [6]. The mobile app provides real-time visualization of movement trajectories during assessments and generates automated daily/weekly reports summarizing key rehabilitation metrics [8,9]. Simultaneously, the companion Research Studio web platform empowers researchers with comprehensive tools for study management, harmonizing raw sensor streams into analysis-ready formats [6,8].

The integrated architecture addresses both technical and regulatory challenges of multimodal rehabilitation research. The mobile app's intuitive interface has demonstrated strong patient adoption, while the web platform's features, including remote consent tracking, compliance monitoring, and configurable study protocols, enable efficient multicenter coordination [8,9]. This infrastructure effectively bridges distributed data collection with centralized research capabilities, supporting the study's goals of both scientific discovery and clinical translation.

3   Preliminary Data Analysis

At this interim stage of the Sensor-S study, we have collected comprehensive wearable sensor data from 27 participants, representing approximately 17% of our target enrollment of 156 subjects. While this initial dataset provides valuable insights, we recognize the need for continued data collection, particularly as the second phase of the project has only recently commenced, limiting our ability to conduct robust cross-phase comparisons at this time.

Despite these limitations, we are actively performing interim analyses on the available data to verify data quality and consistency across recording sessions, refine our analytical pipelines, and identify preliminary trends that may

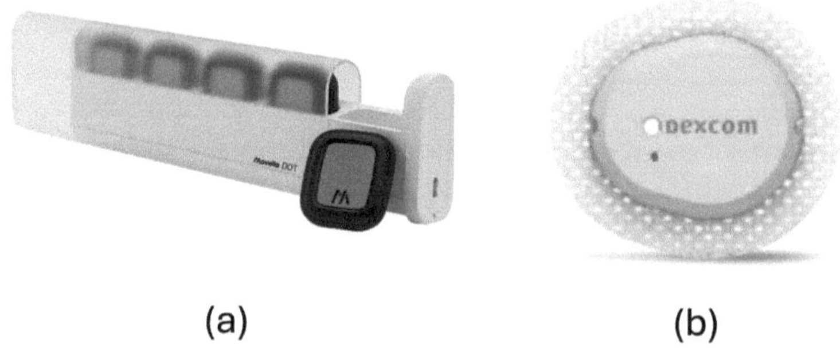

(a)   (b)

Fig. 1. Digital wearables: (a) Movella Xsens DOT, (b) Dexcom G7

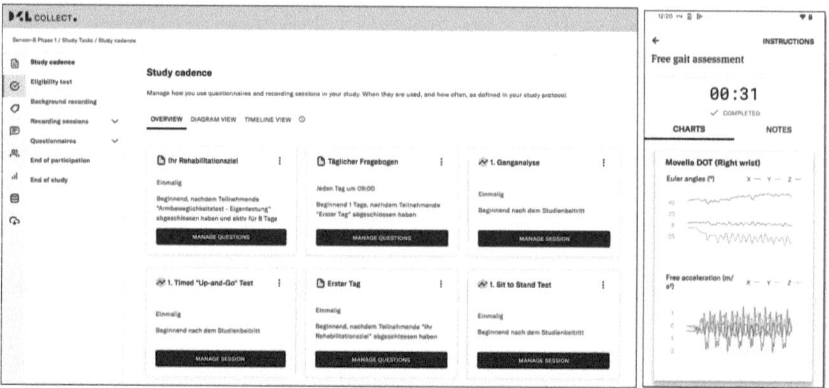

Fig. 2. D4L Research Studio web platform and D4L Collect Android application

inform our final analysis approaches. These ongoing efforts allow us to iteratively improve our protocols while gaining early insights into potential rehabilitation biomarkers.

The following details highlight several important analytical approaches we have implemented thus far.

3.1 Gait Analysis

Our preliminary gait analysis utilizes raw triaxial accelerometer and gyroscope data (120 Hz sampling) from the IMUs to quantify movement asymmetries and recovery patterns in stroke patients [9,13]. The analytical pipeline begins with an adaptive stance detection algorithm that analyzes gyroscope magnitude signals using dynamic thresholding. This detection forms the foundation for calculating detailed foot trajectories (Fig. 3), revealing characteristic deviations in paretic limb movement patterns.

Key spatiotemporal parameters including stride time, stride length, and swing phase duration show statistically significant asymmetries when comparing bilateral measurements within patients. These results align with known hemiparetic gait pathologies and demonstrate our system's sensitivity to stroke-related impairments [7]. For broader context, we benchmark our findings against the open-access Kiel dataset of healthy controls (Fig. 4) [6].

Longitudinal analysis of repeated assessments shows measurable improvement in symmetry indices, though these early trends require verification in our full cohort. All algorithms are implemented in Python using a modular pipeline that will facilitate future expansion as more data becomes available.

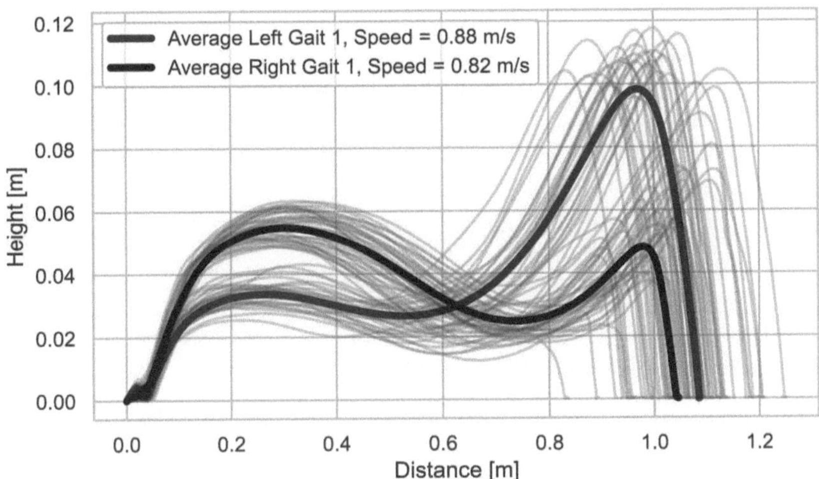

Fig. 3. Gait cycle comparison between left and right foot in a stroke patient

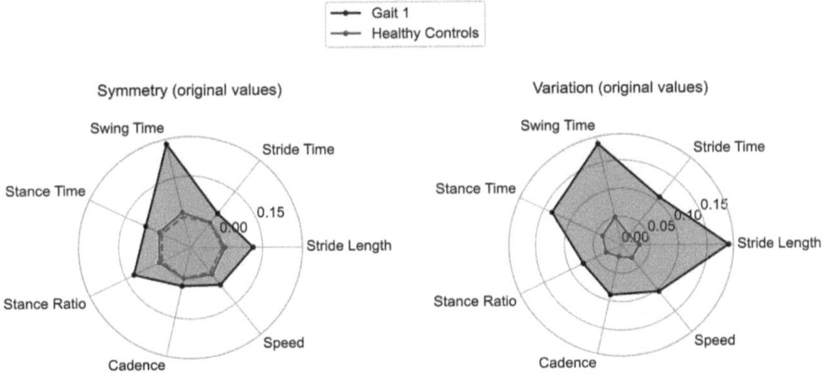

Fig. 4. Radar plot comparing movement parameters between a stroke patient (blue) and healthy controls (red) (Color figure online)

3.2   Signal Smoothness

Movement smoothness serves as a key quantitative biomarker for motor recovery in stroke rehabilitation, reflecting improved neuromuscular control and coordination over time. We quantify smoothness using the normalized jerk metric, calculated as in Eq. (1).

$$J = \frac{1}{2} \cdot \frac{t^5}{L^2} \cdot \int_0^t \left\| \frac{d^3 \mathbf{r}(t)}{dt^3} \right\|^2 dt \tag{1}$$

where:

- J = dimensionless jerk score (lower values indicate smoother motion)
- t = movement duration (s)
- L = path length (m)
- $\mathbf{r}(t)$ = position vector from IMU trajectory integration
- $\frac{d^3 \mathbf{r}}{dt^3}$ = jerk (rate of acceleration change)

This method normalizes for movement duration and amplitude, enabling cross-task comparisons [15]. The jerk metric is particularly sensitive to the small hesitations and corrections characteristic of post-stroke movement disorders [16]. Figure 5 demonstrates these trends, plotting normalized jerk values for 9 participants from intervention group during the sit-to-stand task. The majority show improved smoothness (lower jerk score) for the second visit which is considered as promising results.

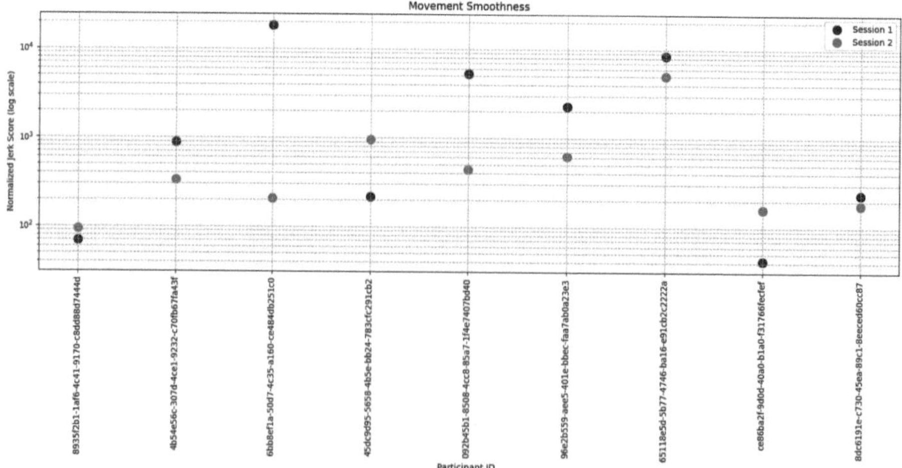

Fig. 5. Normalized jerk score for 9 intervention participants in Visit 1 vs. Visit 2

4   Conclusion

The Sensor-S study demonstrates that multimodal wearable systems can objectively quantify stroke recovery while addressing key implementation challenges in rehabilitation research. Our technical solutions, including adaptive stance detection algorithms, synchronized data capture, and quality control provide a robust framework for continuous motor and physiological monitoring. Interim analyses of 27 participants confirm clinically meaningful sensitivity, detecting improvements in movement smoothness and gait asymmetry reductions, while revealing hardware-specific limitations like IMU packet loss that inform ongoing trial refinements.

As an ongoing study in its early stages, we continue to address critical challenges in data quality (e.g., sensor dropout events), technical reliability (e.g., optimizing IMU firmware), and patient recruitment. Through iterative adjustments such as enhanced pre-session sensor validation and adaptive patient engagement algorithms, we are systematically reducing controllable barriers. Preliminary results, though limited by sample size, align with our hypotheses. Future work will expand our analytical pipelines to include advanced machine learning techniques for personalized rehabilitation profiling.

By rigorously evaluating the integration of wearable sensors with standard care through a randomized controlled design, this study aims to prove the effect of digital wearable on patient engagement in post-stroke rehabilitation. The convergence of technical innovation and clinical translation in this work holds significant potential to redefine post-stroke rehabilitation paradigms [5,8].

Acknowledgements. We gratefully acknowledge Dr. Lin Zhou for her foundational work in wearable-based gait analysis, particularly her framework for IMU signal processing that informed our movement quantification methods.

References

1. Boukhemoufa, I., et al.: Wearable sensors and machine learning in post-stroke rehabilitation assessment: a systematic review. Biomed. Signal Process. Control **71**, 103197 (2022)
2. Zhou, L., et al.: Using transparent neural networks and wearable inertial sensors to generate physiologically-relevant insights for gait. In: 21st IEEE International Conference on Machine Learning and Applications (ICMLA), pp. 1274–1280. IEEE (2022)
3. Spatz, E.S., et al.: Wearable digital health technologies for monitoring in cardiovascular medicine. N. Engl. J. Med. **390**(4), 346–356 (2024)
4. Stock, R., et al.: The potential of wearable technology to support stroke survivors' motivation for home-exercise. Physiotherapy Theory Pract. (2023)
5. Zhou, L., et al.: Monitoring and visualizing stroke rehabilitation progress using wearable sensors. In: IEEE Engineering in Medicine and Biology Conference (EMBC) (2024)

6. Chromik, J., et al.: SensorHub: multimodal sensing in real-life enables home-based studies. Sensors **22**(1), 468 (2022)
7. Zhou, L., Schneider, J., Arnrich, B., Königorski, S.: Analyzing population-level trials as N-of-1 trials: an application to gait. Contemp. Clin. Trials Commun. **38**, 101282 (2024)
8. Sensor-S Study Protocol: Effect of Wearable Sensors on Patient Engagement and Motivation in Post-Stroke Rehabilitation. Version 1.0 (2024)
9. Zhou, L., et al.: How we found our IMU: guidelines to IMU selection and a comparison of seven IMUs for pervasive healthcare applications. Sensors **20**(15), 4090 (2020)
10. Zhou, L., Fischer, E., Brahms, C.M., Granacher, U., Arnrich, B.: Using transparent neural networks and wearable inertial sensors to generate physiologically-relevant insights for gait. In: 21st IEEE International Conference on Machine Learning and Applications (ICMLA), pp. 1274–1280. IEEE (2022)
11. Trautmann, J., et al.: TRIPOD–a treadmill walking dataset with IMU, pressure-distribution and photoelectric data for gait analysis. Data **6**(9), 95 (2021)
12. Dhurgua, L.S., et al.: Use of wearable devices in individuals with or at risk for cardiovascular disease in the US, 2019 to 2020. JAMA Netw. Open **6**(6), e2316634 (2023)
13. Albert, J., Zhou, L., et al.: Using wearable sensors in stroke rehabilitation. Poster Presented at: 11th International Workshop on Sensor-based Activity Recognition and Artificial Intelligence (iWOAR), Potsdam, Germany (2024)
14. Steck, M., et al.: Evaluation of glycemic variability and discharge outcomes in patients with ischemic stroke following thrombolysis. The Neurohospitalist (2023)
15. Teulings, H.L., Contreras-Vidal, J.L., Stelmach, G.E., Adler, C.H.: Parkinsonism reduces coordination of fingers, wrist, and arm in fine motor control. Exp. Brain Res. **116**(2), 269–276 (1997)
16. Rohrer, B., Fasoli, S., Krebs, H.I., et al.: Movement smoothness changes during stroke recovery. J. Neurophysiol. **87**(2), 1235–1240 (2002)

SpaceStriker: A Peer-Assisted Sensor-Based Exergame with Real-Time ML-Driven Feedback

Michal Slupczynski[1(✉)] [iD], Khaleel Asyraaf Mat Sanusi[2] [iD],
Roland Klemke[2,3] [iD], and Stefan Decker[3] [iD]

[1] Computer Science 5, RWTH Aachen University, Aachen, Germany
`slupczynski@dbis.rwth-aachen.de`
[2] Cologne Game Lab, TH Köln, Cologne, Germany
[3] Open University of the Netherlands, Heerlen, The Netherlands

Abstract. Physical inactivity and the lack of meaningful social interaction remain pressing challenges in the increasingly digital environments of today. While exergames offer a promising avenue to encourage movement, they often lack real-time adaptability and social engagement mechanisms. However, few existing systems integrate real-time Machine Learning (ML)-based activity recognition with peer-assisted interaction to enhance both physical and social dimensions of gameplay. We present `SpaceStriker: Exercise Odyssey`, a real-time sensor-based Exergame that combines ML-driven feedback with structured peer interaction modes to promote collaborative and competitive play. The system uses real-time motion recognition to provide immediate feedback, supporting fairness, engagement, and co-regulation between players. Evaluation of user feedback, behavioral observation, and gameplay data across multiple roles reveal that participants found the system usable, motivating, and socially engaging, with peer assistance enhancing awareness and accountability. Our findings demonstrate the feasibility and potential of integrating peer collaboration and ML-based sensor feedback in exergames, paving the way for scalable and, adaptive applications in educational, therapeutic, and social settings.

Keywords: Peer-Assisted Exergaming · Device-free Sensing · Real-time Activity Recognition · Machine Learning · Human-Computer Interaction

1 Introduction

In recent decades, sedentary lifestyles have contributed to the rise of conditions such as obesity, cardiovascular disease, and type 2 diabetes mellitus [2]. These health issues highlight the increasing importance of systems that support physical activity, especially those that are both engaging and accessible. To address these challenges, targeted behavioral and environmental interventions are needed

ⓒ The Author(s), under exclusive license to Springer Nature Switzerland AG 2026
Ö. Durmaz Incel et al. (Eds.): iWOAR 2025, LNCS 16292, pp. 413–421, 2026.
https://doi.org/10.1007/978-3-032-13312-0_27

to overcome common barriers such as lack of time, unclear exercise opportunities, and limited social interaction [8].

One promising intervention is the use of *exergames*, video games that incorporate physical movement into gameplay through full-body interaction [11]. Exergames have been shown to elicit significant physiological responses, making them a valid form of aerobic exercise. Beyond physical benefits, social aspects of exergaming play a crucial role: engaging in physical activity with others enhances motivation and adherence [15], and multiplayer exergaming has been associated with reduced loneliness and improved social connection [6]. Recent advances in Artificial Intelligence (AI), particularly in computer vision and Human Pose Estimation (HPE), enable new forms of real-time activity recognition using standard camera input [10]. These developments pave the way for exergames that are not only hardware-light but also responsive and intelligent in their feedback mechanisms.

1.1   Research Questions

Current exergames often lack social collaboration mechanisms and integrated, real-time ML-based feedback, limiting their interactivity and adaptability. To address this, we formulate the following research questions:

RQ1: How does peer interaction affect player motivation and perception in a sensor-based exergame?

RQ2: How effective is ML-driven, real-time sensor feedback in supporting perceived fairness and activity awareness?

RQ3: How do participants perceive the usability and social dynamics of a peer-assisted, sensor-enhanced exergame?

We present **SpaceStriker**, a prototype exergame that integrates machine learning-based activity recognition, real-time sensor feedback, and peer-assisted interaction. Our key contributions are as follows:

– Design of a real-time exergame with sensor-based activity recognition
– Integration of peer-assistance mechanisms to facilitate cooperative play
– Evaluation of the system's feasibility and usability.

2   Background and Related Work

Exergames have gained attention for promoting physical activity, offering physiological benefits such as improved cardiovascular health [16] and addressing musculoskeletal disorders from sedentary behavior [12]. Interactive feedback is a fundamental component for peer-assisted exergames [9]. Social aspects boost impact of game design: multiplayer exergames improve adherence and enjoyment [5], with cooperative modes encouraging prosocial behavior [7]. Recent advances in computer vision enable real-time HPE using standard cameras [3]. Unlike systems based on Inertial Measurement Units (IMU) or depth sensors, HPE offers accessible, controller-free interaction [4] and device-free sensing. While ML models vary in accuracy and speed [14], they are suitable for tracking multiple users simultaneously [10].

However, few exergames combine real-time ML-based activity recognition with structured peer interaction and feedback. This work addresses that gap by integrating these elements into a unified exergame experience.

3   Methods and Realization

The core concept of this project is a cooperative exergame that leverages real-time HPE to enable full-body interaction without specialized hardware. Real-time activity recognition is implemented via an ML-based HPE pipeline, which processes camera input to detect and track key body joints [3]. This enables immediate in-game feedback and interaction without external controllers. The game design emphasizes peer interaction via cooperative roles and shared performance goals. Players engage in a two-person game designed to foster collaboration and physical engagement through intuitive body movements. Players assume distinct roles: a *Pilot*, who controls the spaceship's movement while dodging obstacles, and a *Gunner*, who aims and fires at enemies; both contribute to a shared score. This setup is structured to promote mutual accountability and coordinated action toward a shared goal.

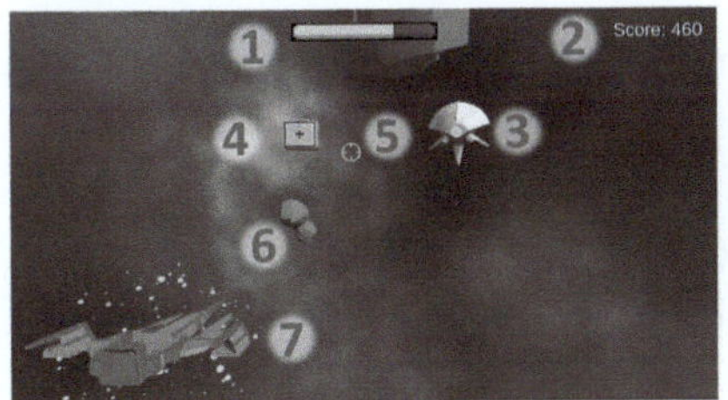
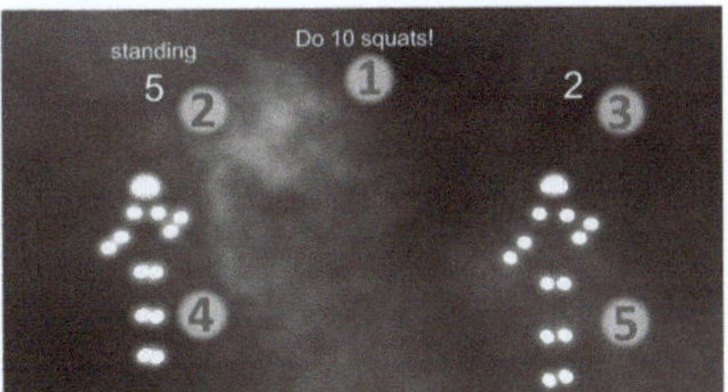

(a) **1**: Healthbar, **2**: Score, **3**: Enemy,
4: Collectible Health Boost,
5: Crosshair (aimed by the *Gunner*),
6: Asteroid to be avoided,
7: Spaceship (controlled by the *Pilot*).

(b) **1**: Exercise instructions,
2 and **3**: Player repetition counts,
4 and **5** Player pose representations.

Fig. 1. *SpaceStriker* game modes: game-stage (left) and exercise-stage (right).

The gameplay is divided in two sections (see Fig. 1): the Game Stage and the Exercise Stage. In the Game Stage (Fig. 1a), players work together to accumulate points by surviving for as long as possible and destroying enemies, encouraging mutual accountability. In this game mode, the spaceship can move within a vertical plane, maneuvering to avoid oncoming asteroids and enemy laser projectiles. A shared score and health bar, visible at the top of the screen, reinforce their mutual dependency (see Fig. 1a) and emphasizes real-time coordination as players must work together to succeed. Collisions with obstacles deplete the spaceship's health, and the game ends when the health reaches zero.

Scoring is calculated by combining survival time and destroyed enemies into a single metric, where t is the time survived, e the number of enemies destroyed, s_t the score per second, and s_e the score per enemy: $\text{score}(t, e) = t \cdot s_t + e \cdot s_e$. Upon reaching a score threshold, both players must perform a set pf physical exercises to progress in the Exercise Stage (see Fig. 1b), reinforcing exertion through collaborative goals. This design aligns with findings that cooperative exergaming boosts motivation and adherence [5], and showcases how ML-based feedback can support immersive, social gameplay.

HPE tracks players' movements, which is then mapped to their assigned controls. The *pilot* navigates the ship using directional input derived from wrist position relative to body center, while the *gunner* aims with hand gestures.

Crosshair position for the *gunner* is derived from the midpoint between both wrists and projected onto a distant plane using raycasting. The system projects a ray from the camera through the midpoint coordinates in screen space. If a ray intersects a target, the crosshair shifts forward to provide depth-based visual feedback. This provides intuitive visual feedback and supports continuous, gesture-based targeting without explicit buttons or controllers.

Spaceship motion for the *pilot* is derived according to Eq. (1) from the angle θ between the body center $\mathbf{c}$ and the midpoint between the wrists $\mathbf{m}$, relative to the vertical axis (see Fig. 2).

$$\theta = \text{atan2}(m_y - c_y, m_x - c_x) - \frac{\pi}{2} \tag{1}$$

This angle is converted into a normalized movement direction:

$$\mathbf{d} = \begin{pmatrix} \cos(\theta) \\ -\sin(\theta) \end{pmatrix} \tag{2}$$

Squat detection is based on the inner angle α_{knee} at the knee, computed from hip - knee - ankle coordinates. Valid squats require alternation between:

$$210° \leq \alpha_{\text{knee}} \leq 290° \quad \text{(squat)}, \quad \text{and} \quad 160° \leq \alpha_{\text{knee}} \leq 190° \quad \text{(stand)}$$

The exergame system was implemented using the Unity 3D engine[1], with a modular architecture separating gameplay logic, movement detection, and network communication. Unity's powerful physics system, advanced graphics rendering, and cross-platform compatibility cater to a wide range of developers. Pose detection is powered by YOLOv8[2], a lightweight model that performs real-time keypoint estimation on webcam input. All components are connected through a modular pipeline, allowing future substitution or refinement of ML models without modifying game logic. A custom Python script continuously transmits

---

[1] https://unity.com/.
[2] https://docs.ultralytics.com/models/yolov8/.

Fig. 2. Visualization of the angle θ used to control the spaceship motion. It is calculated between the body center c and the midpoint between the wrists m.

17 skeleton keypoints via UDP to the Unity backend. On the Unity side, each player object asynchronously receives and decodes keypoint data from the HPE pipeline. Further technical choices such as GPU-based inference, asynchronous networking, and Unity's Netcode for GameObjects ensure low-latency performance and maintainability across platforms.

4 Evaluation

4.1 Participants and Method

The system was evaluated with 11 participants over a two-week period. Eight were aged 25 or younger, while the remaining three were 46 or older. Six participants were students (four in Computer Science), four were employed, and one selected "other" as their occupation. Usability testing was conducted in a controlled lab environment using a mixed-methods approach. Participants interacted with the system in cooperative pairs when possible, or with the one of the evaluators as a fallback partner.

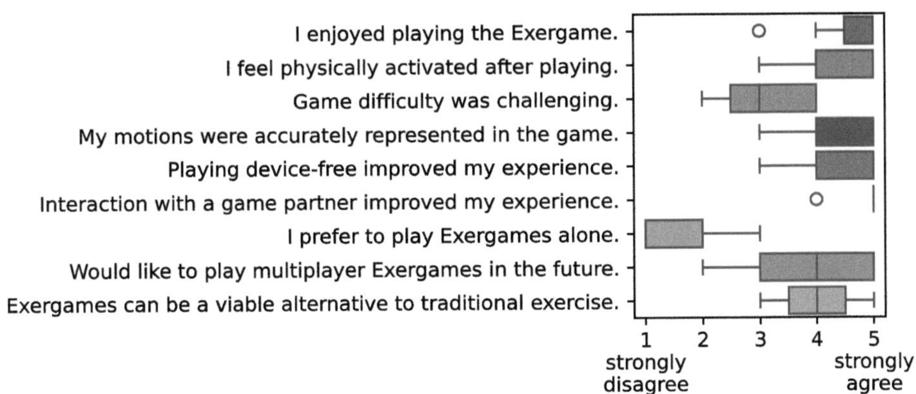

Fig. 3. Game-specific questionnaire results (n = 11)

4.2   Findings

Participants rated the system highly on the System Usability Scale (SUS) [1], with an average score of 80.45, exceeding the threshold for grade A usability. Additionally, participants were asked for game-specific feedback (see Fig. 3), who generally found the game enjoyable and physically activating.

Several users reported mild exhaustion or breaking a sweat, suggesting that even short sessions provided meaningful physical engagement. Difficulty was perceived as appropriate overall, with more experienced gamers adapting quicker to the controls and gameplay mechanics. Real-time motion control was well received, particularly for the pilot role, which most found intuitive. The gunner's controls were seen as slightly less accessible, with some participants expressing minor frustration. Still, most users adapted quickly, and the majority agreed that their movements were accurately reflected in-game. Controller-free interaction was rated positively, with users appreciating the freedom of playing without wearables or handheld devices.

The peer-based gameplay was especially well received: almost all participants indicated that interacting with a partner improved their experience, and most stated a preference for cooperative exergames over solo play. Feedback also indicated strong interest in future use: users see exergames as viable alternatives to traditional exercise, though responses varied in how likely they would be to play again. Additional free-text responses emphasized enjoyment of whole-body control, cooperative gameplay, and the novelty of the interface, while suggesting improvements such as more levels, game modes, and additional visual feedback.

5   Discussion

Real-time HPE allowed for responsive in-game actions without the need for wearables. This minimized user friction and ensured fairness, as players could rely on consistent gameplay behavior to evaluate performance across roles. The cooperative two-role structure encouraged communication and mutual support, which participants cited as a key factor in their enjoyment. The alignment of individual responsibilities with shared outcomes helped sustain motivation and reinforced the sense of joint achievement. Involving non-expert users in system testing provided valuable insights into control clarity, motion interpretation, and social dynamics. This highlights the value of participatory design to informed iterative refinement of ML-driven interactive systems.

RQ1: How does peer interaction affect player motivation and perception in a sensor-based exergame? Participants strongly preferred playing in cooperative mode and consistently reported that peer interaction improved their overall experience. Most disagreed with the idea of playing exergames alone, highlighting the motivational value of shared goals and real-time collaboration.

RQ2: How effective is ML-driven, real-time sensor feedback in supporting perceived fairness and activity awareness? The system's pose-based input was generally perceived as accurate, particularly in the pilot role. ML-based real-time feedback enabled players to link body movement directly to game outcomes, reinforcing activity awareness. While some users found the gunner controls less intuitive, most adapted quickly and reported fair representation of their actions.

RQ3: How do participants perceive the usability and social dynamics of a peer-assisted, sensor-enhanced exergame? The system achieved a high average SUS (80.45), indicating excellent overall usability. Participants valued the controller-free interaction and full-body involvement. Feedback emphasized enjoyment, ease of learning, and appreciation for the cooperative structure, confirming the viability of peer-assisted, sensor-enhanced exergaming as an engaging social activity.

Limitations. The presented study is limited by its small sample size ($n = 11$) and short-term evaluation, without longitudinal follow-up to assess sustained engagement or impact. Additionally, user feedback highlighted areas for improvement, including the addition of more levels, diverse game modes, and enhanced visual feedback. These factors should be addressed in future work to strengthen generalizability and user experience.

6   Summary and Conclusion

SpaceStriker demonstrates the successful integration of ML, sensor-based feedback, and peer interaction within an exergame environment. The system's technical feasibility and strong user reception highlight its potential to foster both physical activity and social engagement. These results underscore the value of combining real-time ML-driven feedback with collaborative gameplay, paving the way for future research and broader applications in health, education, and rehabilitation.

6.1   Future Work

To fully assess the system's effectiveness, future research should be conducted in real-world environments such as schools and rehabilitation centers. Furthermore, a deeper stakeholder engagement loop with users, educators, and clinicians should be established. This feedback will be crucial for refining adaptive ML models, with system applicability and effectiveness being the ultimate goal.

Expanding the game's content is considered a key area for improvement. User feedback indicates that more levels and a variety of new collectible items should be added, such as those that can boost attributes like fire rate or spaceship speed. New enemy types, such as aliens that fly directly toward the spaceship, could also be incorporated to add to the challenge. A greater variety of exercises, including more complex movements like lunges and burpees, would be a welcome addition to the workout experience.

Additionally, a visual representation of both players during gameplay, like a skeleton avatar, should be integrated to provide real-time feedback and increase social engagement. A crucial technical advancement for multiplayer scalability involves implementing HPE on a cloud-based system with a high-end GPU [13]. This would significantly increase the keypoint calculation rate. The main challenge, however, would be to minimize the latency between the server and the client. If a low-latency solution can be found, real-time pose estimation could be made accessible on a wider range of devices, including mobile phones and tablets. This could then pave the way for a new generation of mobile exergames, allowing for a much larger audience to be reached.

Acknowledgments. The research leading to these results has received funding from the German Federal Ministry of Education and Research (BMBF) through the project "Multimodales Immersives Lernen mit künstlicher Intelligenz für Psychomotorische Fähigkeiten" ("MILKI-PSY" (https://milki-psy.de/)) (grant no. 16DHB4015).

References

1. Brooke, J.: SUS: a quick and dirty usability scale. In: Jordan, P.W., Thomas, B., Weerdmeester, B.A., McClelland, I.L. (eds.) Usability Evaluation in Industry, pp. 189–194. Taylor & Francis (1996). https://www.taylorfrancis.com/chapters/edit/10.1201/9781498710411-35/sus-quick-dirty-usability-scale-john-brooke
2. Chai, W., Nigg, C.R., Pagano, I.S., Motl, R.W., Horwath, C., Dishman, R.K.: Associations of quality of life with physical activity, fruit and vegetable consumption, and physical inactivity in a free living, multiethnic population in Hawaii: a longitudinal study. Int. J. Behav. Nutrition Phys. Activity **7**, 83 (2010). https://doi.org/10.1186/1479-5868-7-83
3. Chen, S., Yang, R.R.: Pose trainer: correcting exercise posture using pose estimation. https://doi.org/10.48550/arXiv.2006.11718
4. Rado, D., Sankaran, A., Plasek, J., Nuckley, D.J., Keefe, D.F.: A Real-Time Physical Therapy Visualization Strategy to Improve Unsupervised Patient Rehabilitation (2009). https://www.researchgate.net/publication/267555734_A_Real-Time_Physical_Therapy_Visualization_Strategy_to_Improve_Unsupervised_Patient_Rehabilitation
5. Kaos, M.D., Rhodes, R.E., Hämäläinen, P., Graham, T.N.: Social play in an exergame. In: Brewster, S., Fitzpatrick, G., Cox, A., Kostakos, V. (eds.) Proceedings of the 2019 CHI Conference on Human Factors in Computing Systems, pp. 1–13. ACM, New York (2019). https://doi.org/10.1145/3290605.3300660
6. Li, J., Erdt, M., Chen, L., Cao, Y., Lee, S.Q., Theng, Y.L.: The social effects of exergames on older adults: systematic review and metric analysis. J. Med. Internet Res. **20**(6), e10486 (2018). https://doi.org/10.2196/10486
7. Marker, A.M., Staiano, A.E.: Better together: outcomes of cooperation versus competition in social exergaming. Games Health J. **4**(1), 25–30 (2015). https://doi.org/10.1089/g4h.2014.0066
8. Marmot, M.: Social determinants of health inequalities. Lancet **365**(9464), 1099–1104 (2005). https://doi.org/10.1016/S0140-6736(05)74234-3

9. Mat Sanusi, K.A., Iren, D., Fanchamps, N., Geisen, M., Klemke, R., et al.: Virtual virtuoso: a systematic literature review of immersive learning environments for psychomotor skill development. Educ. Technol. Res. Dev. 1–41 (2025). https://doi.org/10.1007/s11423-025-10449-2

10. Munea, T.L., Jembre, Y.Z., Weldegebriel, H.T., Chen, L., Huang, C., Yang, C.: The progress of human pose estimation: a survey and taxonomy of models applied in 2D human pose estimation. IEEE Access **8**, 133330–133348 (2020). https://doi.org/10.1109/ACCESS.2020.3010248

11. Peng, W., Lin, J.H., Crouse, J.: Is playing exergames really exercising? A meta-analysis of energy expenditure in active video games. Cyberpsychol. Behav. Soc. Netw. **14**(11), 681–688 (2011). https://doi.org/10.1089/cyber.2010.0578

12. Schmidt, A., Shahid, H., Kraft, D., Bieber, G., Fellmann, M.: Interactive exercises for computer-based work using a webcam. In: Proceedings of the 8th International Workshop on Sensor-Based Activity Recognition and Artificial Intelligence, iWOAR 2023. Association for Computing Machinery, New York, NY, USA (2023). https://doi.org/10.1145/3615834.3615840

13. Slupczynski, M.P., Klamma, R.: MILKI-PSY cloud: MLOps-based multimodal sensor stream processing pipeline for learning analytics in psychomotor education. In: MILeS 2022 : Multimodal Immersive Learning Systems 2022: proceedings of the Second International Workshop on Multimodal Immersive Learning Systems (MILeS 2022) at the Seventeenth European Conference on Technology Enhanced Learning (EC-TEL 2022): Toulouse, France, pp. 8–14 (2022). https://doi.org/10.18154/RWTH-2022-09814

14. Toshev, A., Szegedy, C.: DeepPose: human pose estimation via deep neural networks. In: 2014 IEEE Conference on Computer Vision and Pattern Recognition, pp. 1653–1660. IEEE (2014). https://doi.org/10.1109/CVPR.2014.214

15. Warner, L.M., Ziegelmann, J.P., Schüz, B., Wurm, S., Schwarzer, R.: Synergistic effect of social support and self-efficacy on physical exercise in older adults. J. Aging Phys. Act. **19**(3), 249–261 (2011). https://doi.org/10.1123/japa.19.3.249

16. Oh, Y., Yang, S.: Defining exergames & exergaming. In: Meaningful Play Conference (2010)

Voice Privacy in Speech Systems: A Comparative Study of Pitch Shifting and StarGAN-VC

Mehmet Arif Taşlı[1], Eren Akyürek[1,2], and Funda Yıldırım[2]

[1] Department of Computer Engineering, Yeditepe University, Istanbul, Turkey
mehmetarif.tasli@b-tu.de, e.akyurek@utwente.nl
[2] Cognition, Data and Education Section, University of Twente,
Enschede, The Netherlands
f.yildirim@utwente.nl

Abstract. Voice recognition systems facilitate naturalistic human—com-puter interaction. However, spoken input may inherently expose sensitive acoustic features that can threaten user privacy. In particular, raw spoken language data can reveal paralinguistic information such as emotional state, health condition, and speaker identity, which poses a significant privacy risk when the speaker's voice is recognizable, especially within identifiable communities or groups. This study aims to investigate the preservation of acoustic privacy by evaluating two voice transformation techniques: traditional pitch shifting and the StarGAN-VC deep generative model [3], in terms of their effectiveness in obfuscating speaker identity while preserving lexical intelligibility. We measure their performance along two dimensions: lexical accuracy, assessed via an automatic speech recognition (ASR) application programming interface (API), and speaker identifiability, evaluated through subjective human listener studies. Our results show that although both methods degrade ASR performance, StarGAN-VC offers significantly greater privacy protection among individuals within the same social circle, by reducing speaker recognizability with minimal impact on lexical intelligibility. These findings highlight deep generative voice conversion models as viable tools for privacy-preserving solutions in voice-enabled technologies.

Keywords: Voice Privacy · Voice Conversion · Pitch Shifting · Speaker Identity Obfuscation · Automatic Speech Recognition

1 Introduction

The proliferation of Automated Speech Recognition (ASR) technologies has significantly enhanced human—computer interaction, enabling more natural language interfaces across a wide range of platforms. Major technology providers offer robust ASR APIs that support diverse applications, ranging from virtual

Ö. Durmaz Incel et al. (Eds.): iWOAR 2025, LNCS 16292, pp. 422–429, 2026.
https://doi.org/10.1007/978-3-032-13312-0_28

assistants to transcription services. Despite their utility, these systems present serious privacy challenges.

In the context of speech-based systems, privacy concerns can be broadly categorized into two domains: textual privacy and acoustic privacy. Textual privacy relates to the semantic content of speech, such as sensitive medical or proprietary information. Acoustic privacy, on the other hand, pertains to biometric and paralinguistic attributes embedded in the audio signal. These features include, but are not limited to, speaker identity, gender, age, emotional state, accent, and potential health indicators. As acoustic features can uniquely identify individuals, they pose a substantial risk in applications requiring anonymity.

To mitigate these risks, a variety of voice transformation techniques have been proposed. Traditional approaches, such as pitch-shifting algorithms, are computationally efficient but often degrade speech intelligibility and negatively affect ASR performance. In contrast, the StarGAN-VC many-to-many voice conversion model [3] offers improved preservation of intelligibility while enhancing acoustic privacy.

In voice-enabled systems, it is essential to process spoken commands effectively while preserving user privacy. Sensor-based voice recognition often needs to analyze speech types or even content to enable features like command interpretation or emotion-aware responses. However, speech signals carry sensitive paralinguistic information, including speaker identity, emotional state, and health indicators. This creates a need for methods that balance utility and privacy. Recent work has proposed intermediate layers that sanitize speech before it is sent to cloud services, altering biometric or emotional cues while preserving core functionality [14]. Such approaches point to promising directions for privacy-conscious voice systems.

This study evaluates the trade-offs between conventional pitch shifting and the StarGAN-VC voice conversion technique in the context of acoustic privacy. Specifically, we assess the impact of both methods on two key dimensions: speaker identity obfuscation and ASR accuracy. By analyzing how each technique influences the balance between speech utility and identity concealment, we aim to inform the development of privacy-preserving audio processing pipelines that achieve both intelligibility and anonymity.

The proposed system aims to suppress speaker-specific cues to such an extent that even users familiar with each other's accent, prosody, and rhythmic patterns are unable to identify the originating speaker, demonstrating the robustness of the privacy layer in high-stakes scenarios.

2   Related Work

As speech recognition systems become more prevalent, concerns about acoustic privacy have driven research into voice anonymization methods that conceal speaker identity without compromising intelligibility.

Traditional techniques like pitch shifting alter the voice's fundamental frequency [5] and have been used for speaker and gender transformation. For example, a study using SIFT and PSOLA algorithms demonstrated pitch modifications in Arabic speech [2]. However, such methods often degrade linguistic clarity, especially with larger shifts.

More recently, deep learning approaches have shown promise. The Prεεch system [1], for instance, applies client-side acoustic obfuscation before sending audio to cloud-based ASR, offering tunable privacy while preserving transcription quality. These models can obscure biometric cues more effectively than traditional techniques.

Despite this progress, few studies offer direct comparisons between pitch shifting and modern voice conversion models. Moreover, evaluations typically focus on either recognition accuracy or anonymization, rarely both.

This work addresses that gap by comparing pitch shifting and StarGAN-VC [3], assessing both ASR performance and perceived speaker anonymity through a dual objective-subjective framework.

3 Methodology

In this section, we describe our proposed methodology for achieving acoustic privacy while preserving recognition performance, including data preprocessing, voice conversion, and statistical evaluation.

3.1 Data Collection and Preprocessing

Speech data was collected from acquainted participants. To ensure consistency, all recordings were made using the same microphone setup and scripted speech content. The dataset comprises 73 words and several sentences. Preprocessing included normalization and filtering using both high-pass and low-pass filters [4] to enhance clarity and reduce noise.

3.2 Pitch Shifting

Pitch shifting was conducted using Audacity, altering fundamental frequency without changing playback speed [5]. Shifts of $\pm 20\%$ and $\pm 40\%$ were applied. Processed samples were segmented for identity recognition tests.

3.3 StarGAN-VC Voice Conversion

StarGAN-VC enables deep learning-based, zero-shot voice conversion using non-parallel data [3]. The model was trained on the VCTK corpus [13], comprising 20 speakers (10 male, 10 female) with approximately 400 sentences each. It takes a source spectrogram and a target speaker ID to generate the converted spectrogram. Training employed identity loss, cycle consistency loss, and adversarial loss, where the discriminator distinguishes real from converted spectrograms. The model was trained for 100 epochs using the Adam optimizer, achieving a final loss of 0.083. Each test utterance was converted into 10 target voices (5 male, 5 female), resulting in 485 new samples.

3.4   Lexical Voice and Identity Recognition

Voice recognition was performed using the Google Voice Recognition API [7], with performance evaluated via Word Error Rate (WER) [11] across three conditions: original, pitch-shifted, and StarGAN-VC-transformed audio. Samples with high WER were excluded.

Speaker identity recognition was conducted using a custom Java-based application. Participants were asked to identify speakers from randomized samples, including three pitch-shifted and ten StarGAN-VC variants per subject. Trials were split into two sessions to reduce fatigue, and responses were logged to calculate recognition accuracy.

3.5   Evaluation and Statistical Comparison

Pitch shifting and voice conversion were evaluated using two metrics: identity obfuscation and lexical intelligibility. WER from the Google API served as a proxy for ASR compatibility, while subjective recognition tests quantified identity masking. Results illustrate trade-offs between intelligibility and anonymity, informing the privacy-preserving potential of each method in ASR.

4   Experimental Evaluation

This section presents experimental results on lexical integrity and identity recognizability, comparing the Audacity pitch-shifting method with the StarGAN-VC voice conversion model.

4.1   Lexical Integrity

To assess linguistic preservation, we used Google's Speech Recognition API and computed WER on transformed audio.

Audacity pitch shifting was tested at -40%, -20%, $+20\%$, and $+40\%$. Male voices showed higher ASR accuracy with increased pitch (up to 84%), while female voices performed better with decreased pitch (up to 53%). This gender asymmetry likely reflects differences in vocal frequency ranges (see Fig. 1).

StarGAN-VC was tested on ten synthetic target voices (5 male, 5 female). The model achieved up to 90% accuracy on male targets, while performance on female targets plateaued around 78%, possibly due to dataset imbalance in VCTK (see Fig. 2).

4.2   Identity Recognizability

Five participants familiar with the original speakers attempted speaker identification. With six speakers, random guessing yields a 16.7% baseline.

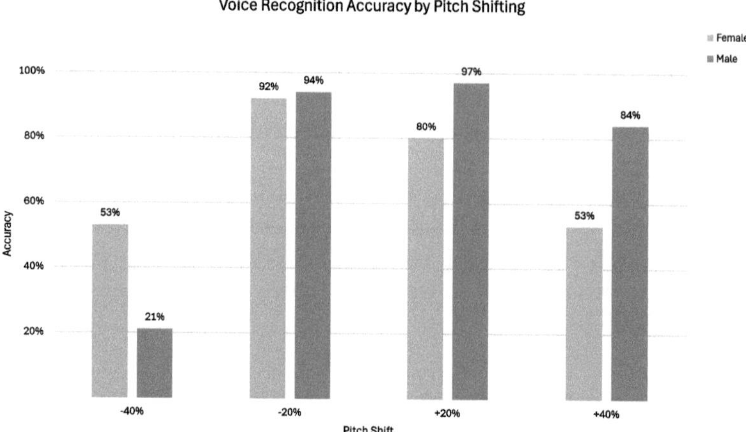

Fig. 1. Voice recognition accuracy after pitch shifting for male and female voices.

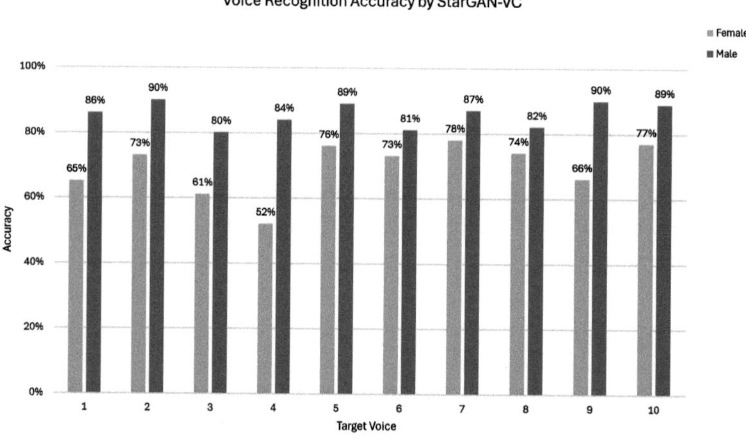

Fig. 2. Voice recognition accuracy across 10 target voices using StarGAN-VC for male and female speakers.

Applying pitch shifts of -20%, $+20\%$, and $+40\%$ yielded an average identification accuracy of 44.5% (see Fig. 3). While better than no transformation, this method fails to provide sufficient identity masking for privacy-oriented applications.

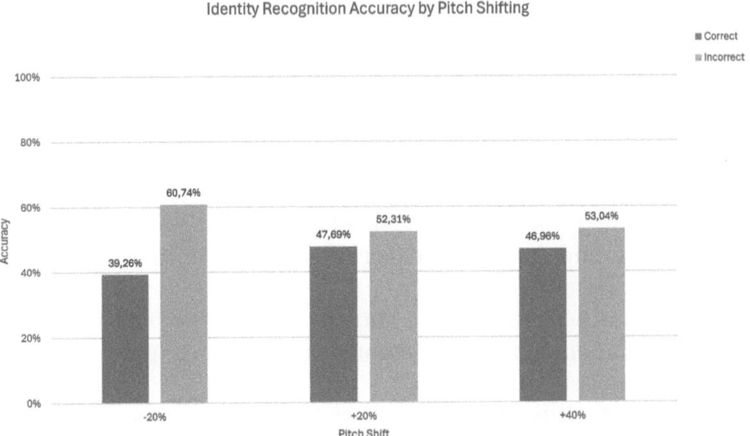

Fig. 3. Identity recognition accuracy under different pitch shift settings using Audacity.

Using 10 voice-converted samples targeting 5 male and 5 female voices, StarGAN-VC achieved a mean identification accuracy of 27% (see Fig. 4), only slightly above chance. This suggests StarGAN-VC effectively obfuscates speaker identity while preserving linguistic content.

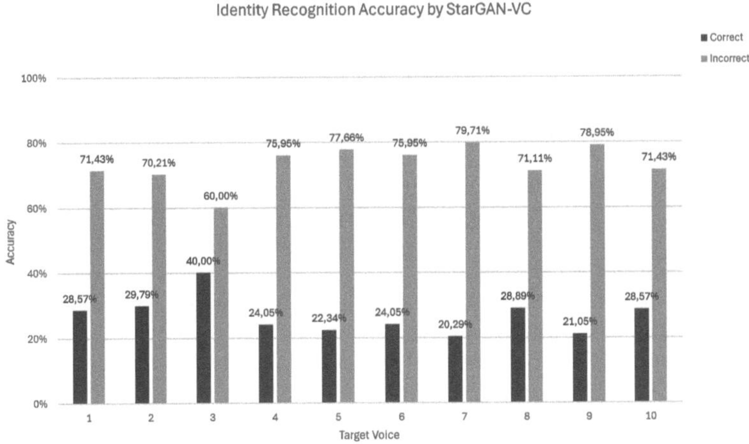

Fig. 4. Identity recognition accuracy across 10 target voices using StarGAN-VC.

4.3   Summary

StarGAN-VC clearly outperforms Audacity in providing a balance between voice obfuscation and linguistic integrity. While pitch-shifting can retain some lexical information, it falls short in concealing speaker identity. StarGAN-VC, by contrast, offers a promising solution for privacy-preserving voice transformation.

5   Conclusion and Future Work

This study compared pitch shifting and StarGAN-VC voice conversion for preserving speech content while masking speaker identity. We evaluated both techniques using ASR and human speaker identification to assess the trade-off between intelligibility and anonymity.

StarGAN-VC outperformed pitch shifting in terms of both recognition accuracy and speaker anonymization, demonstrating strong potential for privacy-preserving voice applications.

The inability of familiar group members to re-identify speakers suggests that the model effectively suppresses subtle vocal cues. This is essential for reducing bias in tasks such as oral assessments, protecting identities in sensitive mental health conversations and in whistleblowing.

Limitations include accent familiarity affecting recognition. Future work could address this by employing more uniform datasets or selecting participant groups with similar language backgrounds.

Further directions include filtering sensitive content in speech and testing more models with larger participant groups to improve generalizability.

References

1. Ahmed, S., et al.: Preech: a system for privacy-preserving speech transcription. arXiv preprint arXiv:1909.04198 (2020)
2. Mousa, A.: Voice Conversion using pitch shifting algorithm by time stretching with PSOLA and re-sampling. J. Electr. Eng. **61**(1), 3–8 (2010). https://doi.org/10.2478/v10187-010-0008-5
3. Kameoka, H., Kaneko, T., Tanaka, K., Hojo, N.: StarGAN-VC: non-parallel many-to-many voice conversion with star generative adversarial networks. arXiv preprint arXiv:1806.02169 (2018)
4. Audacity Team: High Pass Filter/Low Pass Filter. https://manual.audacityteam.org/man/high_pass_filter.html
5. Audacity Team: Pitch Shifting. https://manual.audacityteam.org/man/change_pitch.html
6. Zen, H., et al.: LibriTTS: a corpus derived from LibriSpeech for text-to-speech. arXiv preprint arXiv:1904.02882 (2019)
7. Google Cloud: Speech-to-Text. https://cloud.google.com/speech-to-text
8. Boudreau, T., Glick, J., Greene, S.: NetBeans: The Definitive Guide. O'Reilly Media, Sebastopol (2002)
9. Baken, R.J.: The aged voice: a new hypothesis. J. Voice **19**(3), 317–325 (2005). https://doi.org/10.1016/j.jvoice.2004.07.005
10. Qian, J., et al.: VoiceMask: anonymize and sanitize voice input on mobile devices. arXiv preprint arXiv:1711.11460 (2017)
11. Ali, A., Renals, S.: Word Error Rate Estimation for Speech Recognition: e-WE. https://doi.org/10.18653/v1/P18-2004

12. Kobayashi, K., Toda, T.: Sprocket: open-source voice conversion software. In: Odyssey 2018: The Speaker and Language Recognition Workshop, pp. 203–210 (2018). https://doi.org/10.21437/Odyssey.2018-29
13. Yamagishi, J., Veaux, C., MacDonald, K.: CSTR VCTK Corpus: English Multi-speaker Corpus for CSTR Voice Cloning Toolkit (2019). https://datashare.ed.ac.uk/handle/10283/3443
14. Aloufi, R., Haddadi, H., Boyle, D.: Emotionless: privacy-preserving speech analysis for voice assistants. In: CCS 2019 Workshop. arXiv preprint arXiv:1908.03632 (2019)

Toward Low-Complexity Arrhythmia Classification for Ambient Assisted Living

Hangze Wu[1,2], Ruben Schlonsak[1,3(✉)], and Denys J. C. Matthies[1,3(✉)]

[1] Technical University of Applied Sciences Lübeck, Lübeck, Germany
ruben.schlonsak@th-luebeck.de
[2] East China University of Science and Technology, Shanghai, China
[3] Fraunhofer IMTE, Lübeck, Germany

Abstract. Population aging increases the need for accessible cardiac rhythm screening outside clinical settings. We present a proof-of-concept, low-complexity pipeline for at-home electrocardiogram (ECG) rhythm screening tailored to Ambient Assisted Living (AAL). To mimic single-lead devices, we extract interpretable features from lead II, including ventricular rate, QRS duration, QT/QTc, RR-interval statistics, and simple counts derived from wavelet-based delineation. We compare a compact Fully Connected Neural Network (FCN) against a tree-based model (XGBoost). Models are developed on ChapmanECG under an 11-class label space and evaluated in matched splits; XGBoost yields higher mean accuracy than the FCN. For an external, system-level check, we apply the trained pipeline to short excerpts from the MIT-BIH Arrhythmia Database and harmonize labels via a graded protocol (Correct/Partially Correct/Incorrect) to account for taxonomy differences. Under this protocol, the pipeline attains 82.98% accuracy. While not a diagnostic study, the findings indicate that feature-based, interpretable models can provide practical, low-weight rhythm screening suitable for AAL contexts and merit further validation with clinically curated, single-lead home recordings.

Keywords: ECG · Arrhythmia Classification · Ambient Assisted Living · Feature Engineering · Low-Complexity Models

1 Introduction

The global demographic shift toward population aging is accelerating and will strain healthcare delivery models that were optimized for episodic, clinic-centered care. Cardiovascular diseases (CVDs) remain the leading cause of mortality, accounting for an estimated 32% of all deaths worldwide in 2019, underscoring the need for continuous risk assessment and timely intervention [14]. In high-income countries such as Australia, the proportion of adults aged $\geq$ 65 years is projected to reach 22% by 2057, a transition that is expected to increase healthcare expenditures and disability-adjusted life years attributable to age-related conditions [1,5]. Traditional, reactive care pathways are poorly suited to

Ö. Durmaz Incel et al. (Eds.): iWOAR 2025, LNCS 16292, pp. 430–439, 2026.
https://doi.org/10.1007/978-3-032-13312-0_29

managing chronic, fluctuating CVD risks in older adults, who often present with multimorbidity, polypharmacy, and functional decline.

Ambient Assisted Living (AAL) and Machine Learning (ML) together offer a scalable, preventive alternative. AAL systems embed unobtrusive sensing into the home and community, e.g., wearables, contactless radar, and environmental sensors, to create longitudinal, context-rich physiological and behavioral time series (Fig. 1).

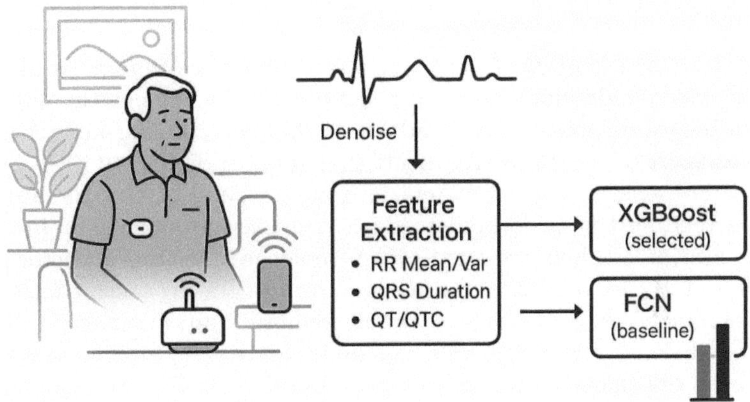

Fig. 1. Overview of the AAL ECG monitoring pipeline: single-lead ECG acquired in a home setting, denoised and processed for feature extraction (RR mean/variance, QRS duration, QT/QTc), followed by lightweight classification (XGBoost selected; Fully Connected Neural Network (FCN) as baseline).

ML methods can transform these multimodal streams into digital biomarkers and individualized risk models, enabling early detection of decompensation (e.g., evolving arrhythmia, heart-failure exacerbation), anomaly detection against personal baselines, and prediction of adverse events to trigger just-in-time interventions. Edge deployment further reduces latency and preserves privacy by processing locally, while periodic, secure aggregation supports population-level model refinement [7,10]. By shifting from episodic to continuous, personalized monitoring and decision support, integrated AAL-ML pipelines have the potential to improve outcomes for older adults living with or at risk for CVDs, while alleviating pressure on overstretched health systems [1,5,14]. The main contributions of this work are:

– A compact feature set and reproducible extraction workflow for single-record ECG analysis.
– A controlled comparison of a Fully Connected Neural Network (FCN) versus an Extreme Gradient Boosting (XGBoost) model under matched train/test splits.

– An integrated MATLAB application demonstrating the end-to-end use of the system from signal input to classification.

2   Related Work

A review of the literature reveals two primary areas of research that are pertinent to this study: the application of Ambient Assisted Living (AAL) technologies for elderly care and the use of deep learning for cardiovascular diagnosis.

Ambient Assisted Living for Cardiovascular Health aims to improve the quality of life for elderly individuals, allowing them to live independently and safely in their own homes for longer. Using advanced Ambient Intelligence technologies, AAL systems create smart environments that support daily activities. These systems integrate sensors, accelerometers, glucometers, and ECG to monitor health, thereby extending the period older adults can live autonomously. In addition, home monitoring can help reduce the inconvenience of visiting a doctor [12]. Triantafyllidis et al. [13] proposed a framework for integrating sensors into Ambient Assisted Living (AAL) systems to enable remote monitoring of patients with chronic conditions, particularly elderly individuals. The architecture relies on wearable sensors that continuously capture physiological parameters and transmit the data via Bluetooth to a smartphone. The smartphone processes the incoming signals and forwards the information to a medical center, where it is reviewed by professional caregivers within the AAL infrastructure. Such a system facilitates reactive services that support patient self-management, while also enabling proactive interventions initiated by the system to enhance patient safety.

Deep Learning in Cardiovascular Diagnosis has emerged as a transformative field over the past decade, with electrocardiogram (ECG) analysis representing one of the most successful applications of artificial intelligence in cardiovascular medicine. Landmark studies trained large CNNs on single-lead or 12-lead recordings and reported cardiologist-level performance for rhythm detection; subsequent benchmarking on PTB-XL confirmed strong results for ResNet/Inception-style architectures [6,11]. However, these gains often require considerable compute, memory, and energy budgets, and models can be brittle under domain shift, which are issues that matter in AAL/edge contexts. Parallel to end-to-end deep learning, feature-based pipelines remain competitive when curated clinical features (e.g., rates, intervals, morphology cues) are available. Gradient-boosted trees, notably XGBoost [3], have shown strong ECG rhythm classification on tabular feature sets and hybrid fusion settings, offering favorable complexity and interpretability compared to deep networks [8]. Several recent studies in cardiology and biomedical signal processing report XGBoost (or ensembles with XGBoost meta-learners) as effective baselines that are easier to deploy on constrained hardware.

3   Methods

This section details the end-to-end pipeline used for ECG rhythm classification in an Ambient Assisted Living (AAL) context: signal preprocessing and wave delineation, feature computation, learning algorithms, a controlled train/test protocol, and a minimal MATLAB application for system integration and usability. The approach emphasizes a compact, clinically motivated feature set and lightweight learners suitable for resource-constrained settings.

3.1   Dataset

The ChapmanECG dataset of Zheng et al. [15] was used for model development. It comprises 12-lead ECG recordings from 10,646 patients with accompanying rhythm and cardiac-condition labels, as well as a per-patient spreadsheet of basic features. Each ECG lead segment contains $N = 5000$ samples. Amplitudes are expressed in μV after conversion from raw ADC counts using the dataset-provided gain g (counts/mV) and baseline b:

$$V_{\mathrm{mV}} = \frac{x - b}{g}, \qquad V_{\mu\mathrm{V}} = 10^3 \, V_{\mathrm{mV}}.$$

For external evaluation, the MIT-BIH Arrhythmia Database [4,9] was employed. It consists of 48 half-hour two-channel ambulatory ECG recordings from 47 subjects, collected between 1975 and 1979 at the BIH Arrhythmia Laboratory. The signals were digitized at 360 samples/s per channel with 11-bit resolution.

3.2   Signal Preprocessing and Wave Detection

We apply wavelet denoising (Biorthogonal 2.6, decomposition level 8) to reduce baseline wander and high-frequency noise. The signal is decomposed into approximation and detail coefficients; low-frequency drift is attenuated by zeroing the lowest-frequency approximation coefficients and high-frequency noise by zeroing detail coefficients, followed by reconstruction. R-peaks are then detected using a wavelet-based procedure, and QRS onsets/offsets as well as T-offsets are delineated to support interval computations used downstream.

From the denoised signal and delineated fiducial points, we compute clinically motivated features: *Ventricular Rate, Atrial Rate, QRS Duration, QT Interval, QTc* (Bazett's correction), *QRS Count, Q Onset, Q Offset, T Offset*, and RR-based statistics (*mean_rr, var_rr*). Age and gender (numeric-mapped) complement the physiologic features. RR statistics derive from inter-R-peak intervals; QTc is computed as $\mathrm{QTc} = \mathrm{QT}/\sqrt{\mathrm{RR}}$ (with RR in seconds). The operational extraction steps for each feature (e.g., counting R-peaks for QRS count, slope-change analysis for Q onset/offset, and T offset) follow the implementation described in the system.

3.3 Model Training

We implemented a compact FCN in TensorFlow 2.1 with ReLU activations and a Softmax output layer. Kernel L2 regularization (λ=0.01) is applied to all dense layers. Training uses Adam (learning rate 10^{-3}) with EarlyStopping and ReduceLRonPlateau monitored on validation loss. We train up to 1,000 epochs with batch size 32 and report test accuracy on held-out data. For comparison, we used a gradient-boosted tree classifier with `multi:softmax` objective for multi-class prediction. Hyperparameters are: `learning_rate` = 0.01, `subsample` = 0.9, and `n_estimators` = 500. The number of classes is set to the number of unique rhythm labels in the training split. This configuration provides a strong tabular baseline with favorable complexity for edge deployment.

To ensure a fair comparison, we used a standardized preprocessing and splitting protocol for both model families. From the ChapmanECG feature table we form X from {*PatientAge, Gender, VentricularRate, AtrialRate, QRSDuration, QTInterval, QTCorrected, QRSCount, QOnset, QOffset, TOffset, mean_rr, var_rr*}, map *Gender* to {0,1}, and encode the target *Rhythm* with a label encoder. We adopt a 70/30 train/test split with a fixed random seed for each run and repeat the experiment for seeds 1..10 so that FCN and XGBoost are compared under matched splits with reduced variance.

4 Results

4.1 Performance on ChapmanECG

Across ten randomized, matched splits, **XGBoost** outperformed the compact **FCN** on accuracy. A paired comparison yielded $p = 1.45594 \times 10^{-11}$ (< 0.01), supporting XGBoost as the selected model. The seed-wise accuracies and summary statistics are shown in Table 1. A more detailed comparison is presented in Fig. 2, where the confusion matrices for both classifiers are shown using a random seed of 3. Both models showed strong performance for SB, SR, ST, SVT, acceptable performance for AFIB, but weak performance for SA; both exhibited several zero-prediction classes (AT, AVNRT, AVRT, SAAWR) owing to sample scarcity. XGBoost produced a non-zero prediction for AF and higher accuracy on AFIB, SA, SVT; FCN was slightly better on SR, ST.

Table 1. Minimum, average, and maximum accuracy comparison

	FCN_accuracy	XGBoost_accuracy
Average	85.43	90.16
Maximum	86.41	91.17
Minimum	84.35	89.32

4.2   External System-Level Evaluation on MIT-BIH

For each MIT-BIH record, the first 10,000 samples were used, matching the development window. Because the MIT-BIH taxonomy differs from the 11-class scheme used during development (e.g., N≡SR, SBR≡SB), predictions were judged using three grades (Appendix: Table 2): *Correct*, *Partially Correct*, and *Incorrect*, following the source's stated criteria and using PhysioNet annotations for verification (cf. Table 6.3 of the source for MIT rhythms [2]). Counting *Partially Correct* as acceptable, the system-level accuracy is **82.98%**; this is lower than the mean development accuracy (90.16%) due to the additional feature-extraction step and cross-dataset taxonomy differences.

On ChapmanECG, XGBoost is consistently superior to FCN across matched splits (mean accuracies 90.16% vs. 85.43%). On MIT-BIH, counting *Partially Correct* as acceptable yields 82.98% system accuracy, with residual errors concentrated in classes affected by taxonomy mismatch and signal/noise-induced feature extraction errors.

5   Discussion

Our results indicate that a compact, feature-based pipeline can achieve practical performance for 11-class rhythm recognition in an AAL setting, even under cross-dataset evaluation. Despite differences between the development (ChapmanECG) and system-level evaluation (MIT-BIH)—including channel configuration, sampling rates, annotation guidelines, patient mix, and noise profiles—the system-level accuracy of 82.98% suggests that clinically motivated features (ventricular rate, QRS duration, RR-interval statistics) provide robust discrimination without relying on large deep networks. This aligns with AAL constraints such as limited device resources, the need for low latency, and strong privacy guarantees through on-device processing.

Misclassifications concentrate among clinically adjacent rhythms that share morphology and rate characteristics in short segments (for example, sinus variants and supraventricular categories). To reflect this nuance, we report a complementary *Partially Correct* metric that treats taxonomically compatible mappings as not fully incorrect, following common merges (e.g., grouping sinus variants SR/SB/ST; aligning AF with AFIB; consolidating SVT-like supraventricular rhythms). This yields a more realistic view of utility in AAL scenarios.

Cross-dataset testing highlights distribution shifts likely to occur in real deployments. While the inductive bias of hand-crafted features mitigates some shift, targeted domain adaptation remains promising: personalized baselines (e.g., subject-specific RR statistics), light-weight calibration with a small number of labeled events, and robust signal-quality indices (SQI) to exclude degraded segments. These strategies should improve transferability without materially increasing model complexity or compute cost.

Short analysis windows reduce latency and energy consumption but may miss transitions. Practical stabilizers include overlapping windows, beat-to-episode aggregation, and simple temporal smoothing (e.g., majority voting) or light sequential models (e.g., HMM/CRF) applied to the discrete label stream. In parallel, harmonized label spaces and a specified evaluation protocol (fixed splits and seeds, consistent windowing) are as critical as model choice for reproducibility and fair comparison.

As a non-diagnostic triage tool, the system can encourage earlier clarification of suspicious rhythms, potentially reducing unnecessary visits while prioritizing cases that warrant clinician review. Clear user guidance and effective communication of uncertainty are essential to minimize false-negative risk and ensure that ambiguous outputs prompt timely follow-up. Overall, our findings support a "low-complexity first" design principle for AAL ECG screening, with a roadmap toward prospective validation, domain adaptation, and seamless integration into home-care and telecardiology workflows.

6   Limitations and Future Work

The model is trained on a single development database (ChapmanECG). Several basic rhythms are rare therein, leading to zero predictions in those classes and limiting generalization to uncommon patterns. Future work should expand training diversity to mitigate these effects.

Evaluation is performed on MIT-BIH, whose taxonomy and annotation practice differ from the 11-class scheme used for development. The study, therefore, introduces a *Partially Correct* grade to acknowledge clinically compatible predictions when labels diverge semantically or temporally. Broader cross-dataset harmonization and label mapping would further reduce such frictions.

Evaluation uses $\approx$30 s excerpts (first 10,000 samples at 360 Hz), matching development-window length. Short windows can under-represent rhythm variability and transitions. Extending or adapting windowing strategies is a direct avenue for improvement.

7   Conclusion

This proof-of-concept AAL system combines clinically motivated ECG features with a lightweight XGBoost classifier. On ChapmanECG, XGBoost surpassed a compact FCN across ten matched splits (paired t-test $p = 1.45594 \times 10^{-11}$) and was therefore integrated into the application. On MIT-BIH (first 10,000 samples per record), the whole pipeline achieved **82.98%** accuracy under an 11-class scheme, with a grading protocol to account for taxonomy and timing differences. The study also motivates a feature-based design via an explicit computational analysis of CNNs on long ECG segments. While limitations arise from class rarity, cross-dataset differences, and feature-extraction sensitivity, the results indicate that a feature-efficient, lightweight approach is viable for AAL-oriented rhythm monitoring and merits further development on broader data with strengthened signal processing.

Acknowledgements. This work was supported by the German Federal Ministry for Economic Affairs and Climate Action (BMWK KK5646401RH4) and by the German Federal Ministry of Research, Technology and Space of Germany (BMFTR 03DPC0711A), whose contributions we gratefully acknowledge.

A   Appendix

Table 2. Label harmonization between ChapmanECG (11 classes) and MIT-BIH record-level rhythms used for grading. 'PC' denotes Partially Correct.

Chapman class	MIT-BIH rhythm(s)	Grade rule
SR (Sinus Rhythm)	N (Normal sinus rhythm)	Correct
SB (Sinus Bradycardia)	SBR (Sinus bradycardia)	Correct
ST (Sinus Tachycardia)	(no direct MIT record label)	PC vs. N/SVT-like[*]
AFIB	AFIB	Correct
AFL	AFL	Correct
SA (Sinus Arrhythmia)	N (with high RR variability)	PC
SVT	SVTA (Supraventricular tachyarr.)	Correct/PC
AT	SVTA	PC
AVNRT	SVTA	PC
AVRT	SVTA	PC
SAAWR	N or NOD (junctional), case-dependent	PC

[*] Short 10–30 s windows with elevated rate but lacking explicit MIT rhythm change are graded PC when consistent with sinus tachy features.

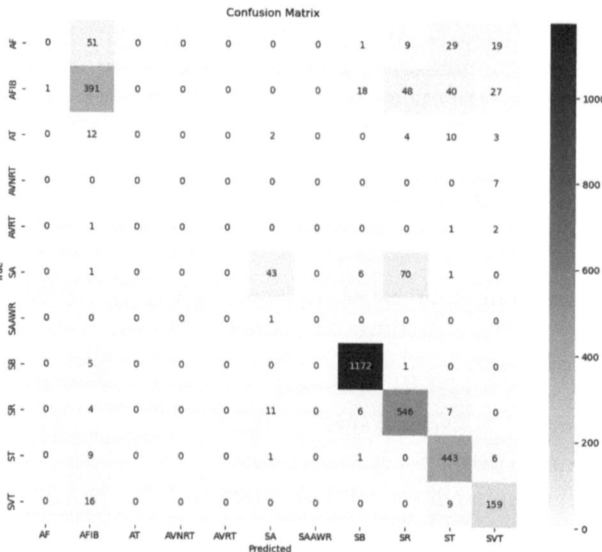

(a) Confusion matrix of the FCN model.

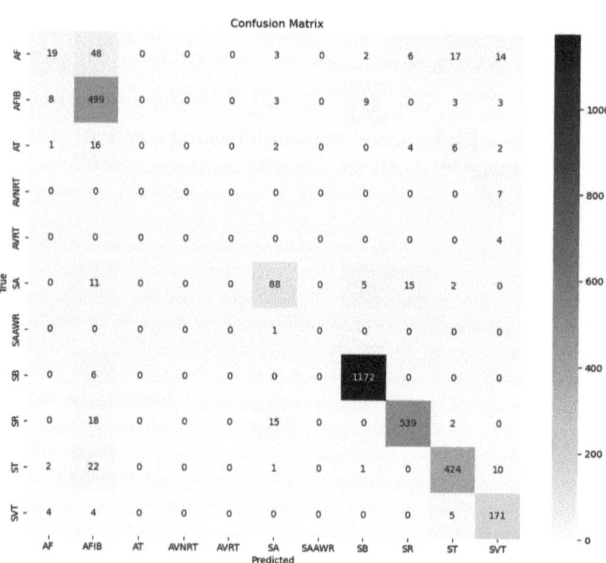

(b) Confusion matrix of the XGBoost model.

Fig. 2. Comparison of classification results for the two approaches.

References

1. Australian Institute of Health and Welfare: Australia's Welfare 2017. Australia's Welfare Series no. 13, AIHW, Canberra (2017). https://www.aihw.gov.au/getmedia/088848dc-906d-4a8b-aa09-79df0f943984/aihw-aus-214-aw17.pdf.aspx?inline=true
2. B.Moody, G.: MIT-BIH arrhythmia database directory (1997). https://archive.physionet.org/physiobank/database/html/mitdbdir/mitdbdir.htm. Accessed 16 May 2024
3. Chen, T., Guestrin, C.: XGBoost: a scalable tree boosting system. In: Proceedings of the 22nd ACM SIGKDD International Conference on Knowledge Discovery and Data Mining, pp. 785–794 (2016)
4. Goldberger, A.L., et al.: PhysioBank, PhysioToolkit, and PhysioNet: components of a new research resource for complex physiologic signals. Circulation $101(23)$, e215–e220 (2000)
5. Ha, N.T., Hendrie, D., Moorin, R.: Impact of population ageing on the costs of hospitalisations for cardiovascular disease: a population-based data linkage study. BMC Health Serv. Res. $14(1)$, 554 (2014). https://doi.org/10.1186/s12913-014-0554-9
6. Hannun, A.Y., et al.: Cardiologist-level arrhythmia detection and classification in ambulatory electrocardiograms using a deep neural network. Nat. Med. $25(1)$, 65–69 (2019). https://doi.org/10.1038/s41591-018-0268-3
7. Huang, Z., et al.: Efficient Edge-AI models for robust ECG abnormality detection on Resource-Constrained hardware. J. Cardiovasc. Transl. Res. $17(4)$, 879–892 (2024)
8. Jahangir, R., Islam, M.N., Islam, M.S., Islam, M.M.: ECG-based heart arrhythmia classification using feature engineering and a hybrid stacked machine learning. BMC Cardiovasc. Disord. $25(1)$, 260 (2025). https://doi.org/10.1186/s12872-025-04678-9
9. Moody, G., Mark, R.: The impact of the MIT-BIH arrhythmia database. IEEE Eng. Med. Biol. $20(3)$, 45–50 (2001). https://doi.org/10.1109/51.932724
10. Rancea, A., Anghel, I., Cioara, T.: Edge computing in healthcare: innovations, opportunities, and challenges. Future Internet $16(9)$ (2024). https://doi.org/10.3390/fi16090329, https://www.mdpi.com/1999-5903/16/9/329
11. Strodthoff, N., Wagner, P., Schaeffter, T., Samek, W.: Deep learning for ECG analysis: benchmarks and insights from PTB-XL. IEEE J. Biomed. Health Inform. $25(5)$, 1519–1528 (2021)
12. Sun, H., De Florio, V., Gui, N., Blondia, C.: Promises and challenges of ambient assisted living systems. In: 2009 Sixth International Conference on Information Technology: New Generations, pp. 1201–1207. IEEE (2009)
13. Triantafyllidis, A.K., Koutkias, V.G., Chouvarda, I., Adami, I., Kouroubali, A., Maglaveras, N.: Framework of sensor-based monitoring for pervasive patient care. Healthc. Technol. Lett. $3(3)$, 153–158 (2016)
14. WHO: Cardiovascular diseases (CVDs) (2021). https://www.who.int/en/news-room/fact-sheets/detail/cardiovascular-diseases-(cvds). Accessed 16 May 2024
15. Zheng, J.: Chapmanecg (2019)

Hacking Rokoko Smart Gloves for Tool Detection Using Recurrent Neural Networks

Zhouyao Yu[1,2], Ruben Schlonsak[1,3], and Denys J. C. Matthies[1,3(✉)]

[1] Technical University of Applied Sciences Lübeck, Lübeck, Germany
{zhouyao.yu,ruben.schlonsak}@th-luebeck.de
[2] East China University of Science and Technology, Shanghai, China
[3] Fraunhofer IMTE, Lübeck, Germany
denys.matthies@th-luebeck.de

Abstract. The prolonged use of tools emitting vibration may cause damage in fingers and hands, known as the Raynaud/White Finger Syndrome. A solution is monitoring the device use for those who work long hours with heavy tools. In this paper, we demonstrate how to hack the Rokoko smart gloves to enable them to detect and monitor the tool in use. We demonstrate how to capture data and how to train a machine learning model. The data collected stems from six 9-DoF IMUs that are placed at each finger and the back of the hand. The model is a Recurrent Neural Network (RNN) with a Long Short-Term Memory (LSTM) layer. In this work-in-progress we show the exemplary discrimination of idle from the use of scissors, knife, and hammer with a precision of 70.75%. As workers already wear gloves, we believe commercial smart gloves to be highly practical for similar applications.

Keywords: Smart Glove · Neural Networks · RRN · LSTM · IMU · Gesture Recognition · Tool Detection

1 Introduction

Prolonged use of heavy tools, such as jackhammer, can lead to nerve damage in fingers and hands. According to research on jackhammer drillers, the longer they use the heavy tools the more they suffer from hand-arm vibration syndrome (HAVS) also called Raynaud or White Finger Syndrome [1]. A monitoring device for tool use is necessary to protect the health of the worker [2]. The current state in tool recognition demonstrates that significant research exists concerning tool recognition or worker activities recognition via computer vision or sensor technology [3]. However it requires extra work to mount cameras in daily work situation, which is a inconvenience. For tracking hand-arm vibration, monitoring the device use can also be done with sensors attached to the drill, but which includes obstructing wires or additional weight from a battery [4].

Ö. Durmaz Incel et al. (Eds.): iWOAR 2025, LNCS 16292, pp. 440–449, 2026.
https://doi.org/10.1007/978-3-032-13312-0_30

On the other hand, workers usually wear protection gloves when operating such devices. Therefore, utilizing a smart glove can be promising and practical approach. Once the tool is known to our system, we can easily calculate the daily doses of vibration based on the HAV intensity ratio, which is usually reported from the tool's datasheet. To demonstrate the feasibility of a tool detection with smart gloves, we hacked the Rokoko smart gloves. In this research, we focus on the data acquisition and final tool detection. For the tool detection, an recurrent neural network containing LSTM layer is used. Data are collected through glove's mounted IMUs, being normalized, and then feed to a NN (Fig. 1).

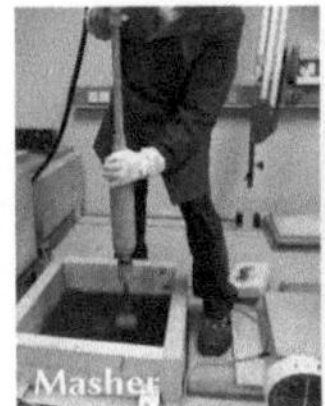

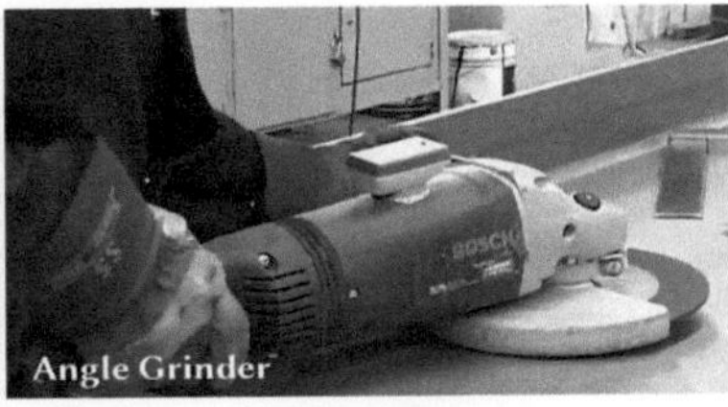

Fig. 1. Typical tools that are used in a various kinds of shop floors may include a masher, grinder, hammer, angle grinder, and many more. All these tools emit considerable hand-arm vibration when used, which is unhealthy and should be tracked by the worker as demanded by legal regulations in European countries such as Germany.

In accrodance to Wobbrock [5], this research is considered an artifact contribution that proposes a feasible and low-cost solution for a working environment tool usage monitoring.

2   Related Work

Plenty of works related to IMU based gesture recognition and tool recognition area have long been conduct in past years, among which there are some inspiring work. The detection used to rely on conventional Bayesian algorithms and state machines, while currently Neural Networks are considered the state-of-the-art for high precision recognition with multi-dimensional data.

Plenty of works have addressed IMU-based gesture and tool recognition. Early approaches relied on Bayesian models and state machines, while neural networks now dominate for high-precision recognition of multidimensional data. Numerous studies have advanced automatic activity recognition across domains, with related contributions from computer-assisted intervention (CAI).

Optical Surgical Workflow Recognition. Sahu et al. [3] proposed tool and surgical phase recognition using CNN features and random forests on the M2CAI16 dataset, achieving ~50% accuracy. While effective in the OR, camera-based solutions are costly and impractical for daily environments with limited visibility.

Attaching Wearable Sensors. Fort et al. [6] suggested embedding accelerometers on the body or tools to monitor hand–arm vibration (HAV) during use of drills, jackhammers, and similar tools, demonstrating feasibility of embedded ML on low-power devices.

Hand–Arm Vibration Exposure in Rock Drill Workers. Clemm et al. [7] compared hand- vs. tool-mounted accelerometers, finding that hand-based sensors may underestimate HAV depending on grip, highlighting limitations of sensor placement.

HAV Estimation with Smartwatches. Matthies et al. [8,9] proposed detecting tool type with smartwatch sensors to estimate HAV dose using manufacturer vibration ratings. They showed that built-in microphones and accelerometers could distinguish tools such as hammer drills, jigsaws, and manual hammers.

Wristband for Activity and Tool Detection. Tao et al. [10] combined IMU and sEMG data via a Myo armband and CNN, achieving up to 98% accuracy for tasks like screwdriver turning or hammering. However, slippage and discomfort of wearable devices limit practical use.

Recognition with Neural Networks. Koch et al. [11] demonstrated that RNNs outperform traditional methods in gesture recognition with shorter sample windows, while LSTM layers enhance robustness for longer sequences. Rivera et al. [12] further showed LSTM-based models achieve $>80\%$ accuracy in daily activity recognition, suggesting strong suitability for IMU-based tool use recognition.

3   Smart Glove

3.1   Commercial Hardware

The hardware used are the Rokoko smart gloves[1]. On each glove, there are six 9-axis IMUs. Each finger features a single IMU while the sixth is attached to the back of the hand. By the hybrid IMU and EMF fusion technology, it can support high accuracy and frequency that up to 100 FPS. In addition, the wireless communication module enables 100 m tracking range, which really fits the labour environment.

As a commercial product, the interface provided to access smart gloves is looks quite sophisticated. Within their software, called Rokoko studio, some black-box algorithms calculate the sensor data and display the tracked hand by a 3d avatar (ses Fig. 6). The software provides a comprehensive platform that allows for device connectivity, real-time gesture representation, streaming capabilities, and animation recording, we are unable to access the raw data.

However, the manufacturer does not currently allow the developer to directly acquire raw sensor data. Thus, the ultimate crucial stage in the development process is to obtain raw sensor data to allow for a more detailed analysis and a customised NN model training.

---

[1] Rokoko: Capture accurate finger motions with Smartgloves (https://www.rokoko.com/products/smartgloves.

3.2 Hacking the Glove

Hacking the software seems quite impossible due to the signed packages and many other unknown factors. So, we decided to attack at a different level. Our starting point is the Rokoko Studio after establishing a wireless network connection to the smart gloves. Notably, it becomes feasible to capture data packets through network packet analysis. By using the tool Wireshark, we can sniff data packages with a 456-byte payload, which are constantly transmitting from gloves by UDP protocol to the computer [13].

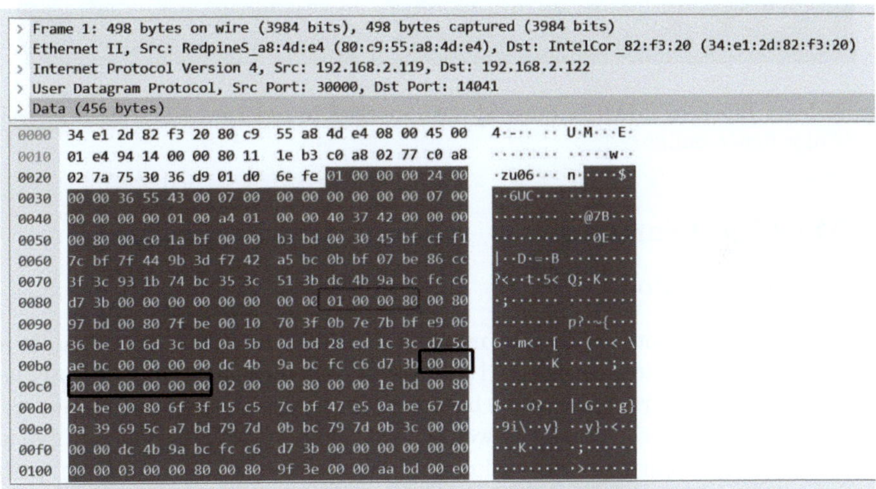

Fig. 2. Rokoko glove data package: Payload is highlighted in blue. Heading code in yellow box. Ending zeros in red box. (Color figure online)

Figure 2 shows the payload highlighted in blue, which is characterized with a split by a series of zeros. Since each glove has six IMUs with the same data format, the payload is apparently divided into six similar blocks, starting with sensor heading code and ending with eight zeros. After rearrange data blocks (Fig. 3), a same row of data is ignored because seldom do two sensors read the same, especially in a resolution of 64 bits. For some most IMUs, we collect data from the accelerometer, gyrometer, magnetometer, and an additional temperature sensor value, which is also embedded [14,15]. Compared to the valid data on the left, it is easy to identify all 10 readings, each consisting of 32 bits.

Finally, a series of motion tests is conducted to identify the id of the IMU. The readings for each sensor and the sequence of bytes present the actual data. In conclusion, each network package composes a header and six IMU data. For each imu, it contains 60 hexdecimal data, starting with IMU sequence number, then following up with a 32-bit accelerometer reading, a 32-bit gyrometer reading, a 32-bit magnetometer reading, a thermometer reading, and finally surrounded by filling zeros.

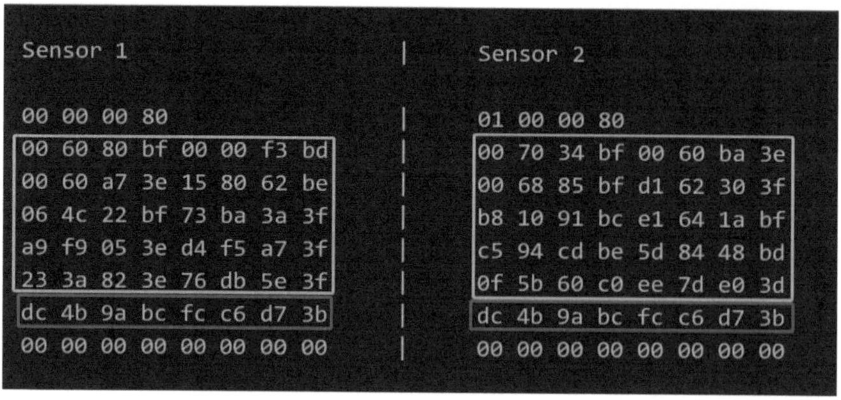

Fig. 3. Data block of 2 IMUs: Ignored data marked in red box. Valid data in yellow box (Color figure online)

4   Machine Learning

4.1   Data Collection

The basis for a machine learning approach is to train a model based on a data set. To establish the data set, we selected four classes, including three commonly used tools, which are scissors, knife and a hammer. The fourth class is the default class containing various other gestures as well as resting motion. The selected motions for testing involve cutting with a knife and scissors, as well as hitting with a hammer. Apparently one is enable to select other motions and devices from the shop floor, such as a drill, grinder etc. However, as this is a work-in-progress and due to practicability, we selected these ones.

During the sampling process, several subjects are tasked to perform these actions while facing various directions and adopting different angles. This deliberate variation in orientation serves the purpose of preventing overfitting during the subsequent model training phase. By incorporating diverse perspectives and angles during sampling, the model can develop a more robust understanding of the targeted motions, enhancing its ability to generalize effectively to various real-world scenarios.

For the purpose of raw data acquisition to support live recognition, the Scapy library has been employed to implement network data capture functionality, seamlessly integrated into the recognition system. Through this library, the script is empowered to capture network packages originating from a specified IP source, while concurrently applying a defined message filter [16]. This integration facilitates real-time data collection, allowing the recognition system to continuously receive and process relevant information for accurate and dynamic motion analysis.

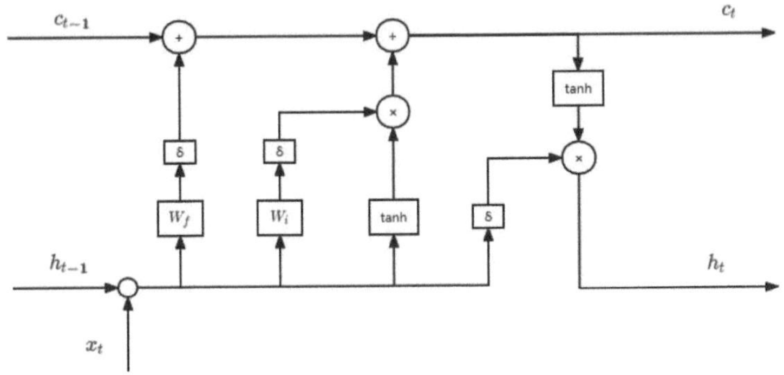

Fig. 4. Our approach of the LSTM cell.

4.2 Signal Processing

Signal Cleaning and Filtering After the data acquisition, the data is still ambiguous to be used, because of unstable frame rate and soiled readings. The frame rate problem is caused by mismatch of sensors and throughput capacity of internet. For each IMU, there is 3-axis gyrometer and accelerometer, which work max to 100 Hz. Moreover, the magnetometer works in lower frequency. However, the incoming data is more frequent than magnetometer updates, which results in a mismatch of readings between magnetometer and current position. Further, due to extra-high frequency, the incoming data sometimes get stuck and are not distributed equably in time. The solution is to lower the frequency and add a validation check in code. The data is refined to 20 Hz update rate. With the help of flag bit in acceleration reading, it is possible to detect whether a frame containing magneto reading. Only the frame with full information can be viewed valid.

For soiled reading, as is mentioned before, excluding thermometer, there are 54 data in one frame. A frame can be viewed as usable only if all readings are valid, which is difficult. During test, phenomenon is common that less than 5 frames are usable in one second that cannot match the requirement of recognition. The solution is to fill the spoiled datum by the former. It is considered not normal if a single datum suddenly goes to zero, given the sample rate is set relatively high. When a new frame is received, it will be compared with two frames of data that are temporally close to each other. If it is invalid, it will be filled by former data.

Extra Data Column. According to the feature of accelerometer, the impact of gravity always reflect on the readings. Take using scissors for instance, the activities of horizontal cutting and vertical cutting will be viewed as two different actions because z-axis is added by gravity reading in former cases and x-axis is the same in the latter case. To decrease the need of sample amount, there are a new column of data added to each IMU, which is the 3d vector norm of acceleration calculated by: $norm = \sqrt{acc_x^2 + acc_y^2 + acc_z^2}$. Thus only the change of acceleration is record, and the data looks like figure. After going through all processing steps, we end up with sequences of 40 samples that reflecting motion in 2 s, which is our chosen window size to feed the neural network.

4.3   Recurrent Neural Network and Long Short-Term Memory

Given the temporal sequence of hand movement, a recurrent neural network is considered better in handling this kind of inputs following related work (see above). In order to get more accurate recognition result, a larger window of input will be better to avoid over-fitting. In this case, LSTM cells are applied in the network as follows:

As is shown in Fig. 4. The memory of context is h_t, with the use of sigmoid function, the network is able to control the memorization and forgetting of context-specific information, and thus the LSTM cell enables the network to process a larger sequential input.

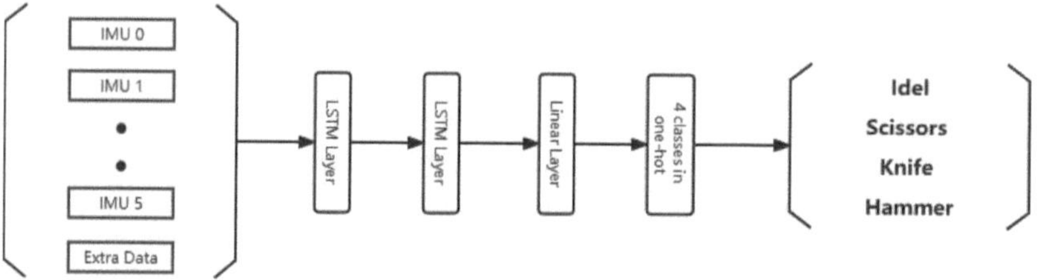

Fig. 5. The Network flow chart of our network layer design used.

The network used in this project consist of two LSTM layers and one linear layers. As is showed in Fig. 5, the input includes the filtered raw data of every imus and some extra data that is calculated according to the raw ones. The input will go through 2 LSTM layers which are fully connected. Then a linear layer will flatten the result as the weight of each tool class.

Fig. 6. Showing the Rokoko Studio's visualisation with different gestural activites.

4.4   Model Training

As previously stated, the algorithm to classify is a RNN. Compared to other classifiers, it is more suitable to handle input in time sequence, and thus pave the way for possible real-time detection. Given the input number of each sample is 40, the LSTM is chosen. Different from traditional RNNs, with its context cell, a LSTM model can handle larger input sample in time sequence. The label of data is encoded in one-hot. In this network, the input data is be fed to a double layers LSTM with a hidden size of 36. The outcome of the sequential input is put into a full connection layer and then the data is flattened to the size of label.

The dataset used to train our model contains five users performing each activity for at least a minute. Our series of data recordings therefore contain different execution styles and thus we do not expect a very high precision. Each series of data match a tool.

5   Evaluation

The test data is generated in the same way as the training data. For our test set, we collected data from a single user and so to speak performed a leave-one-user out to also gain an understanding of the interpersonal feasibility of the trained model. Figure 7 shows the result of test, where the label 0,1,2,3 refer to idle, scissors, knife and hammer respectively. In the test, each tool is used from 10 to 20 s. Overall we achieve a precision of 70.75%, which is fair given the rather small training and test set. As shown, the use of knife is relatively accurate because the execution style did not greatly differ for this activity across users. In this case the motion of using knife is on one platform so it is easy to recognize through the norm of acceleration. To improve the accuracy of other tools, more information should be added. Since the dataset is relatively small for training a stable NN, the model may still overfit to specific users. It is to assume that greater volume of training and test data will most likely result in a substantial boost of accuracy.

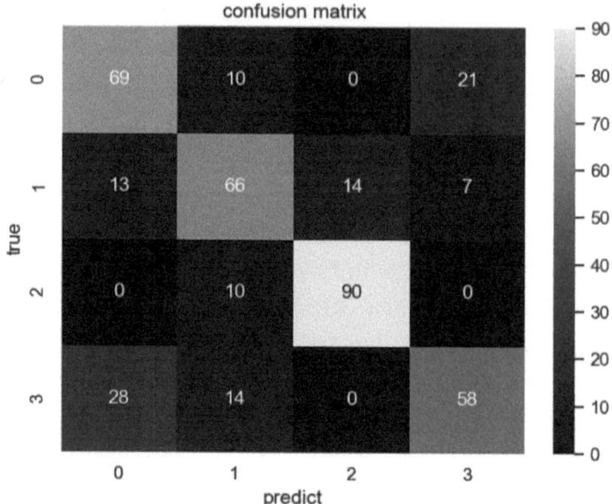

Fig. 7. Confusion matrix generated from our evaluation (Label description: 0 = idle, 1 = scissors, 2 = knife, 3 = hammer)

6   Conclusion and Future Work

In this paper, a tool detection application was developed based on the Rokoko smart gloves. For classification algorithm, a recurrent neural network with two long short-term-memory layers was applied to recognize four classes. Distinguishing the idle state from using scissors, a knife and a hammer resulted in a model precision of 70.75%. The performance looks promising, but should be improved with greater samples in future. Also, applying the glove in a shop floor and training a model with commonly used tools is the next step. Utilizing a commercial smart glove for identifying the hand-arm vibration exposure dosage is a promising approach and should be pursued in future.

Acknowledgement. This work was supported by the German Federal Ministry for Economic Affairs and Climate Action (BMWK KK5646401RH4) and by the German Federal Ministry of Research, Technology and Space of Germany (BMFTR 03DPC0711A), whose contributions we gratefully acknowledge.

References

1. Dasgupta, A.K., Harrison, J.: Effects of vibration on the hand-arm system of miners in India. Occup. Med. **46**(1), 71–78 (1996)
2. zum Vibrationsschutz, A.D.B.: Erstmals grenzwerte für die vibrationsbelastung (2007)
3. Sahu, M., Mukhopadhyay, A., Szengel, A., Zachow, S.: Tool and phase recognition using contextual CNN features. arXiv preprint arXiv:1610.08854 (2016)
4. Kuczyński, J.: Improved methods of assessment of vibration risk (2014)

5. Wobbrock, J.O., Kientz, J.A.: Research contributions in human-computer interaction. Interactions **23**(3), 38–44 (2016)
6. Fort, A., Landi, E., Moretti, R., Parri, L., Peruzzi, G., Pozzebon, A.: Hand-arm vibration monitoring via embedded machine learning on low power wearable devices. In: IEEE International Symposium on Measurements & Networking (M&N), pp. 1–6. IEEE (2022)
7. Clemm, T., Nordby, K.-C., Lunde, L.-K., Ulvestad, B., Bråtveit, M.: Hand-arm vibration exposure in rock drill workers: a comparison between measurements with hand-attached and tool-attached accelerometers. Ann. Work Exposures Health **65**(9), 1123–1132 (2021)
8. Matthies, D.J., Haescher, M., Bieber, G., Nanayakkara, S.: Hand-arm vibration estimation using a commercial smartwatch. In: 14th International Conference on Hand-Arm-Vibration (2019)
9. Matthies, D.J., Bieber, G., Kaulbars, U.: AGIS: automated tool detection & hand-arm vibration estimation using an unmodified smartwatch. In: Proceedings of the 3rd International Workshop on Sensor-based Activity Recognition and Interaction, pp. 1–4 (2016)
10. Tao, W., Lai, Z.-H., Leu, M.C., Yin, Z.: Worker activity recognition in smart manufacturing using IMU and sEMG signals with convolutional neural networks. Procedia Manuf. **26**, 1159–1166 (2018). 46th SME North American Manufacturing Research Conference, NAMRC 46, Texas, USA
11. Koch, P., Dreier, M., Böhme, M., Maass, M., Phan, H., Mertins, A.: Inhomogeneously stacked RNN for recognizing hand gestures from magnetometer data. In: 2019 27th European Signal Processing Conference (EUSIPCO), pp. 1–5. IEEE (2019)
12. Rivera, P., Valarezo, E., Choi, M.-T., Kim, T.-S.: Recognition of human hand activities based on a single wrist IMU using recurrent neural networks. Int. J. Pharma Med. Biol. Sci **6**(4), 114–118 (2017)
13. Beale, J., Orebaugh, A., Ramirez, G.: Wireshark & Ethereal Network Protocol Analyzer Toolkit. Elsevier (2006)
14. Chandrasiri, R., Abhayasinghe, N., Murray, I.: Bluetooth embedded inertial measurement unit for real-time data collection for gait analysis. In: International Conference on Indoor Positioning and Indoor Navigation (2013)
15. Moschevikin, A.P., Sikora, A., Lunkov, P.V., Fedorov, A.A., Maslennikov, E.I.: Hardware and software architecture of multi mems sensor inertial module. In: 2017 24th Saint Petersburg International Conference on Integrated Navigation Systems (ICINS), Saint Petersburg, Russia, pp. 1–3. IEEE (2017)
16. Bansal, S., Bansal, N.: Scapy-a python tool for security testing. J. CS & SB **8**(3), 140 (2015)

Evaluation of the Effect of Camera Viewing Angles on the Quality of Human Pose Estimation in River Surfing

Michael Zöllner[1,2]([✉]) [iD], Moritz Krause[2] [iD], Christian Groth[2] [iD],
Stefan Kniesburges[1] [iD], and Michael Döllinger[1] [iD]

[1] FAU Erlangen, University Hospital Erlangen, 91054 Erlangen, Germany
`michael.zoellner@hof-university.de`
[2] Institute for Information Systems, Hof University, 95028 Hof, Germany

Abstract. Capturing human poses with monocular RGB cameras seems like an uncomplicated compared to extensive motion capturing systems or calibrated multi camera setups. In our application scenario we are capturing the biomechanics of surfers on standing waves in rivers with GoPro cameras. Thereby we identified detection quality issues of the joints on the backside of the surfers' bodies in certain situations.

In this paper we are evaluating different camera positions and angles with regard to the recognition quality of these critical body parts. We are describing the application scenario and the resulting requirements for human pose estimation and hardware setup.

Our evaluation results are identifying patterns of quality issues depending on surfers' stance, skills and motions on the one hand and camera positions and angles on the other hand. We are concluding our paper with further approaches to improve detection quality.

Keywords: Machine Learning · Data Visualization · Pose Estimation · Interactive Systems

1 Introduction

1.1 Introduction

At first glance, river surfing appears like an ideal setting for capturing human poses with monocular RGB cameras. Unlike the large area and the high dynamics in ocean surfing, the situation in rivers is focused on the area of the standing wave. Usually that's a field with a depth of 2 m and a width of the river or channel of 5–12 m. On this standing wave the surfers are surfing with their short boards from side to side while their motion is describing the form of a lazy eight (∞).

Tracking a surfer in the ocean needs a following tele-objective or a camera-drone. Obtaining the exact position of the camera and the target is challenging and lacking

Ö. Durmaz Incel et al. (Eds.): iWOAR 2025, LNCS 16292, pp. 450–458, 2026.
https://doi.org/10.1007/978-3-032-13312-0_31

precision. Whilst in river surfing a static camera at the edge of the river can film the area of interest in high quality.

Nevertheless, we are observing challenges in capturing and reconstructing surfers' poses on river waves. First and foremost, the black matte neoprene wetsuits most surfers are wearing pose a challenge in terms of contrast. Due to their individual and rapid movements there are concealed body parts whose position can't be determined with certainty but only approximated by the human pose estimation models. Surfers stir up water during their turns which is spraying especially around the back side of the body and is overlaying joints. Furthermore, there are classic environmental effects on cameras like backlight and low-contrast areas.

All the arguments mentioned negatively affect the recognition quality of human pose estimation models and thereupon the quality of the data and our resulting conclusions about motion patterns in river surfing.

In this paper we are documenting our evaluation of the effects of camera position and perspective on the quality of human pose estimation. We designed a setup consisting of different camera positions around the surfer and the wave and a set of movement sequences the surfers are performing. We recorded different surfers of different age, weight and gender. Followed by an evaluation of the data and a visual augmentation of the skeleton on top of the video sequences for visual analytics. We are concluding with our results and suggestions about how to improve data quality in human pose estimation in river surfing by optimizing camera placement.

2   Related Work

Thanks to Machine learning based human pose estimation capturing systems do not need any special hardware like time-of-flight cameras anymore. Carnegie Mellon University's OpenPose [1] was a robust solution for 2D and 3D skeleton reconstruction delivering 3D skeleton data in the BODY_25 pose topology. Similar results can be achieved with Google Edge AI's MediaPipe [7] framework. Its Pose Landmarker delivers 33 3D landmarks in the COCO [6] topology superset GHUM3D [13] and a background segmentation mask.

Today there are several open-source toolboxes for human pose estimation utilizing multiple human pose estimation models in their so-called model-zoos. MMPose [2] is an up-to-date solution for 2D and 3D pose estimation for single and multiple humans and animals based on a large set of models and datasets. Similar results can be achieved with the multi-person pose estimator AlphaPose [5].

In order to improve the quality of the resulting human skeleton there are solutions applying inverse kinematics to the detected landmarks. Pose2Sim [11] produces 3D markerless kinematics for humans or animals from multiple calibrated cameras and acts as an alternative to traditional marker-based MoCap methods. Recent models like NVidia GLAMR: Generative Motion Infiller [14] are improving quality by predicting a person's occluded motion and infills the missing frames. A similar quality effect could be achieved with FLK: A filter with learned kinematics for real-time 3D human pose estimation [8] that filters estimation inaccuracy and uses biomechanical constraints of the human body to provide spatial coherency between keypoints.

There are various studies evaluating human pose estimation solutions. To help athletes better analyze the quality of their movements a systematic review study was conducted in five databases including articles for a timeframe of 10 years until 2021. Difini et. al. [3] examined challenges related to pose estimation, usage of estimation methods and specific activities. Dubey et. al. [4] assembled a comprehensive survey on human pose estimation approaches and discussed the evaluation metrics used for estimating human poses. Finally we are refer to a survey covering more than 260 research papers since 2014 with a regularly updated project page [15]. Regarding our own decision using MediaPipe for our evaluation we are mentioning the comparison of the quality of human pose estimation with BlazePose [9] or OpenPose.

3 Experiment Setup

3.1 River Surf Spot

Our evaluation takes place at the river wave in Nuremberg in Bavaria, Germany [10]. The river Pegnitz is split into an 8 m wide channel where the water falls around 120 − 150 cm down a ramp where it is forming a surfable wave. The channel is embedded in concrete walls on which we set up our cameras.

3.2 Hardware Setup

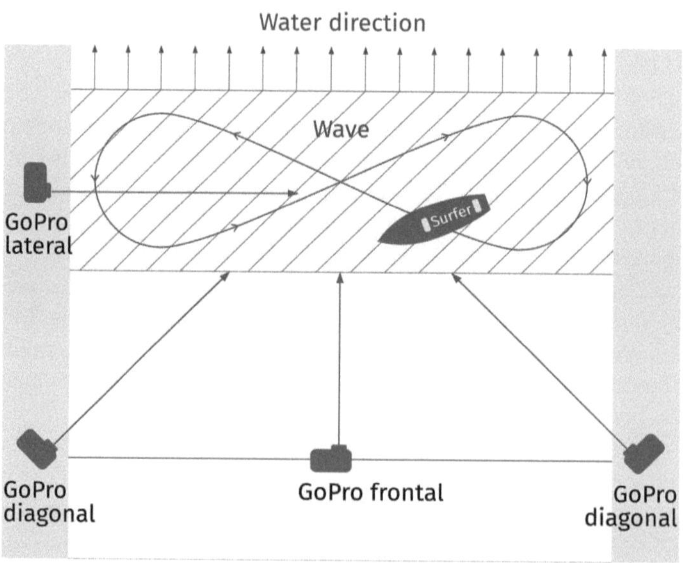

Fig. 1. Diagram of the situation around the wave with the positions and angles of the cameras.

We are using up to three identical GoPro Hero Black 11 cameras. The resolution is set to 5.3K with 16:9 aspect ratio at 5312 x 2988 pixels at 60 fps and linear lens mode.

Their time codes are synchronized via GoPro Labs Precision Date and Time QR code [12] and triggered by the GoPro Remote V3 via Bluetooth. The three positions of the cameras are: frontal filming the surfer from upstream, lateral filming the surfer from the side of the channel and diagonal in a 45 degree angle on the left or right side of the channel (see Fig. 1).

The lateral and diagonal cameras are placed with a GoPro Shory Mini tripod on the concrete walls of the channel. We used a 5 m long carbon extension for positioning the frontal camera in the middle of the 8 m wide channel.

3.3 Human Pose Estimation Software

We are focusing on Google Edge AI's Mediapipe Pose Landmarker in our evaluation to compare the influence of the camera position on the human pose quality. In a previous paper we already compared the results of different pose estimation solutions from a fixed position [16]. For further research we would like to compare our results with MMPose and AlphaPose applying various models in the future.

Mediapipe Pose Landmarker detects landmarks of human bodies from a video resulting in body pose landmarks in image coordinates and in 3-dimensional world coordinates. We used the latest version of the Pose landmarker (Heavy) pose detector ($224 \times 224 \times 3$) and pose landmarker ($256 \times 256 \times 3$) which outputs the human landmarks in the GHUM (3D) topology.

Particularly important for our evaluation are the visibility and presence scores for each joint in the dataset. They are representing if it is visible by the camera and about the detection quality and probability.

We implemented Mediapipe Pose Landmarker in a Jupyter Notebook in Python. Our script was batch processing the videos, generating the GHUM datasets and augmenting the skeleton on top of the video frames. We also generated graphs of the joint positions and visibility scores on the fly.

3.4 Surfers and Motion Routine

In this primary study we selected three surfers with different skill levels and surf stances: a young semi-professional woman with a fast and dynamic surf style (surfer 1, goofy footed, right foot front), a middle-aged male with a progressive surf style (surfer 2, goofy footed, right foot front) and an elderly but sportive male at a beginner level with slower, concentrated movements (surfer 3, regular footed, left foot front).

The surfers surfed several times from the left to the right side and vice versa. At the outer limits they turned with their board into the opposite direction. These are the critical situations where several joints on the backside of the human body become invisible while the body turns pointing to the camera. Since the surfers have different stances (regular, goofy) the positions of the critical joints depend on their stance.

We identified the following critical joints becoming inaccurate during the maneuvers: back hand, back elbow, back shoulder, back hip, back knee, back ankle. Since the surfers' behavior is comparable, we concentrated on the back hand in this evaluation.

4   Results and Interpretation

4.1   Visual Interpretation

Fig. 2. Lateral camera on the left, diagonal camera in the center and frontal camera on the right.

When we are looking at the results and comparison of the three different positions of the camera (see Fig. 2), we can conclude that from the frontal and the diagonal positions all relevant motions are captured by the cameras. The full body of the surfer is always visible in the images, and all joints are present. Although recognize the critical back joints that are concealed by the surfer's body at several times. No body parts are covered by water or objects.

The camera at the lateral position captures the back joints. But it is also cutting the lower body parts due its lower position and the concrete wall of the channel when the surfer is positioned close to it. The water spray the surfer is creating while turning with his board is also covering body parts.

We decided to ignore the lateral camera position and to concentrate on the data evaluation of the diagonal and frontal camera positions.

4.2   Data Interpretation

Our data interpretation consists of the surfers' skeletons rendered on single frames of the video for visual analytics and graphs showing Mediapipe Pose Landmarker's visibility score of the back elbow joint. In the renderings of the skeletons we can verify the correct position of the joint on the body of the surfer. The data plot displays how reliable the elbow joint is detected by the human pose estimation model from the respective camera positions. In a perfect data set both lines would range in the upper part of the graph representing higher visibility scores. When the back elbow is hidden by a body part or water sprays the line drops to a lower visibility score.

The first surfer's style is very fast with dynamic movements of the hands to create momentum. We are observing that the visibility scores of the back elbow differ diametrically from the respective cameras (see Fig. 3). Thus, we can conclude that the elbow is seen by one diagonal camera while it is poorly visible from the camera farther away from the turn. We do not get its location recognized in a decent quality across multiple frames from only one diagonal camera.

The second surfer's style is not as fast as the first one's regarding locomotion. Although the arm movements are very dynamic while generating momentum. In this example we are using one diagonal and one frontal camera. In the graph we can clearly

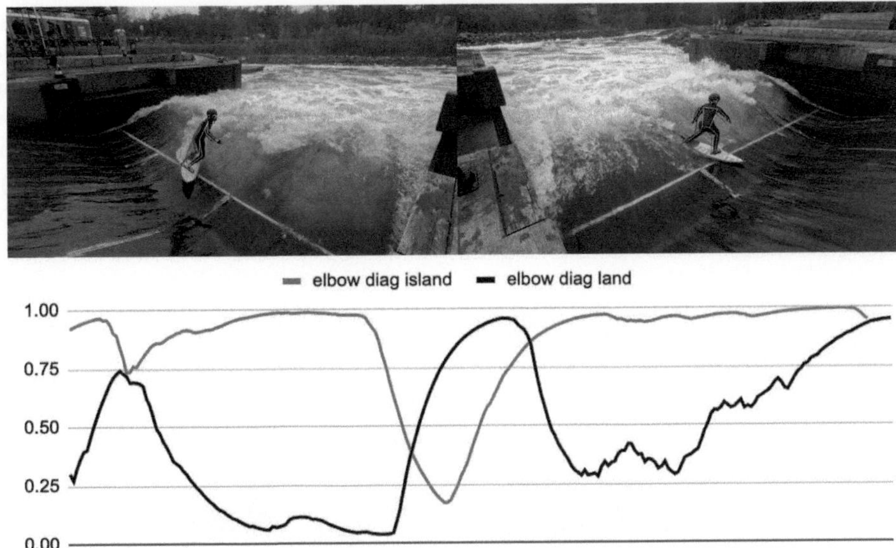

Fig. 3. Surfer 1 – two diagonal cameras and graph of elbow's visibility score

observe the difference to the setup with two diagonal cameras (see Fig. 4). Since the cameras are located closer together there are less diametrically different visibility scores of the back elbow. The scores are running nearly parallel in certain areas with a slight shift. The back elbow is mostly either visible or not visibly by both cameras.

Fig. 4. Surfer 2 – one frontal and one diagonal camera and graph of elbow's visibility score

The third surfer's mellow surfing style is less challenging for the human pose estimation model compared to the previous progressive surfers. The red line shows a reliable recognition of the back elbow from one diagonal camera. In this setup we are observing another challenge regarding quality: The backlight generated by the camera's position relative to the sun reduces the visibility score (see Fig. 5). The black wetsuit is in front of a dark background in the scene caused by the backdrop and the bright water spray. Therefore, the joint is not recognized reliable although it is moving slowly and is not concealed by the body.

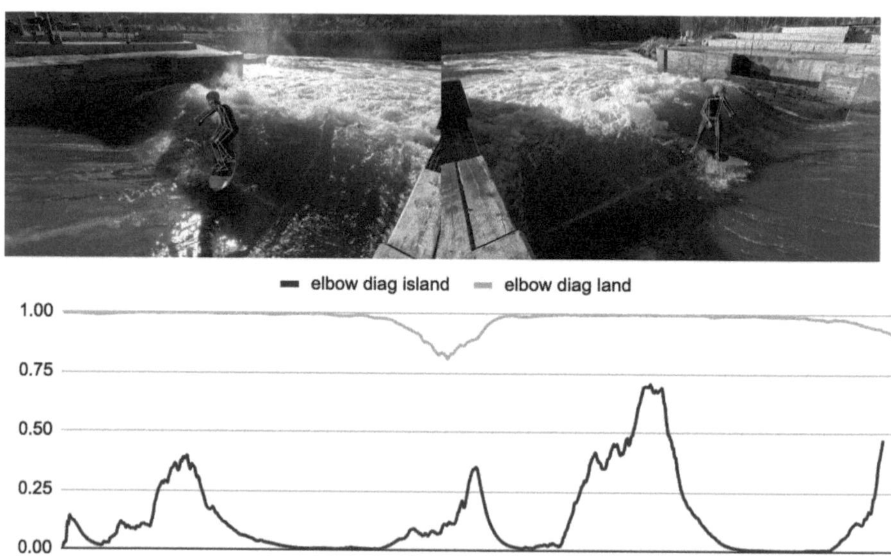

Fig. 5. Surfer 3 – two diagonal cameras and graph of elbow's visibility score

5 Conclusion and Future Work

We have presented three different surfers and our observations of limiting effects in human pose estimation due to obscured body parts. Our evaluation setup examined if the low visibility rates depend on the camera position by processing videos of predefined motion routines with MediaPipe Pose Landmarker. By interpreting the resulting dataset's visibility scores of the back elbow joint we could determine that with a monocular camera setup MediaPipe does not detect a surfer's skeleton in sufficient quality over the whole sequence. The joints on the backside of the body are often concealed while turning the body and the board while filmed from the opposite side. Environmental influences on the lighting conditions like backlight deteriorate the results even further.

We plan to resolve the current limitations focusing on the back elbow with an automated pipeline producing histograms of the visibility scores of all joints. Our goal is to identify all critical joints in different motion situations and depending on the stance of the surfers.

For our next steps we will evaluate a multiple calibrated camera setup with MMPose (Voxelpose) and Pose2Sim. Our evaluation showed that using two diagonal placed cameras should recognize the back joints with the camera closer to the body. Thus, we estimate a more comprehensive skeleton representation.

Another optimization approach could be applying prediction and filters like a Kalman filter on the data and interpolate the missing or uncertain frames. Although while recording fast dynamic surfers at 60 fps the number of missing frames might be too high.

Future approaches of interest are novel models like NVidia GLAMR: Generative Motion Infiller that predicts a person's occluded motion and infills the missing frames. A similar effect could be achieved with FLK: A filter with learned kinematics for real-time 3D human pose estimation that filters estimation inaccuracy and uses biomechanical constraints of the human body to provide spatial coherency between keypoints.

References

1. Cao, Z., Hidalgo, G., Simon, T., Wei, S.-E., Sheikh, Y.: OpenPose: realtime multi-person 2D pose estimation using part affinity fields. arXiv (2019). https://doi.org/10.48550/arXiv.1812.08008
2. Contributors, MMPose. OpenMMLab Pose Estimation Toolbox and Benchmark (2020)
3. Difini, G.M., Martins, M.G., Barbosa, J.L.V.: Human pose estimation for training assistance: a systematic literature review. In: Proceedings of the Brazilian Symposium on Multimedia and the Web, pp. 189–196 (2021)
4. Dubey, S., Dixit, M.: A comprehensive survey on human pose estimation approaches. Multimed. Syst. **29**(1), 167–195 (2023)
5. Fang, H.-S., et al.: AlphaPose: whole-body regional multi-person pose estimation and tracking in real-time. IEEE Trans. Pattern Anal. Mach. Intell. (2022)
6. Lin, T.-Y., et al.: Microsoft COCO: common objects in context. In: Computer Vision–ECCV 2014: 13th European Conference, Zurich, Switzerland, 6–12 September 2014, Part V 13, pp. 740–755 (2014)
7. Lugaresi, C., et al.: Mediapipe: a framework for building perception pipelines. arXiv preprint arXiv:1906.08172 (2019)
8. Martini, E., Boldo, M., Bombieri, N.: FLK: a filter with learned kinematics for real-time 3D human pose estimation. Signal Process. 10959 (2024). https://doi.org/10.1016/j.sigpro.2024.109598
9. Mroz, S., et al.: Comparing the quality of human pose estimation with blazepose or openpose. In: 2021 4th International Conference on Bio-Engineering for Smart Technologies (BioSMART), pp. 1–4 (2021)
10. Nürnberger Dauerwelle – Nürnberg Surft: 2025. https://www.nuernberger-dauerwelle.de/. Accessed 21 July 2025
11. Pagnon, D., Domalain, M., Reveret, L.: Pose2Sim: an end-to-end workflow for 3D markerless sports kinematics—part 1: robustness. Sensors (2021). https://doi.org/10.3390/s21196530
12. Precision Date and Time: 2025. https://gopro.github.io/labs/control/precisiontime/. Accessed 22 July 2025
13. Xu, H., Bazavan, E.G., Zanfir, A., Freeman, W.T., Sukthankar, R., Sminchisescu, C.: GHUM & GHUML: generative 3D human shape and articulated pose models. In: 2020 IEEE/CVF Conference on Computer Vision and Pattern Recognition (CVPR), pp. 6183–6192 (2020). https://doi.org/10.1109/CVPR42600.2020.00622

14. Yuan, Y., Iqbal, U., Molchanov, P., Kitani, K., Kautz, J.: GLAMR: global occlusion-aware human mesh recovery with dynamic cameras. In: Proceedings of the IEEE/CVF Conference on Computer Vision and Pattern Recognition (CVPR) (2022)
15. Zheng, C., et al.: Deep learning-based human pose estimation: a survey. ACM Comput. Surv. **56**(1), 1–37 (2023)
16. Zöllner, M., Krause, M., Gemeinhardt, J., Döllinger, M., Kniesburges, S.: Evaluation of machine learning based pose estimation of surfers on river waves. In: PETRA 2023 - PErvasive Technologies Related to Assistive Environments, Korfu (2023). https://doi.org/10.1145/3594806.3596570

Author Index

A
Aarts, Rhana M.   382
Agac, Sumeyye   77
Akyürek, Eren   422
Ali, Hurriat   308
Anbalagan, Sabari Nathan   364
Arif Taşlı, Mehmet   422
Arnrich, Bert   353, 393, 404

B
Bakanas, V.   1
Barth, Jens   261
Bautmans, Ivan   156
Bemthuis, Rob   343
Bergsma, Ewout   99
Bieber, Gerald   222
Bontempelli, Andrea   287
Botti, Elena   156
Brahimetaj, Redona   156
Burchard, Robin   308
Busso, Matteo   287

C
Cerny, Martin   185
Checherin, Semen   20

D
D'Avis, Noel   116
David, Klaus   373
Decker, Stefan   413
Deters, Jan Kleine   99
Döllinger, Michael   450
Duc, Le Viet   135
Durmaz Incel, Özlem   20, 77

E
Endlicher, Erik   222
Eskofier, Björn   261

F
Faquiri, Silvia   116
Forstner, Timo   222
Fu, Biying   56

G
Gabrecht, Marco   38
Geravand, Milad   222
Giunchiglia, Fausto   287
Groth, Christian   450
Grothe, Lars   116
Gupta, Ankit   185
Güvenatam, Burcu   99

H
Hamann, Tim   261
Hartmann, Hendrik   116
Heinisch, Judith S.   373
Hernlund, Elin   382
Hrovatin, Niki   234

J
Jansen, Bart   156
Janus, Sarah   99
Jetter, Hans-Christian   324

K
Kämpf, Peter   261
Kaynak, Nurcennet   404
Kennel, Valentin   404
Kiefer, Sandra   56
Kirsten, Kristina   353
Klein Brinke, J.   1
Kleine Deters, Jan   196
Klemke, Roland   413
Kniesburges, Stefan   450
Kodur, Krishna   172
Konak, Orhan   393
Kos, Rok   404
Krause, Moritz   450

Ö. Durmaz Incel et al. (Eds.): iWOAR 2025, LNCS 16292, pp. 459–460, 2026.
https://doi.org/10.1007/978-3-032-13312-0

Kyrarini, Maria   172

L
Laumann, Dimitri   250
Li, Jindong   261
Li, Yue   20
Luinge, Arnout   364

M
Malcotti, Leonardo Javier   287
Marin-Perianu, Mihai   382
Marin-Perianu, Raluca   382
Mat Sanusi, Khaleel Asyraaf   413
Mathuseck, Lars   373
Matthies, Denys J. C.   324, 430, 440
Matthies, Denys   38
Milivojčević, Milan   234

N
Naderi, Fatemeh   373
Nägele, Thomas   343
Najem, Ali   196
Nave, Alexander Heinrich   404
Nguyen, Minh Son   135

P
Parmentier, Jeanne I. M.   382
Pöhler, Jonas   250

Q
Qin, Jingwen   20

R
Reyes Leiva, Karla Miriam   185
Rhodin, Marie   382
Rieger, Nikolas   393

S

Sardadvar, Fatemeh   404
Schlonsak, Ruben   38, 324, 430, 440
Schmidt, Felix   404
Sedighi, Mehdi   196
Sharma, Nikita   135
Silva, Jair A. Lima   99
Slupczynski, Michal   413
Straus, Alexa   404
Swinnen, Eva   156

T
Tome, Athina   404
Tošić, Aleksandar   234

V
van der Struijf, Cor   343
Van Laerhoven, Kristof   250, 308
van der Zwaag, Berend-Jan   20
Vičič, Jernej   234

W
Walz, Tim   353
Weese, David   353
Weier, Martin   56
Wörtche, Heinrich   99, 196
Wu, Hangze   430

Y
Yıldırım, Funda   422
Yu, Jiabao   324
Yu, Zhouyao   440

Z
Zanca, Dario   261
Zand, Manizheh   172
Žgank, Zala   382
Zöllner, Michael   450
Zuidema, Sytse U.   99

MIX
Papier aus verantwortungsvollen Quellen
Paper from responsible sources
FSC® C105338

If you have any concerns about our products,
you can contact us on
ProductSafety@springernature.com

In case Publisher is established outside the EU,
the EU authorized representative is:
Springer Nature Customer Service Center GmbH
Europaplatz 3, 69115 Heidelberg, Germany

Printed by Libri Plureos GmbH
in Hamburg, Germany